Native American Cultural and Religious Freedoms

Edited with an introduction by

John R. Wunder
University of Nebraska-Lincoln

GARLAND PUBLISHING, INC.
A MEMBER OF THE TAYLOR & FRANCIS GROUP
New York & London
1999

Library of Congress Cataloging-in-Publication Data

Native American Cultural and religious freedoms / edited with an
  introduction by John R. Wunder.
        p.   cm.
      Includes bibliographical references.
      ISBN 0-8153-3630-6 (pbk. : acid-free paper)
      1. Indians of North America—Civil rights—United States.
    2. Indians of North America—Religion and mythology. 3. Freedom
  of religion—United States. I. Wunder, John R.

    KF8210.C5 N38 1999
    342.73'0872—dc21   99-055731
                                                      CIP

Printed on acid-free, 250-year-life paper
Manufactured in the United States of America

Contents

v   Introduction

1   Discrimination and Native American Religious Rights
Daniel K. Inouye

19   The First Americans and the "Free" Exercise of Religion
Martin C. Loesch

85   Constitutional Law: The Right to Wear a Traditional Indian
Hair Style — Recognition of a Heritage
Peggy Doty

101   The Rights of Reservation Parents and Children:
Cultural Survival or the Final Termination?
David Woodward

131   The Bald Eagle, the Florida Panther and the Nation's Word:
An Essay on the "Quiet" Abrogation of Indian Treaties and the
Proper Reading of *United States* v. *Dion*
Robert Laurence

153   Native American Free Exercise Rights to the Use of Public Lands
Laurie Ensworth

193   Manifest Destiny and American Indian Religious Freedom:
Sequoyah, Badoni, and the Drowned Gods
Howard Stambor

225   *Lyng* v. *Northwest*: Closing the Door to Indian Religious Sites
Stephen McAndrew

253   The Navajo-Hopi Relocation Act and the First Amendment
Free Exercise Clause
Charles Miller

279   Indian Rights: Native Americans Versus American Museums —
A Battle for Artifacts
Bowen Blair

309   One Is Missing: Native American Graves Protection and
Repatriation Act: An Overview and Analysis
June Camille Bush Raines

335   *Employment Division, Department of Human Resources* v. *Smith*:
A Hallucinogenic Treatment of the Free Exercise Clause
Rashelle Perry

353   Trouble in High Places: Erosion of American Indian Rights to
Religious Freedom in the United States
Vine Deloria Jr.

377   Acknowledgments

Introduction

The First Amendment to the Constitution, one would think, would guarantee religious and cultural freedoms for all Americans. This, however, has not been the case historically. Indeed, for Native Americans, freedom to practice one's own religion and freedom to participate in one's chosen culture have never been realized, certainly not without complications.

The primary reason for this disrespect is a fundamental cultural difference between American Indians and the majority society. In testimony before the U.S. Senate, Crow tribal leader Barney Old Coyote explained that Indian religion includes how one lives and one's political, social, and cultural outlook. Religious worship, for Barney Old Coyote, was "an integral part of the Indian way of life and culture which cannot be separated from the whole."[1] He called this the oneness of Indian life, and for Native Americans, religion is life itself. It encompasses their entire being, including their surroundings and their life ways.

During the 1970s, Congress held a series of hearings documenting the abuses of Indian religious liberty. Out of these hearings came the American Indian Religious Freedom Act of 1978 (AIRFA), signed into law by President Jimmy Carter.[2] The act itself has only two paragraphs. The first paragraph charges the United States government to "protect and preserve for American Indians their inherent right to freedom to believe, express, and exercise the traditional religions."[3] This "protection" is to extend to access to sacred sites, cemeteries, sacred objects used in religious ceremonies, and the actual practice of traditional rites. The second section requires federal agencies to evaluate their laws with Native religious leaders, and the president to issue a report on their findings to Congress.[4]

Note what is missing from AIRFA. The act has no enforcement provision. People can continue to deny Indians religious freedoms without sanctions. Only access to sacred sites is protected; the site itself is not. And perhaps most grievous, the law recognizes only past, static, limited Indian religious doctrine. It fails to take into consideration the dynamic holistic philosophy of Native American religion. Thus, it is not surprising that whenever Native American religious practices are in dispute, the American Indian Religious Freedom Act is of minimal assistance.

The essays that follow document the evolution of Native American cultural and religious freedoms. They can be considered in three general sections. One section considers how Indian cultural practices are infringed in American society and their relationships to Native American religious views. Another chronicles how Indian religion relates directly to the land and sacred sites, and how this relationship has not been understood by American courts. And a third considers the actual exercise of religious practices and their relationship to repatriation.

The first essay is authored by one of the most important political officials who has lead the fight for Native American religious freedoms. Senator Daniel K. Inouye of Hawaii explains how Indian religious rights have been infringed. As the former chair of the United States Senate Select Committee on Indian Affairs, he helped shape laws that attempted to protect Native culture and religion, and he is the primary advocate today for revisions to the American Indian Religious Freedom Act. After Senator Inouye's introductory essay, Martin C. Loesch offers an overview of how Native Americans have been treated with the application of the Free Exercise Clause of the First Amendment. This constitutes the primary legal umbrella under which Indians attempt to protect their religious rights.

Religion and culture are synonymous in Native society, and that is seen clearly in the next three essays. First, Peggy Doty explains how Indians sought to prevent the cutting of their children's hair in public schools as an infringement upon their religious and cultural traditions. Next David Woodward discusses how Native American parents were losing their children to Christian religious organizations and how their children were put up for adoption outside of Indian culture. He asks if this is the final termination of Native America? Testimony from tribal leaders and other scholars eventually convinced Congress to pass the Native American Child Welfare Act of 1978,[5] an important legislative provision for the protection of Indian culture and religion that is currently under congressional attack.

The third essay in this grouping is by Robert Laurence. It considers an important U.S. Supreme Court decision, *United States* v. *Dion* (1986).[6] Dwight Dion Sr., a Yankton Sioux, was convicted of illegally shooting four bald eagles on the Yankton Sioux Reservation. He appealed his conviction. Dion argued that eagle feathers were an essential part of traditional Indian religious expression, and that to prevent him from obtaining eagle feathers restricted his right to the free exercise of his religion. Justice Thurgood Marshall, representing the majority of the Court, ruled against Dion and Native American religious freedom. In a decision that dealt a blow to Indian treaty rights and Indian religious rights, Marshall concluded that environmental protection statutes, specifically the Endangered Species Act[7] and the Eagle Protection Act,[8] superseded the Yankton Sioux Treaty of 1858 and by omission any religious arguments seeking the protection of the First Amendment. Laurence explains the ramifications of this ruling for Native American religious freedoms.

The next four essays consider applications of AIRFA to the protection of sacred sites and the land. First, Laurie Ensworth explores the specific application of the Free Exercise Clause as it might be applied to the use of public lands. Then Howard Stambor explains why the American Indian Religious Freedom Act was not applied to disputes in Tennessee and Utah over the damming of rivers and the destruction of Cherokee and Navajo sacred sites.[9] Stephen McAndrew next considers the 1988 attempt of the Yurok, Karok, and Tolowa California Indians to prevent the U.S. Forest Service from paving a road and harvesting timber on the Hoopa Valley Indian Reservation and the Six Rivers National Forest. They argued that this would destroy their sacred sites and infringe upon their exercise of religion, but the Supreme Court was not sympathetic. In an opinion by Justice Sandra Day O'Connor, she formulated a test in order to determine if Native American religious freedoms were violated. In order for such a determination, Indians had to prove that they were coerced into violating their beliefs or they were penalized for their beliefs.[10] The last essay in this section, by Charles Miller, considers the Navajo-Hopi Relocation Act and its ramifications for Indian religious freedoms. In particular, Navajos were forced to move from parts of their reservation to new areas, thereby preventing access to sacred sites.

The last section of this volume includes several essays on the actual practice of Indian religions. Bowen Blair summarizes the disputes over sacred artifacts taken from Indian tribes and placed in museums, and June Camille Bush Raines looks at the religious dimensions to the repatriation of burial remains and funereal objects. Native Americans want the return of their sacred artifacts and relatives. This process, now under the watchful eye of the Native American Graves Protection and Repatriation Act Commission, is happening currently.[11]

This volume concludes with two essays. Rachelle Perry assesses the significant damage done to American Indian religious freedoms, and specifically to the Native American Church, in her essay about *Employment Division, Department of Human Resources of Oregon* v. *Smith* (1990)[12] where the Supreme Court used a firing of two Indians from state jobs to hold that states could regulate peyote as a drug and punish accordingly. AIRFA was eviscerated by this legal determination. Vine Deloria then concludes with a pessimistic warning about the erosion of American Indian religious rights.

NOTES

1. *American Indian Religious Freedom: Hearings on S.J.Res. 102*, U.S. Senate Select Committee on Indian Affairs, 95th Cong., 2nd sess., 1978, 86–87.
2. *U.S. Statutes at Large* 92 (August 11, 1978): 469–70.
3. Ibid., p. 469.
4. Ibib., p. 470.
5. *U.S. Statutes at Large* 92 (November 8, 1978): 3069–78.
6. *United States* v. *Dion*, 476 US 734 (1986).
7. *U.S. Statutes at Large* 87 (December 28, 1973): 884–903.
8. *U.S. Statutes at Large* 54 (June 8, 1940): 250–51.
9. See *Sequoyah* v. *Tennessee Valley Authority*, 620 F.2d 1159 (1980) and *Badoni* v. *Higginson*, 638 F.2d 172 (1980).
10. See *Lyng* v. *Northwest Indian Cemetery Protective Ass'n*, 485 US 439 (1988).
11. *U.S. Statutes at Large* 104 (November 16, 1990): 3048–58.
12. *Employment Division, Department of Human Resources of Oregon, et al.* v. *Alfred L. Smith, et al.*, 494 US 872 (1990).

FURTHER READING

Vine Deloria Jr. and Clifford M Lytle, *American Indians, American Justice* (Austin: University of Texas Press, 1983).

Kathryn Harris, "The American Indian Religious Freedom Act and Its Promise," *American Indian Journal* 5 (June, 1979): 7–10.

Jill E. Martin, "Constitutional Rights and Indian Rites: An Uneasy Balance," *Western Legal History* 3 (Fall-Winter, 1990): 245–70.

Randolf J. Rice, "Native Americans and the Free Exercise Clause," *Hastings Law Journal* 28 (July, 1988): 1509–36.

Dean B. Suagee, "American Indian Religious Freedom and Cultural Resources Management: Protecting Mother Earth's Caretakers," *American Indian Law Review* 10, no. 1, (1942): 1–58.

Charles N. Wilkinson, *American Indians, Time, and the Law: Native Societies in a Modern Constitutional Democracy* (New Haven: Yale University Press, 1987).

John R. Wunder, *"Retained by The People": A History of American Indians and the Bill of Rights* (New York: Oxford University Press, 1994).

DISCRIMINATION AND NATIVE AMERICAN RELIGIOUS RIGHTS

Senator Daniel K. Inouye*

I. Introduction

Mankind has a dark side—the age-old tendency to discriminate against others who are different. This Article shares my perspective as a United States Senator on the problem of discrimination and how it affects Native American human rights issues under the jurisdiction of the Senate Select Committee on Indian Affairs.

A pressing human rights concern of the Committee at this time is the specter of renewed religious discrimination against American Indian tribal religions in the wake of the dramatic retreat from First Amendment protections by the Supreme Court in *Employment Div. Dept. of Human Resources of Oregon v. Smith*.[1] This case is a noteworthy example of the Court's denial of protection for a traditional American Indian religion that predates in antiquity the writing of the First Amendment itself.

The unique cultures of America's Native peoples are inseparable from their religions.[2] Religion pervades the traditional way of life of American Indians.[3] These religions have been historically suppressed by the United States government in ways unprecedented

---

* D-Hawaii. Member of U.S. Senate, Jan. 3, 1963 - Jan. 3, 1993. Member of U.S. House of Representatives, Aug. 21, 1959 - Jan. 3, 1963. Committees: Chairman, Select Committee on Indian Affairs; Appropriations; Commerce; Science & Transportation; Rules & Administration. A.B., University of Hawaii; J.D., George Washington University. Member of the Hawaii Bar.

1. Employment Div. v. Smith, 110 S. Ct. 1595 (1990).

2. *See* the findings of Congress in the American Indian Religious Freedom Act of 1978, 92 Stat. 469 (August 11, 1978), codified at 42 U.S.C.A. 1996.

3. In Wisconsin v. Yoder, 406 U.S. 205, 216-17 (1972) the Court found religion to be a pervasive part of life in the Amish society. This principle applies to the American Indian as well.

for other religions. *Smith* seriously weakened religious freedom in general by discarding long-standing First Amendment standards. This resulted in the immediate banding together of church groups and religious organizations in a move to restore the First Amendment balancing test.[4] The proposed legislation which resulted, however, does not address unique, historical Indian religious discrimination problems. There remains a need for separate legislation to protect free exercise rights of Native Americans, as well as to ensure these citizens the guaranteed protections of all other constitutional provisions.

This Article first discusses the compelling government interest in eliminating discrimination and the necessity for all three branches of the federal government to act together to combat intolerance and prejudice. Secondly, it focuses on the problem of religious discrimination against Native Americans, which has intensified in the wake of recent decisions of the Supreme Court. The issue of religious intolerance and discrimination has been a serious human rights problem for indigenous peoples since Christopher Columbus set foot in the the New World. Congress has now been relegated the responsibility to legislatively grant statutory protection for our original inhabitants.[5]

II. The Government's Interest in Eradicating Discrimination

A. *The Evils of Discrimination*

The human spirit is wonderful thing. At its best, the good qualities of our fellow citizens may serve as an example to inspire us to live up to our lofty ideals and goals. Unfortunately, however, mankind has its frailties. The history of our species is fraught with instances where unwarranted hatred and fear has precipitated great misery upon the innocent. Much of this darkness in the human heart is manifested by discrimination.

Discrimination is defined as "[u]nfair treatment or denial of normal privileges to persons because of their race, age, sex, nationality or religion."[6] When effected through the machinery of the state, it can have devastating impacts upon people, ranging from

---

4. *See* The Religious Freedom Restoration Act of 1991 (H.R. 2797) sponsored *inter alia* by Representative Stephen J. Solarz.

5. *See* Lyng v. Northwest Indian Cemetery Protective Association, 485 U.S. 439, 452-53; *Smith*, 110 S. Ct. at 1606.

6. Black's Law Dictionary 420 (5th ed. 1979). In The Random House Dictionary of the English Language (unabr. ed., Random House, New York, 1983), discrimination is defined to mean treatment of a person based on the group, class,

deep psychological scars upon young schoolchildren,[7] to a separation of the races,[8] to the extreme of racial or cultural genocide. For victims of discrimination, it matters little whether these impacts result from invidious state action, or whether they are inflicted by less obvious applications of facially neutral rules.[9]

In the United States, discrimination is illegal. It is prohibited by the Fifth and Fourteenth Amendments to the Constitution as well as by numerous federal laws. Unfortunately, despite our commitment to these Equal Protection ideals, discrimination has had a long and troubling history in this country. The manner in which America, the world's leading democracy, treats our own racism and prejudice reveals much to the international community concerning our attitude about individual freedom and human rights. This country's challenge in the war against discrimination is an on-going one, as seen from the present resurgence of racism and intolerance. It is a continual struggle to eradicate discrimination—a struggle that requires vigilant commitment from all three branches of government.

Presently there is a disturbing trend in many areas of our country in the direction of intolerance and racism. Especially objectionable is an apparent lack of leadership by all three branches of our government in combating this menace to our society. When the executive branch weakens its resolve to enforce civil rights laws, or the judiciary retreats from prior rules of law and dilutes fundamental

---

or category to which that person. . .belongs rather than on individual merit: *racial and religious intolerance and discrimination.* (emphasis added).

7. Brown v. Board of Education, 347 U.S. 483, 494 (1953).

8. *See* Plessy v. Fergeson, 163 U.S. 539 (1896) (establishing the "separate but equal" doctrine).

9. *See, e.g.*, Yick Wo v. Hopkins, 118 U.S. 356 (1885), where a facially neutral ordinance made laundry businesses illegal in San Francisco, with certain exceptions. Though fair and impartial on its face, it was declared unconstitutional, because the ordinance disparately impacted Chinese residents and was administered discriminatorily.

Though the law be fair on its face and impartial in its appearance, yet, if it is applied and administered by public authority with an evil eye and an unequal hand, so as practically to make unjust and illegal discriminations between persons in similar circumstances, material to their rights, the denial of equal justice is still within the prohibition of the Constitution.

Id. at 373-74.

Discrimination through facially neutral rules is perhaps more invidious than overt discrimination, because it is harder to prove as racially motivated and thus more difficult to ferret out. For example, a rule requiring English-only in public schools seems fair and neutral on its face unless it is enforced, as it was in Lau v. Nichols, 414 U.S. 563 (1974) in a school attended predominantly by Chinese-speaking students.

freedoms enshrined in the Bill of Rights, it falls upon the Congress to increase its vigilance in opposing discrimination through legislation.

History teaches the importance in every society of preventing the occurrence of outbreaks of discriminatory acts and practices and of the need to vigorously enforce human rights guarantees. In those nations which have permitted equal rights for all its citizens to lapse due to lack of government enforcement, serious human violations have quickly appeared. Almost universally, these violations have had rippling effects infringing on the rights of all citizens. Once minority groups fell victim to officially sanctioned discrimination, it was not long before death camps arose in nations such as Cambodia, Nazi Germany and the U.S.S.R. In many newly-established nations that formerly were colonies, while freedom for the majority was achieved, the indigenous population was excluded from the body politic. Widespread cultural and racial genocide was the consequence. This is presently evident in some Central and South American nations, as well as in South Africa.

If America is to provide strong moral leadership in the world today as a much needed beacon for freedom, our indigenous policies need to be vastly different from countries such as South Africa, which have questionable standing in the international community as a result of mistreatment of their original inhabitants. Like us, many nations are former colonies, and the way in which they treat their indigenous populations reflects their intrinsic values. Even if constitutional rights are ensured for a majority of society, a denial of constitutional protections for indigenous people is a heavy moral weight that may cloud a democracy's human rights foreign policy.

America's treatment of its native people is especially important, for domestic and international reasons. Domestically, it is true that all races and ethnic groups have historically faced various forms of discrimination in the United States, but the manner in which our country treats its indigenous native peoples provides a general barometer of our overall commitment to justice and freedom. As Felix S. Cohen, the "father" of Federal Indian law aptly stated in 1953, "[l]ike the miner's canary, the Indian marks the shifts from fresh air to poison gas in our political atmosphere; and our treatment of Indians, even more than our treatment of other minorities, reflects the rise and fall in our democratic faith. . . ."[10] Cohen realized that un-

---

10. FELIX COHEN, HANDBOOK OF FEDERAL INDIAN LAW (The Michie Co., 1982 ed.).

less our government institutions and social policy can protect America's smallest, poorest and weakest minority group from discrimination and injustice, they may also lack the strength and will to accord equal protection for the rest of society. What may be a trickling stream when one constitutional right is lost or the rights of one group are taken away, may become a tidal wave when other rights are also denied.

Cohen's "miner's canary" concern has proven true in the area of religious freedom, where the Supreme Court recently stripped Native Americans of free exercise rights in both *Lyng v. Northwest Indian Cemetery Protective Association*[11] and *Smith*.[12] These troubling cases not only pave the way for unchecked religious discrimination against Native Americans who have already suffered a long and shameful history of government religious suppression, but they also seriously weaken religious liberty for all Americans.

B.   The Equal Protection Remedy

The Fourteenth Amendment to the United States Constitution[13] guarantees that states will not deny individuals either due process or the equal protection of the law. The Fifth Amendment[14] binds the federal government to those same assurances. Equal protection of the law assures that persons who are similarly situated will be treated in a similar manner.[15] The Founding Fathers of our nation perceived that, under our democratic system, there existed a real danger of oppression to which minority groups would be subjected by the rule of the majority. The creation of the Equal Protection Clause was seen as a way to eliminate this threat and correspondingly protect the rights of minorities.

Although the Fifth and Fourteenth Amendments were created to protect minority freedoms, it was not until recently that the courts have construed the Equal Protection Clause in a manner consistent with this original intent. A pertinent example of the narrow

---

11. *Lyng*, 485 U.S. at 439.

12. *Smith*, 110 S. Ct. at 1595.

13. The Fourteenth Amendment provides in pertinent part, "nor shall any State deprive any person of life, liberty, or property, without due process of law; nor deny to any person within its jurisdiction the equal protection of the laws." U.S. Const. amend. XIV.

14. The Fifth Amendment provides in pertinent part, "nor be deprived of life, liberty, or property, without due process of law." U.S. Const. amend. V.

15. Royster Guano Co. v. Virginia, 253 U.S. 412 (1920). *See also*, Joseph Tussman and Jacobus tenBroek, *The Equal Protection of the Laws*, 37 Cal. L. Rev. 341, 344 (1949).

interpretation the judiciary has taken in this regard occurred in 1896 when the Supreme Court approved the "separate but equal" doctrine in *Plessy v. Ferguson*.[16] That antiquated doctrine authorized invidious racial segregation and discrimination against African-Americans to exist as a matter of basic social policy. This fostered immeasurable harm to minorities and demonstrated that sometimes even a revered institution such as the United States Supreme Court cannot rise above prevailing social prejudices of the day. The Court justified the "separate but equal" doctrine with only thinly-veiled judicial sophistry.

> We consider the underlying fallacy of the plaintiff's argument to consist of the assumption that the enforced separation of the two races stamps the colored races with a badge of inferiority. If this be so, it is not by reason of anything found in the act, but solely because the colored race chose to put that construction upon it.[17]

The soul-crushing racism of the "separate but equal" doctrine continued unabated in the United States, without question from the executive and legislative branches until 1953. In that year Thurgood Marshall argued and won the landmark case of *Brown v. Board of Education*.[18] In *Brown*, the Supreme Court recognized that segregation of schoolchildren on the basis of race "generates a feeling of inferiority as to their status in the community that may affect their hearts and minds in a way unlikely ever to be undone"[19] and held that "in the field of public education the doctrine of 'separate but equal' has no place. Separate educational facilities are inherently unequal."[20]

It is difficult today for us to contemplate how our Supreme Court ever resolved to deny important human rights safeguards to many of our citizens, so repugnant is the former interpretation of the Equal Protection Clause to contemporary beliefs. The harm suffered by millions of people was real and remains a permanent scar in the lives of many Americans today. For the sake of those victims and any possible future victims, we must be vigilant against future confusion in affording equal treatment for all citizens under the law.

Other examples demonstrate that breaches in equal protection principles, although they be of brief duration, may have lasting ad-

---

16. *Plessy*, 163 U.S. at 538.
17. *Id.* at 551.
18. *Brown*, 347 U.S. at 483.
19. *Id.* at 494.
20. *Id.* at 494-95.

verse affects upon the casualties of discrimination. At the beginning of World War II, the United States government removed about 120,000 Japanese-Americans from their homes and placed them in internment camps. This mass confinement was a serious curtailment of the civil rights of this minority group, effected solely on the basis of race and without regard for the constitutional rights of American citizens. The United States Congress authorized this unjust policy, and it was in turn implemented by the executive branch of our government. It was reviewed and approved by the Supreme Court in *Mirabayashi v. United States*[21] and in *Korematsu v. United States*.[22] Although it is shocking for us today to realize that an entire ethnic group was incarcerated, at one time in our history, for no reason other than its racial affiliation, it was not until one generation later, in 1988, that this miscarriage of justice was rectified when Congress acted to grant reparations to the internees.[23]

C. The Equal Protection Standard of Review and the American Indian

Traditionally, in analyzing equal protection challenges, the Court applies a two-tier level of review.[24] The extent to which a law must satisfy the Equal Protection Clause is dependent upon a determination of the purpose that was intended by the legislation and the relationship that the different treatment has to achieving the particular governmental aim.[25]

The mere rationality level of review is applied to classifications made on the basis of economics or other social legislation. Such laws are subject only to very limited review. There is a presumption that the law is valid. A challenger must show that the law has no rational relationship to any legitimate government objective.[26]

When a law affects a suspect classification or places a significant burden on the exercise of a fundamental right, it will be strictly scrutinized and upheld only if it is necessary to achieve a compelling state objective and no less burdensome means are available to achieve that end.[27] There is no longer a presumption of constitu-

---

21. Mirabayashi v. United States, 320 U.S. 81 (1943).

22. Korematsu v. United States, 323 U.S. 214 (1944).

23. Japanese Reparations Act, 50 U.S.C § 1989 (1988). Many question the equity of this remedial act.

24. Gerald Gunther, *The Supreme Court 1971 Term Forward: In Search of Evolving Doctrine on a Changing Court: A Model for a Newer Equal Protection*, 86 HARV. L. REV. 1 (1972).

25. Chicago Police Dept. v. Moseley, 408 U.S. 91 (1972).

26. McGowan v. Maryland, 366 U.S. 425, 426 (1961).

27. This standard of review was applied in Shelly v. Kramer, 334 U.S. 1 (1948)

tionality, requiring the government to satisfy a heavy and difficult burden. Classifications based upon race and national origin have been held to be suspect, requiring this stringent type of review.[28]

Suspect classes are determined by considering factors such as a history of pervasive discrimination against the class, the stigmatizing effect of the classification, the fact that the classification is based on an immutable characteristic beyond a person's ability to control, and the consideration that the discrimination is against a discrete and insular minority.[29] In order to qualify as a suspect class, the group of persons affected by the classification must be somehow disadvantaged because of prior discriminatory treatment.[30]

Recently the Court has reviewed several cases in which the judiciary declined to treat with deference legislative determinations creating the affected classifications. An intermediate level of review appears to have been employed—such classifications must be substantially related to an important government interest.[31] This standard of review has been applied to classifications affecting gender and illegitimacy.[32]

It cannot be disputed that the American Indian is entitled to be treated the same as other United States citizens under the Constitution. Early Supreme Court decisions such as *Yick Wo v. Hopkins*[33]

---

where enforcement of a racially restrictive covenant by state court, pursuant to the state's policy for enforcing such agreements, constituted state action for the purpose of the Fourteenth Amendment.

28. *See, e.g., Korematsu*, 323 U.S. at 216 (classifications involving race); Hernandez v. Texas, 347 U.S. 475 (1954) (classifications involving national orgin); Sugarman v. Dougall, 413 U.S. 624 (1973) (classifications involving alienage).

29. *See* United States v. Carolene Product Co., 304 U.S. 144 (1938). Justice Stone stated that courts must protect certain "discrete and insular minorities," who are made victims of prejudicial attitudes and so are denied access to the "political processes ordinarily to be relied upon to protect minorities." *Id.* at 152 n.4. The Justice explained that legislation enacted that affects this type of minority group must be "subjected to more exacting judicial scrutiny under the general prohibition of the 14th Amendment than are most other types of legislation." *Id.*

30. San Antonio School District v. Rodriguez, 411 U.S. 1, 28 (1973) (one of the criteria to qualify as a suspect class is that the particular class be "subjected to such a history of purposeful unequal treatment, or relegated to such a position of political powerlessness as to command extraordinary protection from the majoritarian political process"). *Id.*

31. *See* Trimble v. Gordon, 430 U.S. 762 (1977); Craig v. Boren, 429 U.S. 190 (1976).

32. *See, e.g.*, Reed v. Reed, 404 U.S. 71 (1971) (gender); *Trimble*, 430 U.S. at 762 (illegitimacy); Weber v. Aetna Casualty & Surety Co., 406 U.S. 164 (1972) (illegitimacy); Levy v. Louisiana, 391 U.S. 68 (1968) (illegitimacy).

33. *Yick Wo*, 63 U.S. at 356 (equal protection guarantees contained in the Fourteenth Amendment to the Constitution extend to all persons within the territorial

and *Wong Wing v. United States*[34] clearly established that the guarantees of the Equal Protection Clause applied universally "to all persons within the territorial jurisdiction of the United States."[35] Yet in considering equal protection challenges in cases affecting Indians, the analysis used by the courts differs from the traditional equal protection standard of review, regardless of whether these claims are brought under the United States Constitution or the Indian Civil Rights Act.[36]

Legisation affecting the American Indian is enacted to deal with the "so-called 'Indian problem.' [W]e often talk about the 'Indian problem' as if it were a disease. . . ."[37] Early equal protection cases established that legislation affecting Indians was constitutionally valid as long as it was based, not on race, but instead on "the political or ancestral affiliation of an individual to a tribe. If that affiliation were severed, the individual would no longer be considered an Indian within the meaning of the legislation."[38]

Modern federal court decisions have analyzed equal protection as it applies to Indians in an unusual manner. Rather than considering such legislation as classifications based on race, such laws are held to intend to promote the "trust responsibility" that the federal government has toward Indians who either are members of tribes that fall within the United States' trust relationship, or who have

---

jurisdiction of the United States "without regard to any differences of race, or color, or of nationality.") *Id.* at 369.

34. Wong Wing v. United States, 163 U.S. 223 (1896) ("[A]ll persons within the territory of the United States are entitled to the protection guaranteed by those amendments, and that even aliens shall not be held to answer for a capital or other infamous crime, unless of a presentment to a grand jury, nor be deprived of life, liberty or property without due process of law.") *Id.* at 238.

35. Plyler v. Doe, 457 U.S. 202, 210-12 (1982).

36. Ralph W. Johnson and E. Susan Crystal, *Indians and Equal Protection,* 54 WASH. L. REV. 587, 588 (1979). The Indian Civil Rights Act is codified at 25 U.S.C. §§ 1301-1341 (1976).

37. Rennard Strickland, *Indian Law and Policy: The Historian's Viewpoint,* 54 WASH. L. REV. 475 (1979).

38. *Id.* at 594 (noting early cases such as Montoya v. United States, 180 U.S. 261 (1901) and United States v. Rogers, 45 U.S. (4 How.) 572 (1846)). The author notes that these cases referred to Indians as a "race," although more contemporary cases do not. The contemporary concept of the race of Indians includes Indians from the Caribbean, Latin America and Canada, none of whom enjoy a special status under United States law. In addition, there are United States citizens who, although racially Indian, do not share the special status. Reasons for that lack of status include: (1) the tribe is one with which the United States has never assumed a trust relationship; (2) the tribe has been terminated by Congress, *see, e.g.*, 25 U.S.C. § 564 (1976); and (3) the individual has severed his or her tribal ties, *see* Standing Bear v. Crook, 25 F. Cas. 695 (C.C.D. Neb. 1879) (No. 14,891). *Id.*

ancestral ties to persons who are tribal members. Courts then test this type of legislation with a standard of review that is not applied to other classifications. Laws are valid if they are "rationally" related to achieving Congress' "unique" obligation toward Indians.[39]

My personal opinion is that as long as we profess to strive to maintain democratic principals and seek to provide leadership for the free world, we must not acquiesce to the existence of discrimination against any group within our society, and especially not against our original inhabitants. As stated by one commentator: "What is needed is a new perception of the Indian, a perception of the Indian not as a problem to be corrected, but as peoples with rights, duties, and powers."[40]

III. RELIGIOUS DISCRIMINATION AGAINST NATIVE AMERICANS

A. History

Religious intolerance and supression of tribal religions of Native Americans in the United States is not new. In fact, this form of discrimination has characterized the relationship between our indigenous population and newcomers from Europe for the past 500 years. On his first day in the Western Hemisphere, Christopher Columbus reflected the prevailing view of religious intolerance when he penned his impression of the Indians he encountered: "I believe that they would easily be made Christians because it seemed to me that they had no religion."[41] In the minds of Europeans, tribal religions of the New World were inferior.

> When white men first witnessed Indians impersonating animal spirits in costume and dance, and worshipping rocks and rainbows, they failed to see this as a deep form of religious worship. To their Christian minds, these were deplorable pagan rites. Worship of more than one diety, and sacrificial offerings, directed at the natural world, stamped Indians as a misguided, lesser form of mankind. Here were Christless heathens crying to be rescued from eternal damnation.[42]

Thus, it is not surprising—especially given Europe's own heri-

---

39. Johnson and Crystal, *supra* note 36, at 607. The authors state that this standard of review is "somewhat" greater than the mere rationality level of review, although it seems to be closer to that test than to strict scrutiny. *Id.*

40. Strickland, *supra* note 37, at 478.

41. K. SALE, THE CONQUEST OF PARADISE, 96-97 (1990).

42. P. NABAKOV, NATIVE AMERICAN TESTIMONY: AN ANTHOLOGY OF INDIAN AND WHITE RELATIONS, 60 (1978).

tage of religious discrimination among unpopular Christian denominations and against non-Christian world religions—that intolerance became a basic feature in the Pilgrims' and other colonists' relationship with the Indians. Indeed, although early settlers came to America to escape religious persecution, Old World prejudices were transplanted in the Colonies, where religious discrimination soon became commonplace.[43]

The Establishment Clause of the First Amendment[44] was intended to curb these abuses of the colonists' religious freedom by preventing majoritarian support for popular religious denominations.[45] From the beginning, the federal government's effort to convert Indians to Christianity became a cornerstone of its federal Indian policy.[46] As one commentator noted:

> The government and the religious societies were intertwined in their efforts to civilize and Christianize the Indians throughout the nineteenth Century. The government supported missionaries with funds, assigned agencies to religious societies, and provided land for the building of churches. The question is whether this intermingling consituted an establishment of religion.[47]

As may be expected, government violation of Indian religious freedoms in respect to the Establishment Clause was soon followed by an incursion on these freedoms alternatively protected by the Free Exercise Clause, which prohibits governmental intrusion on the practice of religion. Outright prohibition of tribal religions by the federal government began in the 1890's. Federal troops slaughtered Indian practitioners of the Ghost Dance at Wounded Knee, and systematically suppressed this tribal religion on other Indian

---

43. *See* Everson v. Board of Education, 330 U.S. 1, 8-12 (1946).

44. The First Amendment provides: *"Congress shall make no law respecting an establishment of religion, or prohibiting the free exercise thereof;* or abridging the freedom of speech, or of the press; or the right of the people to peaceably assemble, and to petition the Government for the redress of grievances." (emphasis added). U.S. Const. amend. I.

45. Laurence H. Tribe, American Constitutional Law, § 14-3 at 1158-61 (2d ed. 1988).

46. *See, e.g.*, Quick Bear v. Leupp, 210 U.S. 50 (1908) (government's use of federal funds to establish a Catholic church on the Rosebud Indian Reservation did not violate the Establishment Clause).

47. The American Indian Religious Freedom Act Report, Federal Agencies Task Force, Secretary of the Interior (Department of the Interior, August, 1979) at 3-6. This report recounts the history of government treatment of Indian religions and was part of a study mandated by Section 2 of the American Indian Religious Freedom Act (AIRFA), Pub. L. No. 95-341, Section 1, 92 Stat. 469 (1978). *See also*, Martin, *Constitutional Rights and Indian Rites: An Uneasy Balance, in* 3 Western Legal History 245, 246-252.

Reservations. In 1892 and 1904, federal regulations outlawed the practice of tribal religions entirely, and punished Indian practitioners by either confinement in the agency prisons or by withholding rations.[48]

This ban was not lifted until 1934, more than one generation later. Unfortunately, our government still persisted in infringing upon tribal religious practices. Federal agents arrested Indians for possession of sacred objects such as peyote, eagle feathers, and the cut hair of Indian children. By authority of the federal government, these agents also prohibited schoolchildren from speaking their native languages, prevented native access to holy places located on public lands, destroyed Indian sacred sites, and interfered with tribal ceremonies.[49]

In 1978, Congress sought to reverse this history by creating a resolution establishing a federal policy to preserve and protect Native American religious freedom.[50] The Committees responsible for this measure stated: "America does not need to violate the religions of her native people. There is room for and great value in cultural and religious diversity. We would all be the poorer if these American Indian religions disappeared from the face of the Earth."[51]

However, it requires cooperation from all three branches of government in our system to effectively implement a Congressional policy. Unfortunately, such support was not forthcoming, and the enlightened attitudes expressed in the Act in regard to Indian religious freedom have never been effectuated.[52] The federal courts have since ruled that this policy has no mechanism of enforcement.[53] As a result of recent decisions denying Native Americans religious freedom guaranteed by the First Amendment, it appears that we are regressing to a dark period where once again our gov-

---

48. American Indian Religious Freedom Act Report, *supra* note 47, at 22; Regulations of the Indian Office, effective April 1, 1904, Secretary of the Interior (Washington: Government Printing Office, 1904) at 102-3.

49. *See*, Articles by Vine Deloria, Jr. and Walter Echo-Hawk *in* SPECIAL EDITION ON RELIGIOUS FREEDOM: TODAY'S CHALLENGE, 16 NATIVE AMERICAN RIGHTS FUND LEGAL REVIEW, (No. 2, Summer 1991).

50. AIRFA, *supra* note 47.

51. H.R. Rep. No. 1308, 95th Cong., 2d. Sess. 3 (1978); S. Rep. No. 709, 95th Cong., 2d. Sess. 3 (1978).

52. *See generally*, S. Moore, *Sacred Sites and Public Lands, in* HANDBOOK OF AMERICAN INDIAN RELIGIOUS FREEDOM 81-89 (Christopher Vescey ed., 1991).

53. *See, e.g.*, Wilson v. Block, 708 F. 2d 735, 745-47 (D.C. Cir. 1983). "Thus AIRFA requires federal agencies to consider, but not necessarily to defer to Indian religious values. It does not prohibit agencies from adopting all land uses that conflict with traditional Indian religious beliefs or practices." *Id.* at 747.

ernment is allowing religious discrimination against our indigenous citizens to go unchecked.

B.   *The Lyng and Smith Decisions*

Alarmingly, the Supreme Court has of late exhibited a growing insensitivity toward Native American religious freedom. In *Lyng v. Northwest Indian Cemetery Protective Ass'n*,[54] the Court allowed the Forest Service to virtually destroy an ancient Indian sacred site located on federal land. The Court arrived at this abominable decision by construing the Free Exercise Clause in the most narrow way imaginable, holding that this First Amendment guarantee only provides protection against laws which coerce citizens to violate their religion or punishes them for practicing their beliefs.[55]

As a result of *Lyng*, a growing number of irreplaceable tribal sacred sites are no longer under government protection and are currently being destroyed. The desecration of Indian holy places causes great concern by those citizens interested in the cultural survival of the Indian nations, and distressed at what this loss would mean to our nation's cultural heritage in general. However, the retreat from First Amendment religious protection signified by *Lyng* went largely unnoticed, probably because the worship of the land, including mountain tops and waterfalls, is a practice unique in our country to Native Americans.[56]

It was not until its 1990 decision in *Smith*[57] that the Supreme Court's insensitivity to Native religious rights came to the attention of the general public. In that case, the Court affirmed the decision of an Oregon Employment Appeals Board denying unemployment compensation to two Native Americans who were terminated from their employment as counselors with a substance abuse rehabilitation center because of their participation in a sacramental peyote ceremony.

Peyote, used for centuries by Indians in religious ceremonies, is a cactus plant that grows only along the Rio Grande River, near the Texas and Mexican border. Today, this religion is among the most ancient, largest and most continuously practiced indigenous reli-

---

54. *Lyng*, 485 U.S. at 439.

55. *Id.* at 547.

56. For an explanation of the role of sacred sites in American Indian tribal religions, *see* Vine Deloria, Jr. *Sacred Lands and Religious Freedom*, 16 NATIVE AMERICAN RIGHTS FUND LEGAL REVIEW, 1, 1-6 (No. 2, Summer 1991).

57. *Smith*, 110 S. Ct. at 1595.

gions in the Western Hemisphere.[58] As found in *People v. Woody*:[59]

> Peyotism discloses a long history. A reference to the religious use of peyote in Mexico appears in Spanish historical sources as early as 1560. Peyotism spread from Mexico to the United States and Canada: American anthropologists describe it as well established in this country during the latter part of the nineteenth century. Today, Indians of many tribes practice Peyotism.[60]

Peyote is used as a sacrament, but it is considered by Native Americans to be more important in their religion than the use of wine in Christian services. The court in *Woody* stated: "Although peyote serves as a sacramental symbol similar to bread and wine in certain Christian churches, it is more than a sacrament. Peyote constitutes in itself an object of worship; prayers are devoted to it much as prayers are devoted to the Holy Ghost."[61]

Federal law and twenty-eight states have permitted the religious use of peyote by Native Americans for decades through statutory, administrative, or judicially-created religious exemptions from drug laws, and there has been no discernable law enforcement, public safety or health problem created as a result of this policy. Although the state law of Oregon does not allow for such an exemption, the Supreme Court of Oregon determined that the decision to disallow unemployment benefits to two Native American rehabilitation counselors could not withstand federal constitutional scrutiny.[62]

Prior to *Smith*, it was settled constitutional law that a two-part balancing test would be used to determine the validity of a law which incidentally burdened religion. Once parties challenging legislation demonstrated that their belief was sincere and that the state action imposed a substantial burden on their religious practice, the government was required to show that the law was enacted to achieve a compelling state interest by the least restrictive means available.[63] However, in *Smith*, the Court broke with precedent and

---

58. OMER C. STEWART, PEYOTE RELIGION: A HISTORY (Univ. of Okla. Press, 1987).

59. People v. Woody, 394 P. 2d 813, 817 (1964).

60. *Id.*

61. *Id.*

62. Black v. Employment Div., 301 Or. 221, 721 P.2d 451 (1986); Smith v. Employment Div., 301 Or. 209, 721 P. 2d 445 (1986).

63. RONALD D. ROTUNDA, ET AL., TREATISE ON CONSTITUTIONAL LAW, SUBSTANCE AND PROCEDURE, § 21.8 at 401-402 (1986). *See* Hobbie v. Unemployment Appeals Comm'n, 480 U.S. 136 (1987); Thomas v. Review Board, 450 U.S. 707 (1981); Wisconsin v. Yoder, 406 U.S. 205 (1972); Sherbert v. Verner, 374 U.S. 398, 402-403 (1963).

rejected the traditional balancing test. The protection of the diversity of minority religions in our country was found to be a "luxury," and the extension of First Amendment guarantees to unpopular faiths would be "courting anarchy."[64]

The decision also suggested that the Free Exercise Clause may not protect religious adherents against government intrusion unless some other right guaranted by the First Amendment was also affected.[65] In a concurring opinion, Justice O'Connor nevertheless strongly criticized the majority opinion for not applying the traditional standard of review in this case.[66] Justice Blackmun wrote a strong dissent, joined by Justices Marshall and Brennan.

For Indians, the decision in *Smith* creates the frightening specter of a return to the era when tribal people could be imprisoned for practicing their religion. In the wake of *Smith*, the State of Oklahoma is currently prosecuting an elderly, life-long member of the Native American Church for possession of peyote. As a result of the decision in *Smith* and *Lyng*, all of our indigenous inhabitants who wish to worship according to the dictates of their conscience are in danger. As Peterson Zah, President of the Navajo Nation, in a plea for Indian religious liberty recently stated:

> Indians do not have the same religious freedoms as other Americans, even though their ceremonies developed thousands of years before Europeans—many of them fleeing religious persecution—settled in the United States. . . . Respect should be given to a religion that does not involve going to church one day a week, but which is based on animals, the world and the universe, and whose church is the mountains, rivers, clouds and sky. . . .[67]

After Cohen's allegorical "miner's canary" was in effect snuffed out by these decisions, religious organizations and constitutional scholars finally rose up to call to public attention the fact that a cherished constitutional right was in danger of being extinguished. As stated in a recent Time cover story:

> For all the rifts among religious and civil-libertarian groups, this decision brought a choir of outrage singing full-voice. A whole clause of the Bill of Rights had been abolished, critics charged, and the whole concept of religious freedom was now imperiled. "On the really small and odd religious groups," said University of

---

64. *Smith*, 110 S. Ct. at 1605.
65. *Id.* at 1601.
66. *Id.* at 1610-11.
67. ALBUQUERQUE JOURNAL, Nov. 23, 1991, at 1.

Texas' Laycock, "it's just open season."[68]

As federal courts are now constrained to follow *Smith*, we can expect a rash of decisions denying citizens who are not members of mainstream Judeo-Christian religions the protections of the First Amendment.[69] Although the Solarz Bill,[70] proposed for the purpose of restoring the "compelling state interest" balancing test, is intended to redress this situation, it does not deal with concerns unique to the practice of Native American religions. Also, there is no guarantee that the courts will not attempt to weaken this legislation in future Indian religion cases.

IV. CONCLUSION

The treatment of Native American religious freedom and our government's attitudes toward their civil rights as citizens has been a long-standing problem. Today, 500 years after Columbus arrived on this continent, it is intolerable that our original inhabitants are still not treated as the equal of other citizens under the Constitution. At this juncture in history, we are finally becoming aware that the curtailment of freedoms enshrined in the Bill of Rights in respect to certain minority groups may also affect the rights of all citizens.

Because of the failure of the judicial and executive branches of government in this regard, it is now incumbent upon Congress to begin to focus on this serious human rights problem in our country, with a view towards redressing religious discrimination against Native Americans. It is imperative that we guarantee that their freedom of worship is protected. This is mandated not only by the Constitution, but also by the trust relationship between the federal government and the Indian Tribal governments, which has been honored by all three branches of government since the 1830's.

Today, there is a need for our society to rededicate itself to allowing equal protection of the laws for all citizens. With the col-

---

68. TIME, Dec. 9, 1991, at 68.

69. *See,* Hunafa v. Murphy, 907 F.2d 46, 48 (7th Cir. 1990); International Center for Justice and Peace v. I.N.S., 910 F. 2d 42 (2d Cir. 1990); Salvation Army v. N.J. Dept. of Community Affairs, 919 F.2d 183, 194-95 (3rd Cir. 1990); Salam v. Lockhart, 905 F.2d 1168, 1171 n.1 (8th Cir. 1990); South Ridge Baptist Church v. Indus. Comm'n of Ohio, 911 F.2d 1203, 1213 (6th Cir. 1990); Cornerstone Bible Church v. City of Hastings, Mich., 740 F. Supp 654, 669-70 (D. Mich. 1990); Montgomery v. County of Clinton, 743 F. Supp. 1253, 1259 (W.D. Mich., 1990); Yang v. Sturner, 750 F. Supp. 558, 559 (D. R.I. 1990).

70. Solarz, *supra* note 4.

lapse of communism, historic opportunities exist for us to provide freedom and equality throughout the world. That international challenge cannot be met if America's commitment to liberty for all is not strong. We must take a stand to reject racism, discrimination and prejudice. It is now time for us to accord respect and equality to American Indians, especially in regard to their right to worship in the manner that their ancestors have for centuries before them. If the First Americans cannot be secure in such freedom, the liberty of all Americans stands in danger.

THE FIRST AMERICANS AND THE "FREE" EXERCISE OF RELIGION

*Martin C. Loesch**

Introduction

October 1992 marked the quincentennial of the "discovery" of the North and South American continents by European explorers. The occasion provides a fitting opportunity to review the history of interaction between the people of the Americas and the Europeans. As European greed and populations expanded, their explorers headed west in search of land and wealth. They brought to this hemisphere not only immigrants, but also new political structures, cultures, traditions, religions, technologies, economic systems, biases, diseases, languages, and foods. Those imports radically changed the lives and land of the aboriginal peoples they encountered.

When Columbus arrived in the Caribbean in the fall of 1492, he discovered a land already inhabited by millions of people, organized into distinct political and cultural groups. To him they were only heathen savages suitable for servitude, but in fact centuries of civilization and sophisticated systems of spiritual beliefs had developed among them on a continent rich in resources. The domination of the indigenous people in the Americas began with the first people Columbus encountered, the Arawaks, who were taken "by force in order that they might learn and give [Columbus] information of whatever there is in these parts."[1] After Columbus' second expedition to the area he brought 500 Arawak men, women, and children back to Spain as slaves.

In the 250 years that followed, the population of the Arawaks was cut in half by genocide, slave labor, and disease.[2] The European explorers enslaved, exterminated, or removed these aboriginal people who occupied the land they needed for expansion. The Europeans, like the Arawaks, appreciated the

---

© 1993 Martin C. Loesch

* Associate, Gordon & Polscer, Seattle, Wash. B.A. 1987, University of Notre Dame; J.D. 1991, University of Notre Dame Law School; L.L.M. 1992, University of Notre Dame Law School. Many thanks to Dr. Sharon L. O'Brien and to (Rev.) William M. Lewers, C.S.C., whose friendship, inspiration and support made this article possible.

This article updates material previously published in the September 1993 *Canadian Law Reporter*.

1. HOWARD ZINN, A PEOPLE'S HISTORY OF THE UNITED STATES 1 (1980).

2. In North America, the estimated 10 million Indians inhabiting the continent at the time Columbus arrived would eventually be reduced to one million. *Id.* at 16. More recent scholarship has concluded that the total population of the hemisphere was 75 million to 100 million (with eight million to 12 million people living north of present-day Mexico). DAVID E. STANNARD, AMERICAN HOLOCAUST: COLUMBUS AND THE CONQUEST OF THE NEW WORLD 11 (1992). The Arawak people alone likely numbered close to eight million. *Id.* at 72.

abundance of resources in this land, but to the Spanish these resources meant opportunity for economic gain. In the name of progress and religious enlightenment the entire Arawak way of life was sacrificed. Their history was to be repeated time and time again whenever the Europeans discovered new uses for the land which was the home of the people they called "savages." These civilized Europeans took the land, the culture, the spirituality, the children, and the vitality of the "savages" they conquered. The Native Americans continue to struggle today to regain what has been taken from them.

Because the peoples of the Americas are too many, and their struggles to continue to practice their "religions" are too varied for one article to cover comprehensively, this article will focus on the experience of the northern Native Peoples in what has become the United States. The international influence of the legal system of the United States recommends its history of relationship with its native population as an example of the treatment of indigenous peoples. For all its abuses, the legal relationship between the Indian nations of North America and the United States government is seen as quite positive.[3] Some tribes still retain a semblance of independent legal status, and the political process continues to bring Indian concerns to the fore. The decisions of the United States Supreme Court and the statements of the United States Congress will provide the context for a brief overview of the conditions of the North American indigenous peoples throughout the history of the United States.

This article will trace the legal history of the Native Americans, especially in their fight for respect for their spiritual practices. To set the stage for the drama of this spiritual and cultural tragedy, this article will first draw out the backdrop of the relationship between the first Americans and the European immigrants. The initial section of this article will show that the dominant culture has vacillated between respecting the autonomy of the Native Peoples and compelling their assimilation into United States society. This article will discuss some of the prevailing attitudes and theories that undergirded the frequently brutal and exploitive, and occasionally the benign, actions of the government with respect to these people.

The second section focuses specifically on the legal question of the right of the Native Americans to freely practice their spiritual beliefs.[4] This section will first briefly summarize the history of religious rights in the United States, then describe how evolving free exercise jurisprudence has impacted Native American free exercise claims. The cases and jurisprudence pertaining to

---

3. VINE DELORIA, GOD IS RED 282 (1973). Vine Deloria even says that "[a]mong all the nations of the world the United States, because of its secular concern for justice, has created the best record for dealing with aboriginal peoples." *Id.*

4. "Congress shall make no law respecting an establishment of religion, or prohibiting the free exercise thereof . . . ." U.S. CONST. amend. I.

"sacred site" claims will be the focus of some attention. In these cases, Indians attempt to protect particular places from government actions which threaten to limit the ability of Native Americans to practice their "religion." The *Lyng v. Northwest Cemetery Protective Ass'n*[5] decision is the most recent Supreme Court opinion addressing a sacred site claim, and section three will attend to the questions raised by that case in some detail.

The fourth section attempts to delineate some of the reasons why Native American spiritual practices receive so little protection. Because most of the judicial decisions reflect serious misunderstandings about Indian spiritual beliefs, this section summarizes some of the prominent features of Indian spirituality. There is a wealth of scholarship on this subject which cannot be exhausted in this forum, but this section will highlight some salient differences, because the religions of the majority culture and the spirituality of Native Americans.

There is little cause for hope at the present time. Indian blood is no longer being shed to advance white civilization, but as one Native American said, "They're not killing us on the plains anymore. Now they're killing us in the courts." The result is not substantively different even though the campaign is more subtle.

There are two potential avenues for reform and the fifth section of this article describes their promise. The first requires jurisprudential reform, in the form of a resuscitation of the worn-out Free Exercise Clause of the First Amendment. The Court must recognize that Native American spiritual practice claims are different from the nonreligious practice claims other groups legitimately make upon the state. When Native Americans predicate their claims against the government on religious grounds, they deserve to be treated the same as all others who claim protection for religious practice. No foreseeable judicial reform is on the horizon. The Supreme Court has abdicated its responsibility to protect Native American rights and in *Lyng* stated that the only potential solutions were legislative.[6]

The American Indian Religious Freedom Act (AIRFA)[7] had the potential to provide the kind of protection that Native American religious practices require. The courts have, however, construed the statute very narrowly so as to be "without teeth."[8] Several amendments have been proposed to strengthen AIRFA.[9] Unfortunately, those amendments failed to receive sufficient legislative support. Congress in 1993 has had before it both the Religious Freedom Restoration Act[10] and the Native American Free Exercise of

---

5. 485 U.S. 439 (1988).

6. *Id.* at 458.

7. Pub. L. No. 95-341, 92 Stat. 469 (codified at 42 U.S.C. § 1996 (1988)).

8. *See infra* § II, pt. C.

9. 1990, 1991, 1992.

10. H.R. 1308, 103d Cong., 1st Sess. (1993); S. 578, 103d Cong., 1st Sess. (1993). *See infra*

Religion Act.[11] These bills represent the only realistic hope Native Americans have today for their ability to practice their spiritual beliefs and their way of life. This legislation will provide the legal recourse Native Americans have not found in the Constitution. Although they do not provide the permanent protections that Native Americans deserve, they should both be passed. Congress passed the Religious Freedom Restoration Act and President Clinton signed it into law on November 16, 1993,[12] but the prospects for the passage of the Native American Free Exercise of Religion Act are not good. Only passage of both bills will provide the measure of protection Native American spiritual practices merit.

These recommendations will be supported in due time, but first it is necessary to present some of the history and context of these issues. The history of the first peoples on this continent is important in part because their stories have been silenced, as the stories of women, African-Americans, gays and lesbians, refugees, and other oppressed peoples have been silenced before. The histories of the First Peoples are not often considered in abstract legal debates about jurisprudence, excessive entanglement, compelling interests, or legislative policy. Those stories have not often been told with the honesty and humility that centuries of abuse, deception, and disrespect should engender. Our present political discussion is impoverished if we fail to consider what has transpired in the past. Only with a clear understanding of our collective history can advocates and policy makers begin to appreciate the importance of the issues at hand.

I. The Indigenous Americans

A. The Colonial Period (1492-1776)

Europeans justified the acquisition of land in the Americas two ways: first, as the religious duty of an enlightened and civilized people; and second, as the legal result of "discovering" previously unclaimed land. The colonizing powers secured their interests in the new land by proving to other European powers that they were the first to "discover" a new piece of territory. This rationalization became known as the "Discovery Doctrine," a geographic "first come, first served" theory in which the only relevant players were the competing European countries.[13] The existence of native populations on these territories was irrelevant to colonial claims.

Francisco de Vitoria, the Spanish legal philosopher and theologian, challenged the validity of the doctrine of discovery, arguing that the Indians

---

note 12 and accompanying text.

11. S. 1021, 103d Cong., 1st Sess. (1993).

12. Religious Freedom Restoration Act of 1993, Pub. L. No. 103-141, 107 Stat. 1488.

13. STANNARD, *supra* note 2, at 234-36.

were the true owners of the land. He believed that the "aborigines undoubted-ly had true dominion in both public and private matters, just like Christians and that neither their princes nor private persons could be despoiled of their property on the ground of their not being true owners."[14] Vitoria's views were predicated on a fundamental belief in human equality. Indians were no different from Europeans, he reasoned, and therefore their land could only be taken from them by consent or through conquest resulting from a just war.[15] Since the law between states at that time only recognized discovery as an authoritative source of title when the land was previously uninhabited, discovery of the inhabited territories in the East was inadequate to fend off other claimants.

Based on the "discovery" by Columbus, the Pope legitimized the claims of Spain to the "New World" and proclaimed her dominion over all lands previously unclaimed by other European powers.[16] The intersection between law and religion at this time was significant. Juan Gines de Sepúlveda, at the great debate at Valladolid organized by Charles V in Spain, argued that because the aboriginal people were not Christian, they therefore lacked any legitimate claim to their land, allowing it to be taken for the Church.[17] Sepúlveda, an eminent Spanish scholar, believed that the Indians were inferior barbarians who engaged in human sacrifice and who were destined for servitude.[18] The role of the State and the Church was to Christianize and civilize the "savages," purportedly for their own benefit.[19] The paganism of the "savages" justified the usurpation of their lands. There was no doubt that the new lands could be taken from the natives; the interesting question was whether those acquisitions could be protected from the other colonial powers. The Spanish argued that their discovery of the new continent, plus the papal grants, created an exclusive claim to the new territories.[20]

Bartolomé de Las Casas, the confrontational slave owner-turned-priest and champion of the Indian people, countered Sepulveda's argument. For five days at the debate, Las Casas recounted tales of Spanish cruelty toward the

14. ROBERT N. CLINTON ET AL., AMERICAN INDIAN LAW 139 (1991).

15. S. James Anaya, The Rights of Indigenous Peoples and International Law in Historical and Contemporary Perspective (1989) (symposium paper) in HARVARD INDIAN LAW SYMPOSIUM 211 (Harvard Law School Publications Center 1990).

16. BARTOLOMÉ DE LAS CASAS: THE ONLY WAY 10 (Helen R. Parish ed., Francis P. Sullivan trans., 1992) (citing POPE ALEXANDER VI, BULL OF DONATION (May 3, 1493)). Later popes were to overturn the doctrine of title by discovery or conquests supported by their predecessors. Pope Paul III argued that the Indians "are not to be deprived of their liberty or the right to their property. They are to have, to hold, to enjoy both liberty and dominion, freely, lawfully." *Id.* at 115 (citing SUBLIMIS DEUS (June 2, 1537)).

17. THOMAS R. BERGER, A LONG AND TERRIBLE SHADOW: WHITE VALUES, NATIVE RIGHTS IN THE AMERICAS, 1492-1992, at 20 (1991).

18. *Id.* at 20-21.

19. *Id.* at 3.

20. *Id.* at 17.

American natives. He described the Spaniards as "ravening beasts, killing, terrorizing, afflicting, torturing, and destroying the native peoples, doing all this with the strangest and most varied . . . methods of cruelty, never seen or heard before . . . ."[21] He claimed that the Spanish only had a right to enter Indian land to Christianize the Indians. Las Casas disputed Sepulveda's portrayal of the Indians as savages by describing their spiritual practices, their cultures, and their political organizations.[22]

No formal decision was reached at the debate at Valladolid. The discussion, both about the relationship between the Europeans and the American inhabitants and which, if any, European country held title to the newly acquired lands, continued among other thinkers. Hugo Grotius, the Dutch jurist and statesman, followed Sepulveda's reasoning. He believed that legal authority derived from universal norms rather than the acts of temporal authorities and positive law. Grotius aimed to remove the religious grounds for a just war and rejected title by discovery. Unlike some of the Spanish who viewed the Indians as brutish or inhuman,[23] Grotius acknowledged their ability to make treaties with the Europeans and their fundamental right to self-governance.[24]

The French and English contested the Spanish claims in America because the Spanish had not consummated their discovery with effective occupation and possession. England and France argued that only on those lands where Spain exercised control and maintained settlements could she claim dominion. Once the occupying powers dismissed paganism as grounds for a just war against the natives, colonization became the most acceptable proof of possession.

Unlike their Central and South American counterparts, the North American colonies were primarily English in origin, though the French and Spanish also had substantial land holdings. The relationship between the newly arrived English and the established indigenous people began with a gift and ended in virtual annihilation. The first immigrants were supported by the Indians and taught how to survive in the "new" land. Their generosity was not returned, however. For example, after Richard Greenville landed in Virginia in 1585, his party encountered an Indian who "stole" a silver cup.[25] Greenville plundered and burned the entire Indian village nearby. As more and more refugees from religious intoleration and poverty came to the colonies, land became scarce and the colonists took by force what the natives had earlier given freely.

---

21. *Id.* at 15 (citing BARTOLOMÉ DE LAS CASAS, THE DEVASTATION OF THE INDIES: A BRIEF ACCOUNT (Herma Briffault trans., 1974)).

22. *Id.* at 22.

23. *See* STANNARD, *supra* note 2, at 218.

24. BERGER, *supra* note 17, at 196.

25. ZINN, *supra* note 1, at 12.

The colonies were an export operation designed to return wealth to the European continent and Britain. The private charter companies commissioned by the colonizing powers viewed the New World as a source of raw materials and power. The colonists generally found it easier to cooperate with the local inhabitants, who had already established a system of trade and exchange, than to combat them. As a result, the companies actually purchased the title to land held by the natives and promised to respect Indian land holdings.[26] However, the experience of the natives was far from uniform. After settlement began in earnest, some of the colonies expropriated land by force while others maintained strictly diplomatic relations with the natives. The Crown set the basic policies, but each colony held general authority to manage its own affairs with the Indians.[27]

The Carolinas, for example, were developed by Indian slaves.[28] Early trading in deer skins gave way to trading in Indians after white settlers from Barbados brought the slave trade with them.[29] The Indians wanted guns, metal knives, and cooking utensils which the English offered in exchange for assistance in capturing slaves. In this way the tribes were encouraged to work and fight against one another. Despite condemnation from the government in England and from the Church, the settlers continued their brutal exploitation of Indian slave labor.[30] These English entrepreneurs were not troubled by the issues of the debate between Las Casas and Sepulveda.[31] Theirs was an economic, not an evangelical mission, and the slave trade in Indians was a profitable business.

By the mid-1700s the less exploited tribes of the North were dissatisfied with the persistent land fraud, broken agreements, encroaching white settlement, and trade inequities.[32] Hostilities were frequent. The English government attempted to centralize relations with the Indians by appointing two agents to conduct the relations between the Indian nations and the Crown. The "Albany Conference" was convened in 1754 to address Indian complaints about fraudulent land transactions.[33] With the Royal Proclamation of 1763,[34] the Crown declared all lands west of the crest of the Appalachians to be Indian Territory and forbade English settlers from taking possession of those

---

26. Sharon L. O'Brien, The Application of International Law to the Legal Status of American Indians 21 (1978) (unpublished Ph.D. dissertation, University of Oregon) [hereinafter O'Brien, International Law].

27. CLINTON ET AL., *supra* note 14, at 140.

28. BERGER, *supra* note 17, at 47.

29. *Id.* at 48.

30. *Id.* at 51.

31. *Id.*

32. *Id.* at 60.

33. *Id.*

34. Royal Proclamation of 1763, *reprinted in* R.S.C., No. 1 app. I, at 1 (1985).

or any other lands reserved to the Indians.[35] The most important provision of the Proclamation prohibited land sales by anyone but the Crown.[36] The reservation of land not previously purchased or ceded was absolute.[37] The Appalachian crest became the "Proclamation Line."[38] In the short term, this segregation eased tensions by minimizing interaction.

The principal goals of British policy at this time were to preserve the colonial foothold on Native American soil so that the resources of the new land could continue to flow, and to avoid disruption of trade. The rights of the Indians were observed more often in rhetoric than in practice and the tradition of pushing the Indians further west began. Nonetheless, the property rights of most of the Indian nations were never again to receive as much respect as they did under English occupation.

B. A Change of Government (1776-1789)

During the Revolutionary War, almost every Indian nation fought on the side of the British.[39] The colonists, therefore, struggled valiantly to secure the neutrality of tribes who were not actively fighting. Even Henry Knox, the first Secretary of War, said, "The Indians, being the prior occupants possess the right of the soil."[40] He noted that "[i]t is a melancholy reflection, that our modes of population have been more destructive to the Indian natives than the conduct of the conquerors of Mexico and Peru. The evidence of this is the utter extirpation of nearly all the Indians in the most populous parts of the Union."[41] The first treaty between the emancipated colonists and the natives was signed on September 17, 1778. This treaty with the Delaware Indians guaranteed the territorial integrity of the Delaware lands, established trade relations, and even contemplated the possibility of an Indian state joining the new confederation at some point in the future.[42]

The Articles of Confederation provided for centralized regulation of Indian affairs by the Continental Congress.[43] After the revolution ended, however,

---

35. *Id.* at 5-6.

36. *Id.* at 6.

37. *Id.* at 5.

38. BERGER, *supra* note 17, at 62.

39. ZINN, *supra* note 1, at 124.

40. *Id.*; FRANCIS P. PRUCHA, DOCUMENTS OF UNITED STATES INDIAN POLICY 10 (1975).

41. PRUCHA, *supra* note 40, at 72 (citing HERBERT APTHEKAR, THE EARLY YEARS OF THE REPUBLIC: FROM THE END OF THE REVOLUTION TO THE FIRST ADMINISTRATION OF WASHINGTON (1783-1793) (1976)).

42. COMMISSIONER OF INDIAN AFFAIRS, TREATIES BETWEEN THE UNITED STATES OF AMERICA AND THE SEVERAL INDIAN TRIBES, FROM 1778 TO 1837, at 3 (Kraus Reprint Co., 1975) (1837).

43. ARTICLES OF CONFEDERATION art. IX, cl. 4 (U.S. 1781) ("The United States in Congress shall also have the sole and exclusive power of . . . regulating the trade and managing all affairs with the Indians, not members of any of the States, provided that the legislative right of any State within its own limits be not infringed or violated . . . .").

New York, North Carolina, and Georgia resisted federal control of what they saw as internal issues. The Continental Congress was unable to secure approval for a proposal to limit white encroachment onto Indian lands, and they settled instead on a provision restraining alienation (i.e., forbidding settlement) of Indian lands outside of state boundaries without the express approval of Congress.[44]

The ubiquitous debate over the rights of the immigrants to Indian land rose again during the period in which relationships among the several states were being established.[45] Was discovery enough to justify usurping Indian territory? Did the successful occupation of Indian lands by the colonists secure their claim to the land? Did the colonists' conquest over the Indians in battle give them title to the land? Were reparations to the Indians required for taking their territory? The Continental Congress appointed a committee to discuss these issues. The committee concluded "that it has long been the opinion of the country, supported by Justice and humanity, that the Indians have just claims to all lands occupied by and not fairly purchased from them."[46]

C. The Constitutional Period (1789-1803)

During this period, aboriginal claims to land were embroiled in a developing controversy between the states and the new federal government. This debate was to become the first constitutional issue relating to the Indians considered by the Supreme Court. Early uncertainty and ambiguity account for the numerous Native American land claims which continue to this day.

The Congress acted quickly to bring Indian Affairs under the ambit of its authority. The Trade and Intercourse Act of 1790[47] prohibited the sale of any Indian land to any person or state unless done so through the treaty process of the United States.[48] The new government thereby replicated the policy of the British Royal Proclamation of 1763.[49] The Act was amended or supplemented seven times[50] as the government reinterpreted the policies established by its treaties with the Indians and as the fledgling country struggled against the flood of white immigration in its efforts to enforce the Act.[51] The Act had established a system that simply proved to be unworkable. Too many

---

44. 25 JOURNALS OF THE CONTINENTAL CONGRESS 1774-1789, at 602 (Sept. 22, 1783) (Washington, U.S. Govt. Print. Off. 1904-37).

45. BERGER, *supra* note 17, at 73-74.

46. 33 JOURNALS OF THE CONTINENTAL CONGRESS 1774-1789, at 457 (Aug. 3, 1787) (Washington, U.S. Govt. Print. Off. 1904-37).

47. Ch. 33, 1 Stat. 137 (current versions in scattered sections of 18 U.S.C. & 25 U.S.C.).

48. *Id.* § 4, 1 Stat. at 138.

49. BERGER, *supra* note 17, at 70.

50. 1793, 1796, 1799, 1802, 1817, 1822, 1834.

51. BERGER, *supra* note 17, at 70.

white settlers wanted what the Indians had — land. They also did not want to wait for the wheels of the federal bureaucracy to turn.

Father Francis Paul Prucha, a political and native historian, has described the following fundamental elements of the federal Indian program at this time:

> (1) Protection of Indian rights to their land by setting definite boundaries for the Indian Country, restricting the whites from entering the area except under certain controls, and removing illegal intruders.
>
> (2) Control of the disposition of Indian lands by denying the right of private individuals or local governments to acquire land from the Indians by purchase or by other means.
>
> (3) Regulation of the Indian trade by determining the conditions under which individuals might engage in the trade, prohibiting certain classes of traders, and actually entering into the trade itself.
>
> (4) Control of the liquor traffic by regulating the flow of intoxicating liquor into the Indian Country and then prohibiting it altogether.
>
> (5) Provision for the punishment of crimes committed by members of one race against the other and compensation for damages suffered by one group at the hands of the other, in order to remove the occasions for private retaliation which led to frontier hostilities.
>
> (6) Promotion of civilization and education among the Indians, in the hope that they might be absorbed into the general stream of American society.[52]

These goals constituted the foundation of federal government relations with the Indians. Prodigious effort was expended to establish fixed territorial lines between Indian Country and non-Indian holdings, but the borders fluctuated dramatically. After illegal white settlements were established on Indian land, the federal government negotiated a new grant from the Indians to the United States. As new issues emerged, different aspects of these elements were emphasized and new treaties were drafted and ratified.

The changing policies regarding Indian land were also, in part, governed by simple facts. In 1790, slightly less than 4,000,000 whites occupied the Eastern seaboard of the United States. Fifty years later there were 13,000,000 immigrant non-Indians, 4,500,000 of which had crossed the crest of the Appalachians in violation of the inherited agreement between the Indians and

---

52. FRANCIS P. PRUCHA, AMERICAN INDIAN POLICY IN THE FORMATIVE YEARS 2-3 (1962), *cited in* CLINTON ET. AL., *supra* note 14, at 143.

the British made eighty years earlier. Clearly, population growth of this magnitude required an expanding land base.[53]

The purchase of the Louisiana Territory in 1803 provided some desperately needed land and eliminated competition from France on this continent. Unfortunately, much of this land was presently occupied by Indians who had been pushed off their ancestral homelands in the East. Congress enacted legislation authorizing the president to exchange land with a tribe living east of the Mississippi for lands the United States did not want west of the Mississippi. This solution seemed obvious, but difficulties in coercing the Indians to cooperate were to drag on for decades.

D. The Removal Period (1803-1861)

With the French out of the country and the English defeated in the War of 1812,[54] the Indians were the only remaining competition for territorial resources in the East. In order for whites to enjoy the benefit of the property purchased by President Thomas Jefferson, the Indians would have to leave. The idea of collecting the Indians into a state or states of their own persisted as a solution.[55]

The removal process began diplomatically. The 1817 Treaty with the Cherokees[56] provided that they trade their present lands for territory on the Arkansas and White rivers. This treaty, and others of the period,[57] introduced a new aspect to treaty making with the Indians. The government discovered that treaties could be used to divide the Indians amongst themselves. By destroying communal ownership of land and creating internal competition for land grants that were only awarded to "friendly" tribes or sub-sets of tribes, the federal government could educate the Indians in the civilizing aspects of competition as well as limit their ability to unite. Diplomatic efforts also preserved the foundation of legitimate title to Indian land if the government could show that it had been ceded voluntarily.

Three seminal Supreme Court decisions during this period, *Johnson v. M'Intosh*,[58] *Cherokee Nation v. Georgia*,[59] and *Worcester v. Georgia*,[60]

---

53. "[W]hen the eighteenth century was drawing to its close, less than 5000 native people remained alive in all of eastern Virginia, North Carolina, South Carolina, and Louisiana combined . . . ." STANNARD, *supra* note 2, at 121.

54. The War of 1812 was the last war in which the Indian nations participated militarily in the contest between European nations vying for control of North America. BERGER, *supra* note 17, at 64.

55. *Id.* at 69.

56. July 8, 1817, U.S.-Cherokee Nation, 7 Stat. 156.

57. Treaty with the Choctaws, Oct. 8, 1820, U.S.-Choctaw Nation, 7 Stat. 210; Treaty with the Creeks, Feb. 12, 1825, U.S.-Creek Nation, 7 Stat. 237; Treaty with the Creeks, Jan. 24, 1826, U.S.-Creek Nation, 7 Stat. 286; Treaty with the Western Cherokee, May 6, 1828, U.S.-Cherokee Nation, 7 Stat. 311; Treaties with the Delawares, Aug. 3, 1829 & Sept. 24, 1829, U.S.-Delaware Indians, 7 Stat. 326, 327; Treaty with the Choctaw, U.S.-Choctaw Nation, Sept. 27, 1830, 7 Stat. 333, 340. These treaties are cited in CLINTON ET AL., *supra* note 14, at 145.

58. 21 U.S. (8 Wheat) 543 (1823).

authored by Chief Justice John Marshall, established the relationship between the Indian nations and the federal government.

The first case, *Johnson v. M'Intosh*,[61] settled, for America, the relationship between discovery and title. Marshall acknowledged that the United States' claims to the land were, for the most part, predicated on conquest of the Native Americans, not voluntary succession.[62] The issue was whether the Illinois and Piankeshaw Indians held title to land that was freely alienable. Justice Marshall found that the rights of the original inhabitants were necessarily impaired by European development saying:

> [The natives] were admitted to be the rightful occupants of the soil, with a legal as well as just claim to retain possession of it, and to use it according to their own discretion; but their rights to complete sovereignty, as independent nations, were necessarily diminished and their power to dispose of the soil at their own will, to whomsoever they pleased, was denied by the fundamental principle that discovery gave exclusive title to those who made it.[63]

The economic vitality and structure of the United States was at stake in this case; to have found that the Indians did hold valid title would have undercut the entire market for the land companies flourishing at the time. The Court refused to uphold the transfers made by the Indians and thereby established the rule that the United States can determine what Indians can and cannot do with their land.

The second case, *Cherokee Nation v. Georgia*,[64] defined the character of the Indian Nations relative to the federal government and set in motion an understanding of Native Americans as subjugated peoples. The case focused on the nature and extent of Indian sovereignty. After the State of Georgia annexed the federally established land they also dissolved all the Cherokee organs of government. When one Cherokee man was indicted for the murder of another the state supreme court held that Georgia criminal courts and not the Cherokee tribal courts had jurisdiction because the Cherokee "savages" could not, by definition, have a lawful grant.[65] Marshall summarized the issue of the case by asking, "Do the Cherokees constitute a *foreign* state in the sense of the constitution?"[66] Marshall held that they were not foreign states,

---

59. 30 U.S. (5 Pet.) 1 (1831).
60. 31 U.S. (6 Pet.) 515 (1832).
61. 21 U.S. (8 Wheat) 543 (1823).
62. *M'Intosh*, 21 U.S. (8 Wheat) at 574.
63. *Id.*
64. 30 U.S. (5 Pet.) 1 (1831).
65. BERGER, *supra* note 17, at 76 (citing *Cherokee Nation*, 30 U.S. (5 Pet.) at 19).
66. *Cherokee Nation*, 30 U.S. (5 Pet.) at 16 (emphasis added).

but rather "domestic dependent nations."[67] He described their relationship with the United States as resembling "that of a ward to his guardian."[68] This description led to the "trust relationship" later accepted between the United States and the Indian nations. Because the Cherokees were neither a state admitted to the Union nor a foreign state, Article III, Section 2 of the Constitution did not give the Supreme Court jurisdiction to hear the case. The fact that Marshall described this "state of pupilage" as between the Indians and the federal government indicated who was to win the federal/state conflict operating behind the facts of this case.

The third case, *Worcester v. Georgia*,[69] originated from a Georgia criminal prosecution of four religious missionaries who deliberately broke a law requiring them to have a state license to live on Indian lands. Recall that the state had annexed the Indian territory and required the Cherokee Indians who lived there to submit to Georgia law. Marshall found that the Georgia laws were an unconstitutional interference with the treaty relationships established between the Cherokee Nations and the United States, and, therefore, reversed the Georgia judgment.[70] Marshall described the Indian relationship with the federal government as follows: "[B]y declaring treaties already made, as well as those to be made, to be the Supreme law of the land, has adopted and sanctioned the previous treaties with the Indian nations, and consequently admits their rank among those powers who are capable of making treaties."[71] Marshall analogized the Indian nations to small European nations who sought the protection of greater powers.[72] By this reasoning, the laws of Georgia could have no force on Cherokee territory.[73]

The State of Georgia correctly understood, however, that President Andrew Jackson, veteran of military campaigns against the Indians, would not interfere in state assertion of authority over the tribes.[74] A constitutional crisis, prompted when Jackson refused to execute the judgment of the Supreme Court, was only narrowly averted. To avoid the embarrassment and ensuing conflict, the Court simply ended its session and put off the issue because an improper writ was issued. The case did not overrule *M'Intosh* or *Cherokee*

---

67. *Id.* at 17.
68. *Id.*
69. 31 U.S. (6 Pet.) 515 (1832).
70. *Id.* at 557-58.
71. *Id.* at 558.
72. *Id.* at 560.
73. *Id.*
74. Jackson is purported to have said in response to Marshall's judgment in the *Worcester* decision: "John Marshall has made his decision, now let him enforce it." 1 HORACE GREELEY, THE AMERICAN CONFLICT: A HISTORY OF THE GREAT REBELLION IN THE UNITED STATES OF AMERICA 1860-64, at 106 (Hartford, O.D. Case & Co.; Chicago, G. & C.W. Sherwood, 1864-66), *cited in* CLINTON ET AL., *supra* note 14, at 28.

Nation, but it did affirm Indian sovereignty by accepting some limited jurisdiction supremacy for Indians on Indian land.

The affirmation was not to last long, however. The Choctaws, Chickasaws, and Creeks had already given in to removal pressure. The Seminoles had lost their desperate attempt to fight off the white military. The Cherokees had not fought back, but had resisted removal by trying to adapt to the white way, taking on European political structures and styles of living. When the pressures on their land became too great, their government was dissolved, their newspaper was suppressed, and their land was given away.[75] Their experience in Georgia was repeated. They were summoned to sign a removal treaty in 1836,[76] but only five hundred of the seventeen thousand Cherokees showed up for the signing. The treaty was signed in any case, ratified by the Senate, and the Cherokees were rounded up and pushed westward.[77] Estimates are that 4000 to 8000 people died on what came to be known as the Trail of Tears.[78]

In a speech to Congress in December 1838, President Martin Van Buren said: "It affords sincere pleasure to apprise the Congress of the entire removal of the Cherokee Nation of Indians to their new homes west of the Mississippi. The measures authorized by Congress at its last session have had the happiest effects."[79] The policy of removal of Indians to areas beyond state lines lasted until at least 1861.

E. The Reservation System (1861-1887)

The period of time between 1830 and 1855 was a time of tremendous growth for this young country. By 1853, the present boundaries of the United States were established and people were moving west. The settlers moved through the Great Plains and into California in search of gold and land, manifestly destined to conquer all human and geographic obstacles to development of the "new" lands. The pressure on the Indians, who had been "removed" to the Great Plains states, increased.

As California's population increased, federal agents experimented with the creation of smaller Indian land holdings within the state in exchange for guarantees of territorial permanence, social services, and guarantees of self-governance.[80] Congress withheld immediate approval of these "reservations," because they departed from the removal policy, but despite the vastly increased size of the country, land was becoming scarce. Finally, the Enabling

---

75. STANNARD, *supra* note 2, at 122.
76. Treaty of New Echota, Dec. 29, 1835, U.S.-Cherokee Nation, 7 Stat. 478.
77. STANNARD, *supra* note 2, at 123.
78. BERGER, *supra* note 17, at 86; *see also* STANNARD, *supra* note 2, at 124.
79. ZINN, *supra* note 1, at 144-46.
80. BERGER, *supra* note 17, at 87.

Act for the Kansas Territory[81] established a policy of respect for the jurisdictional integrity of the Indian lands within the state.

This Act established a pattern whereby newly admitted states would renounce jurisdiction over the Indians, and would grant the Indians some independent sovereignty for activities occurring on their own lands. The states, in turn, received vast land holdings that had previously been promised to the Indians in perpetuity. Most of the famous Indian battles during this time occurred as the government attempted to force Indians onto reservation lands or to keep them there.[82]

Under the reservation system, other aspects of Indian life began to change as well. In 1871, the government ended all treaty making with the Indian tribes.[83] In 1882, Secretary of the Interior, Henry M. Teller, initiated a policy to end Indian religious ceremonies and later to imprison Indians engaging in traditional rites.[84] In 1885, the Congress passed the Major Crimes Act,[85] providing federal court jurisdiction over seven enumerated crimes committed by Indians on or off Indian reservations.[86] For the first time, this statute provided federal jurisdiction over intratribal affairs.[87] Much of previously settled Indian policy began to be reconsidered during the 1880s.

F. Allotment and Assimilation (1887-1934)

The importance of the Dawes Act[88] is difficult to overestimate.[89] Its purpose was intimately tied to the view that promoting Indian separatism was not working, and the solution to the "Indian problem" was to turn them into "white people." Aboriginal people still combat this problem today, as do other minority cultures in contact with a dominant culture.

The following policy objectives guided legal developments during this period in 1877: (1) assimilation of the Indians to white economic life through termination of communal ownership of land, (2) elimination of the Indian community, culture, and political structure, and (3) coercion of the Indians to

---

81. Ch. 20, 12 Stat. 126 (1861).

82. BERGER, *supra* note 17, at 87-92.

83. Act of Mar. 3, 1871 (Appropriations Act), ch. 120, § 1, 16 Stat. 544, 566 (codified in part at 25 U.S.C. § 71 (1988)).

84. Sharon L. O'Brien, *A Legal Analysis of the American Indian Religious Freedom Act, in* THE HANDBOOK OF AMERICAN INDIAN RELIGIOUS FREEDOM 28 (Christopher T. Vecsey ed., 1991) [hereinafter HANDBOOK].

85. Act of Mar. 3, 1885 (Appropriations Act), ch. 341, § 9, 23 Stat. 362, 385 (1885) (codified at 18 U.S.C. § 1153 (1988)).

86. *Id.*

87. CLINTON ET AL., *supra* note 14, at 148.

88. General Allotment Act of 1887 (Dawes Act), ch. 119, 24 Stat. 388 (codified as amended at 25 U.S.C. §§ 331-334, 339, 341-342, 348-349, 354, 381 (1988)) (named after Sen. Henry L. Dawes (D.-Mass.), who advocated its passage).

89. BERGER, *supra* note 17, at 102.

adopt habits of civilized life exhibited by the white race.[90] The Dawes Act is directly related to the first two of these objectives and indirectly related to the third.

Previously, all Indian land had been assigned to the tribes and generally held in common. The Dawes Act assigned particular parcels of sixty-four hectares of land to each family head of household and thirty-two hectares to each single person over eighteen years of age in each tribe.[91] These parcels were to be permanent, could be passed on through inheritance, and were inalienable for twenty-five years.[92] The Act aimed to induce the Native Americans to adopt a European, profit-generating agrarian lifestyle, instead of their traditional, more communal, and subsistence-based life. The early allotment efforts had been predicated on voluntary acceptance of these terms, but the Act anticipated coercing the Indians to accept allotment and the eventually dissolving the tribes and the reservations.[93] The Act envisioned that the Indians would become subject to state law at the end of the inalienation period and provided that any lands not distributed through the allotment process would be ceded to the federal government.[94] The government sold those lands to anxious white settlers.

During the first twenty-five years of the allotment program, the Indians lost almost two-thirds of their previous land holdings and eighty-seven percent of their "good land,"[95] through government sales of "surplus" land and fraudulent land deals with whites. Much of this land passed to non-Indian owners through state property tax foreclosures.[96] President Theodore Roosevelt claimed that the Act would be "a mighty pulverizing engine to break up the tribal mass."[97] Despite previous treaties promising political autonomy and territorial permanency, the government openly aimed to destroy the Native American society.

The second and third goals were primarily achieved through educational and religious reorientation. Federally administered schools and religious education instructed Indians in the habits of civilized life. Boarding schools were an important instrument for effecting assimilation.[98] Native American

---

90. EDWARD H. SPICER, THE AMERICAN INDIANS 183-90 (1980).

91. BERGER, *supra* note 17, at 102.

92. Though the Secretary of the Interior and many statutes which followed created shorter restraints on alienation. The history of the Menaminee reservation is a famous example of the resulting "checkerboard" effect.

93. BERGER, *supra* note 17, at 102.

94. *Id.*

95. CLINTON ET AL., *supra* note 14, at 152. The amount went from 138 million acres to 48 million acres. *Id.* Of the remaining 48 million acres, 20 million were desert or semi-desert. *Id.*

96. BERGER, *supra* note 17, at 103.

97. President Theodore Roosevelt, Mesage to the Senate and House of Representatives (Dec. 3, 1901), *in* 10 A COMPILATION OF THE MESSAGES AND PAPERS OF THE PRESIDENTS, 1789-1908, at 450 (James D. Richardson ed., 1902).

98. O'Brien, International Law, *supra* note 26, at 79.

children were taken from their parents, sometimes after federal officials threatened to withhold food rations if the parents did not cooperate, and sent to schools where they learned English, practiced white cultural traditions, and were taught that Indian culture was inferior.[99] Oftentimes the children were sent to live with white families during the summer so that they would not be influenced by their parents to pick up Indian ways.[100] Christian religious groups were also active in the schools and on the reservations recruiting Indians to their systems and denigrating Indian religious practices.

The second and third goals were also implemented in a series of institutions created by regulations of the Bureau of Indian Affairs (BIA).[101] The BIA created Courts of Indian Offenses and an Indian Service of the Bureau Police. Both served to create an alternative power structure within the Indian community to compete with the traditional tribal organization. The Code of Indian Offenses implemented by the Bureau Police and Courts of Indian Offenses proscribed many traditional Indian cultural and religious practices.[102] Through these two institutions and others like them,[103] white political relations made great inroads into Indian life.

BIA administrators assumed that, after adopting the way of life of the white people, the Indians would shed their culture and meld into the white culture as the European immigrant groups had done. The one major difference between the immigrants and the Indians, however, was that the immigrants had voluntarily left their own communities, cultures, and homeland in search of what they considered to be better opportunities in the United States. The Indians never made that choice.[104]

The last major legislation of the period conferred citizenship on all "noncitizen" Indians born within the United States.[105] The Indian nations that survived allotment now found themselves assimilated by the dictates of the occupying power. The assimilation campaign was officially complete, but the inadequacies and injustice of the previous fifty years began to become more manifest. A report sponsored by the Brookings Institute,[106] however, concluded that "the assimilation campaign had failed to realize its objectives and that the Indians lived in conditions of extreme poverty, with poor health

---

99. *Id.*

100. *See* SPICER, *supra* note 90, at 188.

101. Created in 1824.

102. CLINTON ET AL., *supra* note 14, at 151.

103. Legislation such as the Act of June 28, 1898 (Curtis Act), ch. 542, 30 Stat. 567, which dissolved the Cherokee and Choctaw tribal governments as legal institutions, also combined to affect change in Indian life.

104. BERGER, *supra* note 17, at 151.

105. Act of June 2, 1924, ch. 233, 43 Stat. 253.

106. *See* INSTITUTE FOR GOV'T RESEARCH, STUDIES IN ADMINISTRATION, THE PROBLEM OF INDIAN ADMINISTRATION (Lewis Merriam et al. ed., 1928). This work is popularly known as the *Merriam Report.*

and inadequate education."[107] The BIA, under John Collier as Commissioner of Indian Affairs, reflected the changing attitudes toward Indians that began to arise. Collier abolished official prohibitions against Indian religious practices and instituted other reforms that helped to ease government discrimination against Indians.[108] Slowly, the situation began to improve.

G. The Reorganization Act Period (1934-1940)

If the allotment and assimilation period marked the nadir of the relationship between the Native American peoples and the federal government, then the period which followed indicated a general improvement. The Indian Reorganization Act (IRA)[109] formalized a rejection of the policies that had guided Indian policy for more than fifty years. "By 1934, there was a sense that something very serious was wrong with the direction of federal policy based on the [Dawes] Act and the principles that undergirded it."[110] When President Franklin Roosevelt chose John Collier as Commissioner of Indian Affairs, a new era of Indian policy began. The new system implemented policies reflecting Marshall's emphasis on allowing the Indians to govern themselves within their own territory and allowed the tribes to choose to adopt new institutions based on the model of a liberal, European, constitutional democracy. The sense of choice was limited, however. Some of the tribes experienced substantial pressure to accept the IRA and the consequences of refusing to vote whether or not to accept it were severe.[111]

The Act ended land allotments and authorized the Secretary of the Interior to purchase additional lands for Indian use. Further, it required that timber harvesting on Indian lands be designed with the goal of long-term yield, rather than the quick gains brought by clear cutting. The decision about whether or not to harvest remained with the federal government, not the Indians. One of the most important provisions of the IRA allowed the Indian tribes to develop constitutions and corporate charters. Even though these constitutions and the corporate structure were established on white terms, the limited autonomy they brought revived the sense of tribal government and control. These corporations developed widely and became instruments of social change in the tribes.[112] Irrigation systems were built, communally owned cattle herds were established, and the exploration of mineral and oil resources began. Not all of the changes "development" generated were positive, but some good effects did come as a result.

---

107. SPICER, *supra* note 90, at 189-90.

108. *See* O'Brien, International Law, *supra* note 26, at 28.

109. Indian Reorganization Act of 1934 (Wheeler-Howard Act), ch. 576, 48 Stat. 984 (codified at 25 U.S.C. §§ 461-479 (1988 & Supp. II 1990)).

110. CLINTON ET AL., *supra* note 14, at 152.

111. *See Wheeler-Howard Act — Exempt Certain Indians: Hearings Before the House Comm. on Indian Affairs on S. 2103*, 76th Cong., 3d Sess. 22 (1940).

112. SPICER, *supra* note 90, at 193.

Importantly, IRA also defined the term, "Indian," which established the following qualification for election, acceptance, and benefits under the Act:

> The term 'Indian' as used in [the IRA] shall include all persons of Indian descent who are members of any recognized Indian tribe now under Federal jurisdiction, and all persons who are descendants of such members who were, on June 1, 1934, residing within the present boundaries of any Indian reservation, and shall further include all other persons of one-half or more Indian blood. For the purposes of [the Act], Eskimos and other aboriginal peoples of Alaska shall be considered Indians.[113]

Eventually, 258 tribal elections were held to decide whether or not to accept the Act. A total of 181 tribes, including 129,750 individual Indians, accepted organization under the Act. Seventy-seven tribes, with 86,365 Indians, rejected it.[114] IRA and its effects marked a new era in Indian affairs.

H. The Termination Era (1940-1962)[115]

The controversy between assimilation and autonomy was not ended by the IRA. Within Congress there was strong support for the notions that reservations were places of forced internment that should be closed, and that America should cease to deal with the Indians differently from any other minority group. In the name of freeing tribes from federal supervision, Congress undertook a policy "terminating"[116] the special relationship between the Native Americans and the United States.

House of Representatives Concurrent Resolution 108[117] states that the policy of Congress was that the Indians should be treated identically with all other citizens. Several tribes were "designated"[118] as subjects of study, the end result of which was legislation placing the individuals of the tribes fully under state authority. Eventually, 109 tribes were terminated; 1,362,155 acres of reservation land and 11,466 Indians were affected, comprising 3% of all federally managed Indians and 3.2% of the trust land.[119] Congress also

---

113. 25 U.S.C. § 479 (1988).

114. CLINTON ET AL., *supra* note 14, at 154.

115. For a comprehensive analysis of this period, see DONALD FIXICO, TERMINATION AND RELOCATION: FEDERAL INDIAN POLICY, 1945-1960 (1986).

116. Act of June 17, 1954 (Termination Act), ch. 303, 68 Stat. 250, 252 (codified as amended at 25 U.S.C. §§ 891-902 (1970) (repealed 1973)), stated that "all statutes of the United States which affect Indians because of their status as Indians shall no longer be applicable to the members of the tribe . . . ." *Id.*, *cited in* Sharon L. O'Brien, *Tribes and Indians: With Whom Does the United States Maintain a Relationship?*, 66 NOTRE DAME L. REV. 1461, 1471 n.49 (1991) [hereinafter O'Brien, *Tribes & Indians*].

117. H.R. Con. Res. 108, 83d Cong., 1st Sess., 67 Stat. B132 (1953).

118. *Id.* The Flathead, the Klamath, the Menominee, the Potowatamie, and the Chippewa. *Id.*

119. CLINTON ET AL., *supra* note 14, at 158.

adopted Public Law 280,[120] which transferred jurisdiction over crimes and civil causes of action previously held by federal and tribal authorities to the states.[121]

I. Assertions of Sovereignty (1962-Present)

In recent years court decisions and congressional enactments have diminished the impact of termination. Two terminated tribes, the Menominee and Klamath, challenged the termination of fishing and hunting rights that conflicted with treaty provisions.[122] The Supreme Court held that the termination legislation did not abrogate their tribe's treaty rights. Congress has restored some tribes to federal recognition and included other terminated tribes in benefit programs aimed at federally recognized tribes.[123]

Native Americans benefitted in the 1960s from President Lyndon Johnson's War on Poverty and from legislation that gave Indians the opportunity to sue in federal court.[124] In the 1970s, Native Americans challenged infringement of land, hunting, and fishing rights in court. They challenged federal authority more directly by taking over the Bureau of Indian Affairs Office in Washington in 1972 and by resisting police control at Wounded Knee in 1973. The Indian Civil Rights Act of 1968[125] also gave Indians guarantees under the Bill of Rights that they had not previously known, including federal *habeas corpus* jurisdiction, and retrocession of Public Law 280 jurisdiction to the federal government.[126] Though this Act has been very controversial in the Native American community, it permitted Indians to raise individual and collective rights claims in federal court. Also passed during this time were the Indian Self-Determination and Education Assistance Act of 1975[127] and the Indian Child Welfare Act of 1978,[128] which strengthened the role of the tribes in making decisions about their members.

---

120. Act of Aug. 15, 1953, ch. 505, 67 Stat. 588 (Pub. L. No. 83-280) (codified as amended at 18 U.S.C. § 1162, 25 U.S.C. §§ 1321-1326, 28 U.S.C. § 1360 (1988)).

121. *Id.*

122. *See* Menominee Tribe of Indians v. United States, 391 U.S. 404 (1967); Kimball v. Callahan, 493 F.2d 564 (9th Cir.), *cert. denied*, 419 U.S. 1019 (1974).

123. Indian Child Welfare Act of 1978, Pub. L. No. 95-608, 92 Stat. 3069 (codified at 25 U.S.C. §§ 1901-1963 (1988 & Supp. II 1990)); Indian Health Care Improvement Act, Pub. L. No. 94-437, 90 Stat. 1400 (1976) (codified in scattered sections of 25 U.S.C.); Indian Education Act, Pub. L. No. 92-318, 86 Stat. 334 (1972) (codified in scattered sections of 20 U.S.C.). These authorities are cited in O'Brien, *Tribes & Indians, supra* note 116, at 1472 nn. 50-52.

124. Act of Oct. 10, 1966, Pub. L. No. 89-635, 80 Stat. 880 (codified at 28 U.S.C. § 1362 (1988)) (making court challenges possible).

125. Pub. L. No. 90-284, 82 Stat. 77 (codified in part at 25 U.S.C. §§ 1301-1303 (1988)).

126. CLINTON ET AL., *supra* note 14, at 160.

127. Pub. L. No. 93-638, 88 Stat. 2203 (codified as amended at 25 U.S.C. §§ 450-450n (1988)).

128. 25 U.S.C. §§ 1901-1963 (1988 & Supp. II 1990).

These assertions of sovereignty and statutory gains in autonomy reawakened latent questions about the nature of federal trust responsibility for
Indians. Because Justice Marshall's infamous guardian/ward characterization
was formalized in the Dawes Act, requiring the federal government to
administer the allotment process for the benefit of Indian land recipients, a
trust relationship between the government and the Indians developed. The
government was seen as the trustee of a body of assets to which the Indians
were entitled and for which they needed the administrative capacities of the
federal government. The government, through the Department of the Interior
and the Bureau of Indian Affairs, argued that this trust relationship only
extended to property and only for federally recognized tribes.[129] In 1974, the
National Tribal Council claimed that the trust responsibility included not only
these obligations, but also the requirement that the federal government protect
the sovereignty of the Indian tribes.[130] Some scholars have noted that the
trust responsibility works both for and against Native American sovereignty
efforts.[131] Care by a trustee allows a beneficiary to enforce her rights to trust
assets, but it also necessarily entails a strong sense of control and paternalism.
The sword cuts both ways.

In the later part of the 1970s, Native Americans and Native American
policy experienced a backlash against what were viewed as excesses of the
1960s. Citizens groups, such as the Montanans Opposed to Discrimination
and the Interstate Congress for Equal Rights and Responsibilities, lobbied
Congress to return to the assimilation policies of the past. Bills were
introduced calling for a reevaluation of Indian law, limitations on hunting and
fishing rights, and even an end to all treaties entered into with the Indians by
the United States.[132]

These groups and the change of political agenda that took place in the
1980s set the stage for an increased focus on the financial relationship
between the government and the Indians. President Ronald Reagan, in an
effort to limit federal expenditures for Indian support, issued a Statement on
Indian Policy proclaiming that "[i]t is important to the concept of self-
government that tribes reduce their dependence on Federal funds by providing
a greater percentage of the cost of their self-government."[133] This policy,
however, may be little more than the "termination" wolf in the "sovereignty"
sheep's clothing. Congress, nonetheless, called for extensive economic

---

129. FRANCIS P. PRUCHA, THE GREAT FATHER: THE UNITED STATES GOVERNMENT AND
THE AMERICAN INDIANS 399 (1984).

130. *Id.*

131. *Id.* at 400.

132. CLINTON ET AL., *supra* note 14, at 162.

133. President Ronald Reagan, Statement on Indian Policy (Jan. 24, 1983), *in* [1983] 1 PUB.
PAPERS 96-97.

development on the reservations, though the tribes were expected to provide most of the capital to fund this development.

Since President Richard Nixon's famous call for congressional support of Indian autonomy efforts,[134] all subsequent presidents have, with varying degrees of credibility, asserted interest in developing Native American self-governance measures. After a meeting with indigenous leaders President George Bush stated, "Today we move forward toward a permanent relationship of understanding and trust, a relationship in which the tribes of the nation sit in positions of sovereignty along with other governments that compose the family that is America."[135] A project was initiated in 1988 by Congress to support a test group of tribes who participate in a three-year attempt at self-governance. Although the tribes must still negotiate with the Bureau of Indian Affairs for their funding, their relationship approximates that of one sovereign to another.

Conditions on the reservations today, however, are still not good. Estimates are that unemployment on the reservations runs as high as 80% and alcoholism is nearly as widespread. The average annual income is less than $7000. Nonetheless, there is hope among the tribes who have joined the self-determination project[136] that new jobs, better schools, and a new pride in Indian culture will be engendered by a return to self-governance.

The Native Americans continue to face many struggles today. The extermination policies have ended and their children are no longer being forced into boarding schools, but the challenges of alcoholism, unemployment, and the battle to maintain their culture are all very real. One of the greatest threats to the Native American community continues to be the assault on their spiritual practices. This assault is no longer military but is instead legal. The stakes, however, are just as high. The following sections discuss the general environment of protection of religious rights in the United States and a focus on how the standards continue to work to the detriment of Native Americans.

II. Constitutional Protection of Religion

"Congress shall make no law respecting an establishment of religion, or prohibiting the free exercise thereof . . . ."[137] These two clauses of the First

---

134. President Richard Nixon, Special Message to the Congress on Indian Affairs (July 8, 1970), 1970 PUB. PAPERS 564, 576, *cited in* PRUCHA, *supra* note 129, at 379 ("We have concluded that Indians will get better programs and that public monies will be more effectively expended if the people who are most affected by these programs are responsible for operating them.").

135. Martha Williams, *Some Native Americans Begin Push for Self-Determination*, SEATTLE TIMES, June 30, 1991, at A1.

136. Seven tribes are currently participating: in Washington, the Quinault Indian Nation, the Jamestown Klallam Tribe, the Lummi Indian Tribe; in California, the Hoopa Valley Tribe; in Oklahoma, the Absentee-Shawnee Tribe, the Cherokee Tribe; and in Minnesota, the Mille Lacs Chippewa.

137. U.S. CONST. amend. I.

Amendment are collectively known as the Religion Clauses and individually known as the Establishment Clause and the Free Exercise Clause. These parts of the First Amendment have been made applicable to the states by the Fourteenth Amendment.[138] Each clause can be implicated by government action that either helps or hinders religion. In the context of Native American religious freedom, Indians claim that the government has violated these constitutional protections when a government action has unduly burdened their spiritual practices. Generally, a free exercise claim is at issue, but occasionally the government will claim that even if a free exercise violation is found the requested government accommodation of Native American spiritual practice would amount to an Establishment Clause violation. "There is a natural antagonism between a command not to establish religion and a command not to inhibit its practice."[139] A principle of "neutrality" has guided the Court's analysis of Religion Clause claims, but, as this article will show, neutrality has worked almost without exception to the detriment of Native Americans. The next section outlines the standards and method of analysis employed by courts in these cases.

A. The Establishment Clause

Most of the religious rights issues that arise involve the second part of the "Religion Clauses" of the Constitution, rather than the first. Establishment Clause analysis is implicated, however, when the government improperly involves itself in support of a particular religious group. In the Native American context, Establishment Clause issues arise when courts worry that the protection they are asked to afford Indian religious practices require that the government be more than neutral toward Native American spirituality.

The traditional Establishment Clause standards are set forth in *Lemon v. Kurtzman.*[140] In *Lemon*, the Court established a three-part test for determining the validity of state statutes granting financial aid to church related schools. The law in question must: (1) reflect a clearly secular purpose; (2) have a primary effect that neither advances nor inhibits religion; and (3) avoid excessive government entanglement with religion. Justice Sandra Day O'Connor has called for a reformulation of the Establishment Clause test that would put the court in the position of an "objective observer."[141] Her two-prong test would first ask whether the court has "endorsed" a particular

---

138. Everson v. Board of Educ., 330 U.S. 1, 14-15 (1947), *reh'g denied*, 330 U.S. 855 (1947); Cantwell v. Connecticut, 310 U.S. 296, 303-04 (1940).

139. JOHN E. NOWAK ET AL., CONSTITUTIONAL LAW 1031 (1986).

140. 403 U.S. 602 (1971).

141. Wallace v. Jaffree, 472 U.S. 38, 76 (1985) (holding that an Alabama statue authorizing a period of silence of meditation or voluntary prayer violated the Establishment Clause requirement of neutrality toward religion). The Supreme Court has recently announced its intention to reevaluation the *Lemon* test by accepting certiorari of Grumet v. Board of Educ., 618 N.E.2d 94 (N.Y. 1993), *cert. denied*, 62 U.S.L.W. 3368 (Nov. 29, 1993).

religion or religious belief.[142] The second prong of her test would investigate whether the challenged statute requires the government to become excessively entangled with religious institutions.[143] Though this test seems to be gaining favor on the Court in recent years, it has not yet become the standard of analysis.[144]

In the 1992 term, the Supreme Court further muddied the already turbid waters of Establishment Clause analysis by refusing to reconsider *Lemon* while affirming the unconstitutionality of a rabbinical prayer at a public middle school graduation ceremony. By a 5-4 majority, the Court held in *Lee v. Weisman*[145] that a school could not provide for a "nonsectarian" prayer to be led by a member of the clergy selected by the school.[146] The Court held that the conduct of the school principal, in deciding that an invocation and benediction should be given and in selecting a religious participant, constituted state action.[147] The Court languished over the "state-imposed character of an invocation and benediction by clergy selected by the school"[148] and found that the "conformity required of the student in this case was too high an exaction to withstand the test of the Establishment Clause."[149]

After acknowledging the "delicate and fact-sensitive" character of Establishment Clause jurisprudence, Justice Anthony Kennedy, writing for the majority, clearly limited this decision to the school graduation context.[150] Despite his characterization of the decision, however, scholarship has already noted the Court's snub of the *Lemon* test analysis in favor of an expanded focus on coercion as a determinative principal.[151] Whether this change portends a reinvigorated future for the Establishment Clause or is the harbinger of further confusion remains to be seen. For Native American religious freedom, the situation could not get much worse.

Courts evaluating Native American free exercise claims have found Establishment Clause problems when asked to protect religious freedom on government lands.[152] In *Inupiat Community of Arctic Slope v. United*

---

142. Board of Educ. v. Mergens, 496 U.S. 226, 248 (1990).

143. Lynch v. Donnelly, 465 U.S. 668, 687-88 (1984) (holding that the inclusion of a nativity scene in a city display does not violate the Establishment Clause).

144. Laurence H. Tribe, Comments on Proposed Legislation to Protect Native American Religious Freedom, Memorandum to Native American Tribal Leaders and Academics Meeting at Harvard Divinity School (Nov. 13, 1990) (on file with author).

145. 112 S. Ct. 2649 (1992).

146. *Id.* at 2655.

147. *Id.* at 2655-56.

148. *Id.* at 2660.

149. *Id.* at 2661.

150. *Id.*

151. *See The Supreme Court, 1991 Term — Leading Cases*, 100 HARV. L. REV. 163, 259 (1992).

152. Though not in a Native American rights context, the Supreme Court's statement in Lee v. Weisman, 112 S. Ct. 2649 (1992), tells the tale. The Court said, "The principle that

States,[153] the court observed that the Inupiat claims sought to deprive the public of normal use of the seas at issue and therefore created serious Establishment Clause problems. The court in *Crow v. Gullet*[154] noted that other courts had expressed concern about affording special treatment to Indians and so becoming excessively entangled with religion.[155] Not all courts have shared this concern One court found that "where government action violates the Free Exercise Clause, the Establishment Clause ordinarily does not bar judicial relief."[156]

Because the bulk of Native American Religion Clause claims are based on a perceived threat to the right to freely engage in their spiritual practices, the next section delves into the specific details of free exercise jurisprudence in some detail.

B. *Free Exercise Jurisprudence in American History*

The framers of the Bill of Rights gave the protection of religious freedom priority in their list of protections which citizens reserved for themselves in this country. The objective of this First Amendment was unqualified federal government neutrality regarding religious beliefs and governmental accommodation of religious practices where its actions burdened them.[157] Since the Fourteenth Amendment extended this protection to the states, state action has generated most of the conflict between government interests and the rights of individuals to practice their religious beliefs freely. A brief survey of the history of free exercise jurisprudence reveals three prominent perspectives.

1. *Belief and Practice*

In the first free exercise case, *Reynolds v. United States*,[158] the Supreme Court upheld an anti-polygamy law against the claim of a Mormon plaintiff that his religious beliefs required such marriages. The Court stated that "Congress was deprived of all legislative power over mere opinion, but was left free to reach actions which were in violation of social duties or subversive of good order."[159] Because polygamy was in "violation of social duties" and

---

government may accommodate the free exercise of religion does not supersede the fundamental limitations imposed by the Establishment Clause." *Id.* at 2655.

153. 548 F. Supp. 182, 189 (D. Alaska 1982), *aff'd*, 746 F.2d 570 (1984).

154. 541 F. Supp. 785, 794 (D.C. S.D. 1982).

155. *Id.* at 794 (citing Widmar v. Vincent, 454 U.S. 263, 263 (1981)).

156. Wilson v. Block, 708 F.2d 735, 747 (1983) (citing Wisconsin v. Yoder, 406 U.S. 205, 220-21 (1972); Sherbert v. Verner, 374 U.S. 398, 409 (1963)).

157. Gillette v. United States, 401 U.S. 437, 449-50 (1971). "[W]hen government activities touch on the religious sphere, they must be secular in purpose, evenhanded in operation, and neutral in primary impact." *Id.* at 450.

158. 98 U.S. 145 (1878).

159. *Id.* at 164.

subversive of good order,"[160] Congress was free to make a law to outlaw this offensive practice, despite its infringement on the plaintiff's religious practice.

This opinion required the government to protect only religious *belief*, not religious practice. The Court reasoned that any other position would subordinate law to religious belief allowing every citizen to construct his or her own law based on religious conviction.[161] After 1940, the Court deemphasized the distinction between belief and practice and established new standards for permissible burdens on religious practice.

In *Cantwell v. Connecticut*,[162] the Court expanded protection for religious conduct.[163] The *Cantwell* Court reversed the conviction of several Jehovah's Witnesses for failing to obtain government approval before soliciting money. In addition to supporting its absolute ban on governmental interference with beliefs,[164] the Court held that the government could not inhibit the plaintiff's "chosen form of religion."[165] This decision protected not only the freedom to believe, but also, in some circumstances, the freedom to act on those beliefs.[166]

Three years later, in *West Virginia State Board of Education v. Barnette*,[167] the Court supported the *Cantwell* standard and rejected a weaker test outlined in *Minersville School District v. Gobitis*.[168] Acknowledging that the First Amendment limited permissible government action, the *Barnette* Court recognized as valid only those restrictions on freedom of speech and of the press, of assembly and of worship only to the extent necessary protect a legitimate state interest from "grave and immediate danger."[169]

---

160. *Id.* at 159.

161. *Id.* at 166-67; *see also* Kenneth Marin, Employment Division v. Smith: *The Supreme Court Alters the State of Free Exercise Doctrine* 40 AMER. U.L. REV. 1431, 1436 (1991).

162. 310 U.S. 296 (1940).

163. *Id.* at 303-04.

164. *Id.* at 303. This protection has been maintained throughout the history of the Court. *See* Torcaso v. Watkins, 367 U.S. 488 (1961) (striking down a state constitutionally required declaration of belief in God as a prerequisite for holding public office).

165. *Cantwell*, 310 U.S. at 303.

166. *Id.* Justice Owen Roberts stated that "[t]he first is absolute but, in the nature of things, the second cannot be." *Id.* at 303-04.

167. 319 U.S. 624 (1943).

168. 310 U.S. 586 (1940), *overruled by* West Virginia St. Bd. of Educ. v. Barnette, 319 U.S. 624 (1943). Here, the Court supported a school board expulsion of a Jehovah's Witness who refused to salute the flag, finding that the expulsion was not directed at the student's belief, but at his refusal to follow school rules. *Gobitis*, 310 U.S. at 594, 599-600. That decision excluded from free exercise strict scrutiny any "general law not aimed at the promotion or restriction of religious beliefs." *Id.* at 594. It established a general "rational basis" test for government action affecting religious belief. *Id.* at 598-600.

169. *Barnette*, 319 U.S. at 639.

2. Setting the Standard

The major free exercise decision of the Earl Warren Court was *Sherbert v. Verner*.[170] *Sherbert* used the two-part balancing test established in *Braunfeld v. Brown*,[171] which required that the plaintiff first establish that an action of the government has burdened a sincerely held[172] religious belief.[173] After the plaintiff established an infringement on religious rights, the burden shifted to the government to show that its infringement was justified by a compelling interest. The Court upheld a state law requiring that businesses close on Sunday, despite the burden on merchants whose religion also required them to rest on days other than Sunday.[174] Because this burden was indirect in that its purpose was not to impede religious observance or discriminate between religions, the Court found that it did not amount to a compulsion to act contrary to religious beliefs.[175]

In *Sherbert*,[176] the Court increased the level of scrutiny applied to indirect burdens on the free exercise of religion.[177] The Court again rejected the rational basis standard of review[178] and held that even incidental burdens on religious practice had to be justified by a compelling state interest.[179] Once the plaintiff established the prima facie requirements of sincere belief and burden on religion, the infringement was unconstitutional unless the government could show that the infringement on religious practice was justified by a compelling governmental interest which could not be protected by less restrictive means.[180] The Court found that even economic burdens of the *Braunfeld* type amounted to "the same kind of burden . . . as would a fine imposed . . . for . . . Sunday worship."[181]

The Court next expanded its application of the free exercise clause in *Wisconsin v. Yoder*,[182] in holding that Wisconsin could not require members of the Old Order Amish religion and the Conservative Mennonite Church to send their children to school after the eighth grade.[183] The Court followed

---

170. 374 U.S. 398 (1963).

171. 366 U.S. 599 (1961).

172. For a discussion of sincerity assessment, see John T. Noonan, *How Sincere Do You Have to Be to Be Religious?*, 1988 U. ILL. L. REV. 713, which analyzes United States v. Ballard, 322 U.S. 78 (1944), which is the origin of sincerity assessment addressed by the Court.

173. *Braunfeld*, 366 U.S. at 606-07.

174. *Id.* at 605-06.

175. *Id.*

176. 374 U.S. 398 (1963).

177. *Id.* at 406.

178. *Id.*

179. *Id.* at 403.

180. *Id.* The state had to show that "no alternative forms of regulation" could pass constitutional muster. *Id.* at 407.

181. *Id.* at 404.

182. 406 U.S. 205 (1972).

183. *Id.* at 232-34.

its familiar balancing test and found that the Amish and Mennonites sincerely held a religiously-based belief that sending their children to secondary school would expose them to worldly influences that ran counter to their religious emphasis on different values.[184] Justice Warren Burger, writing for the majority, emphasized that the Amish way of life was intimately related with their religious beliefs.[185] The Amish and Mennonites could claim an exemption from the school obligation since they had shown that this government behavior had a coercive effect on the practice of their religion due to the burden it placed on that practice.[186]

The state requirement at issue in *Yoder* could only be justified by a compelling state interest in imposing modern society upon the Amish.[187] The state failed to demonstrate an interest of significant importance and the Court saw that there were less burdensome means of achieving the state articulated goal of training good citizens.[188] The Court also reasoned that the Amish and Mennonite system of education was ideal for training their children for life in their community.[189] This facially neutral statute was found to unduly burden the free exercise of the Amish and Mennonite religions; the Court, therefore, exempted Amish and Mennonite children from attending public school beyond the eighth grade.[190]

With these cases, the Court established the two-prong test for evaluating indirect burdens on the free exercise of religion which exists to this day: a plaintiff must first show that a government action coerced her to violate religious beliefs or penalized her for a religious practice, and second prove that those beliefs are sincere, deeply rooted in religion, and shared by others. If both prongs are satisfied, the government bears the burden of showing a compelling need for its action. Direct burdens on religious freedom are still absolutely prohibited.[191] In recent years, however, the Court has tended to interpret state interests broadly and individual religious interests narrowly.[192]

3. The Scope Narrows

In *United States v. Lee*,[193] the Court denied an Amish employer's right to refuse to withhold social security taxes from his Amish employees. Though the Court recognized the genuine burden that participating in the social

---

184. *Id.* at 211.
185. *Id.* at 235-36.
186. *Id.* at 234.
187. *Id.* at 235.
188. *Id.* at 224-25.
189. *Id.* at 223.
190. *Id.* at 234.
191. Braunfeld v. Brown, 366 U.S. 599, 603 (1961).
192. *See, e.g.*, Lyng v. Northwest Indian Cemetery Ass'n, 485 U.S. 439 (1988).
193. 455 U.S. 252 (1982).

security system placed on the plaintiff's religious liberty,[194] it found that compulsory payments were necessary for the maintenance of the system and that an exemption would be unduly difficult to administer. Efficiency in the "social security system justified forcing Lee to comply with the law in violation of his faith."[195] This decision marked a movement away from an expansive view of the governmental duty to refrain from infringing upon individual religious practices.

The Court has continued to move in that direction in recent decisions. In *Bowen v. Roy*,[196] the Court refused to exempt a Native American child from identification by a social security number. It characterized her father's claim as a demand that government "conduct its own internal affairs in ways that comport with [his] religious beliefs . . . ."[197] Some commentators have suggested that this decision implies a heightened level of scrutiny by the Court of government actions that require a choice between adherence to a religious belief and enjoyment of a government benefit.[198] Those government actions which make the practice of a particular faith more difficult or costly, on the contrary, require a less substantial government interest to overcome burdens to the free exercise of religion.

The Court's attack on judicial enforcement of the right to free religious exercise continued in *Employment Division, Department of Human Resources v. Smith*.[199] In that case the Court upheld Oregon's denial of unemployment compensation to two drug counselors who were fired from their jobs after ingesting peyote in an annual sacramental ritual of the Native American Church.[200] Consumption of peyote was a crime under Oregon law. The state unemployment agency denied their application for benefits based on its conclusion that they were fired for work-related misconduct. The Supreme Court upheld the constitutionality of the denial of benefits against a free exercise challenge, finding that if a "generally applicable and otherwise valid"[201] across-the-board criminal statute exists, any impact on a person's ability to freely practice his or her religion is "merely the incidental effect"[202] of the statute. Such an incidental effect does not violate the First Amendment.[203] In order to "trigger free exercise balancing analysis, the object of a criminal statute on its face must proscribe the exercise of

---

194. *Id.* at 259-61.
195. Nowak et al., *supra* note 139, at 1078.
196. 476 U.S. 693 (1986).
197. *Id.* at 699.
198. Laurence H. Tribe, American Constitutional Law § 14-13, at 1262-64 (2d ed. 1988).
199. 494 U.S. 872 (1990).
200. *Id.* at 890.
201. *Id.* at 878.
202. *Id.*
203. *Id.*

religion."[204] This holding virtually guarantees that any general criminal statute that is opposed on free exercise grounds will not be open to balancing by a reviewing court. As a result, the Court will never get to the question of whether the state interest asserted is compelling enough to warrant an infringement on religious rights, nor will the state have to show that its means of achieving that interest are the least intrusive possible. Implicitly, the Court is saying that any police power interest bars free exercise analysis by the courts. This development leaves minority religious claims at the mercy of majoritarian politics without the check of the judiciary.[205]

The result of these sobering developments is that the First Amendment restriction on government activities which prohibit the free exercise of religion means:

(1) The government cannot directly act to proscribe religious belief.[206]

(2) To qualify for judicial review of a government action which allegedly implicates Religion Clause protections, the claimant must show:

(a) That the religious beliefs burdened are held in good faith; and

(b) The affected religious practice is rooted in religious belief and furthers this belief; and

(c) The practice is central or important to the practice of her or his religion.[207]

(3) Regulation of religious conduct is permissible if the motive of the legislation is not discriminatorily directed at religion.[208]

(4) Neutral civil laws or government conduct which directly burden the ability of citizens to engage in sincere religious practices are subject to strict scrutiny.[209]

(5) Neutral and generally applicable criminal laws are not open to free exercise challenge.[210]

---

204. John Delaney, *Police Power Absolutism and Nullifying the Free Exercise Clause: A Critique of* Oregon v. Smith, 25 IND. L. REV. 80 (1991) (citing *Smith*, 494 U.S. at 878-84).

205. Justice Harry Blackmun acknowledges, in his dissent, that the majority's instruction for plaintiffs like these to look to the political process for redress "will place at a relative disadvantage those religious practices that are not widely engaged in." *Smith*, 494 U.S. at 890 (Blackmun, J., dissenting).

206. Braunfeld v. Brown, 366 U.S. 599, 603-04 (1961).

207. *See* Wisconsin v. Yoder, 406 U.S. 205, 216-19 (1972).

208. Cantwell v. Connecticut, 310 U.S. 296, 303-04 (1940).

209. Sherbert v. Verner, 374 U.S. 398, 403 (1963).

210. *Smith*, 494 U.S. at 872. The Supreme Court recently applied and upheld this standard in Church of the Lukumi Babalu Aye v. City of Hialeah 113 S. Ct. 2217 (1993). In *Hialeah*, the Court struck down a Florida statute for violating both the neutrality toward religion and general applicability arms of the *Smith* test. *Id.* at 2226. As a result of the failure to meet those two requirements, the enactments were given compelling interest scrutiny. *Id.* at 2227. The ordinances at issue failed to meet the requirements of the most rigorous judicial scrutiny and were invalidated. *Id.*

(6) Government actions which indirectly make it "more difficult to practice certain religious beliefs" will not require a compelling governmental justification, but instead some lower level of justification.[211]

As recently as June 24, 1992, the Supreme Court has said that "[t]he First Amendment's Religion Clauses mean that religious beliefs and religious expression are too precious to be either proscribed or prescribed by the State."[212] Nonetheless, if recent court opinions are any indication, it will be very difficult for a plaintiff to establish a direct government burden on the practice of religion. The current Court favors restrictions on the claims that individuals can make on the government when it comes to protection of religious practices. These restrictions have profoundly affected Native American religious rights' claims.

C. The Free Exercise Clause and Native Americans

The Free Exercise Clause has been invoked by Native Americans to protect their right to ingest sacred peyote,[213] to practice their spirituality at sacred sites,[214] to gather and keep sacred objects,[215] to hunt and fish,[216] to protect the spirits of their children,[217] and to express their spirituality through traditional dress while in prison.[218] A complete exposition of all the Native American free exercise cases would extend far beyond the scope of this article. A brief survey of the impact of free exercise jurisprudence on Native Americans follows. To further limit the scope of this analysis, this article will only consider free exercise jurisprudence within the context of Native American "sacred site" claims. Where these lands are claimed by the United States government, conflicts between the government's intended use and ceremonial use by Indians often arise.

Five cases will demonstrate the difficulties of applying the *Sherbert* and *Yoder* tests to sacred site claims. In all these cases, Native American claims failed the analysis required by the court. After studying these cases, one can see that the balance is weighted against Native Americans. Even when the religious nature of the claim is accepted, it is very difficult for an Indian

---

211. Lyng v. Northwest Indian Cemetery Protective Ass'n, 485 U.S. 439, 452 (1988).

212. Lee v. Weisman, 112 S. Ct. 2649, 2656 (1992).

213. People v. Woody, 40 Cal. Rptr. 69 (1964).

214. *See* Lyng v. Northwest Indian Cemetery Protective Ass'n, 485 U.S. 439 (1988). See also *Lyng's* ancestors and progeny.

215. United States v. Dion, 762 F.2d 674 (8th Cir. 1985).

216. Frank v. State, 604 P.2d 1068 (Alaska 1979).

217. Bowen v. Roy, 476 U.S. 693 (1986).

218. Standing Deer v. Carlson, 831 F.2d 1525 (9th Cir. 1987).

religious right to outweigh the government's interest. Ethnocentrism,[219] rather than objective analysis, pervades judicial commentary on these decisions.

These cases can usefully be broken down into three categories.[220] First, in *Badoni v. Higginson*,[221] the court found that the government interest outweighed the plaintiff's religious interest.[222] Second, in *Sequoyah v. TVA*[223] and *Inupiat Community of Arctic Slope v. United States* (*Inupiat Community I*),[224] the courts found that the practices which the Indians claimed to be protected by the First Amendment were not religious.[225] Third, in *Crow v. Gullet*[226] and *Wilson v. Block*,[227] the court found no burden on Native American religious practices.[228] All of these cases framed their discussion of the question presented in *Sherbert* and *Yoder* terms, but the character of the analysis varied widely.

1. The Government's Interest Outweighs Indian Religious Claims

The creation of the Glen Canyon Dam and Reservoir, known as Lake Powell, on the Colorado river flooded land fifty-eight miles upstream. Eventually, these waters entered the Rainbow Bridge National Monument which is surrounded by the Navajo reservation in southern Utah and is managed by the National Park Service. The rising waters of Lake Powell flooded areas previously used by the Navajo for prayer ceremonies for at least a hundred years. The Navajo also believe that some of their gods live in the area of Rainbow Bridge that is now underwater. Tourists have desecrated the sacred nature of the site with graffiti, alcohol consumption, and general failure to respect the importance of the area to Native Americans. As a result of these changes to a once isolated and pristine area, the Navajo are no longer able to engage in practice their spiritual practices in the area.

Among other claims, the Navajo plaintiffs in *Badoni*[229] sought declaratory and injunctive relief for the violation of their First Amendment rights. The trial court granted summary judgment for the government because it believed that the plaintiff's lack of a property interest in the Monument was disposi-

---

219. "Ethnocentrism" is defined as: "1: Having race as a central interest 2: characterized by or based on the attitude that one's own group is superior." WEBSTER'S NEW COLLEGIATE DICTIONARY 389 (1981).

220. *See* Erica Rosenberg, *Native American's Access to Religious Sites: Underprotected Under the Free Exercise Clause?*, 26 B.C. L. REV. 463, 475 (1985).

221. 638 F.2d 172 (10th Cir. 1980).

222. *Id.* at 177-78

223. 620 F.2d 1159 (6th Cir. 1980).

224. 548 F. Supp. 182 (D. Alaska 1982), *aff'd*, 746 F.2d 570 (9th Cir. 1984) (*Inupiat Community I*).

225. *Id.* at 188-89.

226. 706 F.2d 856 (8th Cir. 1983).

227. 708 F.2d 735 (D.C. Cir. 1983), *cert. denied*, 464 U.S. 956 (1983).

228. *Crow*, 706 F.2d at 858; *Wilson*, 708 F.2d at 746.

229. 455 F. Supp. 641 (D. Utah 1977).

tive.[230] The *Badoni* court rejected the "no property interest" argument,[231] stating that the "government must manage its property in a manner that does not offend the Constitution."[232] It did, however, affirm the lower court judgment for different reasons.[233]

The *Badoni* court acknowledged the *Yoder* two-step free exercise analysis.[234] Though it did not explicitly state that the Native Americans had been burdened in their religious practice, it did cite the changed circumstances at the Monument and the destructive effects these changes had on the ability of the Navajo to engage in their spiritual practices.[235] The court then stated, without actually balancing the burden on the Navajo, that the government interest in maintaining Lake Powell outweighed the religious interest of the plaintiffs.[236] Any accommodation of the Navajo claims would have required a reduction in the water level of Lake Powell. Because the court found that maintaining the level of Lake Powell is a compelling government interest, it did not "reach the question [of] whether the government action involved infringe[d upon] plaintiffs' free exercise of religion."[237]

The court failed to address the second part of the second prong of the *Sherbert/Yoder* test, which requires the government to show that its compelling interest cannot be satisfied by a less intrusive means. It did find that it was "reasonable to conclude that no action other than reducing the water level would avoid the alleged infringement of the plaintiffs' beliefs and practices."[238] No argument or discussion of possible alternatives supported that finding.

The balance was never struck in *Badoni*. The court cited the proper authorities and stated the rule correctly, but failed to apply the test to the facts. A proper adjudication of these issues would have first evaluated the burden on religious practice and assessed whether it was sincere and substantial. In this case, the court found that there was a substantial burden of a sincerely held religious belief brought about by the flooding of Navajo sacred sites. Had the court followed the *Sherbert/Yoder* test, the second step would have studied the nature of the government's interest in its activity and how substantial the interests involved were. Those interests would have been weighed against a fundamental religious right to determine whether or not there was a violation. Finally, even if the government's interest was found to outweigh the plaintiff's religious rights, the court should have required the

230. *Id.* at 644-45.
231. Badoni v. Higginson, 638 F.2d 172, 176 (10th Cir. 1980).
232. *Id.*
233. *Id.*
234. *Id.* at 176-77.
235. *Id.* at 177.
236. *Id.* at 177-78.
237. *Id.* at 177 n.4.
238. *Id.* at 177.

government to prove that its interest could not be satisfied by any less intrusive means.

In legal realist terms, the religious rights of the Navajo lost to economic development interests. Economic development for the benefit of the majority outweighed the fundamental religious rights of the minority.

2. Not All That Is Claimed To Be Religious Will Be Respected As Such

Native Americans have to worry not only that their religious rights will not be valued by the courts, but also that their actions and beliefs will not be recognized as religious at all. Two courts failed to protect Indian religious practices because they did not believe them to be, in fact, religious. In *Sequoyah*[239] and *Inupiat Community I*[240] the courts found themselves in the "confusing and essentially uncharted waters"[241] of First Amendment free exercise law. Neither of these cases, unfortunately, did much to help clear up these challenging issues.

Since 1965 the Cherokee Indians had been challenging the construction of the Tellico Dam on the Little Tennessee River in Tennessee. Like the Glen Canyon Dam discussed above, the completion of the Tellico Dam would have resulted in the flooding of a vast area upstream from the dam. Some of that area included Cherokee sacred sites, prayer spots, holy places, and cemeteries.[242] The Cherokee complaint stated that the Indians would "suffer injury by the infringement of their right to worship the religion of their choice in the manner of their choosing by the destruction of sites which they hold in reverence . . . ."[243] The court also noted that particular locations are more important to Indian religions than they are to most other religions.[244]

Despite the Indian claims, the *Sequoyah* court concluded that what was at issue was actually cultural and traditional interests and not religious interests.[245] It struggled with the notion that the destruction of a particular place could deny the plaintiffs the ability to freely exercise their religion. The court also required some sense that the contested government action inhibited some practice or belief that was *central* to the plaintiffs' religion.[246] It stated the following:

> Granting as we do that the individual plaintiffs sincerely adhere to a religion which honors ancestors and draws its spiritual strength from feelings of kinship with nature, they have fallen

239. 620 F.2d 1159 (1980).
240. 548 F. Supp. 182 (D. Alaska 1982), *aff'd*, 746 F.2d 570 (9th Cir. 1984).
241. Sequoyah v. TVA, 620 F.2d 1159, 1165 (6th Cir. 1980) (Merrit, J., dissenting).
242. *Id.* at 1160.
243. *Id.*
244. *Id.* at 1163.
245. *Id.* at 1164-65.
246. *Id.* at 1164.

short of demonstrating that worship at *the particular geographic location in question* is inseparable from the way of life, the cornerstone of their religious observance, or plays a central role in their religious ceremonies and practices.[247]

The court based its interest in centrality and particularity on *Wisconsin v. Yoder*,[248] *Frank v. State*,[249] and *People v. Woody*.[250] The *Sequoyah* court found that the impairment the Cherokee would suffer by the flooding of the Little Tennessee Valley would be cultural, rather than religious.[251] Because no religious interest was threatened, the rest of the *Yoder* analysis did not apply.

The *Sequoyah* court misconstrued the case law it used to support its opinion. The *Frank* opinion expressly stated that "[i]t is sufficient that the practice be deeply rooted in religious belief to bring it within the ambit of the free exercise clause and place on the state its burden of justification."[252] The *Frank* court decidedly rejected centrality as the standard for constitutional review.[253]

The Inupiat people faced a similar problem in their claim to title of the Beaufort and Chukchi Seas of the Arctic Ocean. They attempted to prevent the lease-sale of oil exploration rights in the seas that they traditionally used for fishing and whaling. They also claimed that the government action would deny them access to sacred sites.[254] Though this case was predominantly decided on sovereignty grounds, the Inupiat were also making an important religious exercise claim. The Ninth Circuit opinion[255] is very brief and relies heavily upon the District Court decision.[256] The religious exercise analysis of that decision focused upon the *Yoder* and *Sequoyah* decisions.

As in *Sequoyah*, the *Inupiat* court failed to find support for the religious character of the plaintiffs' claims. They revealed a lack of understanding regarding site-specific or place-based religious traditions in the following statements:

> In essence, the Inupiats claim that their religious beliefs are inextricably inter-twined with their hunting and gathering life-

---

247. *Id.* (emphasis added) (citations omitted).
248. 406 U.S. 205 (1972).
249. 604 P.2d 1068 (Alaska 1979).
250. 40 Cal. Rptr. 69 (1964).
251. *Sequoyah*, 620 F.2d at 1165.
252. *Frank*, 604 P.2d at 1072-73 (citations omitted).
253. *Id.* at 1074-75.
254. Inupiat Community of Arctic Slope v. United States, 548 F. Supp. 182, 183 (D. Alaska 1982) (*Inupiat Community I*).
255. *See* Inupiat Community of Arctic Slope v. United States, 746 F.2d 570 (9th Cir. 1984) (*Inupiat Community II*).
256. *Inupiat Community I*, 548 F. Supp. at 188.

style, and since all exploratory activities [in the contested area] negatively affect some portion of their subsistence area, all such activity should be interdicted on free-exercise grounds. Carried to its ultimate, their contention would result in the creation of a vast religious sanctuary over the Arctic seas beyond the state's territorial waters. A claim to such a large area based on such non-specific grounds cannot provide the sort of 'serious obstacle' contemplated by *Yoder*.[257]

The court found that the Inupiat had offered no explanation for the religious significance of the area at issue and for how the defendants' activities would interfere with their free exercise of religion.[258] Based on the geographic scope and religious unfamiliarity of their claim, the Native Americans were denied access to the free exercise test.

The Inupiat, however, did submit evidence of the integration of their religion and subsistence living.[259] In their culture, ice, sea, whale, and seal are all part of the religion. Any interference with their natural relations, therefore, affects the ability of the Inupiat to practice their religion. Because the court did not understand or could not appreciate this interdependence, they found no burden on religion.

Since they found no burden on religious practice, the court should not have reached the second prong of the *Yoder* test.[260] To correctly apply the second prong of *Yoder*, the court would have first had to find an Inupiat religious interest in the Beaufort and Chukchi Seas. Only then should they have balanced that religious interest against the government interest in selling oil exploration leases.[261] In this confused analysis the court skipped to the balancing test without first finding a religious burden.

These two cases show the clash between dominant and minority religions and traditions. In the Native American and Native Alaskan communities, the religious and cultural aspects of the individual and the community cannot be separated. The *Yoder* test has not adapted well to this difference between dominant culture religions and Native American religions. Unfortunately, even when the *Yoder* test might usefully have been employed, courts have frequently misapplied the analysis.

---

257. *Id.* at 188-89.

258. *Id.*

259. Plaintiffs' Memorandum in Opposition to Defendants' Motions for Judgment on the Pleadings at 126, Inupiat Community of Arctic Slope v. United States, 548 F. Supp. 182 (D. Alaska 1982) (No. A 81-19 CIV.) (*Inupiat Community I*), *cited in* Rosenberg, *supra* note 220, at 480 n.235.

260. *Inupiat Community I*, 548 F..Supp. at 189.

261. Rosenberg, *supra* note 220, at 481.

3. When Government Actions Do Not Infringe on Religion

Even when courts recognize that Native American interests in particular areas are religious, they are not always willing to accept that government action infringes upon religious practice. These cases generally turn on factual determinations made by courts that contradict claims made by plaintiff Indians. The *Yoder* balancing test is often misapplied by these courts as they balance government interest against religious interests after determining that the contested government actions do not infringe on religious rights. Two cases will illustrate the improper application of the *Yoder* standards.

In *Crow v. Gullet*,[262] the Lakota and Tsistsistas plaintiffs sought declaratory and injunctive relief against development in Bear Butte State Park in South Dakota. This area had been used by the Lakota and Tsistsistas Indians for vision quests, sweat lodge ceremonies, and the rite of isolation and deprivation. The beauty of the Black Hills had also attracted tourists and the state constructed a state park. The case at issue arose when the state made plans to develop this park by adding more roads and visitor facilities. The plaintiffs claimed that these developments and the restrictions necessary for construction of the new facilities diminished the spiritual value of the Butte and impaired their religious ceremonies.

The district court was not convinced by the Lakota and Tsistsistas claims and concluded that they had "failed to establish any infringement of a constitutionally cognizable first amendment right."[263] The court based its opinion, in part, on the fact that the plaintiffs had no "property interest" in the park.[264] The court also compared the total infringement suffered in *Badoni*[265] and noted that the impact suffered by the present plaintiffs was only partial and temporary.[266] Finally, the district court compared the temporary restrictions on the ability of the Lakota and Tsistsistas to practice their religion with the "compelling state interest[] in preserving the environment and the resource from further decay and erosion, in protecting the health, safety, and welfare of park visitors, and in improving public access to this unique geological and historical landmark."[267] In short, the state interest in maintaining this park outweighed the religious rights of the Lakota and Tsistsistas.

This extraordinary opinion was affirmed by the Eighth Circuit[268] as not clearly erroneous. Although the district court found no religious burden, it mistakenly proceeded to the second step of the *Yoder* analysis. Finding no

---

262. 706 F.2d 856 (8th Cir. 1983).
263. Crow v. Gullet, 541 F. Supp. 785, 794 (D.C. S.D. 1982).
264. *Id.* at 791.
265. *See supra* text accompanying notes 229-39.
266. *Crow*, 541 F. Supp. at 792.
267. *Id.* at 794.
268. *Crow*, 706 F.2d at 856.

burden should have ended the analysis. The comparison with *Badoni* is similarly misplaced because the plaintiffs in this case had not, according to the court, met their burden of proving the "indispensability" of overnight camping.[269] Lastly, the lack of property interest of the plaintiffs, while possibly a valid factor to be considered, is clearly not dispositive of whether or not citizens can complain about governmental uses of public land that infringe upon individual rights.[270]

The Navajo and Hopi tribes of northeastern Arizona protested similar development in the Coconino National Forest in *Wilson v. Block*.[271] The San Francisco Peaks lie adjacent to the Navajo and Hopi reservations and are believed by them to be the home of specific deities who are invoked in Navajo religious ceremonies. The Hopis believe the Peaks to be the home of "Kachinas" who are emissaries sent by the creator to communicate with human beings. The tribes believe that development of the area would impair the healing power of the Peaks and insult the Kachinas and the creator.

The Forest Service had used a portion of the Peaks for downhill skiing since 1937, though the facilities were limited. In 1977 the Forest Service transferred the permit to operate the ski facilities to a private company who wanted to expand the operations. The Navajo and Hopi protested this planned expansion because it would cause the Peaks to lose their healing power and, therefore, their religious efficacy to the tribes. They also noted that expansion of the ski facilities would make it more difficult to teach their people that these places were sacred. The chair of the Hopi tribe stated, "[t]he destruction of these [religious] practices will also destroy our present way of life and culture."[272]

The court acknowledged that the claims of the Navajo and Hopi were legitimately religious. It also correctly summarized the *Cantwell*, *Sherbert*, and *Thomas* line of analysis. The court, however, rejected the plaintiffs' application of *Sherbert* and *Thomas* because "[t]he government here has not conditioned any benefit upon conduct proscribed or mandated by plaintiffs' beliefs."[273] Because the religious practices and beliefs of the Navajo and Hopi are site specific, they argued that development would "severely impair the practice of [their] religions if it destroyed the natural conditions necessary for the performance of ceremonies . . . ."[274] The court backed away from the *Sequoyah* centrality requirement, but said that "[i]f the plaintiffs cannot demonstrate that the government land at issue is indispensable to some

269. *Id.* at 858. Overnight camping had been restricted during the construction of the park improvements. *Id.*

270. *See* Sequoyah v. TVA, 620 F.2d 1159, 1164 (1980).

271. 708 F.2d 735 (D.C. Cir. 1983), *cert. denied*, 464 U.S. 977 (1983).

272. *Id.* at 740 n.2.

273. *Id.* at 741.

274. *Id.* at 742.

religious practice, whether or not central to their religious practice, they have not justified a First Amendment claim."[275]

The Navajo and Hopi produced evidence that peaks were sacred and indispensable to their religious practice.[276] The government argued that the limited proposed development would only impact on a portion of the character of the Peaks and that a guarantee of access to the Peaks should permit continuation of "all essential rituals."[277] The court held that the plaintiffs had not met their burden of demonstrating that the government's proposed land use "would impair a religious practice that could not be performed at any other site."[278] Because the court found that the plaintiffs had not shown a burden on their religious practice, it did not reach the question of whether the government's interest in the proposed expansion was compelling or not.[279]

Wilson reveals the danger of allowing courts to determine whether an infringement on religious rights meets the *Yoder* "burden" standard. *Wilson* was reduced to a contest of experts. The Navajo and Hopi affidavits spoke of the tragic effects this development would have on their ability to practice their religion. The government experts testified that the effects would not be all that bad. The court was impressed by the government's experts and required the plaintiffs to prove the indispensability of the particular area at issue. It ignored the Navajo and Hopi claims that the Peaks are "sacred" and that their religious practices required "natural conditions."[280] Indispensability, in this case, became only a thin mask for the *Sequoyah* centrality requirement. The decision was meant to take the court out of making doctrinal judgments about religious claims, but this case shows that the judgment of what is and is not indispensable will still require government approval of religious claims. Even if the "indispensable" standard is preferable to the "centrality" standard, the opportunity for a court to apply culturally dominant perspectives to its analysis of a minority religion is too difficult to avoid.

D. Free Exercise Conclusions

Analysis of the history and development of free exercise jurisprudence, focusing especially on the conflicts that arise between the government and Native Americans, reveals that the Indians almost always lose. Sometimes the government refuses to recognize the religious character of Indian religious claims. Other times the government recognizes that the Native American interests are religious but does not acknowledge that the government actions at issue actually burden religious practice. In other instances the government

---

275. *Id.* at 743.
276. *Id.* at 744.
277. *Id.* (quoting a government expert on Hopi and Navajo religion).
278. *Id.* at 744.
279. *Id.* at 745.
280. *Id.* at 742.

acknowledges its burden on Native Americans' religious practices but believes that the interests of the majority culture trump the religious rights of the Indians. In all these cases the courts have failed to protect the religious exercise claims of Native Americans.

In *Northwest Indian Cemetery Protective Ass'n v. Peterson*,[281] the Ninth Circuit held out the promise of a brighter future for Native Peoples. Unfortunately, that decision was overturned by the Supreme Court in *Lyng*.[282] Because the *Lyng* decision captures the essence of the conflict over religious rights, the next section focuses on it exclusively.

III. Lyng v. Northwest Indian Cemetery Protection Ass'n and an Evolving Understanding of Judicial Responsibility for Individual Rights

The Supreme Court continues to be engaged in an historical debate concerning the protection of individual rights and the scope of the role of the judiciary. Recently, the Supreme Court held that the Free Exercise Clause of the First Amendment to the United States Constitution did not prohibit the government from harvesting timber or constructing a road through land considered sacred to three Northern California Indian tribes.[283] The differences between the majority opinion and the dissent characterize some of the salient features of the process of questioning the role of the judiciary in resolving these conflicts.

After presenting the facts and analysis of *Lyng* in detail, this section will discuss some of the ways in which the decision exemplifies current trends in the Supreme Court and what those trends might mean for Native American religious liberty.

A. Facts

The towns of Gasquet and Orleans are approximately sixty miles apart in the northwest corner of California, twenty miles from the Pacific Ocean and thirty miles south of the Oregon border. Between them lies the Six Rivers National Forest. The Forest Service first planned to link these towns in the late 1940s. A standard jeep road was constructed in the mid-1960s and was paved in parts over the next twenty years. The primary purpose of the road was to facilitate logging efforts in the area, though it also helped in forest fire protection and provided increased recreational access to the area.

In 1972, the Forest Service began preparing a multiple-use management plan for a 67,500 acre area known as the Blue Creek Unit of the Six Rivers National Forest. The plan called for the harvesting of 733,000,000 board feet

---

281. 764 F.2d 581 (9th Cir. 1985), *withdrawn and aff'd on reh'g*, 795 F.2d 688 (9th Cir. 1986).

282. 485 U.S. 439 (1988).

283. *Peterson*, 764 F.2d at 586.

of timber over an eighty year period, the paving of the remaining six mile segment of the road between Gasquet and Orleans (the G-O road), and the construction of an additional two hundred miles of logging roads. The Blue Creek Unit Plan, adopted in 1976, was the origin of the dispute which arose between the Yurok, Karok, and Tolowa Indians and the Forest Service.

These tribes call the area known to the United States government as the Blue Creek area, the High Country. For at least two hundred years, and possibly longer, they have gone to the High Country for religious purposes. Though these three communities have somewhat different religious beliefs, they all share some common beliefs and practices. The High Country, they believe, is where the prehuman spirits went when human beings arrived on earth. These spirits are a source of religious power and medicine. Through interaction with the spirits of these places, individual practitioners attain spiritual and curative power which is shared with other members of their community. The communities at large depend on the spirits of the High Country to prepare their tribal leaders for ceremonies and to provide them with healing power. These tribes also believe that their religious practices have important "World Renewal" functions as well. The welfare of the tribe and indeed all humanity depend on the ability of individual practitioners to communicate with the spirits of the High Country.

Of special importance in the Blue Creek area are rock outcroppings called Chimney Rock, Doctor Rock, and Peak 8. The importance of these peaks has grown as others have been developed or desecrated. These sites themselves are believed to be sacred, as they provide the environment where spiritual rituals may take place. The qualities of "silence, the aesthetic perspective, and the physical attributes, are an extension of the sacredness of [each] particular site."[284] The pristine, undisturbed natural environment, privacy and silence that have characterized the High Country, and especially these particular peaks, for the preceding centuries are essential for spiritual use of the area. The G-O Road plan called for construction within a mile of these sacred areas.

After administrative remedies failed, the plaintiff Indians[285] and the State of California sought a preliminary injunction against the Forest Service to prevent, among other things, the construction of the final six mile segment of road, known as the Chimney Rock section. Their request for injunctive relief was denied,[286] but a trial on the merits found that the Forest Service plan

---

284. DORTHEA THEODORATUS ET AL., CULTURAL RESOURCES OF THE CHIMNEY ROCK SECTION, GASQUET-ORLEANS ROAD, SIX RIVERS NATIONAL FOREST 101-02 (1979), *reprinted in* FOREST SERVICE, U.S. DEP'T OF AGRICULTURE, FINAL ENVIRONMENTAL IMPACT STATEMENT, GASQUET-ORLEANS ROAD, CHIMNEY ROCK SECTION app. K, at 14 (1982), *cited in* Lyng v. Northwest Indian Cemetery Protective Ass'n, 485 U.S. 439, 459 (1987).

285. Including four Indian individuals, seven conservation groups, two individual conservationists, and the Northwest Indian Cemetery Protective Association.

286. Northwest Indian Cemetery Protective Ass'n v. Peterson, 552 F. Supp. 951 (N.D. Cal.

violated the First Amendment of the Constitution,[287] several federal environmental acts,[288] and the fishing and water rights of the Hoopa Valley Indian
Reservation residents and the federal government's trust responsibilities to the
Hoopa Valley Indians. The district court judge permanently enjoined the
Forest Service from constructing the Chimney Rock section of the G-O Road
or engaging in timber harvesting until they produced a new environmental
impact statement.[289]

While appeal to the Ninth Circuit was pending, the United States Congress
passed the California Wilderness Act of 1984.[290] The Act protected most of
the contested area from timber harvesting but left open a corridor for the
construction of the Chimney Rock section of the G-O Road. The Ninth
Circuit affirmed the district court in nearly all respects.[291] It did, however,
vacate the district court order as it applied to the federal government's trust
responsibility to the Indians of the Hoopa Valley Reservation, because the
trust responsibility issue could not be decided properly without the tribe being
represented.[292] It also withdrew that part of the order relating to the violation
of the federal Wilderness Act that had been made moot by the passage of the
California Wilderness Act. The other parts of the district court order,
including the constitutional issue, were affirmed.

The Supreme Court, in a 5-3 decision,[293] reversed the Ninth Circuit.[294]
Justice O'Connor wrote for the majority[295] and held that the First Amendment did not prohibit the government from permitting timber harvesting and
road construction in the Blue Creek/High Country area.[296] The majority
viewed this question to be controlled by the Court's analysis in *Bowen v.
Roy*[297] where the Court rejected an Indian's constitutional challenge to the

---

1982).

287. "Congress shall make no law respecting an establishment of religion, or prohibiting the
free exercise thereof . . . ." U.S. CONST. amend. I.

288. National Environmental Policy Act (NEPA) of 1969, Pub. L. No. 91-190, 83 Stat. 852
(1970) (codified as amended at 42 U.S.C. §§ 4321-4370(b) (1988)); Wilderness Act of 1964, Pub.
L. No. 88-577, 78 Stat. 890 (codified as amended at 16 U.S.C. §§ 1131-1136 (1988); Federal
Water Pollution Control (Clean Water) Act, Pub. L. No. 92-500, 86 Stat. 880 (codified as
amended at 33 U.S.C. §§ 1251-1387 (1988)).

289. Northwest Indian Protective Ass'n v. Peterson, 565 F. Supp. 586, 606 (N.D. Cal. 1983).

290. Pub. L. 98-425, 98 Stat. 1619 (codified as amended at 16 U.S.C. §§ 1131-1132 (1988)).

291. *See* Northwest Indian Cemetery Protective Ass'n v. Peterson 764 F.2d 581 (9th Cir.
1985), *withdrawn and aff'd on reh'g*, 795 F.2d 688 (9th Cir. 1986), *rev'd sub nom.* Lyng v.
Northwest Indian Cemetery Protective Ass'n, 485 U.S. 439 (1987).

292. Northwest Indian Cemetery Protective Ass'n v. Peterson, 795 F.2d 688, 697 n.10.

293. Newly appointed Justice Anthony Kennedy did not participate in this decision.

294. *See* Lyng v. Northwest Indian Cemetery Protective Ass'n, 485 U.S. 439 (1988).

295. Chief Justice William Rehnquist and Justices O'Connor, Antonin Scalia, John Paul
Stevens, and Byron White.

296. *Lyng*, at 440.

297. 476 U.S. 693 (1986).

assignment of a social security number to his daughter.[298] He believed that the use of a social security number by government agencies would "rob the spirit" of his daughter and prevent her from becoming a holy person.[299] The *Lyng* Court stated that the use of a social security number could not be distinguished from the building of a road or the harvesting of timber on government land.[300] For the majority, the key point was that these actions did not coerce an individual to act in opposition to his or her religious beliefs or penalize him or her by prohibiting the receipt of some governmental benefit. They reasoned that any other decision in this context would amount to "beneficial ownership of . . . public property" and "diminution of the Government['s] property rights."[301]

The dissent[302] described the majority reading of the Free Exercise Clause as narrow, emphasizing the form rather than the effect of government action.[303] Where the majority required that the plaintiffs show affirmative coercion, Justice Brennan, writing in dissent, called for a test that focuses on government action that poses a real and substantial threat of frustrating religious practices.[304] The Brennan test would require that claimants would have to show a sincere belief and a substantial threat to religious practice. Upon such a showing the government would have to justify the infringement upon religious exercise with a compelling state interest.

B. Sacred Places and Free Exercise of Religion

As a result of the *Lyng* decision, the sole inquiry in a free exercise conflict is whether a government action coerces an individual into violating his or her religious beliefs. An infringement can be either indirect coercion or a penalty, but the effect of a government action upon the ability of a particular group to practice its religion is not relevant to the determination of constitutionality.[305] The dissent protests that "[b]oth common sense and our prior cases teach us . . . that governmental action that makes the practice of a given faith more difficult necessarily penalizes that practice and thereby tends to prevent adherence to religious belief."[306] Justice Brennan explained, "The incongruous result is that when the government forces an individual or group to chose between their beliefs and a benefit, it is an impermissible burden, yet when the government prevents a practice and entirely eliminates the element of choice, no burden exists."[307]

298. *Id.* at 710-12.
299. *Id.* at 696.
300. *Lyng*, 485 U.S. at 449.
301. *Id.* at 453.
302. Justices William Brennan, Thurgood Marshall, and Blackmun.
303. *Lyng*, 485 U.S. at 466-67 (Brennan, J., dissenting).
304. *Id.* at 459.
305. *Id.* at 451.
306. *Id.* at 456.
307. Nancy Akins, *New Direction in Sacred Lands Claims:* Lyng v. Northwest Indian

C. The Role of the Judiciary

1. The Judiciary and Native Americans

The previous sections have developed the history and analysis of the *Lyng* case in some detail because these issues point to what is the primary precipitate of the *Lyng* decision. *Lyng* is rightly seen as a case about the Free Exercise Clause and Native American claims to sacred lands. Underlying the analysis in *Lyng*, however, is the central issue of the role of the judiciary in protecting individual rights and its interaction with the other branches of government.

Justice O'Connor raises this issue in her response to Justice Brennan's dissent when she asserts that his proposal "would cast the Judiciary in a role that [it] was never intended to play."[308] Her opinion reflects her own significant deference to other branches of government on constitutional issues, one that seems to be gaining greater acceptance by other members of the Court.[309] Justice Brennan described this abdication to the legislature as bestowing "on one party . . . the unilateral authority to resolve all future disputes in its favor, subject only to the Court's toothless exhortation to be 'sensitive' to affected religions."[310]

Justice O'Connor sees the claimants as asking the Court "to satisfy every citizen's religious needs and desires."[311] In a pluralistic society with many religious beliefs, she anticipates competing demands on government to conform to the mandates of each religious group. Since neither the Constitution nor the courts are equipped to reconcile these competing demands, that task is left to the legislature. To support her claim, she cites *The Federalist No. 10*, which suggests that competition among religious and political factions will temper these demands.[312]

This decision has profound implications for all litigation of constitutional claims. Her statement puts the religious interests of minorities in the hands of the majoritarian dominated branches of government to protect them from infringement on fundamental rights by those same branches. *Roy*,[313] upon which the majority decision heavily relies, centers upon the fact that the claimant was asking the government to change one of its internal procedures to avoid offending his religious beliefs. That case focused on *how* the

---

Cemetery Protective Association, 29 NAT. RESOURCES J. 593, 605 (1989).

308. *Lyng*, 485 U.S. at 458.

309. Donald Falk, Lyng v. Northwest Indian Cemetery Protective Association: *Bulldozing First Amendment Protection of Indian Sacred Lands*, 16 ECOLOGY L.Q. 515, 561 (1989).

310. *Lyng*, 485 U.S. at 473.

311. *Id.* at 453.

312. *Id.* (citing THE FEDERALIST No. 10, at 58-59 (James Madison) (Jacob E. Cooke ed., 1961)).

313. 476 U.S. 693 (1986).

government conducted its own affairs. The issue in the *Lyng* case centers upon *what* effect the government is having on the ability of the claimants to practice their religion. By characterizing all government agency action as same as *Roy* internal procedures, the Court confers absolute discretion on executive and congressional agencies with respect to the effect of their actions on fundamental rights.

For Native Americans, this decision means that there is no constitutional review of government actions that fail to prohibit outright rituals or require violation of beliefs. Actions which make it impossible or meaningless for Indians to practice their faith cannot be reviewed. The severity of this ruling is exacerbated by the fact that Indians are dependent upon so many federal agencies and subject to the actions of so many public land managers.[314] The Court encourages land managers to accommodate religious practices of Native Americans,[315] but also assures the agencies that their determination of what is an acceptable level of deleterious effect will receive unfavorable review.

When one branch of government abdicates its responsibility, the three-footed stool of American democracy cannot stand. A government which does not check cannot balance. James Madison warned against the gradual accumulation of power in one of the departments of government. Madison saw that the legislative branch was most prone to power grabbing in a republican government. A government which allows the power of majority factions to dominate minority groups is, in his mind, no different from the pre-social contract community. He said:

> Justice is the end of government. It is the end of civil society. It ever has been, and ever will be pursued, until it be obtained, or until liberty be lost in the pursuit. In a society, under the forms of which the stronger faction can readily unite and oppress the weaker, anarchy may as truly be said to reign, as in a state of nature where the weaker individual is not secured against the violence of the stronger.[316]

The *Lyng* decision returns Native Americans to the state of nature in regards to religious liberty. Unless some bulwark can be established against the strength of the majority, their religious freedom will not be secure against the violence of intolerance.

2. *Constitutional Rights and the Judiciary*

That Justice O'Connor and Justice Brennan, along with their fellow justices, should disagree about what is the proper role of the judiciary in resolving an issue of this complexity is not surprising. These questions require herculean

---

314. Falk, *supra* note 309, at 564.
315. *Lyng*, 485 U.S. at 453.
316. THE FEDERALIST No. 51, at 352 (James Madison) (Jacob E. Cooke ed., 1961).

effort to dissect and have been the source of immense conflict throughout the history of the modern liberal state. Since Jean Jacques Rousseau and the Baron de Montesquieu derived different understandings of the nature of the state and the relationship of the judiciary to the other constituent parts of the state, there has been widespread disagreement on these points.

The interesting aspect of this problem in *Lyng* is more *how* the Court arrived at its decision than *what* its decision held. The two opinions in the case reach substantially different results through generally different approaches, even though they do manifest some similarity. Loosely, Justice O'Connor appears to favor a restrained judiciary that defers substantially to legislative determinations in all areas save for those directly relegated to the care of the Court. Justice Brennan, on the other hand, calls the Court to be more active in protecting individual liberty against the excesses of the representative branches. In this sense, both Justices agree with Montesquieu that the different branches need to be separated from one another and with the Federalists that they should also serve as some form of check on the power of the other. Justice O'Connor seems to share Rousseau's optimism that the general will of the people will produce a legal culture that will respect minority rights, while Justice Brennan appears more skeptical.

Justice O'Connor relies on a variety of methods of legal reasoning to justify her decision: appeal to fundamental principles, reference to general policy goals, and reliance upon established precedent. These three approaches are interwoven throughout her discussion of the impact of the Free Exercise Clause of the Constitution on this case. She relies on the interpretation of the scope of the Free Exercise Clause discussed in *Bowen v. Roy* to limit the breadth of the Court's discussion.[317] She points to the potential conflict between a wide range of government policies and the fundamental rights asserted by the *Lyng* plaintiffs.[318] She discusses the central principles which give order to the relationship among the governmental branches.[319]

D. Lyng and What It Portends

Lyng is a tragic defeat for the Native American population in this country, who saw it as an opportunity for vindication and protection of what they understood to be their rights as United States citizens. Their disappointment is also a loss for other minority groups, who might otherwise have sought the protection of the judicial system from over-zealous legislatures. The Court has restricted its own ability to protect individual rights by limiting the questions it will consider. Part of this decision is an only slightly subtle intertextual discussion of which body among the governmental entities is best equipped to respond to this claim. The *Lyng* Court has held that unless there is a clear and

---

317. *Lyng*, 485 U.S. at 457-58.
318. *Id.* at 452.
319. *Id.* at 457-58.

unambiguous violation of the plain meaning of the Free Exercise Clause, it will not interfere in legislative or administrative decisions. This decision reflects a heavy deference to majoritarian decision making, with all its attendant difficulties.

IV. Native American Spirituality

At the center of all the controversy expressed in the cases discussed in this article Indian peoples are struggling desperately to maintain their spiritual beliefs, their culture, their ethnic identity, and their way of life. Two problems appear between the majority Indian communities. The first difficulty Native American communities have faced in presenting their legal challenges to the actions of the invading peoples is that they, like most insular minorities, tend to be viewed as one and similar. Because they are different from Europeans, all Indians are seen as a mass or a unit. Most people fail to see that individual tribal groups and indeed individual Indians have different experiences of spirituality and different belief systems. Native Americans are quick to point out that their traditions are as complex and varied as the multiplicity of their cultures would suggest. The first problem Native Peoples face is that judges fail to accept that Native American belief and practice is itself pluralistic and varied.

The second problem Native Americans face when they present constitutional challenges to government action is that they are asking judges to protect religious beliefs and traditions fundamentally different from their own. If courts are to make insightful decisions about Native American religious exercise disputes, they must have some understanding of the nature of Indian life and of its differences from that of the dominant culture.

This section attempts to illuminate some of those differences, to describe some of the general characteristics of Native American spirituality, and in particular to draw out the significance of sacred places. Of necessity, this discussion will simplify a complex subject. Not all Native American groups would ascribe to all of the beliefs portrayed here, but this level of generalization will usefully capture some of the most salient points of interest. Other scholars have written on this subject with particular virtuosity and should be consulted for a more detailed description of the spirituality of America's original peoples.[320]

---

320. *See, e.g.,* DELORIA, *supra* note 3; SEEING WITH A NATIVE EYE (Walter H. Capps ed., 1976); JOHN (FIRE) LAME DEER & RICHARD ERDOES, LAME DEER: SEEKER OF VISIONS (1972); JOHN G. NEIHARDT, BLACK ELK SPEAKS (1932); AKE HULTKRANTZ, THE RELIGIONS OF THE AMERICAN INDIANS (1967); RUPERT ROSS, DANCING WITH A GHOST (1992).

A. Differences Between Europeans and Americans

Before courts can protect Indian sacred sites and practices, they must first appreciate the spiritual character of their claims. The many differences between the spiritual life of Native Americans and the descendants of immigrants challenges understanding and toleration. These differences arise from several factors.

As discussed earlier,[321] the general assumption by Europeans when they encountered Native Peoples was that the natives knew no religion. Out of ignorance and intolerance of theologies different from their own, the Europeans called the indigenous peoples pagans, savages, brutes, and heathens. The process of cultural destruction began with the first Columbian contacts.

> [E]ach time the Spanish encountered a native individual or group in the course of their travels they were ordered to read to the Indians a statement informing them of the truth of Christianity and the necessity to swear immediate allegiance to the Pope and the Spanish crown. . . . As one Spanish conquistador and historian described the routine: 'After they had been put in chains, someone read the *Requerimento* without knowing their language and without any interpreters, and without either the reader or the Indians understanding the language they had not opportunity to reply, being in immediately carried away prisoners, the Spanish not failing to use the stick on those who did not go fast enough.'[322]

As it was at that time, language is currently one of the primary obstacles. Because the dominant society has not accepted native spirituality on its own terms, all Indian traditions and beliefs must be translated, in order for their petition to be heard in the American judicial system.[323]

This necessity might seem only practically expedient, but it has significant consequences. The result is that the plaintiff Indians in *Smith* had to describe their use of peyote as "sacrament," even though that word has no currency in Indian spirituality. Indians describe their sacred places as churches or altars in order to help non-Indians understand their significance. They have analogized moose meat used in a funeral ceremony to the "wine and wafer of Christianity."[324] All these phenomena are understood, if at all, only in translation, not in their original terms. Indeed, Native American traditional languages do not even have a word to express the European notion of

---

321. *See supra* text accompanying notes 14-38.
322. STANNARD, *supra* note 2, at 65-66.
323. *See* Christopher T. Vecsey, *Prologue, in* HANDBOOK, *supra* note 84, at 12.
324. Frank v. State, 604 P.2d 1072, 1072 (Alaska 1979).

"religion."[325] These differences frustrate any discussion of spiritual practices.

Other factors are equally significant. Native American spiritual practices manifest great diversity from group to group. They also tolerate substantially more internal diversity than does the Judeo-Christian tradition. Within Native American life there are no accepted canonical texts, no sense of orthodoxy. The *Lyng* court saw in this lack of uniformity a source of doubt as to the validity of the claims of the plaintiffs.[326] In reality, however, Indian traditions simply allow a greater sense of pluralism than do others. Unfortunately, this diversity has not been accepted by non-Indians as an essential aspect of tribal beliefs.[327]

Native American spiritual traditions tend to be more spatially oriented and less time-oriented. Western European religions are based on a different relationship to space and an "assumption that time proceeds in a linear fashion."[328] The result for Judeo-Christian religions is that "[r]evelation has generally been considered as a specific body of truth related to a particular individual at a specific time."[329] For Native Americans, "[r]evelation [is] a particular experience at a particular place, [with] no universal truth emerging . . . ."[330] Some Judeo-Christian religions, unlike Indian religions, are arranged hierarchically.[331] There is a clear line of authority; some people decide what other people should believe. Though Native American communities also have shamans, priests, and medicine men and women, their relationship to the people is much different. They are viewed not as teachers or missionaries, but as people who have some special "proximity and access to the sacred beings and forces."[332]

Finally, Native American spiritual practices are mystifying because they are generally conducted in secret and in remote places. Most non-Indians have never witnessed an authentic Indian spiritual ceremony. Because they have been remembered through the oral history of discrete communities, there has been little opportunity even for those with interest in Native American spirituality to understand and appreciate them.

---

325. HULTKRANTZ, *supra* note 320, at 9.

326. *See* Lyng v. Northwest Indian Cemetery Protective Ass'n, 485 U.S. 439 (1988).

327. Vecsey, *supra* note 323, at 12.

328. DELORIA, *supra* note 3, at 76.

329. *Id.* at 80.

330. *Id.*

331. JERRY MANDER, THE ABSENCE OF THE SACRED: THE FAILURE OF TECHNOLOGY AND THE SURVIVAL OF THE INDIAN NATIONS 209 (1991).

332. Deward E. Walker, Jr., *Protection of American Indian Sacred Geography, in* HANDBOOK, *supra* note 84, at 105.

B. *Characteristics of Native American Spiritual Traditions*

Being rooted in and connected to the natural world are two fundamental characteristics of Indian spirituality. Indian religions are "religions of nature." Through the myths, legends, stories, and rituals that carry the religious beliefs through history, Indians learn that they are part of the environment around them. "Mysterious but real power dwells in nature — in mountains, rivers, rocks, even pebbles. White people may consider them inanimate objects, but to the Indian, they are enmeshed in the web of the universe, pulsating with life and potent with medicine."[333] Indians also acknowledge their dependence upon the earth.

> We all start out in this world as tiny seeds — no different from our animal brothers and sisters, the deer, the bear, the buffalo, or the trees, the flowers, the winged people. Every particle of our bodies come from the good things Mother Earth has put forth. Mother Earth is our real mother, because every bit of us truly comes from her, and daily she takes care of us.[334]

They hunted and farmed, took life and sustained it, but they attributed their success to the generosity of nature.[335] Out of this reverence for nature grows the sense that places can be sacred.

Native American spiritual beliefs are also based on a related spirit of "connectedness." All of Indian life is interrelated and dependent. All aspects of reality, earth, animals, spirits, stars, humans, and plants, are one. The past is contained in the present. The earth which gives life to people today is the body of people who have died. A Crow chief said: "The soil you see is not ordinary soil — it is the dust of the blood, the flesh and the bones of our ancestors. . . . You will have to dig down through the surface before you can find nature's earth, as the upper portion is Crow."[336] In the Indian world it is impossible to "separate religious reality from other aspects of communal experience."[337] The spiritual aspect of life is intimately tied to the political, the economic, and the social.[338] Every human action, hunting, weaving, prayer, and dance is "a recognition and affirmation of the sacredness of life."[339]

333. RICHARD ERDOES & ALPHONSO ORTIZ, AMERICAN INDIAN MYTHS AND LEGENDS at xi (1984).

334. ED McGAA, EAGLE MAN, MOTHER EARTH SPIRITUALITY: NATIVE AMERICAN PATHS TO HEALING OURSELVES AND OUR WORLD 203 (1990).

335. Christopher T. Vecsey, *American Indian Environmental Religions, in* CHRISTOPHER T. VECSEY ET AL., AMERICAN INDIAN ENVIRONMENTALISTS: ECOLOGICAL ISSUES IN NATIVE AMERICAN HISTORY 15 (1980).

336. DELORIA, *supra* note 3, at 166.

337. *Id.* at 82; *see also* Barre Toelken, *Seeing with a Native Eye: How Many Sheep Will it Hold?, in* SEEING WITH A NATIVE EYE, *supra* note 320, at 14.

338. MANDER, *supra* note 331, at 208.

339. Annie L. Booth & Harvey L. Jacobs, *Ties that Bind: Native American Beliefs as a*

Native American spirituality is also communal. Christianity, on the other hand, is premised upon an individual response to revelation.[340] Indian tribal culture is dominated by religion. "Ceremonies of community wide [sic] scope are the chief characteristic feature of religious activity."[341] The interdependence of subsistence living requires that every aspect of the community be integrated. There is, of course, a deep individual dimension to Indian spirituality, but the religions remain inherently communal.[342] The communal character of belief and practice informs the connection to the natural world and the connectedness of reality. It allows the Navajo in *Wilson v. Block*[343] to believe that the San Francisco Peaks are a living deity and that they are essential to the survival of the Navajo people.

Deward E. Walker, Jr. has summarized the "core features" of traditional Native American spirituality as follows:

1. A body of mythic accounts explaining cultural origins and cultural development as distinctive peoples.
2. A special sense of the sacred that is centered in natural time and natural geography.
3. A set of critical and calendrical rituals that give social form and expression to religious beliefs and permit the groups and their members to experience their mythology.
4. A group of individuals normally described as shamans (medicine men and medicine women) who teach and lead group(s) in the conduct of their ritual life.
5. A set of prescriptive and proscriptive (ethical) guidelines establishing appropriate behavior associated with the sacred.
6. A means of communicating (dreams and visions) with sacred spirits and forces.
7. A belief in dreams and visions as the principal sources of religious knowledge.
8. A belief that harmony must be maintained with the sacred through the satisfactory conduct of rituals and adherence to sacred prescriptions and proscriptions.
9. A belief that while all aspects of nature and culture are potentially sacred, there are certain times and geological locations that together possess great sacredness.
10. The major goal of religious life is gaining the spiritual power and understanding necessary for a successful life,

---

Foundation for Environmental Consciousness, 12 ENVTL. ETHICS 40 (1990).

340. DELORIA, *supra* note 3, at 63, 198.
341. *Id.* at 200.
342. *Id.* at 200-08.
343. *See supra* note 227.

by entering into the sacred at certain sacred times/
places.[344]

These norms would not be likely to achieve universal approval, but they are
generally descriptive of the common attributes of Native American spirituality.

C. Sacred Places

The sacredness of place captures all of these characteristics of Native
American life. When Indians claim that particular sites are sacred they say,

> [O]ur ancestors arose from the earth here; our parents are buried
> here, we receive revelation here; . . . we make pilgrimages and
> vision quests here; our gods dwell here; our religion requires that
> we have privacy here; . . . [and] hence, this sacred site must
> remain undisturbed, or we must have unlimited access to this
> place.[345]

They say that when they speak of land, they "are speaking of something
sacred,"[346] and they say that some areas are more sacred than others.[347]

To Native Americans the sanctity of land and places is the reference point
for their understanding of the world.[348] The Indians chose to live close to
their sacred places: there the power and mystery of life are concentrated. The
sacred sites are sources of insight and meaning. They are regarded as
"essential for human survival."[349]

D. Conclusions

The history of Indian interaction with whites has been a struggle for land.
European immigrants wanted land to occupy and develop, to exploit and
civilize. For the Indians, this struggle has been not only a territorial issue, but
also a spiritual issue, and a question of cultural survival. This section has
shown that the Indian relationship with the land is intimately spiritual.
Because relationship with the earth pervades the entire Indian existence, any
damage to the land affects the entire people. The contests portrayed in the
cases discussed herein are, as a result, not simple battles over resources, not
merely logging interests against wilderness preservation. At their core, they
are about the survival of the Indian nations, the identity of the plaintiffs as
Indians, and the well being of all people.

---

344. Walker, *supra* note 332, at 102.
345. Vecsey, *supra* note 323, at 22.
346. PETER MATHIESSON, INDIAN COUNTRY 119 (1984).
347. Dewald Walker identifies 30 sacred sites that are currently in use, out of an
accumulating list of approximately 300. Walker, *supra* note 332, at 108-09.
348. DELORIA, *supra* note 3, at 75.
349. Walker, *supra* note 332, at 25.

V. What Can We Do?

The unwillingness of the Supreme Court to entertain Indian free exercise challenges to government actions when Indians ask the Court to protect sacred sites creates a completely novel situation in the history of fundamental rights in this country. Native Americans have been told by the court in *Lyng*[350] and *Smith*[351] that they should look to legislative solutions for their problems with the federal government's use of its own land.[352] The Bill of Rights was drafted to protect fundamental individual rights from the whims of majoritarian politics, but the Supreme Court has told Indians that it will not protect those rights against actions by the other branches of government. Justice O'Connor, the author of the *Lyng* opinion, in her earlier concurrence in *Smith* quoted Justice Jackson's memorable words:

> The very purpose of [the] Bill of Rights was to withdraw certain subjects from the vicissitudes of political controversy, to place them beyond the reach of majorities and officials and to establish them as legal principles to be applied by the courts. One's right to life, liberty, and property, to free speech, a free press, freedom of worship and assembly, and other fundamental rights may not be submitted to vote; they depend on the outcome of no elections.[353]

Native Americans are forced to ask the very people they believe to be infringing on their rights to protect them. In this situation there is little cause for hope.

Any solution must advocate some substantial changes in approach. Two possible solutions are (1) reformation of the free exercise jurisprudence of free exercise, and (2) legislative action.

A. Jurisprudential Reform

The *Lyng* and *Smith* Courts read the Free Exercise Clause protections very narrowly.[354] As a result, Indian claims have not even been successful when

---

350. The *Lyng* Court stated:

The Constitution does not, and courts cannot, offer to reconcile the various competing demands on government, many of them rooted in sincere religious belief, that inevitably arise in so diverse a society as ours. That task, to the extent that it is feasible, is for the legislatures and other institutions.

Lyng v. Northwest Indian Cemetery Protective Ass'n, 485 U.S. 439, 452 (1988).

351. Employment Div., Dep't of Human Resources v. Smith, 494 U.S. 872 (1990).

352. *Id.* at 890.

353. *Id.* at 903 (O'Connor, J., concurring) (quoting West Virginia St. Bd. of Educ. v. Barnette, 319 U.S. 624, 638 (1943)).

354. "[D]ecisions of the United States Supreme Court . . . have narrowed the scope of Native American religious free exercise rights under the free exercise clause of the First Amendment of the Constitution of the United States . . . ." S. 1979, 101st Cong., 1st Sess. pmbl. (1989)

the Court has accepted that the proposed government action would "virtually destroy"[355] the ability of the Indians to practice their religion. Because the action at issue was seen to have only an "incidental" effect and did not directly coerce individuals to act contrary to their beliefs, the *Lyng* Court held that the Free Exercise Clause was not violated.

A different standard for infringement would be required in order to protect the rights of Native Americans. Dewald Walker has argued that the "centrality" standard, which requires that a sacred site be deemed essential, indispensable, or required for the practice of a religion, be replaced with an "integrity" standard.[356] An integrity standard would view an infringement on religious exercise as a forced or undesired change in the customary practice of a religion. This standard would find an infringement if the physical conditions required for a customary ritual had been so altered that performance was prevented.[357] This standard would clearly benefit Native Americans, but the case law has demonstrated that even when the plaintiffs can prove an infringement on religious rights, courts easily outweigh religious interests with almost any government interest.[358]

Perhaps a better response to the judicial practice of "passing the buck" is to abolish the incidental/direct harm dichotomy. After *Smith*, the government is free to harm religious practice if it does so indirectly. Only overt intention to harm religious practice is prohibited. A framework whereby a violation of the First Amendment would be found whenever a governmental action adversely affected the ability of an individual to practice his or her religion could be usefully and constitutionally applied. The plaintiff would still initially be required to demonstrate the religious character of her belief and that it was sincerely held. If that burden is met, whether the governmental action directly targets religious believers or whether it only incidentally affects the ability of believers to practice their beliefs, the government would then have to demonstrate a compelling interest to justify the interference with free exercise rights. Many new claims would be open to free exercise balancing as a result. Courts would be required to undergo the same factual assessment that they already perform in the free speech context. This suggestion is, however, susceptible to the same criticism as is Walker's, but it avoids potential problems with the ability of the judiciary to evaluate both when the integrity of a religious practice is disturbed and Establishment Clause conflicts that might result.

(introduced by Sen. Inouye).
355. *Lyng*, 485 U.S. at 451.
356. Walker, *supra* note 332, at 112.
357. *Id.* at 113.
358. *See supra* text accompanying notes 229-61.

Because neither of these suggestions are likely to be heeded by the present Supreme Court, Native Americans might do better to accept Justice O'Connor's suggestion to look to the legislature for assistance.

B. Legislative Possibilities

Shortly after the *Lyng* decision was rendered, Rep. Morris Udall (D.-Ariz.) introduced a bill calling for amendments to the AIRFA,[359] to prohibit federal agencies from managing government land in a manner that poses a "substantial and realistic threat to undermine and frustrate traditional Native American practices."[360] Representative Udall had been widely quoted by courts for referring to AIRFA as a bill that conferred no "special religious rights on Indians" and which in fact had "no teeth in it."[361] Courts have accepted this reading of the Act, even though other less restrictive readings are possible.[362]

AIRFA was the first legislative attempt to protect and preserve the rights of American Indians to believe, express, and practice their traditional religions. The Act was meant to accomplish the protections that the First Amendment had not been able to achieve.[363] Although AIRFA established a governmental *policy* of protecting Native American religious practice, it did nothing to affect the *practice* of federal land management. In the years since the passage of AIRFA, the ability of Indians to practice their religion on government lands has been limited.

Since that time, various other amendments to the AIRFA have been proposed. Representative Udall, Sen. John McCain (R.-Ariz.), and Sen. Daniel Inouye (D.-Haw.) have all introduced bills to amend the AIRFA. Senator Inouye's bill[364] was reintroduced on January 14th, 1991 and showed the most promise of early passage. This bill directed the Executive branch to develop rules and regulations which will guarantee Native American free exercise of religion.[365] It encouraged cooperation between Federal agencies on accommodating both Native American religious needs and the other management goals for federal land.[366] It also established administrative procedures for Indians to complain when federal activities "disturb the integrity of Native American religious places, sacred places, or the sanctity thereof, or interfere with the access thereto, or use thereof, or adversely affect the exercise of the Native American religions, as *determined* by the affected Native American

---

359. Pub. L. No. 95-341, 92 Stat. 469 (codified at 42 U.S.C. § 1996 (1988)).

360. H.R. 1546, 101st Cong., 1st Sess., § 3(a) (1989).

361. 124 Cong. Rec. 21,444-45 (1978) (statement of Rep. Udall); *see also Lyng*, 485 U.S. at 455.

362. *See* O'Brien, *Tribes & Indians, supra* note 116, at 1471.

363. *See supra* note 359.

364. S. 110, 103d Cong., 1st Sess. (1991).

365. *Id.*

366. *Id.*

practitioners."[367] The bill aimed to involve Native American input into federal land management decisions and to give them recourse when their rights are not adequately protected.

Concerns were raised at the time that this bill was languishing in Congress that it could implicate Establishment Clause conflicts. Professor Laurence Tribe proposed several revisions of the amendment to avoid the Establishment Clause problems raised by the involvement and authority of Native American religious leaders in determining when a government activity infringes on religious liberty.[368] Professor David Williams also evaluated the appearance of an Establishment Clause violation and determined that the amendments fell into a category of accommodation of religion that is neither proscribed nor prescribed.[369] In any event, the Inouye amendments to AIRFA were never passed.

Other legislative possibilities have been discussed. Jack Trope has suggested that Native Americans could consider using the National Historic Preservation Act[370] to register sacred sites as "landmarks" to protect them from other government actions.[371] Religious sites are not generally included within the designation of landmark, but Indian religious places may qualify because Indians do not segregate religion from the other aspects of their culture. This suggestion would require that Native Americans identify particular sacred areas, something tribal groups such as the Hopi would surely resist. They have continuously asserted that the location of their sacred places are secret. If protection cannot be found elsewhere, there may be no other legislative alternative.

The National Environmental Policy Act (NEPA) of 1969[372] is also a possible avenue for protection of Native American religious sites. NEPA requires an environmental impact statement for any government action which significantly affects the "quality of the human environment."[373] Effects on historical or cultural sites are included within the parameters of the environmental impact statement, and actions adversely affecting landmarks on the

367. *Id.* § 6(a) (emphasis added).

368. Laurence H. Tribe, Comments on Proposed Legislation to Protect Native American Religious Freedom, Memorandum to 1990 Meeting of Native American Tribal Leaders and Academics (on file with author).

369. *David C. Williams, Constitutionality of Proposed Amendments to the American Indian Religious Freedom Act, Written Testimony Before the Senate Select Committee on Indian Affairs,* 101st Cong., 1st Sess. 369 (commenting on the first Inouye bill, S. 1979, 101th Cong., 1st Sess. (1987), which was resubmitted as S. 110).

370. Pub. L. No. 89-664, 80 Stat. 915 (codified as amended at 16 U.S.C. § 470 (1988)).

371. Jack F. Trope, Alternative Approaches to the Protection of Sacred Sites, Association of American Indian Affairs Memo (Jan. 16, 1991) (on file with author).

372. 42 U.S.C. §§ 4321-4370(b) (1988).

373. *Id.* § 4332.

National Register must also be noted.[374] Native Americans should consider using these two acts in combination, if other options are not available.[375]

Two bills were introduced in the 103d Congress in 1993 that have the potential of providing the protection which the Supreme Court has failed to provide and which has not yet been forthcoming legislatively. The Religious Freedom Restoration Act[376] was introduced in the House of Representatives by Rep. Charles E. Schumer (D.-N.Y.) and in the Senate by Sen. Edward M. Kennedy (D.-Mass). The purpose of the bill is "to restore the compelling interest test as set forth in Sherbert v. Verner... and Wisconsin v. Yoder... and to guarantee its application in all cases where free exercise of religion is burdened."[377] The bill also aims "to provide a claim or defense to persons whose religious exercise is burdened by government."[378] This bill legislatively "overturns" the *Smith* decision by requiring the government to justify burdens on religious exercise even if those burdens are imposed by laws which are facially neutral toward religion. Initially, several groups opposed the bill, fearing that the bill might impact upon the right of religious organizations to receive public funds for social service programs and might create a "religious" right to abortion. After those issues were resolved and the most significant opposition to the bill agreed to support it, the bill passed the Congress and was signed by President Clinton on November 16, 1993. Unfortunately, it alone will not adequately protect free exercise rights peculiar to Native Americans.

The Native American Free Exercise of Religion Act of 1993[379] was introduced in the Senate by Senator Inouye. This bill acknowledges the "chilling and discriminatory effect on the free exercise of Native American religions"[380] of the *Lyng* decision. In response, it creates specific protection for Native American sacred sites, the traditional use of peyote, Native American prisoners' rights to practice their religion while incarcerated, and the religious use of eagles and other animals and plants. A very important component of this bill is a section which gives any federal court jurisdiction over Native American claims that a governmental action would restrict the petitioner's free exercise of religion. If the petitioner can show "any evidence that a restriction upon the practitioner's free exercise of religion exists as a result of federal or state action,"[381] then "the governmental authority shall refrain from such action unless it can demonstrate that application of the restriction to the practitioner is essential to further a compelling governmental

374. 40 C.F.R. §§ 1508.8, 1508.27(8) (1991).

375. Trope, *supra* note 368.

376. H.R. 1308, 103d Cong., 1st Sess. (1993); S. 578, 103d Cong., 1st Sess. (1993).

377. H.R. 1308, § 2(b)(1); S. 578, § 2(b)(1).

378. H.R. 1308, § 2(b)(2); S. 578 § 2(b)(2).

379. S. 1021, 103d Cong., 1st Sess. (1993).

380. *Id.* § 101(9).

381. *Id.* § 501(2).

interest and the application is the least restrictive means of furthering that compelling governmental interest."[382]

The provisions of this bill cure some of the Establishment Clause issues raised about the amendments to AIRFA. The previous legislation, which allowed the Native American petitioners to define a violation, even if they did not violate the Establishment Clause, left too much ambiguity to be practically workable. The new bill provides more clarity.

Together these bills would undo much of the damage done to the free exercise rights of the first Americans. Legislative remedies, though not satisfying, are necessary responses to the failure of the judicial system to protect Native American religious rights. Legislative whims change with the political wind. Protections afforded today can be eroded by future representatives. While the current jurisprudence refuses to acknowledge the religious integrity and cultural necessity of the spiritual practices of Native Peoples, legislation is probably the best protection available. Protection today, although ephemeral, is better than no protection at all.

The Native American Free Exercise of Religion Act of 1993 and the Religious Freedom Restoration Act appear to afford the most substantial guarantees for Native American religious practice. Other possibilities do exist, though they would not provide the full range of protection afforded under these acts. Congress should provide a clear mandate to restore the "full scope of rights and remedies . . . available under the free exercise of the Constitution of the United States . . . ."[383] Nothing less befits the tradition of religious toleration with which this country began and nothing less befits the special responsibility owed to the first Americans.

Conclusion

The United States has had a troubled relationship with the first Americans. Alexis de Tocqueville described the European majority in the young country he observed as "omnipotent."[384] Native Americans experienced that power as they struggled to maintain their homelands and even their identity throughout hundreds of years of abuse. The United States policy has shifted from respect for the autonomy of aboriginal peoples to attempting to assimilate them into the dominant culture. Presently, Native Americans stand on the threshold of a new era that might return them to the status of the self-governing communities they enjoyed before the arrival of white people.

Indigenous people all over the globe have begun to organize themselves politically, to be recognized by the established governmental powers, and to

---

382. *Id.* § 501(1).

383. S. 110 at pmbl.

384. ALEXIS DE TOCQUEVILLE, DEMOCRACY IN AMERICA 246 (George Lawrence trans., 1966).

gain support for their demands of autonomy and protection. They raise the international agreements which pertain to them in their domestic court battles and press for new developments on the international front. The years to come hold the possibility of developing the respect for their rich cultural heritage.[385]

Indigenous people are one of the least protected minorities in the world today. They struggle against political regimes that still for the most part do not allow them to live their traditional lifestyle and do not provide the protection that their cultures need and deserve. National governments do not give Native Peoples equal opportunities to choose the benefits of development and at the same time they do not permit them to remain the same. One of the most common conflicts is over the rights of indigenous peoples to practice their traditional spiritual beliefs. The native North Americans have found their ability to exercise their beliefs limited in many ways.

This article has reviewed the history of the battle for religious rights that Native Americans continue to wage to this day. Indian sacred places are still not protected from the economic development interests of federal land managers who do not value Native American culture. The judiciary has washed its hands of this question. Without significant jurisprudential reform, courts will not provide the fundamental Constitutional rights to Indians that they do to other United States citizens. The Supreme Court has pointed Native Americans to the door of the legislature as a possible source for religious protection. Though we all should be concerned about the Court's willingness to abdicate their mandate as champion of individual rights and fundamental freedoms, there are possibilities for Native Americans within the political sphere. The AIRFA should be given the "teeth" it never received in the form of the Native American Free Exercise of Religion Act. The Religious Freedom Restoration Act should be passed to put the Native Peoples on the same footing, with the same standards of protection, as all other religious groups. Other current legislation should be examined for its potential to defend Indian sacred places. Protection of the ability of Native Americans to practice their beliefs is not only a matter of principle. It is a matter of cultural survival. Their struggle should be the concern of every citizen of this country, for until the first Americans are equal Americans, the wounds of years past will continue to stain all of our hands with guilt.

---

385. See the appendix to this article.

APPENDIX

Indigenous People in International Perspective

The history of the indigenous Americans is but one story among many similar stories throughout the history of the world. Indigenous people have generally lost in their relations with European powers. They have lost their lives, their territory, their culture, their autonomy, and their spirituality. The Native Americans are one example of the system of exploitation that has become common worldwide. Still, the system in the United States is seen internationally as a success. The treatment of Indians in this country, while at times genocidal and inhumane, has become the measure against which other systems are assessed. Though it may challenge credulity, Native Peoples in the United States, in general, have been better treated than those in other countries.

To this day, no universally accepted international standards exist to guide relations with indigenous people. The current international system remains predominantly state centered; states are therefore reluctant to support indigenous rights claims which might conflict with their assertions of sovereignty.[386] To establish an international legal system that guarantees indigenous rights will take great effort. First, the content of those rights must be established and agreed upon. Second, indigenous people must gain the support of those rights by states, despite state fears of diminution in sovereignty.[387] A brief discussion of the relationship between the modern organized international community and Native Peoples will demonstrate the difficulty of this task.

Hundreds of years of history are relevant to this discussion, but for purposes of this short history, the period after the formation of the United Nations in 1948 will only be discussed. In 1949, Bolivia proposed setting up a United Nations subcommission to study the "situation of the aboriginal population of the American continent."[388] A number of American countries did not support this idea, and no other similar proposals were made for two decades.[389]

During the period of the late sixties and seventies, the special problems of indigenous peoples began attracting more and more international attention. In 1970, the U.N. recommended that a detailed study of discrimination against

---

386. Anaya, *supra* note 15.

387. *Id.* at 215.

388. José R. Martinez Cobo, United Nations, Economic and Social Council, Commission on Human Rights, Sub-Commission on Prevention of Discrimination and Protection of Minorities, Study of the Problem of Discrimination Against Indigenous Populations, U.N. Doc. E/CN.4/Sub.2/1986/7 & Adds.1-4 (1987).

389. Hurst Hannum, *New Developments in Indigenous Rights*, 28 Va. J. Int'l L. 649, 657 (1988).

indigenous peoples be prepared. Nongovernmental organizations began to get involved in the problem and a number of major conferences were called to discuss indigenous issues. The first international conference of nongovernmental organizations on indigenous issues was held in 1977. In 1981, the U.N. Sub-Commission on Prevention of Discrimination and Protection of Minorities appointed a Special Rapporteur to study discrimination against indigenous people.[390]

All this attention resulted in the establishment, in 1981, of a Working Group on Indigenous Populations of the U.N. Sub-Commission on the Prevention of Discrimination and Protection of Minorities. Since its founding the Working Group has been seen as innovative on a number of levels. It allowed oral and written contributions by all indigenous peoples organizations who wished to participate, and more than fifty organizations participated in its fifth session in 1987.[391] The group has seen itself as the primary center for the collection of information about the condition of indigenous people around the world. They have documented numerous killings, arrests, tortures, land deprivations, and desecration of religious sites.[392] They have pointed to the link between autonomy and self-determination on the one hand and peace and development on the other.[393] The group's primary effort since 1985, however, has been the production of a draft declaration of the rights of indigenous populations.

The Draft Declaration[394] is now in its third revision. The Working Group on Indigenous Populations completed its work in July and submitted the draft to the U.N. Subcommission on Prevention of Discrimination and Protection of Minorities. From the Subcommission the Declaration moves to the U.N. Human Rights Commission in March of 1994, then to the Economic and Social Council and finally, to the General Assembly.[395]

In many ways the Declaration is a revolutionary document. One of its primary objectives is the protection of the right of indigenous groups to exist and to preserve their own culture. It calls for the right to "full and effective enjoyment of all human rights and fundamental freedoms," as well as the

---

390. ROBERT N. CLINTON ET AL., AMERICAN INDIAN LAW 1295 (1991).

391. *Id.* at 1296.

392. *Id.* at 1297.

393. *Discrimination Against Indigenous Peoples, Report of the United Nations Technical Conference on Practical Experience in the Realization of Sustainable and Environmentally Sound Self-Development of Indigenous Peoples*, U.N. ESCOR Comm. on Human Rights, 44th Sess., Agenda Item 15, at 6, U.N. Doc. E/CN.4/Sub.2/1992/31 (prov. ed. 1992) [hereinafter *Report*].

394. *Discrimination Against Indigenous Peoples: Report of the Working Group on Indigenous Populations on its Tenth Session, United Nations Sub-Commission Draft Declaration on the Rights of Indigenous Peoples*, U.N. ESCOR Comm. on Human Rights, 44th Sess., Agenda Item 15, U.N. Doc. E/CN.4/Sub.2/1993/29 (1993) [hereinafter *Declaration*].

395. INDIAN RIGHTS, HUMAN RIGHTS (Indian Law Resource Center Memorandum, Helena, Mont.), No. 4, Summer 1993, at 2.

observance of the corresponding responsibilities, "which are recognized in the Charter of the United Nations, the Universal Declaration of Human Rights and international human rights law."[396] It also emphasizes collective rights,[397] which the indigenous people overcome the limitations of individually-focused rights norms. The Declaration also attempts to protect land holdings of indigenous people from governmental confiscation.[398] Perhaps most importantly, the Declaration consistently refers to aboriginal populations as "peoples," a deeply controversial title that troubles governmental representatives because of its meaning within the U.N. Charter.

In the United Nations Charter, "peoples" are entitled to "equal rights and self-determination."[399] Indigenous groups must attain the title "peoples" because it identifies them as primarily a community, rather than an amalgamation of individuals.[400] The current draft of the Declaration states in part:

> Indigenous peoples have the right of self-determination, in accordance with international law by virtue of which they may freely determine their political status and institutions and freely pursue their economic, social and cultural development. An integral part of this is the right to autonomy and self-government.[401]

Identification as "distinct peoples" is existence in the international arena. As international law now stands, *peoples* have enforceable rights under international law, *people* are governed by national law. If the Declaration can state that indigenous peoples are "peoples," then many of the international protections which have previously been denied them would be secured.

The most direct statement on the rights of indigenous people can be found in the 1989 International Labour Organization Convention of Indigenous and Tribal Peoples. This convention revised a 1957 convention which represented a mixture of assimilationist policies and protection for indigenous people. The previous convention aimed to facilitate the progression of indigenous populations into their national communities,[402] but became inadequate as the

---

396. *Declaration, supra* note 394, at 46 (Annex I, pt. I, para. 2).

397. "Indigenous peoples have the collective right to live in freedom, peace and security as distinct peoples and to full guarantees against genocide or any other act of violence, including the removal of indigenous children from their families and communities under any pretext." *Id.* at 46 (Annex I, pt. II, para. 5).

398. *Id.* at 48-49 (Annex I, pt. IV, paras. 26, 27).

399. U.N. CHARTER art. 1, par. 2.

400. "Indigenous peoples have the collective and individual right to maintain and develop their distinct ethnic and cultural characteristics and identities, including the right to self-identification." *Declaration, supra* note 394, at 47 (Annex I, pt. II, para. 6).

401. *Id.* at 46 (Annex I, pt. I, para. 1).

402. International Labour Organization Convention (No. 107) Concerning the Protection and Integration of Indigenous and Other Tribal and Semi-Tribal Populations in Independent Countries pmbl., June 26, 1957, 328 U.N.T.S. 247 (entered into force June 2, 1959).

consensus of international opinion shifted toward helping indigenous communities to maintain their unique cultural identities. Although international opinion on how to respond to indigenous peoples has changed since 1957, the ILO deserves credit for adopting the first international legal instrument to protect the rights of indigenous peoples.

The present ILO Convention speaks in terms of respecting "the special importance for the cultures and spiritual values of the peoples concerned of their relationship with the lands or territories . . . which they occupy or otherwise use, and in particular the collective aspects of that relationship."[403] Clearly, the tenor of the 1989 Convention reflects developments in the understanding of indigenous peoples. The 1989 Convention, unfortunately, has not yet entered into force, and so carries no weight in international law at this point. Despite its impotence, the ILO Convention is being considered in the development of the Declaration of Indigenous Rights mentioned earlier.[404]

Other recent developments indicate that collective rights of ethnic minorities, such as indigenous peoples, are beginning to get more respect. The United Nations Conference on Environment and Development held in Rio de Janiero during the summer of 1992 addressed many pressing indigenous and environmental issues. Agenda 21 of the Conference Declaration states:

> Indigenous peoples and their communities, and other local communities, have a vital role in environmental management and development because of their knowledge and traditional practices. States should recognize and duly support their identity, culture and interests and enable their effective participation in the achievement of sustainable development.[405]

Indigenous people are making their presence felt at international decision-making forums and have even gained consultative status at a number of United Nations bodies.[406] In 1985, the General Assembly of the United Nations established the Voluntary Fund for Indigenous Populations to provide financial assistance to representatives of indigenous communities and organizations attending Working Group sessions. In 1992, Rigoberta Menchu, the first indigenous person ever to be recognized for her work defending the human rights of indigenous peoples, won the Nobel Peace Prize. She has been appointed the United Nations Ambassador at Large and as such convened the first Summit of Indigenous Peoples in Guatemala in May of 1993. Each of

---

403. *Id.* at art. 13.

404. *Trends, ILO Takes Up Indian Cause; Latin American Legislation "In the Vanguard,"* WR-93-22 LATIN AM. WKLY. REP. 258 (issue dated June 10, 1993), *available in* LEXIS, Nexis Library, Omni File.

405. *Report, supra* note 393, at 5 (quoting principle 22 of United Nations Conference on Environment and Development (UNCED), Rio de Janeiro, Braz., 1992)).

406. United Nations Economic and Social Council and others.

these steps are important in the long road to respect for the rights of indigenous peoples, but even they are not sufficient.

The United Nations made a powerful statement on December 10, 1992, when it declared 1993 to be the International Year for the World's Indigenous People.[407] In his statement on the opening celebration of the Year of Indigenous Peoples, Secretary General Boutros Boutros-Ghali said, "Unity through diversity is the only true and enduring diversity."[408] He also acknowledged that there "could be no protection of human rights without preserving cultural authenticity."[409]

The second World Conference on Human Rights, which opened in Vienna on June 14, 1993, gave special attention to the rights of indigenous peoples in its deliberations. The results were a mixture of successes and failures. The indigenous delegates succeeded in securing a recommendation from the conference that the General Assembly declare a Decade of Indigenous Peoples beginning in 1994 to give special attention to the world's 300,000,000 indigenous people. The indigenous peoples in attendance at the conference also sought to solidify their right to self-determination within the nation-state system and renewed the argument over whether they should be known as "peoples" or simply "people." On the latter score, nations again failed to protect indigenous rights as the crucial "s" was deleted from every paragraph referring to indigenous peoples in the concluding document by the Brazilian president of the drafting committee, Gilberto Saboia, on June 20, 1993.[410] As a result, the Conference only recognized the variety of peoples represented by 200 delegates from all over the globe as one people, despite differences in culture, language, religions, and native lands.

While the United Nations World Conference on Human Rights was going on, a Nongovernmental Organization-Forum was also held in Vienna. The NGO-Forum was attended by 2000 people representing 1000 human rights NGOs. The NGO-Forum provided an opportunity for human rights organizations to evaluate the performance of the United Nations in promoting human rights. The organizations present also made recommendations on how to improve the United Nations' human rights programs. One working group evaluated the state of indigenous peoples rights and made recommendations for improvement. They contributed the following to the final statement of the NGO-Forum:

---

407. G.A. Res. 45/164, U.N. GAOR, 45th Sess., 69th plen. mtg., at 277-78, U.N. Doc. No. E/CN.4/1992/2 (1990).

408. *United Nations: Indigenous Year Gets Off to a Bumpy Start*, INTER PRESS SERVICE, Dec. 10, 1992, *available in* LEXIS, Nexis Library, Omni File.

409. *Id.*

410. Carmen A. Fernandez & Alecia McKenzie, *Human Rights: Indigenous Peoples Disappointed With Conference*, INTER PRESS SERVICE, June 25, 1993, *available in* LEXIS, Nexis Library, Omni File.

The members of the working group B stress the distinct characteristics of indigenous peoples which distinguish them from minorities. They urge that indigenous peoples be recognized as nations with inherent collective rights of self-determination, development, self-government and autonomy.

Recommendations include the proclamation of the International Decade of the World's Indigenous Peoples, the establishment of a High Commissioner, a Special Rapporteur or another permanent UN body with adequate resources for the protection of the rights of indigenous peoples. Furthermore, they urge the UN to adopt, without further delay, the strongest possible draft of the Universal Declaration of the Rights of Indigenous Peoples and to ensure full participation of representatives of indigenous peoples in the drafting process and related activities.[411]

These recommendations, if adopted by the United Nations, would be a good start toward the protection of the rights of indigenous peoples.[412]

The International Year of Indigenous People is only a start. Even a Decade of Indigenous People and a Declaration of Indigenous Rights are but a beginning. The road to a more just future will be secured only when the international community both acknowledges the terrible history of oppression that is the story of the relationship between indigenous peoples and the dominant societies, and affirms the inherent right of all indigenous peoples to the protection of their culture, land, religion, and ethnicity. Today's efforts are essential, but much remains to be done. They are, however, cause for hope. Though indigenous people lack substantive guarantees of their rights even today, the rosy fingers of a new dawn are visible on the horizon.

411. Final Statement at the World Conference on Human Rights, NGO-Forum (All Human Rights for All), Vienna, Aus. (June 12, 1993) (on file with author).

412. These references are current as of July 1, 1993. The Drafting Committee for the Universal Declaration of the Rights of Indigenous Peoples was scheduled to meet in mid-July 1993. A third draft of the Universal Declaration was expected in the fall of 1993.

CONSTITUTIONAL LAW: THE RIGHT TO WEAR A TRADITIONAL INDIAN HAIR STYLE— RECOGNITION OF A HERITAGE

Peggy Doty

In recent years there has been an increase in awareness of the American Indian's historical, cultural, and religious traditions. Not surprisingly, attempts to revitalize these customs have often resulted in litigation.[1] One area in particular where this has occurred is in efforts of Native American students and inmates of penal institutions to claim cultural and religious rights to wear traditional Indian hair styles in violation of institutional regulations.[2] There are arguments for allowing such hair styles, even though to do so violates the appearance codes of the regulated school or prison environment. Nevertheless, except in one case, *Teterud v. Gillman*,[3] the courts so far have been reluctant to recognize any rights in this particular area.[4]

Theories and Arguments

Related to Religion

The argument for wearing long hair as an exercise of religion, with the right protected under first amendment freedom of religious expression,[5] most often stems from the view that the Indian's daily secular activities are interrelated and integrated with his religious beliefs.[6] This view of the interaction of daily activities and religion is part of the heritage of many Indians[7], as well as the particular Indians already involved in litigation.[8] There is, however, some difference of opinion on the importance and validity of this theory.[9]

Another religious argument with substance concerns the taking of a "Ceremonial Indian Vow."[10] This position emphasizes the seriousness and sincerity of the vow in conjunction with strong beliefs about breaking such a solemn oath, and is only pertinent to the religious right issue if the subject matter of the vow is of a religious nature. Again, as in the first view, there is disagreement as to the importance and effect of such a vow and the believed consequences for breaking it.[11] Other than these two grounds, there is apparently no other substantial religious basis for wearing long braided hair,[12] and even the grounds espoused have not received much legal recognition.[13]

Another issue that has been raised in the Indian religion issue involves the extent to which the first amendment applies to a traditional Native American religion, *i.e.*, one that is fundamentally

105

different from the Judeo-Christian religions the first amendment was designed to protect.[14] On its face, this interrogatory indicates that a Native American religion would be excluded from the intended protection of the first amendment. This, however, would seem to be unlikely considering the purpose behind constitutionally guaranteed freedom of religion. The purpose was to protect such an exercise of religion from being unreasonably controlled by the government,[15] a situation in England that helped prompt the early settlement of the United States by colonists rebelling against such religious restrictions. Thus, the motivation behind this constitutional guarantee would indicate that perhaps the first amendment might be more liberally extended to protect Native American religious beliefs.

Related to Culture

Another argument for the right to wear a traditional Indian hair style centers upon the cultural significance of such a right. Although each tribe or group of Indians should be considered individually, generally, the traditional style of long, braided hair was a common cultural characteristic among the many different Indian tribes.[16]

Although there is no legally recognized right to preserve and assert a particular cultural heritage, there have been several arguments supporting the idea of allowing Indians to follow traditional cultural practices even while in such controlled environments as school or prison. One of these arguments covers the possible detrimental effects stemming from regulations that discourage any display of cultural pride such as wearing a traditional Indian hair style.

In the schools, the effects of policies directed at suppressing and discouraging Indian culture and tradition have often resulted in Indian student frustration and alienation, along with a loss of pride, initiative, and identity.[17] This consequence is reported not only as a personal observation, but as a statistical fact throughout the transcripts of the hearings before the United States Senate Special Subcommittee on Indian Education,[18] as well as in the report of that subcommittee.[19] The findings of the subcommittee illustrate that the enforcement of such school hair style regulations prohibiting the wearing of a traditional Indian hair style[20] in effect results in defeating an often claimed justification for those hair codes. This justification, espoused by some school officials and recognized by at least one court,[21] supports enforcement of appearance codes by arguing that such regulations encourage the state objective of instilling pride and initiative among students, leading to scholastic achievement. The results of the hearings point out, however, that instead of

106

instilling pride in Indian students, the policies frustrate pride and discourage motivation.

This detrimental effect is recognized among Indian prison inmates, and as contributing significantly to at least one Indian inmate's problems which led to his incarceration,[22] as well as being counterproductive to the rehabilitation goals of modern prisons.[23] In light of these undesirable effects caused by a seemingly innocuous appearance code, a practical problem arises as to developing and enforcing a hair code that would not harmfully affect any ethnic or racial groups. A suggested solution to this problem would be either to have no hair style regulations at all or to develop an "appearance" code that does not restrict any appearance reflecting a person's ethnic or racial culture, possibly by providing reasonable exceptions appropriate for the groups represented in a particular school or prison population.

Recognition of Indian culture is further encouraged in a discussion of the effect of the current growing interest in cultural patterns and values of America's past and the relevance it should have to Indian culture.[24] After noting that the objective of preserving cultural values in the United States presents the question of *whose* cultural values, the authors go on to comment, in reference to a congressional act dealing with cultural preservation,[25] that "[t]he declaration of Congress that the 'historical and cultural foundations of the nation' should be preserved in order 'to give a sense of orientation to the American people' is inclusive. It speaks to and of all Americans—not only white Americans but . . . American Indians as well."[26]

Another cultural argument for allowing Indians to wear traditional hair styles involves the claim that the first amendment protection for freedom of speech[27] extends to actions that so specifically convey a particular message that they can be considered analogous to speech. In *Tinker v. Des Moines Independent School District*,[28] the Supreme Court recognized that the wearing of black armbands by students in protest of the Viet Nam War was an expression closely akin to pure speech and was entitled to first amendment protection.[29] A case even more in point with these Indian rights issues is *Braxton v. Board of Public Instruction*,[30] where a Florida court found that the first amendment protected a black school teacher's right to wear a beard as "an appropriate expression of his heritage, culture, and racial pride."[31] In accordance with the lines of reasoning in *Tinker* and *Braxton*, the wearing of long braided hair has been claimed to be a definite expression of pride in being an Indian[32] and, therefore, is also entitled to protection under the first amendment. The wearing of a traditional American Indian hair style, viewed as an attempt to convey a distinct and specific message, can be distinguished from

107

other "school hair-length" cases denying the wearing of long hair as merely a broad symbol of general discontent, rather than as a sign of a particular communication.[33] Thus, the wearing of a traditional hair style as part of an Indian's cultural heritage and as a clear expression of that culture can legitimately be argued to be protected under the first amendment through application of the decisions of *Tinker* and *Braxton*.

The foregoing seems to give support to a view that Native Americans should be allowed to wear traditional hair styles. The goal of institutions such as schools and prisons for the development of self-worth would be furthered by such tolerance.

However, a contrary view arguing against the recognition of different cultures in public schools should be mentioned. That view contends that an integrated school system cannot favor different ethnic and racial groups and remain one organization.[34] While, on its face, this position may seem to have a logical and practical strength, it nevertheless seems contrary to the accepted idea that one of the functions of American education is to provide exposure to and exchange of many different ideas.[35] One of the acknowledged conclusions of the landmark school desegregation case, *Brown v. Board of Education*,[36] was that "only by amalgamating children of various races, colors, cultural, ethical, and environmental backgrounds can the public schools become the effective 'market place of ideas' for the benefit of all students."[37] As Justice Douglas observed in *Tinker v. Des Moines Independent School District*,[38] "our constitutional system repudiates the idea that a state may conduct its school 'to foster a homogeneous people.' "[39] Finally, *Keyishan v. Board of Regents*[40] further emphasized the importance of education, including a wide exposure to many different views.[41]

Court Decisions

There are four reported cases concerning the wearing of a traditional Indian hair style by an American Indian.[42] They deal with challenges to school or prison dress and hair regulations[43] with the Indians asserting primarily their religious right, and secondarily, their cultural right to wear a traditional Indian hair style. This tendency to focus on the religious issue is based on the legal strength of the first amendment right to free exercise of religion,[44] while the culturally based arguments lack such a legal basis.[45] Furthermore, any legal acknowledgment of cultural customs is usually related to a religion, and culture itself is not really challenged except in its connection with religious beliefs.[46]

108

Two of the reported cases deal with American Indian students' hair length and public schools' appearance codes. In *New Rider v. Board of Education*,[47] three Pawnee Indian junior high school students claimed the prerogative of wearing traditional Indian hair styles in violation of the school's hair code[48] as part of their freedom of religion right,[49] as well as part of other rights protected under the first and fourteenth amendments of the United States Constitution.[50] Although substantial evidence was presented on the freedom of religion right argument,[51] the Tenth Circuit Court of Appeals never really discussed that issue specifically. The court affirmed the trial court's reversal of its original holding[52] and found that no substantial constitutional questions were presented by the students' attack on the hair regulation.

The appeals court, relying on several other prior holdings,[53] went on to state that the regulation and management of state schools should be left in the hands of the school authorities and state courts, and that a federal court should avoid getting involved with the operations of a state's public school system unless the exercise of a constitutional right is impinged. The court skirted the religious exercise issue during its argument, negating the free speech issue by citing as authority an earlier non-Indian student hair-length case, *Freeman v. Flake*.[54] The court pointed out that it recognized that *Freeman* specifically did not concern a claim of any racial or religious discrimination, and that although the *New Rider* students argued this distinction, the decision in *Freeman* would be reaffirmed. This indicated that although the *Freeman* holding concerned only the first amendment right of free speech, the precedent would apply equally to any other first amendment rights.[55] In other words, the decision implied that because it has been held that long hair is not protected under the freedom of speech clause of the first amendment, it follows that long hair, even though related to religion and racial heritage, also is not protected under the freedom of religion clause of the first amendment. Finally, after balancing the claimed constitutional right and the public interest,[56] the court further found that the hair code involved in this case[57] bore a rational relationship to the state objective of "instilling pride and initiative among the students leading to scholarship attainment and high school spirit and morale," as well as helping maintain order and discipline in operation of the school.[58] As discussed earlier, it is somewhat irrational to believe that pride and initiative can be instilled in American Indian students by forbidding the wearing of a traditional Indian hair style which in fact is claimed to be an expression of pride in their culture and heritage.[59]

109

Hatch v. Goerke[60] varies from the other cases in that the challengers of the school's hair regulation[61] were the student's parents. The plaintiffs, the mother being an American Indian, argued generally that the enforcement of the code infringed on their rights to rear their children according to their own religious, cultural, and moral values. In this case, the Tenth Circuit Court of Appeals partly answered the religious freedom question in finding an important distinction between this case and that of *Wisconsin v. Yoder*.[62] *Yoder* allowed Amish parents to withdraw their children from compulsory public education after a certain grade on the basis that such continued education created conflicts with the basic religious tenets and practices of the Amish faith.[63] In distinguishing *Hatch* from *Yoder*, the court found that the school appearance regulations in this case did not create a clash with religious beliefs like the all-encompassing, religiously based concept of rearing children recognized in *Yoder*. However, the Tenth Circuit Court of Appeals, as in *New Rider*, again avoided addressing the religious freedom question fully by once more relying on such decisions as *Freeman*,[64] with additional authority this time of the *New Rider* decision which reaffirmed *Freeman*. Based on those decisions, the federal court abstained from getting involved in state operations of public schools, leaving the regulation of student hair length to be handled through state procedures.[65]

The other two cases in this area concern the reforcement of prison hair regulations against inmates. *United States ex rel. Goings v. Aaron*[66] deals with an Oglala Sioux Indian inmate's right to wear long hair as part of his religion and culture. However, the decision in this case deals more with the importance of the inmate's taking of a "Ceremonial Indian Vow" to be more religious, with the plaintiff claiming that to force him to cut his hair would break his vow and subject him to serious consequences. Opposing evidence was presented as to the beliefs surrounding the severity of breaking such a vow.[67] The Minnesota District Court decided that since the prisoner was being released in 55 days from the time of the decision, he could just renew the vow after his release, but that until his release, he would be subject to the prison regulations.[68] Thus, the court treated the issue as moot and chose to enforce the prison regulations in keeping with the majority of cases on prison regulations and constitutional rights.[69] Moreover, the court found that the evidence presented indicated a lack of sincerity in Goings' recently acquired religious beliefs.[70] In contrast, the more recent decision of *Teterud v. Gillman* found that the Indian inmate's sincerity in his also recently awakened religious beliefs was not sufficiently contradicted by the evidence and

110

the court seemed to apply a more lenient standard.[71] Finally, in balancing the interests in *Goings*, the court found that even if the prisoner had had a sincere religious belief, his religious freedom, as in most cases with non-Indian inmates,[72] is subject to reasonable limitations in the prison environment.[73]

The most recent case, *Teterud v. Gillman*,[74] discusses and answers the religious rights question in more depth and more directly[75] than any of the other three cases. Interestingly enough, this case is the only one that recognizes any rights of an American Indian to wear a traditional hair style in a case concerning a one-half Cree Indian inmate's challenge to the enforcement of the Iowa State Penitentiary's hair regulation against himself and other American Indian inmates. Under the Supreme Court's definition of religious beliefs followed in *United States v. Seeger*,[76] the Iowa court here concluded that Teterud's religious views came within that interpretation and constituted a valid religion worthy of recognition.[77] Based on evidence emphasizing various religious and cultural functions that an Indian's traditional hair style could fulfill,[78] the court found that hair plays a central role in a religion of the Plains Indians[79] and that therefore "[a]n Indian's hair length can have a sufficient religious significance to make a forced cutting of that hair an encroachment on the Indian's First Amendment rights."[80] Acknowledging Teterud's sincerity in his beliefs, the court further held that "if an individual Indian's belief in the Indian Religion is honest, made in good faith, and sincere, he should be allowed to wear his hair in the traditional style."[81] Unlike most other prison hair code cases,[82] this decision held that the enforcement of the particular prison hair regulations against Teterud was not justified on the grounds that "long hair was unsanitary, created hazards around machinery, increased difficulty in identifying inmates, or could hide contraband."[83] Finally, after reviewing *Goings* and *New Rider*, the court in *Teterud* specifically disagreed with those holdings and went on to declare that Teterud's "interest in wearing the traditional Indian hair style is predicated upon a sincere religious belief which must be constitutionally protected."[84]

Religious Aspects

A review of the cases points out that in focusing on the religious aspects of the four cases, there are similarities as well as distinctions. The two school-related cases, *New Rider* and *Hatch*, basically decided the issue of protection under the first amendment freedom of religion clause, finding no solid claim of constitutional restraint.[85] The decisions in *New Rider* and *Hatch* both relied on an earlier

111

non-Indian student hair-length case that did not involve religious or racial issues at all, with *New Rider* implying that freedom of expression and freedom of religious exercise are essentially the same issue. As discussed previously, the court in *New Rider* indicated that since *Freeman* had held long hair not to be protected under the first amendment free speech clause, then long hair was not protected under the freedom of religion clause either, regardless of any distinctions.[86]

The two prison cases show more distinction in their decisions. Dealing with the religious issue, *Goings* found no protection under the first amendment because the prisoner's newly acquired religious beliefs were not considered by the court to be sincere. On the other hand, the *Teterud* decision held that, based on the evidence, the inmate's religious beliefs were valid, sincere, and entitled to constitutional protection under the first amendment freedom of religion clause.

Since *Teterud* is the only case that recognizes a religious right to wear a traditional Indian hair style, it is understandable that it varies in several ways from the other three cases. *Teterud* is the only decision that found the hair regulations not to satisfy the claimed justification.[87] In contrast, *Goings* found that religious freedom was subject to reasonable rules of conduct in and out of prison.[88] As discussed *supra*, *New Rider* held that the hair code was in keeping with the state's school objective of instilling pride, encouraging scholarship and morale, and maintaining discipline.[89] The *Hatch* decision merely found that the regulation did not create a clash with any significant religious beliefs, and thus should be enforced.[90]

Both the plaintiffs in *New Rider* and the plaintiff in *Teterud* presented evidence as to the interrelatedness of religion and the traditional Indian hair style as well as to other daily activities.[91] The court in *New Rider* hesitated to recognize such an all-encompassing religion[92] and found the evidence to be insufficient in supporting the validity of that belief. In *Teterud*, the court disagreed with *New Rider* and found the belief of an interrelation between religion and the daily aspects of living to be valid, sincere, and worthy of constitutional protection, according to the evidence presented which was very similar in theory to the evidence offered in *New Rider*.[93]

Cultural Aspects

As indicated before, it is difficult to separate the acknowledgment of culture or the lack of it from religious rights.[94] Although this is true in the four cases dealt with, there are some distinguishable cultural aspects.

Hatch is the only one of the four that specifically includes cultural values in the alleged rights asserted by the plaintiff parents, and then it is only generally included in the broad allegations[95] with no substantial argument discussed or answered in the court's decision. In comparison, the plaintiffs in *New Rider* did not specifically allege a cultural right, but a subtle claim was included incidental to the other issues, particularly the right to religious exercise.[96] *Goings* dealt with some cultural aspects in focusing part of the discussion on Goings' taking of a "Ceremonial Indian Vow" to return to the old Indian traditions and religion.[97] Finally, in contrast to the other cases, the decision in *Teterud* seemed to deal more directly with cultural rights because the court determined one of the issues to be "whether or not an Indian's cultural and traditional beliefs constitute a religion...,"[98] but this was again in connection with religion. However, the court goes beyond the religious point in saying that an Indian may wish to wear a traditional hair style for a variety of reasons, and it is not the court's duty to speculate as to the reasons.[99] The court qualifies this in relation to religious beliefs by stating that as long as an Indian's belief in an Indian religion is in good faith, honest, and sincere, that Indian should be allowed to wear a traditional hair style.[100] Nevertheless, none of these cases seem to clearly recognize any cultural rights separately from religious rights as justifying an Indian's wearing his hair in a traditional style.

There does seem to be some legal recognition of a cultural right that should be acknowledged, at least as argued in the dissent to the denial of certiorari in *New Rider*.[101] That dissent, along with other sources such as the hearings before the United States Senate Special Subcommittee on Indian Education[102] and the report of that subcommittee,[103] recognized the detrimental effect of suppressing Indian culture[104] and, therefore, in addition to other reasons,[105] encouraged the acknowledgment and allowance of an Indian cultural right to wear a traditional hair style. However, this was a dissent and only represents a legal minority. Nevertheless, there was similar evidence presented and recognized in *Teterud*[106] which indicated at least a stronger minority opinion which could become that of the majority.

Conclusion

Although the majority of court decisions hold that an Indian has no constitutionally protected rights to wear a traditional Indian hair

113

style as part of a cultural heritage or a religious belief, the holding in *Teterud*, plus the dissent opinion in *New Rider*, indicate the possible beginnings of a change in attitude. Furthermore, arguments expressing the importance of a right to a cultural expression and traditional identity encourage the recognition of less prohibitive attitudes toward allowing Indians to show pride in their specific cultures and to freely exercise their traditional religions. Following these modes of thinking, perhaps Indians in the future will be allowed or even encouraged to wear traditional hair styles as the exercise of a cultural and/or religious right.

NOTES

1. *In re* Grady, 69 Cal. App. 2d 887, 394 P.2d 728, 50 Cal. Rptr. 912 (1964).

2. New Rider v. Board of Educ., 480 F.2d 693 (10th Cir. 1973), *cert. denied*, 414 U.S. 1097, *reh. denied*, 415 U.S. 939 (1974); Hatch v. Goerke, 502 F.2d 1189 (10th Cir. 1974); Teterud v. Gillman, 385 F. Supp. 153 (S.D. Iowa 1974); United States *ex rel.* Goings v. Aaron, 350 F. Supp. 1 (D. Minn. 1972). These cases deal with the more commonly recognized hair style of land hair parted in the middle with a braid on each side. However, it should be pointed out that there are many different traditional hair styles depending on the particular tribe or group of Indians. *See, e.g.,* R. SPENCER, J. JENNING, ET AL., THE NATIVE AMERICANS (1965) [hereinafter cited as SPENCER ET AL.]; J. STOUTENBURGH, Jr., DICTIONARY OF THE AMERICAN INDIAN 136 (1960) [hereinafter cited as STOUTENBURGH]; J. TERRELL, AMERICAN INDIAN ALMANAC (1971) [hereinafter cited as TERRELL]; C. WISSLER, INDIANS OF THE UNITED STATES (1940) [hereinafter cited as WISSLER].

3. 385 F. Supp. 153 (S.D. Iowa 1974) (allowed an Indian inmate to wear a traditional Indian hair style as part of his religious beliefs and culture although in violation of the prison hair code). For similar non-Indian cases, *see* Kuyumjian v. Grandway Dep't Stores, CCH EMPLOYMENT PRACTICES 5086 (1972) (recognized long hair as a symbol of the plaintiff's personally developed religion); Braxton v. Board of Public Instruction, 303 F. Supp 958 (S.D. Fla. 1969) (allowed a black male teacher to wear a beard as an expression of his culture and racial pride).

4. New Rider v. Board of Educ., 480 F.2d 693 (10th Cir. 1973), *cert. denied*, 414 U.S. 1097, *reh. denied*, 415 U.S. 939 (1974); Hatch v. Goerke, 502 F.2d 1189 (10th Cir. 1974); United States *ex rel.* Goings v. Aaron, 350 F. Supp. 1 (D. Minn. 1972). For cases dealing with non-Indians, *see* Marshall v. District of Columbia, 392 F. Supp. 1012 (D.C. Cir. 1975); Cupit v. Baton Rouge Police Dep't, 277 So. 2d 454 (C.A. La. 1973) (both of these cases did not allow violation of the hair codes even though the hair was grown for religious purposes.).

5. U.S. CONST. amend. I: "Congress shall make no law respecting an establishment of religion, or prohibiting the free exercise thereof . . . ."

6. *See* cases cited in note 2, *supra.*

7. *See, e.g.,* SPENCER ET AL., STOUTENBURGH, TERRELL, WISSLER, *supra* note 2.

8. Arapaho, Crees, Oglala Sioux, and Pawnees.

9. This disagreement is illustrated by contrasting evidence presented in several of the cases concerned. In *Teterud*, an anthropologist testified to the interrelatedness of the Plains Indians' religion and daily lives, and pointed out that one of the spiritual customs of these Indians is to cut off their hair to show grief or humility after a close

114

94

relative has died. Another anthropologist, noting that long braided hair was a traditional Cree custom, explained the importance of the physical appearance of the Cree Indians in relation to spiritual matters, stating that the Cree would unbraid their hair on very serious religious occasions. While in contrast to this, a fullblooded Yankton Sioux Indian testified that male Indians' hair length was a matter of individual preference, and noted that her experiences attending many Indian religious ceremonies across the United States indicated that Indian males do not necessarily wear long hair in those ceremonies. Teterud v. Gillman, 385 F. Supp. 153, 155 (S.D. Iowa 1974).

In *Goings*, the petitioners testified that although the Indian inmates met regularly to discuss Indian culture and to engage in religious services, he was the only one wearing long hair. In addition, an Oglala Sioux testified that as a former military pilot, he had had short hair and that he annually participated in religious ceremonies. United States *ex rel.* Goings v. Aaron, 350 F. Supp. 1 (D. Minn. 1972).

In *New Rider*, an anthropologist testified as to the religious and cultural significance of long braided hair as well as the frequently reported warrior style of a hair ridge among the Pawnees. She explained that not only was the hair style traditional, but it was related to specific Pawnee dance and religious beliefs that everything a Pawnee does each day has religious significance. While, on the one hand, another anthropologist and author also testified that the Pawnee culture and religion are highly integrated with most of the tribal practices and traditions, she went on to say this did not include a particular custom of wearing long braided hair. New Rider v. Board of Educ., 480 F.2d 693, 697 (10th Cir. 1973), *cert. denied*, 414 U.S. 1097, *reh. denied*, 415 U.S. 939 (1974).

10. This argument was an issue in *United States ex rel. Goings v. Aaron*, which concerned the enforcement of the Minnesota State Penitentiary hair code against an Oglala Sioux Indian inmate. 350 F. Supp. 1 (D. Minn. 1972).

11. An Oglala Sioux Indian testified that "a vow of the type petitioner had taken . . . was certain to be important to petitioner, particularly in view of the Indian teachings that to break a vow of this sort would make him fearful that great misfortune would be nearly certain to follow." In contrast to this, a Jewish rabbi, aware of the tradition of long hair in Judaism, testified that a broken vow to cut one's hair could be renewed and such would in effect amount to a reinstatement. 350 F. Supp. 1, 3 (D. Minn. 1972).

12. SPENCER ET AL., STOUTENBURGH, TERRELL, and WISSLER, *supra* note 2; Dr. William Bittle, professor of anthropology, University of Oklahoma; Ms. Judy Jordon, anthropologist specializing in American Indian studies. Dr. Bittle also suggested that the scalplock, sometimes with an amulet braided into it, which was worn by some Indians, could be considered religious in a very broad sense, but that hair style was really tied in with the warrior status and war.

13. *See* cases cited in note 2 *supra*.

14. This was included in the petition for writ of certiorari made by the plaintiffs in *New Rider* that was denied at 414 U.S. 1097 (1973). Petition for Writ of Certiorari to the United States Supreme Court, on file at the Oklahoma Indian Rights Association, Norman, Okla.

15. *See, e.g.*, Despain v. DeKalb County Community School Dist. 428, 384 F.2d 836, *cert. denied*, 390 U.S. 906 (1967).

16. SPENCER ET AL., STOUTENBURGH, TERRELL, WISSLER, *supra* note 2.

17. *See* Petition for Writ of Certiorari, note 14 *supra*. See also the dissent to the denial of the petition at 414 U.S. 1097 (1973).

18. *Hearings Before the Special Senate Subcomm. on Indian Education of the Senate Comm. on Labor & Public Welfare*, 90th Cong. 1st and 2d. Sess. (1968). *See, e.g.*, at Walker, *Problems of American Indian Education*, at 2002, and Patterson,

115

De Facto Segregation and the American Indian, at 1657.

19. *Senate Special Subcomm. on Indian Education: A National Tragedy,* S. Rep. No. 91-501, 91st Cong., 1st Sess. (1969).

20. The hair regulation concerned in *New Rider* was that "Hair should have no odd coloring or style. It should be tapered or blocked in the back and cannot touch the shirt collar or ears and should be one-fourth inch above the eyebrows; sideburns must be no lower than the earlobe and face clean shaven . . ." 480 F.2d 693, 695 (10th Cir. 1973).

The hair code involved in *Hatch* included a provision that boys' hair should be kept trim and neatly groomed and should not extend below the eyebrows or the collar. 502 F.2d 1189, 1191 (10th Cir. 1974).

21. In *New Rider,* the Tenth Circuit Court of Appeals emphasized the testimony of Marvin Stokes, Superintendent of Schools at Byng, Okla., on the relationship between compliance with similar school dress-hair regulations and scholarship attainment, as well as instilling pride and initiative in students and found that "the hair code regulation bears a rational relationship to a state objective, i.e., that of instilling pride and initiative among the students leading to scholarship attainment and high school spirit and morale." 480 F.2d 690, 697 (10th Cir. 1973).

22. In *Teterud v. Gillman,* the psychiatrist that treated Teterud, the Cree Indian inmate, described him "when he first came for treatment as having a passive-aggressive personality which was based in part upon childhood rejection, including feeling of being 'unworthy as an Indian' and being 'just another God-damn Indian Kid.' " Furthermore, in accordance with the view that an Indian should be allowed to recognize his culture rather than perpetuating policies of suppression, "Dr. Johnson advised Teterud that his low opinion of himself could change and that he should 'start taking pride in being a red man, or an Indian, as opposed to feeling bad about it.' " 385 F. Supp. 153, 155 (S.D. Iowa 1974).

23. In *Teterud,* "Dr. Johnson further testified that the compelled cutting of Teterud's hair would generally be counter-productive to rehabilitation and, therefore, that the cutting of Teterud's hair would have no beneficial effect." Other testimony in this case pointed out the positive effect instilling racial and cultural pride had on successful rehabilitation among inmates that are members of minority groups.

"Robert Sarver, the former Commissioner of Corrections of Arkansas and West Virginia, testified that from the standpoint of criminology and penology, the instilling of racial and cultural pride in a member of a racial minority would be an important factor in successful rehabilitation." *Id.* at 155.

24. Wilson and Zingg, *What is America's Heritage? Historic Preservation and American Indian Culture,* 22 Kan. L. Rev. 413 (1974) [hereinafter cited as Wilson & Zingg].

25. National Historic Preservation Act of 1966, 16 U.S.C.A. § 470 (1970) as cited in Wilson & Zingg, *supra* note 24, at 413.

26. *Id.* at 415.

27. U.S. Const. amend. I: "Congress shall make no law . . . abridging the freedom of speech. . . ."

28. 393 U.S. 503 (1968).

29. It is important to point out that this was the holding in *Tinker* where at least there was no finding that the operation of the school was substantially endangered by the symbolic speech.

30. 303 F. Supp. 958 (M.D. Fla. 1969).

31. *Id.* at 959.

32. *See, eg.,* New Rider v. Board of Educ., 480 F.2d 693 (10th Cir. 1973).

116

33. Freedman v. Flake, 448 F.2d 258 (10th Cir. 1971). For such a distinction *see,* *e.g.,* the dissent to New Rider v. Board of Educ., where cert. denied, 414 U.S. 1097 (1974).

34. 480 F.2d 693, 698 (10th Cir. 1973).

35. *See, eg.,* Keyishan v. Board of Regents, 385 U.S. 589 (1967); Brown v. Board of Educ., 347 U.S. 483 (1954).

36. Brown v. Board of Educ., 347 U.S. 483 (1954).

37. 480 F.2d 693, 699 (10th Cir. 1973). It is interesting to note that this summary of the *Brown* conclusion is cited in the very case that the argument against favoring different ethnic and racial groups is raised, although not in relation to each other.

38. 393 U.S. 503 (1968). *See also* discussion on *Tinker* in Folsom, *Equal Opportunity for Indian Children—the Legal Basis for Compelling Bilingual and Bicultural Education,* 3 AM. INDIAN L. REV., 51, 71-72 (1975).

39. 414 U.S. 1097, 1098 (1974).

40. 385 U.S. 589 (1967).

41. " 'The vigilant protection of constitutional freedoms is nowhere more vital than in the community of American Schools.' Shelton v. Tucker, [364 U.S. 479] at 487 [81 S.Ct. 247, 5 L.Ed.2d 231]. The classroom is peculiarly the 'market-place of ideas.' The Nation's future depends upon leaders trained through wide exposure to that robust exchange of ideas which discovers truth 'out of a multitude of tongues, [rather] than through any kind of authoritative selection. United States v. Associated Press, D.C., 52 F. Supp. 362, 372 (S.D.N.Y. 1943)." 385 U.S. 589, 603 (1967).

42. Cited at note 2, *supra,* and the subjects of this note.

43. The hair regulation concerned in *New Rider* was that "[h]air should have no odd coloring or style. It should be tapered or blocked in the back and cannot touch the shirt collar or ears and should be one-fourth inch above the eyebrows; sideburns must be no lower than the earlobe and face clean shaven. . . ." 480 F.2d 693, 695 (10th Cir. 1973).

The hair code in *Hatch* included a provision that boys' hair should be kept trim and neatly groomed and should not extend below the eyebrows or the collar. 502 F.2d 1189, 1191 (10th Cir. 1974).

The hair code concerned in *Goings* was ". . . .[h]air cuts must be in accordance with the following guidelines: Hair must not extend over the ears on the sides, over the collar in the back, over the eyebrows in the front . . ." 350 F. Supp. 1, 2 (D. Minn. 1972).

The hair code in *Teterud* was "hair length may grow at the shirt collar, and bottom on the ears. May grow over the ears if desired." 385 F. Supp. 153, 154 (S.D. Iowa 1974).

44. U.S. CONST. amend. I.

45. However, it could be broadly argued that under the fourteenth amendment, a freedom or liberty to follow a traditional culture cannot be deprived without due process of law and that as part of the equal protection of the law, an Indian has just much right to follow his cultural beliefs as do other Americans of the more recognized Judeo-Christian religions and cultures:

". . . nor shall any state deprive any person of life, liberty, or property without due process of law; nor deny any person within its jurisdiction the equal protection of the laws." U.S. CONST. amend. XIV § 1.

46. *See, e.g.,* Wisconsin v. Yoder, 406 U.S. 205 (1972); Shaffield v. Northrop Worldwide Aircraft Serv., Inc., 373 F. Supp. 937 (Ala. 1974); *In re* Grady, 61 Cal. App. 2d 88, 394 P.2d 728, 50 Cal. Rptr. 912 (1964).

47. 480 F.2d 693 (10th Cir. 1973).

117

48. *New Rider* hair code, *see* note 43 *supra*.

49. U.S. Const. amend I.

50. U.S. Const. amend. I: "Congress shall make no law . . . abridging the freedom of speech . . ."; U.S. Const. amend. XIV § 1.

51. *See* arguments note 9 *supra*.

52. The trial court originally found in issuing a preliminary injunction, that the wearing of long braided hair is an expression of Pawnee Indian tradition and heritage as well as a symbol of their religious identity. 480 F.2d 693, 696 (10th Cir. 1973).

53. San Antonio Indep. School Dist. v. Rodriguez, 411 U.S. 1 (1973); McGowan v. Maryland, 366 U.S. 420 (1961); Freeman v. Flake, 448 F.2d 258 (10th Cir. 1971).

54. Freeman v. Flake, 448 F.2d 258 (10th Cir. 1971).

55. 480 F.2d 693, 698 (10th Cir. 1973).

56. For authority to apply balancing test, see the following cases: Barker v. Wingo, Warden, 407 U.S. 514 (1972); Dunn v. Blumstein, 405 U.S. 330 (1972); McGowan v. Maryland, 366 U.S. 420 (1961); Shelton v. Tucker, 364 U.S. 479 (1960); Christian Echoes Nat'l Ministry, Inc. v. United States, 470 F.2d 849 (10th Cir. 1972).

57. *See* discussion at note 20, *supra*.

58. *See* discussion at note 21, *supra*. The superintendent also explained that better groomed students generally created less trouble and that a dress-hair code that recognized each ethnic group would create a disruptive atmosphere.

59. See notes 17 through 23 *supra* and accompanying text.

60. 502 F.2d 1189 (10th Cir. 1974).

61. For an explanation of the hair code, see note 20 *supra*.

62. 406 U.S. 205 (1972).

63. *Id.*

64. The court in this decision found that the duty of supervising a student's hair length was for the state and should be handled through state procedures. 448 F.2d 258 (10th Cir. 1971).

65. 502 F.2d 1189, 1192 (10th Cir. 1974).

66. 350 F. Supp 1 (D. Minn. 1972).

67. See note 11 *supra*.

68. 350 F. Supp. 1, 4 (D. Minn. 1972). The hair code concerned was ". . . [h]air cuts must be in accordance with the following guidelines: Hair must not extend over the ears on the sides, over the collar in the back, over the eyebrows in the front . . ." *Id.* at 2.

69. *See, e.g.*, Long v. Parker, 390 F.2d 816 (3d Cir. 1968); Evans v. Ciccone, 377 F.2d 4 (8th Cir. 1967); Poe v. Werner, 336 F. Supp. 1014 (M.D. Pa. 1974); Holt v. Hutto, 363 F. Supp. 194 (E.D. Ark. 1973); Barnett v. Rodgers, 410 F.2d 995 (C.A.D.C. 1969).

70. 350 F. Supp. 1, 4 (D. Minn. 1972): "A prime consideration in the case obviously is whether the petitioner is sincere in pressing his claim on the grounds of his religious beliefs insofar as regards long hair, and on this issue the court is constrained to find that there is substantial doubt and to hold against petitioner. According to his testimony, he had gone 26½ years of his life without following Indian customs, the last ten of which he has spent in confinement. No other Indians at the Institution are motivated by religious customs the way he claims to be. . . . Further, he did submit to the cutting of his hair after his furlough. . . . Nevertheless, the court cannot believe that in such a short period of time the petitioner has become so devoutly religious in his own tribal ways that he cannot forego growing his hair to the desired length for another brief period."

71. 385 F. Supp. 153, 157 (S.D. Iowa 1974): "It suffices to say that if an individual

118

Indian's belief in the Indian religion is honest, made in good faith, and sincere, he should be allowed to wear his hair in the traditional style. . . .

". . .Warden Brewer . . . seems to indicate that Teterud was sincere in his beliefs. On the other hand, the Court must note that Teterud was raised a Catholic in an orphanage during his youth. The record further discloses that it was not until adulthood that Teterud became interested in his Indian ancestry and heritage. In addition, prior to trial Teterud was an active member of the Church of the New Song, a religious organization which this court recognized as such. . . . The thrust of the defendants' challenge of Teterud's sincerity stems from the fact that the plaintiffs' reawakened interest in Indian customs and life appears to be of very recent vintage. This challenge must be viewed, however, in light of the additional fact that Teterud has spent the bulk of his life in various institutions wherein his active desire to pursue the Indian way of life may have been somewhat constrained. The Court can never know with assurance whether Teterud is sincere or insincere. The defendants, however, have not presented sufficient evidence to show that Teterud's beliefs are not made in good faith."

72. See cases at note 69 *supra*.

73. 350 F. Supp. 1, 5 (D. Minn. 1972).

74. 385 F. Supp. 153 (S.D. Iowa 1974).

75. *Id.* at 154: "Hair length may grow to the shirt collar, and bottom on the ears. May grow over the ears if desired."

76. *Id.* at 153: "In United States v. Seeger, . . . 380 U.S. [163] at 176, 85 S.Ct. [850] at 859, [13 L.Ed.2d 733 (1965)], the Supreme Court interpreted religious beliefs as follows: "Within that phrase would come all sincere religious beliefs which are based upon a power or being, or upon a faith, to which all else is subordinate or upon which all else is ultimately dependent."

77. *Id.* at 156: "The Indians' beliefs are based upon the existence of a Great Spirit, a power or being greater than man and, thus definition."

78. *Id.* at 155.

79. *Id.* at 157. It should be noted that the decision is not limited only to Cree Indians, but is extended to include Plains Indians generally.

80. *Id.* at 156.

81. *Id.*

82. See cases at note 69 *supra*.

83. 385 F. Supp. 153, 157 (S.D. Iowa 1974).

84. *Id.*

85. 502 F.2d 1189, 1192 (10th Cir. 1974); 480 F.2d 693, 698 (10th Cir. 1973).

86. 480 F.2d 693, 698 (10th Cir. 1973).

87. The justification was based on the grounds "that long hair was unsanitary, created hazards around machinery, increased difficulty in identifying inmates or could hide contraband." 385 F. Supp. 153 (S.D. Iowa 1974).

88. 350 F. Supp. 1, 5 (D. Minn. 1972).

89. See discussion at notes 21 and 56 *supra*.

90. 502 F.2d 1189, 1192 (10th Cir. 1974).

91. See discussion at note 9 *supra*.

92. 480 F.2d 693, 700 (10th Cir. 1973): "We believe that we would create a veritable quagmire for school boards . . . were we to hold that the subject dress-hair regulation implicates basic constitutional values. We need only ponder . . . what exceptions beyond those urged here might be constitutionally mandated upon the appellees should the appellants prevail here. . . . [W]e might ask how a school board could draft a dress-hair regulation . . . which would not impinge upon or interfere with

119

a personal held belief that is sincere and meaningful in the life of its possessor (a student), parallel to that filled by the orthodox belief in God."

93. See discussion of evidence presented at note 9 *supra*.

94. *See, e.g.,* 406 U.S. 205 (1972); 373 F. Supp. 937 (S.D. Ala. 1974); 394 P.2d 728 (Cal. 1964).

95. The parents claimed the enforcement of the hair regulation violated their right to raise their children according to their own religious, cultural, and moral values. 502 F.2d 1189, 1191-92 (10th Cir. 1974).

96. Sidney Moore, Sr., age 69, testified that "[w]hen he was a boy he wore long braided hair. . . . He referred to such hair style as the 'old traditional ways.' He sees a resurgence among the young Indian people to 'regain their tradition, to learn their culture.' " 480 F.2d 693, 696 (10th Cir. 1973). *See also* note 9 *supra*.

97. 350 F. Supp. 1, 3 (D. Minn. 1972)

98. 385 F. Supp. 153, 156 (S.D. Iowa 1974).

99. *Id.*

100. *Id.*

101. 414 U.S. 1097 (1973).

102. See note 18 *supra*.

103. See note 19 *supra*.

104. See text accompanying notes 17 through 23 *supra*.

105. "Petitioners were not wearing their hair in a desired style simply because it was the fashionable or accepted style, or because they somehow felt the need to register an inchoate discontent with the general malaise they might have perceived in our society. They were in fact attempting to broadcast a clear and specific message to their fellow students and others—their pride in being Indian. This, I believe, should clearly bring this case within the ambit of Tinker . . . where we struck down a school policy which refused to allow students to wear black armbands in protest of the Vietnam War. We recognized that such armbands were closely akin to pure speech and were entitled to First Amendment protection, . . . at least where, as here . . . there was no finding that the operation of the school was substantially endangered by the symbolic speech. . . ." 414 U.S. 1097, 1098 (1973).

106. See discussion at notes 22 and 23 *supra*; 385 F. Supp. 153, 157 (S.D. Iowa 1974).

THE RIGHTS OF RESERVATION PARENTS AND CHILDREN: CULTURAL SURVIVAL OR THE FINAL TERMINATION?

David Woodward*

Introduction

> [F]reedom to differ is not limited to things
> that do not matter much. That would be a mere
> shadow of freedom. The test of its substance
> is the right to differ as to things that touch
> the heart of the existing order.[1]

Justice Jackson's words, written more than a quarter century ago, were offered in defense of the refusal by the children of Jehovah's Witnesses to salute the American flag. The import of these words is, however, much broader, for Justice Jackson defined a right that is both fundamental and revolutionary, one that still endures in a country with a revolutionary beginning: the right to be different, to live differently. That right should include what some have called the "right to cultural integrity,"[2] an essential part of which is the right of American Indian parents living on reservations to rear their children within their own culture.[3] A meaningful right to cultural survival,[4] in turn, depends upon recognition by the non-Indian community, and especially by its judicial system, first, of the fundamental and personal right of Indian parents to control the care of their children, and second, of tribal court jurisdiction over the Indian parent-child relationship as the primary safeguard of that right. This article is offered as a modest step toward establishing that right and enhancing that recognition.

The Crisis

The current plight of the reservation Indian child is critical because of its magnitude and its destructive impact on the very survival of the tribe. A recent survey of states with large Indian populations, conducted by the Association on American Indian Affairs (AAIA), reveals that 25-35 per cent of all Indian children are removed from their homes and channeled into foster homes, adoptive

* J.D. 1975, University of California; B.A. 1971, St. Cloud State College, Minn.

21

homes, or institutions.[5] Of those destined for foster care, 85 per cent are placed in non-Indian homes.[6] The family suffering submerged in these figures quickly surfaces when attention shifts from numbers to people. Three brief examples should suffice. On January 9, 1973, Delphine Foote, a 24-year-old mother from the Standing Rock Sioux Reservation, left her infant son, Christopher, with the South Dakota Welfare Department and her signature on a form which stated explicitly that relinquishment of custody was strictly temporary. That statement was reinforced by the oral understanding between Ms. Foote and her assigned social worker that Christopher would be immediately returned upon demand. The mother subsequently made that demand only to have the Department institute a neglect and dependency proceeding against her in an attempt to terminate her parental rights to Christopher and thereby facilitate his adoption by the non-Indian foster parents with whom he had been placed.[7]

California social workers, convinced that an Indian reservation is no place to rear a child, pursued their convictions by placing Blossom Lavonne, a three-year-old Rosebud Sioux, in a preadoptive home. Pursuant to her mother's request, Blossom had been taken to California by her aunt. When, as planned, the mother arrived one week later, Blossom had already been placed by social workers, who argued not that the natural mother was in any way unfit, but that reservation life was harmful to a child, and that the preadoptive parents were in a far better position financially to provide a better quality life than was her mother.[8]

The desire to provide an Indian child mainstream American opportunities probably also motivated two Wisconsin women visiting South Dakota's Pine Ridge Indian Reservation during the Christmas season in 1972. They asked the Indian mother of three-year-old Benita Rowland if they could take her child on a short trip to Wisconsin. Benita's mother gave them what she thought to be written permission for the trip, only to be informed later that the paper she signed was actually an agreement to relinquish her parental rights to Benita. Willing to purchase the child if her parents continued to insist upon her return, the Wisconsin women sent the following consoling explanation to Benita's mother: "We have not taken Benita from you; you gave her physical birth, which we could not give, and we can give her opportunities which you could not give—so she belongs to both of us. But far more, she belongs to the Lord."[9]

The disintegration of Indian family life documented by the foregoing statistics and illustrations may be traced to the fear by the non-

22

Indian community of a " 'foreign community' within its borders,"[10] or to the tendency of the dominant society to insist that a different culture is an inferior one,[11] or to other origins. But regardless of the cause, failure within the non-Indian community, particularly within its judicial system, to recognize the basic right of reservation Indian parents to bring up their own children in their own culture poses a fundamental threat to the future of the reservation itself. As its children leave, so too does its capacity to perpetuate itself. That threat becomes fatal when combined with the accompanying failure to recognize that vesting primary responsibility for control of the reservation Indian parent-child relationship with the tribe itself is essential if it is to be able "to provide for the care and upbringing of its young, a *sine qua non* to the preservation of its identity."[12] Removing that threat by drawing recognition to the rights first, of reservation Indian parents and children and, second, of Indian tribes, is difficult without some understanding of what law governs today's reservation Indian family. As one commentator has thoughtfully observed, "It is doubtful that justice can be secured for Indians until America better understands the laws under which the Indian lives."[13]

The Jurisdictional Enigma

Emerging Principles

Arriving at that better understanding is not easy. The initial difficulty is the sheer quantity of what must be understood: "the vast hodgepodge of treaties, statutes, judicial and administrative rulings, and unrecorded practice in which the intricacies and perplexities, confusions and injustices of the law governing Indians lay concealed."[14] A recent estimate suggests that the hodgepodge includes at least "389 treaties, an entire volume of special federal statutes, over 2,000 regulations, some 500 opinions of the Attorney General and Interior Department Solicitor, and hundreds of court decisions."[15]

Considering its vast content alone, it is not surprising that confusion has dominated Indian law from its inception. Nineteenth-century American courts characterized the rapidly developing law governing the relationship between Indian and non-Indian communities as "an anomalous one . . . of a complex character,"[16] one "marked by peculiar and cardinal distinctions which exist nowhere else."[17] Twentieth-century American courts concur: confusion continues to reign over Indian law.[18]

It shares its throne with vacillation within the dominant society

23

as to how best to solve the "Indian problem." Congressional policy in the latter part of the nineteenth century, embodied in the General Allotment Act,[19] was geared toward assimilation of the Indian into mainstream America.[20] In 1934, Congress stood that policy on its head by passing the Indian Reorganization Act,[21] designed ".to rehabilitate the Indian's economic life and to give him a chance to develop the initiative destroyed by a century of oppression and paternalism."[22] The 1950's brought yet another reversal by a Congress convinced that termination of federal responsibilities and services coupled with assimilation was the best solution. However, the termination thrust of the 1950's policy has since yielded to a federal program to promote Indian political and cultural autonomy.[23]

Congressional vacillation in formulating and executing a consistent federal policy toward the American Indian thus fed judicial confusion in developing a coherent body of Indian law, which in turn nurtured further congressional fluctuation. Fortunately, a few fundamental jurisdictional principles emerged despite this cyclical development of the hodgepodge. The first is the view of Indian tribes as physically within the states in which they reside, yet politically beyond them. The earliest expression of this view was *Worcester v. Georgia*,[24] in which the Supreme Court characterized the Cherokee Nation as "a distinct community, occupying its own territory . . . in which the laws of Georgia can have no force, and which the citizens of Georgia have no right to enter. . . ."[25] Although hardly free from attack,[26] that characterization has survived the more than 140 years that have passed since its formulation.

Its corollary principle constitutes a second cornerstone of Indian law: the exclusivity of federal jurisdiction absent an express congressional grant of state jurisdiction.[27] The roots of this principle are also anchored in *Worcester v. Georgia*,[28] and its branches matured early in the development of Indian law to shield tribes from the imposition of state law.

A third jurisdictional point permeating those already discussed is the wardship theory. Its origins have been traced to Chief Justice Marshall's creative yet infinitely ambiguous denomination of Indian tribes as "domestic dependent nations" who "are in a state of pupilage" and who stand to the federal government in a relationship that "resembles that of a ward to his guardian."[29] Fifty-five years later the Supreme Court decided that the American Indian had ceased to resemble a ward and had actually become one.[30] Despite its unmistakably imperialistic cast, wardship thinking continued to dominate late nineteenth- and early twentieth-century judicial approaches toward solving the jurisdictional puzzle.

24

Williams v. Lee[31] articulated the following jurisdictional test in holding that Arizona had no jurisdiction over an action by a non-Indian owner of a store located on the Navaho Reservation to collect for goods sold on credit to a Navaho couple:

> Essentially, absent governing Acts of Congress, the question has always been whether the state action infringed on the right of reservation Indians to make their own laws and be ruled by them.[32]

In applying this test, the Court concluded that the exercise of state jurisdiction under the circumstances then before it "would undermine the authority of tribal courts over Reservation affairs and hence would infringe on the right of the Indians to govern themselves."[33]

Perhaps because of the inherent ambiguity in the *Williams* test, the Supreme Court declined to apply it six years after its formulation.[34] In denying Arizona the power to impose a tax on income derived from a trading post on the Navaho Reservation, the Court in *Warren Trading Post Co. v. Arizona Tax Commission* bypassed the obvious infringement test and instead reasoned that "comprehensive federal regulation of Indian traders" by Congress had so preempted the area as to leave "no room . . . for state laws imposing additional burdens upon traders."[35] *Warren* has been viewed by one commentator as marking a return to the old principle of federal exclusivity through preemption rather than the tribal sovereignty emphasis of *Williams*.[36]

By focusing attention upon a pervasive federal regulatory scheme governing the conduct of traders on the reservation, *Warren* foreshadowed the Supreme Court's most recent approach, exclusive analytical reliance upon applicable federal statutes and treaties. *Kennerly v. District Court of Montana*[37] exemplified that analysis and established the current jurisdictional test. Confronted with an action against members of the Blackfeet Indian Tribe to recover the price of food sold on credit at plaintiff's store, located within the boundaries of the reservation in the incorporated town of Browning, *Kennerly* grounded its analysis on Public Law 280.[38] Since the state had not made any effort to take advantage of the jurisdictional opportunities presented by that law as initially passed in 1953, and since a tribal code provision purporting to confer concurrent state jurisdiction in those cases where the defendant was a tribal member was held not to "comport with the explicit requirements" of the Civil Rights Act of 1968,[39] Montana had no jurisdiction to decide the

25

controversy. The *Kennerly* Court did not find a violation of the *Williams* infringement test. In view of the tribe's own provision attempting to permit the exercise of concurrent jurisdiction by the state in certain cases, perhaps the Court could not logically find such a violation.[40] Nevertheless, state jurisdiction was denied on the theory that neither the state nor the tribe had satisfied the explicit statutory procedures embodied in Public Law 280 and the Civil Rights Act of 1968 for state assumption of jurisdiction. *Kennerly* has generally been construed to mean that state jurisdiction over actions arising on a reservation and involving an Indian litigant hinges upon strict compliance with requisite federal procedures.[41]

Recent Supreme Court decisions, while clearly affirming that construction,[42] have been less precise in coming to grips with two ensuing issues: first, whether the *Kennerly* requirement of strict compliance with federal legislation is absolute, and second, to what extent, if any, the *Williams* infringement test remains good law.

Mescalero Apache Tribe v. Jones[43] confirmed that state jurisdiction does attach to Indian activity occurring outside reservation boundaries. Consequently, the failure of a state to satisfy the provisions of Public Law 280 or the failure of the state and/or tribe to comply with the Civil Rights Act of 1968 would presumably not preclude state assertion of jurisdiction over such activity. However, a companion case, *McClanahan v. Arizona State Tax Commission*,[44] mentioned the following categories in the Court's "brief statement of what this case does not involve": "Indians who have left or never inhabited reservations" or "who do not possess the usual accoutrements of tribal self-government," activity among non-Indians on the reservation, and activity by reservation Indians occurring on nonreservation land.[45] While *Mescalero* supports state jurisdiction in the latter situation, the *McClanahan* Court's exclusion of the remaining categories from its consideration makes their present status uncertain.

Two possible interpretations are immediately apparent. One is that by explicitly avoiding these categories, the Court is sub silentio undermining their validity as exceptions both to the principle of federal exclusivity absent a specific congressional grant of state jurisdiction, and to *Kennerly*'s insistence upon strict compliance with the terms of that grant. However, since prior case law arguably supports state jurisdiction in those areas untouched by the *McClanahan* Court,[46] a more reasonable interpretation is that the Court's silence merely requires independent inquiry for precedent in these instances to determine whether state jurisdiction applies. If so, the rule articulated in *Kennerly* would not be absolute; *McClanahan*'s exclusions

26

would still be implied exceptions, so that state jurisdiction in these areas is independent of compliance with relevant congressional statutes governing state assumption of jurisdiction.[47]

Determining the status of the *Williams* infringement test after *McClanahan* and *Mescalero* is more difficult than gauging *Kennerly*'s scope, because the guidance offered by the Court on this issue is not only ambiguous, but contradictory. In *Mescalero*, Justice White cited *Williams* to support what is referred to as the "upshot" of Supreme Court Indian jurisdictional precedent, *i.e.*, the proposition that "even on reservations, state laws may be applied unless such application would interfere with reservation self-government."[48] Yet, in *McClanahan*, Justice Marshall first emphatically declined Arizona's invitation to apply the *Williams* test, then suggested that it had always been invoked in situations "involving non-Indians."[49] Thus, assuming *Mescalero* and *McClanahan* are entitled to equal weight on the issue of the present status of the infringement test, Justice White's apparent broad reaffirmation of the *Williams* test does not square with its relegation by Justice Marshall to situations involving non-Indians. However, primary attention must be centered upon Justice Marshall's treatment of *Williams* if for no other reason than it is both more direct and more extensive.

Doing so dispenses with the inconsistency, but not the ambiguity. The *McClanahan* Court was unmistakably clear in indicating that even where tribal self-government would not be infringed by state assumption of jurisdiction, the Public Law 280—Civil Rights Act of 1968 procedures must still be followed step by step. What is not clear, however, is whether proper observance of federal procedures would necessarily lead to state jurisdiction in a case involving reservation activity of a non-Indian litigant where assumption of such jurisdiction would clearly infringe tribal self-government. A forceful argument has been made that it does, based on the premise that the *Williams* test is merely a synopsis of other exceptions, and not itself a separate exception to the principle of federal exclusivity absent an express congressional grant of state jurisdiction coupled with exact satisfaction of the grant's conditions.[50] However, this argument ignores the real possibility that by repeatedly referring to "the *Williams* test" and by limiting that test to a prescribed sphere (*i.e.*, situations where at least one party is a non-Indian), the Court is presupposing its separate character. More significantly, the argument ignores the fact that the policy basing the *Williams* test, the goal of promoting the autonomy of tribal government, is overwhelmingly endorsed by current federal policy.[51] It is therefore at least arguable that even where the federal statutory avenue to state as-

27

sumption of jurisdiction has been strictly followed, a state may still lack jurisdiction over reservation activity of a non-Indian litigant when asserting its jurisdiction would infringe upon the tribe's right to self-government.

But while arguably applicable in the foregoing instance, the *Williams* test has otherwise yielded to that expressed in *Kennerly*, so that state jurisdiction now generally depends not upon whether its exercise would infringe upon reservation self-government, but upon exact compliance by the state with Public Law 280 or by both the state and the tribe with the Civil Rights Act of 1968. Absent such compliance, the state has no jurisdiction unless one of the exceptions alluded to in *McClanahan* applies, *i.e.*, unless the case involves (1) Indians who do not live on a reservation, (2) Indians who do not possess "the usual accoutrements of tribal self-government," (3) the activity of non-Indian litigants on the reservation, or (4) the activity of reservation Indians off the reservation.

Who Governs?

Present Law: The Jurisdictional Answer

The foregoing jurisdictional analysis provides the first of two conceptual frameworks within which the question of which system has the power to adjudicate controversies involving the well-being of the reservation Indian child can be answered: the tribe, the state, or the federal government. Application of that analysis largely turns upon a determination of first, whether custody of the reservation Indian child is obtained on the reservation, and second, whether the state is what will be referred to as a "Public Law 280 state."[52]

To illustrate, assume child custody is obtained within the boundaries of a reservation located in a non-Public Law 280 state by the non-Indian prospective parents. *Kennerly v. District Court of Montana* dictates that state jurisdiction hinges upon strict compliance with applicable federal statutes establishing the procedure for state assumption of jurisdiction. Thus, the state would have jurisdiction over a parental rights termination proceeding only if one of the implicit *McClanahan* exceptions to the *Kennerly* rule applies. It seems, however, that none does. This is not a case dealing with the activity of Indians who live off the reservation or who are "without the accoutrements of tribal self-government." Nor does it involve conduct of only non-Indian litigants on the reservation or the activity of reservation Indians off the reservation. Absent compliance or the applicability of any exception to the compliance requirement, the state is thus without jurisdiction.

28

On the other hand, where custody is obtained off the reservation in either a Public Law 280 or a non-Public Law 280 state, the previously outlined criteria point toward state jurisdiction. When an Indian parent temporarily leaves a reservation situated in a Public Law 280 state and entrusts the temporary custody of her child to a state welfare agency which then wrongfully places the child in a foster care or adoptive home, state jurisdiction derives from full satisfaction of the federally established procedure for state assumption of jurisdiction pursuant to *Kennerly*. And since both *Mescalero* and *McClanahan* make clear that state jurisdiction attaches in any event to activity of reservation Indians occurring off the reservation, changing the situs of the activity to a non-Public Law 280 state does not alter the result.[53]

The more difficult case, however, arises with factual patterns somewhere between the above pair of hypotheses. The procurement of custody of a reservation Indian child, when accomplished on a reservation located in a Public Law 280 state by non-Indian prospective parents, creates precisely the one situation in which it is at least arguable that the *Williams* infringement test has survived *Kennerly* and *McClanahan*. Assuming *Williams* applies to such a situation, the critical question becomes whether the assertion of state jurisdiction would infringe on "the right of reservation Indians to make their own laws and be ruled by them."[54] The answer depends upon whether tribal court jurisdiction over reservation Indian children is an essential matter of reservation self-government. For two reasons, both questions can be answered only in the affirmative. First, it is difficult to imagine a matter more essential to reservation self-government than a tribe's control over its youth which, as previously noted, has been rightfully recognized as the *sine qua non* of tribal identity.[55] Without that control, the integrity of the tribe as a distinct political and cultural community is threatened. Second, even a cursory review of relevant case law reveals that subjects far less central than a tribe's control over its own children have been deemed to be essential matters of self-government into which the state cannot intrude.[56] Thus, there is little doubt that the reservation Indian parent-child relationship constitutes an area essential to reservation self-government and, therefore, is one immune from state jurisdiction under the infringement test of *Williams v. Lee*.

Even if *Williams* is found *not* to be controlling, so as to preclude state jurisdiction over a proceeding to terminate the parental rights of a reservation Indian parent where custody of the child was obtained by non-Indian prospective parents while on a reservation located in a Public Law 280 state, the jurisdictional inquiry should not

29

end. The more profound question of whether a state court having jurisdiction *should* exercise that jurisdiction remains. Several reasons dictate that it should decline to do so.

Ignoring the disturbing constitutional implications possibly attendant upon the exercise of state jurisdiction over an Indian child whose parents have temporarily entrusted his care to a state welfare agency off the reservation,[57] there remains a persuasive reason why a state should decline to exercise its jurisdiction, regardless of how it has been established. It can be found in a recurrent theme in Indian case law since the nineteenth century—the policy of vesting responsibility over reservation affairs with tribal government to the exclusion of not only state, but also federal control. A careful reading of the early Supreme Court decisions now regarded as the linchpins of contemporary Indian law discloses the origins of this policy. For example, a close look at the language of *Worcester v. Georgia* reveals the following principle: "The settled doctrine of the law of nations is, that a weaker power does not surrender its independence—its right to self-government, by association with a stronger, and taking its protection."[58] Chief Justice Marshall's articulation of the principle that political destruction of the conquered is not, and should not be, the inevitable consequence of conquest goes hand in hand with his characterization of Indian nations as distinct political communities. More importantly, it goes straight to the jugular of the entire wardship mentality. Unable to find "any attempt, on the part of the crown, to interfere with the internal affairs of the Indians," Marshall went on to touch the Achilles heel of wardship thinking: "Protection does not imply the destruction of the protected."[59]

Worcester's preference for reservation control of reservation matters was later implicitly confirmed in *United States v. Kagama,*[60] where Justice Miller emphasized that Indian tribes "were, and always have been, regarded as . . . a separate people, with the power of regulating their internal and social relations."[61] In *Ex Parte Crow Dog,*[62] the Supreme Court offered perhaps its most morally laden rationale for that preference. It concluded that trying criminal defendants who mature in one culture by the laws of another is unconscionable:

> It tries them, not by their peers, nor by the customs of their people, nor the law of their land, but by superiors of a different race, according to the law of a social state . . . which is opposed to the traditions of their history [and] to the habits of their lives. . . .[63]

These nineteenth-century manifestations of the policy of leaving

30

internal reservation affairs free from state and federal interference were subsequently embodied in two interrelated doctrines developed by twentieth-century courts. The first, the doctrine of tribal sovereignty, was perhaps best articulated by Felix Cohen:

> The whole course of judicial decision on the nature of Indian tribal power is marked by adherence to three fundamental principles: (1) An Indian tribe possesses, in the first instance, all the power of any sovereign state. (2) Conquest renders the tribe subject to the legislative power of the United States and, in substance, terminates the external powers of sovereignty of the tribe, e.g., its power to enter into treaties with foreign nations, but does not by itself affect the internal sovereignty of the tribe, i.e., its powers of local self-government. (3) These powers are subject to qualification by treaties and by express legislation of Congress, but, save as thus expressly qualified, full powers of internal sovereignty are vested in the Indian tribes and their duly constituted organs of government.[64]

The second doctrine, the intra-tribal affairs doctrine, may be viewed as a corollary of the first in that its pivotal concept is that courts should abstain from interfering in litigation stemming from problems purely internal to the tribe, such as defining the criteria of tribal membership.[65]

While neither doctrine has gone unchallenged,[66] there can be little doubt that their foundational policy supporting the cultural and political autonomy of the tribe is currently sound.[67] The clearest manifestation of this policy from the executive branch is former President Nixon's 1970 message to Congress:

> It is long past time that the Indian policies of the Federal Government began to recognize and build upon the capacities and insights of the Indian people. Both as a matter of justice and as a matter of enlightened social policy, we must begin to act on the basis of what the Indians themselves have long been telling us. The time has come to break decisively with the past and to create the conditions for a new era in which the Indians' future is determined by Indian acts and Indian decisions. . . . This, then, must be the goal of any new national policy towards the Indian people: To strengthen the Indians' sense of autonomy without threatening his sense of community.[68]

Congressional endorsement of the "new national policy" becomes readily apparent when the Civil Rights Act of 1968, with its provision conditioning state assumption of jurisdiction upon the consent

31

of the tribe(s) to be affected, is contrasted with its 1953 predecessor, Public Law 280, which contained no such provision, but instead unilaterally conferred state jurisdiction upon five states and opened the door for others to assume jurisdiction independent of tribal sentiment toward such assumption.[69] Furthermore, the federal judiciary has convincingly demonstrated in two ways its assent to the same national Indian policy: first, by evidencing a strong preference for a general requirement of exhaustion of tribal remedies as a prerequisite to suit under the Indian Civil Rights Act;[70] and second, by applying the provisions of the Act in a fashion marked with increasing flexibility and sensitivity to tribal customs and traditions, thereby lessening the profound cultural tension its enactment invited.[71]

This current federal policy embraced by all three branches of our nation's government provides the most persuasive reason why the exercise of state jurisdiction over the reservation Indian child should be declined in deference to tribal jurisdiction. When that overwhelming policy is coupled with its historical antecedent, the persistent judicial theme of tribal management of tribal affairs to the exclusion of both state and federal control, that deference becomes not only sound, but compelling.

Future Law: Toward Cultural Survival

A better way of reaching the conclusion that primary responsibility over the reservation parent-child relationship ought to remain in the tribe is by focusing upon the interests threatened by the current Indian child custody crisis. Such an approach offers more than simplicity; it provides a more rational and humane approach than the territorial perspective so characteristic of the present Supreme Court's vision. Rather than resolving the issue by determining whether custody of the reservation child was obtained on or off the reservation and in a Public Law 280 or non-Public Law 280 state, thereby inviting what has been aptly called (although in a different context) "tape measure justice,"[72] centering attention upon the interests at stake helps to insure that common sense policy, not territorial quirks, will be determinative.

What, then, are these interests? The two that are in need of greatest protection are (1) the interests of individual Indian parents in rearing their children within the family framework of their own culture, and (2) the corresponding interests of individual Indian children to live in their own culture with their own parents. Measured by the yardstick of established constitutional doctrine, both these interests meet the dimensions of protected constitutional rights.

32

More than a quarter of a century ago, the Supreme Court characterized the rights to marry and have children as fundamental, "basic rights of man."[73] Since then, the Court has classified a mother's right to the custody of her child as a personal right far more precious than property rights,[74] and has emphasized that "[c]hildren have a very special place in life which law should reflect."[75] It has also elevated the American family unit to an almost sacred status. *Stanley v. Illinois*[76] firmly establishes the broad constitutional basis supporting this nation's traditional respect for the family: "The integrity of the family unit has found protection in the Due Process Clause of the Fourteenth Amendment . . ., the Equal Protection Clause of the Fourteenth Amendment . . ., and the Ninth Amendment. . . ."[77]

In forcefully defending home and family, the Court has not overlooked the importance of the role parents play in the challenge of rearing children. Its consistent position has been that "[i]t is cardinal with us that the custody, care and nurture of the child reside first in the parents."[78] Chief Justice Burger's recent remarks in *Wisconsin v. Yoder*[79] crystallized this position:

> The history and culture of Western civilization reflect a strong tradition of parental concern for the nature and upbringing of their children. This primary role of the parents in the upbringing of their children is now established beyond debate as an enduring American tradition.[80]

It is but a small, almost imperceptible step from recognition of the ascendancy of the home, the family unit, and the parental role in child-rearing to a correlative recognition of the Indian home, the Indian family unit, and the essential role of Indian parents in bringing up their children within the confines of their own culture.

Admittedly, constitutional family law evolved primarily within the context of non-Indian culture; nevertheless, cultural orthodoxy has never been required in American jurisprudence. On the contrary, the Supreme Court has unequivocally stated that "[o]ur whole constitutional heritage rebels at the thought of giving government the power to control men's minds,"[81] just as it "repudiates the idea that a State may conduct its schools 'to foster a homogeneous people.'"[82] Furthermore, the Court has readily applied "the limitations of the Constitution with no fear that freedom to be intellectually and spiritually diverse or even contrary will disintegrate the social organization."[83] Perhaps the most eloquent expression of American judicial repulsion against coerced uniformity can be found in the words of Justice Jackson:

33

If there is any fixed star in our constitutional constellation, it is that no official, high or petty, can prescribe what shall be orthodox in politics, nationalism, religion, or other matters of opinion or force citizens to confess by word or act their faith therein.[84]

The light of that fixed star has illuminated the thinking of both state and federal courts confronted with Indian child custody cases. For example, the Alaska Supreme Court demonstrated laudable sensitivity to the cultural differences graphically presented in *Carle v. Carle*.[85] Confronted with the critical question of whether a young son should continue to be brought up in the traditional native village culture of his father or in his mother's modern urban culture, the lower court in *Carle* decided that since "village way of life is inevitably succumbing to the predominate [*sic*] Caucasian, urban society of the land," the boy could better make the transitional adjustment with his mother in Juneau.[86] The Alaska Supreme Court reversed, leaving no doubt that cultural bias must not motivate decisions involving Indian child custody determinations:

> We think it is not permissible, in a bicultural context, to decide a child's custody on the hypothesis that it is necessary to facilitate the child's adjustment to what is believed to be the dominant culture. . . . It is not the function of our courts to homogenize Alaskan society.[87]

An equally sophisticated approach to the cultural schism posed by many Indian child custody proceedings was recently demonstrated by a juvenile court in Utah. The state Welfare Department filed a petition to terminate the parental rights of a Navaho father to his 10- and 12-year-old daughters, both of whom had been in the Department's "temporary" custody for four years pursuant to a prior court order. In *State of Utah ex rel. Goodman*,[88] the state attempted to show that (1) the father failed to make repeated inquiries concerning the well-being of his children, and (2) during several visits of the social worker to the father's Navaho family camp on the Navaho Reservation, the father appeared "somewhat hostile and he stated that [the social worker] had no business with [his] children."[89] Conceding that the father did ask that his children be returned, the state nevertheless argued that he had neither home nor mother to offer them, but only their grandmother's care.

The father's legal services attorneys countered by establishing, through expert testimony on the characteristics of Navaho culture, that the parental role in child care responsibilities is shared among

34

members of the extended family, that a father whose wife was deceased would ordinarily rely upon his parents and other relatives in caring for his children, that it was not at all derelict of him to do so, and that given the entrenched distrust of the Anglo community and the language and cultural barriers involved, it would not be unusual for a Navaho father to be reluctant to express concern over his children to the very Anglos he regards as having taken them from him initially. The *Goodman* court was convinced:

> [W]e are here dealing with members of a culture whose motivations and methods and perceptions, while appropriate for that culture, may not fit patterns of expected behavior in the Anglo culture. Respondent's evidence tends to show that in the context of his culture, Mr. Goodman's lack of initiative in making demonstrations of interest in, or providing some support for his children, and his non-cooperativeness or apparent hostility with those who sought to evaluate his attitudes and home situation may well have been a matter or [*sic*] pride.[90]

The court went on to hold that considering the preciousness of the rights involved, proof of conduct indicative of abandonment or neglect in Anglo culture was not enough to carry the state's heavy burden, primarily because the significance of such conduct must be appraised to the extent possible from the cultural context in which it occurred.

The lesson of cultural sensitivity was reiterated even more powerfully in *Wisconsin Potawatomies of the Hannahville Indian Community v. Houston.*[91] After a state court hearing instigated by an adoption petition filed by the children's Indian great-uncle, three orphaned Potawatomie children were placed first with the state Welfare Department and then in the adoptive home of a non-Indian Florida couple. The tribe filed suit in federal court to regain custody.

The *Wisconsin Potawatomies* court squarely faced the core issue by defining it not as a question of which litigants might be the better parents or which is the preferable culture for the children's growth, but as the more profound question of whether the tribal or state system of government is entitled to make those determinations. In answering in favor of exclusive tribal jurisdiction, the court first noted that Michigan had not assumed jurisdiction under Public Law 280 over the plaintiff tribe, then went on to find that even though custody of the children was obtained outside reservation boundaries, the domicile of the children followed that of the mother, which was on the reservation despite her frequent travels beyond its limits.

35

Wisconsin Potawatomies first noted that Public Law 280 was not applicable; it then focused on the policy choice of who ought to govern, considering the interests at stake:

> If tribal sovereignty is to have any meaning at all at this juncture of history, it must necessarily include the right, within its own boundaries and membership, to provide for the care and upbringing of its young, a *sine qua non* to the preservation of its identity.[92]

The court's ultimate finding in *Wisconsin Potawatomies* that "the care and custody of Indian children is a matter of Indian concern and interest"[93] is a tribute not only to the American judiciary's flexibility, but to its common sense.

Indeed, the sensitivity to cultural differences expressed in *Carle, Goodman,* and *Wisconsin Potawatomies,* as well as the almost sacrosanct respect shown by the Supreme Court for the integrity of the family unit, can be viewed on a higher plane as judicial soundings of a traditional American theme that is of critical relevance to the entire "who governs" question generally, and the current child custody crisis specifically. The early rhythm of that theme was struck by Jefferson when he wrote of self-evident truths, of the equality of man, and of inalienable rights, including life, liberty, and the pursuit of happiness. Its melody was underscored by the perceptive identification of the Preamble to the Declaration of Independence as both "the single most concentrated expression of the revolutionary intellectual tradition" and the embodiment of "the idea that liberty was man's inalienable right to self-determination."[94] The same respected student of America's revolutionary tradition also observed that that tradition "took as its point of departure not property, but conscience. . . ."[95]

Given this point of departure, it is not surprising to find the nation's highest court bringing the integrity of family life within the fold of several constitutional guarantees, particularly that afforded by due process. Nor is it surprising to discover that the Court's pronouncement that "[t]he fundamental theory of liberty upon which all governments in this Union repose excludes any general power of the state to standardize its children"[96] has been extended by bold state court declarations that a parent's right to his or her child is "a fundamental, natural right,"[97] and that the corresponding right of the child to enjoy the care of his natural parents is an "inherent constitutionally protected" liberty.[98]

These, then, are the interests jeopardized by today's child custody crisis that threatens the extinction of reservation Indian cultures across the country. When American courts move to protect those in-

36

terests by recognizing the primacy of tribal court jurisdiction over the reservation Indian child, they are doing nothing more than maintaining continuity with the nation's tradition, a tradition rooted in conscience and in liberty.

Suggestions for a More Humane Future

The Constitutional Right To Cultural Integrity

The Supreme Court recently had the opportunity to sustain that continuity by recognizing a constitutional right to cultural integrity. Unable to convince the Tenth Circuit Court of Appeals that the suspension from an Oklahoma junior high school of two male Pawnee Indian students for wearing their hair in braids (the traditional hairstyle for male Pawnees) denied them their constitutional rights to speech, free exercise of religion, and equal protection,[99] the Native American Rights Fund (NARF) unsuccessfully petitioned for certiorari. In its petition for a rehearing of the denial of certiorari, NARF argued "that this is an appropriate case for the Court to recognize an implied constitutional right to cultural integrity."[100] To invoke this right, NARF contended, the plaintiff might be required to show first the existence of a firmly established culture, and second, that the conduct involved represented a specific characteristic of that culture. To date, the Supreme Court has declined to consider this implied constitutional right to cultural integrity and the two-pronged test designed by NARF to invoke it.

Considering the fact that *New Rider v. Board of Education* unfortunately may have been viewed simply as one of many "long hair cases"[101] inviting judicial infringement upon the domain of public school authorities rather than as a dispute steeped in the profound constitutional issues of freedom of speech, freedom of religion, and equal protection, the Supreme Court's refusal to grant certiorari was predictable, if not justifiable. However, if again presented with the opportunity to consider the same right to cultural survival in a different context, the Court should not fail to evaluate and establish the right. Given what that tribunal has said about the sacredness of the home, the integrity of the family, the repugnancy of compelled cultural orthodoxy, the emphasis that Western civilization and culture have traditionally placed upon the parental role in child-rearing, and the fundamental nature of a parent's right to the custody of his or her child, it could not but extend constitutional protection to the essence of the right to cultural survival: the right of reservation Indian parents to rear their children according to the customs and traditions of their culture, and the correlative right of reservation

37

Indian children to be raised by their own parents in their own culture. To withhold recognition of that right would be to ignore overwhelming precedent, thereby repudiating the humanistic basis of that precedent—the enduring judicial respect for the sacredness of those intimate relationships between man and woman that often ripen into marriage, home, and family.

On the other hand, the Supreme Court would have no more difficulty resting on that humane basis by endorsing a constitutional right to cultural survival than a reservation Indian parent caught in the web of a parental rights termination proceeding would have in invoking its benefit. Such a parent could easily satisfy NARF's two-pronged test requiring evidence, first, of a well-defined culture, and second, that the conduct involved is characteristic of that culture. Given the ancient origins of the American Indian, the first requirement lends itself more to judicial notice than to proof. For reluctant judges, Wisconsin v. Yoder,[102] invalidating a state compulsory school attendance law as applied to Amish children as violative of the first amendment, could be cited to illustrate the Supreme Court's willingness to extend constitutional protection to a way of life whose identity has been forged during no less than three centuries of self-perpetuation. Surely the way of life of the American Indian is no less identifiable, no less enduring, and no less entitled to constitutional protection. As the Supreme Court cautioned in McClanahan, "[i]t must always be remembered that the various Indian tribes were once independent and sovereign nations, and that their claim to sovereignty long predates that for our own Government."[103] In delivering his indictment of past Bureau Indian policy, Felix Cohen was even more specific:

> Through four centuries the Spanish, English, and American Indian Bureaus have tried to turn Indians into submissive peasants. So far they have failed. To that failure we owe much that is precious in our American way of life.[104]

The extended family concept offers a useful vehicle to reach the second requirement of the NARF test, proof of conduct characteristic of the culture previously identified. The concept itself is not difficult to appreciate, assuming one is not inflexibly devoted to the American nuclear family as not only the best, but the only way to rear a child. In the extended family, the child-rearing functions are typically distributed beyond the sphere of the non-Indian family nucleus (mother, father, and siblings) so that grandparents, uncles, aunts, and other relatives and even friends within the tribal com-

38

munity often share the responsibilities and joys of bringing up the children.

The widespread prevalence of the extended family and of reliance upon it by Indian parents, who are often desperately in need of its assistance because of financial or marital difficulties, or the death of a loved one, unquestionably renders that reliance conduct characteristic of Indian culture. For instance, the Navaho father whose paternal rights were at stake in Goodman[105] relied upon members of his own family and of his deceased wife's family for help in caring for his minor children. Such reliance was shown to be a characteristic response to such a situation by a Navaho man living in a Navaho family camp.[106] Similarly, in seeking restoration of custody of the three orphaned children in Wisconsin Potawatomies, their paternal great-uncle was merely following the traditional Potawatomie duties of blood relatives in times of family crisis.[107] When Mr. Carle urged the Alaska Supreme Court to permit his son to live with the son's paternal aunt next door to the father, he was in effect inviting judicial recognition of the child care unit characteristic of Alaska village culture, the extended family.[108] Finally, a conscientious Cheyenne River Sioux parent in need of child care will look first to members of the extended family, not to a non-Indian temporary care facility, however well managed or well meaning.[109] As these illustrations demonstrate, the extended family plays such a pervasive role in the upbringing of reservation Indian children that reliance upon it by an Indian parent in need of child care assistance may clearly constitute conduct characteristic of the Indian culture under scrutiny.

Once the Indian parent threatened with termination of parental rights has shown the existence of a well-defined Indian culture, as well as conduct essential to it (e.g., reliance upon the extended family), that parent has brought himself or herself within the scope of the proposed constitutional right to cultural survival. However, the inquiry does not end there. The right of any parent to the custody of his or her child is not absolute,[110] but the fact that the American legal system has deemed parental rights to be fundamental marshals an additional safeguard from the ranks of constitutional doctrine—the Supreme Court's repeated insistence that a fundamental, personal liberty will be subordinated only to governmental action either shown to be necessary to further a compelling governmental interest,[111] or demonstrated to constitute the least drastic available means of promoting a substantial governmental purpose.[112] While "compelling governmental interests," "necessary connections," and "least drastic alternatives" at best are hardly gems of judicial precision, and

39

at worst seem wholly conclusionary, the simple idea they often obscure is that because personal freedoms are so very essential, only governmental goals of far greater significance will justify restricting them.

It is hard to imagine a governmental purpose of such magnitude implicated in Indian child custody cases. Surely a state's interest in providing for children believed to be abandoned or neglected cannot justify the devastating consequence of repeated state court terminations of Indian parental rights—the wholesale eradication of the reservation's cultural base. A state or federal interest in fostering a culturally homogeneous populace is an equally insufficient justification, for the Supreme Court itself has said that the homogeneity goal, while understandable, cannot sanction an invasion of fourteenth amendment liberty.[113] The same statement logically extends to invasions of what should be another integral component of due process liberty, the proposed constitutional right to cultural survival. While it is difficult to envision a governmental interest any court could reasonably find important enough to override that right, it is impossible to conclude that a court would also find that the current widespread siphoning of reservation Indian children constitutes a necessary, let alone least drastic, means of promoting that interest.

Statutory Reforms

Supreme Court recognition of a constitutional right to cultural survival is the first of three needed steps toward the protection of fundamental rights too long neglected, and toward reviving the egalitarian heritage of this country. Congress must take the second step. A clear statutory directive is needed to insure not only that procurement of a tribal court order be a prerequisite to the placement of a reservation Indian child,[114] but that litigation stemming from the reservation parent-child relationship be initiated in tribal court. These changes would serve three vital functions. First, they would both reaffirm and promote the current federal commitment to Indian cultural and political autonomy. Second, they would weave a thread of clarity into the tangled jurisdictional web spun by Public Law 280 and its progeny. Third, they would vest primary responsibility for the adjudication of the rights of Indian parents and children in the tribunal most attuned to the customs and traditions of Indian family life.[115]

Attitudinal Reforms

While recognition by the Supreme Court of a constitutional right

40

to cultural survival and by Congress of the primacy of Indian ju-dicial control of the reservation parent-child relationship are two steps in the right direction, they are meaningless unless their sounds are heard and heeded at a more concrete level, the point at which the interests of the Alaska native parent, the Navaho father, or the Sioux mother touch the interests of the state's social services agency. Con-sequently, the third step toward the protection of reservation In-dian family life can only be taken by social workers willing to radical-ly rethink their role so that poverty alone will no longer be considered a possible ground for the termination of parental rights,[116] so that cultural differences will no longer be equated with cultural inferi-ority, and so that the primary function of social services will be the service of all society, and especially the energetic promotion of the unity of happy family life, be it Indian or non-Indian.

Conclusion

In 1964 the California Supreme Court paid this eloquent tribute to American Indian culture in upholding the right of Native Ameri-can Church members to use peyote in their religious ceremonies:

> The varying currents of the subcultures that flow into the main-stream of our national life give it depth and beauty. We preserve a greater value than an ancient tradition when we protect the rights of the Indians who honestly practiced an old religion in using peyote....[117]

The statement would apply with equal force to a firm commitment by the non-Indian community to protecting the rights of reservation Indian parents and children to Indian family life so that the future of those rights will be one of respect, not termination. Once the Supreme Court embraces a constitutional right to cultural survival, once Congress vests in tribal courts the primary power to adjudicate reservation Indian child custody disputes, and once social workers expand their sensitivities beyond the limits of non-Indian culture, we as a nation will be preserving more than an ancient Indian tradi-tion. By breathing fresh life into the words of Justice Jackson, that freedom to differ must include the right to differ "as to things that touch the heart of the existing order," we will be preserving the American tradition as well.

NOTES

1. West Virginia Bd. of Educ. v. Barnette, 319 U.S. 624, 641-42 (1943).
2. The Native American Rights Fund (NARF) recently urged the Supreme

41

Court to squarely endorse this right. Declining to do so, despite the strong dissent of Justices Douglas and Marshall, the Court summarily denied certiorari. *See* New Rider v. Bd. of Educ., 480 F.2d 693 (10th Cir.), *cert. denied*, 94 S.Ct. 733 (1973).

3. Bertram Hirsch, counsel for the Association on American Indian Affairs (AAIA), succinctly defines the right to cultural integrity as follows: "In short, cultural integrity is the preservation of the way of life of the family in the context of the society in which it exists." Brief of Amici Curiae at 7, Hootch v. Alaska State-Operated School System, No. 72-2450 (Alas. 1974).

4. Given the devastating impact upon the very future of tribal life inherent in the current reservation Indian child crisis, the right to cultural integrity can be more accurately and urgently denominated as the "right to cultural survival."

5. 1 ASSOCIATION ON AMERICAN INDIAN AFFAIRS, INC., INDIAN FAMILY DEFENSE 1 (Winter 1974).

6. *Id.* at 2. Focusing on local illustrations, the AAIA study estimates that in Wisconsin, Indian children are placed in foster homes at 10 times the rate of non-Indian children (*id.* at 5), while in Minnesota, foster home placement of Indian children exceeds that of non-Indian children by a factor of four and one-half (*id.* at 7). Depressingly similar patterns can be found in Montana, where Indian children constitute 96 per cent of all foster care placements, and in North and South Dakota, where 17 times more Indian than non-Indian children are growing up in foster homes. *Id.* at 3.

7. Habeas Corpus Hearing, Mobridge, S.D. (Cir. Ct. 6th Jud. Dist., Apr. 1974).

8. 1 ASSOCIATION ON AMERICAN INDIAN AFFAIRS, INC., INDIAN FAMILY DEFENSE 3 (Winter 1974).

9. *Id.* at 1.

10. M. PRICE, LAW AND THE AMERICAN INDIAN 44 (1973) [hereinafter cited as M. PRICE]. An early manifestation of this fear was Georgia's refusal to comply with the Supreme Court's holding that the Cherokee Nation was "a distinct community" exempt from the application of state laws. Worcester v. Georgia, 31 U.S. 515, 561 (1832). More than half a century after *Worcester*, the Supreme Court indicated that the hostility surrounding Indian communities had not lessened: "Because of the local ill feeling, the people of the States where they are found are often their deadliest enemies." United States v. Kagama, 118 U.S. 375, 384 (1886).

Overt expressions of that sentiment today, although far less frequent, do occur. One example not only of the fear, but of the polarization it engenders, was sparked by the remark of South Dakota Governor Richard Kniep that South Dakota is not "a place of racial intolerance or hatred." The following day the American Indian Movement voiced its disagreement by declaring South Dakota a war zone, announcing a national boycott against tourism in the state, and warning "all tourists if they travel in South Dakota [that] Indian people will assume they are either there to kill Indians or help Indians." Rapid City Journal, May 9, 1974, at 2, col. 1.

Indirect expressions of this fear are, of course, more difficult to identify. However, some representatives of the non-Indian judicial system perceive the vesting of primary control of the Indian parent-child relationship in the Indian judicial system as the first step toward either Indian control of non-Indian affairs [Brief of Respondent Poyhonen at 11, Comenout v. Burdman, 82 Wash. 2d 192, 525 P.2d 217 (1974)] or the creation of "an island of amnesty within the territory of the State, flight to which will shield an Indian person from the operation of the law" [United States *ex rel.* Cobell v. Cobell, C.A. No. 3123, at 6 (D. Mont. Dec. 6, 1972)]: Given these reactions, it is difficult to avoid the conclusion that the overt fears of America's nineteenth-century non-Indian community are still covertly shared by its twentieth-century successor.

42

11. Such was the logic of the 1944 House Select Committee on Indian Affairs when it declared that "[t]he goal of Indian education should be to make the Indian child a better American rather than to equip him simply to be a better Indian." S. REP. No. 91-501, 91st Cong., 1st Sess., 13-14. More than 20 years later, the 91st Congress characterized its earlier policy as "self-righteous intolerance of tribal communities and cultural differences." *Id.* at 21.

Modern judicial opinions are not devoid of traces of the same intolerance. *See* Carle v. Carle, 503 P.2d 1050, 1053 (Ala. 1972), discussed at notes 85-87 and accompanying text, *infra*, where the trial court's award of custody of an Indian child was based in part on the tacit assumption that the Alaskan "village way of life is inevitably succumbing to the predominate (*sic*) Caucasian urban society of the land." Non-Indian superiority surfaces most often, however, in the daily practice of social workers. Examples have already been mentioned of the common value judgment that Indian children can only look toward a brighter future if they are raised off the reservation. *See* notes 4-13 and accompanying text, *infra*. *See also*, Wisconsin Potawatomies of the Hannahville Indian Community v. Houston, M-56-72 C.A., at 15 (W.D. Mich., Nov. 16, 1973), where testimony indicated that a state social worker responded to an inquiry by a relative of recently orphaned Indian children by flatly declaring "that it would be best if she didn't try to locate the children" and that the social worker "did not want the children to be on the reservation."

A related though somewhat more subtle manifestation of the attitude that cultural differences are equivalent to cultural deficiencies is the repeated failure of non-Indian welfare agencies to recognize the existence and effectiveness of child-rearing alternatives to the American nuclear family. For example, the all too frequent response of social workers to the customary Indian practice of sharing child care responsibilities among members of the extended family is not merely the refusal to acknowledge its legitimacy, but the argument that reliance upon it by Indian parents is indicative of abandonment or neglect. *See, e.g., In re* Cantrell, 495 P.2d 179, 181 (Mont. 1972) and Deprivation Petition, at 2; *In re* Patricia Alexis and Karen Alexis, No. 44642 (Super. Ct., Juv. Dep't., King Co., Wash., filed Dec. 6, 1973). Thus, parental participation in a communal approach to raising children becomes grounds for terminating parental rights.

The ultimate purpose underlying many of the dependency-neglect proceedings initiated by social service agencies is to facilitate adoption of the reservation Indian child by a non-Indian couple in whose foster care he has oftentimes already been placed. *See, e.g.,* Brief of Parents at 26, *In re* the Comenout Children, No. 3565 (Juv. Ct., Grays Harbor Co., Wash., Aug. 6, 1973); Brief of Mr. and Mrs. Chiquiti and the Squamish Tribal Court, at 21; *In re* Patricia Alexis and Karen Alexis, No. 44642 (Super. Ct., Juv. Dep't., King Co., Wash., filed Dec. 6, 1973). Taken together, these welfare practices reveal a startling dichotomy between the role social services are presumably designed to play, that of striving to promote family unity, and the role these agencies too often play in actual practice, that of advancing the disintegration of Indian family life.

12. Wisconsin Potawatomies of the Hannahville Indian Community v. Houston, M-56-72 C.A. (W.D. Mich., Nov. 16, 1973).

13. Echohawk, *Justice and the American Indians,* 3 CONTRACT 33, 35 (1973).

14. F. COHEN, FEDERAL INDIAN LAW, v (1971), quoting Felix Frankfurter without further citation.

15. Echohawk, *Justice and the American Indians,* 3 CONTACT 33 (1973).

16. United States v. Kagama, 118 U.S. 375, 381 (1886).

43

17. Cherokee Nation v. Georgia, 30 U.S. 1, 16 (1831).

18. For example, the Supreme Court recently acknowledged that the "anomalous . . . and complex character" of nineteenth-century Indian law has retained its imprint on current law. McClanahan v. Arizona State Tax Comm'n., 411 U.S. 164, 173 (1973).

19. 24 Stat. 388, *as amended*, 25 U.S.C. § 331-358 (1887).

20. *See* Comment, *The Indian Battle For Self-Determination*, 58 CAL. L. REV. 445, 471 (1970).

21. Wheeler-Howard Act, 25 U.S.C. § 476 (1934).

22. H.R. REP. No. 1804, 73d Cong., 2d Sess., 6 (1934).

23. *See* notes 62-66 and accompanying text, *infra*.

24. 31 U.S. 515 (1832).

25. *Id.* at 561.

26. In Organized Village of Kake v. Egan, 369 U.S. 60, 72 (1962), for example, Justice Frankfurter concluded that the *Worcester* view of an Indian reservation as a separate community exempted from state law "has yielded to closer analysis when confronted . . . with diverse situations." For a critique of *Kake* as "a tribute to the power of a scholarly opinion, even where that scholarship is faulty," *see* M. PRICE, *supra* note 10, at 193.

27. The constitutional source of federal plenary power over Indians are those provisions vesting in the President the power to make treaties (U.S. CONST., art. 11, § 2, cl. 2), and in Congress, the power to make war (*id.* art. 1, § 8, cl. 11) and to regulate commerce "with the Indian tribes" (*id.* art. 1, §8, cl. 3). Although the guardian-ward theory (*see* text and note 26 *supra*) and federal ownership of tribal occupied land have been cited as other recognized sources (*see* Comment, *The Indian Battle For Self-Determination*, 58 CAL. L. REV. 445, 447-52 (1970)), the Supreme Court's most recent emphasis has been upon the constitutional sources, specifically the treaty-making provision and the commerce clause. *See* McClanahan v. Arizona State Tax Comm'n., 411 U.S. 164, 172 n.7 (1973).

28. 31 U.S. 515, 561 (1832).

29. Cherokee Nation v. Georgia, 30 U.S. 1, 17 (1831). *See also* Comment, *The Indian Battle For Self-Determination*, 58 CAL. L. REV. 445, 449 (1970).

30. United States v. Kagama, 118 U.S. 375, 384-85 (1886).

31. 358 U.S. 217 (1959).

32. *Id.* at 220.

33. *Id.* at 223.

34. Although the *Williams* test was intended as a safeguard of tribal control of reservation affairs, it has been criticized, even by those sympathetic to that purpose, as being so ambiguous as to invite state courts to assert their jurisdiction simply by finding that doing so does not constitute infringement. M. PRICE, *supra* note 10, at 188.

35. 380 U.S. 685, 690 (1965).

36. Comment, *The Indian Battle For Self-Determination*, 58 CAL. L. REV. 445, 476 (1970).

37. 400 U.S. 423 (1971).

38. 25 U.S.C. § 1321 *et seq.*, as amended, (1953). Passed with other "termination legislation" by a Congress determined to solve "the Indian problem" by minimizing federal responsibilities and shifting the burden to the states, Pub. L. 280 originally extended state civil and criminal jurisdiction over all Indian Country within five states: California, Nebraska, Oregon, Minnesota (excluding the Red Lake Reservation), and

44

Wisconsin (excluding the Menominee Reservation). In addition to this unilateral extension of state jurisdiction, Pub. L. 280 also prescribed how the remaining states might assume jurisdiction over Indian Country located within their boundaries if they so desired. These states were divided into two groups, with a separate section of Pub. L. 280 devoted to each. The first group consisted of those states having obstacles to assumption of jurisdiction embodied in their constitutions or enabling acts, *i.e.*, disclaimer clauses in which the citizens of the state disclaimed jurisdiction over Indian land located within the state and acknowledged that federal control over such land was exclusive. The second group was comprised of those states without such impediments.

The pertinent civil jurisdictional provisions of the 1968 revision of Pub. L. 280, 25 U.S.C. §§ 1322-24 (1974 Supp.), now read as follows:

"§ 1322. Assumption by State of Civil jurisdiction—Consent of United States; force and effect of civil laws

"(a) The consent of the United States is hereby given to any State not having jurisdiction over civil causes of action between Indians or to which Indians are parties which arise in the areas of Indian country situated within such State to assume, with the consent of the tribe occupying the particular Indian country or part thereof which would be affected by such assumption, such measure of jurisdiction over any or all such civil causes of action arising within such Indian country or any part thereof as may be determined by such State to the same extent that such State has jurisdiction over other civil causes of action, and those civil laws of such State that are of general application to private persons or private property shall have the same force and effect within such Indian country or part thereof as they have elsewhere within that State.

"Alienation, encumbrance, taxation, use and probate of property

"(b) Nothing in this section shall authorize the alienation, encumbrance, or taxation of any real or personal property, including water rights, belonging to any Indian or any Indian tribe, band, or community that is held in trust by the United States or is subject to a restriction against alienation imposed by the United States; or shall authorize regulation of the use of such property in a manner inconsistent with any Federal treaty, agreement or statute, or with any regulation made pursuant thereto; or shall confer jurisdiction upon the State to adjudicate, in probate proceedings or otherwise, the ownership or right to possession of such property or any interest therein.

"Force and effect of tribal ordinances or customs

"(c) Any tribal ordinance or custom heretofore or hereafter adopted by an Indian tribe, band, or community in the exercise of any authority which it may possess shall, if not inconsistent with any applicable civil law of the State, be given full force and effect in the determination of civil causes of action pursuant to this section.

"§ 1324. Amendment of State constitutions or statutes to remove legal impediment; effective date

"Notwithstanding the provisions of any enabling Act for the admission of a State, the consent of the United States is hereby given to the people of any State to amend, where necessary, their State constitution or existing statutes, as the case may be, to remove any legal impediment to the assumption of civil or criminal jurisdiction in accordance with the provisions of this subchapter. The provisions of this subchapter shall not become effective with respect to such assumption of jurisdiction by any such State until the people thereof have appropriately amended their State constitution or statutes, as the case may be."

For an extensive and critical analysis of Pub. L. 280, *see* Goldberg, *P.L. 280: State Jurisdiction Over Indian Country*, 22 U.C.L.A. L. Rev. — (1975).

45

39. Kennerly v. Dist. Court of Montana, 400 U.S. 423, 427 (1971). Title IV of the Civil Rights Act of 1968 repealed § 7 of Pub. L. 280, which dealt with those states without constitutional or statutory barriers to assumption of jurisdiction (*see* note 38 *supra*), and added the prospective requirement of tribal consent as a prerequisite to future state assumptions of either civil or criminal jurisdiction over Indian country lying within state borders. The tribal consent requirement, together with the procedure Congress established to satisfy it, are contained in 25 U.S.C. § 1326 (1968), which provides: "State jurisdiction acquired pursuant to this subchapter with respect to criminal offenses or civil causes of action, or with respect to both, shall be applicable in Indian country only where the enrolled Indians within the affected area of such Indian country accept such jurisdiction by a majority vote of the adult Indians voting at a special election held for that purpose. The Secretary of the Interior shall call such special election under such rules and regulations as he may prescribe, when requested to do so by the tribal council or other governing body, or by 20 per centum of such enrolled adults."

40. M. PRICE, *supra* note 10, at 188.

41. *Id.* at 209. *See also* Sullivan, *State Civil Power Over Reservation Indians*, 33 MONT. L. REV. 291 (1972).

42. McClanahan v. Arizona State Tax Comm'n., 411 U.S. 164, 178 n.19 (1973).

43. 411 U.S. 145, 148-49 (1973).

44. 411 U.S. 164, 167-68 (1973).

45. *Id.* at 167-68.

46. *See* cases cited in McClanahan at *Id.*, 164, 168.

47. Class discussion led by M. Price, Seminar: Indian Legal Problems, UCLA School of Law, Feb. 5, 1974.

48. 411 U.S. 145, 147 (1973).

49. 411 U.S. 164, 179 (1973), citing Organized Village of Kake v. Egan, 369 U.S. 60 (1962), in which the Court refused to enjoin enforcement against two incorporated communities of Tlinget Indians, of an Alaska statute barring the use of salmon traps. Since a non-Indian party, the state, was implicated in both *Kake* and *McClanahan*, Justice Marshall's reference to non-Indians arguably was meant to apply to private non-Indian litigants, *i.e.*, to situations where at least one party is a non-Indian individual. This was not the case in *McClanahan*. *See* note 41, *supra*.

50. Class discussion led by M. Price, Seminar: Indian Legal Problems, UCLA School of Law, Feb. 5, 1974.

51. *See* text at p. 24.

52. One which either assumed jurisdiction between 1953 and 1968 by directly receiving it in 1953 under Pub. L. 280 or subsequently complying with its provisions, or assumed jurisdiction after 1968 by satisfying, together with the tribe, the requirements of the Civil Rights Act of 1968. *See* note 35, *supra*.

53. However, approaching the jurisdictional issue from the perspective contended for in the section headed *Future Law* of this comment, that of asking who ought to govern given the vital personal liberties at stake in child custody determinations, a contrary conclusion may well be reached regardless of whether a Pub. L. 280 state is involved. *See, e.g.*, Wisconsin Potawatomies of the Hannahville Indian Community v. Houston, M-56-72 C.A. (W.D. Mich., Nov. 16, 1973), where tribal court jurisdiction was held to be exclusive despite the fact that custody was obtained off the reservation in a non-Pub. L. 280 state.

54. Williams v. Lee, 358 U.S. 217, 220 (1959).

46

55. Wisconsin Potawatomies of the Hannahville Indian Community v. Houston, M-56-72 C.A. (W.D. Mich., Nov. 16, 1973) at 31.

56. The broad spectrum of state action that has been deemed violative of the infringement test of Williams v. Lee includes, *inter alia*: state taxation, Comm'r. of Taxation v. Brun, 286 Minn. 43, 174 N.W.2d 120 (1970); extradition, Arizona *ex rel.* Merrill v. Turtle, 413 F.2d 683 (9th Cir. 1969); and commercial transactions between Indians and non-Indians, Williams v. Lee, 358 U.S. 217 (1959) and Kain v. Wilson, 83 S.D. 482, 161 N.W.2d 704 (S.D. 1968). In the domestic relations area, *Williams* has been used to deny a non-Pub. L. 280 state jurisdiction over the divorce of a tribal couple married on a reservation. Whyte v. Dist. Court of Montezuma County, 140 Colo. 334, 346 P.2d 1012 (1959). The same conclusion should logically apply to an oftentimes integral part of the divorce proceeding, the child custody determination.

57. It is now well established that the right to travel is a constitutionally protected right. *See* Edwards v. California, 314 U.S. 160 (1941) (Douglas concurring); Kent v. Dulles, 357 U.S. 116 (1958); Shapiro v. Thompson, 394 U.S. 618 (1969). *Accord*, State v. Wylie, 516 P.2d 142 (Alaska 1973). In Kent v. Dulles, 357 U.S. 116, 125-26 (1958), Justice Douglas offered this explanation for extending constitutional protection to freedom of movement: "Travel abroad, like travel within the country . . ., may be as close to the heart of the individual as the choice of what he eats, or wears, or reads. Freedom of movement is basic in our scheme of values. . . . 'Our nation,' wrote Chafee, 'has thrived on the principle that, outside of plainly harmful conduct, every American is left to shape his life as he thinks best, do what he pleases, go where he pleases.' " As state action effectively penalizing a fundamental right lying "close to the heart" of an oftentimes extremely mobile reservation Indian community, the exercise of state jurisdiction in such circumstances would clearly undermine the policy of allowing Americans the freedom to go where they please. The tribal court structure offers a forum in which the state may further its interest in the well-being of purportedly neglected children without infringing upon the rights of both Indian parent and child to travel freely beyond the confines of the reservation.

58. 31 U.S. 515, 561 (1832).

59. *Id.* at 231, 236.

60. 118 U.S. 375 (1886).

61. *Id.* at 381.

62. 109 U.S. 556 (1883).

63. *Id.* at 571.

64. F. COHEN, FEDERAL INDIAN LAW, 123 (1971). *See also* Colliflower v. Garland, 342 F.2d 369 (9th Cir. 1965); Iron Crow v. Oglala Sioux Tribe of the Pine Ridge Reservation, 129 F. Supp. 15 (D.S.D. 1955), *aff'd*, 231 F.2d 89 (8th Cir. 1956).

65. Martinez v. Southern Ute Tribe of Southern Ute Reservation, 249 F.2d 915 (10th Cir. 1957). For other illustrations, *see* Prairie Band of Potawatomie Tribe of Indians v. Puckkee, 321 F.2d 767 (10th Cir. 1963); Oliver v. Udall, 306 F.2d 819 (D.C. Cir. 1962).

66. In McClanahan v. Arizona State Tax Comm'n., Justice Marshall refused to rely upon "platonic notions of Indian sovereignty" and chose instead to center analysis upon "the applicable treaties and statutes which define the limits of state power." 411 U.S. 164, 172 (1973). Furthermore, the intra-tribal affairs doctrine has been substantially eroded by the enactment of the Indian Bill of Rights, 25 U.S.C. § 1302 (1968). Passed as part of the Civil Rights Act of 1968, the Indian Bill of Rights protects persons suffering deprivations of certain constitutional rights by tribal gov-

47

ernment. It incorporates within its provisions the first amendment as well as amendments four through eight, but with some variations. The establishment clause of the first amendment is deleted; assistance of counsel in a criminal proceeding is guaranteed only if the defendant can afford it; infliction of criminal penalties by tribal courts is limited to the imposition of not more than a $500 fine and/or imprisonment for six months per offense; and, while there is no provision for grand jury indictment, the right to trial by a jury of not less than six persons is afforded to a defendant accused of an offense punishable by imprisonment. It is difficult to construe the individual constitutional guarantees of the Indian Bill of Rights as anything less than a frontal attack upon the line of federal court decisions in which the intra-tribal affairs doctrine evolved. *See generally* Note, *The Indian Bill of Rights and the Constitutional Status of Tribal Governments*, 82 HARV. L. REV. 1343 (1969). Nevertheless, the doctrine's underlying policy, the promotion of tribal cultural and political autonomy, has survived. *See* note 67, *infra*.

67. The *McClanahan* Court itself concluded its discussion of the sovereignty doctrine by emphasizing: "[I]t must always be remembered that the various Indian tribes were once independent and sovereign nations, and that their claim to sovereignty long predates that of our own Government." 411 U.S. 164, 172 (1973). As for the sustained vitality of the doctrinal basis of the intra-tribal affairs concept, the avoidance of such affairs traditionally demonstrated by federal courts has been correctly recognized as being "consistent with the *present federal objective* of preserving the Indian tribes as self-governing, culturally autonomous units." McCurdy v. Steele, 353 F. Supp. 629, 632 (D. Utah 1973) (emphasis added). But see note 66, *supra*.

68. Presidential Message to Congress on Indian Affairs, July 8, 1970.

69. A more recent example of congressional efforts toward furthering the current federal policy of promoting tribal cultural and political autonomy is the Indian Financing Act of 1974, Pub. L. 93-262, 88 Stat. 77 (1974), which was expressly enacted to achieve "the long sought goal of Indian self-sufficiency." H.R. REP. No. 93-907, 93d Cong., 2d Sess., as reported in No. 4 U.S. CODE CONG. & ADMIN. NEWS, 722 (May 15, 1974).

70. "A general exhaustion requirement . . . would do much to strengthen tribal governments, including tribal courts, and, thereby aid the reservation Indian in maintaining a distinct cultural identity." O'Neal v. Cheyenne River Sioux Tribe, 482 F.2d 1140, 1148 (8th Cir. 1973). *Accord*, Clark v. Land & Forestry Comm. of the Cheyenne River Sioux Tribal Council, C.A. 74-3021 (D.S.D. Aug. 9, 1974). *Cf.* Dodge v. Nakai, 298 F. Supp. 17 (D. Ariz. 1968); McCurdy v. Steele, 353 F. Supp. 629 (D. Utah 1973).

71. The seminal article assessing the devastating impact a rigid application of such Anglo-American concepts as due process and equal protection would have upon the future survival of tribes as distinct ethnic communities is Note, *The Indian Bill of Rights and the Constitutional Status of Tribal Governments*, 82 HARV. L. REV. 1343 (1968). The "essential fairness" standard there propounded was explicitly adopted in McCurdy v. Steele, 353 F. Supp. 629, 640 (D. Utah 1973), where the Court held that "[e]ssential fairness in the tribal context, not procedural punctiliousness, is the standard against which the disputed actions must be measured." *Id.* at 633. "It would thus appear that the Indian Civil Rights Act is properly considered in the context of federal concern for Indian self-government and cultural autonomy: Its guarantees of individual rights should, where possible, be harmonized with tribal cultural and governmental autonomy." *Id.*, *accord*, O'Neal v. Cheyenne River Sioux Tribe, 482 F.2d 1140, 1144 (8th Cir. 1973): "[I]t is clear to us that Congress wished to protect and

48

preserve individual rights of the Indian peoples, with the realization that this goal is best achieved by maintaining the unique Indian culture and necessarily strengthening tribal governments."

72. *See generally* Brief for Appellant, DeCoteau v. Dist. Court for the Tenth Judicial Dist., 211 N.W.2d 843 (S.D. 1973).

73. Skinner v. Oklahoma, 316 U.S. 535, 541 (1942).

74. May v. Anderson, 345 U.S. 528, 533 (1953).

75. *Id.* at 536 (Frankfurter, concurring).

76. 405 U.S. 645 (1972).

77. *Id.* at 651. *See also* Poe v. Ullman, 367 U.S. 497, 522 (Harlan, dissenting): "The home derives its pre-eminence as the seat of family life. And the integrity of that life is something so fundamental that it has been found to draw to its protection the principles of more than one explicitly granted Constitutional right."

78. Prince v. Massachusetts, 321 U.S. 166 (1944).

79. 406 U.S. 205 (1972).

80. *Id.* at 232.

81. Stanley v. Georgia, 394 U.S. 557, 565 (1969).

82. New Rider v. Bd. of Educ., 480 F.2d 693 (10th Cir. 1973), *cert. denied*, 94 S.Ct. 733, 753 (1973) (Douglas, dissenting).

83. West Virginia Bd. of Educ. v. Barnette, 319 U.S. 624, 641 (1943).

84. *Id.* at 642.

85. 503 P.2d 1050 (Ala. 1972). The father, a Haida Indian from the village of Hydaburg, appealed from the tribal court's award of custody of his seven-year-old son to the mother, originally a Tlinget Indian raised in the village of Klawock but living in Juneau. The father's job as a commercial fisherman necessitated that he leave his son and native community during the summer; however, he spent the winter off-seasons in Hydaburg living "the traditional subsistence existence of village Alaska," primarily including hunting, trapping, and berrying. *Id.* at 1051.

86. *Id.* at 1053.

87. *Id.* at 1055.

88. Case No. 630231, 232 (Dist. Juv. Ct., Grand Co., Utah, Feb. 15, 1973).

89. *Id.*, Petition at 1.

90. State of Utah *ex rel.* Goodman, Case No. 630231, 232 (Dist. Juv. Ct., Grand Co., Utah, Feb. 15, 1973) at 8.

91. M-56-72 C.A. (W.D. Mich., Nov. 16, 1973).

92. *Id.* at 31.

93. *Id.* at 43.

94. S. LYND, INTELLECTUAL ORIGINS OF AMERICAN RADICALISM 4, 59 (1968). Those inclined to view the Declaration as more of an historical anachronism than a present reality would do well to note an insight the author persuasively supports: "Distant and archaic as it may often appear, the language of the Declaration of Independence remains relevant as an instrument for social transformation." *Id.* at 10.

95. *Id.* at 163.

96. Pierce v. Society of Sisters of Holy Names, 268 U.S. 510, 534-35 (1925).

97. *In re* A.N., 201 N.W.2d 118, 119 (N.D. 1972).

98. Stubbs v. Hammond, 257 Ia. 1071, 135 N.W.2d 540, 543 (1965). *Accord*, State v. Whaley, 246 Minn. 535 at 75 N.W.2d 786, 794 (1956).

99. New Rider v. Bd. of Educ., 480 F.2d 693 (10th Cir. 1973), *cert. denied*, 94 S.Ct. 733 (1973).

100. *Id.*, Petition for Rehearing at 2.

49

101. *See, e.g.*, Freeman v. Flake, 448 F.2d 258 (10th Cir. 1971), *cert. denied*, 405 U.S. 1032 (1972).

102. 406 U.S. 205 (1972).

103. 411 U.S. 164, 172 (1973).

104. F. COHEN, THE LEGAL CONSCIENCE: SELECTED PAPERS OF FELIX S. COHEN, 316-17 (1 Cohen ed. 1960).

105. Case No. 630231, 232 (Dist. Juv. Ct., Grand Co., Utah, Feb. 15, 1973).

106. The Navaho family camp is an extended family differing from the American nuclear family in that the parental role is shared by many extended family members; the child often feels a closer attachment to aunts and uncles specifically and to the family group, generally, and the grandparents stand in a position of ultimate respect as group leaders. *Id.* at 7-8.

107. Wisconsin Potawatomies of the Hannahville Indian Community v. Houston, M-56-72 C.A. (W.D. Mich., Nov. 16, 1973) at 41.

108. The *Carle* court accepted the invitation: "The evidence indicated that it is not unusual in the village culture for the relatives of a child, such as the paternal aunt here, to provide a home and care for a child where for some reason the natural parents are not suitably situated to do so." Carle v. Carle, 503 P.2d 1050, 1054 n.8 (1972).

109. Interview with Mrs. Flies By, Cheyenne River Sioux mother, in Eagle Butte, S.D., May, 1974. Such reliance upon the extended family by Sioux parents is not surprising considering the fundamental position the sacredness of the relationship has traditionally held in Sioux culture. In fact, since all of creation is regarded as one interrelationship in Sioux religion, the Sioux people once referred to one another according to relationship determined by age, not blood. BLACK ELK, THE SACRED PIPE, 15, n.5 (Penguin ed. 1971).

110. Prince v. Massachusetts, 321 U.S. 166, 166-67 (1944).

111. *See, e.g.*, Dunn v. Blumstein, 405 U.S. 330, 337 (1972); Oregon v. Mitchell, 400 U.S. 112, 238 (1970); Griswold v. Connecticut, 381 U.S. 479, 497 (1965) (Goldberg, concurring).

112. *See, e.g.*, Oregon v. Mitchell, 400 U.S. 112, 238 (1970); Shelton v. Tucker, 364 U.S. 479, 488 (1960).

113. Meyer v. Nebraska, 262 U.S. 390, 402 (1923).

114. 1 ASSOCIATION ON AMERICAN INDIAN AFFAIRS, INC., INDIAN FAMILY DEFENSE, 4 (Winter 1974).

115. Given such a congressional directive, no further legislation would be needed to safeguard these individual rights from abusive practices of any government, including that of the tribe. The due process clause of the Indian Civil Rights Act [25 U.S.C. § 1302(8) (1968)] would already offer an adequate federal remedy to Indian parents or children who are convinced that their constitutional right to cultural survival has been abridged by their own tribal government. *See* note 61 *supra*. The flexible interpretation of that clause by contemporary federal courts, increasingly sensitive to the dangers of rigidly applying non-Indian legal concepts within an Indian cultural context (*see* notes 62 and 66 and accompanying text *supra*), will help insure that constitutional protection of the reservation Indian child and parent and will not entail a lethal threat to Indian tribal government.

116. For judicial recognittion of this point, *see* State v. Whaley, 246 Minn. 535, 75 N.W.2d 786, 792 (1956).

117. People v. Woody, 394 P.2d 813, 821-22 (1964).

50

THE BALD EAGLE, THE FLORIDA PANTHER AND THE NATION'S WORD: AN ESSAY ON THE "QUIET" ABROGATION OF INDIAN TREATIES AND THE PROPER READING OF *UNITED STATES V. DION*

ROBERT LAURENCE*

When animals become endangered, the nation, we have come to believe, should rally to their defense. Sadly enough, but not uncommonly, those protective statutes are in conflict, either directly or indirectly, with old promises made by the nation to Indian tribes in exchange for their land and sovereignty. When such a conflict arises, which wins out: the endangered species or the nation's word? This essay explores that question in the context of the Endangered Species Act, the Bald Eagle Protection Act and treaty promises to the Sioux and Seminole tribes. Professor Laurence argues for a very careful and restrictive reading of United States v. Dion *and concludes with an unflattering critique of the cases in which Chief Billie of the Florida Seminoles was prosecuted for shooting a Florida panther.*

Caught in a "sting" operation mounted by the United States Fish and Wildlife Service, four Indian men, residents of the Yankton Indian reservation in South Dakota, were arrested, prosecuted and convicted of criminal violations in the killing and trading of parts of bald and golden eagles and scissor-tailed flycatchers, all protected birds under federal environmental laws. The men appealed on several grounds. Of salient interest to this article, Dwight Dion, Sr. claimed his right to

---

* Professor of Law, University of Arkansas; Visiting Professor of Law, Florida State University. This article overlaps in subject matter, and in some cases complete thoughts, with the last third of Hanna & Laurence, *Justice Thurgood Marshall and the Problem of Indian Treaty Abrogation*, 40 ARK. L. REV. 797, 829-39 (1987). The input and influence of Tassie Hanna, of the New Mexico bar, on the ideas put forth there were so great it is almost illegal to publish them here as my own. In fact, the "proper reading" of *Dion* mentioned in the title and urged in this article was originally Ms. Hanna's reading, not mine, a circumstance I happily here acknowledge. Of course, any errors and infelicities are my responsibility alone.

hunt and sell the birds was protected by an old Indian treaty between his tribe and the United States. Two long Eighth Circuit opinions resulted: a panel decision on the entrapment issue[1] and an *en banc* decision on the treaty issue,[2] affirming the convictions on some of the counts and reversing on others. Certiorari was sought and obtained by the United States on the treaty issue alone. The circuit court was reversed and the conviction was partially reinstated.[3] The purpose of this essay is to discuss the Supreme Court's opinion in *Dion* and to put forward what I think to be the correct reading of the test for treaty abrogation obtained therein.

First, a little background on Indian treaties and the law that governs them. The domestic law of the United States recognizes that Indian tribes are unique aggregations of people who governed themselves long before the ratification of our Constitution[4] and retain, even today, some of these important rights of self-governance.[5]

---

1. United States v. Dion, 752 F.2d 674 (8th Cir. 1985). Lyle Dion, Jr., and others claimed they had been entrapped by federal officers, who represented themselves as dealers in bird parts and quietly offered some fairly substantial sums of money to persons willing to deliver. In *Dion* a panel of the Eighth Circuit reversed the convictions and wrote an opinion that might be characterized as very friendly to the notion of entrapment. *See id.* While the federal prosecutor sought a rehearing before the Eighth Circuit on the entrapment issue, the Solicitor General informed the Supreme Court that no appeal on that issue would be taken, nor would the government seek to try Lyle Dion, Jr. again. *See* United States v. Dion, 476 U.S. 734 (1986), Petition by the United States for Writ of Certiorari at II. The entrapment issue was apparently never reheard by the Eighth Circuit and, in any case, is well beyond the scope of this article.
2. United States v. Dion, 752 F.2d 1261 (8th Cir. 1985). The *en banc* decision preceded the panel decision cited in the previous note. The full court, in fact, remanded to the panel on many non-treaty issues, including entrapment.
3. United States v. Dion, 476 U.S. 734, *on remand*, 800 F.2d 771 (8th Cir. 1986).
4. McClanahan v. Arizona State Tax Comm'n., 411 U.S. 164, 172 (1973): "[I]t must always be remembered that the various Indian tribes were once independent and sovereign nations, and that their claim to sovereignty long predates that of our own Government."
5. Cases upholding the principle of self-determination include Kerr-McGee, Inc. v. Navajo Tribe, 471 U.S. 195 (1985) (tribes have the power to tax non-members); Merrion v. Jicarilla Apache Tribe, 455 U.S. 130 (1982) (sovereignty includes the power to tax); Santa Clara Pueblo v. Martinez, 436 U.S. 49 (1978) (tribes have sovereign immunity); United States v. Wheeler, 435 U.S. 313 (1978) (tribes have the power to punish members independently of a federal prosecution for the same acts, with no double jeopardy difficulties); and United States v. Mazurie, 419 U.S. 544 (1975) (tribes have sufficient sovereignty to accept congressional delegation). *Cf.* White Mountain Apache Tribe v. Bracker, 448 U.S. 136, 143-44 (1980) (tribal sovereignty leads to special rules of treaty and statutory construction); *McClanahan*, 411 U.S. 164, 172 (1973) (tribal sovereignty is a "backdrop" against which federal statutes are to be read). The origins of the doctrine of federal recognition of self-determination are found in Cherokee Nation v. Georgia, 30 U.S. (5 Pet.) 1 (1831) where Chief Justice Marshall, in dicta, called the Cherokee tribe a "domestic, dependent nation." *Id.* at 17. As is implicit in Chief Justice Marshall's characterization, the recognition of tribal sovereignty is not without its limits. *See, e.g.*, Montana v. United States, 450 U.S. 544 (1981) (tribes do not have the power to restrict non-Indians' rights to hunt and fish on their own fee simple land on the reservation); Oliphant v. Suquamish Indian Tribe, 435 U.S. 191 (1978) (tribes do not have the power to criminally punish a non-Indian). Congress

Federal law has recognized various aspects of tribal sovereignty from the earliest days, although there has been considerable give and take over the years in government policy toward the tribes.[6] Early on, the state-to-state model of United States relations with the tribes included treaty-making; while this practice ended in 1871,[7] the treaties remain the supreme law of the land[8] and are a kind of protection rarely available to non-Indian groups of American citizens.

In the past quarter-century, the Supreme Court of the United States has spent an extraordinary amount of time laboring over the meaning of Indian treaties.[9] While the field of Indian law contains a remarkable variety of fascinating issues, there are few cases that make no mention at all of treaty rights, and many put the construction of a treaty at the center of the analysis. In those cases in which a treaty plays a central role, a common problem involves the suspected abrogation of Indian treaty rights by the government. Notwithstanding Justice Black's admonition that "[g]reat nations, like great men, should keep their word,"[10] the United States has, with some regularity, sought to go back on its word and restructure the government-tribe relationship.

---

and the Executive, also, continue to recognize Indian tribal sovereignty. *See, e.g.*, Indian Self-Determination and Education Assistance Act, 25 U.S.C. 450-50n, 455-58e (1982); President Nixon's Special Message to Congress on Indian Affairs, 6 WEEKLY COMP. OF PRES. DOC. 894 (July 8, 1970).

6. It is fair to say that support for Indian self-determination from each of the three branches of government has varied from time to time over the years, *see* F. COHEN, HANDBOOK OF FEDERAL INDIAN LAW at 47-206 (1982), and that the courts have not always been synchronized with the more political branches. For example, Cherokee Nation v. Georgia, 30 U.S. (5 Pet.) 1 (1831), and Worcester v. Georgia, 31 U.S. (6 Pet.) 515 (1832), were quite respectful of Indian rights, even while the Jackson administration was fulfilling its pledge to remove the Indians from east of the Mississippi. *See* COHEN, *supra*, at 78-91. Likewise Williams v. Lee, 358 U.S. 217 (1959), held an on-reservation transaction could not be heard in state court, at the same time that the Eisenhower administration was pursuing a policy of terminating the tribes and giving all jurisdiction to the states. *See* COHEN, *supra*, at 152-179. In the other direction, Oliphant v. Suquamish Indian Tribe, 435 U.S. 191 (1978), was grudging in its acceptance of tribal power during a time when the Carter administration, following the lead of President Nixon, was advancing the interests of tribal self-determination. *See* COHEN, *supra*, at 180-206.

7. Act of Mar. 3, 1871, Ch. 120, § 1, 16 Stat. 566 (codified at 25 U.S.C. §71 (1982). *See also* COHEN, *supra* note 6, at 105-07.

8. U.S. CONST. art. VI, cl. 2.

9. C. WILKINSON, AMERICAN INDIANS, TIME, AND THE LAW: NATIVE SOCIETIES IN A MODERN CONSTITUTIONAL DEMOCRACY at 2, 125-32 (1987). Charles F. Wilkinson lists sixty-five United States Supreme Court Indian law cases decided since 1970, most, but not all of which have some treaty implicated directly or indirectly in the decision. Professor Wilkinson notes "the Court has become more active in Indian law than in fields such as securities, bankruptcy, pollution control and international law." *Id.* at 125.

10. Federal Power Comm'n. v. Tuscarora Indian Nation, 362 U.S. 99, 142 (1960). *Tuscarora* was a treaty abrogation case and Justice Black's stirring quotation came in dissent.

Often this restructuring was done with forethought. Many times in the latter part of last century and early in this one, the United States, having decided that a treaty promise had been improvidently made, went back to the tribe concerned and renegotiated the deal.[11] In many treaty construction and abrogation cases, a court must interpret these renegotiations to determine exactly which promises remained intact.[12]

Not uncommonly, however, the government chose to abrogate a treaty unilaterally. Both with respect to Indian and non-Indian treaties, the law is established that governments have the *power* to change their minds; treaties may be abrogated by one side acting alone.[13]

---

11. One common occasion for renegotiation was called for by the allotment acts late in the nineteenth century. Those acts, whose purpose was to place land in the hands of individual Indians in hopes of "civilizing" them, and not incidently to transfer ownership of much so-called surplus lands to white hands, usually required restructuring of treaty rights. *See* COHEN, *supra* note 6, at 127-44. Lone Wolf v. Hitchcock, 187 U.S. 553 (1903), made it clear that consent of the Indians was not required in order to abrogate the treaty, but nevertheless in many cases the government did attempt to reach new agreements with the Indians. *See, e.g.*, Rosebud Sioux Tribe v. Kneip, 420 U.S. 584 (1977).

12. *See, for example*, Solem v. Bartlett, 465 U.S. 463 (1984); Rosebud Sioux Tribe v. Kneip, 430 U.S. 584 (1977); DeCoteau v. District County Court, 420 U.S. 425 (1975); Mattz v. Arnett, 412 U.S. 481 (1973); Seymour v. Superintendent, 368 U.S. 351 (1962). *See generally* Hanna & Laurence, *Justice Thurgood Marshall and the Problem of Indian Treaty Abrogation*, 40 ARK. L. REV. 797, 802-29 (1987).

13. Fong Yue Ting v. United States, 149 U.S. 698, 720-21 (1893); Lone Wolf v. Hitchcock, 187 U.S. 553, 566 (1903). That is not to say that abrogation of treaty rights, and in particular Indian treaty rights, imposes no liability on the government. It took many more years to establish the obligation to compensate than it did the power to abrogate, but it is now equally well settled. The power to abrogate was affirmed in *Lone Wolf*. The obligation to compensate for a bad faith abrogation was finally established in United States v. Sioux Nation, 448 U.S. 371 (1980). *Lone Wolf* had rather expressly suggested that all abrogations, even bad faith abrogations, would be political questions and complaints should be addressed to the Congress. 187 U.S. at 568. An unflattering appraisal of *Sioux Nation* is found in Newton, *The Judicial Role in Fifth Amendment Takings of Indian Lands: An Analysis of the Sioux Nation Rule*, 61 OR. L. REV. 245 (1982).

Sioux Nation held that the question of whether the government owes the Indians money for the abrogation turns on the government's intent at the time of the abrogation. If a good faith attempt to compensate was made at the time of the abrogation, then the presumption is that the government was acting in its trustee capacity and was not taking the Indians' property. No compensation is due in such cases, unless the government violated a fiduciary obligation. *See, e.g.*, Seminole Nation v. United States, 316 U.S. 286 (1942). If good faith was lacking then the abrogation was a taking and the government owes the Indians money, plus interest from the time of the abrogation. The largest judgment ever entered by the Court of Claims is one for a treaty abrogation where there had been no good faith attempt to compensate. The judgment was for $17.1 million plus simple interest at 5% from 1877, and 4% post-judgment interest for the period of Supreme Court review. The total was well in excess of $100 million and was nearly four times the previous largest judgment of the Court of Claims. No case on the present docket of the court, now called the United States Claims Court, threatens to reach more than half of the *Sioux Nation* judgment. All of this information, and more, came to me in a fascinating telephone conversation of March 30, 1988 with Frank Peartree, the present and longtime clerk of the Claims Court. With respect to treaty abrogation, see the colloquy between Professors Henkin

Hence, there is little litigation any more over the question of whether the power to walk away from a treaty is within Congress's power.

Goldwater v. Carter[14] is an interesting case in this regard. Late in 1978 President Carter announced to the nation that, as of January 1, 1979, the United States would recognize the People's Republic of China as the sole legitimate government of China and that the Mutual Defense Treaty with the Republic of China (Taiwan) would be terminated unilaterally on that day.[15] The treaty contained a provision for unilateral abrogation, but required one year's notice. Senator Goldwater and other legislators brought suit in federal court challenging the termination unless it was supported by congressional action. The district court granted the relief,[16] but the circuit court reversed,[17] finding the President's abrogation of the treaty effective. A widely divided Supreme Court granted certiorari and vacated the judgment.[18] Chief Justice Burger and Justices Rehnquist, Stewart and Stevens, in an

---

and Westen in the *Harvard Law Review* over the question of the status of international treaties before federal courts: Henkin, *The Constitution and United State Sovereignty: A Century of Chinese Exclusion and Its Progeny*, 100 HARV. L. REV. 853 (1987); Westen, *The Place of Foreign Treaties in the Courts of the United States:A Reply to Louis Henkin*, 101 HARV. L. REV. 511 (1987); Henkin, *Lexical Priority or "Political Question": A Response*, 101 HARV. L. REV. 524 (1987). Professor Westen addresses the question of the abrogation of Indian treaties at some length. His conclusion is that treaties are "lexically superior" to, that is to say "unabrogated" by, subsequent inconsistent statutes, but are nonetheless treated by the nation's courts as "constitutionally nonjusticiable." WESTEN, *supra* at 517-21. That this distinction is a fine one is shown by his discussion of the *Sioux Nation* case:

> If the United States truly had the "prerogative" under the Constitution to "abrogate" its treaty obligations, the Sioux would have been forced to seek relief from Congress as a supplicant, basing their plea on something that, legally, was a "nonquestion." Their claim would have had the same status under American law as that of a claimant who seeks relief under statute *A* after it has been repealed by statute *B*. Instead, the Sioux based their claim on the continuing validity of the Fort Laramie Treaty—a treaty that, although judicially unenforceable, was still perceived as imposing legal obligations on the United States. [Footnote omitted].

Id. at 520-21. In the omitted footnote, Professor Westen notes the procedural history behind the *Sioux Nation* case that required the Indians to turn to Congress at least three times to gain permission to sue under the treaty in question. *Id.* at 520 n.32.

Cf. Harbour Cold Stores, Ltd. v. Ramson, Ltd., L.R.C. (Commercial) 308, 316 (Ct. App. Jamaica 1982):

> The effect of a fundamental breach (of contract) is that it relieves the other party of any further obligation to perform what he . . . for his part . . . has undertaken. And perhaps more precisely, the contract is not put out of existence though all further performance of certain obligations undertaken by each party in favor of the other may cease. It survives for the purpose of measuring the claim arising out of the breach.

(Carey, J.A., quoting Viscount Simon in Heyman v. Darwin's, Ltd. A.E.R. 337, 341 (1942).

    14. 617 F.2d 697 (D.C. 1979), *vacated*, 444 U.S. 996 (1979).

    15. *Id.* at 700.

    16. 481 F. Supp. 949 (D.D.C. 1979).

    17. 617 F.2d 697 (D.C. Cir. 1979).

    18. *Id.*

opinion by Rehnquist, thought the case presented political questions not fit to be addressed by the Court.[19] Justice Powell would have dismissed the case as moot,[20] but did not agree it was political.[21] Justices Blackmun and White would have set the case for argument,[22] and Justice Brennan would have affirmed the circuit court dismissal.[23] Justice Marshall concurred in the vacation and remand, without opinion.[24] The plurality opinion, then, is Justice Rehnquist's, finding that the dispute between the President and the Congress over the *mechanics* of the abrogation is a political one. However, the Justices did not question the *power* of the United States to abrogate the treaty with Taiwan.

It is not always so clear that an abrogation has, in fact, taken place. In some cases, and especially it seems with respect to Indian treaties, Congress may merely enact a statute of broad national application with little or no awareness of its impact on treaty rights. These are the "quiet" abrogations of this article's title. In these cases, before determining the extent of the abrogation, the court has to determine whether the later statute works a treaty abrogation at all. The Indians, in other words, will still claim their treaty rights are intact and represent an exception to the otherwise broad application of the statute.

For example, in *United States v. Dion*,[25] Dwight Dion, Sr. attempted to shield himself from federal prosecution, using a treaty between his tribe and the United States ratified in 1858, and the Court was asked to decide whether the treaty survived enactment of the statutes under which Dion was being prosecuted. The first step in the analysis might be to determine whether Dion, in fact, had a treaty right to hunt and sell eagles. However, the Supreme Court, looking ahead and foreseeing the full abrogation of any such right, was able to assume this first step away.[26] The Eighth Circuit expressly discussed the question,[27] and that exploration merits a mention here.

---

19. Goldwater v. Carter, 444 U.S. 996, 1002-06 (1979).
20. *Id.* at 997-98.
21. *Id.* at 998-1002.
22. *Id.* at 1006.
23. *Id.* at 1006-07.
24. *Id.* at 996.
25. Treaty with the Yankton Sioux, April 19, 1858, 11 Stat. 743. It is clear that individual members of a tribe may clothe themselves in the treaty rights reserved by their tribe. United States v. Winans, 198 U.S. 371 (1905). *See also Dion*, 476 U.S. at 738, n.4 and cases cited therein. Two of the *Dion* defendants, Terry Fool Bull and Asa Primeaux, Sr., were not able to raise a treaty defense because they were not members of the tribe on whose reservation the eagles were killed. *See Dion*, 752 F.2d at 1262, n.4.
26. 476 U.S. at 738.
27. 752 F.2d 1261, 1263-65.

Whether Dion was possessed of a treaty right to hunt bald eagles and the other birds might be seen as an especially difficult question. The treaty with the Yankton Sioux does not mention either hunting or eagles. However, the rules of Indian treaty construction require treaties to be construed as the Indians would have understood them and should be liberally construed to the advantage of the Indians.[28] The Eighth Circuit was certainly correct in concluding the treaty's silence was no bar.[29] The Yankton had reserved land for themselves under the treaty and the Indians very likely assumed hunting rights were appurtenant to the land.[30]

The government raised several objections before the Eighth Circuit against the asserted treaty right. First, it argued, the treaty should be interpreted in the light of legitimate conservation policies.[31] This notion flows from Justice Douglas's famous dictum: "[a] treaty does not give the Indians a federal right to pursue the last living steelhead [trout] until it enters their nets."[32]

As a broad general proposition, the "conservation-as-limiting-factor" argument is specious. The Indian parties to a treaty are just as capable of applying conservation principles as are the federal and state governments[33] and, in any case, it is their treaty-recognized resource to conserve. Of course, there are obvious limitations to this response. There are mitigating factors favoring a narrower proposition respecting conservation policies as treaty construction aids. For

---

28. *See* COHEN, *supra* note 6, at 221-28.

29. United States v. Dion, 752 F.2d at 1264.

30. *See* Reynolds, *Indian Hunting and Fishing Rights: The Role of Tribal Sovereignty and Preemption*, 62 N.C. L. REV. 743, 747-56 (1984). *See also* Oregon Dep't of Fish and Wildlife v. Klamath Indian Tribe, 473 U.S. 753 (1985). In *Klamath*, the tribe was claiming a treaty-protected right to hunt and fish on land off their present reservation but once included in a treaty reservation. It was clear in that case the tribe's 1864 treaty had been abrogated and the reservation reduced in size. The Indians had, in fact, been paid for the abrogation. The tribe argued, however, there had been no intent to abrogate the treaty to the extent of the now off-reservation fishing rights, and that those federal rights preempted state law. *See* Solem v. Bartlett, 465 U.S. 463 (1984). The State of Oregon prevailed before the Supreme Court. One question was whether the right to fish is appurtenant to or independent of the land on which the fishing is to be done. The Court conceded that the separation of the right from the land is possible. 473 U.S. at 765-66. Citing Washington v. Washington State Commercial Passenger Fishing Vessel Ass'n., 443 U.S. 658, 675-76 *modified*, 444 U.S. 816 (1979) and Carpenter v. Shaw, 280 U.S. 363 (1930), the Ninth Circuit had decided the case on this basis. *See* Klamath Indian Tribe v. Oregon Dep't of Fish and Wildlife, 729 F.2d 609, 612 (9th Cir. 1984). However, the Supreme Court determined that in the *Klamath* case, the right to fish was appurtenant to the land and was relinquished by the Indians when they surrendered the land for a cash payment. Justice Marshall, who wrote *Dion*, dissented along with Justice Brennan. 473 U.S. at 775.

31. 752 F.2d at 1267-69.

32. Department of Game v. Puyallup Tribe, 414 U.S. 44, 49 (1973).

33. *See, e.g.*, New Mexico v. Mescalero Apache Tribe, 462 U.S. 324 (1983); discussed *infra* note 36.

example, if the hunting right was not reserved exclusively to the Indians but was shared between the Indians and others, the rights of those others, reflected in their government's conservation policies, should be a factor in the treaty's interpretation. The same analysis is appropriate if the right was protected off-reservation as well as on. Supreme Court cases reflect this limitation.[34]

If the species is a migratory one, but the treaty right is exclusive and on-reservation, then the outcome from the non-Indian population's viewpoint is just as clear. "Those are our eagles (or salmon, elk, or, maybe, oil, gas or groundwater), too. We should have a say in how you hunt them." The problem is, of course, that the non-Indians *did* have a say—in their government's negotiation and ratification of the treaty—and they, through their representatives, agreed to the retention by the Indians of exclusive on-reservation rights. How can the treaty now be construed otherwise?

The answer lies in the "as the Indians understood the treaty" rule of construction. It would have been beyond the expectations of all the parties in the nineteenth century to anticipate the destruction of the resource and hence the treaty should not protect the right to that extent. This argument gains force in relation to the Indian control of an off-reservation resource by their on-reservation activities. When the reservation sits astride a stream where a species migrates every year, the entire off-reservation population could be decimated in one season by exploitative on-reservation fishing. Such is the case of the steelhead, and explains Justice Douglas's dictum.[35] When the species roams freely across the country, including Indian reservations, the argument has less strength.[36] The eagle's is a case between two extremes.

---

34. *See, e.g.*, Washington v. Washington State Commercial Passenger Fishing Vessel Ass'n, 443 U.S. 658 (1979), *modified*, 444 U.S. 816 (1979); Puyallup Tribe, Inc. v. Department of Game, 433 U.S. 165 (1977); Antoine v. Washington, 420 U.S. 194 (1975); Department of Game v. Puyallup Tribe, Inc. 414 U.S. 44 (1973); Puyallup Tribe, Inc. v. Department of Game, 391 U.S. 392 (1968). *See also* Reynolds, *supra* note 30, at 767-73. Professor Reynolds' focus in her article is on state, not federal, conservation and sports regulation. The issue is the same however, for the legitimacy of the state regulation depends first on its not being preempted by federal law. *See id.* at 771-81.

See also Lac Courte Oreilles Band of Lake Superior Chippewa Indians v. Wisconsin, 653 F. Supp. 1420, 1435 (W.D. Wisc. 1987), which distinguished *Dion* on the basis suggested by this text.

35. Department of Game v. Puyallup Tribe, Inc. 414 U.S. 44 (1973). In case it does not go without saying, there is not and never has been the slightest indication that the Puyallup Tribe had any intention of pursuing the last steelhead into its nets.

36. *See* New Mexico v. Mescalero Apache Tribe, 462 U.S. 324 (1983) in which the Court held the state's ability to control the hunting of elk on the reservation to be preempted by the tribe's legitimate and federally-sanctioned control of the same resource. Although the tribe's regulations were unclear as to whether conservation or economic purpose dominated, they were

The eagle migrates in large numbers across the reservation to a sanctuary bordering the reservation. The sanctuary is necessary because most of the off-reservation eagle habitat has been destroyed by non-Indians. The Eighth Circuit answered by finding hunting by Indians did not in fact threaten the eagle with extinction, and so the "conservation as limiting factor" argument lost on the facts.[37] The Supreme Court found any treaty right that did exist had been abrogated. The court did not reach this other issue.[38]

The government also argued before the Eighth Circuit that while the treaty might protect the right to shoot an eagle, it did not protect any right to sell the carcass or otherwise engage in commercial activity in the feathers.[39] Once again under the traditional notions of Indian treaty interpretation, the question is whether the Indian parties to the treaty would have understood that the latter right was protected. The question can be stated to make the answer appear easy. Did the Yankton chiefs imagine in 1858 that the treaty-protected activities would include the wholesaling of eagle feathers to non-Indians for shipment to New Mexico to be made into *objets d'art*, ultimately destined to grace the offices of East Coast accountants? No, they did not.

On the other hand, were eagles hunted in the nineteenth century only for individual consumption? Was there trade in eagle feathers? Between Indians? Between Indians and others? Such matters should be open for proof at trial; it is not unlikely that some trade in eagle parts took place[40] and is treaty-protected activity. *Dion*, as addressed by the Eighth Circuit, and other cases accept the legitimacy of the

---

somewhat more generous to hunters than were the state's. One suspects both purposes dominated. The Supreme Court, in ratifying the tribe's ability to control the on-reservation hunting of a resource that roamed freely across reservation boundaries, implicitly rejected the standard set by a panel of the Ninth Circuit: "As to such hunting and fishing [by non-tribal members on the reservation] *the more severe restrictions, whether originating with the State or Tribe, control.*" United States v. Montana, 604 F.2d 1162, 1171 (9th Cir. 1979), *reversed on other grounds*, 450 U.S. 544 (1981) (emphasis added). *See also* Confederated Tribes of Colville Indian Reservation v. Washington, 591 F.2d 89, 92 (9th Cir. 1979), *Rev. denied*, 452 U.S. 911 (1981). The passage of the Ninth Circuit's "the more severe restrictions win" rule from Indian law jurisprudence is unlamented. It appeared to have been premised on the notion that "conservation" in all cases means "conservative" and that a government could not legitimately determine that conservation interests required the harvesting of a resource to reduce numbers but improve the health of the resource as a whole.

37.   752 F.2d at 1268, n.14.
38.   476 U.S. at 738, n.5.
39.   752 F.2d at 1264-65.
40.   A fictional account of such a trade in sacred or quasi-sacred medicine bundles between Indians is found in J. WELCH, FOOLS CROW (1986) at 109. While Mr. Welch is a Blackfeet and Gros Ventre Indian and has assured me that he understands that such transactions indeed took place in the old days, I am unable to cite to any particular non-fiction source.

inquiry,[41] and before the Supreme Court, at least with respect to Northwest Coast fishing, the argument has carried the day.[42]

It is interesting to note that the issue of the protection *vel non* of commercial trading in eagles can become closely related to the issue of first amendment protection of the activity. On one hand, the religious use of eagle parts may be protected, both by treaty and by the Constitution. On the other hand, the crass commercial dealings in our endangered national bird (endangered, it is admitted, almost entirely by past and present non-Indian activity) are not "religious" nor, as has been shown, treaty-protected. Between these cases lies the harder case where an eagle is felled by one Indian and traded or sold to another for use in a religious ceremony. The resolution of the treaty issues in such a case would require historical evidence to determine what the Indians understood the treaty to mean; mere conclusions concerning "commercial" or "non-commercial" activity will not do.[43] The Supreme Court avoided resolving the first ammendment issues in *Dion*, therefore they will not be addressed here.[44]

The conclusion to here, then, is the 1858 treaty with the Yankton should be construed—as the Eighth Circuit did expressly and the Supreme Court did by implication—to protect at least some hunting of eagles, even though the birds have become symbolic and, to a lesser but still important extent, endangered.[45] Furthermore, a court should be hesitant to proclaim only "non-commercial" activity is protected.

As has already been noted, all of the foregoing was assumed away by the Supreme Court, leaving the abrogation issue directly presented.[46] Given that the Yankton were once promised the right to hunt on the reservation, including the right to hunt eagles and other now-

---

41. *See* the discussion in *Dion*, 752 F.2d at 1264. *See also* United States v. Top Sky, 547 F.2d 486 (9th Cir. 1976).

42. *See Dion*, 752 F.2d at 1265 and cases cited *supra* n. 11.

43. The Eighth Circuit in *Dion* concluded that "the Yankton Sioux would not have understood the treaty as reserving in them a right to sell eagles . . . ." 752 F.2d at 1264. As the text indicates, I think this statement is much too broad and must be read in the context of the facts of *Dion*, where the feathers from the Yankton reservation appeared to be ending up in New Mexico craft shops. The Supreme Court assumed that the case before it concerned non-commercial dealings in eagles. 476 U.S. at 736, n.3.

44. The Eighth Circuit had rejected the religion claim, 752 F.2d at 1264-65, and it was abandoned by the defendants before the Supreme Court, 476 U.S. at 736, n. 2. *See* United States v. Abeyta, 632 F. Supp. 1301 (D.N.M. 1986) and *Dion*, 476 U.S. at 746. *See also* United States v. Billie, 667 F. Supp. 1485 (S.D. Fla. 1987) and State v. Billie, 497 So. 2d 889 (Fla. 2d DCA 1986), cases concerning the shooting of an endangered Florida panther, which are discussed in detail *infra* text and notes 63-90 and accompanying text.

45. The golden eagle, though protected under the Bald Eagle Protection Act, 16 U.S.C. § 668 (1982), is not endangered. *See Dion*, 476 U.S. at 740-41 and United States v. Abeyta, 632 F. Supp. 1301, 1307 (D.N.M. 1986).

46. 476 U.S. at 738.

protected birds, was that promise put aside when Congress passed the laws to protect the birds?

One approach to this question would be to require that Congress place its intent to abrogate an Indian treaty on the face of the abrogating statute; to make it so there could be no "quiet" abrogations.[47] It has for some time been clear that the test is not that demanding. Prior to *Dion*, the Eighth Circuit had established its *White* test that "statutory abrogation of treaty rights can only be accomplished by an express reference to treaty rights in the statute *or in the statute's legislative history*."[48] The Ninth Circuit's test was a less stringent one which looked to surrounding circumstances as well as the statute itself and its express legislative history.[49] The United States, before the Eighth Circuit in *Dion*, urged the abandonment of the *White* test, but the Eighth Circuit stuck to its guns, preferring the "greater clarity and more consistent results" of the *White* test.[50]

The government next suggested that the *White* test be modified in the case of natural resource conservation, citing *New York ex rel. Kennedy v. Becker*[51] and the *Puyallup* cases.[52] The court was unpersuaded, however, and read the cited cases narrowly: *Kennedy* as an off-reservation fishing case,[53] and the *Puyallup* cases as ones involving fishing rights held by the Indians in common with non-Indians.[54]

The Supreme Court reversed the Eighth Circuit, reformulating the *White* test.

> What is essential is clear evidence that Congress actually considered the conflict between its intended action on the one hand and Indian treaty rights on the other, and chose to resolve that conflict by abrogating the treaty.[55]

---

47. *See, e.g.*, Wilkinson & Volkman, *Judicial Review of Indian Treaty Abrogation*, 63 CALIF. L. REV. 601 (1975). *See also* Wilkinson, *supra* note 9, at 52 and n.97.

48. *Dion*, 752 F.2d at 1265 (emphasis in original). The test originated in the case of United States v. White, 508 F.2d 453 (8th Cir. 1974).

49. *See* United States v. Fryberg, 622 F.2d 1010 (9th Cir. 1980), *cert. denied* 449 U.S. 1004 (1980).

50. *Dion*, 752 F.2d at 1267. The court suggested rather strongly that this might be the test only for criminal cases such as *Dion*. *Id*.

51. 241 U.S. 556 (1916).

52. Puyallup Tribe, Inc. v. Department of Game, 433 U.S. 165 (1977); Department of Game v. Puyallup Tribe, Inc. 414 U.S. 44 (1973); and Puyallup Tribe, Inc. v. Department of Game, 391 U.S. 392 (1968).

53. *Dion*, 752 F.2d at 1267-68.

54. *Id*. at 1268-69.

55. 476 U.S. at 740.

The Supreme Court in *Dion* found such an "actual consideration" and the resulting "choice" to abrogate.[56]

The *Dion* "actual consideration and choice" test should be read to be strong and demanding and has much to recommend it. The word "actual" has a special place in the law, reserved for those occasions where a court seeks evidence that something *in fact* occurred, not that something "constructively" occurred. The "actual consideration and choice" test makes it clear that the question is not merely whether Congress would have been adverse to the notion that it was abrogating an Indian treaty, had it been brought to its attention.

Where will a court turn for evidence of Congress's "actual consideration and choice"? Justice Thurgood Marshall was careful to begin his opinion for the Court with a consideration of the language of the Bald Eagle Protection Act, a signal to lower courts that the first place to look is always to the statute itself.[57] Next, the legislative history must be inspected, for direct evidence of congressional choice often is found there.

The Eighth Circuit's *White* test stopped here, demanding express and direct evidence in the legislative history of Congress's intent to abrogate the treaty.[58] To some extent that test was preferable to *Dion*'s. It is satisfying when one is sure that Congress knew that the proposed legislation would have the effect of going back, unilaterally, on the national word.

The applicable legislative history in *Dion* contained nothing that express, and the Supreme Court's reversal shows nothing that express is required. It would be a mistake, however, to read *Dion* as establishing a tremendously different standard for "quiet" abrogations than had been contained in the *White* test. It is true enough the *Dion* "actual consideration and choice" test does not require *direct* evidence of the

---

56. *Id.* at 774-77. The Eighth Circuit had found no intent to abrogate expressed in either the statute or its legislative history, and further:

> even if we ignore the express reference test and, instead, look for congressional intent to abrogate or modify treaty rights in less reliable sources, we reach the same conclusion. . . . [T]he fact that the acts are broadly worded conservation measures is inconclusive as to intent to abrogate Indian treaty rights. The plaudible purpose behind conservation statutes gives rise to strong emotions, especially where bald eagles are concerned, but does not necessarily reveal a congressional intent to eliminate rights protected by federal treaties.

Dion, 752 F.2d at 1269-70.

57. *Dion*, 476 U.S. at 740: "[C]ongressional intent to abrogate Indian treaty rights to hunt bald and golden eagles is certainly strongly suggested on the face of the Eagle Protection Act." *See generally* WILKINSON, *supra* note 9, at 52 and cases cited therein. "But the modern cases have generally hewed to the standard of express language as a benchmark and have rarely dispensed with the requirement." WILKINSON, *supra* note 9, at 52.

58. *Dion*, 752 F.2d at 1269.

consideration and choice; Justice Marshall's opinion indicates that circumstantial evidence will do. But, by way of emphasis, Justice Marshall for the unanimous Court made the point that it is *"essential"* any such circumstantial evidence "clear[ly]" indicate congressional consideration and choice to abrogate before an abrogation will be found.[59]

With respect to the Bald Eagle Protection Act the circumstantial evidence was strong. The hunting of eagles by Indians was directly discussed by the legislators, showing actual consideration of the impact of the proposed legislation on Indians. While direct mention of Indian treaties and their abrogation is not found, it is clear some members of Congress were concerned with the rights of Indians.[60] Furthermore, the talk of Indians hunting eagles was not abstract discussion, far removed from the details of the proposed legislation. Congress recognized some Indian eagle hunting is legitimate and a protected activity, even if it was thinking of the first amendment and no one precisely brought to its attention that such legitimacy and protection also flows from treaties.[61] More important, Congress took action following this discussion and established a permit scheme to

---

59. *Dion*, 476 U.S. at 739.

60. Before the Eighth Circuit in *Dion* there had been no need to inspect the legislative history of the Bald Eagle Protection Act. *White* was a case interpreting the terms of that Act and, as the Act had not been amended, that case was stare decisis. *Dion*, 752 F.2d at 1269. With respect to the Endangered Species Act, the Eighth Circuit wrote: "[W]e cannot find an express reference to Indian treaty hunting rights showing congressional intent to abrogate or modify such rights in either the statutory language or legislative history of this Act." *Id.*

The Supreme Court appeared to agree with the Eighth Circuit that the intent to abrogate is much less clear under the Endangered Species Act than it is under the Eagle Protection Act: "[T]he Endangered Species Act and its legislative history, [*Dion*] points out, are to a great extent silent regarding Indian hunting rights." *Dion*, 476 U.S. at 745. Nevertheless, the Court held that the prosecution under the Endangered Species Act was proper: "[W]e have held, however, that Congress in passing and amending the Eagle Protection Act divested Dion of his treaty right to hunt bald eagles. He therefore has no treaty right to hunt bald eagles that he can assert as a defense to an Endangered Species Act charge." *Id.* Thus the Court made clear that its test in *Dion* was something more than the determination that when a treaty and a statute conflict the statute controls. Rather, the statute represents an abrogation of the treaty in the true sense of the word and the treaty right is gone.

As Ms. Hanna and I discussed in the earlier article, this interpretation of Dion's rights under the Endangered Species Act makes the costs of a court's error in determining whether Congress intended a "quiet" abrogation greater. *See* Hanna & Laurence, *Justice Thurgood Marshall and the Problem of Indian Treaty Abrogation*, 40 ARK. L. REV. 797, 833-35 (1986). This greater cost, in turn, argues in favor of the stricter, bright line rule of *White*.

61. Why would Congress be less concerned with treaty-protected hunting than with hunting for religious purposes? Given its acknowledged power to abrogate treaty rights unilaterally, *see* Lone Wolf v. Hitchcock, 187 U.S. 553 (1903) and United States v. Sioux Nation, 448 U.S. 371 (1980), and note 13 *supra*, and given its acknowledged lack of power to abrogate first amendment rights, *see* U.S. CONST. amend. 1 and the American Indian Religious Freedom Act, 42 U.S.C. § 1996 (1981), Congress might well spend more time avoiding the latter than the former.

protect Indian religious rights. It is impossible to read *Dion* without being impressed by the importance Justice Marshall placed on this permit scheme.[62] The presence of the permit scheme shows Congress actually considered Indian rights and made that consideration tangible. Admittedly, the link to Indian treaty rights is still circumstantial, but seems to be a distinction too legalistic for the Court.[63]

Thus, even though *Dion* found the treaty abrogated, it established a very stringent test for "quiet" abrogations. Under Justice Marshall's opinion, a court must keep in mind its *"essential"* task is to find *"clear"* evidence the Congress *"actually considered"* the Indians' treaty rights and *"chose"* to abrogate the treaty.[64] In seeking this evidence, the court should look first, as Justice Marshall did, to the face of the statute and the legislative history. While circumstantial evidence of the congressional consideration and choice may occasionally convince a court an abrogation was intended, the *Dion* case itself argues for a limited role for this part of the test. The importance to the Court of the permit scheme should guide lower courts, when they turn to

---

62. The provision allowing taking of eagles under permit for the religious purposes of Indian tribes is difficult to explain except as a reflection of an understanding that the statute otherwise bans the taking of eagles by Indians, a recognition that such a prohibition would cause hardship for the Indians, and a decision that that problem should be solved not by exempting Indians from the coverage of the statute, but by authorizing the Secretary to issue permits to Indians where appropriate. 476 U.S. 742-43. And again, "Congress expressly chose to set in place a regime in which the Secretary of the Interior had control over Indian hunting, rather than one in which Indian on-reservation hunting was unrestricted." *Id.* at 743.

63. Strictly speaking, before the statute in question was passed, Indian rights fell into two catagories. First, there were treaty-protected rights, usually geographically restricted to the reservation; these rights were raised by Dion as a defense. Second, there were the rights of Indians, in common with non-Indians, to engage in otherwise unregulated activity. It is not difficult to decide that Congress intended to ban the previously unregulated off-reservation activity of both Indians and non-Indians. But did it intend to ban the treaty-protected right? Here the inquiry becomes almost metaphysical, for recall that, with respect to the Yankton Sioux, there is no mention of the right to hunt in the treaty at all.

All of the legislative history cited by the Court is consistent with the notion that the eagle shooting being regulated was unprotected by treaty. The existence of the religious purposes permit scheme, for example, is explainable as an attempt to save the constitutionality of the system from attack by an Indian claiming the right to be free of federal regulation of the religious hunting of birds where no treaty protects the hunter. For example, some of Dion's co-defendants, charged with hunting eagles off their own reservations, might have raised this defense. This was the Eighth Circuit's approach. "[A]s the majority in *White* revealed, the religious purposes' exception is not limited to the taking of eagles by Indians or to the taking of eagles on Indian reservations." United States v. White, 508 F.2d at 458. "In other words, it could have been deemed necessary to permit non-Indians to hunt eagles, on or off a reservation, in order for the Indian tribes to obtain enough eagle parts for their religious needs." *Dion*, 752 F.2d at 1270. With respect to the hunting of eagles as protected religious activity, *see* United States v. Abeyta, 632 F. Supp. 1301 (D.N.M. 1986). The Supreme Court did not reach Dion's religious freedom argument. 476 U.S. at 736 n.3.

64. *Id.* at 740 (emphasis added).

inspect evidence that is not found expressly in the statute or legislative history, to seek the same kind of clarity and definiteness. With this sort of careful consideration, a court may be comfortable that it may avoid inadvertent upsets of carefully constructed tribal-federal relations and imposing liability for money damages on the United States, all in the name of a "quiet" abrogation.

The days are happily gone when the United States, with its divine arrogance of the last century, purposefully fails to keep its word to its Indian citizens as if there was something in the status of Indians that made promises to them meaningless.[65] More common these days is the choice of some otherwise worthy national goal—such as the protection of eagles—that runs afoul of a treaty-made promise to an Indian tribe. Congress's choice of whether to abrogate the treaty or not is one that should be done soberly, carefully and, one would hope, with some considerable disquietude regarding abrogation. Furthermore "quiet" abrogations raise all of the obvious problems of inadvertence and injustice. Similarly, when a court faces what is argued to be such a "quiet" abrogation, it ought to be hesitant, indeed reluctant, to reach the conclusion that the treaty right has been cast aside. The proper reading of the *Dion* opinion shows that the Supreme Court's approach is fully consistent with that hesitancy and reluctance.

The earliest receptions of *Dion* were inauspicious. In December of 1983, James E. Billie, Chief of the Seminole Tribe in Florida, killed a *felis concolor coryi,* or Florida panther, an endangered species, protected under both state and federal law. Dual prosecutions commenced. The state trial court dismissed the information against Billie, but the Florida District Court of Appeal reversed and remanded for trial.[66] In the federal prosecution, the federal district court denied Billie's motion to dismiss.[67] Both cases purported to use the Supreme

---

65. Some will find this sentence in the text to be hopelessly optimistic, enough so to make me as arrogant as any nineteenth century Indian country missionary, calvary officer or federal law-maker. I confess to some optimism, not unlimited, in this field, and have done so publicly. *See* Laurence, *Learning to Live with the Plenary Power of Congress over the Indian Nations, to be published at* 30 ARIZ. L. REV. (1988). Those less optimistic, and toward whom that essay was one volley in a so-far friendly debate, include Professor Robert A. Williams, Jr. of the University of Arizona and Professor Milner S. Ball of the University of Georgia. *See* Williams, *Jefferson, the Norman Yoke, and American Indian Lands,* 29 ARIZ. L. REV. 165 (1987); Ball, *Constitution, Court, Indian Tribes,* 1987 AM. BAR FOUND. RES. J. 1; Williams, *The Algebra of Federal Indian Law,* 1986 WIS. L. REV. 219.

66. State v. Billie, 497 So. 2d 889 (Fla. 2d DCA 1986). At trial, Billie was acquitted, N.Y. Times, October 9, 1987, at 29, col. 1.

67. United States v. Billie, 667 F. Supp. 1485 (S.D. Fla. 1987). Billie's first trial in federal court ended in a mistrial, the jury deadlocked at 7-5 in favor of acquittal. N. Y. Times, August 28, 1987, at 32, col. 1. Following the verdict of acquittal in the state prosecution, *see* note 66, *supra,* the Justice Department dropped the federal prosecution. N. Y. Times, October 11, 1987, at 28, col. 2.

Court's test for "quiet" abrogations from *Dion*; both used it superficially and rather off-handedly found a treaty abrogation.

The first concern for both courts, of course, had to be whether Billie's right to hunt the Florida panther was treaty-protected. Both equivocated, citing to the "conservation as a limiting factor" rule,[68] discussed above.[69] Both courts even went so far as to paraphrase Justice Douglas's steelhead trout dicta: "[Congress] could not have intended that the Indians would have the unfettered right to kill the last handful of Florida panthers," said the federal court.[70] "The Seminoles do not have the right to hunt the very last living Florida panther," the state judge offered.[71]

It is difficult for me to believe that Justice Douglas, even the conservationist that he was, would have entirely approved of such glib and casual restatements of his thoughts from the *Puyallup* litigation. South Florida has surely become an inhospitable range for an animal as wild and predatory as the panther, but it is self-evident that circumstance follows white, not Indian, greed, exploitation and shortsightedness. Panthers are truly in short supply. But to suggest in such an easy fashion that the Seminoles in general or Chief Billie in particular are out to exterminate the species, or indeed that the Chief's taking of one panther for religious purposes represents such a threat, either by itself or in some unstated aggregation, is certainly more phrase-making than legal analysis.

The state court's analysis of whether Billie's right to hunt on the Big Cypress Reservation[72] is limited by conservation concerns does not go much beyond this phrase-making. It seems entirely contained in the conclusion: ". . . however, the United States Supreme Court has said that an Indian's right to hunt pursuant to executive order can be regulated by the need to conserve a species," citing the *Puyallup* cases.[73] As mentioned above,[74] the analysis is not that simple. Panthers are not steelhead trout. Steelhead trout are an anadromous species of fish that migrates along particular and exact routes, and is much more sensitive to Indian harvesting than a predatory mammal of the sub-tropics. The

---

68. *See* United States v. Billie, 667 F. Supp. at 1489; State v. Billie, 497 So. 2d at 892.

69. *See supra* notes 31-38 and accompanying text.

70. United States v. Billie, 667 F. Supp. at 1492.

71. State v. Billie, 497 So. 2d at 895.

72. While there were many treaties between the United States and the Seminole Tribe, the Big Cypress Reservation, the main home of the Tribe in Florida, was established by executive order, not treaty. *See* United States v. Billie, 667 F. Supp. at 1488 n.2. The fact that the reservation is not a treaty reservation should have no impact on the case. *See Dion,* 476 U.S. at 745 n.8.

73. State v. Billie, 497 So. 2d at 892.

74. *See* United States v. Billie, 667 F. Supp. at 1496.

panther is apt to roam over a fifty to three hundred square mile area, only part of which is on the reservation. On the other hand, a fish that lays thousands of eggs may be less vulnerable than a mammal that bears only a few offspring each year. The District Court of Appeal's discussion falls far short of the Eighth Circuit's analysis in *Dion*, which rightly assigns the government the task of proving Indian eagle hunting threatened the animal with extinction.[75]

The federal district court's analysis of the question of treaty abrogation is more careful. That court also recognized that when a federal prosecution is involved, the question of the interpretation of the treaty right and the question of the right's abrogation merge. In other words, once we know that the Congress has the power to abrogate treaty rights to hunt, the issue is whether the federal conservation statute did so—the *Dion* issue. Only if it is found that the federal statute left the treaty intact would it be necessary to determine whether the treaty protects the right and then only for the purposes of prosecution under state law. The structure of *Dion* itself supports this approach. Hence, the federal court reached the conclusion that

> where conservation measures are necessary to protect endangered wildlife, the Government can intervene on behalf of other federal interests. The migratory nature of the Florida panther gives Indians, the states, and the federal Government a common interest in the preservation of the species. Where the actions of one group can frustrate the others' efforts at conservation . . . reasonable, nondiscriminatory measures may be required to ensure the species' continued existence.[76]

The key words in that passage are "necessary" and "can frustrate", and the district court should have devoted some time to the factual question of whether Seminole hunting of panthers for religious purposes *necessarily frustrates* legitimate conservation aims. Nevertheless, the court was correct in turning immediately to the Endangered Species Act, to determine if it was written by Congress to abrogate any treaty hunting right that existed. The evidence is not great that it did.

Both courts noted that the Supreme Court in *Dion* was able to leave open the question of whether the Endangered Species Act is a treaty-abrogating act of Congress.[77] That is technically correct, but it is difficult not to read some approval into the Court's language when it

---

75. *See Dion*, 752 F.2d at 1268.
76. United States v. Billie, 667 F. Supp. at 1490 (citations omitted).
77. *Dion*, 476 U.S. at 745. *See* State v. Billie, 497 So. 2d at 893; United States v. Billie, 667 F. Supp. at 1487. *See also* note 45, *supra*.

noted that "[t]he Endangered Species Act and its legislative history, [Dion] points out, are to a great extent silent regarding Indian hunting rights."[78]

The federal district court in *Billie* made all it could of the legislative history, but in the end was able to point to precious little indication in the Endangered Species Act that hints of an intent to abrogate Indian treaties:

> [The Endangered Species Act's] general comprehensiveness, its nonexclusion of Indians, and the limited exceptions for certain Alaskan natives . . . demonstrate that Congress considered Indian interests, balanced them against conservation needs, and defined the extent to which Indians would be permitted to take protected wildlife.[79]

The Alaskan natives the court referred to, it should be noted, are not protected by any treaty and would need federal statutory protection to have any rights at all, other than their rights in common with other Alaskan citizens.[80]

The federal district court did not really object to Dion's observation, with the apparent approval of the Supreme Court, that the legislative history of the Endangered Species Act is mostly silent on the subject of Indian hunting rights. The court, instead, based much of its holding on some legislative history of a bill before the House of Representatives in a previous Congress—a bill that never passed—the relevance of which is not entirely clear.[81] All in all, when compared with *Dion*, the congressional "demonstration" found by the federal court falls well short of *Dion*'s mark.

The most telling bit of the federal court's "evidence" of Congress's intent to abrogate is its continued reference to "the Act's general comprehensiveness,"[82] for it is at this exact point that *Dion* requires more. In *all* cases of "quiet" treaty abrogations, a generally comprehensive statute will be weighed against the terms of an Indian treaty.

---

78. *Dion*, 476 U.S. at 745.

79. United States v. Billie, 667 F. Supp. at 1490.

80. *See generally*, Cohen, *supra* note 6, at 739-46.

81. United States v. Billie, 667 F. Supp. at 1490-91. As described in *Billie*, the House bill was H.R. 13081, 92d Cong. 2d Sess. A companion bill in the Senate was S. 3199, 92d Cong. 2d Sess., which also failed to pass. It seems that ever since then Justice Rehnquist's creative use of unpassed legislation in Oliphant v. Suquamish Indian Tribe, 435 U.S. 191 (1978), the use of such non-statutes in Indian law cases has been on the rise.

82. United States v. Billie, 667 F. Supp. at 1491. *See also id.* at 1488 and 1492. The Florida state court was impressed, too, by the comprehensiveness of the federal statute. *See* State v. Billie, 497 So. 2d at 893 and 895. Neither court seems daunted by the commitment of the United States to keep its word to the Indian parties to a treaty.

The fact that Congress has sought to regulate an area of national concern is not enough, however, to conclude that Congress at the same time means to go back on an old and important promise:

> What is *essential* is *clear evidence* that Congress *actually considered* the conflict between its intended action on the one hand and Indian treaty rights on the other, and *chose* to resolve that conflict by abrogating the treaty.[83]

The Florida state court picked out of *Dion* a weaker "sufficiently compelling evidence" test.[84] It then appeared to use an even weaker test: "[t]he Endangered Species Act abrogates any inherent rights the Seminole Indians may have for hunting the Florida panther, *since only Alaskan native Indians are specifically exempt from the Act. In expressly exempting only Alaskan Indians, we must presume* Congress did not intend to exempt any other Indian tribes."[85] Then a non-Indian case was cited.[86]

---

83. *Dion*, 476 U.S. at 739-40 (emphasis added).

84. "The Supreme Court concluded that while an express statement of Congress may be preferable, it would not rigidly interpret that preference as a per se rule where the evidence of congressional intent to abrogate was sufficiently compelling." State v. Billie, 497 So. 2d at 893. In *Dion*, the "sufficiently compelling" language occurs just before the "[W]hat is essential . . ." passage quoted immediately above in the text, which I have characterized as the case's test. *See Dion*, 476 U.S. at 739-40.

85. State v. Billie, 497 So. 2d at 894 (emphasis added and citations omitted). The Florida court has made a technical mistake here by equating Alaskan natives with Alaskan Indians, to the possible offense of Inuits and Aleuts. *See* COHEN, *supra* note 6, at 739. The error is probably forgivable, though, for a court so far from Alaska.

86. 497 So. 2d at 894, citing Tennessee Valley Authority v. Hill, 437 U.S. 153 (1978), a leading case on the Endangered Species Act. It is reasonably clear that both the state and federal judges saw *Billie* as first involving panthers and only secondarily concerning Indians. For example, the federal court in *Hill* began its analysis by noting that the Endangered Species Act is "the most comprehensive legislation for the preservation of endangered species ever enacted by any nation." United States v. Billie, 667 F. Supp. at 1488 (quoting *Hill*, 437 U.S. at 180). Then, for good measure, the court quoted the same passage again at the close of its analysis. United States v. Billie, 667 F. Supp. at 1492. The cases might have been decided differently if the courts had been made to see them first as cases involving the nation's solemn word, which has, unhappily, come into conflict with the future of a proud and endangered beast. Imagine if the federal district court's first quotation had been not from *Hill*, but from *Tuscarora*: Justice Black on word-keeping, quoted *supra* at note 10. From this vantage point, it becomes much clearer that the first question must be the extent of the conflict between the treaty and the environment: just exactly how much will the panther be harmed by a decision that keeps the government's word? If the answer is "substantially" then the result in *Billie* might be justified. But the government should be put to the proof, or, alternatively, must prove that Congress has already *actually* considered the question and made the choice to abrogate.

This conflict between first viewing the case as a panther case or an Indian case is seen most clearly in one part of the state court opinion. Turning at the end to an "additional aspect" of the case, the court briefly studied Florida Statute § 380.055(8) which permits the Seminole Tribe, under state law, to hunt in its usual and customary way on the Big Cypress Reservation. This

Any "sufficiently compelling" test collapses upon itself and ultimately begs the question. And a presumption that treaty-protected Seminoles are covered merely because certain non-treaty Alaskan natives are not turns *Dion* on its head. However, my real complaint with the state court decision is not that it substituted one black-letter statement of the law for another. The mistake is in black-letterizing the *Dion* case in the first place. Divorcing *Dion* from its facts and leaving the test quoted above floating in a vacuum does not do justice to the Court's opinion.

The federal district court did little better in this regard. It paid lip service to the correct test from *Dion*,[87] but it, too, treated the test as if it were a black-letter statement, divorced from the facts of the case that gave rise to the test. In particular, the court failed to consider the importance of the permit scheme Congress put into place under the Bald Eagle Protection Act and left off the Endangered Species Act.[88] The importance of that scheme, remember, was that it made the circumstantial evidence of congressional consideration and choice *clear* rather than presumed. It decreased markedly the chances that the Court was guessing wrong in finding that the nation's word was being recanted.

Instead, the federal district court found circumstantial evidence in the exemption for Alaskan natives. But note how much weaker this evidence is than that in *Dion* itself. As I noted above,[89] the permit scheme under the Bald Eagle Protection Act did not directly address treaty rights, but at least Congress knew, or should have known, that it was dealing with Indians who had substantial treaty rights covering, in most cases, hunting and fishing. However, the exemption in the Endangered Species Act applies to Indians *without* treaty rights, as Congress knew or should have known. The exemption in the latter act is more consistent, much more consistent, with the continued recogni-

---

would appear to be a good defense to the state prosecution, but the court held that the state endangered species act governed, as the more specific statute, "because it specifically addresses the subject of an endangered species, i.e., the Florida panther." *Id.* It is not at all clear to me why a statute mentioning panthers but not Seminoles is more specific than one that mentions Seminoles but not panthers. In fact, § 380.055(8) specifically mentions both hunting and "traditional tribal ceremonials."

87.   667 F. Supp. at 1489, 1491-92.

88.   Billie had argued in the federal prosecution that a permit scheme such as Congress placed in the Bald Eagle Protection Act was necessary to save the Endangered Species Act from an attack under the first amendment free exercise clause for overbreadth on its face and as applied. United States v. Billie, 667 F. Supp. at 1494. The court rejected the argument, though with little discussion of the permitting scheme. *Id.* at 1494-97. I will leave discussion of the religious freedom issue for another day.

89.   *See supra* at notes 60-63 and accompanying text.

tion of treaty rights than the permit scheme for the taking of eagles.

All of this shows, perhaps, that the Eighth Circuit was correct in *White* and in *Dion*.[90] The Supreme Court's test as stated and applied in *Dion* is stringent, but it lacks the bright line clarity of the *White* test. Bright lines, perhaps, should be avoided for their inflexibility.[91] But when the slope is as slippery as legislative history and treaty construction tend to be, and when the costs are as dear as those involved when treaty rights and endangered animals are at stake, then there is much to be said for certainty. And, as the *Billie* cases show, a little Supreme Court flexibility can go a long way in the hands of lower court judges. Is a mention in the legislative history that a treaty is at stake too much to ask? Surely not. But the Supreme Court unanimously chose otherwise. There lies ahead, I fear, ample litigation where effective advocates will have to urge that the line be held against further quiet degradation of the nation's word. "Indian treaty rights are too fundamental to be easily cast aside."[92]

---

90. The federal district court in *Billie* noted that the Eighth Circuit in *Dion* had found that the Endangered Species Act did not abrogate Indian treaties, United States v. Billie, 667 F. Supp. at 1487, but held that it was not bound by that out-of-circuit opinion. True enough, but the court later gave considerable deference to a Tenth Circuit opinion of much less relevance. *See id.* at 1490, discussing Northern Arapahoe Tribe v. Hodel, 808 F.2d 741 (10th Cir. 1987).

91. "Our entire profession is trained to attack 'bright lines' the way hounds attack foxes." Robbins v. California, 453 U.S. 420, 443 (1981) (Rehnquist, J. dissenting).

92. Dion, 476 U.S. at 739.

NATIVE AMERICAN FREE EXERCISE RIGHTS TO THE USE OF PUBLIC LANDS

I. INTRODUCTION

Native Americans have become increasingly visible litigants in the state and federal courts. Tribes have claimed lands under ancient treaties in South Dakota, Maine, and New York.[1] Tribes in Washington, Oregon, and Michigan have also contested limitations on their fishing rights.[2]

Long-standing pressures toward the assimilation of Native Americans have generated much of this recent litigation. Over the years, United States' Indian policy has vascillated between paternalistic toleration of tribal culture,[3] and legislative interference with Native American lifestyles.[4] Many

---

[1] *See* Rosebud Sioux Tribe v. Kneip, 430 U.S. 584 (1977) (declaratory judgment settling boundaries of Rosebud Sioux Reservation according to an 1889 treaty and three subsequent acts of Congress); Joint Tribal Council of Passamaquoddy Tribe v. Morton, 528 F.2d 370 (1st Cir. 1975) (declaratory judgment action to compel the United States Attorney General to sue the state of Maine on behalf of Passamaquoddy Indians pursuant to a 1794 land treaty); Oneida Indian Nation v. Oneida County, 434 F. Supp. 527 (N.D.N.Y. 1977) (damages action for state's wrongful divestment of five million acres of Indian land in violation of various treaties and federal statutes).

[2] *See* Washington v. Washington State Commercial Passenger Fishing Vessel Ass'n, 443 U.S. 658 (1979) (state of Washington brought suit on behalf of seven tribes seeking an interpretation of fishing rights under several treaties); Puyallup Tribe, Inc. v. Department of Game, 433 U.S. 165 (1977) (Puyallup Indians sought exemption from conservation measures restricting the manner in which tribal fishing could be conducted); Kimball v. Callahan, 590 F.2d 768 (9th Cir. 1969) (declaratory judgment action to clarify fishing rights of Klamath Indians who sold their tribal property and withdrew from the tribal group), *cert. denied,* 444 U.S. 826 (1980); United States v. Michigan, 471 F. Supp. 192 (W.D. Mich. 1979) (Indians attempted to preserve right to fish in the Great Lakes reserved to them by treaty), *aff'd on rehearing,* 653 F.2d 277 (6th Cir. 1981), *cert. denied,* 102 S. Ct. 971 (1982).

[3] *See, e.g.,* Squire v. Capoeman, 351 U.S. 1, 6-7 (1956) (" 'Doubtful expressions are to be resolved in favor of the weak and defenseless people who are the wards of the nation, dependent on its protection and good faith.' " (quoting Carpenter v. Shaw, 280 U.S. 363, 367 (1930))); Worcester v. Georgia, 31 U.S. 512, 552-59 (1832) (describing Cherokee Indians as a dependent people).

[4] *See, e.g.,* Indian Allotment Act of 1887, ch. 119, § 1, 24 Stat. 388 (current

153

Native Americans view social integration as cultural obliteration.[5] It is therefore not surprising that many tribes are resorting to the courts for help in preserving a heritage that is difficult to retain.

This Note will analyze one aspect of Native American culture that has become the subject of constitutional debate. Two cases recently raised the question whether Native Americans have a right under the free exercise clause of the first amendment[6] to be free from governmental interference with their access to religious sites located on public lands. In *Sequoyah v. Tennessee Valley Authority*[7] and *Badoni v. Higginson*,[8] Native Americans unsuccessfully challenged the constitutionality of congressional decisions to build major development projects on lands that plaintiffs considered holy.[9] This Note evaluates the first amendment analysis which the district and appellate courts employed in these cases and concludes that each court improperly rejected Native American claims.

Part II examines these cases and describes the constitutional balancing test developed by the Supreme Court in *Wisconsin v. Yoder*[10] to evaluate free exercise claims. After discussing the nature of Native American interests in public lands, Part III concludes that these interests should have received constitutional protection in *Sequoyah* and *Badoni*. Part IV uses the *Yoder* balancing test to weigh Native American rights against competing government interests and illustrates the inadequacies of the *Sequoyah* and *Badoni* approaches to this problem. Finally, the Note develops an approach which adapts the *Yoder* balancing test to the Native American situation, thereby helping to resolve the conflict between the religious rights of Native Americans and the legitimate land-related needs of the whole of the American public.

---

version at 25 U.S.C. §§ 331-351 (Supp. IV 1980)) (legislation breaking up communal tribal property and distributing it to individual Indians); Act of Mar. 3, 1871, ch. 120, § 1, 16 Stat. 566 (current version at 25 U.S.C. § 71 (1976)) (statute depriving Indian tribes of their status as independent nations with capacity to contract by treaty). *See generally* A. JOSEPHY, INDIAN HERITAGE OF AMERICA 345-65 (1969) (providing a brief history of legislative policy concerning Native Americans, including a description of the Indian Allotment Act). *But see* Indian Self-Determination Act, 25 U.S.C. § 450(a)-(n) (1976) (statute authorizing HEW to make grants to and contracts with Indian tribes; Indian Reorganization Act, 25 U.S.C. §§ 461-492 (1976) (reversing policies underlying the Indian Allotment Act).

[5] *See* Means, *Fighting Words on the Future of the Earth*, MOTHER JONES, Dec. 1980, at 25 (leader of the American Indian Movement refers to Indian assimilation into the American mainstream as "cultural genocide").

[6] U.S. CONST. amend. I, provides: "Congress shall make no law respecting an establishment of religion or prohibiting the free exercise thereof . . . ."

[7] 480 F. Supp. 608 (E.D. Tenn. 1979), *aff'd*, 620 F.2d 1159 (6th Cir.), *cert. denied*, 449 U.S. 653 (1980).

[8] 455 F. Supp. 641 (D. Utah 1977), *aff'd*, 638 F.2d 172 (10th Cir. 1980), *cert. denied*, 452 U.S. 954 (1981).

[9] *Badoni*, 638 F.2d at 177; *Sequoyah*, 620 F.2d at 1165.

[10] 406 U.S. 205 (1972).

II. CURRENT JUDICIAL APPROACHES TO NATIVE AMERICAN SUITS CLAIMING ACCESS TO PUBLIC LANDS

In *Sequoyah*[11] and *Badoni*,[12] the United States Courts of Appeals for the Sixth and Tenth Circuits analyzed the question of Native American access to sacred sites on public lands within a constitutional framework provided by two recent Supreme Court cases.[13] The *Sequoyah* and *Badoni* courts ultimately held these right of access claims invalid.[14] Close examination of these cases reveals that the *Sequoyah* and *Badoni* courts erred in failing to recognize that Native Americans have a constitutional right to use public lands for religious purposes.

A. *Native American Free Exercise Claims:* Sequoyah v. Tennessee Valley Authority *and* Badoni v. Higginson

In *Sequoyah*, Cherokee Indians, alleging infringement of their first amendment rights,[15] petitioned the United States District Court in Tennessee for an injunction prohibiting the completion of the Tellico Dam.[16] Con-

---

[11] 620 F.2d 1159 (6th Cir.), *cert. denied*, 449 U.S. 653 (1980).

[12] 638 F.2d 172 (10th Cir. 1980), *cert. denied*, 452 U.S. 954 (1981).

[13] Wisconsin v. Yoder, 406 U.S. 205 (1972); Sherbert v. Verner, 374 U.S. 398 (1963). For a discussion of these cases, see *infra* Section II B.

[14] *Sequoyah*, 620 F.2d at 177; *Badoni*, 638 F.2d at 1165. Congress also addressed the issue of Native American access to public lands for religious purposes when it passed the American Indian Religious Freedom Act, Pub. L. No. 95-341, § 1, 92 Stat. 469 (current version at 42 U.S.C. § 1996 (Supp. IV 1980)). The Act requires administrative agencies to adopt procedures in the administration of laws that protect American Indians' religious practices. Although the Act does not confer a private right of action on Native Americans for violations of its terms, it does provide useful insight into the nature of the free exercise problem in this context. For example, the Act contains a congressional determination that Native Americans have an "inherent right" to use public lands for religious purposes. 42 U.S.C. § 1996 (Supp. IV 1980). This determination casts serious doubt on the *Badoni* and *Sequoyah* district courts' summary conclusion that, absent a property right, Native Americans may not claim a right of access to these lands under the first amendment. For a discussion of the Act, see *infra* notes 69-76 and accompanying text.

[15] 480 F. Supp. at 610.

[16] *Sequoyah*, 620 F.2d at 1160. Plaintiffs included two bands of the Cherokee Nation and three individual Cherokee, one of whom is a religious leader and a direct descendant of Sequoyah, the inventor of the Cherokee writing system. *Id.* at 1162. This class action was brought on behalf of "all those present or future Cherokee Indians who practice the traditional Cherokee religion and adhere to Cherokee Indian tradition and culture." *Id.* at 1160. In *Sequoyah*, affidavits of anthropologists, Cherokee religious leaders, and members of the tribe helped establish the nature of Cherokee religious belief. These affidavits are available from the Native American Law Library, Boulder, Colorado.

gress first appropriated funds for the dam's construction in 1966.[17] Plaintiffs claimed that the dam, by flooding the Little Tennessee Valley, would destroy sacred burial grounds and preclude access to sites used for gathering ceremonial medicines.[18] The Cherokee also believed that the waters would prevent them from contacting the supernatural world through the worship of sacred sites located in the Little Tennessee Valley.[19]

The District Court dismissed the suit, holding that the free exercise clause does not create a right to use another's property to advance one's own religious purposes.[20] On appeal, the Sixth Circuit retreated from this approach, noting that lack of a property interest in the Little Tennessee Valley was not conclusive of the plaintiffs' right to first amendment protection.[21] The court denied the injunction, however, because it found the plaintiffs had failed to demonstrate a substantial religious interest in preserving the sites in question.[22] The court held that worship at these sites was neither central to Cherokee religious belief nor essential to effective religious practice.[23] It

---

[17] *Id.* The Sixth Circuit had previously enjoined completion of the dam for its failure to comply with the provisions of the Endangered Species Act, 16 U.S.C. §§ 1531-1542 (Supp. IV 1980). *See* Hill v. T.V.A., 549 F.2d 1063, 1075 (6th Cir. 1977). Construction resumed in 1979 only after Congress exempted Tellico from this Act and from the "provisions of any other law." *Sequoyah*, 480 F. Supp. at 610.

[18] *Id.* at 610. The Little Tennessee Valley contains hundreds of Cherokee ancestral graves. Affidavit of Dr. Duane King, at 8 (Oct. 10, 1979). The Cherokee consider graves sacred because they believe that, after death, everything a person knows is buried in the ground along with the person's body. Affidavit of Ammoneta Sequoyah, at 2 (Oct. 11, 1979). This knowledge is an object of worship for the Cherokee. Some religious leaders believe they will lose their own knowledge of medicine if these gravesites are destroyed. *Id.; see* Affidavit of Lloyd Sequoyah, at 3 (Oct., 1979) ("If the homeland of our forefathers is covered with this water it will cover the medicine and the spiritual strength of our people . . . .").

[19] For a detailed discussion of Cherokee beliefs about sacred sites, see *infra* notes 110-115, 121 and accompanying text.

[20] *Sequoyah*, 480 F. Supp. at 612.

[21] *Sequoyah*, 620 F.2d at 1164. The court based this holding both on the unique character of the Cherokee religion and on the fact that the United States government had forcibly expelled the Cherokee from Southern Appalachia, extinguishing their aboriginal title. The Cherokee were compelled to journey west along a "Trail of Tears" to Oklahoma. *Id.; see* United States v. Michigan, 471 F. Supp. 192, 211 (W.D. Mich. 1979) (recounting some of the hardships Native Americans endured traveling west when President Andrew Jackson ordered their removal from lands east of the Mississippi), *aff'd on rehearing,* 653 F.2d 277 (6th Cir. 1980), *cert. denied,* 102 S. Ct. 971 (1981).

[22] *Sequoyah*, 620 F.2d at 1164.

[23] *Id.* In addition to holding that the contested sites were not central to Cherokee religion, the Sixth Circuit indicated that Cherokee beliefs about natural objects are cultural and historical rather than religious. Because the court characterized Cherokee interests as secular, it did not consider these interests protected under the free exercise clause. *Id.* at 1164-65.

therefore held that the flooding did not abridge Cherokee rights to religious freedom.[24]

The Tenth Circuit also faced the issue of Native American rights to the use of public lands for religious practices in *Badoni v. Higginson*.[25] The plaintiffs, religious leaders of the Navajo Nation, sought to enjoin the federal government from operating the Glen Canyon Dam at a water level damaging to Navajo religious interests.[26] The dam was erected as part of the Colorado Water Storage Project, a comprehensive plan to develop the Colorado River for power generation, irrigation, mineral development, and maintenance of municipal and industrial water supplies.[27] The plan contemplated the partial flooding of the Rainbow Bridge National Monument, a national park surrounded by the Navajo reservation.[28] The park contains a 309-foot natural sandstone arch which the Navajo consider sacred.[29] Plaintiffs believed that Navajo gods inhabited several natural phenomena submerged by the Glen Canyon Project. The creation of a reservoir had already drowned some of these gods,[30] and plaintiffs asserted that their remaining religious ceremonies would be ineffective if not held near the homes of their surviving

---

[24] *Id.* at 1165.

[25] 638 F.2d 172 (10th Cir. 1980), *cert. denied*, 452 U.S. 954 (1981).

[26] *Badoni*, 455 F. Supp. at 643-44. The action was filed by eight individual Navajo and three Chapters of the Navajo Nation. *Id.* at 642.

[27] *Badoni*, 638 F.2d at 177. In Friends of the Earth v. Armstrong, 485 F.2d 1 (10th Cir. 1973), *cert. denied*, 414 U.S. 1171 (1974), the court provides a detailed description of the project, its purposes, and the legislation authorizing its implementation. The project involved complex negotiations among seven states and the Mexican government. It required extensive cooperation between these sovereignties in building and operating water storage and utilization facilities. *Id.* at 4-5.

[28] *Badoni*, 638 F.2d at 175.

[29] *Id.*
The park was specifically set aside to preserve this arch, Rainbow Bridge. In planning the Glen Canyon Dam, Congress originally directed the Secretary of the Interior to avoid impairing Rainbow Bridge and the monument surrounding it. 43 U.S.C. § 620 (1956). In Friends of the Earth v. Armstrong, 485 F.2d 1 (10th Cir. 1973), *cert. denied*, 414 U.S. 1171 (1974), the Tenth Circuit held that Congress had subsequently repealed this directive by implication when it enacted measures calling for the operation of the dam at its highest capacity. *Id.* at 11; *see Badoni*, 455 F. Supp. at 647.

[30] *Badoni*, 638 F.2d at 176-77.
One of the drowned Navajo gods was Talking Rock who resided near a creek in the floor of the canyon. Talking Rock was a collection of eight Rock People who are Talking Gods, and who hear every word uttered in their immediate vicinity. These Rock People repeated words back in an echo effect to the people who originally said them. K. LUCKERT, NAVAJO MOUNTAIN AND RAINBOW BRIDGE RELIGION 53-54 (1977). For a description of Navajo beliefs about other natural objects in the Glen Canyon area, see *infra* notes 96, 99, 105-09 and accompanying text.

spirits. They claimed the inundation abridged their constitutional rights to religious free exercise by denying them access to these sacred sites.[31]

The *Badoni* district court rejected Navajo claims on grounds similar to those articulated by the *Sequoyah* district court—the plaintiffs had no property interest in the disputed holy lands.[32] Moreover, the district court found that, because the sites destroyed in *Badoni* had no deep religious significance to any organized group, the Indians were not entitled to first amendment protection.[33] Finally, the district court concluded that the nation's vital interest in the Colorado Water Storage Project heavily outweighed whatever interests the Indians might have had in continuing their traditional practices.[34] On appeal, the Tenth Circuit agreed that the government had a compelling need to maintain and increase the water level surrounding Rainbow Bridge. It therefore affirmed the lower court's decision without reaching the question whether Navajo free exercise rights were implicated.[35]

B.   *The Constitutional Context:* Wisconsin v. Yoder *and* Sherbert v. Verner

In *Wisconsin v. Yoder*[36] and *Sherbert v. Verner,*[37] the Supreme Court developed a method for evaluating free exercise claims. These cases illustrate circumstances in which free exercise relief will be granted. The *Sequoyah* and *Badoni* courts relied on these cases in deciding whether to protect Native American interests. *Sherbert* and *Yoder* are therefore important to a discussion of whether the *Sequoyah* and *Badoni* courts correctly analyzed Native American free exercise claims.

Yoder represents the Court's current approach to claims of religious abridgment. In *Yoder,* a group of Amish citizens sought exemption from prosecution under a Wisconsin statute that required school attendance until

---

[31] *Badoni,* 638 F.2d at 176. The plaintiffs also objected to the area's desecration by tourists who began visiting it after the creation of Lake Powell. *Id.*

[32] *Badoni,* 455 F. Supp. at 644. The court suggested that protection of Navajo interests in this case might lead to absurd consequences. It reasoned that if religious interests could entitle the Navajo to exercise dominion over Rainbow Bridge, someone claiming a profound religious attachment to the Lincoln Memorial could likewise enjoin its sacrilegious use. *Id.*

[33] *Id.* at 646. The court held that plaintiffs failed to show a history of consistent religious use of the Glen Canyon area. Deriving a standard from a description of religion it found in Wisconsin v. Yoder, 406 U.S. 205 (1972), the court concluded that access to the canyon was unimportant to Navajo religion. Ceremonial practices at sacred sites were found not to be intimately related to daily living among the Navajo. *Badoni,* 455 F. Supp. at 646; *see infra* Section III A (discussing whether the court's use of this "standard" was appropriate).

[34] *Badoni,* 455 F. Supp. at 646.

[35] *Badoni,* 638 F.2d at 177 & n.4.

[36] 406 U.S. 205 (1972).

[37] 374 U.S. 398 (1963).

the age of sixteen.[38] The Amish refused to send their children to school beyond the eighth grade because they believe integration into their religious community can only be accomplished through vocational training on the farm and in the home.[39] The Supreme Court exempted the Amish from prosecution under the statute because it found that mandatory high school attendance interfered with the defendants' ability to adhere to their fundamental religious tenets.[40] Wisconsin failed to show that its interest in educating Amish children justified this interference.[41]

Under *Yoder*'s analysis, a person claiming free exercise protection must first prove that the government has abridged important religious interests.[42] If this is established, the burden shifts to the government to show "there is a state interest of sufficient magnitude to override the interests claiming protection."[43] *Yoder* thus sets out a balancing test under which the Court weighs the severity of the religious abridgment against the importance of a state's competing policies.[44]

---

[38] WIS. STAT. § 118.15(1)(a)(1969); *Yoder*, 406 U.S. at 207.

[39] *Yoder*, 406 U.S. at 211. The Amish believe that ultimate salvation depends on the individual's assumption of a simple, agrarian lifestyle. This lifestyle is strictly ordered by religious belief, requiring existence in a community separate and aloof from the modern world. Vocational education is believed necessary to develop the skills required for life in the Amish community. During adolescence, children prepare to assume an adult role by fulfilling the requirements for adult baptism. They learn to enjoy physical labor, and to conform their daily conduct to the tenets of the Amish faith. *Id.* at 210-11. The Amish reject a secular high school education because it exposes children to the modern values of material success and competition which their faith discourages. *Id.*

[40] *Id.* at 219. The Court also noted that the future existence of the Amish community would be jeopardized if the Amish were prevented from effectively passing their beliefs and practices on to their children. *Id.* at 218.

[41] *Id.* at 234. The Court found that an eighth grade education plus a few years of Amish vocational training adequately protected Wisconsin's interests in promoting self-sufficiency and a responsible exercise of the voting franchise. *Id.*

[42] *Id.* at 214. The challenger has the burden of proving two things: 1) that he or she is asserting a protectible religious interest, and 2) that this interest has been abridged by government action. *Id.*

In deciding whether an interest is protectible under the first amendment, the Court has looked to a number of factors. These include whether the practice is religious, *see* Welsh v. United States, 398 U.S. 333, 340-43 (1970) (plurality opinion); United States v. Seeger, 380 U.S. 163, 184 (1965), whether it is important to the practitioner's scheme of religious belief, *see infra* notes 125-46 and accompanying text, and whether these beliefs are sincerely held by the religious observer, *see* United States v. Ballard, 322 U.S. 78, 84-85 (1944).

[43] *Yoder*, 406 U.S. at 214.

[44] *Id.*

Commentators suggest that a free exercise balancing process is problematic and easily manipulated because it contains no standards for quantifying the importance of individual religious needs or larger social policies. Even if these conflicting interests

Sherbert, decided almost ten years before *Yoder*, is crucial to free exercise analysis. It held that states may not impose substantial indirect burdens on religious practice unless a compelling state interest justifies the state's activity.[45] *Sherbert* involved a challenge by a Seventh Day Adventist to a South Carolina statute which denied the plaintiff unemployment benefits because she refused to accept available work.[46] Plaintiff's observance of a Saturday Sabbath caused her to be fired from her job and prevented her from accepting employment which required a six-day work week.[47] Plaintiff claimed that by withholding statutory benefits, South Carolina had unconstitutionally forced her to choose between observing the precepts of her religion and accepting benefits under the program.[48] Without deciding whether the state's interest was sufficiently important to support a religious infringement,[49] the Supreme Court agreed,[50] and required South Carolina to compensate the plaintiff because her unavailability for work was motivated by

---

could be quantified, they are qualitatively different and therefore difficult to compare. *See* Gianella, *Religious Liberty, Nonestablishment and Doctrinal Development*, 80 HARV. L. REV. 1381, 1384-86 (1967); Pepper, Reynolds, Yoder *and Beyond: Alternatives for the Free Exercise Clause*, 1981 UTAH L. REV. 341, 341-45; *accord* Clark, *Guidelines for the Free Exercise Clause*, 83 HARV. L. REV. 327, 329-30 (1969).

[45] *Sherbert*, 374 U.S. at 406. Unlike the plaintiff in *Sherbert*, most free exercise challengers have sought exemption from regulatory statutes which prohibit rather than inhibit religious practice, *see, e.g.*, Reynolds v. United States, 98 U.S. 145 (1878) (upholding statute prohibiting Mormons from practicing polygamy); People v. Woody, 61 Cal. 2d 716, 394 P.2d 813, 40 Cal. Rptr. 69 (1964) (exempting Native Americans from statute prohibiting the possession and use of peyote), or which require conduct offensive to the practitioner's religious ideology, *see, e.g.*, Jehovah's Witnesses v. King County Hosp., 390 U.S. 598 (1968) (per curiam) (requiring religiously objectionable blood transfusions to save a child's life); Jacobson v. Massachusetts, 197 U.S. 11 (1905) (upholding compulsory vaccination requirement over religious objections). *Yoder* illustrates this last type of challenge—the Amish sought relief from a statute requiring specific behavior. *See supra* notes 38-41 and accompanying text. *Sequoyah* and *Badoni* are similar to *Sherbert*, however, because the government prevented religious practice without directly prohibiting it. *See supra* notes 15-18, 25-31 and accompanying text.

[46] The South Carolina Unemployment Compensation Act, S.C. CODE ANN. §§ 41-35-110, 41-35-120 (Law. Co-op 1976), rendered claimants ineligible for unemployment benefits for a period of five weeks if they failed to apply for or accept suitable, available employment. *Sherbert*, 374 U.S. at 400 n.3.

[47] *Sherbert*, 374 U.S. at 399.

[48] *Id.* at 404.

[49] South Carolina's asserted interest in *Sherbert* was to protect its unemployment fund from fraudulent claims by insincere applicants. *Id.* at 407. This interest was not raised below, so the Court refused to decide whether it was sufficiently important to support a religious infringement. *Id.* The state had no other adequate justification for imposing a burden on plaintiff's religion.

[50] *Id.* at 406.

religious convictions.[51] The Court thus required the state either to confer direct benefits on the plaintiff or to abandon its unemployment benefits program altogether.[52] *Sherbert* thereby establishes that the first amendment sometimes requires the government to refrain from acting unless it affirmatively protects religious practices.[53]

In addition to holding that both direct and indirect religious burdens will be balanced against government interests, *Sherbert* and *Yoder* illustrate how the *Yoder* balancing test should be applied. Although both cases concede that the government may burden religious practices[54] to serve an important government interest, they also require courts to closely scrutinize government programs before permitting religious abridgments.[55] Moreover, the government, in proving the predominance of its interests, must do more than assert a general need to effectuate an important policy. It must show that an accommodation of religious practices would specifically harm its interests.[56]

---

[51] *Id.* at 409.

[52] *Id.* at 406.

[53] The Court reaffirmed *Sherbert's* prohibition of indirect religious infringements in Thomas v. Review Bd., Ind. Employment Sec. Div., 450 U.S. 707 (1981). In *Thomas,* Indiana denied unemployment benefits to a factory worker who had terminated his employment for religious reasons. Relying on *Yoder* and *Sherbert,* the Court held that the state's interests in protecting its unemployment program were insufficiently compelling to justify placing a burden on plaintiff's religious liberty. *Id.* at 718-19.

[54] *Yoder,* 406 U.S. at 218; *Sherbert,* 374 U.S. at 402-03.
The Court acknowledged a distinction between religious belief and religious practice that dates back to the nineteenth century. *See* Reynolds v. United States, 98 U.S. 145, 166 (1898). In Cantwell v. Connecticut, 310 U.S. 296 (1940), the Court restated this distinction, noting that the free exercise clause "embraces two concepts—freedom to believe and freedom to act. The first is absolute but, in the nature of things, the second cannot be." *Id.* at 303-04.

[55] *Yoder,* 406 U.S. at 221; *Sherbert,* 374 U.S. at 407-07. In *Yoder,* the Court manifested an intent to "searchingly examine" the gravity of the state's interest and the necessity of using religiously intrusive means for carrying it out. 406 U.S. at 221. This "close look" marked a retreat, however, from *Sherbert's* "strict scrutiny" approach. In *Sherbert,* the Court held that a state interest must be compelling to justify a religious infringement, 374 U.S. at 406; *Yoder* only requires the state interest to be more important than the religious interest claiming protection. *See Yoder,* 406 U.S. at 214. *But see* Thomas v. Review Bd., Ind. Employment Sec. Div., 450 U.S. 707, 718-19 (1981) (returning to *Sherbert's* definitional balancing approach).

[56] *See Yoder,* 406 U.S. at 221; *Sherbert,* 374 U.S. at 407. In *Yoder,* the Court found Wisconsin's admittedly strong interest in education insufficient to compel the Amish to send their children to high school. 406 U.S. at 236. It held that, because no one, not even the Amish children, would be harmed if the Amish were exempted from the statute, Wisconsin's showing of a general interest was not strong enough to overcome plaintiffs' religious claims. *Id.* at 230, 236.
In *Sherbert,* the Court noted that South Carolina's general interest in its unem-

Finally, *Sherbert* and *Yoder* demand that before the government may burden religious practice, it must prove that it could not have implemented its policy by adopting less religiously intrusive means. The Court stated in *Sherbert* that to justify its burdening of plaintiff's religion, South Carolina would be required "to demonstrate that no alternative forms of regulation would combat . . . abuses without infringing first amendment rights."[57] *Yoder* appears to have incorporated this requirement into its balancing process— the Court found that Wisconsin's interest in educating the Amish could be adequately met without interfering with fundamental Amish practices.[58]

III.   A Closer Look at Native American Theology: Were Protected Religious Interests Abridged in *Sequoyah* and *Badoni?*

Each of the trial and appellate courts in *Sequoyah* and *Badoni* purported to use the *Yoder* free exercise analysis in deciding whether to grant relief to

---

ployment fund would not have justified a religious infringement absent specific proof that fraudulent claims would substantially and unavoidably harm the program. 374 U.S. at 407.

[57] *Sherbert,* 374 U.S. at 407; *see* Thomas v. Review Bd., Ind. Employment Sec. Div., 450 U.S. 707, 718 (1981).

Pursuant to this "least restrictive alternative" test, the Court balances the cost in effectiveness of implementing an alternative regulation against the benefits to religion the alternative would afford. Where the alternative's benefit to religion outweighs its costs to the government, the Court will invalidate the existing regulation. *Cf.* Ely, *Flag Desecration: A Case Study in the Roles of Categorization and Balancing in First Amendment Analysis,* 88 HARV. L. REV. 1482, 1484-87 (1975) (discussing the Court's use of various forms of this test in the context of free speech). For free exercise cases applying this test, see *Sherbert,* 374 U.S. at 409 (indicating that a religious exemption would not have unduly burdened the statutory scheme); Braunfield v. Brown, 366 U.S. 599, 609 (1961) (holding that an exemption from regulation would produce insurmountable administrative difficulties).

[58] The Court did not explicitly apply the "least restrictive alternative" test in *Yoder* because Wisconsin had no important interest in forcing the Amish to attend school. 406 U.S. at 235; *see supra* note 41. Although the plaintiffs did not directly raise the issue of alternatives, the Court did note that the state might wish to reach a compromise with the Amish, whereby children would receive limited academic training from members of the Amish community. 406 U.S. at 208 n.3, 236 n.23. The Court appeared to prefer this alternative to the prospect of frustrating Amish religious practices. *Id.*

Even though the "least restrictive alternative" test was not essential to *Yoder's* holding, *Yoder's* balancing process requires courts to address the question of alternative regulations. If an important government goal can be achieved by less intrusive means, the importance of the state's interest in its restrictive regulation is reduced to the extent that the alternative's benefits to religion outweigh its marginal cost to the government. In cases where individual and state interests are close to each other in degrees of importance, this discounting of the government's interest could tip the scale in favor of protecting religion, thereby requiring the state to adopt the alternative measure. Courts might reach this same result where an alternative would produce great savings to religion with comparatively minor costs to the state.

the Native Americans. These courts disagreed, however, as to which aspect of this approach precluded protection of Native American interests.[59] Contradictions between the *Sequoyah* and *Badoni* opinions illustrate that the courts lack a coherent method for using *Yoder* to evaluate Native American claims to public lands. This Section demonstrates that each of these courts either ignored or misinterpreted the evidence the Cherokee and Navajo submitted. It then concludes that, under *Yoder*, the *Sequoyah* and *Badoni* courts should have balanced Native American interests against the government's competing policies.

A. *Do Native American Land Claims Qualify for First Amendment Protection?*

Litigants asserting free exercise claims must satisfy a number of criteria before courts will weigh their interests against the importance of government action. First, the Supreme Court has decided that the practice abridged must further a bona fide religious belief.[60] Second, this belief must be sincerely held by the individual asserting it.[61] Finally, the Court has required observance of the practice to be important to the claimant's religious ideology.[62]

---

[59] The district court in *Badoni* was the most emphatic in its denial of protection to Native American interests. It held that these interests were not of sufficient importance to be protected, that plaintiffs' lack of a property interest precluded a finding of religious abridgment, and that the government's interest outweighed plaintiffs' asserted needs. *Badoni,* 455 F. Supp. at 644-47. The Tenth Circuit affirmed, but based its decision solely on *Yoder's* balancing process, holding that the government's interest outweighed Navajo interests. *Badoni,* 638 F.2d at 177. The *Sequoyah* district court, after finding that Cherokee interests were religious, held that no abridgment resulted from the flooding. *Sequoyah,* 480 F. Supp. at 612. The Sixth Circuit, on the other hand, found an abridgment, but rejected Cherokee beliefs as lacking importance and as having a secular character. *Sequoyah,* 620 F.2d at 1164-65.

[60] Thomas v. Review Bd., Ind. Employment Sec. Div., 450 U.S. 707, 716 (1981) (function of reviewing court to determine whether litigant is expressing an honest religious conviction); *Yoder,* 406 U.S. at 215 (to receive protection under the religion clauses, a practice must be "rooted in religious belief").

[61] United States v. Ballard, 322 U.S. 78, 84-88 (1944) (Court held that jury may evaluate a religious claimant's sincerity but may not consider the truth of the claimant's religious beliefs).

[62] The requirement of showing importance or centrality may best be explained as a means for preventing the application of *Yoder's* troublesome balancing process to religious interests that may turn out to be trivial. *See supra* note 44. The Supreme Court has never explicitly adopted importance as a requirement for free exercise balancing, but it did stress the importance of Amish religious practices in *Yoder,* 406 U.S. at 216, and treated importance as a threshhold issue in *Sherbert,* 374 U.S. at 399 n.1. Several lower courts have also required a showing of importance. *See Sequoyah,* 620 F.2d at 1164; Teterud v. Gilman, 385 F. Supp. 153, 156-57 (S.D. Iowa), *aff'd sub nom.* Teterud v. Burns, 522 F.2d 357 (8th Cir. 1975); Frank v. Alaska, 604 P.2d 1068, 1072-73 (Alaska 1979); People v. Woody, 61 Cal. 2d 716, 720-22, 394 P.2d 813, 817-18, 40 Cal. Rptr. 69, 73-74 (1964); *infra* notes 131-35 and accompanying text.

The Sixth Circuit in *Sequoyah* and the *Badoni* district court rejected Cherokee and Navajo claims on the basis of these factors. This Section analyzes each of these requirements in detail and reconsiders Cherokee and Navajo claims in light of this analysis.

1. Religious Character of Indian Beliefs About Public Lands

The Sixth Circuit in *Sequoyah* and the *Badoni* district court found Native American practices at sacred sites to be insufficiently religious to warrant first amendment protection.[63] The Sixth Circuit found that Cherokee practices were essentially cultural,[64] while the *Badoni* district court found no "history of consistency" in Navajo use of sacred sites.[65] The courts thought that these findings precluded them from characterizing Cherokee and Navajo practices as religious. Neither Congress nor the Supreme Court has directly addressed the question of what practices are religious for first amendment purposes.[66] The Supreme Court has defined religion in a statutory context,[67] however, and Congress specifically considered the religious nature of Native American practices when it passed the American Indian Religious Freedom Act.[68] These definitions provide insight into the question of whether Navajo and Cherokee practices are "religious" within the meaning of the first amendment.

(a) *The American Indian Religious Freedom Act.* Congress passed the American Indian Religious Freedom Act[69] in an attempt to eradicate, within a limited sphere, its own past insensitivity to American Indian religious freedom.[70] The Act directs administrative agencies to examine their policies

---

[63] *Sequoyah,* 620 F.2d at 1164-65; *Badoni,* 455 F. Supp. at 646.

[64] *Sequoyah,* 620 F.2d at 1164.

[65] *Badoni,* 455 F. Supp. at 646.

[66] The Court's failure to define religion may be a deliberate attempt to avoid restricting the scope of the free exercise clause in a manner that would exclude unusual religious rituals. In Fowler v. Rhode Island, 345 U.S. 67, 69-70 (1953), the Court noted that apart from narrow exceptions, "it is no business of the courts to say that what is a religious practice or activity for one group is not a religion under the first amendment."

[67] *See infra* notes 78-83 and accompanying text.

[68] Pub. L. No. 95-341, 92 Stat. 469 (1978) (currently codified at 42 U.S.C. § 1996 (Supp. IV 1980)).

[69] *Id.*

[70] *See id.* Congress found that religious abridgments had resulted from its own failure to consider whether its actions would have an adverse impact on Native American religious practice. H.R. REP. NO. 1308, 95th CONG., 2d SESS. 1-2 (1978), *reprinted in* 1978 U.S. CODE CONG. & AD. NEWS 1262, 1263-64. It found that the absence of a clear federal policy protecting Native American religious practices, ignorance about Indian religious needs, and an inflexibility in government regulations had contributed to interference with Native American religious practices. *Id.*

and procedures[71] and to make changes necessary to avoid government interference with American Indian religious practice.[72] The Act does not confer a right of action on Native Americans,[73] and neither the *Sequoyah*

---

[71] *Id.* Pursuant to § 2, the President set up a Task Force which prepared a report documenting areas of conflict and procedural changes under contemplation. *See Federal Agencies Task Force,* AMERICAN INDIAN RELIGIOUS FREEDOM ACT REPORT (1979). The Task Force was composed of thirty government agencies that acknowledged that their activities might affect Native American free exercise. *Id.* The Assistant Secretary for Indian Affairs for the Department of the Interior directed this group, which included representatives from the Department of Energy, the National Forest Service, the National Park Service, the Tennessee Valley Authority, the Bureau of Land Management, the Department of the Navy, and the Interagency Archaeological Service. *Id.* After conducting internal agency evaluations and attending ten meetings with Native American religious leaders, members of the Task Force uncovered many regulations interfering with Native American access to sacred sites. *Id.* Problems concerning access were found to exist in twenty states; these problems affected over forty Native American tribes. *Id.*

[72] 42 U.S.C. § 1996. To fulfill this requirement, several agencies adopted procedural mechanisms for preventing future religious abridgments. For example, the National Forest Service, the Department of the Navy, the National Park Service, and the Bureau of Land Management set up continuing communications networks so that Indian religious interests could be fully considered before land use decisions were made. *See Federal Agencies Task Force,* AMERICAN INDIAN RELIGIOUS FREEDOM ACT REPORT (1979). The Tennessee Valley Authority and the Department of Energy agreed to address Native American religious needs in drawing up environmental impact statements. *Id.* The Department of the Navy, the National Park Service, and the Tennessee Valley Authority have relaxed access regulations for religious ceremonies where existing land uses are compatible with Native American religious exercise. *Id.* The Department of the Navy has made arrangements to accommodate Native American access to missile and bomb impact areas at China Lake, California and on a small island off the coast of Maui, Hawaii. *Id.*

[73] In Cannon v. University of Chicago, 441 U.S. 677, 688-89 n.9 (1979), the Court indicated that it would use four factors to determine whether Congress intended the courts to imply a right of action under a federal statute. These factors, which the Court first adopted in Cort v. Ash, 422 U.S. 66, 78 (1975), include (1) whether the statute was intended to benefit a particular class of plaintiffs, (2) whether the legislative history indicates an intent for a right of action to exist, (3) whether a right of action is consistent with the purpose of the legislative scheme, and (4) whether the area is one traditionally relegated to state law. *Cannon,* 441 U.S. at 688-89 n.9; *Cort,* 422 U.S. at 78; *see* HART & WECHSLER'S THE FEDERAL COURTS AND THE FEDERAL SYSTEM 192-94 (2d ed. Supp. 1981). Native Americans are obviously intended beneficiaries of the American Indian Religious Freedom Act. However, the legislative history does not disclose an intent to confer a right of action on individual Indians. In addition, the language of the Act indicates that violations of Native American religious rights were intended to be remedied through changes in administrative policies and procedures. *See* 42 U.S.C. § 1996. Because Congress intended the Act to provide administrative remedies, a private right of action by individuals appears to be beyond the scope of the Act and inconsistent with its purpose.

nor the *Badoni* courts used the Act to evaluate Cherokee and Navajo claims.[74] In identifying certain Native American practices as religious, however, the Act does provide courts with guidance for determining whether the free exercise clause protects Native American interests in public lands.

The American Indian Religious Freedom Act explicitly recognizes that Indians' "inherent right to . . . exercise [their] religion[ ]" includes the right of "access to sites."[75] The Act's legislative history notes that denial of access to sacred sites involves far more than a mere abridgment of cultural practices. Instead, Congress indicated that such a denial is "analogous to preventing a non-Indian from entering his church or temple."[76] The Act thus acknowledges that, although Native American practices are unconventional, they are religious and entitled to protection. This congressional finding suggests that courts should not be misled by the unconventionality of Native American practices in determining these practices' religious character.

(b) *Judicial Approaches to Defining Religion.* When Congress characterized Native American use of sacred sites as religious under the American Indian Religious Freedom Act, it acted in a manner consistent with the Supreme Court's practice of avoiding restrictive definitions of religion. The Court has never explicitly defined religion for constitutional purposes.[77] However, two cases which define religion in a statutory context—*United States v. Seeger*[78] and *Welsh v. United States*,[79]—support the conclusion that the unconventional nature of a given practice has little relevance to whether the practice is religious. Both cases involved a statute that granted draft exemptions to those who objected to war on "religious" grounds.[80] The statute, which focused on religious belief, defined this belief as "an individual's relation to a Supreme Being involving duties superior to those arising from any human relation."[81]

---

[74] *Sequoyah* and *Badoni* are the only cases in which the Act has been asserted as a basis for protecting Native American religion. In *Sequoyah,* the Act was rendered inapplicable by a provision of the Tellico authorizing amendment which approved the dam notwithstanding the provisions of any other law. *Sequoyah,* 620 F.2d at 1161. The Tenth Circuit refused to consider the Act in *Badoni* because it had not been passed in 1977 when proceedings in the trial court began. *Badoni,* 638 F.2d at 180.

[75] 42 U.S.C. § 1996.

[76] H.R. REP. NO. 1308, 95th CONG., 2d SESS. 2 (1978), *reprinted in* 1978 U.S. CODE CONG. & AD. NEWS 1262, 1263. The legislative history states that "there is no overriding reason to deny Indians the right to inter their dead in sanctified ground." *Id.* Congress was here referring to the fact that some Indians have been denied access to lands put under federal supervision *because* they are Indian cemeteries. *Id.*

[77] *See supra* note 66.

[78] 380 U.S. 163 (1965).

[79] 398 U.S. 333 (1970) (plurality opinion).

[80] Universal Military Training and Selective Service Act, § 456(j) (1951) (codified at 50 U.S.C. App. § 456(j) (1976)).

[81] *Id.; Seeger,* 380 U.S. at 165.

In *Seeger*, the Court indicated that this language did not require belief in an orthodox god. The Court held that Congress intended belief in a Supreme Being to include any belief that "occup[ied] the same place in the life of the objector as an orthodox belief in God holds in the life of one clearly qualified for exemption."[82] In *Welsh*, the Court extended its definition of "religious . . . belief" to include all beliefs that the applicant characterized as religious, provided he held them with the strength of traditional religious convictions.[83] *Welsh* eliminated the requirement of belief in God from the Court's interpretation of religious belief under the statute. *Welsh* and *Seeger* therefore made the strength and fundamentality of a belief, not its conventionality, determinative of its religious character.

The Court stated in *Seeger* that it was not defining religion for constitutional purposes.[84] However, the Court has adopted a deferential approach to characterizing beliefs and practices under the first amendment which is consistent with the Court's statutory construction of religion in *Welsh* and *Seeger*.[85] Historically, the Court has acknowledged the religious nature of many unusual creeds,[86] and has scrupulously avoided imposing ideological

---

[82] 380 U.S. at 184. This language has been called a "functional" test for religion. *See* Note, *Toward a Constitutional Definition of Religion*, 91 HARV. L. REV. 1056, 1066-67, 1072-75 (1978). To clarify this standard, the Court quoted extensively from the works of Dr. Paul Tillich, a Protestant theologian who identifies god as what the individual "take[s] seriously without reservation." 380 U.S. at 187.

[83] 398 U.S. at 342-43. The plurality included moral convictions in its construction of "religious training and belief," thereby reversing its exclusion of these beliefs in *Seeger*. *Id.* These beliefs would qualify an applicant for exemption, regardless of whether they addressed themselves to a notion of God, if they were not essentially matters of policy, pragmatism, or expediency. *Id.*

[84] 380 U.S. at 174.

[85] *See supra* note 66; *infra* notes 86-88 and accompanying text. In addition, several lower courts have used *Welsh* and *Seeger* to characterize beliefs as religious for first amendment purposes. *See, e.g.*, Founding Church of Scientology v. United States, 409 F.2d 1146, 1162 (D.C. Cir. 1969) (holding that the Science of Dianetics is a religion under the free exercise clause), *cert. denied*, 396 U.S. 963 (1969); Malnak v. Yogi, 440 F. Supp. 1284, 1313-14 (D.N.J. 1977) (court found transcendental meditation to be a religion under the establishment clause), *aff'd*, 592 F.2d 197 (3d Cir. 1977).

[86] *See, e.g.*, Heffron v. International Soc'y for Krishna Consciousness, 452 U.S. 640, 647 (1981) (Court found proselytization requirement of Krishna sect religious); *Yoder*, 406 U.S. at 216 (Court found Amish educational practices to be religious); United States v. Ballard, 322 U.S. 78, 87-88 (1944) (Court suggested that, if sincerely held, beliefs of members of "I AM" movement would be protected even though they seem "preposterous"); Reynolds v. United States, 98 U.S. 145, 161 (1878) (Court acknowledged religious character of Mormon beliefs about polygamy).

The lower courts have also refused to make conventionality the test for free exercise protection. For example, courts have granted religious exemptions from property taxes and federal regulatory legislation to groups that do not profess devo-

requirements as a prerequisite to first amendment protection.[87] Under the free exercise clause, the Court has focused on whether a practitioner describes a belief or practice as fulfilling a religious function.[88] The Court's constitutional approach to characterizing beliefs and practices thus parallels the approach to religion it adopted in interpreting the Selective Service Statute.

The Court's deferential approach to defining religion has provided the lower courts with little guidance for determining which beliefs and practices are religious for free exercise purposes. As a result, the lower courts have considered a range of factors in deciding whether to protect religious practice. They have considered, for example, whether the belief underlying a practice serves a religious purpose for the individual.[89] Whether the belief is expressed through a structure of open practice by members of an organized cult has also been important in distinguishing theology from personal, pragmatic, or political preferences.[90]

(c) *Religious Character of Cherokee and Navajo Beliefs About Public Lands.* Courts have gone to great lengths to define religion in a manner that

---

tion to any deity. *See, e.g.,* Founding Church of Scientology v. United States, 409 F.2d 1146, 1146 (D.C. Cir. 1969), *cert. denied,* 396 U.S. 963 (1969); Washington Ethical Soc'y v. District of Columbia, 249 F.2d 127, 128-29 (D.C. Cir. 1957); Fellowship of Humanity v. County of Alameda, 153 Cal. App. 2d 673, 698, 315 P.2d 394, 409-10 (1957). Thus, nontheistic beliefs appear to be religious under the Constitution as well as under the Selective Service Statute. *See supra* note 82 and accompanying text.

[87] *See* Thomas v. Review Bd., Ind. Employment Sec. Div., 450 U.S. 707, 714 (1981) ("[R]eligious beliefs need not be acceptable, logical, consistent or comprehensible to others to merit First Amendment protection."); Ballard v. United States, 322 U.S. 78, 87 (1974) (The Constitution gave man the right "to answer to no man for the verity of his religious views."); *supra* note 66.

[88] Thomas v. Review Bd., Ind. Employment Sec. Div., 450 U.S. 707, 715-16 (1981) (individual characterization controls even where church members disagree about content of religious doctrine); *see supra* notes 86-87 and accompanying text.

[89] Founding Church of Scientology v. United States, 409 F.2d 1146, 1146 (D.C. Cir. 1969) (religion described as a theory of "man's nature or his place in the Universe," analogous to beliefs held by recognized religions), *cert. denied,* 396 U.S. 963 (1969); Washington Ethical Soc'y v. District of Columbia, 249 F.2d 127, 129 (D.C. Cir. 1957) (Religion includes "devotion to some principle; strict fidelity or faithfulness; conscientiousness, pious affecting or attachment."); Fellowship of Humanity v. County of Alameda, 153 Cal. App. 2d 673, 693, 315 P.2d 394, 406 (1957) (Religion is belief that "fills a void that exists in the lives of most men.").

[90] Washington Ethical Soc'y v. District of Columbia, 249 F.2d 127, 128 (D.C. Cir. 1957) (regularity of organized services relevant to a finding of religion); Fellowship of Humanity v. County of Alameda, 153 Cal. App. 2d 673, 693, 315 P.2d 394, 406 (1957) ("Religion simply includes: (1) a belief, not necessarily referring to supernatural powers; (2) a cult, involving a gregarious association openly expressing belief; (3) a system of moral practice directly resulting from an adherence to the belief; and (4) an organization within the cult designed to observe the tenets of the belief.").

encompasses almost every ideology having an arguable relation to an individual's fundamental beliefs. They have acknowledged that beliefs about a Supreme Being are religious,[91] and have extended this definition to other beliefs which the individual characterizes as fundamental.[92] In determining the religious character of Native American practices, courts should be guided by the flexible definition of religion required by the free exercise clause. However, in evaluating Native American practices, courts should also consider whether these practices and their underlying beliefs meet the criteria the courts have found relevant to a religious characterization.

Although it appears that spiritual practice need not be organized for courts to characterize this practice as religious,[93] some courts have considered a group's organization in deciding whether to afford it constitutional protection.[94] For example, the *Badoni* district court rejected Navajo claims in part because it found Navajo practices insufficiently organized under the first amendment.[95] To determine whether organizational requirements should present an obstacle to the protection of Native American spiritual practice, it is useful to examine the general organization of Native American tribes.

---

[91] None of the statutory or constitutional cases question that beliefs in God are religious. In fact, courts often compare unconventional beliefs to theistic beliefs in determining their religious character. *See* Founding Church of Scientology v. United States, 409 F.2d 1146, 1160 (D.C. Cir. 1969), *cert. denied,* 396 U.S. 963 (1969); Malnak v. Yogi, 440 F. Supp. 1284, 1322 (D.N.J. 1977) (court compared "creative intelligence" with Christian, Buddhist, and Hindu concepts of God), *aff'd,* 592 F.2d 197 (3d Cir. 1977); *supra* note 82 and accompanying text.

[92] *See supra* notes 77-90 and accompanying text.

[93] At least one court has excluded organization from the factors it will consider in determining whether a practice is religious. *See Sequoyah,* 620 F.2d at 1163 ("[T]here is no requirement that a religion meet any organizational or doctrinal test in order to qualify for first amendment protection."). In addition, *Welsh* and *Seeger* indicate that even idiosyncratic beliefs and practices can be religious if an individual adheres to them with sufficient fervor. *See supra* notes 82-83 and accompanying text.

[94] Courts often consider a group's organization to be a useful factor when the practices asserted are unconventional, *see, e.g., Yoder,* 406 U.S. at 216 (Court noted that Amish beliefs were "shared by an organized group" in concluding that beliefs were religious); Washington Ethical Soc'y v. District of Columbia, 249 F.2d 127, 128 (D.C. Cir 1957) (court referred to organization in evaluating nature of nontheistic practice); *cf.* Fellowship of Humanity v. County of Alameda, 153 Cal. App. 2d 673, 693, 315 P.2d 394, 406 (1957) (court included organization in its definition of religion). A finding of organization helps courts compare an asserted practice with practices adhered to by recognized religious groups. *Washington Ethical Soc'y,* 249 F.2d at 128; *Fellowship of Humanity,* 153 Cal. App. 2d at 689-93, 315 P.2d at 403-06. Organization is therefore relevant to a discussion of religion but is not a necessary element of a religious characterization.

[95] *Badoni,* 455 F. Supp. at 646 (court rejected Navajo claims because it found plaintiffs had failed to establish that well-attended ceremonies were frequently conducted in Glen Canyon).

Native American religion differs from the conventional concept of "organized religion" because tribes often do not congregate at specified times to participate in organized services.[96] Nevertheless, anthropologists have demonstrated that a high degree of internal cohesiveness exists within many Native American spiritual communities.[97] Studies indicate that Native American spiritual traditions are held in common by members of organized tribes.[98] Hierarchical religious structures exist in many tribes,[99] and many

---

[96] Navajo religious leaders, for example, conduct ceremonies only as the need arises. Often, only those individuals who are soliciting protection from the gods attend these ceremonies. *See* K. LUCKERT, *supra* note 30, at 89-91.

[97] *See generally* H. DRIVER, INDIANS OF NORTH AMERICA (1962); K. LUCKERT, NAVAJO MOUNTAIN AND RAINBOW BRIDGE RELIGION (1977); W. POWERS, OGLALA RELIGION (1975); J. SWANTON, INDIANS OF THE SOUTHEASTERN UNITED STATES (1946); R. UNDERHILL, PAPAGO INDIAN RELIGION (1946); R. UNDERHILL, RED MAN'S RELIGION (1965).

[98] *See supra* note 97.

The federal government has recognized the organization of many Native American tribes; only those tribes that are sufficiently organized to implement a constitutional government are certified under federal statute. *See* 25 U.S.C. §§ 476-477 (1976). Certification, which is similar to incorporation, enables the tribe to act as an independent legal entity. Most tribes apply for certification to obtain desirable rights and powers.

By granting class status to the Cherokee as a tribe, and conferring standing to sue on three Chapters of the Navajo Nation, the *Sequoyah* and *Badoni* courts also recognized a congruence between Native American tribal and spiritual communities. A class may be certified only when "the class is so numerous that joinder of all members is impracticable," and "where there are questions of law or fact common to the class." FED. R. CIV. P. 23(a). In allowing a collective cause of action, the courts must have found a commonality of interest among the members of two organized tribes sufficient to allow these groups to assert a free exercise claim.

Examination of the *Sequoyah* affidavits, *see supra* note 16, indicates, moreover, that many members of the Cherokee tribe hold similar beliefs concerning the significance of sites in the Little Tennessee Valley. *Compare* Affidavit of Myrtle Driver (Oct. 10, 1979) (discussing legend of the Beaded Belt and various prophesies about technological advancements of white culture) *with* Affidavit of Goliath George, at 2 (Oct. 10, 1979) (describing technological prophesies) *and* Affidavit of Lloyd Sequoyah, at 2-3 (Oct. 1979) (recounting legend of Beaded Belt); *compare* Affidavit of Ela Jackson, at 1 (Oct. 11, 1979) (discussing sacred burial grounds) *and* Affidavit of Bailey Coleman, at 1-2 (Oct. 9, 1979) (discussing significance of Cherokee graves) *and* Affidavit of Robin Toineeta, at 2 (Oct. 9, 1979) (discussing Cherokee graveyards) *with* Affidavit of Iva Rattler, at 1 (Oct. 11, 1979) (containing description of Cherokee beliefs about gravesites) *and* Affidavit of Ammoneta Sequoyah, at 2 (Oct. 11, 1979) (discussing beliefs about graves). This similarity documents the existence of a complex pattern of belief peculiar to the Cherokee.

[99] For example, in some tribes religious leaders are individuals who possess a more detailed knowledge of spiritual doctrine than other members of the tribe. *See, e.g.,* Affidavit of Professor Albert L. Warhaftig, at 2 (Oct. 8, 1979) (indicating that

Native Americans maintain their beliefs and practices over time through use of an oral tradition.[100] These aspects of tribal existence, in addition to substantial evidence of organization on the records of *Sequoyah* and *Badoni*,[101] should have satisfied the courts as to the organized nature of Cherokee and Navajo spiritual life.

The Supreme Court has held that to be religious, a practice must be "rooted in religious belief."[102] Thus, courts have considered whether a practice is related to religious belief in deciding whether the practice deserves free exercise protection.[103] Anthropologists have described consistently the ways in which Indian tribes translate their beliefs into spiritual practice.[104] Moreover, the records in *Sequoyah* and *Badoni* contained evidence of a strong link between the beliefs the Cherokee and Navajo hold and the rituals these groups perform.

The Navajo believe that many of their gods inhabit natural objects in the

---

Cherokee religious leadership is determined by the extent of the individual's religious knowledge).

The knowledge necessary to become a religious leader is passed down through the family or the community in some tribes. *See* K. LUCKERT, *supra* note 30, at 87-89, 93. It is revealed to the potential leader in trances or visions in other tribes. *See* W. POWERS, *supra* note 97, at 59-63; R. UNDERHILL, RED MAN'S RELIGION, *supra* note 97, at 82-85.

[100] *See infra* note 115 and accompanying text.

[101] *See supra* notes 96, 98-99.

[102] *Yoder*, 406 U.S. at 215.

[103] *See id.; cf.* Fellowship of Humanity v. County of Alameda, 153 Cal. App. 2d 673, 693, 315 P.2d 394, 406 (1957) (Religion involves a "system of moral practice directly resulting from an adherence to the belief.").

[104] Although practices differ widely from tribe to tribe, many tribes throughout the country conduct ceremonies which, in the aggregate, govern almost every aspect of tribal existence. Generally, these ceremonies are designed to procure assistance and protection from supernatural entities believed capable of influencing daily life. Complex ceremonies exist for healing the sick, H. DRIVER, *supra* note 97, at 399, 411-12; W. POWERS, *supra* note 97, at 147-54; J. SWANTON, *supra* note 97, at 782, safety on a voyage, W. POWERS, *supra* note 97, at 146, luck in confrontation with authority, K. LUCKERT, *supra* note 30, at 81-83, bringing of rain, H. DRIVER, *supra* note 97, at 102; R. UNDERHILL, PAPAGO INDIAN RELIGION, *supra* note 97, at 41-67; *infra* note 108 and accompanying text, purification preparatory to hunting, H. DRIVER, *supra* note 97, at 44; R. UNDERHILL, PAPAGO INDIAN RELIGION, *supra* note 97, at 85-115; R. UNDERHILL, RED MAN'S RELIGION, *supra* note 97, at 117-26, interment of the dead, H. DRIVER, *supra* note 97, at 409; R. UNDERHILL, RED MAN'S RELIGION, *supra* note 97, at 62-72, fertility, H. DRIVER, *supra* note 97, at 427, safety during pregnancy, K. LUCKERT, *supra* note 30, at 82, success in agriculture, H. DRIVER, *supra* note 97, at 102; R. UNDERHILL, PAPAGO INDIAN RELIGION, *supra* note 97, at 69-84, and for maintaining the social fabric of the community, particularly insofar as this helps to instill traditional values in Native American youth, K. LUCKERT, *supra* note 30, at 55.

Glen Canyon area.[105] Ceremonies are directed to these objects to elicit divine assistance.[106] For example, Rainbow Bridge is a spirit which brings rain and protects the Navajo from tangible and spiritual danger.[107] The Navajo are an agricultural people who depend on steady rainfall for prosperity. Before the flooding, whenever the tribe experienced inadequate rainfall, songs, gifts, and ceremonies were offered at the foot of Rainbow Bridge or otherwise given to the tangible forms of canyon spirits.[108] Ceremonies directed to other gods are still conducted, to bring health, financial success, and luck in confrontation with the United States government.[109]

---

[105] This belief may result from the fact that several of the canyon's rock formations resemble human beings with Native American facial characteristics. *See* K. LUCKERT, *supra* note 30, at 13, 14, 17 (photos). The Navajo believe that Holy People, Navajo gods, began to inhabit natural phenomena when these gods retreated into the canyon after they had previously been living harmoniously with humans. *Id.* at 11-12. Navajo Rock People carved themselves into the canyon walls, while other Navajo gods transfigured themselves into a variety of natural phenomena. Water People include Springs, Rivers, Serpents and Rainbows; these gods collaborate in bringing rain. Navajo Mountain, located near Rainbow Bridge and called Head of Earth by the Navajo, is considered the crown of the earth god. It is also the dwelling place of Monster-Slayer and his sister, Born-for-Water, two gods who played an important role in rescuing original settlers from the onslaught of the U.S. Cavalry. *Id.* at 30-37, 56.

[106] Because Talking Rock can speak to humans, *see supra* note 30, he is responsible for telling the Navajo when ceremonies should be performed. K. LUCKERT, *supra* note 30, at 95. These revelations occur in dreams, and offerings must be given to Talking Rock to ensure his continued vigilance on behalf of the Navajo community. *Id.* at 95, 125.

[107] K. LUCKERT, *supra* note 30, at 30. Rainbow Bridge is believed to contain two Rainbow People, one male and one female. These gods turned themselves into stone after helping two Navajo children cross the canyon from the land of the gods back to the land of the humans. *Id.* at 46, 112, 120.

[108] One way the Navajo requested rain was by taking water from a sacred spring in the canyon floor and ceremonially depositing it in another spring located on the top of Head of Earth, thereby inspiring divine precipitory collaboration. *Id.* at 144-45. Another rain ceremony is carried out at the junction of the Colorado and San Juan Rivers, where these male and female tributaries unite and give birth to rain-giving clouds and spirits. *Id.* at 44-45.

The effectiveness of these ceremonies has been sharply curtailed by government action. The erection of a radio tower on Head of Earth has interfered with the spiritual cycle between the two springs. *Id.* at 70-71, 107. The flooding of the area has hidden the juncture of the two rivers, preventing the Navajo from leaving offerings there. *Id.* at 45.

[109] Monster-Slayer and Born-for-Water, *see supra* note 105, were born and raised to maturity in one day. They are therefore appealed to when relief from a calamity must come within a twenty-four hour period, such as when an individual needs emergency medical treatment. *Id.* at 81-83. "Protectionway" ceremonies are offered to Navajo gods when the tribe needs help in sparing the life of a person with a

In contrast to Navajo ideology, Cherokee beliefs about natural phenomena only marginally involve the deification of natural objects in the Little Tennessee Valley.[110] The Cherokee are basically monotheistic; they believe one spirit, the U ne tla nv hi, controls the destiny of the Cherokee people.[111] The religious significance of the Little Tennessee Valley inheres in the Cherokee belief that the valley is the birthplace of the Cherokee Nation, its religion, culture, and tradition.[112] The Cherokee practice their religion, in part, by worshipping the valley itself; they believe that prayer to and at sacred sites facilitates direct communication with the supernatural world.[113]

---

terminal illness, in ensuring the safety of Navajo criminal defendants facing confrontations with the courts or police, in protecting someone from exposure to evil ghosts and witches, in curing the flu, and in preventing harm to Navajo who have been drafted into the armed forces. *Id.* at 81-83, 105.

[110] The Little Tennessee River is the only phenomena in the valley that was documented in *Sequoyah* as containing a spiritual entity. The Cherokee believe the river is a living being which constitutes "the road to the inexhaustible renewal of the underworld." Letter from Professor Charles Hudson to Ben Bridgers, at 2 (Oct. 8, 1979). They considered the river to be a source of fertility and longevity, *id.*, and often performed purification rituals in it before the federal government built the Tellico Dam. Affidavit of Dr. Duane King, at 7-8 (Oct. 10, 1979).

[111] *See* Affidavit of Emmaline Driver, at 1 (Oct. 10, 1979) (indicating that U ne tla nv hi can provide the Cherokee people with spiritual strength); Affidavit of Myrtle Driver, at 1 (Oct. 10, 1979) (the U ne tla nv hi watches over the Cherokee and provides for their livelihood); Affidavit of Goliath George, at 1-3 (Oct. 8, 1979) (indicating that the U ne tla nv hi is an omniscient being who created heaven and earth).

[112] The Little Tennessee Valley contains the sites of several ancient Cherokee cities. Affidavit of Mary G. Ross, at 1 (Oct. 7, 1979). Chota is one of these cities, *id.*; it is considered the religious homeland of the Cherokee people and is analogous to a Cherokee Jerusalem. *See* Affidavit of Richard Crowe, at 1-2 (Oct. 10, 1979); Affidavit of Emmaline Driver, at 1-2 (Oct. 10, 1979); Affidavit of Lloyd Sequoyah, at 1-3 (Oct. 1979). Before construction of the Tellico Dam flooded the area, many Cherokee made pilgrimages to the valley to worship and receive spiritual strength. *See* Affidavit of Emmaline Driver, at 1-2 (Oct. 10, 1979); Affidavit of Robert Blankenship, at 1 (Oct. 9, 1979); Affidavit of John A. Crowe, at 1 (Oct. 8, 1979). In addition, Cherokee prophecies and myths of creation are closely related to specific sites in the Little Tennessee Valley. *See, e.g.,* Affidavit of Goliath George, at 1 (Oct. 8, 1979); Affidavit of Dr. Duane King, at 2-6 (Oct. 10, 1979); Affidavit of Dr. Albert L. Warhaftig, at 2-3 (Oct. 8, 1979).

[113] *See* Affidavit of Roy D. French, at 1 (Oct. 11, 1979) (containing statement by affiant that he can almost hear his forefathers talking to him when he visits Tellico); Affidavit of Ammoneta Sequoyah, at 2 (Oct. 11, 1979) (stating that survival of tribe's knowledge of medicine depends on preservation of Little Tennessee Valley); Affidavit of Robert Blankenship, at 1 (Oct. 9, 1979) (stating that Chota and Little Tennessee River are the only two tangible objects left which the Cherokee worship); Affidavit of Richard Crowe, at 1-2 (Oct. 7, 1979) (indicating that Chota is the connection between the Cherokee people and the Great Spirit).

In addition, to help preserve their religious beliefs, the Cherokee often make pilgrimages to sacred sites where they believe important events occurred.[114] During their pilgrimages, the Cherokee recount the legends associated with these events, thereby refreshing their memories concerning religious doctrine.[115]

Anthropological evidence thus suggests that members of the Cherokee and Navajo tribes engage in practices inspired by beliefs they consider religious. However, spiritual practice alone may be insufficient to support free exercise protection of the beliefs underlying these practices.[116] To receive protection under the first amendment, Native Americans must prove that the beliefs which generate spiritual practice are similar to beliefs which non-Indians hold concerning a god or an ultimate concern.[117]

For the Cherokee and Navajo Indians religious beliefs about natural objects fill the same role as a conventional belief in God. For the Navajo, natural objects are gods, and beliefs about these objects are beliefs in their divine powers.[118] Cherokee beliefs about sites in the Little Tennessee Valley are also related to notions of theism; the Cherokee believe that communication with the Great Spirit is accomplished by worship at sacred places.[119] Although Native American beliefs are viewed as unconventional in the United States, the courts have held that conventionality is not the test for religion under the first amendment.[120] Given the wide range of activities over

---

[114] The tribe believes that many events of spiritual significance occurred at Chota before the Cherokee were removed to Oklahoma in the 19th century. *See* Affidavit of Emmaline Driver, at 1 (Oct. 10, 1979) (at a site in the valley, prophet revealed how the U ne tla nv hi wanted the Cherokee to live and worship); Affidavit of Dr. Duane King, at 2-4 (Oct. 10, 1979) (stating that several sacred explanations of the world's origin relate specifically to Little Tennessee Valley).

[115] One anthropologist has indicated that "to understand or maintain Cherokee religion without access to [sacred] sites . . . would be like attempting to understand or practice Judaism or Christianity without the Book of Genesis." Affidavit of Professor Albert L. Warhaftig, at 4 (Oct. 8, 1979). Visiting Chota is analogous to reading a Christian bible because these visits document and maintain the content of Cherokee religious tradition. Affidavit of Professor Albert L. Warhaftig, at 3-4 (Oct. 8, 1979). Cherokee religious beliefs are not reduced to writing; they are transmitted orally between generations of tribal members. *Id.* at 3. Thus, the perpetuation of Cherokee religious doctrine depends on the practice of communicating religious beliefs during pilgrimages to the Little Tennessee Valley.

[116] *See supra* notes 87-90 and accompanying text.

[117] *See supra* notes 78-88 and accompanying text.

[118] *See supra* notes 105-09 and accompanying text.

[119] *See supra* notes 110-115 and accompanying text.

[120] *Sequoyah,* 620 F.2d at 1163 ("Orthodoxy is not an issue."); Washington Ethical Soc'y v. District of Columbia, 249 F.2d 127, 129 (D.C. Cir. 1957) ("To construe exemptions so strictly that unorthodox or minority forms of worship would be denied the exemption benefits granted to those conforming to the majority beliefs might well raise constitutional issues.").

which Native American gods exercise control, beliefs associated with these gods are beliefs about a power or being to which all else is subordinate and upon which all else ultimately depends.[121] Thus, Cherokee and Navajo beliefs about sacred sites, and the land-related practices arising pursuant to these beliefs, appear to be religious under the free exercise clause.

2. Sincerity and Centrality

In addition to requiring that beliefs be religious to be protected under the first amendment, the Court has required a showing of the sincerity and importance of these beliefs as part of the challenger's burden of proof. Although the sincerity of Cherokee and Navajo beliefs went uncontested in *Sequoyah*[122] and *Badoni*,[123] the Court of Appeals in *Sequoyah* and the

---

[121] *See Seeger*, 380 U.S. at 174; *supra* notes 82-83 and accompanying text.

Native Americans believe that the survival of their communities is threatened by disruptions of religious worship. K. LUCKERT, *supra* note 30, at 148 (statement of Lamar Bedonie); *see* Means, *supra* note 5, at 22-38. The Cherokee believe, for example, that their god, the U ne tla nv hi, will punish the Cherokee people if they allow the white man to destroy sacred sites or desecrate sacred burial grounds. Affidavit of Dr. Duane King, at 7 (Oct. 10, 1979) (destruction of the valley is a violation of religious concept; those who permit it to happen will suffer for their acts). Cherokee religious leaders have historically prophesied that the Cherokee Nation will be all but destroyed through the encroachments of white America. Affidavit of Dr. Duane King, at 5 (Oct. 10, 1979) (religious leader prophesied that Cherokee will remain viable as an ethnic group only as long as waters of valley are allowed to run downhill). They view this eventual demise of the Cherokee people as a form of divine retribution against religiously disloyal Cherokee. Affidavit of Professor Albert L. Warhaftig, at 2 (Oct. 8, 1979) (prophesies state that "as a result of their failing to have kept sacred laws established for them in the time of Creation, [the Cherokee] will be reduced as a people . . . their riches will be lost or stolen, and, in general, all that they hold precious will be taken"). Thus, many Cherokee believe that the flooding is both a punishment for past religious digressions and a means for testing the religious loyalty of the Cherokee people.

[122] *Sequoyah*, 620 F.2d at 1163 ("The sincerity of the adherence of individual plaintiffs to [their] religion is not questioned."); *Sequoyah*, 480 F. Supp. at 612 (because the court found no free exercise claim stated in the complaint, it did not need to consider the sincerity of plaintiffs' beliefs).

[123] *Badoni*, 638 F.2d at 176-77; *Badoni*, 455 F. Supp. at 645. The Tenth Circuit did not address the sincerity of plaintiffs' beliefs because it found these beliefs would be outweighed even if they did qualify for protection. In so doing, the court reversed the order in which religious and government interests are usually evaluated. Although the district court acknowledged plaintiffs' sincerity, in dicta it found that the Navajo had failed to demonstrate a history of consistent ceremonial use of the Glen Canyon area. The court thought this lack of consistency undermined plaintiffs' contention of sincerity.

The trial court's findings concerning the consistency of Navajo practice not only contradicted its own acceptance of plaintiffs' sincerity, but also ignored a substantial

district court in *Badoni* rejected Native Americans' access to public lands as an inessential element of effective religious practice.[124] An analysis of "centrality"[125] indicates, however, that these courts misapplied this requirement. Courts have placed the burden of proving the centrality of a religious practice on the party who asserts that the interest should be protected.[126] To receive first amendment relief, challengers must prove that government action has interfered with fundamental practices of their religious creeds.[127]

Beyond holding that practices required by "fundamental tenets"[128] and "cardinal principles"[129] qualify for constitutional protection, the Supreme Court has not explained what makes a practice central for free exercise

---

amount of evidence on the record in *Badoni*. Navajo ceremonies have been conducted near Rainbow Bridge for over one hundred years. *See* K. LUCKERT, *supra* note 30, at 5, 9. Ceremonies are not carried out regularly because they are performed only as needed by members of the Navajo community. *Id.* at 89-91. The federal government's inconsistent use of sacred sites may be partially responsible for the infrequency of some ceremonies. *See supra* note 108.

[124] *Sequoyah*, 620 F.2d at 1164 (The court found the "centrality of the valley to the practice of traditional Cherokee religion . . . missing from this case."); *Badoni*, 455 F. Supp. at 645-46 (plaintiffs had not demonstrated that religious belief and daily conduct were "inseparable and interdependent").

[125] The courts phrase this requirement differently—some focus on the importance of a religious practice, some on its centrality, and some use another formulation of this requirement. *See infra* notes 126-35 and accompanying text.

[126] *See Yoder*, 406 U.S. at 215 (appellants showed that their practices were essential to the survival of their religious creed); *Sherbert*, 374 U.S. at 399 n.1 (there was no question that the statute violated a basic tenet of appellant's religious creed); *Sequoyah*, 620 F.2d at 1164 (plaintiffs failed to prove centrality of worship at ancestral graves); Teterud v. Gilman, 385 F. Supp. 153, 157 (S.D. Iowa 1974) (Native American plaintiff proved wearing hair in braids was central to his religion), *aff'd sub nom.* Teterud v. Burns, 522 F.2d 357 (8th Cir. 1975); Frank v. Alaska, 604 P.2d 1068, 1072 (Alaska 1979) (appellants successfully proved use of moose meat in funeral potlatch was deeply rooted in religious belief); People v. Woody, 61 Cal. 2d 716, 720, 394 P.2d 813, 817, 40 Cal. Rptr. 69, 73 (1964) (appellants proved use of peyote "plays a central role in the ceremony and practice of the Native American Church").

[127] The Court has never articulated the policies underlying the centrality requirement. One might conclude, however, that this aspect of the free exercise clause is grounded in efficiency interests and interests in protecting government policies from ill-advised invalidation. Under the *Yoder* balancing test, it appears that few government programs will be outweighed by a religious practice considered unimportant by the people who engage in it. A centrality requirement avoids time-consuming balancing of legislative policies against religious practices which may turn out to be insubstantial. In addition, placing the burden of proof on the claimant insulates a challenged statute from an unnecessary application of *Yoder*'s ambiguous balancing process.

[128] *Yoder*, 406 U.S. at 218 (suggesting that Amish practices are fundamental because their abridgment carried a "very real threat of undermining the Amish community and religious practice as they exist today").

[129] *Sherbert*, 374 U.S. at 406.

purposes.[130] Other courts have discussed this requirement in more detail, however, in evaluating Native American religious interests.[131] In *Teterud v. Gilman*,[132] a federal district court held that the Indian practice of wearing hair in braids was central because "the wearing of traditional hairstyles [is] an important aspect of the spiritual life of Indians, and a fundamental spiritual custom."[133] Other courts have held that a practice is central if it is the cornerstone of religious observance,[134] or if its prohibition "results in a virtual inhibition of the practice of claimant's religion."[135] These cases illustrate a range of interpretations of centrality with respect to Native American free exercise claims.

Given the substantial anthropological evidence submitted in *Sequoyah* and *Badoni*,[136] it is surprising that two of these courts refused to find plaintiffs' interests in public lands central to Cherokee and Navajo ideology.[137] To reach this result, the Sixth Circuit in *Sequoyah*[138] and the *Badoni*

---

[130] The Court has either stated that a practice is important, *Sherbert*, 374 U.S. at 399 n.1 (noting as a threshold matter that "the prohibition against Saturday labor is a basic tenet of the Seventh Day Adventist creed"), or described the practice in sufficient detail to make its importance self-evident, *see Yoder*, 406 U.S. at 215-19; Murdock v. Pennsylvania, 319 U.S. 105, 108-09 (1942) (describing evangelical practices of Jehovah's Witnesses). Frequently, the government declines to contest the importance of a claimant's religious practices, so this issue is not addressed. *See Yoder*, 406 U.S. at 219 (describing Amish practices in dicta); *Sherbert*, 374 U.S. at 399 n.1; *Murdock*, 319 U.S. at 109.

[131] *See, e.g., Sequoyah*, 620 F.2d at 1164 (discussing centrality of Cherokee practices at sacred sites); Teterud v. Gilman, 385 F. Supp. 153, 156-57 (S.D. Iowa 1974) (discussing centrality of Indian religious custom of wearing hair in braids), *aff'd sub nom.* Teterud v. Burns, 522 F.2d 357 (8th Cir. 1975); Frank v. Alaska, 604 P.2d 1068, 1072-73 (Alaska 1979) (evaluating the importance of consuming moose meat at a funeral potlatch); People v. Woody, 61 Cal. 2d 716, 720-22, 394 P.2d 813, 817-18, 40 Cal. Rptr. 69, 73-74 (1964) (discussing role of peyote in worship of Native American Church). For a general discussion of Native American free exercise claims, see Note, *Native Americans and the Free Exercise Clause*, 28 HASTINGS L.J. 1509 (1977).

[132] 385 F. Supp. 153 (S.D. Iowa 1974), *aff'd sub nom.* Teterud v. Burns, 522 F.2d 357 (8th Cir. 1975).

[133] *Id.* at 156. Plaintiff objected to hair length restrictions in force at the penitentiary in which he was incarcerated. *Id.* at 154.

[134] Frank v. Alaska, 604 P.2d 1068, 1071-73 (Alaska 1979) (moose meat found to be an essential requirement of the Athabascan Indians' most important religious ceremony).

[135] People v. Woody, 61 Cal. 2d 716, 721, 394 P.2d 813, 818, 40 Cal. Rptr. 69, 73 (1964) (peyote found to be an object of worship—without it religious practice by members of the Native American Church would be meaningless).

[136] *See supra* notes 105-15 and accompanying text (describing Cherokee and Navajo beliefs and practices concerning sacred sites).

[137] *Sequoyah*, 620 F.2d at 1164-65; *Badoni*, 455 F. Supp. at 645-46. These courts found Cherokee and Navajo interests neither religious nor important.

[138] *Sequoyah*, 620 F.2d at 1164.

district court[139] derived a test for centrality from language they found in *Yoder*.[140] In *Yoder*, the Court described Amish educational practices as matters of "deep religious conviction, shared by an organized group, and intimately related to daily living."[141] The *Sequoyah* and *Badoni* courts denied relief to Cherokee and Navajo interests because they found that Native American practices were not intimately related to their daily lives.[142]

Analysis of the nature of the centrality requirement in other free exercise cases suggests that the *Sequoyah* and *Badoni* courts probably erred in using the *Yoder* intimate relation language to test the centrality of Cherokee and Navajo interests. Most courts use centrality to measure the importance a practice has within the context of a larger religious belief system.[143] Although a religious practice may affect the manner in which a practitioner orders his or her life, the impact of the religious belief on the adherent's daily activities is not necessarily analogous to the role the practice plays in the overall religious scheme. Church attendance on important religious holidays, for example, may determine a practitioner's ultimate salvation within his or her religious creed; however, this occasional attendance might only minimally affect the conduct of the practitioner's daily affairs.

Centrality and an intimate relation between belief and daily conduct are thus two different concepts.[144] In describing Amish practices as intimately related to daily living, the *Yoder* Court did not manifest an intent to expand or modify the requirements for a finding of centrality.[145] It therefore appears

---

[139] *Badoni*, 455 F. Supp. at 645-46.

[140] The *Badoni* district court relied exclusively on *Yoder* to assess the centrality of Navajo practices. *Id.* The *Sequoyah* appeals court based its holding on two other formulations of centrality in addition to the *Yoder* language—Frank v. Alaska, 604 P.2d 1068 (Alaska 1979), and People v. Woody, 61 Cal. 2d 716, 394 P.2d 813, 40 Cal. Rptr. 69 (1964). *Sequoyah*, 620 F.2d at 1164. *Yoder*'s impact on the holding in *Sequoyah* is therefore difficult to assess.

[141] *Yoder*, 406 U.S. at 216.

[142] The *Sequoyah* court held that worship in the Little Tennessee Valley is not central to Cherokee religious observance because it is not inseparable from the Cherokee lifestyle. 620 F.2d at 1164. Similarly, Navajo interests were held not protected in *Badoni* because plaintiffs had failed to demonstrate "a vital relationship of the practice in question with the Navajo way of life." 455 F. Supp. at 646.

[143] *See supra* notes 125-35 and accompanying text (discussing centrality).

[144] Although these concepts are analytically distinct, application of the intimate relation language may be helpful in ascertaining the centrality of religious practice in some situations. If a court finds that religious belief substantially determines the content of a practitioner's daily life, this finding may constitute strong evidence that the beliefs underlying daily conduct are central. Using this language to prove the centrality of a belief differs, however, from using the absence of an intimate relation to disprove centrality.

[145] Educational practices were central in *Yoder* because of the "vital role that belief and daily conduct play in the continued survival of the Old Order Amish . . . religious organization." 406 U.S. at 235.

the *Sequoyah* and *Badoni* courts misconstrued *Yoder*'s language by equating the centrality of a religious practice with a showing of an intimate relation between belief and daily conduct.[146]

However the test for centrality is phrased, Cherokee and Navajo practices would seem to satisfy even the strictest interpretation of this requirement. Under a strict interpretation, religious practices will only be central if they are essential to the continued existence of a claimant's religion.[147] Cherokee and Navajo practitioners can only communicate with the supernatural through worship at holy lands.[148] The ability to engage in religious practice at sacred sites is essential to the survival of Cherokee and Navajo religion.[149] It is therefore evident that the *Sequoyah* and *Badoni* courts should have found Cherokee and Navajo beliefs and practices sufficiently central to merit first amendment protection.

B. *Were Native American Interests Abridged in* Sequoyah *and* Badoni?

Once Native Americans establish that their practices are protected, they must prove that government action has abridged these practices before a

---

Even if the *Yoder* language can be characterized as a test for centrality, it appears that Native American interests in public lands are intimately related to daily living. Ceremonies may not occur on a daily basis, but Native Americans believe their ceremonies influence a wide variety of daily experiences. *See supra* notes 104-15. Some tribes believe that their daily existence will be seriously disrupted unless practitioners strictly adhere to religious doctrine. *See supra* note 121. Arguably, cultural survival and religious integrity are as mutually interdependent for Native Americans as they are for the Old Order Amish. *See Yoder*, 406 U.S. at 209-19; *supra* notes 104-15, 121.

[146] Use of the intimate relation language as a test for centrality is also inconsistent with *Yoder*'s overall import. Throughout its opinion, the *Yoder* Court emphasized the idiosyncratic nature of the practices it was describing. 406 U.S. at 217, 226, 235-36. It noted that few other religions had beliefs with an impact on daily life similar to those of the Old Order Amish. *Id.* If Amish religion were to serve as a model for centrality, it appears that many recognized religious practices would no longer be entitled to first amendment protection. It is unlikely that the *Yoder* Court intended to withdraw religious status from all but the most orthodox of these conventional practitioners. Thus, it appears courts should not construe *Yoder*'s intimate relation language to be a new formulation of the centrality requirement.

[147] *Yoder*, 406 U.S. at 218; People v. Woody, 61 Cal. 2d 716, 721, 394 P.2d 813, 818, 40 Cal. Rptr. 69, 73 (1964).

[148] *See supra* notes 105-15 and accompanying text.

[149] *Id.* In addition to frustrating Navajo ceremonies, government flooding of sacred sites may actually interfere with religious belief. It is not useful to believe in gods who no longer have the power to influence life. Similarly, because the Little Tennessee Valley is an object of worship for the Cherokee, the many practices associated with the area will become meaningless if it is destroyed by government flooding. *See supra* note 135 and accompanying text.

court will apply the *Yoder* balancing test.[150] Although the government in *Sequoyah* and *Badoni* did not dispute that the floodings had precluded Cherokee and Navajo access to submerged areas,[151] the district courts in these cases refused to acknowledge that cognizable religious abridgments had taken place.[152] Examination of these holdings demonstrates that the *Yoder* balancing test should have been applied.

The *Sequoyah* and *Badoni* district courts rejected Cherokee and Navajo claims of religious abridgment because the plaintiffs could not assert a property interest in the lands to which they demanded access.[153] These courts believed the free exercise clause does not require the federal government to maintain public property in a condition suitable for religious use.[154] They indicated the government may freely use its land without fear of intruding upon constitutionally protected rights.[155] Given the scarcity and value of land, it is understandable that the *Sequoyah* and *Badoni* district courts were reluctant to restrict federal uses of public lands. These courts did not explain, however, why the absence of an ownership interest should preclude a finding of religious abridgment. When the government floods sacred burial grounds, it frustrates Native American religious practice, regardless of whether the land is owned by the tribe or the federal government. Consequently, the *Sequoyah* and *Badoni* courts should have found an abridgment unless federal ownership of sacred sites permits otherwise unconstitutional religious interference.

Although the Supreme Court has never stated that the federal government must tailor use of its property to individual religious needs, it has repeatedly held that the free exercise clause and the fourteenth amendment require states to allow religious proselytization on public streets.[156] These cases

---

[150] *See Yoder*, 406 U.S. at 214. The Court noted that if a challenged state action is to be upheld, "it must appear either that the State does not deny the free exercise of religious belief . . . or that there is a state interest of sufficient magnitude to override the interest claiming protection." *Id.*

[151] *Sequoyah*, 480 F. Supp. at 610; *Badoni*, 455 F. Supp. at 642.

[152] *Sequoyah*, 480 F. Supp. at 612; *Badoni*, 455 F. Supp. at 644.

[153] *See supra* note 152.

[154] *Id.*

[155] *Sequoyah*, 480 F. Supp. at 612; *Badoni*, 455 F. Supp. at 644-45. On appeal, however, the Sixth and Tenth Circuits held that Native Americans need not prove property rights in sacred lands to raise a free exercise challenge. *Badoni*, 638 F.2d at 176; *Sequoyah*, 620 F.2d at 1164.

[156] The Court has held that a state may not prohibit religious speech and practice on public property without a compelling justification. Kunz v. New York, 340 U.S. 290, 294 (1951) (possibility of public disorder insufficient justification for imposing a license requirement on religious speech); Prince v. Massachusetts, 321 U.S. 158, 170-71 (1943) (state had compelling interest in preventing children from engaging in religious street solicitation, but could not prohibit such behavior in adults); Cantwell v. Connecticut, 310 U.S. 296, 307 (1940) (state interest in public safety did not justify permit requirement for religious street solicitation); *cf.* Heffron v. International

suggest that the first amendment requires the government to permit some access to public lands. While these cases do not guarantee first amendment plaintiffs a right of access to any particular piece of land, they do undermine the contention that Native Americans' lack of a property interest in contested lands *a fortiori* defeats their free exercise claims. Moreover, summary dismissal of free exercise claims on the grounds that Native Americans have no property interest in the federal lands is anomalous in light of the language and purpose of the American Indian Religious Freedom Act.[157] Indeed, the Act states that Native Americans' "inherent" right to exercise their religion includes a right of access.[158] Courts should not confuse the government's right to limit access to federal lands when they have a sufficient interest in doing so with an absolute right to foreclose access without consideration of either the government's interest or the importance of the religious practices abridged.

Religious abridgment occurs whenever government action frustrates protected religious practice. The *Sequoyah* and *Badoni* district courts departed from conventional free exercise doctrine in holding that federal property rights may preclude a finding that a religious abridgment has occurred. These courts were unable to cite any constitutional authority for the limitations they imposed.[159] The absence of constituitional support for the holdings in the *Sequoyah* and *Badoni* cases suggests that the district courts should have refused to distinguish federal property rights from other kinds of government interests. Because the Cherokee and Navajo established that the Tellico and Glen Canyon Dams prevented them from engaging in important religious ceremonies, the courts should have applied the *Yoder* balancing test to Cherokee and Navajo religious claims.[160]

Soc'y for Krishna Consciousness, 452 U.S. 640, 647, 651 (1982) (dicta) (first amendment protects religious proselytization on public streets). In addition, the Court has required states to commit resources to a religious practitioner where a failure to do so would unjustifiably obstruct religious observance. Thomas v. Review Bd., Ind. Employment Sec. Div., 450 U.S. 707, 717-18 (1980) (Court required state to grant unemployment benefits to Jehovah's Witness who left his job because of transfer to weapons manufacturing assignment); *Sherbert,* 374 U.S. at 404-06; *supra* notes 50-53 and accompanying text (discussing this aspect of *Sherbert*). These cases indicate that religious activities on public lands are entitled to a first amendment balancing analysis. Interference with such activities will comprise an unconstitutional religious abridgment unless adequately justified by an important secular goal.

[157] 42 U.S.C. § 1996 (Supp. IV 1980); *see supra* notes 69-76 and accompanying text.

[158] 42 U.S.C. § 1996.

[159] *See supra* notes 20, 32 and accompanying text.

[160] Enjoining the projects would not raise a problem under the establishment clause by impermissibly dedicating public resources to an identifiable religious group. *See* Walz v. Tax Comm'n, 397 U.S. 664, 674 (1970) (government violates establishment clause when it becomes excessively entangled with religion); School Dist. of Abington Township v. Schempp, 374 U.S. 203, 222 (1963) (establishment clause

IV. THE *Yoder* BALANCING TEST

A. *Applications of* Yoder *in* Sequoyah *and* Badoni

If the *Sequoyah* and *Badoni* courts had found Cherokee and Navajo practices to be protected religious expression, they would have applied the *Yoder* balancing test to Native American free exercise claims. *Yoder* would have required the government to prove that its interests outweighed Native American interests in public lands.[161] To meet its burden, the government would have had to establish that the general policies it sought to achieve through construction of the Tellico and Glen Canyon Dams were important[162] and that the projects would have actually furthered these policies.[163] Moreover, if alternative means were available that did not intrude upon religious rights, the government would have had to show that the cost of implementing these means outweighed the benefits to religion that these alternatives afforded.[164] Examination of each of these factors in *Sequoyah* and *Badoni* indicates that the outcome in these cases is inconsistent with a proper balancing of Native American and government interests.

---

prohibits government from supporting religion). In *Sherbert,* the Court pointed out that government actions designed to prevent religious infringement "reflect nothing more than the governmental obligation of neutrality in the face of religious differences" and do not violate the establishment clause. 374 U.S. at 409. The federal government has, for a long time, authorized the use of public lands for religious services where this helps to avoid burdening first amendment rights. For example, the government owns and/or operates over one hundred active churches on federal lands for the convenience of tourists visiting remote recreational areas. Information received under the Freedom of Information Act available from the Native American Youth Council, Albuquerque, New Mexico. It has also authorized the use of military bases to provide religious services for members of the armed forces. United States Army Reg. No. 60-5 (1944); United States Navy Reg. Ch. 1 § 2 & Ch. 34 §§ 1-2 (1920); *see also* School Dist. of Abington Township v. Schempp, 374 U.S. 203, 226 (1963) (dicta) (indicating that these Army and Navy regulations are valid under the establishment clause). *Accord* Illinois *ex rel.* McCollum v. Board of Educ., 333 U.S. 203, 254 (1948) (Reed, J., dissenting) (noting that first amendment does not prohibit government use of military facilities for religious services). If the *Sequoyah* and *Badoni* courts had enjoined the flooding of Cherokee and Navajo sacred sites, they would have merely extended this principle of government neutrality to Native American religious practice.

[161] *See supra* notes 43-44 and accompanying text.

[162] *Yoder,* 406 U.S. at 215 ("[O]nly those interests of the highest order . . . can overbalance legitimate claims to the free exercise of religion."); *Sherbert,* 398 U.S. at 403 (infringement of free exercise rights must be justified by a compelling state interest).

[163] *See supra* note 56 and accompanying text.

[164] *See supra* notes 57-58 and accompanying text.

1. Importance of Government Policies and Tailoring Means to Ends

The importance of the government's interest in constructing the Tellico and Glen Canyon projects is incontrovertible. Congress designed both dams to increase energy production and water utilization efficiency in two areas of the United States.[165] Plans for the projects were drawn up at a time when the development of domestic energy supplies was at the top of the list of national priorities.[166] Thus, the general policies asserted in *Sequoyah* and *Badoni* were sufficiently important to satisfy the first aspect of the government's burden of proof.

Although the Glen Canyon Project in *Badoni* clearly furthered congressional energy goals,[167] the Tellico Dam in *Sequoyah* does not appear to have advanced these policies. In *Sequoyah,* neither the Sixth Circuit nor the district court required the government to prove that the Tellico Dam promoted the fulfillment of national energy goals.[168] However, the legislative history surrounding Tellico's authorizing amendment indicates that the government might have had difficulty meeting its burden under *Yoder.* An examination of this legislative history demonstrates that national interests in energy and water might not have been harmed had the *Sequoyah* court enjoined Tellico's completion.

Congress authorized completion of the Tellico Dam by approving an

---

[165] *See* Tennessee Valley Authority v. Hill, 437 U.S. 153, 157 (1978) (discussing the policies underlying Tellico); Friends of the Earth v. Armstrong, 485 F.2d 1, 3-4 (10th Cir. 1973) (discussing the Glen Canyon Project), *cert. denied,* 414 U.S. 1171 (1974).

[166] Congress gave its final approval to the Tellico dam on September 25, 1979, just 2 1/2 years after President Carter characterized the energy crisis in the United States as "the greatest domestic challenge our country will face in our lifetime," and "the moral equivalent of war." N.Y. Times, Apr. 21, 1977, at B8, col. 1 (quoting President Carter's Address to a Joint Session of Congress).

Although Congress began to plan the Colorado Water Storage Project in 1956, before the country had encountered major energy shortages, energy production was an important national interest in 1977 when the Navajo initiated the *Badoni* suit.

[167] The Glen Canyon Dam was a vital link in a comprehensive interstate water delivery system. *See* Friends of the Earth v. Armstrong, 485 F.2d 1, 4-6 (10th Cir. 1973), *cert. denied,* 414 U.S. 1171 (1974). The dam allowed water from the Colorado River to reach downstream participants in the project who would not otherwise have been able to benefit from the project. *Id.; see Badoni,* 638 F.2d at 177. The Glen Canyon Dam therefore furthered the congressional goal of facilitating interstate cooperation in the implementation of this scheme; enjoining its construction would have upset the delicate balance of water delivery that extensive multistate negotiations had achieved. *See Friends of the Earth,* 485 F.2d at 4-6.

[168] Neither court in *Sequoyah* balanced Cherokee interests against the government's need to build the Tellico dam; both courts disposed of Cherokee claims by finding that a religious abridgment had not occurred. *See Sequoyah,* 620 F.2d at 1165; 480 F. Supp. at 612; *supra* notes 20-24 and accompanying text.

amendment to the Energy and Water Development Appropriations Bill.[169] The amendment specifically overrode the Endangered Species Committee's decision to prohibit further construction of the dam.[170] The Committee, which was empowered to exempt important projects from the provisions of the Endangered Species Act, had refused to exempt Tellico because the project would incur large costs without adding significantly to the energy producing capacity of the T.V.A. system.[171] Moreover, it appears that Congress did not carefully consider the Committee's findings before passing the amendment, as discussion in the House lasted only forty seconds.[172] Indeed, some members of Congress later noted that the greatest benefit that would accrue from the Tellico project was the incidental creation of recreational facilities for Tennessee residents.[173]

Given the dam's history, it appears that a decision to forego the project probably would not have seriously jeopardized important interests in water and energy development. At the very least, the *Sequoyah* courts should not

---

[169] H.R. 4388, 96th Cong., 1st Sess. (1979); *see* 125 CONG. REC. H7215 (daily ed. Aug. 2, 1979). The amendment provided that "notwithstanding the provisions of [the Endangered Species Act] or any other law, the [T.V.A.] is authorized and directed to complete construction, operate and maintain the Tellico Dam and Reservoir."

[170] *See* 125 CONG. REC. H7217 (daily ed. Aug. 2, 1979) (statement of Rep. Dingell) (indicating that adoption of the amendment would overrule Committee's decision to deny an exemption); 125 CONG. REC. S9627 (daily ed. July 17, 1979) (statement of Sen. Culver) (noting the amendment's effect).

The Endangered Species Committee is a seven-member cabinet level committee that was set up by a special amendment to the Endangered Species Act. 16 U.S.C. § 1536(h) (Supp. IV 1980). It is composed of environmentalists and members of the construction industry, and is empowered to grant exemptions from the Act to important projects otherwise in conflict with the Act's provisions. *Id.*

[171] 125 CONG. REC. H7218 (daily ed. Aug. 2, 1979) (statement of Rep. Conte) (summarizing Letter from the Committee Chairman, Interior Secretary Andrus); 125 CONG. REC. H7216 (daily ed. Aug. 2, 1979) (statement of Rep. Breaux) (stating that the project was economically unsound). *But see* 125 CONG. REC. S12273 (daily ed. Sept. 10, 1979) (statement of Sen. Sasser) (indicating that Tellico would supply electricity to 20,000 homes).

The Committee also found that the dam would pose a danger of flooding in the area because it was too small to handle anticipated runoffs and failed to meet current dam safety standards. 125 CONG. REC. H7218 (daily ed. Aug. 2, 1979) (Letter from Secretary Andrus to the Speaker of the House).

[172] 125 CONG. REC. H7217 (daily ed. Aug. 2, 1979) (statement of Rep. Dingell).

Congress did debate the amendment after the fact, however, when several members moved to delete the amendment claiming it had been improperly introduced. *See id.;* 125 CONG. REC. H2215 (daily ed. Aug. 2, 1979) (statement of Rep. Breaux); 125 CONG. REC. S9629-30 (daily ed. July 17, 1979) (statement of Sen. Culver).

[173] *See* 125 CONG. REC. H7217 (daily ed. Aug. 2, 1979) (statement of Rep. Dingell); 125 CONG. REC. S9632 (daily ed. July 17, 1979) (statement of Sen. Heinz) (noting that "this benefit is made somewhat ludicrous when one realizes that there are 22 large recreation reservoirs within a 50 mile radius of the Tellico project").

have assumed that the Tellico Dam furthered the government's interest. These courts should have required the government to prove that the project advanced important national policies before disallowing Cherokee religious claims.

2. Availability of Alternative Means

Once the government proves that an accommodation of religious rights would harm its policies, *Sherbert* and *Yoder* indicate that courts must balance this harm against the religious benefit an accommodation would afford.[174] As part of this balancing process, courts must evaluate whether the government could have adopted alternative means for implementing its policies that would have reduced the intrusion on religious interests.[175] Unless the government establishes that reasonable alternative means were unavailable,[176] and that a failure to implement its selected means would unduly harm important interests,[177] courts must invalidate the government action that caused the religious abridgment.[178]

In *Sequoyah,* neither the Sixth Circuit nor the district court balanced Cherokee interests against government needs. Therefore, neither court discussed the existence of alternatives to the Tellico Dam. The amendment's legislative history indicates that a decision to forego construction probably would not have appreciably harmed the government's interest in developing power supplies.[179] Further, Tellico's questionable contribution to the fulfillment of energy needs indicates that almost any alternative would have provided analogous benefits to government interests without abridging religious rights.[180] Because government interests would not have been harmed if the *Sequoyah* court had enjoined Tellico, it appears that under *Yoder,* legitimate Cherokee interests in preserving their religious homeland heavily outweighed the government's interest in completing the Tellico Dam.

In *Badoni,* the Tenth Circuit attempted to balance Navajo religious needs against the importance of the government project.[181] The Tenth Circuit was probably correct in its finding that a failure to flood Glen Canyon would have

---

[174] *See supra* notes 57-58 and accompanying text.

[175] *Id.*

[176] *Sherbert,* 374 U.S. at 407 (It is "plainly incumbent upon the [government] to demonstrate that no alternative forms of regulation would combat . . . abuses without infringing first amendment rights."); *see supra* note 57 and accompanying text.

[177] *See supra* notes 56-58 and accompanying text.

[178] *Id.*

[179] *See supra* notes 171-73 and accompanying text.

[180] Possible alternatives might have included construction of other hydroelectric projects, development of solar energy facilities or implementation of coal-fired generating plants.

[181] The *Badoni* court merely stated the *Yoder* balancing test and then concluded that government interests in the dam outweighed Navajo religious interests. 638 F.2d at 176-77.

harmed important government interests.[182] However, the court misapplied
Yoder because it did not evaluate the existence of alternatives in refusing to
enjoin completion of the Glen Canyon project. To meet its burden of proof
under *Yoder,* the government should have been required to demonstrate that
the costs of alternatives would outweigh their resulting benefit to religion.[183]

Instead of balancing the costs of alternatives against the benefits of accommodation, the Tenth Circuit in *Badoni* did not reach the question
whether Navajo interests in public lands could be protected.[184] This court
merely assumed that the Glen Canyon project as implemented justified an
abridgment of religious rights.[185] The court may have viewed the flooding of
Glen Canyon as so important that it would clearly outweigh any interest
advanced by any religious group. However, without analyzing the nature
and content of Navajo interests, this court could not have compared the
importance of these interests with the costs of adopting alternative means.[186]
The *Yoder* balancing test provides a viable mechanism for protecting national and individual interests only when applied in a manner which affords
due weight to both religious and government needs. The *Badoni* court's
failure to specifically address Navajo interests undermines the legitimacy of
its decision to deny first amendment relief.

B.   *An Application of* Yoder *that Protects Native American Religious Rights*

As the *Sequoyah* and *Badoni* cases illustrate, the issue of when Native
Americans have a constitutional right of access to religious sites on public
lands poses a difficult dilemma for the federal courts. The free exercise
clause requires courts simultaneously to protect the religious liberties of all
American citizens, including members of Native American tribes, and to
avoid interfering with important national policies. The *Sequoyah* and *Badoni*
courts faced this dilemma; they attempted to weigh the importance of the
Tellico and Glen Canyon dams against the constitutional rights of members
of a small minority.

Confronted with the unconventional nature of Native American religious
practices, it appears the *Sequoyah* and *Badoni* courts reacted by protecting
the interests they believed were relevant to a larger segment of the American
public. Unfortunately, to reach this result, these courts made questionable

---

[182] *See supra* notes 27, 167 and accompanying text.

[183] *See supra* notes 57-58.

[184] *Badoni,* 638 F.2d at 177 n.4 ("Because we agree with the trial court that the
government's interest . . . is compelling, we do not reach the question whether the
government action involved infringes plaintiffs' free exercise of religion.").

[185] *Id.* at 177.

[186] Minor alterations in the Glen Canyon project might have produced substantial
savings to Navajo religious rights. For example, the government might have removed
some of the Rock People from the canyon before it completed the flooding, thus
enabling the Navajo to continue practicing many of their important ceremonies.

findings concerning the nature of Native American interests.[187] They also misapplied the *Yoder* balancing test by failing to question the existence of alternative government means.[188] The *Sequoyah* and *Badoni* courts' insensitivity to Native American religion is inconsistent with the policy of religious toleration that has developed over many years of constitutional litigation.[189]

Perhaps one reason that Native American claims meet resistance in the federal courts is that the *Yoder* balancing test becomes difficult to apply by the time these claims reach the courts. For example, in *Sequoyah* and *Badoni*, Cherokee and Navajo plaintiffs did not attempt to enjoin construction of the dams until after these projects were substantially completed.[190] Once a project is under construction, courts have difficulty justifying the costs of altering a proposed plan or preventing a project's completion.[191]

---

[187] *See supra* notes 22-24, 33 and accompanying text.

[188] *See supra* notes 20, 184 and accompanying text.

[189] *See* Thomas v. Review Bd., Indus. Employment Sec. Div., 450 U.S. 707, 718 (1980) (" '[O]nly those interests of the highest order . . . can overbalance legitimate claims to the free exercise of religion.' " (quoting Wisconsin v. Yoder, 406 U.S. 205, 218 (1972))); Walz v. Tax Comm'n, 397 U.S. 664, 669 (1970) (stating that Court will not tolerate governmental interference with religion); Sherbert v. Verner, 374 U.S. 398, 410 (1963) (state may not deny benefits to a citizen on basis of religious practice); Fowler v. Rhode Island, 345 U.S. 67, 70 (1953) (courts have no constitutional competence to approve, disapprove, classify or regulate religious sermons); United States v. Ballard, 322 U.S. 78, 87 (1944) (first amendment affords preferred treatment to all religions); Cantwell v. Connecticut, 310 U.S. 296, 303 (1940) (law cannot restrict individual's freedom to choose form of worship or religious association).

[190] *See supra* notes 15-19, 25-31 and accompanying text.

Native Americans are sometimes not informed about how a project will affect their interests until it is too late to object effectively. *See* Affidavit of Robert Blankenship, at 1-2 (Oct. 1979) (indicating that the T.V.A. requested advice from the Cherokee concerning proper disposal of ancestral remains only a few days before flooding was scheduled to take place). At the same time, Native Americans often do not act because they have been politically powerless for centuries and believe it is futile to challenge government action. *See* Affidavit of John A. Crowe, at 1 (Oct. 8, 1979) ("Many people have resigned themselves to the fact that the valley will be flooded . . . . They cannot fight the mighty TVA."); Affidavit of John M. Kanott, at 1 (Oct. 1979) (stating that the Tellico Dam "is the TVA's way of showing the world they can do what they please any time they feel like it").

[191] In the context of assessing the environmental impact of a nuclear reactor, the United States Court of Appeals for the District of Columbia Circuit stated that once "irreversible and irretrievable commitment[s] of resources have already been made [an assessment of costs and benefits] . . . may become a hollow exercise." Calvert Cliffs Coordinating Comm., Inc. v. United States Atomic Energy Comm'n, 449 F.2d 1109, 1128 (D.C. Cir. 1971). This court also noted that "[o]nce a facility has been completely constructed, the economic cost of any alteration may be very great." *Id.*

Realistically, the increased costs of adopting an alternative plan begin to outweigh the alternative's marginal benefit to religion as soon as the government spends a substantial amount of money on the project's implementation.

Sherbert and *Yoder* require the government to prove that it could not have prevented an abridgment of religious practice by adopting reasonable alternatives to a development project.[192] Yet, analyzing alternatives after the government expends substantial resources exaggerates, for first amendment purposes, the government's interest in building a project on sacred lands. The government will automatically satisfy its burden of proof whenever the controversy involves a substantially completed project.[193] Consequently, applying the *Yoder* balancing test to measure the government's interest in a project that is under construction virtually eliminates the least restrictive alternative requirement from first amendment analysis in these cases.

Courts can be sensitive to the resources spent on a nearly completed project without distorting the balancing process they apply under the free exercise clause. By applying the doctrine of laches, courts could bar Native American claims whenever inexcusable delay in asserting these claims unduly prejudices the government.[194] Properly applied, laches adequately protects the government's interest in the resources it has expended without skewing the results of the *Yoder* first amendment analysis.[195] By resolving the problem of prejudice caused by delay, laches would enable courts to focus directly on the strength of the government's interest in building a project on sacred lands. This doctrine does not, however, remove the difficulties inherent in applying the least restrictive alternative test to a substantially completed project.

---

[192] *See supra* notes 56-58 and accompanying text.

[193] In the words of Robert Moses, New York State's most influential public works developer, "[o]nce you sink the first stake . . . they'll never make you pull it up." Robert Moses Obituary, N.Y. Times, Thurs., July 30, 1981, at B18, col. 6.

[194] Laches is an equitable doctrine which bars assertion of a claim where the defendant shows: "(1) a delay in asserting a right or claim; (2) that the delay was not excusable; and (3) that there was undue prejudice to the party against whom the claim was asserted." Environmental Defense Fund v. Alexander, 614 F.2d 474, 478 (5th Cir. 1980).

[195] *Id.* Laches should justify dismissal of Native American constitutional claims only in extraordinary circumstances. Where the government seeks to assert the defense of laches against a challenge to its own action, the government must prove that the plaintiffs "were or should have been aware of the questionable nature of the governmental activity." *Id.* at 479. In the context of Native American religion, this requirement may be difficult for the government to meet. The government often fails to inform Native Americans about how a project will affect their interests until a project is well under way. *See supra* note 190. In addition, many Native Americans may be unaware that the courts can provide an effective vehicle for the protection of religious rights. *Id.* The U.S. government's historic insensitivity to Indian needs, *see*

If the constitutional requirement of assessing alternatives is read in conjunction with the policies underlying the American Indian Religious Freedom Act, an approach to free exercise claims emerges which fully implements the *Yoder* test. The American Indian Religious Freedom Act requires agencies to avoid abridgments by addressing Indian religious interests during the planning stages of government projects.[196] *Sherbert* and *Yoder* require the courts to invalidate religiously intrusive actions if the government could have avoided an abridgment by using available alternative means.[197] A synthesis of these two concepts would allow courts to apply the *Yoder* balancing test to the planning stages of government projects—a time when alternative means are still available.

If courts were to apply the *Yoder* test to the planning stages of government projects, they would enjoin intrusive projects unless the government proved that careful planning could not have avoided a religious abridgment. To implement a retrospective application of *Yoder*, courts would require the government to establish that no reasonable alternatives were available prior to the onset of a project's construction. One way the government might meet this burden would be by engaging in activities similar to those required by the American Indian Religious Freedom Act. The government would find it difficult to prove that alternatives were unavailable at the planning stages unless it had actually investigated alternatives before committing resources to a project's implementation. Government proof that relevant agencies timely considered Indian religious interests[198] and attempted to accommodate them[199] would help to establish the unavailability of reasonable alternatives. Evidence of a prior analysis of alternative schemes would also indicate that the government's rejection of an available alternative was based on an intelligent assessment of government costs and religious benefits.[200]

A. JOSEPHY, *supra* note 4, at 345-65, has discouraged many Native Americans from challenging government activity. *See supra* note 190. Thus, in most cases, courts should use their equitable discretion to avoid frustrating Native Americans' legitimate attempts to vindicate their constitutional rights.

[196] *See supra* notes 71-72 and accompanying text.

[197] *See supra* notes 57-58 and accompanying text.

[198] *See supra* note 71 and accompanying text. For example, it would be helpful to show that agencies consulted Native American religious leaders early in a project's planning stages.

[199] *See supra* note 72 and accompanying text. Pursuant to the American Indian Religious Freedom Act, the Tennessee Valley Authority and the Department of Energy developed procedures for addressing Indian religion while drawing up environmental impact statements. To meet its burden of proof under *Yoder*, the government could show it had conducted a cost-benefit analysis of alternative plans that did not abridge Native American religious rights.

[200] If the government were required to document the economic and social costs involved in implementing an alternative plan, courts would be better able to ascertain whether the alternative's benefit to religion would outweigh these detriments to government interests.

If the government demonstrated that no reasonable alternative means were available at the time it planned a project, courts would still have to balance government interests against Native American constitutional rights.[201] Pursuant to such an approach, courts would compare the importance of general government policies with the centrality of asserted religious interests.[202] A retrospective application of *Yoder* would facilitate this balancing process by providing a workable context for addressing the costs and benefits of alternative means.[203] Such an approach would require courts to enjoin a project whenever the government failed to specifically prove that the costs of adopting alternatives available at the planning stages outweighed the benefits to religion these alternatives would afford.

An application of *Yoder* to the planning stages might require a court, at some point, to enjoin further implementation of a substantially completed project. Although this action would produce social costs, its long-term benefits to religion would ultimately outweigh any initial waste of public resources. Faced with the threat of a future injunction, government agencies would pay careful attention to Native American religious needs when making land use decisions, thus obviating the need for repeated injunctive relief. The American Indian Religious Freedom Act independently requires this careful attention.[204] Consequently, a constitutional duty of careful planning would not substantially increase the government's responsibility to be sensitive to religious interests. If the courts enforced this duty under the free exercise clause, they could decrease judicial involvement in this troublesome area while preventing abridgments of Native American religious rights.

V. Conclusion

In *Sequoyah v. Tennessee Valley Authority* and *Badoni v. Higginson*, two federal appellate courts attempted to resolve the question whether, under

---

[201] Under *Sherbert* and *Yoder*, an analysis of available alternatives is only one aspect of the government's burden of proving the importance of a challenged project. In addition, the government must demonstrate that its general policies are important, that a failure to build the project would have substantially harmed these policies, and, finally, that the benefits of the project as a whole outweigh the costs it produces to religious practice. *See supra* notes 56-58 and accompanying text.

[202] Even if the government proves it could not have adopted alternative means, courts must still decide whether the importance of the government's general policy justifies an abridgment of religious rights. For, example, the government's interest in building recreational facilities would probably not justify a serious religious infringement, even if such facilities could only be built on lands which Native Americans hold sacred.

[203] Proof of compliance with procedures designed to prevent religious abridgments would provide courts with concrete evidence that would be useful in quantifying the costs and benefits that a religious accommodation would produce. *See supra* notes 57-58. This approach would eliminate many of the ambiguities involved in comparing religious interests with government needs under *Yoder*. *See supra* note 44.

[204] *See supra* notes 71-72 and accompanying text.

the free exercise clause, Native Americans can prevent the government from using lands in a manner that precludes access to sacred sites. In addressing this issue, these courts ignored substantial evidence concerning the religious character of Native American land-related practices. In order to protect government interests in completed projects, these courts also misapplied established constitutional standards and retreated unnecessarily from a long line of constitutional precedent which ensures free exercise protection to even the most unconventional religious practices.

If Native Americans are to receive first amendment protection, courts must recognize that development projects cannot be distinguished for free exercise purposes from other kinds of government action. Courts must apply traditional constitutional analysis in a manner capable of affording Native Americans meaningful first amendment relief. The American Indian Religious Freedom Act may serve as a useful mechanism for preventing abridgments of religious rights. However, unless courts incorporate similar policies into the *Yoder* test, Native American religious practices will remain subject to official discretion, to be subordinated to the demands of administrative convenience and fluctuating dominant political interests. Hopefully, the courts will reconsider the importance of Native American religious freedom in the near future. In doing so, they should apply the Constitution in a manner that extends its protections to all classes of American citizens.

LAURIE ENSWORTH

MANIFEST DESTINY AND AMERICAN INDIAN RELIGIOUS FREEDOM: *SEQUOYAH, BADONI,* AND THE DROWNED GODS

*Howard Stambor**

Introduction

The area of worship cannot be delineated from social, political, culture, and other areas of Indian lifestyle, including his general outlook upon economic and resource development . . . . [W]orship is . . . an integral part of the Indian way of life and culture which cannot be separated from the whole. This oneness of Indian life seems to be the basic difference between the Indian and non-Indians of a dominant society.[1]

In his statement before the Senate Select Committee on Indian Affairs, Mr. Barney Old Coyote of the Crow Tribe of Montana underlined the issues that continue to vex legislative, administrative, and judicial efforts to deal with matters relating to the religious practices of American Indians. The various tribal religions practiced by native peoples in the United States are almost without exception inextricably linked with what non-Indian society regards as *culture*.[2] This unity of culture and religion makes American Indian forms of worship alien and difficult for the non-Indian to understand[3] and poses difficult questions for

---

* B.A., 1971, McGill University (Canada); M. Phil., 1976, Yale; J.D., 1982, University of Pennsylvania. Associate, Davis, Wright, Todd, Riese & Jones, Seattle, Wash.

1. *American Indian Religious Freedom: Hearings on S.J. Res. 102 Before the Senate Select Comm. on Indian Affairs*, 95th Cong., 2d Sess. 86-87 (1978) [hereinafter cited as *Hearings on S.J. Res. 102*] (statement of Barney Old Coyote, Crow Tribe, Montana).

2. *See, e.g.*, the remarks of Chief Oren Lyons of the Onondaga Tribe appearing in the ARTS ADVOCATE, Jan. 1975, at 2, col. 4, and cited in Note, *Native Americans Versus American Museums—A Battle for Artifacts*, 7 AM. INDIAN L. REV. 125, 127 (1979): "Religion, as it has been and is still practiced today on the reservation, permeates all aspects of tribal society. The language makes no distinction between religion, government, or law. Tribal customs and religious ordinances are synonymous. All aspects of life are tied in to one totality."

3. D. GETCHES, D. ROSENFELT, & C. WILKINSON, CASES AND MATERIALS ON FEDERAL INDIAN LAW 504 (1979) [hereinafter cited as GETCHES]:
Much of Indian religious life does not include the existence of a church, periodic meetings, ritual, and identifiable dogma. Instead, there is a pervasive quality to Indian religion which gives all aspects of Indian life and society a spiritual significance. In pursuit of traditional Indian religion, an Indian may feel compelled to relate to nature and

courts[4] that must decide whether certain arguably religious practices of American Indians lie within the shelter of the free exercise
clause of the first amendment.[5] Various courts have responded to
this challenge with conflicting conclusions about which American
Indian practices are indeed religious and which are merely expressions of culture or personal preference unprotected by the first
amendment.[6]

The conquest and oppression of the American Indian tribes by
the white man was a shameful episode in our national history, an
enterprise so unworthy of a nation that holds itself forth as the
champion of liberty and democracy that it is difficult to imagine
any but the most hardened and cynical disciple of manifest
destiny who today would be unwilling to join in the consensus
that regards the treatment of the American Indian by the white
man with shame and horror.[7] What is not as widely recognized or
understood, however, is that the lingering effect of oppression
has had a lasting and pervasive impact on Indian religions as they

---

to others in a particular way. Unfamiliarity with Indian spiritual life and an inherent
suspicion of fraud when religious doctrine and practice are not crisply defined by ancient writings or a central authority are obstacles to judicial understanding and protection of Indian religion.

See also Harris, *The American Indian Religious Freedom Act and Its Promise*, 5 AM. IN-
DIAN J. 7 (June 1979): "Non-Indians can comprehend worship in a church or synagogue,
but not on a mountaintop or with an eagle feather." *See generally* FEDERAL AGENCIES
TASK FORCE, AMERICAN INDIAN RELIGIOUS FREEDOM ACT REPORT P.L. 95-341, 8-12 (1979)
[hereinafter cited as TASK FORCE REPORT] for a thorough and sensitive analysis of the
nature of American Indian tribal religion and its intimate relation (if not identity) with
tribal culture.

4. GETCHES, *supra* note 3, at 507-08: "the struggle to categorize neatly what Indians are moved to do by their traditions . . . [illuminates] the difficulty our legal system
has in applying constitutional protections to a strange culture's value system and spiritual
life."

5. U.S. CONST. amend. I: "Congress shall make no law respecting an establishment
of religion, or prohibiting the free exercise thereof; . . ."

6. *Compare* People v. Woody, 61 Cal. 2d 716, 394 P.2d 813, 40 Cal. Rptr. 69
(1964) (state law banning possession and use of peyote may not be enforced against practicing member of Native American Church) *with* State v. Soto, 21 Or. App. 794, 537 P.2d
142 (1975), *cert. denied*, 424 U.S. 955 (state law banning possession and use of peyote
may be enforced against practicing member of Native American Church). *Compare*
Teterud v. Burns, 522 F.2d 357 (8th Cir. 1975) (wearing of long hair by Indian is a
religious practice protected against state interference by the first amendment) *with* New
Rider v. Board of Educ., 480 F.2d 693 (10th Cir.), *cert. denied*, 414 U.S. 1097 (1973)
(wearing of long hair by Indian is not a religious practice and is therefore not protected
against state interference by the first amendment). *See generally id.* (Douglas, J., dissenting from denial of certiorari); Note, *The Right to Wear a Traditional Indian Hair
Style—Recognition of a Heritage*, 4 AM. INDIAN L. REV. 105 (1976).

7. *See e.g.*, TASK FORCE REPORT, *supra* note 3, at 1-17.

are practiced today and on the ability of American Indians to carry on what remains of their religious practices.[8] All too often, ignorance and inadvertence have come to replace the avarice and malice that formerly inspired government attitudes toward the American Indian.[9] As Senator James Abourezk, Chairman of the Senate Select Committee on Indian Affairs, has noted, "[I]n recent years, there have been increasing incidents of infringement of the religious rights of American Indians. New barriers have been raised against the pursuit of their traditional culture, of which the religion is an integral part."[10] Senator Dewey F. Bartlett warned that "[w]e do not need to add continued violation of American Indian religious freedom to the long list of rights consistently abridged by the Federal government."[11]

The long history of oppression of the American Indian continues today. It is a bitter irony that this history makes it increasingly difficult for American Indians to assert successfully the right to practice their religion free from government interference, government interference having already so effectively alienated them from their tribal religions.[12] Much of this interference has been incidental to the goals of the legislation or regulation that has impinged on the religious practices of American Indians, but the impact is real nevertheless:

> A lack of U.S. governmental policy has allowed infringement in the practice of native traditional religions. These infringements came about through the enforcement of policies . . . which are basically sound and which the large majority of Indians strongly support. . . . But, because such laws were not

---

8. T. Pressly, *Freedom of Religion for the American Indian in the Twentieth Century*, in STUDIES IN AMERICAN INDIAN LAW 285, 294 (R. Johnson ed. 1970): "The total impact of the white man's religion upon the red man is hard to ascertain at this time. Certainly it has affected and changed many Indian tribal practices and has also driven many rituals underground."

9. See *Native Americans' Right to Believe and Exercise Their Traditional Native Religions Free of Federal Government Interference: Report to Accompany S.J. Res. 102*, S. REP. No. 709, 95th Cong., 2d Sess. 4-5 (1978) [hereinafter cited as S. REP. 709, 1978]. "Lack of knowledge, unawareness, insensitivity, and neglect are the keynotes of the Federal Government's interaction with traditional Indians' religions and cultures."

10. *Hearings on S.J. Res. 102, supra* note 1, at 1.

11. *Id.* at 7.

12. See GETCHES, *supra* note 3, at 509:
Perhaps the process [Justice] Douglas [dissenting from the denial of certiorari in New Rider v. Board of Educ., 414 U.S. 1097, 1101-1103 (1973)] describes has been so effective in suppressing Indian culture that traditional practices emerge only in isolated instances, lacking in the consistency that generally marks a religious practice.

intended to relate to religion and because there was a lack of awareness of their effect on religion, Congress neglected to fully consider the impact of such laws on the Indians' religious practices.

It is only within the last decade that it has become apparent that such laws, when combined with more restrictive regulations, insensitive enforcement procedures and administrative policy directives, in fact, have interfered severely with the culture and religion of American Indians.[13]

This article will discuss two recent appellate court decisions[14] that have had precisely this impact on the religious practices of two great Indian nations, the Cherokee and the Navajo. In each case, tribal representatives alleged that the inundation by federal water projects of sites sacred to the traditional tribal religions was an unconstitutional infringement of their first amendment right freely to exercise their religion. In both cases the courts ruled against the Indians. This article will suggest that the results of both cases were, in a practical sense, inevitable, though both courts failed to address the constitutional question raised by the Indians in a principled and constitutionally defensible manner. This article will also examine briefly the American Indian Religious Freedom Act of 1978,[15] raised by both tribes as a statutory claim, concluding that the statute is no more than a statement of good intentions and otherwise impotent as an instrument for righting the constitutional wrongs suffered by American Indians in their efforts to practice their religion free from government interference.

I.   *The Cherokee Claim: Sequoyah v. Tennessee Valley Authority*

In 1979 three Cherokee Indians acting as individuals and two Cherokee tribal organizations jointly petitioned the District Court for the Eastern District of Tennessee for an injunction to restrain the Tennessee Valley Authority from closing the floodgates of

---

13. S. REP. 709, 1978, *supra* note 9, at 2.

14. Sequoyah v. TVA, 620 F.2d 1159 (6th Cir.), *cert. denied* 449 U.S. 953 (1980) and Badoni v. Higginson, 638 F.2d 172 (10th Cir. 1980), *cert. denied sub nom.* Badoni v. Broadbent, 452 U.S. 954 (1981).

15. Act of Aug. 11, 1978, Pub. L. No. 95-341, 92 Stat. 469 (codified in part at 42 U.S.C. § 1996).

Tellico Dam on the Little Tennessee River.[16] The TVA's action would begin the impoundment of water to form the Tellico Reservoir, flood the valley of the Little Tennessee, and inundate burial grounds and sites sacred to the followers of the traditional Cherokee religion.[17] The lead plaintiff, 78-year-old Ammoneta Sequoyah, a practicing Cherokee medicine man, testified that the impoundment of the Tellico Reservoir would destroy the source of his medicine and make it impossible for him to continue to practice his traditional religious healing art.[18] Numerous other Cherokee affiants testified as to the sacred nature of the lands scheduled for inundation.[19] However, the court denied plaintiffs' motion for a preliminary injunction and granted defendant's motion to dismiss for failure to state a claim upon which relief can

---

16. Writing in the 1978 *Supreme Court Review*, Martin E. Marty expressed surprise at how the "snail darter case," TVA v. Hill, 437 U.S. 153 (1978), had upstaged two important religion cases the Supreme Court had decided in the 1977-78 term. *See* Marty, *Of Darters and Schools and Clergymen: The Religion Clauses Worse Confounded*, 1978 Sup. Ct. Rev. 171 (1978). *In TVA v. Hill*, environmentalists' concern for the fate of a small fish had succeeded in blocking the completion of the mighty Tellico Dam project on the Little Tennessee River. The two religion cases were McDaniel v. Paty, 435 U.S. 618 (1978) and New York v. Cathedral Academy, 434 U.S. 125 (1977). It is little short of ironic that the same Tellico Dam project was soon to generate its own litigation grounded in the free exercise clause of the first amendment.

17. Sequoyah v. TVA, 480 F. Supp. 608 (E.D. Tenn. 1979).

18. *Id.*, Plaintiffs' Memorandum, Exhibit D (Affidavit of Ammoneta Sequoyah):

If the water covers Chota and the other sacred places of the Cherokee along the River, I will lose my knowledge of medicine.

If the lands are flooded, the medicine that comes from Chota will be ended because the strength and spiritual power of the Cherokee will be destroyed . . . .

If this land is flooded and these sacred places are destroyed, the knowledge and beliefs of my people who are in the ground will be destroyed.

19. *See id.*, Exhibits C-GG, Affidavits of Affiants. Albert L. Wahrhaftig, Chairman, Department of Anthropology, Sonoma State University, testified:

In short, to attempt to understand or maintain Cherokee religion without access to known and significant sites in the 'old country' would be like attempting to understand and practice Judaism or Christianity without the Book of Genesis. These sites represent the ultimate foundation of Cherokee belief and practice, now, and for the future.

Emmaline Driver stated: "If they are flooded, our spiritual strength from our forefathers will be taken away from us, along with the origin of our organized religion. The white man has taken nearly everything away from us, our heritage, culture, traditions, and our way of life that is our religion."

Richard Crowe stated:

This land is sacred to me and my people, and it is hard for me to talk about how I feel about this land.

I have been going to the lands at Tellico for many years, for at least more than thirty (30) years. Before I went myself, I used to hear my people, my parents, speak of the land. My people referred to it in the Cherokee language. They said: *di ga ta le no hr* [in Cherokee script in original]. This means, "This is where WE began."

be granted pursuant to Federal Rule of Civil Procedure 12(b)(6) after hearing oral argument on the motions.[20]

The Tennessee Tellico Dam has had a stormy history.[21] Judge Robert L. Taylor, in his memorandum opinion denying plaintiffs the injunctive relief they had sought, indicated that since 1966, when Congress first appropriated money for the construction of the dam, nine lawsuits have been brought at the district court level and that progress on the dam had been impeded by two injunctions, though the project had been free from injunction for nine of its fourteen years of existence.[22]

The Court characterized plaintiffs' claim as follows:

> The land . . . which will be flooded . . . is sacred to the Cherokee religion and a vital part of the Cherokee religious practices. . . . The plaintiffs contend that impoundment of the reservoir will violate their constitutional right to free exercise of their religion, in addition to their claimed statutory rights of access to lands of religious and historical significance.[23]

After rejecting plaintiffs' statutory arguments, the court addressed plaintiffs' constitutional claims.[24]

The court assumed that "the land to be flooded is considered sacred to the Cherokee religion and that active practitioners of that religion would want to make pilgrimages to this land as a precept of their religion."[25] Nevertheless, it held that the free exercise clause of the first amendment did not require that injunctive relief be granted to the Cherokee plaintiffs.[26] Citing eight Supreme Court free exercise decisions, the court summarized the elements of a free exercise claim in two short sentences: "An essential element to a claim under the free exercise clause is some form of governmental coercion of actions which are contrary to religious belief" and "This governmental coercion may take the form of pressuring or forcing individuals not to participate in religious practices."[27]

---

20. Sequoyah v. TVA, 480 F. Supp. 608, 612 (E.D. Tenn. 1979).

21. For a history of the controversy generated by the decision to build the Tellico Dam, as well as a sketch of the historical significance of the region, *see* TVA v. Hill, 437 U.S. 153, 156-59 (1978).

22. Sequoyah v. TVA, 480 F. Supp. 608, 610 (E.D. Tenn. 1979).

23. *Id.*

24. *Id.* at 611.

25. *Id.*

26. *Id.* at 612.

27. *Id.* at 611.

The court first found that the impoundment of the Tellico Reservoir would have no coercive effect on plaintiffs. Instead of proceeding systematically to determine if closing the dam would be a form of "pressuring or forcing individuals not to participate in religious practices," the court framed the second level of inquiry in terms so broad that it effectively encompassed the first inquiry. "The question thus becomes whether the denial of access to government-owned land considered sacred and necessary to plaintiffs' religious beliefs infringes the free exercise clause."[28] The inquiry thus posed delved no farther than the finding on the first question.

Having dodged the difficult second question, the court leaped to a legal non sequitur by holding that the absence of a property interest in the lands about to be inundated barred plaintiffs from asserting a free exercise claim in regard to those lands. "The Court has been cited to no case that engrains the free exercise clause with property rights."[29] The second telling question the court had posited for analysis of free exercise claims remained unasked and unanswered. In support of its property interest analysis, the court cited precedent that held that the first amendment does not grant a right of entry to federal property that is normally closed to the public.[30] The inapt analogy is particularly troubling when one considers the historical reasons for the Cherokees' inability to assert a property interest in lands on which their sacred sites and burial places lie: these former Cherokee lands were taken from them by a powerful government bent on conquest.[31] The court's reliance on this lack of a property interest is an insensitive, inequitable, and irresponsible evasion of the more difficult constitutional claim that the Indians raised.

---

28. *Id.* at 612.

29. *Id.*

30. *Id., citing* Downing v. Kunzig, 454 F.2d 1230 (6th Cir. 1972).

31. "The Cherokee race was removed from Tennessee by the federal government in a series of political and military steps, but not before the Cherokees had developed deep religious, cultural and historical ties with their homeland." Plaintiffs' Memorandum, *supra* note 18, at 2. These lands are not now closed to the public. When they were in private hands, plaintiffs had no difficulty in gaining access to them. They will now be closed to the public only because government action will cause them to be inundated. Thus, the court's analogy to prison and military reservation cases in which plaintiffs sought to establish a first amendment forum in a place where none had been previously available to them or to others, and where reasonable time, place, and manner regulation would not permanently or substantially impair the exercise of a constitutionally protected right, does not persuade. *See* Shuttlesworth v. Birmingham, 394 U.S. 147 (1969); Fowler v. Rhode Island, 345 U.S. 67 (1953).

On appeal, the Sixth Circuit, with one judge dissenting, affirmed the district court's denial of plaintiffs' motion for injunctive relief. Because the district court had considered matters outside the pleadings, the court of appeals treated the district court's judgment granting defendant's motion for dismissal as one for summary judgment.[32] The appellate court, however, explicitly rejected the district court's holding that plaintiffs could not assert a first amendment claim to enjoin TVA from flooding the sacred valley because plaintiffs had no property interest in the lands that would be flooded.[33] The court of appeals then analyzed the troubling question avoided by the district court—whether the action of the Tennessee Valley Authority, in flooding land conceded to be sacred to the Cherokee, "pressur[ed] or forc[ed] individuals not to participate in religious practices."[34]

The court began its inquiry by setting forth evidence in the record that tended to show that the claims of the plaintiffs were cultural rather than religious,[35] implicitly accepting the dubious assumption that Indian culture may be distinguished from Indian religion.[36] The court concluded from the more than twenty affidavits submitted in support of plaintiffs' motion for injunctive relief that plaintiffs' claims were fundamentally cultural rather than religious.[37] A careful reading of the affidavits, however, suggests that the court summarized carefully selected portions in order to undercut the religious foundation of plaintiffs' claim.[38] The court's strategy is clear: to address the free exercise question raised by plaintiffs and effectively ignored by the trial court, yet still affirm the trial court's judgment, it would have to show that plaintiffs' claims did not satisfy the constitutional standards for determining whether a belief is religious. The court erroneously assumed that characterization of plaintiffs' claims as cultural as

---

32. Sequoyah v. TVA, 620 F.2d 1159 (6th Cir. 1980).

33. *Id.* at 1164: "While this [lack of a property interest] is a factor to be considered, we feel it should not be conclusive in view of the history of the Cherokee expulsion from Southern Appalachia followed by the 'Trail of Tears' to Oklahoma and the unique nature of plaintiffs' religion."

34. *Sequoyah*, 480 F. Supp. at 611, *citing* McDaniel v. Paty, 435 U.S. 618 (1978). Compare *supra* text accompanying notes 27-31.

35. *Sequoyah*, 620 F.2d at 1162: "the documents in the record indicate that the Cherokee objections to the Tellico Dam were based primarily on a fear that their cultural heritage, rather than their religious rights, would be affected by flooding the Little Tennessee Valley."

36. Compare *supra* text accompanying notes 1-12.

37. *Sequoyah*, 620 F.2d at 1162.

38. *Sequoyah*, 480 F. Supp. 608, Plaintiffs' Memorandum, Exhibits C-GG.

well as religious would place them beyond the bounds of the free exercise clause. But the Supreme Court has never held that a belief must be exclusively religious in order to qualify for first amendment protection.[39]

The court's emphasis on the nonreligious element of plaintiffs' claims could not wholly obscure their religious content.[40] Forced to acknowledge a religious component, the court shifted its approach in an attempt to minimize the significance of that component by trivializing it.[41] A misreading of the affidavits submitted to the trial court buttressed that trivialization.[42] Having rendered plaintiffs' claim a hybrid of culture and religion, the court ventured into an area it mistakenly believed constitutionally gray. It conceded without discussion that plaintiffs had met the threshold requirements that they did in fact have a religion and that they sincerely adhered to it.[43]

"Centrality": A Spurious Constitutional Test

The court opened its analysis of the constitutional question by asserting that *Sherbert v. Verner*[44] and *Wisconsin v. Yoder*[45] required a two-step analysis in evaluating a free exercise claim.

First, it must be determined whether the governmental action does in fact create a burden on the exercise of the plaintiff's re-

---

39. *See* Callahan v. Woods, 658 F.2d 679, 684 (9th Cir. 1981).

40. See *supra* text accompanying note 25.

41. *Sequoyah*, 620 F.2d at 1162-63: "The Cherokees who are plaintiffs in this action obviously have great reverence for their ancestors and believe that the places where their ancestors lived, gathered medicines, died and were buried, have cultural and religious significance. *Similar feelings are shared by most people to a greater or lesser extent.*" (Emphasis added.)

42. *Sequoyah*, 620 F.2d at 1163:

There is no showing that any Cherokees other than Ammoneta Sequoyah and Richard Crowe ever went to the area for religious purposes during [the 100 years prior to TVA's acquisition of the land] . . . . At most, plaintiffs showed that a few Cherokees had made expeditions to the area, prompted for the most part by an understandable desire to learn more about their cultural heritage.

Compare notes 18 and 19 *supra*. Indeed, the failure of plaintiffs' affiants to satisfy the court may well be simply a matter of felicity of language because it is particularly difficult to express the religious nature of an experience in words that convey clear meaning to someone who has not shared that experience. This predicament intensifies when the other sees the religious experience as something that corresponds more closely to his notion of culture than of religion. In this regard, consider the remarks of GETCHES, *supra* note 3.

43. *Sequoyah*, 620 F.2d at 1163.

44. 374 U.S. 398, 402-03 (1963).

45. 406 U.S. 205, 214-15 (1972).

ligion. If a burden is found it must be balanced against the governmental interest, with the government being required to show an overriding or compelling reason for its action.[46]

This first step assesses the "quality of the claims"[47] for which litigants are seeking free exercise protection.

In addressing this first question, the court relied on language in *Yoder*[48] and two state cases, *Frank v. Alaska*[49] and *People v. Woody*,[50] to support its thesis that even if plaintiffs' claims were religious, they were not entitled to free exercise protection unless the disputed practices were central to the religion.[51] None of the cases, however, provides solid authority for the court's "centrality" test. Initially, simply on its facts, it is hard to see how the claim raised in *Yoder* can be said to be more "central" (and thus more *religious* for free exercise purposes) than the claim of the *Sequoyah* plaintiffs. In *Yoder*, unlike *Woody*, the court dealt with practices that were not worship or religious ritual. These practices could be seen as religious only by indulging in a generous and lengthy implicit syllogism: the survival of the Amish religion depends on the successful inculcation of Amish values in each new generation; if Amish children attend public school, they may fail to acquire sufficient Amish values so as to make them adhere to the faith; if young people do not adhere to the Amish faith, the Amish religion will not survive; therefore, inculcation of Amish values is a central tenet of the Amish religion. As this syllogism makes clear, the *Yoder* "centrality" test offered by the *Sequoyah* court is spurious at best. The truly *central* tenets of the Amish faith concern matters of ritual and faith, not the practical problems of guiding children through adolescence.

In contrast, the *Sequoyah* plaintiffs have asserted a much

---

46. *Sequoyah*, 620 F.2d at 1163.

47. Wisconsin v. Yoder, 406 U.S. 205, 215 (1972).

48. *Id.* at 215-16: "[For the Amish, religion and life-style are] . . . inseparable and interdependent . . . . The traditional way of life of the Amish is not merely a matter of personal preference, but one of deep religious conviction, shared by an organized group, and intimately related to daily living."

49. 604 P.2d 1068 (Alaska 1979).

50. 61 Cal. 2d 716, 394 P.2d 813, 40 Cal. Rptr. 69 (1964).

51. The court might also have relied on language in *Sherbert*, 374 U.S. at 406, to support its "centrality" argument, as there the Supreme Court found that Sherbert's belief that she could not work on Saturdays was "a cardinal principle of her religious faith." However, *Sherbert* did not establish a "centrality" rule. The *Sherbert* Court used "centrality" as useful evidence of *sincerity*; in *Sequoyah*, the court has readily conceded plaintiffs' sincerity. In *Sherbert's* terms, then, the "centrality" inquiry in *Sequoyah* is superfluous.

stronger claim to religious centrality. Their claims concern the home of their gods and the ultimate origins of the Cherokee people. Surely the *Yoder* claims are more *"cultural"* than those presented in *Sequoyah*. Moreover, if the Cherokee practices are no longer "intimately related to daily living"[52] except for a few devoted believers, it is only because the government, which now seeks to reject the Cherokee claims as not sufficiently central to the Cherokee faith to qualify for first amendment protection, had in the past systematically worked to deprive the Cherokees of their connection with the land and their sacred religion, which has always been tied to the land. It is remarkable that the Cherokee religion has survived at all, given the powerful forces historically arrayed against it.

The *Woody*[53] and *Frank*[54] courts found that certain practices of American Indians fell within the ambit of the free exercise clause. The *Sequoyah* court, however, used these cases not for their holdings but for their negative implications. *Woody* was a ground-breaking case. It recognized a free exercise exemption from a state ban on the use of peyote by a religious minority, the Native American Church, thus expanding free exercise thinking to encompass non-mainstream religions. Nevertheless, the holding was clearly a logical consequence of the *Sherbert*[55] decision.

Because the use of hallucinogenic drugs is a far more controversial issue than, say, the right to unemployment benefits claimed in *Sherbert*, the California court was careful to couch its opinion in narrow terms in order to preclude all but the strongest claims from staking out territory within the exemption. The *Sequoyah* court correctly remarked that *Woody* found peyote to "play a central role in the ceremony and practice of the Native American Church," that the peyote ceremony comprised "the cornerstone of the religion,"[56] and that "'[t]o forbid the use of peyote is to remove the theological heart of Peyotism.'"[57] A degree of "centrality" equal to that of the practice examined in *Woody* should not be a necessary condition to a finding that a religious practice falls within the shelter of the free exercise clause of the first amendment, particularly in a case not involving the

52. Wisconsin v. Yoder, 406 U.S. 205, 216 (1972).
53. People v. Woody, 61 Cal. 2d 716, 394 P.2d 813, 40 Cal. Rptr. 69 (1964).
54. *Frank*, 604 P.2d 1068.
55. *Sherbert*, 374 U.S. 398 (1963).
56. *Sequoyah*, 620 F.2d at 1164.
57. *Id.*, citing *Woody*, 61 Cal. 2d at 722, 394 P.2d at 817-18, 40 Cal. Rptr. at 74.

controversial use of hallucinogenic drugs. *Woody* does not foreclose the possibility of a lower standard of significance for the protection of less controversial religious practices against secular interference.[58]

Frank v. Alaska[59] poses even more difficult problems for the *Sequoyah* court. In *Frank* the Alaska Supreme Court held that an Athabascan Indian was not subject to prosecution under the state game laws for taking a moose out of season in order to provide food for a traditional funeral feast.[60] The court found that "[w]hile moose itself is not sacred, it is needed for proper observance of a sacred ritual which must take place soon after death occurs. Moose is the centerpiece of the most important ritual in Athabascan life and is the equivalent of sacred symbols in other religions."[61] The eating of moose meat at a funeral feast appears no more centrally religious than worshipping and gathering traditional medicinal plants at the site of the origin of the Cherokee people and their religion.

Furthermore, although *Frank* speaks in the language of "centrality," it clearly does not *require* "centrality" as a necessary condition to free exercise protection. The *Frank* court cited a 1975 Eighth Circuit opinion, *Teterud v. Burns*,[62] as sole federal authority speaking directly to the "centrality" issue. The *Teterud* court stated:

> The appellant's argument appears to be premised on the theory that Teterud was required to prove that wearing long braided hair was an absolute tenet of the Indian religion practiced by all Indians. This is not the law. Proof that the practice is

---

58. *See* Note, *Dubious Intrusions—Peyote, Drug Laws, and Religious Freedom*, 8 AM. INDIAN L. REV. 79, 95 (1980). The student commentator suggests that the *Woody* "centrality" standard is constitutionally suspect and a dead end for future free exercise claims. The commentator argues that "present attitudes and legal standards constitute a distortion of first amendment religious liberties . . ." because the *Woody* "centrality" test sanctions intervention into religious life and freedom. The commentator contends that courts would better serve first amendment values if they followed Justice Jackson's advice "[to] have done with this business of judicially examining other people's faiths." United States v. Ballard, 322 U.S. 78, 95 (1944) (Jackson, J., dissenting).

Furthermore, suggests the commentator, if the Yoder family's "life-style," 406 U.S. at 215, is sheltered by the free exercise clause of the first amendment, so too is American Indian culture. Indian religion and culture are at least as closely interrelated as the religion and culture of the Amish.

59. 604 P.2d 1068 (Alaska 1979).

60. *Id.* at 1073.

61. *Id.*

62. *Id.*, citing *Teterud*, 522 F.2d 357 (8th Cir. 1975).

deeply rooted in religious belief is sufficient. It is not the province of government officials or court to determine religious orthodoxy.[63]

The *Sequoyah* court dismissed *Teterud* as arising in an inapposite factual context not applicable to *Sequoyah*.[64] However, it failed to explain how *Teterud* differs conceptually from *Yoder*, *Woody*, *Frank*, and *Sequoyah*.[65]

The court found that the Little Tennessee River valley was neither the "cornerstone" nor the "theological heart" of the Cherokee religion. Because the Cherokee plaintiffs established neither the "centrality or indispensability" of the valley to the practice of their religion nor the inseparability of their religious practices from their way of life, the court held that they failed to state a claim for which relief could be granted under the free exercise clause of the first amendment.[66] The court found that plaintiffs had instead merely stated a "personal preference" that did not rise to constitutional dimensions:

> The overwhelming concern of the affiants appears to be related to the historical beginnings of the Cherokees and their cultural development. It is damage to tribal and family folklore and traditions, more than particular religious observances, which appears to be at stake. The complaint asserts an "irreversible loss to the culture and history of the plaintiffs." Though cultural history and tradition are vitally important to any group of people, these are not interests protected by the Free Exercise Clause of the First Amendment.[67]

To the contrary, the affidavits that plaintiffs provided to the trial court[68] demonstrate that their concern was primarily and pro-

---

63. 522 F.2d at 360.

64. *Sequoyah*, 620 F.2d at 1163 n.2: "Typically they concern some official regulation of individual activity which infringes the right of a particular group or person to the free exercise of religion. *E.g.*, *Teterud v. Burns*, 522 F.2d 357 (8th Cir. 1975) (prison regulation against long, braided hair)."

65. Recent decisions confirm that the "centrality" test plays no part in free exercise analysis. *See, e.g.*, Callahan v. Woods, 658 F.2d 679 (9th Cir. 1981) (religiously based objection to Social Security numbering as a condition of qualifying children for public assistance sustained); Tooley v. Martin-Marietta Corp., 648 F.2d 1239 (9th Cir. 1981) (statutory rule of accommodation permitting religionists to pay equivalent of union dues to charity not a violation of the establishment clause) (implicit free exercise grounding of statutory exemptions).

66. *Sequoyah*, 620 F.2d at 1164-65.

67. *Id.*

68. See *supra* text accompanying note 32.

foundly religious.[69] Further, even assuming that the court was correct on the facts, it was wrong on the law. There is no authority for its assertion that, in order to merit the protection of the free exercise clause of the first amendment, a religious practice must have its source exclusively in religious belief.[70] The Cherokee plaintiffs thus failed to pass the "quality of the claims" test, which the court set forth as the first of two steps in analyzing free exercise claims.[71] The court concluded that "plaintiffs have not alleged infringement of a constitutionally cognizable First Amendment right."[72] Since plaintiffs failed to satisfy the first step of the analysis, the court did not consider the second, the balancing test: "In the absence of such an infringement, there is no need to balance the opposing interest of the parties or to determine whether the government's interest in proceeding with its plans for the Tellico Dam is 'compelling.' "[73] On this basis, the court affirmed the trial court's judgment denying plaintiffs' motion for injunctive relief.[74]

II. *The Navajo Claim: Badoni v. Higginson*

Rainbow Bridge National Monument is a 160-acre tract in southern Utah, entirely surrounded by the Navajo Indian Reservation. Within this tract is a remarkable sandstone arch, 309 feet high and spanning 278 feet, sacred to Navajos who adhere to the traditional tribal religion.[75] Glen Canyon Dam, located fifty-eight miles below the sandstone arch on the Colorado River, was completed in 1963. The waters rising behind the dam to form the Lake Powell Reservoir have risen to reach the Monument. When the Lake Powell project is complete, there will be forty-six feet of water underneath the Bridge. Under the supervision and management of the National Park Service, boating facilities have been supplied to assist tourists in visiting the Monument as part of the

69. See *supra* text accompanying notes 18-19.

70. *See Callahan*, 658 F.2d 679 and text accompanying note 42 *supra*.

71. See *supra* text accompanying notes 27-28.

72. *Sequoyah*, 620 F.2d at 1165.

73. *Id.*

74. Judge Merritt dissented only on the ground that the case should be remanded for "plaintiffs to offer proof concerning the centrality of their ancestral burial grounds to their religion." *Id.* Judge Merritt fully accepted the "centrality" test and the majority's reasoning; he simply believed that summary judgment was not an appropriate resolution of this matter in which the record indicated that the factual matter of the "centrality" of plaintiff's religious practice allegedly infringed by the closing of the dam was in dispute.

75. *See Badoni v. Higginson*, 638 F.2d 172 (10th Cir. 1980).

Park Service's operation of the adjacent Glen Canyon National Recreation Area.[76]

In 1974 eight individual Navajos, three of them medicine men recognized by their people, brought suit to enjoin the Bureau of Reclamation, the National Park Service, and the Department of the Interior from continuing to act in such a manner as to destroy and desecrate the Navajo gods and sacred sites threatened by the rising waters of Lake Powell and by the influx of tourists.[77] The Navajo grounded their principal claim in the free exercise clause of the first amendment.[78] Intervening as defendants, agencies of the states of Utah and Colorado moved for judgment on the pleadings. The court treated the motion as one for summary judgment and granted it.[79]

The pleadings of the Navajo plaintiffs set forth an elaborate ground for their first amendment claim for injunctive relief.[80] However, the court dismissed plaintiffs' claims on two alternative grounds.[81] First, the court found that plaintiffs had no property interest in Rainbow Bridge National Monument and held that this lack of a property interest was dispositive of plaintiffs' claims. It cited no authority for the holding, stating only that "[t]he court feels that the lack of a property interest is determinative of the First Amendment question and agrees with defendants that plain-

---

76. *Id.* at 175.

77. Badoni v. Higginson, 455 F. Supp. 641 (D. Utah 1977).

78. U.S. Const. amend. I. In addition, the Navajo raised two statutory issues not pertinent to the present discussion. *See Badoni*, 455 F. Supp at 643 (violations of the Colorado River Storage Project Act and of the National Environmental Policy Act).

79. *Badoni*, 455 F. Supp. 641 (D. Utah 1977).

80. *Id.* at 643-44:

Certain geological formations in the Rainbow Bridge area have held positions of central importance in the religion of the Navajo people . . . for at least 100 years. These shrines, which are regarded as the actual incarnate forms of Navajo gods, have performed protective and rain-giving functions for generations of Navajo singers. . . . Plaintiffs allege that the flooding of Bridge Canyon in the vicinity of Rainbow Bridge and the greatly increased tourist traffic due to defendants' actions have resulted in the following specific infringements upon plaintiffs' First Amendment rights: the destruction of holy sites; the drowning of entities recognized as gods by the plaintiffs; prevention of plaintiffs from performing religious ceremonies; desecration of holy sites, especially abodes of gods of the plaintiffs, by tourists; and, by virtue of all of this, injury to the efficacy of plaintiffs' religious prayers, and entreaties to their remaining gods . . . Plaintiffs request this court to order defendants to take appropriate steps to operate Glen Canyon Dam and Reservoir in such a manner that the important religious and cultural interests of plaintiffs will not be harmed or degraded, and to issue rules and regulations to prevent further destruction and desecration of the Rainbow Bridge area by tourists.

81. *Id.* at 644.

tiffs have no cognizable claim under the circumstances presented.''[82] The court held out as persuasive a hypothetical situation proposed by defendants that involved a plaintiff who petitioned a federal court to restrict public access to the Lincoln Memorial because he had had an intense religious experience there.[83] The facile acceptance of defendants' hypothetical situation, however, ignores the difference between the claims of American Indians seeking to protect their religion and the situation described in the hypothetical. The Indians sought to vindicate old claims on territory that was once theirs for a religion that has its roots in the very origins of the Indian people; the Lincoln Memorial litigant could make no such claim. Recognition of the Navajo plaintiffs' first amendment claims would not have required a judgment in favor of defendants' hypothetical plaintiff.[84]

The court then presented an alternative ground of decision. Its cramped view of the free exercise test required by *Yoder*,[85] the difficulty of dismissing as nonreligious a claim that is on its face religious, and the superficial analysis and casual use of language in its first ground of decision led it into logical difficulties from which it failed to extricate itself.

The court began its analysis with the following statement: ''[E]ven if plaintiffs' claims were cognizable First Amendment claims . . . the interests of defendants would clearly outweigh the interests of plaintiffs.''[86] The court believed that even if plaintiffs

---

82. *Id.*

83. *Id.* at 645.

84. See TASK FORCE REPORT, *supra* note 3, at 8-12, for an analysis of the nature of the belief structure of American Indian religions. Defendants' analogy to an individual's spontaneous and contemporary religious experience is inappropriate, *see id.* at 88-98, although as a hypothetical case, it admittedly does raise troubling first amendment questions.

Id. at 12 states:

When the freedom of religion is discussed in the context of the tribal traditions, it is the right to adjust to and maintain relationships with the natural world and its inhabitants that is addressed . . . . The ceremonies and rites themselves set fairly precise rituals and reveal in the performance of the acts their continuing efficacy. While no future revelations can be ruled out, it would be the rarest of events for a new ceremony to be introduced. Except in the most remote areas of Indian country, the urbanization of North America has precluded both Indian and non-Indian from the constant relationship with the natural world that would be conducive to the revelation of further ceremonies.

85. 406 U.S. at 214.

86. *Badoni*, 455 F. Supp. at 645.

had been found to have standing under the property interest test, the religious claims they advanced were clearly outweighed by defendants' interests. However, the court then undercut the logic of this analysis by finding that plaintiffs' claims failed to pass the *Yoder* "centrality" test and therefore *were not religious claims* worthy of first amendment protection:

> It is apparent that these interests do not constitute "deep religious conviction[s], shared by an organized group and intimately related to daily living. . . ."[87] [T]here is nothing to indicate that at the present time the Rainbow Bridge National Monument and its environs has [sic] anything approaching deep, religious significance to any organized group, or has in recent decades been intimately related to the daily living of any group or individual.
>
> . . .
>
> Plaintiffs fail, however, to demonstrate in any manner a vital relationship of the practices in question with the Navajo way of life or a "history of consistency" which would support their allegation of religious use of Rainbow Bridge in recent times.
>
> . . .
>
> In sum, the alleged interests of plaintiffs have not been established.[88]

Applying the "deep religious significance," "intimately related to daily living," and "vital relationship" standards of *Yoder*, the court purported to hold that the Navajo lost the balancing test, when in fact it had held that the Navajo had not stated a religious claim under the free exercise clause. In support of its findings, the court pointed to two dispositive facts: first, the plaintiff medicine men were not "recognized by the Navajo Nation as such," their training was not "tribally organized," and it took place years ago; and second, the ceremonies were held too infrequently to qualify for constitutional protection.[89] The first assertion, however, was explicitly contradicted by a prior finding of the court[90] and, in any case, is meaningless when the relationship between tribal government and tribal religion is properly under-

---

87. *Id.*, *citing Yoder*, 406 U.S. at 216.
88. *Id.* 455 F. Supp. at 646.
89. *Id.*
90. *Id.* at 642: "Three of the individual plaintiffs are qualified and recognized among their people as medicine men—i.e., religious leaders of considerable stature among the Navajo, learned in Navajo history, mythology and culture, and practitioners of traditional rites and ceremonies of ancient origin."

stood.[91] The second assertion may be of some significance when considering a religious claim within the mainstream Judaeo-Christian tradition, but it is irrelevant when applied to traditional religions of the American Indian.[92]

The Tenth Circuit affirmed the district court's denial of relief and grant of defendants' motion for summary judgment. However, it substituted for one of the district court's alternative grounds of decision one of its own.[93] The court cited *Sequoyah* to support its rejection of the district court's conclusion that the Navajos' lack of a property interest in the Monument denied them standing to claim free exercise protection. Further, the court implicitly rejected the notion that *Yoder* required the application of a "centrality test"[94] to free exercise challenges to government activity.[95] The court did not attempt to demonstrate,

---

91. *See, e.g., Hearings on S.J. Res. 102, supra* note 1, at 242-43 (letter of Rev. Caleb Holetstewa Johnson, Personal Representative, Hopi Traditional Kikmongwis, Feb. 21, 1978):

> On many reservations there are two group [sic] of Indians. On the one hand, there are the progressive Indians who are active in the Tribal Councils. On most reservation [sic], they have nothing to do with traditional Indians . . . . In fact, on the Hopi reservation, it is the progressive tribal council which is making problems for the Traditional Hopis. It is the progressive tribal Council who is breaking down and interfering with the Hopi traditions and customs . . . the so-called progressives . . . in most cases, know nothing about the traditional ceremonials and traditional rites of the Indian Tribes.

See also S. REP. 709, 1978, *supra* note 9, at 5:

> It is the intent [of Congress in enacting the American Indian Religious Freedom Act] that that source [of information concerning Indian religious practices] be the practitioner of the religion, the medicine people, religious leaders, and traditionalist [sic] who are Natives—and not Indian experts, political leaders, or any other nonpractitioner.

92. *See* TASK FORCE REPORT, *supra* note 3, at 10-11:

> The tribal religions do not incorporate a set of established truths but serve to perpetuate a set of rituals and ceremonies which must be conducted in accordance with the instructions given in the original revelation of each particular ceremony or ritual . . . . Unlike the larger religions, the ceremonial year did not commemorate specific chronological historical events, and some ceremonies were reserved for occasions that warranted them. Not all ceremonies needed to be performed each year in the manner that the Christian year follows the life and passion of Jesus, for example.

93. Badoni v. Higginson, 638 F.2d 172 (10th Cir. 1980).

94. *Id.* at 176-77.

95. *Id.* at 176:

At the outset, we reject the conclusion that plaintiffs' lack of property rights in the Monument is determinative. The government must manage its property in a manner that does not offend the Constitution. *See Sequoyah v. TVA*, 620 F.2d 1159, 1164 (6th Cir. 1980) (lack of property interest not conclusive, but is a factor in weighing free exercise and competing interests).

as had the district court,[96] that the Navajo claims were not sufficiently "central" to qualify for first amendment protection, but rather held directly that "Rainbow Bridge and a nearby spring, prayer spot and cave have held positions of *central importance* in the religion of some Navajo people living in the area for at least 100 years."[97]

The court then applied the balancing test mandated by *Yoder*[98] to the first of two injuries alleged by plaintiffs. Without extensive analysis, the court found that "the government's interest in maintaining the capacity of Lake Powell at a level that intrudes into the Monument outweighs plaintiffs' religious interest . . . . In these circumstances we believe the government has shown an interest of a magnitude sufficient to justify the alleged infringements."[99] The court saw no delicate balance. The interests of an entire section of the nation in managing scarce water resources simply could not be overborne by religious claims of American Indians.

Plaintiffs had also contended that the National Park Service's inadequate regulation of tourist behavior had infringed the free exercise of their religion. They sought "some measured accommodation"[100] by means of regulations to control the behavior of tourists at the Monument and thereby reduce the injury done to the Monument itself and to their religious practices. The court accepted that tourists had "desecrated [the Monument] by noise, litter and defacement of the Bridge itself."[101] After briefly surveying several free exercise cases, it decided that the rule of accommodation of *Wisconsin v. Yoder*,[102] *Wooley v. Maynard*,[103] *McDaniel v. Paty*,[104] and *Sherbert v. Verner*[105] did not require the government here to take special steps because it "has not prohibited plaintiffs' religious exercises in the area of Rainbow Bridge; plaintiffs may enter the Monument on the same basis as other people."[106] To the contrary, the court found that any government initiative to control the behavior of tourists to the

96. See *supra* text accompanying notes 85-88.
97. *Badoni*, 638 F.2d at 177 (emphasis added).
98. *Yoder*, 406 U.S. at 214.
99. *Badoni*, 638 F.2d at 177.
100. *Id.* at 178, *citing* Appellants' Brief at 8.
101. *Id.*
102. 406 U.S. 205 (1972).
103. 430 U.S. 705 (1977).
104. 435 U.S. 618 (1978).
105. 374 U.S. 398 (1963).
106. *Badoni*, 638 F.2d at 178.

Monument for the benefit of the Navajo in the exercise of their traditional religion would run afoul of the establishment clause of the first amendment.[107]

The court supported its argument by noting that regulation of tourist behavior in order to protect Navajo religious practices at the Monument would infringe the right of the public to use the Monument for its own purposes.[108] The case law upon which the court relied to reach these two conclusions points consistently to contrary propositions. In support of its conclusion that there was danger of an establishment clause violation, the court cited only one case, *School District of Abington v. Schempp*.[109] The court there held that "there must be a secular legislative purpose and a primary effect that neither advances nor inhibits religion."[110] For the proposition that the public had a right of access that may not be regulated for the benefit of an individual's free exercise rights, the court cited a line of cases that stands for a precisely contrary conclusion.[111] The sections that follow will discuss each of these conclusions.

The Establishment Clause Misapplied

Government defendants have traditionally raised the establishment clause as a defense to free exercise claims.[112] However, recent jurisprudence suggests an integrated view of the two religion clauses of the first amendment that would posit the common goal that all religions prosper or decline without the help or interference of government. The two religion clauses should not operate as a system of checks and balances, one upon the other. Chief

---

107. *Id.*: "But what plaintiffs seek in the name of the Free Exercise Clause is affirmative action by the government which implicates the Establishment Clause of the First Amendment."

"Issuance of regulations to exclude tourists completely from the Monument for the avowed purpose of aiding plaintiffs' conduct of religious ceremonies would seem a clear violation of the Establishment Clause . . . . Were it otherwise, the Monument would become a government-managed religious shrine." *Id.* at 179.

108. "Exercise of First Amendment freedoms may not be asserted to deprive the public of its normal use of an area . . . . We must also deny relief insofar as plaintiffs seek to have the government police the actions of tourists lawfully visiting the Monument." *Id.*

109. 374 U.S. 203 (1963).

110. *Id.* at 222.

111. *Badoni*, 638 F.2d at 179.

112. *See, e.g.*, Widmar v. Vincent, 454 U.S. 263 (1981); McDaniel v. Paty, 435 U.S. 638 (1978); Sherbert v. Verner, 374 U.S. 398, 409-10 (1963).

Justice Burger has recognized that such a view requires the resolution of apparent conflict between the two clauses:

> The Court must not ignore the danger that an exception from a general obligation of citizenship on religious grounds may run afoul of the Establishment Clause, but that danger cannot be allowed to prevent any exception no matter how vital it may be to the protection of values promoted by the right of free exercise.[113]

The Court has recognized that at least since *Everson v. Board of Education*,[114] government may provide religious institutions with the basic services normally available to all other citizens without compromising establishment clause values.[115] In the present case, Navajo plaintiffs sought protection from damage and desecration of a religious site located on federally managed land. Had the Navajo requested the same measures in order to protect an esthetic, economic, or ecological interest, the government would have had unquestioned authority to act. Yet the *Badoni* court held that the establishment clause barred the government from acting to protect a landmark geological structure simply because religious beliefs motivated the Navajo plaintiffs. Indeed, the Navajo plaintiffs did not actually seek affirmative government action on their behalf. Rather, they sought only that the government take steps to minimize the destructive impact of its management policies. In effect, the Navajo plaintiffs sought not to have their religion favored by government action, but only to have the impact of *hostile* government action reduced.[116]

The Supreme Court has consistently found that affirmative government action which has only the incidental effect of benefiting religious believers and institutions falls safely within the limits of the establishment clause.[117] This rule of accommoda-

---

113. *Yoder*, 406 U.S. at 220-21. *See also* Justice Brennan's concurrence in School Dist. of Abington v. Schempp, 374 U.S. 203, 296-99 (1963).

114. 330 U.S. 1 (1947).

115. *See, e.g.,* Roemer v. Board of Public Works, 426 U.S. 736, 747 (1976).

116. *See* Petition for Certiorari at 1-3 (Mar. 1981). *See especially id.* at 3:

But it turns the First Amendment completely on its head to hold, as the Court of Appeals did here, that the Establishment Clause prevents the Government from tailoring its activities in otherwise unobjectionable ways—and in ways it might well have been employed in this very case if religion had not been involved—so as to minimize the Government's own positive inroads upon practices protected by the Free Exercise Clause.

117. *See, e.g.,* Roemer v. Board of Public Works, 426 U.S. 736 (1976); Tilton v. Richardson, 403 U.S. 672 (1971); Board of Educ. v. Allen, 392 U.S. 236 (1968); Zorach

tion is not, of course, unlimited; the three-part test most fully articulated in *Nyquist*[118] sets the outer limit for government accommodation under the establishment clause.

The *Badoni* court was simply wrong in its conclusion that government action to protect Navajo religious practices would have converted the Monument into "a government-managed religious shrine."[119] The *Nyquist* test demonstrates otherwise. As the Navajo plaintiffs observed, "[T]he whole point is that Rainbow Bridge is a religious shrine; it was that long before it was declared to be a national monument."[120] The court held that the accommodation that the Navajo requested would violate the second prong of *Nyquist*, which prohibits government action that has a primary effect of advancing one religion above all others.[121] The second part of the *Nyquist* test, however, is framed in the alternative: The primary effect of the challenged government action must *neither* advance *nor* inhibit religion.[122] The court loaded the dice against the Navajo in its framing of the question. The government is now acting in a manner that impairs the practice of the Navajo religion. Rather than ask whether acceding to the Navajo request would implicate the government in action that has as its primary effect the advancement of the Navajo religion, the court should have inquired whether government refusal to modify its injurious activity impermissibly inhibited the Navajo in the free exercise of their religion. The trial court's factual findings, which the appellate court accepted, make it abundantly clear that the government action, or refusal to modify its action, fell short of the standard set forth in the second part of the *Nyquist* test.[123]

---

v. Clauson, 343 U.S. 306 (1952); Everson v. Board of Educ., 330 U.S. 1 (1947), for illustrative cases in which the Supreme Court has permitted local government to provide certain services and benefits to parochial schools and their students in the face of establishment clause challenges.

118. *See* Committee for Public Educ. & Religious Liberty v. Nyquist, 413 U.S. 756, 773 (1973). Under *Nyquist*, governmental action will survive an establishment clause challenge if it can be shown that the action is motivated by a secular legislative purpose, that its primary effect neither advances nor inhibits religion, and that it does not require excessive government entanglement with religious institutions and practices.

119. *Badoni*, 638 F.2d at 179.

120. Petition, *supra* note 116.

121. *Badoni*, 638 F.2d at 179.

122. *Nyquist*, 413 U.S. at 773.

123. For a recent district court decision that follows *Badoni* and inappropriately applies the second part of the *Nyquist* test, *see* Hopi Indian Tribe v. Block, No. 81-0841; Navajo Medicinemen's Ass'n v. Block, No. 81-0493; Wilson v. Block, No. 81-0558, 8 I.L.R. 3073 (D.D.C., June 15, 1981), *aff'd* No. 81-1912 (D.C. Cir. May 20, 1983).

The Public Forum Cases Misconstrued

The court held alternatively that regulations to protect Navajo practitioners from intrusion by tourists would be an impermissible burden on the right of those tourists to free access to the Monument.[124] In support of this proposition the court cited a familiar line of freedom of assembly and freedom of expression cases.[125] Implying that government regulation of the tourist crowds at the Monument to minimize interference with the practice of the traditional Navajo religion would violate a first amendment right of the tourists, the court insisted that the case law supported such a proposition: "Government action has frequently been invalidated when it has denied the exercise of First Amendment rights compatible with public use."[126]

These cited cases, however, stand for a proposition quite contrary to that for which the court sought support. They stand instead for the proposition that the public right to free access to public forums must sometimes yield to the exercise of first amendment rights. In other words, these cases present a cogent argument for government intervention to protect the Navajo in their efforts to exercise their first amendment right to practice their religion. They do not support the government's refusal to act in order to avoid interfering with a tenuous first amendment right of tourists to the Monument.[127] Such an accommodation would not run afoul of the establishment clause. Indeed, read in tandem, the religion clauses demand it. When government action directly burdens the free exercise of a particular religion, the government does not offer favored treatment to that religion when it acts to lift that burden.[128]

By choosing to balance the constitutional equities in favor of encouraging tourism, the court has effectively denied the Navajo the practice of their traditional religion. The court framed a choice between maintaining the Monument as a shrine or destroying it. Since it wrongly believed that the establishment clause of the first amendment barred the government from acting to preserve the Monument as a shrine, it voted for its destruction.

---

124. See note 108 *supra*.
125. *Badoni*, 638 F.2d at 179, *citing* Shuttlesworth v. Birmingham, 384 U.S. 147, 152 (1969); Amalgamated Food Employees Union v. Logan Valley Plaza, Inc., 391 U.S. 308, 320 (1968); Cox v. Louisiana, 379 U.S. 536, 554-55 (1965); Niemotko v. Maryland, 340 U.S. 268, 271 (1951); Hague v. C.I.O., 307 U.S. 496, 515-16 (1939).
126. *Badoni*, 638 F.2d at 179.
127. *See* Niemotko v. Maryland, 340 U.S. 268, 271 (1951).
128. *See, e.g.*, Fowler v. Rhode Island, 345 U.S. 67 (1953).

III.   *The Illusory Protections of the American Indian Religious Freedom Act*

Indian plaintiffs in both *Sequoyah*[129] and *Badoni*[130] invoked the protection of the recently enacted American Indian Religious Freedom Act.[131] In *Sequoyah* the court dismissed the Cherokee claim under the Act as overborne by superseding legislation and thus did not examine the substance of the Act.[132] In *Badoni* the court curtly refused even to consider the Navajo claims under the Act.[133] If the Act does not apply to the situations presented by the Indian plaintiffs in *Sequoyah* and *Badoni*, it is difficult to imagine what import it might have beyond its praiseworthy but ineffective statement of policy and expression of good will. As the following examination of the legislative history of the Act reveals, Congress never seriously intended to put teeth into the Act. Despite Senator Abourezk's protests, the executive branch took the hint. It has not construed the Act to modify any existing state or federal law,[134] but has seen its purpose as merely to state

---

129. *Sequoyah*, 620 F.2d at 1161.

130. *Badoni*, 638 F.2d at 180.

131. Act of Aug. 11, 1978, Pub. L. No. 95-341, 92 Stat. 469 (codified in part at 42 U.S.C. § 1996). See Appendix for full text.

132. *Sequoyah*, 620 F.2d at 1161:
Relief under the . . . Act . . . is foreclosed by a provision of the Energy and Water Development Appropriation Bill, Pub. Law No. 96-69 . . . . "[N]otwithstanding provisions of 16 U.S.C., Chapter 35 [The Endangered Species Act] *or any other law*, the Corporation [TVA] is authorized and directed to complete construction, operate, and maintain the Tellico Dame . . . ." (Emphasis added.) No clearer congressional command is imaginable. No law is to stand in the way of the completion and operation of the dam.

133. *Badoni*, 638 F.2d at 180: "But we do not have before us the constitutionality of . . . [the Act] or of any action taken by defendants in alleged violation of them."

134. *See Hearings on S.J. Res. 102, supra* note 1, at 132-33 (colloquy between Larry L. Simms, Office of the Legal Counsel, Department of Justice, and Senator Abourezk, Chairman, U.S. Senate Select Committee on Indian Affairs):
Abourezk: What you are saying is, the administration—the Justice Department—would not want to see Congress overrule anything that happened before. I don't have to tell you that if Senate Joint Resolution 102 passes, it does overrule anything previously conflicting. Is that right?
Simms: Well, we are also here to find out what the intent is. . . . That is another thing we are unclear about.
See also, e.g., President Jimmy Carter, *Statement on Signing S.J. Res. 102 Into Law*, Weekly Comp. Pres. Doc. 1417-18 (Aug. 12, 1978): "This act is in no way intended to alter that guarantee [to worship freely] or override existing laws. . . ." *See also* S. Rep. 709, 1978, *supra* note 9, at 11 (statement by George Goodwin, Deputy Assistant Secretary of the Interior for Indian Affairs): "We recommend passage of Senate Joint Resolution 102 with clarifying language . . . [which] would insure that no provision of the resolution

federal policy and announce an agenda for administrative and regulatory reform.[135]

In his statement before the Senate Select Committee on Indian Affairs, Larry L. Simms, an attorney from the Department of Justice, raised the administration's concerns about what he identified as establishment clause and federalism problems with the proposed Act.[136] Simms advanced an administration proposal that Congress resolve the federalism problem and the question of the status of prior conflicting legislation by inserting limiting

---

would be construed as amending existing law." *See id.* at 12 (conclusion of committee):

The resolution does direct the administration to change its regulations and enforcement practices wherever necessary to protect and preserve native American religious cultural rights and practices. If changes cannot be made consistent with present statutory intent, then the President must report back to Congress his recommendations for changes in existing law which will require further legislative action.

This conclusion comports substantially with the position taken by the Justice Department. *See id.* at 11 (remarks by Larry L. Simms):

Where conflicts arise that cannot be resolved within the existing statutory framework the proper course for the executive branch would be to seek legislation permitting Congress to declare its intent with regard to the balance to be struck between preservation of religious freedom and the achievement of the objectives of the specific programs involved.

Congressman Udall, sponsor of the Act in the House, made it abundantly clear that Congress intended to limit the authority of the Act. *See* 124 CONG. REC. H6871-73 (daily ed. July 18, 1978):

It is not the intent of my bill to wipe out laws passed for the benefit of the general public or to confer special religious rights on Indians . . . . It has no teeth in it. It is the sense of the Congress . . . it is the Department's [of Justice] understanding that this resolution . . . does not change any existing State or Federal law. That, of course, is the committee's understanding and intent.

See also, Indian Rights, supra note 2, at 141: "[The Act] does not seek to correct any express federal policy which infringes upon Indians' religious practices. Instead, it attempts to rectify injustices which occurred from a lack of federal policy."

The United States Commission on Civil Rights has taken a similarly benign view of the Act. *See* U.S. COMM'N ON CIVIL RIGHTS, AMERICAN INDIAN CIVIL RIGHTS HANDBOOK (2d ed. 1980), at 6: "It is hoped [that] this process [specified in Section 2 of the Act] will ensure that government policies and practices take into account and do not unnecessarily interfere with Indian religious practices."

135. President Jimmy Carter, *Statement, supra* note 134, at 1417: "This legislation sets forth the policy of the United States to protect and preserve the inherent right of American Indian, Eskimo, Aleut, and Native Hawaiian people to believe, express, and exercise their traditional religions." *See also American Indian Religious Freedom: Report to Accompany H.J. Res. 738,* H.R. REP. No. 1308, 95th Cong., 2d Sess. 1 (1978):

The purpose of House Joint Resolution 738 . . . is to insure that the policies and procedures of various Federal agencies, as they may impact upon the exercise of traditional Indian religious practices, are brought into compliance with the constitutional injunction that Congress shall make no laws abridging the free exercise of religion.

136. S. REP. 709, 1978, *supra* note 9, at 10-11 (statement of Larry L. Simms).

language into section 2 of the Act[137] and adding a third section.[138] Though the Committee accepted neither amendment, it appears to have accepted the *sense* of the amendments as part of the Act.[139] The Committee closed its report with the following finding: "In compliance with subsection 4 of rule XXIX of the Standing Rules of the Senate, the Committee notes that no changes in existing law are made by Senate Joint Resolution 102 as reported."[140] It thus required no leap of the judicial imagination for the *Badoni* and *Sequoyah* courts to find that the American Indian Religious Freedom Act had no bearing on the resolution of the free exercise claims advanced by the Indian plaintiffs. Congress's toothless expression of special concern for problems of Indian access to sacred sites, precisely the problem addressed in both *Sequoyah* and *Badoni*, was insufficient.[141]

Simms also expressed the Justice Department's concern that the Act might pose establishment clause problems, suggesting that the Act might be read so as "to give preferential treatment to Indian religious freedom beyond that afforded to other non-Indian religions."[142] However, Simms did not offer any concrete examples as to how this concern of the Justice Department might materialize.

---

137. *Id.* at 11: "We would suggest that section 2 of the resolution be amended to read as follows: '. . . to implement such changes *as may be consistent with existing statutes.*'" (Emphasis added.)

138. *Id.*: "Section 3. Nothing in this resolution shall be construed as affecting any provision of State or Federal law."

139. See *supra* text accompanying notes 134-135.

140. S. REP. 709, 1978, *supra* note 9, at 12.

141. *See id.* at 2-3:

The first restrictions are denials of access to Indians to certain physical locations. Often, these locations include certain sites . . . which are sacred to Indian religions . . . . To deny access to them is analogous to preventing a non-Indian from entering his church or temple . . . . Federal agencies such as the Forest Service, Park Service, Bureau of Land Management, and others have prevented Indians in certain cases from entering onto these lands. The issue is not ownership or protection of the lands involved. Rather, it is a straightforward question of access in order to worship and perform the necessary rites.

142. *See id.* at 10:

This is not to say that the unique characteristics of Indian religious practices may not call for and permit accommodations different from those reached with respect to non-Indian religions. It is to say that there may be some situations in which a conscious preference accorded to some Indian religious practices [may] raise establishment clause and due process clause problems.

Apparently the Justice Department is willing to recognize the rule of free exercise accommodation. However, for reasons that are not apparent, Simms cites Kennedy v. B.N.D.D., 459 F.2d 415 (9th Cir. 1972), to support his establishment clause concerns.

The Committee responded by clarifying its purpose: "[The Act] is in no way intended to provide Indian religions with a more favorable status than other religions, only to insure that the U.S. Government treats them equally."[143]

Congress could not attempt to create by statute an exemption from the establishment clause strictures of the first amendment.[144] The only reported decision that deals with the substance of the Act takes precisely this position.[145]

The draftsmen of the *Task Force Report*[146] were sensitive to the possibility of establishment clause challenges to the Act, as well as challenges to the administrative and legislative action that would be taken pursuant to the Act. The *Report*'s first defense against such challenges, however, reveals only a superficial understanding of the implications of the establishment clause:

> The establishment of a religion is not a problem when viewed from within the tribal context . . . . Establishment is fundamentally the imposition by the political institution of forms of belief and practice which are in conflict with or are distasteful to people of a different tradition. Protecting Indian religious practices from curiosity seekers, casual observers, and administrative rules and regulations is the only practical way that religious freedom can be assured to Indian Tribes and Native groups. It is not the establishment of their religion because their religions, not being proselytizing religions, seek to preserve the ceremonies, rituals and beliefs, not to spread them.[147]

---

143. S. REP. 709, 1978, *supra* note 9, at 6.

144. *But cf.* Katzenbach v. Morgan, 384 U.S. 641 (1966); Cox, *The Supreme Court, 1965 Term—Foreword: Constitutional Adjudication and the Promotion of Human Rights*, 80 HARV. L. REV. 91 (1966).

145. *See* Navajo Medicinemen's Ass'n v. Block, No. 81-0493, 8 I.L.R. 3073, 3076 (D.D.C. June 15, 1981), *aff'd*, No. 81-1912 (D.C. Cir. May 20, 1983). The court stated that the Act is a guarantee of first amendment rights of American Indians and does not grant any rights not already found in the amendment. Once again, Indian plaintiffs lost a land access question, with the court holding that the Act does not require that access to publicly owned property be granted to Indians without consideration for other users or activities (in this case the development of the Snow Bowl ski resort in the sacred San Francisco Peaks area of Arizona).

See also U.S. Dept. of Agriculture, Forest Service, Chief's Decision on Request for Administrative Review of Southwestern Regional Forester's Decision Involving Arizona Snow Bowl Skiing Facilities and the Snow Bowl Road, Coconino National Forest, 8 I.L.R. 5011 (Dept. of Agric., Dec. 31, 1980).

146. TASK FORCE REPORT, *supra* note 3.

147. *Id.* at 12.

The *Report* suggests that only proselytizing religions can be "established" by government action. But the government cannot offer support to a religion without violating the establishment clause under the rule of *Nyquist*.[148] The *Report* offers no further establishment clause analysis, but merely reiterates that establishment clause strictures do not apply to traditional Indian religion:

> Protecting the boundaries of state and church are certainly important, but to guarantee religious freedom to American Indians does not necessarily mean the establishment of traditional Native religions over and above other religions . . . . It is possible to state that traditional Native religions have little chance of creating a national crisis in the church-state relationship.[149]
>
> [The Act] does not constitute the establishment of a religion. The premises of Native tribal religions differ so fundamentally from the religions of the majority in perspective and practice that the traditional dangers against which the establishment clause guards do not exist.[150]

Whether this is in fact true remains to be seen, since *Navajo Medicinemen's Association*[151] is the only reported federal court decision which addresses the substance of the Act. Given the extreme caution revealed by the legislative history,[152] it seems unlikely that any agency of the federal government will seek to apply the Act in a controversial manner and thereby pose any difficult constitutional questions. Rather, the Act will more probably remain a benign statement of government policy and a direction to federal agencies to examine carefully their policies, regulations, and procedures which may have an impact on the practice of traditional American Indian religions.[153]

Conclusion: A Proposal for Judicial Candor

Both *Badoni* and *Sequoyah* offer unprincipled resolutions of difficult and troubling situations in which government action has severely impaired the ability of American Indians to practice their

148. 413 U.S. 756.

149. TASK FORCE REPORT, *supra* note 3, at 89 and 98.

150. *Id.*

151. Navajo Medicinemen's Ass'n v. Block, No. 81-0493, 8 I.L.R. 3073, 3076 (D.D.C. June 15, 1981), *aff'd*, No. 81-1912 (D.C. Cir. May 20, 1983).

152. See *supra* notes 135-138 and accompanying text.

153. *See* American Indian Religious Freedom Act, Act of Aug. 11, 1978, Pub. L. No. 95-341, 92 Stat. 469, § 2 (codified in part at 42 U.S.C. § 1996). See Appendix for full text.

traditional tribal religions. Neither court advances first amendment jurisprudence in its analysis. Relying on a dubious "centrality" test, the *Sequoyah* court wrongly found that the Cherokee had failed to state a religious claim under the free exercise clause of the first amendment. The *Badoni* court assumed that competing interests would have outweighed any religious interests the Navajo might have asserted. It therefore declined to analyze the religious interest the Navajo had alleged. The court buttressed its holding with a poorly reasoned establishment clause attack on the Navajos' argument. Both courts affirmed summary judgments, foreclosing any possibility of an evidentiary hearing on factual matters relating to the Indians' claims. Neither decision offers any concrete guidance on the difficult free exercise issues these cases present. It still remains for a federal court to admit candidly that massive federal water projects that affect millions of people and large sections of the country will consistently weigh more heavily in the balance than the competing religious claims of isolated groups of American Indians. The historical inevitability of this result will not make the underlying hierarchy of values any more palatable.

Unfortunately, the American Indian Religious Freedom Act will likely continue to provide little aid to Indian plaintiffs such as those in *Sequoyah* and *Badoni*. Perhaps the Act will remind government officials responsible for formulating and applying the rules, regulations, and procedures of federal administrative agencies to be more solicitous of Indian religious interests. But the Act, an impotent statement of good intentions, will have no impact on the power relationship between white society and Indian society that is at the core of the problems relating to traditional Indian religious practice.

(Appendix follows)

Appendix

American Indian Religious Freedom Act:

PUBLIC LAW 95-341—AUG. 11, 1978

Public Law 95-341
95th Congress

Joint Resolution

American Indian Religious Freedom.

Whereas the freedom of religion for all people is an inherent right, fundamental to the democratic structure of the United States and is guaranteed by the First Amendment of the United States Constitution:

Whereas the United States has traditionally rejected the concept of a government denying individuals the right to practice their religion and, as a result, has benefited from a rich variety of religious heritages in this country;

Whereas the religious practices of the American Indian (as well as Native Alaskan and Hawaiian) are an integral part of their culture, tradition and heritage, such practices forming the basis of Indian identity and value systems;

Whereas the traditional American Indian religions, as an integral part of Indian life, are indispensable and irreplaceable;

Whereas the lack of a clear, comprehensive, and consistent Federal policy has often resulted in the abridgment of religious freedom for traditional American Indians;

Whereas such religious infringements result from the lack of knowledge or the insensitive and inflexible enforcement of Federal policies and regulations premised on a variety of laws;

Whereas such laws were designed for such worthwhile purposes as conservation and preservation of natural species and resources but were never intended to relate to Indian religious practices and, therefore, were passed without consideration of their effect on traditional American Indian religions;

Whereas such laws and policies often deny American Indians access to sacred sites required in their religions, including cemeteries;

Whereas such laws at times prohibit the use and possession of sacred objects necessary to the exercise of religious rites and ceremonies;

Whereas traditional American Indian ceremonies have been intruded upon, interfered with, and in a few instances banned: Now, therefore, be it

Resolved by the Senate and House of Representatives of the United States of America in Congress assembled, That henceforth it shall be the policy of the United States to protect and preserve for American Indians their inherent right of freedom to believe, express, and exercise the traditional religions of the American Indian, Eskimo, Aleut, and Native Hawaiians, including but not limited to access to sites, use and possession of sacred objects, and the freedom to worship through ceremonials and traditional rites.

Sec. 2. The President shall direct the various Federal departments, agencies, and other instrumentalities responsible for administering relevant laws to evaluate their policies and procedures in consultation with native traditional religious leaders in order to determine appropriate changes necessary to protect and preserve Native American religious cultural rights and practices. Twelve months after approval of this resolution, the President shall report back to the Congress the results of his evaluation, including any changes which were made in administrative policies and procedures, and any recommendations he may have for legislative action.

LYNG V. NORTHWEST: CLOSING THE DOOR TO INDIAN RELIGIOUS SITES

I. INTRODUCTION

The first amendment to the Constitution provides that "Congress shall make no law . . . prohibiting the free exercise [of religion]."[1] The United States Supreme Court has held that the first amendment's free exercise clause prohibits any government activity that has a "coercive effect" on a religion or religious practice.[2] The government activity need not expressly prohibit religion to have a "coercive effect." It is a sufficient religious prohibition if the activity directly or indirectly impedes a the religious practice.[3] The free exercise clause thus proscribes legislation or government actions that are facially neutral yet discriminatory in effect.[4] The protection afforded by the first amendment is intended to apply to unorthodox as well as orthodox religions. "[R]eligious beliefs need not be acceptable, logical, consistent, or comprehensible to others in order to merit First Amendment protection."[5] However, that protection

---

1. U.S. CONST. amend. I. The full text of the Religion Clauses provides: "Congress shall make no law respecting an establishment of religion, or prohibiting the free exercise thereof. . . ." Although the establishment clause is implicated in several of the cases discussed herein, this article will address only the free exercise claims. The test employed by the U.S. Supreme Court in analyzing establishment clause cases was clarified in Lemon v. Kurtzman, 403 U.S. 602 (1971). To be constitutionally valid, governmental action must satisfy three tests. First, it must reflect a secular purpose; second, its primary effect must neither advance nor inhibit religion; third, it must not foster an excessive entanglement with religion. *Id.* at 612-13.

2. School Dist. v. Schempp, 374 U.S. 203 (1963). The purpose of the free exercise clause "is to secure religious liberty in the individual by prohibiting any invasions thereof by civil authority. Hence it is necessary in a free exercise case for one to show the coercive effect of the enactment as it operates against him in the practice of his religion." *Id.* at 223.

3. *See* Sherbert v. Verner, 374 U.S. 398, 404 (1963) ("If the purpose or effect of a law is to impede the observance of one or all religions or is to discriminate invidiously between religions, that law is constitutionally invalid even though the burden may be characterized as being only indirect.") (quoting Braunfeld v. Brown, 366 U.S. 599, 607 (1961)).

4. *See, e.g.,* Wisconsin v. Yoder, 406 U.S. 205 (1972) (state statute requiring parents to send children to school until the age of 16 violated free exercise rights of Amish parents). "A regulation neutral on its face may, in its application, nonetheless offend the constitutional requirement for governmental neutrality if it unduly burdens the free exercise of religion." *Id.* at 220.

5. Thomas v. Review Bd., 450 U.S. 707, 714 (1981) (denial of unemployment benefits to a Jehovah's Witness who quit his job manufacturing military tanks because it conflicted with his religious beliefs violated his free exercise rights).

is not absolute.[6] To determine whether the plaintiff's religious practice warrants constitutional protection, the United States Supreme Court applies a test which balances the infringement on the plaintiff's religion against the competing government interest.[7]

In recent years, a number of claims presenting a new first amendment issue have been brought by American Indians. The Indians have alleged violations of their free exercise rights because governmental land use decisions have interfered with Indian use of sacred religious ceremonial sites.[8] In each case, the court denied the Indians' claims and upheld the government's actions.[9] The issue finally reached the United States Supreme Court in *Lyng v. Northwest Indian Cemetery Protective Ass'n*,[10] and again the Indians' claims were denied.[11] In *Lyng*, the Court had an opportunity to afford constitutional protection to the Indian religions, but failed to do so. The Court upheld the government's plan to construct a paved highway and to permit timber harvesting in a national forest that had sacred value to certain Indian tribes.[12] The Court utilized a very narrow interpretation of the free exercise clause by holding that the proposed activity neither coerced tribe members into violating their religious beliefs nor penalized their religious activity.[13] The result indicates that

---

6. *See* United States v. Lee, 455 U.S. 252, 259 (1982) (stating that "to maintain an organized society that guarantees religious freedom to a great variety of faiths requires that some religious practices yield to the common good.").

7. *Id.* at 256-59. The balancing test is applied in two steps. First, the plaintiff must establish that the government has interfered with the free exercise of his religion. If the plaintiff meets this burden, the government must show that its action is essential to accomplish a compelling interest in order to justify the interference. *See also infra* notes 18-40 and accompanying text.

8. *See, e.g.*, Crow v. Gullet, 541 F. Supp. 785 (D.S.D. 1982) (Lakota and Tsistsistas Indians claimed that state action restricting and regulating access to a religious site in a state park violated free exercise rights), *aff'd*, 706 F.2d 856 (8th Cir. 1983) (per curiam), *cert. denied*, 464 U.S. 977 (1983); Inupiat Community v. Alaska, 548 F. Supp. 182 (D. Alaska 1982) (Inupiat tribe objected to U.S. leasing seas off Alaska coast to oil companies because it interfered with their religious activities), *aff'd*, 746 F.2d 570 (9th Cir. 1984), *cert. denied*, 474 U.S. 820 (1985); Hopi Indian Tribe v. Block, 8 Indian L. Rep. 3073 (Am. Indian Law Training Program) (D.D.C. June 15, 1981) (denied Navajo and Hopi Indians claim that the expansion of a ski resort permitted by the U.S. Forest Service violated their free exercise of religion), *aff'd sub nom.* Wilson v. Block, 708 F.2d 735 (D.C. Cir. 1983), *cert. denied sub nom.* Hopi Indian Tribe v. Block, 464 U.S. 1056 (1984); Sequoyah v. TVA, 480 F. Supp. 608 (E.D. Tenn. 1979) (flooding by TVA that would bury sacred Indian sites did not violate plaintiff's religious beliefs or practices), *aff'd*, 620 F.2d 1159 (6th Cir. 1980), *cert. denied*, 449 U.S. 953 (1980); Badoni v. Higginson, 455 F. Supp. 641 (D. Utah 1977) (Navajo Indians' claim that flooding by the Glen Canyon Dam drowned Navajo Gods and destroyed a sacred prayer site did not give rise to a cognizable first amendment free exercise claim), *aff'd*, 638 F.2d 172 (10th Cir. 1980), *cert. denied sub nom.* Badoni v. Broadbent, 452 U.S. 954 (1981).

9. *See infra* notes 51-149 and accompanying text.

10. 485 U.S. 439 (1988).

11. *Id.* at 458.

12. *Id.*

13. *Id.* at 417-458.

the government, at least in cases where its actions interfere with the religious practices of American Indians, may take such action even where the negative impact on the religion is very significant and the government's interest in the action is less than compelling.

In each of the cases cited,[14] and again in *Lyng*,[15] the test enunciated by the United States Supreme Court has been varied, and has been misapplied by lower courts when analyzing the free exercise claims.[16] This Note will examine the reasons for those misapplications. Part II will discuss the development of the Court's test and its application in the Indian cases, Part III will analyze the *Lyng* decision and its impact, and Part IV will examine the reasons for the incorrect analysis in the Indian cases and will make recommendations to improve future decisions.[17]

II. The Free Exercise Clause

A. Development of the Modern Test of the Free Exercise Clause

The first amendment clearly states that Congress may not prohibit the free exercise of religion. Early decisions under the free exercise clause indicated that Congress was free to enact any legislation that did not formally prohibit religion, regardless of its effect on the religion.[18] However, modern cases have given the clause a broader reading. Since 1963, the Court has held that legislation or government activity may be declared unconstitutional even if its effects on religion are incidental or indirect.[19] In subsequent decisions, the Court has established a balancing test to determine whether legislation or government activity violates the free exercise clause.[20]

The two-prong test first enunciated in *Sherbert v. Verner*[21] and elab-

---

14. *See supra* note 8 and *infra* notes 51-149 and accompanying text.

15. 485 U.S. 439 (1988).

16. *See infra* notes 51-149 and accompanying text.

17. This article will only address the cases in which American Indians claim that governmental land use decisions violate their first amemndment rights. It will not discuss cases in which Indians claim that restrictions on their use of drugs, wild game, or other activities violate their rights. *See, e.g.,* Frank v. Alaska, 604 P.2d 1068 (Alaska 1979) (reversing conviction of Athabascan Indian under state game laws for using moose meat in a religious ceremony); People v. Woody, 61 Cal. 2d 716, 394 P.2d 813, 40 Cal. Rptr. 69 (1964) (reversing drug conviction of Navajo Indian who used peyote during religious ceremony).

18. *See, e.g.,* Reynolds v. United States, 98 U.S. 145, 166 (1878) (upholding prohibition of polygamy over the claims of a Mormon whose religion required him to engage in that practice).

19. *See infra* note 3.

20. *See infra* note 7 and *supra* notes 21-23.

21. 374 U.S. 398 (1963) (denial of state unemployment benefits to a Seventh Day Adventist who refused to work on Saturday due to her religious beliefs held unconstitutional). A similar test was applied in a plurality opinion by Chief Justice Warren in Braunfeld v. Brown, 366 U.S. 599, 606-

orated upon in *Wisconsin v. Yoder*[22] balances the burden on the plaintiff's religion against the competing state interest.[23] As a threshold requirement, the plaintiff must show that the practice in question is based on a sincerely[24] held "religious belief"[25] that is important to that religion.[26] The Court has indicated that the plaintiff's subjective assertions of importance[27] and sincerity[28] are generally accepted unless there is objective evidence to the contrary.

First, the plaintiff must show that the government has actually infringed upon the exercise of his religion.[29] The Court has held that to infringe upon a religion, the government action must have a "coercive effect"[30] that either directly or indirectly impedes the religious practices.[31] An infringement was found where the state disqualified a woman from receiving unemployment benefits because she refused a job which would have required her to work on Saturday in violation of her Seventh-Day Adventist beliefs.[32] A state statute requiring Amish parents to send their children to public or private school until they reached the age of sixteen was held to violate the free exercise clause.[33] Another violation was found where payment of social security taxes and receipt of benefits violated Amish religious beliefs.[34]

If the plaintiff establishes an infringement upon his religion, the sec-

---

607 (1961) (upholding Pennsylvania statute forbidding retail sale of certain items on Sundays over constitutional challenge of Orthodox Jews).

22. 406 U.S. 205 (1972) (state statute requiring parents to send their children to school until the age of 16 violated the free exercise rights of Amish parents).

23. *Id.* at 214.

24. *See* United States v. Lee, 455 U.S. 252, 257 (1982).

25. *Yoder*, 406 U.S. at 215 (stating that "to have the protection of the Religion Clauses, the claims must be rooted in religious belief.").

26. *Sherbert*, 374 U.S. at 406 (finding that practice in question was important because it constituted a "cardinal principle" of the claimant's faith).

27. *See, e.g.*, Thomas v. Review Bd., 450 U.S. 707, 716 (1981) (the "[c]ourts are not arbiters of scriptural interpretation.").

28. *See, e.g.*, *Lee*, 455 U.S. at 257.

29. *Sherbert*, 374 U.S. at 403 (question of whether disqualification for unemployment benefits imposed any burden on the free exercise of the claimant's religion).

30. School Dist. v. Schempp, 374 U.S. 203, 223 (1963) (requiring plaintiff to show the coercive effect of the government action on his religion).

31. *See supra* note 3.

32. *Sherbert*, 374 U.S. at 401-02.

33. Wisconsin v. Yoder, 406 U.S. 205 (1972). Amish parents believed that by sending their children to high school they would risk censure by the church community and endanger both their own and their children's salvation. *Id.* at 209.

34. United States v. Lee, 455 U.S. 252 (1982): An Amish plaintiff believed that the payment of social security taxes and receipt of benefits conflicted with his "religiously based obligation to provide for their fellow members the kind of assistance contemplated by the social security system." *Id.* at 257.

ond prong requires the court to examine the nature of the competing government interest causing the infringement.[35] The government interests are subject to strict scrutiny.[36] Thus, only "compelling" state interests justify the infringement of a first amendment right.[37] Indeed, the Court has stated, "only those interests of the highest order and those not otherwise served can overbalance legitimate claims to the free exercise of religion."[38] If the court determines that the state interest is not compelling, then it does not outweigh the religious interest, and the government's action is held unconstitutional. Even if the state interest is sufficiently compelling to outweigh the religious interest, the statute is invalid unless it burdens religion no more than is necessary to accomplish its purpose. The existence of less restrictive alternatives will also defeat the statute.[39]

B.   The Indian/Land Use Decisions

In 1978, Congress passed the American Indian Religious Freedom Act (AIRFA), which provides:

> On and after August 11, 1978, it shall be the policy of the United States to protect and preserve for American Indians their inherent right of freedom to believe, express, and exercise the traditional religions of the American Indian, Eskimo, Aleut, and Native Hawaiians, including but not limited to access to sites, use and possession of sacred objects, and the freedom to worship through ceremonial and traditional rites.

The Joint Resolution of Congress proposing the act stated that the motivating reasons included "the lack of a clear, comprehensive, and consistent Federal policy"[40] which "often resulted in the abridgement of religious freedom for traditional American Indians."[41] The proponents believed that the infringements resulted from a "lack of knowledge or the insensitive and inflexible enforcement of Federal policies."[42] Moreover, the resolution stated that laws concerning the environment were passed

---

35. See, e.g., Sherbert, 374 U.S. at 406.

36. Thomas v. Review Bd. 450 U.S. 707, 718 (1981) (stating that "[t]he state may justify an inroad on religious liberty by showing that it is the least restrictive means of achieving some compelling state interest.").

37. Id. An example of a "compelling state interest" is the government's need to maintain the social security tax system See United States v. Lee, 455 U.S. 252, 260 (1982).

38. Yoder, 406 U.S. at 215.

39. Thomas, 450 U.S. at 718 (state must use the "least restrictive means" to achieve its interest).

40. American Indian Religious Freedom Act, Pub. L. No. 95-341, 92 Stat. 469-70 (1978).

41. Id.

42. Id.

without considering the effects on the Indian religions and that "american Indian ceremonies have been intruded upon, interfered with, and in a few instances banned."[43]

Section 2 of the resolution requires the President to direct the various administrative departments and agencies to evaluate their policies and to make appropriate changes to reflect the new policy.[44] While the act does not create a statutory cause of action, its purpose is to ensure that the traditional Indian religions are constitutionally protected.[45] In fact, the United States Supreme Court has interpreted the act as "accurately identif[ying] the mission of the Free Exercise Clause itself."[46]

Since the act was passed, a number of cases have arisen in which American Indians have claimed that governmental land use decisions interfere with their use of land in religious ceremonies and thereby violates their free exercise rights.[47] The cases demonstrate that the courts are unwilling to apply the proper tests and analysis to assess the Indians' claims.[48]

1. Failure to Find a Religious Interest

In *Sequoyah v. TVA*,[49] *Badoni v. Higginson*,[50] and *Inupiat Community v. United States*,[51] the courts found that religious interests worthy of first amendment protection did not exist despite substantial evidence in each case supporting the presence of religion sufficient to meet the *Sherbert* standard.[52]

In *Sequoyah*, two bands of the Cherokee Nation and three individual Cherokee Indians brought a class action suit seeking an injunction to prevent the completion of the Tellico Dam on the Little Tennessee River in Monroe County, Tennessee.[53] The complaint alleged that the im-

---

43. *Id.*

44. *Id.*

45. H.R. 95-1308, 95th Cong., 2d Sess. (1978).

46. Bowen v. Roy, 476 U.S. 693, 700 (1986) (statutory requirement that a state agency utilize Social Security numbers in administering Aid to Families with Dependent Children and Food Stamp programs did not violate the free exercise rights of Indian parents). *See also infra* notes 181-185 and accompanying text.

47. *See supra* note 8 and *infra* notes 51-149 and accompanying text.

48. *See supra* notes 18-40 and accompanying text.

49. 480 F. Supp. 608 (E.D. Tenn. 1979), *aff'd*, 620 F.2d 1159 (6th Cir. 1980), *cert. denied*, 449 U.S. 953 (1980).

50. 455 F. Supp. 641 (D. Utah 1977), *aff'd*, 638 F.2d 172 (10th Cir. 1980), *cert. denied sub nom.* Badoni v. Broadbent, 452 U.S. 954 (1981).

51. 548 F. Supp. 182 (D. Alaska 1982), *aff'd*, 746 F.2d 570 (9th Cir. 1984), *cert. denied*, 474 U.S. 820 (1985).

52. Sherbert v. Verner, 374 U.S. 398 (1963).

53. *Sequoyah*, 480 F. Supp. at 610.

poundment created by the dam would destroy Indian religious sites and prevent the plaintiffs from having access to those sites.[54] The district court began its discussion with the assumption that the land in question was considered sacred by the Cherokee religion and was utilized as a precept of that religion.[55] The court cited *Yoder, Sherbert,* and other cases for the proposition that governmental coercion of actions contrary to the claimant's belief is an essential element of a free exercise claim.[56] "This governmental coercion may take the form of pressuring or forcing individuals not to participate in religious practices."[57] Nevertheless, the court concluded that preventing access to the land had no coercive effect on the religious practices.[58] The court ruled that a free exercise claim had not been stated because the Indians had failed to claim a legal property interest in the site.[59]

Denying a first amendment claim on the grounds that the state, and not the plaintiffs, held a legal property interest in the land implies that the government may use its land in any manner, regardless of the effects on individual religious freedom. This decision by the district court is inconsistent with United States Supreme Court decisions under the modern free exercise test.[60]

Notwithstanding this inconsistency, the Court of Appeals for the Sixth Circuit affirmed on appeal.[61] The court held that the plaintiffs had not shown a constitutionally cognizable first amendment claim because they failed to establish that the particular valley in question was "central" or indispensible to their religious observances despite the district court's finding to the contrary.[62] The court of appeals disagreed with the district court's conclusion that a lack of a property interest in the land was dispositive of the claim.[63] However, it diverged from the traditioal religion tests by adding the requirement that the land be "central" to the religion.[64]

---

54. *Id.*
55. *Id.* at 611.
56. *Id.*
57. *Id.* at 611-12 (citing McDaniel v. Paty, 435 U.S. 618 (1978) which declared unconstitutional a Tennessee statute barring members of the clergy from serving as delegates to the state constitutional convention).
58. *Id.* at 612.
59. *Id.*
60. *See supra* notes 18-39 and accompanying text. The test developed by the Court over the last twenty-five years emphasizes that the indirect burdens of any government action on religion violates the first amendment unless an overriding government interest justifies the burden.
61. 620 F.2d 1159 (6th Cir. 1980).
62. *Id.* at 1164.
63. *Id.*
64. *Id. See also supra* notes 18-40 and accompanying text and text accompanying note 56. No

The court first examined the contents of twenty-five affidavits filed by the plaintiffs describing the religious significance of the valley to the Cherokee people.[65] The affidavits explained the plaintiffs' belief that the valley was the birthplace of the Cherokee.[66] The plaintiffs believed that several specific sites were important to their religion, including a town that once was "the capital of the Cherokee Nation and a 'peace town' or sanctuary."[67] The "peace town" was considered a holy and sacred place where the Cherokees first connected "with the Great Spirit."[68] Affidavits and testimony of anthropologists specializing in American Indian studies confirmed the religious importance of the valley, and added that the actual damming of the river conflicted with the Indians' beliefs.[69]

After acknowledging the religious importance of the land and accepting the assertions as true, the court phrased the issue as "whether the plaintiffs [had] shown a constitutionally cognizable infringement of a First Amendment right."[70] It initially stated the correct test applied under the *Yoder* and *Sherbert* line of cases.[71] However, the court varied the test by using language from *Yoder*[72] and two state supreme court decisions[73] to require a finding that the Little River Tennessee Valley was "central" or indispensible to the religion.[74] It held that the claim of centrality was missing.[75]

After analyzing the "quality of the claims" as required by *Yoder*,[76] the court concluded that the claims asserted were "cultural" and "traditional", rather than religious claims protected under the first amendment.[77] By so concluding, the court declined to balance the competing

---

statement of free exercise analysis by the Court has included the "centrality" requirement. *See, e.g.,* United States v. Lee, 455 U.S. 252, 257 (1982) (compulsory participation in the Social Security system interfered with the plaintiff's free exercise rights).

65. *Sequoyah*, 620 F.2d at 1162.

66. *Id.* ("This is where WE begun.").

67. *Id.* at n. *.

68. *Id.*

69. *Id.* The anthropologists testified that it was important for the Indians to live in harmony with nature, and that interference with natural objects, such as damming rivers, was wrong.

70. *Id.* at 1163.

71. *Id. See also supra* notes 20-39 and accompanying text.

72. *See supra* note 4.

73. *See supra* note 17.

74. *Sequoyah*, 620 F.2d at 1164.

75. *Id.*

76. Wisconsin v. Yoder, 406 U.S. 205, 215 (1972).

77. *Sequoyah*, 620 F.2d at 1164-65. After alleging that the proposed action would infringe upon the plaintiff's rights by destroying the religious significance of the land and prevent the plaintiffs from having access to the land, the complaint further alleged that the dam would cause "irreversible loss to the culture and history of the plaintiffs." *Id.* at 1160.

interest of the government.[78] Judge Merritt argued in dissent that since the "centrality" standard had not previously been articulated, the case should have been remanded to the district court to allow the plaintiffs an opportunity to meet this burden.[79]

The *Sequoyah* court's analysis of the claims was incorrect in two respects. First, the requirement that a claimant assert an interest "central" to his religion is not part of the United States Supreme Court's free exercise test.[80] The *Yoder* court did not establish a requirement that the practice be "central" to the religion. It distinguished religious beliefs from purely secular beliefs in determining which practices were protected by the first amendment.[81] This distinction is made only to determine whether a plaintiff has satisfied the threshold requirement that the practice in question is based on a religious belief.[82]

Second, the court's finding that the claims represented cultural and historical—not religious—interests represented an analysis that should not be performed by a court. The United States Supreme Court has ruled on several occasions that lower courts should not endeavor to determine the truth or falsity of religious beliefs.[83] The fact that injury to cultural and historical sites was alleged in addition to allegations of religious injury does not preclude a finding that religious interests were at stake. The plaintiffs' religious assertions were supported by substantial evidence and should have been accepted by the court as true.

In *Badoni v. Higginson*[84], the district court denied a similar claim on the grounds that the Indians held no legal property interest in the land to which Indian access was impeded by the challenged state practice. The

---

78. *Id.* at 1165.

79. *Id.* (Merritt, J., dissenting).

80. Subsequent United States Supreme Court decisions considering the Free Exercise Clause have not imposed the "centrality" standard. *See, e.g.*, Hobbie v. Unemployment Appeals Comm'n, 480 U.S. 136, 140 (1987) (requiring only a burden on the free exercise of religion); Thomas v. Review Bd., 450 U.S. 707, 717-18 (1981) (burden exists if government conduct pressures one to modify behavior and violate religious beliefs).

81. *Yoder*, 406 U.S. at 215-16.

82. *Id.* at 215. ("To have the protection of the Religion Clauses, the claims must be rooted in religious belief.").

83. *See, e.g.*, United States v. Ballard, 322 U.S. 78 (1944). The Court explained this concept by saying:

"The religious views espoused by respondents might seem incredible, if not preposterous, to most people. But if those doctrines are subject to trial before a jury charged with finding their truth or falsity, then the same can be done with the religious beliefs of any sect. When the triers of fact undertake that task, they enter a forbidden domain."

Id. at 87. *See also* Thomas v. Review Bd., 450 U.S. 707, 716 (1981) ("courts are not arbiters of scriptural interpretation.").

84. 455 F. Supp. 641, 644-45 (D. Utah 1977), *aff'd*, 638 F.2d 172 (10th Cir. 1980), *cert. denied sub nom.* Badoni v. Broadbent, 452 U.S. 954 (1981).

Badoni court held that the religious interest asserted was outweighed by the state's interest in operating the Glen Canyon Dam on the Colorado River in Southern Utah.[85]   As a result, the court misapplied the established test by failing to consider the religious interest of the plaintiffs.

In *Badoni*, eight individual Navajo Indians and three Navajo community organizations sought injunctive relief to prevent further destruction and desecration of the Rainbow Bridge National Monument.[86] The plaintiffs also sought to enjoin further major actions in the operation of the dam and reservoir pending completion of a final environmental impact study.[87] Included among the plaintiffs were three "medicine men" who were religious leaders learned in the history, mythology, and culture of the Navajo Indians, and who were also practitioners of traditional rites and ceremonies.[88] The medicine men alleged that the dam operations caused destruction and desecration of holy sites, the drowning of Navajo gods, injury to the efficacy of prayers and entreaties to the remaining gods, and prevented the performance of religious ceremonies as well.[89] Moreover, the plaintiffs claimed that these actions would result in severe emotional and spiritual distress to the Navajo people.[90]

The court held that even if all of the assertions were true, there was no first amendment protection because the plaintiffs held no legal property interest in the land.[91] Again, this holding is inconsistent with the constitutional guarantee of religious freedom. It also illustrates the difficulty courts experience in applying first amendment religious protection to claims involving land use. The court then misapplied the *Yoder* test by concluding that, even if the plaintiffs' claims were cognizable under the first amendment, the state interests outweighed those claims.[92]

The court confused the threshold requirement of presenting a sincerely held religious belief with the first part of the two-part balancing test—examination of the infringement upon the claimant's religion. If the court found that the plaintiffs had presented a constitutionally cognizable claim, it should have examined the burden placed on the exercise of the religion by the state. The government should then have been required to come forward with a "compelling" state interest that justified

---

85. *Id.* at 645.

86. *Id.* at 642-43.

87. *Id.* at 643.

88. *Id.* at 642. Interestingly, the court's use of the word mythology permits an inference that it does not consider the doctrines religion, but merely "myths."

89. *Id.* at 644.

90. *Id.*

91. *Id.* at 644-45.

92. *Id.* at 645.

the action and the resulting infringement.[93]

Badoni was affirmed on appeal by the Court of Appeals for the Tenth Circuit,[94] however, the court of appeals again disagreed with the district court's ruling that a lack of a legal property interest in the land disposed of the plaintiffs' claims.[95] The tenth circuit did as the sixth circuit had done in Sequoia; it announced the proper test but promptly misapplied it. Since maintaining the water level of the lake was deemed a compelling government interest, the court refused to consider the infringement on the plaintiffs' religion.[96]

This analysis fails to apply the first prong of the test and implies that the state need not consider burdens on religious freedom resulting from its actions. Under this application, no free exercise claim challenging government action can succeed. Even where the state interest is compelling, the courts must properly apply the test to ensure that the government's burden on religion is no more than is necessary to achieve its goal. "The state may justify an inroad on religious liberty by showing that it is the least restrictive means of achieving some compelling state interest."[97]

The *Badoni* court also addressed the issue of whether the presence and behavior of tourists in the area desecrated sacred Indian sites and prevented the plaintiffs from performing ceremonies.[98] The court denied the plaintiffs' claims by holding that there was "no basis in the law ordering the government to exclude the public from public areas to insure privacy during the exercise of First Amendment rights."[99] This conclusion ignores the fact that the government designated the area as a national park and allowed the tourists to enter, even though the land had been used for religous ceremonies for over 100 years.

The *Badoni* court denied the claims because they did not fall within the two types of claims previously brought under the free exercise clause.[100] Those claims arise 1) when the government compels individuals to violate the tenets of their religion,[101] or, 2) when the state condi-

---

93. *See supra* notes 18-40 and accompanying text.
94. Badoni v. Higginson, 638 F.2d 172 (10th Cir. 1980), *cert. denied sub nom.* Badoni v. Broadbent, 452 U.S. 954 (1981).
95. *Id.* at 176. "The government must manage its property in a manner that does not offend the Constitution." (citing *Sequoyah*, 620 F.2d 1159, 1164 (6th Cir. 1980), *cert. denied*, 449 U.S. 953 (1980)).
96. *Id.* at 177 n.4.
97. Thomas v. Review Bd., 450 U.S. 707, 718 (1981).
98. *Badoni*, 638 F.2d at 177. *See also* text accompanying notes 54-84
99. *Id.* at 179.
100. *Id.* at 178.
101. *See, e.g.*, Wisconsin v. Yoder, 406 U.S. 205 (1972) (state statute requiring parents to send their children to school until they reach the age of sixteen conflicted with Amish religious beliefs).

tions receipt of a benefit on renunciation of a religious practice.[102] The court concluded that the government had not interfered with the plaintiffs' free exercise of their religion because it had not prohibited their religious practices.[103] This narrow definition of "prohibit" in constitutional analysis is inconsistent with previous free exercise decisions.[104]

In *Inupiat Community v. Alaska*,[105] the court again overlooked evidence of a religious interest and held that the plaintiffs' claims were not specific enough to establish a constitutionally protected interest.[106] The Inupiat tribe sought injunctive relief, damages, and declaration of their title to an area of sea ice off the coast of Alaska.[107] They claimed that a government lease of the area to oil companies violated their first amendment rights because oil exploration interfered with their hunting and gathering lifestyle which was inextricably intertwined with their religious beliefs.[108] The court concluded that the claim failed because it met neither of the two elements established by *Wisconsin v. Yoder*.[109]

The court's first conclusion was that the government action did "not create a serious obstacle to the exercise of the plaintiff's religion."[110] It reached this conclusion without first recognizing a religious interest, holding that a claim based "on such non-specific grounds cannot provide the sort of 'serious obstacle' contemplated by *Yoder*."[111] The court declined to recognize a religious interest because it felt that the plaintiffs had not adequately explained or defined the manner in which their religion was burdened.[112] While there must be some minimal requirement in pleading a claim,[113] the court's finding is inconsistent with the Supreme Court's free exercise decisions.[114] In dismissing the plaintiffs'

---

102. *See, e.g.*, Sherbert v. Verner, 374 U.S. 398 (1963) (held unconstitutional state statute requiring woman to accept employment in which she would have to work on Saturday, contrary to her Seventh-Day Adventist religious beliefs).

103. *Badoni*, 638 F.2d at 178. The plaintiffs could enter the site on the same basis as other people.

104. *See supra* notes 18-39 and accompanying text.

105. 548 F. Supp. 182 (D. Alaska 1982), *aff'd*, 746 F.2d 570 (9th Cir. 1964), *cert. denied*, 474 U.S. 820 (1985).

106. *Id.* at 188-89.

107. *Id.* at 185.

108. *Id.* at 188-89.

109. *Id.* at 188.

110. *Id.*

111. *Id.* at 189.

112. *Id.* at 188.

113. The Court has not established a test to determine whether an asserted interest is "religious" and merits consideration under the first amendment. For a discussion of the difficulty in making that determination, see generally Clark, *Guidelines for the Free Exercise Clause*, 83 HARV. L. REV. 327 (1969); Choper, *Defining Religion in the First Amendment*, 1982 U. ILL. L. REV. 579 (1982).

114. *See, e.g.*, Thomas v. Review Board, 450 U.S. 707 (1981). "Courts should not undertake to

case, the *Inupiat* court failed to recognize a religion practiced by the Inupiat people for hundreds of years. The court then assessed the government's interest under the second prong of *Yoder* and concluded that it outweighed the religious interest asserted.[115] However, this conclusion cannot be legitimately reached under *Yoder* without first recognizing that a religious interest is burdened.

2. Failure to Find a Burden

In two other cases,[116] courts have recognized religious interests worthy of constitutional protection but have found that government use of the land did not burden the exercise of those religions.

In *Crow v. Gullett*,[117] traditional chiefs and spiritual leaders of the Lakota and Tsistsistas Nations challenged the constitutionality of restrictive access measures taken by the Department of Game, Fish, and Parks. The Department had restricted the plaintiffs' access to Bear Butte State Park in the Black Hills region of South Dakota.[118] The plaintiffs presented numerous affidavits and several witnesses to establish the religious significance of the area.[119] The Lakota Indians considered the park the most significant site of their religious ceremonies.[120] Moreover, the Tsistsistas made pilgrimages to Bear Butte to receive powers and benefits of the Great Spirit.[121] The plaintiffs alleged a burden on the free exercise of their religion because construction of roads, parking lots, viewing platforms, and buildings allowed tourists to disrupt religious practices.[122] The court considered these allegations together with the religious assertions and somehow concluded that the defendants had not infringed upon the plaintiffs' religion.[123]

---

dissect religious beliefs because . . . [they] are not articulated with the clarity and precision that a more sophisticated person might employ." *Id.* at 715.

115. *Inupiat*, 548 F. Supp. at 189.

116. Crow v. Gullett, 541 F. Supp. 785 (D.S.D. 1982) (denying Indian plaintiffs' claimed free exercise violation by state actions restricting and regulating access to traditional religious ceremonial grounds), *aff'd*, 706 F.2d 856 (8th Cir. 1983) (per curiam), *cert. denied*, 464 U.S. 977 (1983); Hopi Indian Tribe v. Block, 8 Indian L. Rep. 3073 (Am. Indian Law Training Program) (D.D.C. June 15, 1981), (denying Hopi Indian Tribe challenge on free exercise grounds to the decision of the Agricultural Department authorizing development of a ski area), *aff'd sub nom.* Wilson v. Block, 708 F.2d 735 (D.C. Cir. 1983), *cert. denied sub nom.* Hopi Indian Tribe v. Block, 464 U.S. 1056 (1984).

117. 541 F. Supp. 785 (D.S.D. 1982), *aff'd*, 706 F.2d 856 (8th Cir. 1983) (per curiam), *cert. denied*, 464 U.S. 977.

118. *Id.* at 787.

119. *Id.* at 788.

120. *Id.*

121. *Id.*

122. *Id.*

123. *Id.* at 791.

Crow demonstrates another example of a court confusing the first prong of the balancing test with the ultimate conclusion to be reached. Certainly, in light of the Supreme Court's ruling that even indirect infringements are subject to constitutional scrutiny,[124] the Department's action burdened the plaintiffs' religious practices by inviting disruptions of the Indians' religious ceremonies. Whether the burden on plaintiffs' religion was justified by some overriding state interest is to be decided under the second part of the test. The district court held that the first amendment requires only that the state not prohibit religion, but that it does not impose a duty to facilitate the practice.[125]

This narrow interpretation of the free exercise clause is inconsistent with the modern test. The Supreme Court has held that prohibition of religion under a first amendment analysis includes indirect burdens on religion as well as outright prohibitions of religious practices.[126] The *Crow* court's ruling also misstates the facts of the case. The state was not providing an environment for the practice of religion. It was infringing upon religious practices that had been performed in the area for many years. The Court of Appeals for the Eighth Circuit affirmed, holding that the district court was not clearly erroneous in either its factual determinations or legal analysis.[127]

In *Hopi Indian Tribe v. Block*,[128] the district court followed *Badoni*[129] and *Sequoyah*[130] in denying Indian claims because the plaintiffs failed to establish that the site in question was "central" to their religion. The Navajo and Hopi Indian plaintiffs sought to enjoin the proposed expansion of a ski resort in the San Francisco Peaks area of the Cococino National Forest in Arizona. The plaintiffs alleged that the expansion would violate their free exercise rights by desecrating sacred religious sites.[131] Further, the defendants stipulated that the Navajos believed the Peaks were actually a "sacred body and a spiritual being or god," that they prayed to the Peaks as a "living deity," and that con-

---

124. *See supra* notes 29-34 and accompanying text.

125. *Crow*, 541 F. Supp. at 791.

126. *See supra* notes 3, 29-34 and accompanying text.

127. Crow v. Gullett, 706 F.2d 856 (8th Cir. 1983), *cert. denied*, 464 U.S. 977 (1983).

128. 8 Indian L. Rep. 3073 (Am. Indian Law Training Program) (D.D.C. June 15, 1981), *aff'd sub nom.* Wilson v. Block, 708 F.2d 735 (D.C. Cir. 1983), *cert. denied sub nom.* Hopi Indian Tribe v. Block, 464 U.S. 1056 (1984).

129. 455 F. Supp. 641 (D. Utah 1977), *aff'd*, 638 F.2d 172 (10th Cir. 1980), *cert. denied sub nom.* Badoni v. Broadbent, 452 U.S. 954 (1981).

130. 480 F. Supp. 608 (E.D. Tenn. 1979), *aff'd*, 620 F.2d 1159 (6th Cir. 1980), *cert. denied*, 449 U.S. 953 (1980).

131. *Hopi*, 8 Indian L. Rep. at 3073.

struction caused the deity to lose its power.[132] There was substantial evidence that the Peaks held equal religious significance to the Hopi tribe, including the locations of holy shrines that were visited by religious leaders.[133] The court noted that the Hopi people had existed in the area for over a thousand years.[134]

The court considered the evidence and agreed with the Forest Service that the first amendment did not protect the Indians from the development.[135] The *Hopi* court followed the *Bandoni* analysis by denying the plaintiffs' claims because they did not fall within one of the two traditional types of free exercise claims.[136] Since the plaintiffs had not been forced to say or to believe anything contrary to their religion, nor had they been forced to choose between their religion and receiving a public benefit, there had been no "coercion" and therefore no cognizable infringement.[137] The court compared the infringement alleged in *Hopi* with that alleged in *Sequoyah*, and concluded that the burden was less severe in the instant case because the plaintiffs had not been totally denied access to the sites as the plaintiffs in *Sequoyah* had been.[138] The court added that the indirect effects on the religion were not prohibited by the free exercise clause.[139]

The Court of Appeals for the District of Columbia affirmed, holding that plaintiffs asserting a free exercise claim in opposition to government land use must, at a minimum, prove that the government use would impair a religious practice that could not be performed at any other site.[140] In reaching this conclusion, the court of appeals restricted *Sherbert* and *Thomas* to their facts and interpreted *Sequoyah* as holding that the site, rather than the practice performed at the site, must be indispensible to some religious practice.[141]

The court ruled that the plaintiffs had failed to meet their burden[142] despite noting earlier that "[the Indians] must have access to the San Francisco Peaks to practice their religions,"[143] and that "development of

---

132. *Id.* at 3074.
133. *Id.*
134. *Id.* at 3073.
135. *Id.* at 3074.
136. *Id. See also supra* notes 95-97 and accompanying text.
137. *Hopi,* 8 Indian L. Rep. at 3074.
138. *Id.* at 3075.
139. *Id.*
140. Wilson v. Block, 708 F.2d 735, 744 (D.C. Cir. 1983), *cert. denied sub nom.* Hopi Indian Tribe v. Block, 464 U.S. 1056 (1984).
141. *Id.* at 743.
142. *Id.* at 744.
143. *Id.* at 742.

the Peaks would severely impair the practice of the religions . . . ."[144] Although the court noted the religious significance of the area to the plaintiffs, it nevertheless concluded that expansion of the ski resort would not unduly interfere with that practice.[145]

Thus, under *Hopi*, a plaintiff must prove, at a minimum, that a governmental action with respect to alleged religious sites impairs a religious practice that cannot be performed at another site.[146] However, the court indicated that such proof alone will not necessarily establish a burden on the free exercise of religion.[147] Since the *Hopi* plaintiffs had failed to meet this burden of proof, the court declined to state what additional factors might be necessary to establish a burden worthy of constitutional eradication.[148] Thus, the *Hopi* court not only imposed upon the Indians another difficult burden of proof, but simultaneously diluted the significance of successfully meeting that burden.

III.   THE *LYNG* DECISION AND ITS IMPACT

In *Lyng v. Northwest Indian Cemetery Protective Ass'n,*[149] the United States Supreme Court had an opportunity to settle the issue and provide constitutional protection to Indians using land for religious purposes. Instead, the Court reversed lower court decisions in favor of the Indians because the government activity neither coerced violation of the plaintiffs' beliefs nor penalized their religious activity.[150]

A.   *Facts of* Lyng

In 1977, the U.S. Forest Service commissioned a study of American Indian cultural and religious sites in the Hoopa Valley Indian Reservation and Six Rivers National Forest in Northern California.[151] The purpose of the study was to determine the impact of the proposed upgrade of an existing unpaved road and of possible timber harvesting in the Chimney Rock area of the forest.[152] The area had long been held sacred by the Yurok, Karok, and Tolowa Indian tribes.[153] The study found the entire

---

144. *Id.*
145. *Id.* at 744-45.
146. *Id.* at 744.
147. *Id.* at n.5.
148. *Id.*
149. 485 U.S. 439 (1988).
150. *Id.* at 448-53. In so holding, the Supreme Court aligned itself with some of the more narrow decisions discussed above. *See supra* text accompanying notes 101-105 and 137-140.
151. *Id.* at 442-45.
152. *Id.* at 442.
153. *Id.*

area "significant as an integral and indispensible [sic] part of Indian religious conceptualization and practice."[154] The study concluded that constructing the road "would cause serious and irreparable damage to the sacred areas which are an integral and necessary part of the belief systems and lifeway of the Northwest California Indian peoples."[155] The report recommended that the proposed road not be completed.[156] In 1982, the Forest Service rejected the recommendation and prepared a final environmental impact statement, intending to proceed with the construction.[157] Consequently, individual Indians and various organizations brought suit seeking an injunction to prevent the construction and timber harvesting.[158]

In *Northwest Indian Cemetery Protective Ass'n v. Peterson*,[159] the District Court for the Northern District of California became the first federal court to properly apply and analyze the free exercise test in a case involving Indian claims to land use for religious purposes.[160] The court found that the plaintiffs' claims were based on a sincerely held religious belief.[161] It analyzed the burden imposed upon the religion by the proposed action, and found that the "[d]egradation of the high country and impairment of such training would carry 'a very real threat of undermining the [tribal] commmunit[ies] and religious practice[s] as they exist today.' "[162] The court concluded that the proposed action imposed a burden on the free exercise of their religion.[163]

The court then weighed the government's interest in completing the road and in permitting the timber harvesting against the plaintiffs' religious interest. Completion of the road, said the court, would not materially serve the primary interests asserted by the government because the road would not improve access to timber or increase the number of jobs in the area.[164] It also found that increased recreational access could not

---

154. *Id.*
155. *Id.*
156. *Id.*
157. *Id.* at 443.
158. *Id.*
159. 565 F. Supp. 586 (N.D. Cal. 1983), *modified*, 764 F.2d 581 (9th Cir. 1985), *aff'd on rehearing*, 795 F.2d 688 (9th Cir. 1986), *rev'd sub nom.* Lyng v. Northwest Indian Cemetery Protective Ass'n, 485 U.S. 439 (1988) (*Peterson* was *Lyng's* predecessor).
160. In a previous decision concerning this case, the district court denied a request for a preliminary injunction by incorrectly ruling that because the proposed activity did not impose an "unlawful" burden on religion, it need not determine whether the state asserted an "overriding" interest. *Northwest Indian Cemetery Protective Ass'n v. Peterson*, 552 F. Supp. 951 (N.D. Cal. 1982).
161. *Northwest Indian Cemetery Protective Ass'n*, 565 F. Supp. at 594.
162. *Id.* (quoting Wisconsin v. Yoder, 406 U.S. 205, 218 (1971)).
163. *Id.* at 595.
164. *Id.* at 595-96.

justify infringement of constitutional rights.[165] According to the court, the remaining interests asserted by the government fell "far short of constituting the 'paramount interests' necessary to justify infringement of plaintiffs' freedom of religion."[166] Accordingly, the court held that the proposed activity was unconstitutional.[167]

The Ninth Circuit affirmed the unconstitutionality of the government action.[168] Although the court initially stated the proper test,[169] it ultimately followed *Wilson, Sequoyah,* and *Crow* in applying the "centrality" standard.[170] The majority found that the plaintiffs met the standard.[171] Relying on the study by the Forest Service, it concluded that the construction would have significant, though largely indirect, adverse effects on Indian religious practices.[172] The court found that the government failed to demonstrate a compelling interest in the completion of the road that would justify upholding its proposed action.[173]

While the government's appeal was pending before the Ninth Circuit, Congress passed legislation[174] which designated much of the area in question a wilderness area in which timber could not be harvested.[175] As a result, the court found that the timber harvesting became a less significant issue in the case.[176]

B.   The Lyng *Decision*

In *Lyng v. Northwest Indian Cemetery Protective Ass'n,*[177] the United States Supreme Court refused to acknowledge the constitutional infringement suffered by the Indians because it did not fit into one of the two narrowly defined injuries previously recognized by the Court. It concentrated on the form of the challenged government action rather than its effects. Consequently, a 5-3 majority of the Court upheld the proposed government action because it neither coerced the Indians into violating

---

165. *Id.* at 596.

166. *Id.* (quoting Sherbert v. Verner, 374 U.S. 398, 406 (1962)).

167. *Id.* at 597.

168. Northwest Indian Cemetery Protective Ass'n v. Peterson, 795 F.2d 688, 695 (9th Cir. 1986).

169. "To establish a constitutionally valid free exercise claim, the Indian plaintiffs have the initial burden of demonstrating that govermental actions create a burden on their rights." *Id.* at 691.

170. *Id.* at 692.

171. *Id.*

172. *Id.* at 693.

173. *Id.* at 694-95.

174. California Wilderness Act of 1984, Pub. L. No. 98-425, 98 Stat. 1619 (1984).

175. *Id.*

176. *Northwest Indian Cemetery Protective Ass'n,* 795 F.2d at 692-93.

177. 485 U.S. 439 (1988).

their religious beliefs nor penalized them for practicing their religion.[178]

In an opinion written by Justice O'Connor, the majority refused to follow the *Sherbert-Yoder*[179] line of cases, and instead relied heavily on *Bowen v. Roy.*[180] *Roy* denied the free exercise claims of American Indians in a different factual setting. The Court there considered a claim by Abenaki Indian parents that a federal statute requiring the assignment and use of a Social Security number for each member of the family by state welfare agencies administering federal aid programs violated their religious beliefs.[181] The couple alleged that the assignment of a number to their 2-year old daughter and subsequent use by the agencies would "rob the spirit" of the girl and prevent her from "becoming a holy person" with "greater spiritual power."[182]

The Court in *Roy* declined to balance the competing interests because the government action did not trigger the protection of the first amendment.[183] It denied the Roys' constitutional challenge, holding that "[t]he [f]ree [e]xercise [c]lause affords an individual protection from certain forms of governmental compulsion; it does not afford an individual a right to dictate the conduct of the Government's internal procedures."[184]

The *Lyng* court began its analysis by finding that the Indians' alleged infringement was similar to the claim in *Roy.*[185] The Court reiterated its holding in *Roy* by saying "[t]he Free Exercise Clause simply cannot be understood to require the Government to conduct its own internal affairs in ways that comport with the religious beliefs of its particular citizens."[186] Remarkably, the Court then stated that "[t]he building of a road or the harvesting of timber on publicly owned land cannot meaningfully be distinguished from the use of Social Security numbers in *Roy.*"[187] Its reasoning was that, although in both cases the government action significantly interfered with religion, in neither case did it coerce individuals to violate their beliefs, nor penalize them for practicing their religion.[188]

The two cases, however, can and should be distinguished. *Roy* focused on the internal nature of a government procedure utilized to ad-

---

178. *Id.* at 449.
179. *See supra* notes 18-39 and accompanying text.
180. 476 U.S. 693 (1986).
181. *Id.* at 695.
182. *Id.* at 696.
183. *Id.* at 706-08.
184. *Id.* at 700.
185. *Lyng,* 485 U.S. at 448.
186. *Id.* (quoting *Roy,* 476 U.S. at 699).
187. *Id.* at 449.
188. *Id.*

minister an insurance program. In *Lyng*, the proposed action was an external manifestation of the government's efforts to improve access to timber and recreational areas in a forest.[189] The action involved significant intrusion into the sacred grounds of the Indians, making it virtually impossible for them to practice their religion.[190] By confining constitutionally protected injuries to those in which the government either coerces violation of beliefs or causes forbearance of the receipt of certain benefits, the Court implies that the government can indirectly prevent people from practicing their religion without even raising a constitutional issue. This result is contrary to the Court's previous holdings that even indirect burdens are prohibited by the free exercise clause.[191]

The Court declined to follow the *Sherbert-Yoder* line of cases because they were inconsistent with *Roy*.[192] The Court conceded that it "has repeatedly held that indirect coercion or penalties on the free exercise of religion, not just outright prohibitions, are subject to scrutiny under the First Amendment."[193] However, the Court reasoned that this does not require the government to bring forward a compelling interest to justify actions which may have an incidental effect of making it more difficult for people to practice their religion.[194]

The opinion did not explain the distinction between "indirect coercion" and the "incidental effect" of making it more difficult to practice a religion without coercing one into acting in a manner contrary to his or her beliefs. It seems that by making the practice of religion more difficult, or as in this case, nearly impossible,[195] the government is in fact coercing individuals into acting contrary to their beliefs. By characterizing the infringement as an "incidental effect" not worthy of first amendment recognition, the Court trivializes the Indians' injuries and arbitrarily refuses to accord them constitutional protection.

---

189. *See supra* notes 175-77 and accompanying text. The passage of the California Wilderness Act of 1984 made the timber a less important consideration. Also, the district court found that the degradation of the environment resulting from the construction would decrease the area's suitability for the primitive recreation that the government purported to serve. *See Northwest Indian Cemetery Protective Ass'n*, 565 F. Supp. at 596.

190. *Northwest Indian Cemetery Protective Ass'n*, 565 F. Supp. at 595. Quoting the study report, the court found that the "[i]ntrusions on the sanctity of the Blue Creek high country are potentially destructive of the very core of Northwest [Indian] religious beliefs and practices." *Id.*

191. *See supra* notes 18-39 and accompanying text.

192. *Lyng*, 485 U.S. at 450-53. The Court did not explain why the inconsistency with *Roy* rendered the precedent cases inapplicable to the *Lyng* decision.

193. *Id.* at 450.

194. *Id.*

195. The Ninth Circuit had found that such proposed actions "would virtually destroy the Indians' ability to practice their religion . . . ." *Northwest Indian Cemetery Protective Ass'n*, 795 F.2d at 693.

The majority concluded this line of reasoning by noting that the key word in the free exercise clause is "prohibit,"[196] and that the clause "is written in terms of what the government cannot do to the individual, not in terms of what the individual can exact from the government."[197] This characterization misstates the case and reverses the parties' roles. By intruding on sacred Indian grounds, the government is "doing" something to the Indians. The government is disrupting religious practices that have been performed there for over 200 years. The Indians on the other hand, are not trying to exact anything from the government. The Indians seek only to continue those practices unfettered by government intrusion.

In further defining its holding, the Court stated that the "line between unconstitutional prohibitions on the free exercise of religion and the legitimate conduct by government . . . cannot depend on measuring the effects of a governmental action on a religious objector's spiritual development."[198] This reasoning is contrary to the Court's modern free exercise test,[199] and contradicts the Court's statement in *Roy* that "the nature of the burden is relevant to the standard the government must meet to justify the burden."[200]

After noting the "devastating" and "extremely grave" effects the proposed actions could have on the religion,[201] and after accepting the Ninth Circuit's finding that the government's actions would "virtually destroy the Indians' ability to practice their religion,"[202] the Supreme Court ruled that "the Constitution simply does not provide a principle that could justify upholding respondents' legal claims."[203] Yet, the Constitution does provide such a principle because the free exercise clause of the first amendment has been interpreted for the past twenty-five years as providing this type of protection.[204] Nevertheless, the Court supported its holding by arguing that requiring the government to satisfy the religious needs of every citizen would restrict government operations, would impose a religious servitude upon government land, and would diminish

---

196. *Lyng*, 485 U.S. at 451.
197. *Id.* (quoting Sherbert v. Verner, 374 U.S. 398, 412 (1963) (Douglas, J., concurring)).
198. *Id.*
199. *See supra* notes 21-40 and accompanying text.
200. *Roy*, 476 U.S. at 707.
201. *Lyng*, 485 U.S. at 451.
202. *Id.* at 451-452. The majority treated this finding by the Ninth Circuit as a "prediction." However, Justice Brennan explained in his dissent that this treatment violates the principles of judicial review, and is inconsistent with the rule that the Court will not disturb findings of fact made by the lower courts unless they are clearly in error. *Id.* at 1333 n.3 (Brennan, J., dissenting).
203. *Id.* at 452.
204. *See supra* notes 18-40 and accompanying text.

the government's property rights.[205] Extending the results of a decision to such possibilities cannot justify the denial of a legitimate constitutional claim.

In the end, the majority based its decision on the belief that the government may do what it pleases with its own land.[206] Moreover, the Court relied on a narrow definition of the word "prohibit" that ignores previous Supreme Court decisions.[207] The *Lyng* holding undermines the purpose of the first amendment and dilutes its protection of religious liberty.

Justice Brennan's dissent criticizes the majority's emphasis on the form rather than on the effect of the government actions.[208] He argues that the Constitution does not prohibit only the two types of religious restraint recognized by the majority, but rather, it forbids any governmental frustration or inhibition of religious practices.[209] Ironically, the dissent advocates application of the "centrality" standard to require a showing of substantial frustration of religious freedom. Apparently, Justice Brennan would not neccessarily require the threatened extinction of the religion.[210] The majority, however, refused to adopt the "centrality" standard.[211]

C. The Impact of Lyng

The result of *Lyng* is that the U.S. Forest Service may destroy for nearly 5,000 individuals a religion that has been performed in the same place for over 200 years. The primary benefit to the state is that a road will be paved that has little value to either government or private interests. Additionally, this decision will permit very limited but unnecessary timber harvesting despite a Congressional prohibition against timber harvesting in the area.[212] In essence, the government may take any action that does not fall within the Court's narrowly prescribed limits. Thus, *Lyng* allows government interference with Indian religious practices even where the government interest is less than compelling, and despite the significant adverse effects on the individual's religion.

---

205. *Lyng*, 485 U.S. at 452.

206. *Id.* at 453. "Whatever rights the Indians may have to the use of the area, however, those rights do not divest the Government of its right to use what is, after all, *its* land." *Id.* at 456 (emphasis original).

207. *Id.* at 456.

208. *Id.* at 466-67 (Brennan, J., dissenting).

209. *Id.* at 459.

210. *Id.* at 475.

211. *Id.* at 457-58.

212. *See supra* notes 175-77 and accompanying text.

The plaintiffs in *Lyng* presented a constitutional challenge that was as strong, if not stronger, than any other Indian case before it. The *Lyng* plaintiffs' defeat may have eliminated any possibility that Indians may successfully challenge governmental land management that interferes with their practice of religions on public lands. For example, in *United States v. Means*,[213] the Court of Appeals for the Eighth Circuit reversed a district court's granting to Sioux Indians of a special use permit. The Indians requested use of the Black Hills National Forest as a religious, cultural, and educational community. The district court held that denial of the use permit violated the Indians' free exercise rights. The court of appeals, citing *Lyng* as support for its ruling, held that the government had not coerced the Indians into violating their religious beliefs, had not compelled them to refrain from religious conduct, nor had it caused them to act in a manner contrary to their religious beliefs.[214] The court also cited *Lyng* for the proposition that lower courts have been reluctant to invalidate governmental land use decisions challenged by the Indians.[215] This interpretation of *Lyng* and demonstrates the substantial impact it may have on future decisions.

For example, in denying a free exercise challenge to a New York statute, a district court cited *Lyng* to support its statement that "not all governmental actions that burden religious practices must be justified by a compelling state interest."[216] This reading implies that *Lyng* lowered the level of scrutiny applied to free exercise claims. If this is a correct interpretation of the *Lyng* decision, it represents another dilution of first amendment religious protection.

Lyng may have significant impact on other areas as well. The Court of Appeals for the Second Circuit cited *Lyng* in support of the proposition that "the Government's important interest in controlling federal property has been found to prevail over individuals' First Amendment rights."[217] Such a broad reading of *Lyng* seriously undermines well settled first amendment guarantees. The government's interest in forest management in *Lyng* should not qualify as the type of compelling inter-

---

213. 858 F.2d 404 (8th Cir. 1988).

214. *Id.* at 407.

215. *Id.*

216. Blackwelder v. Safnauer, 689 F. Supp. 106, 129 (N.D.N.Y. 1988), *aff'd*, 866 F.2d 548 (2d Cir. 1989) (upholding New York state statute governing minimum standards of instruction that had to be provided to school-aged children outside public schools).

217. Serra v. United States General Servs. Admin., 847 F.2d 1045, 1049 (2d Cir. 1988) (upholding government's decision to relocate a sculpture it had purchased over the constitutional challenge of the artist who had created it).

est required by *Sherbert* and its progeny.[218] The court also cited *Lyng* when it said that "[w]hatever [free exercise] rights the Indians may have to the use of [the National Park], those rights do not divest the Government of its right to use what is after all, *its* land."[219] The first amendment is supposed to guarantee freedom of thought and religion in our society.[220] Its protection therefore should not be weighed against the mere fact of government ownership, but instead should be weighed against the government's interest in using the land in such a way as to impede religious practices. Allowing the government to manage its property in any manner, without considering the effects on the rights of the people it represents, undermines the Constitution's guarantees of liberty. Further, such a shallow standard means that unrestrained use by the government of public lands could never be curbed justifyably for any reason, because, after all, it *is* the government's land.

IV. REASONS FOR INCORRECT ANALYSIS AND RECOMMENDATIONS

The cases discussed above present difficult issues involving one of the most fundamental rights protected under the Constitution. This Note has not attempted to argue with the results of these cases, but rather with the legal principals adopted by the courts in resolving the issue. Requiring the courts to follow the mechanical application of an established test may not be desirable in all areas of the law, but in the analysis of free exercise claims clearly articulated and binding rules would better enable courts to achieve proper results. In the cases discussed above, asserted religious interests were not recognized as such and thus not accorded constitutional protection. If this treatment was applied to all religious claims brought to the courts, the guarantees of the first amendment would become meaningless. Proper application of the test established in *Sherbert*[221] and its progeny would guarantee preservation of those first amendment liberties.

If the United States Supreme Court is going to follow *Lyng* and focus on the form rather than the effect of the government action, it should allow the Indian claims to fit into its narrow definition of "infringement." In *Lyng*, the Court decided that the free exercise clause only prohibits

---

218. *See supra* notes 35-39 and accompanying text. In prior cases, lower courts found that the proposed government actions were of marginal value and did not justify the infringement on religion. *See supra* notes 160-168 and accompanying text.

219. *Serra*, 847 F.2d at 1049-50 (quoting Lyng v. Northwest Indian Cemetery Protective Ass'n, 485 U.S. 439, 453 (1988) (emphasis original).

220. *See* United States v. Ballard, 322 U.S. 78, 86-87 (1943) (holding that the truth or falsity of individual's religious beliefs cannot be submitted to a jury).

221. *See supra* notes 3-8 and accompanying text.

the government from coercing an individual into violating his religious beliefs or from penalizing his religious activity by denying the rights, benefits, and privileges enjoyed by other citzens.[222] Certainly, finding that the proposed activity would virtually destroy the plaintiffs' religion should qualify their claim for scrutiny at least, as a denial of rights, benefits and privileges enjoyed by other citizens. Alternatively, by making it impossible for the Indians to practice their religion, the Indians are coerced by trespass laws into violating their beliefs by staying away from traditional sacred grounds. In some cases, Indians are punished, or threatened with punishment for trespassing on restricted area once a sacred religious site to the Indians. Short of an express prohibition, it is difficult to imagine a more burdensome infringement.

The Indian cases are often seen as "all or nothing" decisions with little or no room for accommodating opposing interests. For example, to uphold the Indians' claims in *Sequoyah*[223] may have ultimely required the government to forego use of the dam altogether. While economic interests theoretically should yield to fundamental rights in constitutional analysis, it is likely that the *Sequoyah* court was mindful that the government had invested over 100 million dollars in the project. Because the asserted religious interest was not recognized by the court, it was not balanced against the competing government interest. However, given the economic circumstances, the court probably would have had difficulty holding for the Indians.

In *Badoni*,[224] there was evidence that the government had available less restrictive means of furthering its interest. Among the relief sought by the Indians were reasonable restrictions on alcoholic beverage consumption in the area, and occasional closing of the bridge area to allow for private religious ceremonies without public intrusion.[225] Because the court concluded that no constitutionally cognizant burden on religion existed, no accommodation was ordered.[226] Moreover, it is interesting to note that no "compelling" state interest was advanced to support the state's unwillingness to facilitate the religious practice. The *Badoni* decision demonstrates how important it is for the lower courts properly to apply the Supreme Court's two-part test.

A strict rule requiring a finding of a religious interest, weighing the

---

222. *Lyng*, 485 U.S. at 449. *See also supra* notes 186-208 and accompanying text.

223. Sequoyah v. TVA, 480 F. Supp. 608 (E.D. Tenn. 1979), *aff'd*, 620 F.2d 1159 (6th Cir. 1980), *cert. denied*, 449 U.S. 953 (1980). *See also supra* notes 51-84 and accompanying text.

224. 638 F.2d 172 (10th Cir. 1980). *See also supra* notes 85-104 and accompanying text.

225. 638 F.2d at 178.

226. *Id.* at 178-79.

infringement on plaintiffs' religious interest caused by the government against the competing government interest would allow the lower courts properly to assess the conflicts. Courts will be better able to protect religious interests where necessary, and to formulate an accommodation whenever possible.[227]

The lower courts seem to be concerned with avoiding setting precedents that would result in the government's loss of property rights. Indeed, in *Inupiat* part of the relief requested was a declaration of Indian title to the land at issue.[228] In *Lyng*, the Court seemed very concerned with the precedential value of a decision in favor of the Indian plaintiffs, which could possibly result in the Indians holding *de facto* beneficial ownership of public land.[229] Again, however, lower court concern with government property rights should not interfere with judicial enforcement of first amendment guarantees.

The unique role of land in the Indian religions continues to present problems for the courts. In several of the cases discussed above, the courts either found no cognizable religious interest or no significant infringement on religion, despite the presentation of substantial evidence to the contrary. It is interesting to note that in *Yoder*, an important part of the Amish religion recognized in the decision and ultimately protected by it was "their devotion to a life in harmony with nature and the soil . . . ."[230] It is a similar type of relationship with the land in Indian religions that apparently presents difficulties in these cases. "American Indians hold their lands—places—as having the highest possible meaning, and all their statements are made with this reference point in mind."[231]

As discussed above, the courts are permitted a cursory inquiry into the sincerity of asserted religious beliefs, but should not question the truthfulness of the assertions.[232] The courts must acquire some understanding of the importance of land to the Indian religions if Indian's religious interests are to be protected. The analysis should focus more on the nature of the state actions and less on a skeptical inquiry (express or implied) into the beliefs of the individual.

Equally as important in understanding the role of land is acceptance

---

227. The concept of accomodation was first discussed in Wisconsin v. Yoder, 406 U.S. 205 (1972). It allowed the Amish an exemption under the state statute while allowing the state to achieve its interest in maintaining education standards.

228. Inupiat Community v. United States, 548 F. Supp. 182, 183 (D. Alaska 1982), *aff'd*, 746 F.2d 570 (9th Cir. 1984), *cert. denied*, 474 U.S. 820 (1985).

229. *Lyng*, 108 S. Ct. at 453.

230. *Yoder*, 406 U.S. at 210.

231. V. DELORIA, JR., GOD IS RED 75 (1973).

232. *See supra* note 84 and accompanying text.

of that role as fundamental to Indian religions. The courts should accept as fact a claimant's assertion of importance if the assertion is supported by sufficient evidence. In *Sequoyah*,[233] the court found the plaintiffs' interests to be cultural rather than religious, despite the plaintiff's assertions and evidence that their use of the land had religious as well as cultural implications. This type of finding is inconsistent with the Supreme Court's ruling in *Thomas v. Review Board*[234] that "religious beliefs need not be acceptable, logical, consistent, or comprehensible to others in order to merit First Amendment protection."[235] Consideration of the importance of land to the Indian religions and the sincerity of Indian beliefs may enable the courts to recognize infringements imposed upon these religions by government activities.

V. CONCLUSION

The Indian claims in the cases described have not been properly analyzed, and therefore, Indian religions have not been given adequate constitutional protection. Because these claims are important to the Indian community and are likely to continue as our population expands into areas utilized as religious sites, the issues should be resolved. Until they are, the American Indian Religious Freedom Act and the free exercise clause of the first amendment will hold no meaning for American Indians trying to preserve their traditional religious practices.

Unfortunately, the *Lyng* decision may have settled the issue without resolving the difficult problems presented in the cases. *Lyng*'s narrow focus on form rather than on effect of government actions may make it impossible for Indians, or anyone else, to succesfully challenge governmental land management that interferes with religious practices.

Stephen McAndrew

---

233. *See supra* notes 51-84 and accompanying text.
234. 450 U.S. 707 (1981).
235. *Id.* at 714.

The Navajo-Hopi Relocation Act and the First Amendment Free Exercise Clause

Introduction

SINCE 1974, OVER 11,000 Navajo have been relocated off their traditional lands in northern Arizona.[1] This relocation is pursuant to the Navajo-Hopi Relocation Act of 1974, which was enacted to resolve a decades old dispute between the Navajo and Hopi over the ownership of these lands.[2]

In an attempt to halt the Navajo relocation, forty-six full blooded Dineh, or Navajo Indians, have filed a complaint to enjoin the forced relocation.[3] The complaint asserts seven claims for relief against various defendants.[4] The core, however, of the Navajo's argument is that because the practice of their religion is inextricably tied to these lands, the forced relocation violates their first amendment free exercise rights.[5]

---

1. Whitson, *A Policy Review of the Federal Government's Relocation of Navajo Indians Under P.L. 93-531 and P.L. 96-305*, 27 Ariz. L. Rev. 371, 372 n.8 (1985).

2. Navajo-Hopi Relocation Act, Pub. L. No. 93-531, 88 Stat. 1714 (1974), *amended by* Navajo-Hopi Relocation Amendments Act, Pub. L. No. 96-305, 94 Stat. 930 (1980) (codified at 25 U.S.C. §§ 640d to 640d-28 (1982)).

3. Manybeads v. United States, No. 88 Civ. 0181, slip. op. at 32 (D.D.C. filed Jan. 26, 1988). Venue was subsequently changed to the United States District Court for the District of Arizona pursuant to the district court's order of February 19, 1988.

4. The complaint asserts the following claims for relief: (1) violation of right to free exercise of religion; (2) violation of the American Indian Religious Freedom Act, 42 U.S.C. § 1996; (3) violation of equal protection; (4) violation of federal trust responsibility; (5) violation of right of freedom of religion under customary international law and the United States Charter; (6) violation of plaintiff's right to protection against genocide as provided in international law and in the Genocide Convention; (7) violation of plaintiffs' rights as a "self governing people" under article 73 of the United Nations Charter. Manybeads v. United States, No. 88 Civ. 0181, slip. op. at 51-54 (D.D.C. filed Jan. 26, 1988).

In addition to the United States, the named defendants are: Donald P. Hodel, Secretary of the Department of the Interior; United States Department of Interior; Ross O. Swimmer, Assistant Secretary of the Department of Interior; United States Bureau of Indian Affairs; Hawley Atkinson, Chairman of the Navajo Hopi Indian Relocation Commission; and the Navajo Hopi Indian Relocation Commission. *Id.* at 29-32.

5. *Id.* at 51.

In recent years, many Native American free exercise claims have failed.[6] Further, the Navajo's task in pursuing their claims has been made more difficult by the United States Supreme Court's decision of *Lyng v. Northwest Indian Cemetery Protective Association*.[7] In *Lyng*, the Court declared that even if the construction of a road through sacred grounds would destroy the Indian's ability to practice their religion, the "Constitution simply does not provide a principle that could justify upholding [their] legal claims."[8]

Part I of this Comment examines the Supreme Court's analyses of free exercise claims leading up to its decision of *Lyng v. Northwest Indian Cemetery Protective Association*. Part I also examines lower federal court decisions on Native American free exercise claims. Part II sets forth the history of Navajo occupation in the relocation area and Navajo religion.[9] Part III discusses the principal arguments on both sides of the relocation issue as it relates to free exercise: whether forced relocation constitutes a burden on Navajo free exercise of religion; whether forced relocation is supported by a compelling government interest; and whether the establishment clause is implicated in forced relocation.

This Comment concludes that forced relocation of traditional Navajo constitutes an infringement of their free exercise of religion. Therefore, this Comment urges that traditional Navajo who face relocation be permitted to remain on their land to practice the religion they have practiced for centuries.[10]

---

6. *See infra* notes 45-57 and accompanying text.

7. 108 S. Ct. 1319 (1988).

8. *Id.* at 1326-27.

9. The word "religion" is used cautiously because it may connote traditional western religions, in which, as one author has noted, "the emphasis is on conformity of individual behavior to religious dogma, and not on communal involvement in ceremonies and continual renewal of relationships with holy places." Comment, *Indian Worship v. Government Development: A New Breed of Religion Cases*, 1984 UTAH L. REV. 313, 320. Although there are similarities between Native American and western beliefs, such as a belief in a supernatural power, the distinctive emphasis in Native American religions is the significance of place. Barsh, *The Illusion of Religious Freedom for Indigenous Americans*, 65 OR. L. REV. 363, 364-65 (1986).

10. The Navajo's claims also face procedural challenges that have profound free exercise implications. These challenges include whether the plaintiffs have standing and whether their claims are barred by res judicata.

Congress passed the Act of July 22, 1958, which provided that the Navajo and Hopi tribes "acting through the chairmen of their respective tribal councils *for and on behalf of said tribes*" were authorized to commence an action in United States District Court for the

I. THE CONSTITUTIONAL ISSUES

A. *The Supreme Court and Free Exercise of Religion*

The test for determining whether an individual's free exercise right had been infringed was previously stated in axiomatic fashion.[11] First, the individual must have asserted a religious belief rather than a mere personal philosophy.[12] If a religious belief was

---

District of Arizona "for the purpose of determining the rights and interests of said parties in and to said lands and quieting title thereto . . . . " Pub. L. No. 85-547, 72 Stat. 403 (1958) (emphasis added). Subsequent decisions have interpreted this language to mean that "the Tribe represents the interests of all members in the dispute." Sekaguaptewa v. MacDonald, 544 F.2d 396, 403 (9th Cir. 1976), cert. denied, 430 U.S. 931 (1977); see also Sidney v. Zah, 718 F.2d 1453, 1457 (9th Cir. 1983). Therefore, the argument is that individual Navajos lack standing to present first amendment claims because Congress has conferred representation for all issues relating to relocation on the tribe.

This argument is supposedly buttressed by the passage of the Navajo-Hopi Relocation Act of 1974, which provided for the creation of tribal negotiating teams to partition the disputed lands. Each team would "have full authority to bind its tribe with respect *to any other matter* concerning the joint use area within the scope of this subchapter." 25 U.S.C. § 640d-1(a) (1982) (emphasis added).

However, the Navajo-Hopi Relocation Act of 1974, and its predecessor, the Act of July 22, 1958 were limited to intertribal suits, *and* were not intended to apply to individual claims. See Sidney v. Zah, 718 F.2d 1453, 1457 (9th Cir. 1983); Sekaquatewa v. MacDonald, 591 F.2d 1289, 1292 (9th Cir. 1976), cert. denied, 430 U.S. 931 (1977).

Further, to find that the plaintiffs do not have standing would in essence mean that they have waived their right to bring such claims. This would be contrary to the well settled principle that waiver of a constitutional right requires "an intentional relinquishment or abandonment of a known right or privilege." Brookhart v. Janis, 384 U.S. 1, 4 (1966); see also 16 AM. JUR. 2D Constitutional Law § 619 (1979). Here, there is no evidence that individual tribal members knowingly waived their right to bring constitutional claims.

The Ninth Circuit court has held that Healing v. Jones II, 210 F. Supp. 125 (D. Ariz. 1962), aff'd per curiam, 373 U.S. 758 (1963), was res judicata as to all Navajo claims to the land, aboriginal, or otherwise. United States v. Kabinto, 456 F.2d 1087, 1090 (9th Cir. 1972). However, that ruling must be read in light of the limited jurisdiction conferred on the courts by the 1958 and 1974 acts, which was only to quiet title and approve relocation. First amendment issues have not been addressed by the United States District Court of Arizona, nor could they have been pursuant to the statutory authority under which the cases subsequent to Healing were decided. See Plaintiffs' Memorandum of Law in Opposition to Defendants' Motion to Dismiss at 11-29, Manybeads v. United States, No. 88 Civ. 410 (D. Ariz. filed Jan. 26, 1988).

To hold against the traditional Navajos on procedural grounds would result in a finding that Congress could strip away the right to bring first amendment claims without assent. Therefore, this writer proposes that decisions on these procedural issues be decided in the context of the first amendment claims.

11. U.S. CONST. amend. I. The free exercise clause provides in pertinent part: "Congress shall make no law[s] . . . prohibiting the free exercise [of religion] . . . ." Id.

12. Wisconsin v. Yoder, 406 U.S. 205, 216 (1972) (upholding Amish claim that mandatory school attendance violated their free exercise rights). Subsequently, the Supreme

demonstrated, then the court had to determine whether the government action burdened that belief.[13] Where a burden was found, the government action could only be justified if it was rooted in a "compelling state interest."[14] Further, the government action could be held invalid even though it merely impeded the religious practice.[15]

The Supreme Court's decisions evidenced a trend toward broadening the scope of free exercise protection. This trend appears to have reached its zenith with the Court's decision of *Wisconsin v. Yoder*.[16]

Wisconsin v. Yoder presented the Court with a claim by traditional Amish that Wisconsin's mandatory school attendance law violated their first amendment free exercise rights.[17] In analyzing this claim, the Court looked to the "impact that compulsory high school attendance could have on the continued survival of the Amish communities."[18] The Court noted that the Amish belief was based on a view of life in "harmony with nature and the soil"[19] and that this belief, which had existed for centuries,[20] pervaded and determined their mode of life.[21] These considerations led the Court

---

Court in Thomas v. Review Bd., 450 U.S. 707, 716 (1981), observed that "courts are not arbiters of scriptural interpretation," leading at least one commentator to point out that the court will accept at face value the plaintiff's assertion of religious belief. Comment, *supra* note 9, at 315. Given the Supreme Court's reluctance to question whether a belief is protected or not, this Comment is predicated upon the assumption that traditional Navajo religion is a protected religion under the first amendment.

13. Sherbert v. Verner, 374 U.S. 398, 403 (1963) (upholding Seventh-Day Adventist claim that her disqualification for employment benefits because she would not work on Saturdays, her Sabbath day, violated her free exercise of religion).

14. Wisconsin v. Yoder, 406 U.S. 205, 215 (1972). "[O]nly those interests of the highest order and those not otherwise served can overbalance legitimate claims to the free exercise of religion." *Id.*

15. *Id.* (quoting Braunfeld v. Brown, 336 U.S. 599, 607 (1961) ("[I]f the purpose or effect of a law is to impede the observance of one or all religions . . . that law is constitutionally invalid.")).

16. 406 U.S. 205 (1972).

17. *Id.* at 209.

18. *Id.*

19. *Id.* at 210. Harmony with nature is also at the core of traditional Navajo belief. R. UNDERHILL, RED MAN'S RELIGION: BELIEFS AND PRACTICES OF THE INDIANS NORTH OF MEXICO 228 (1965).

20. Wisconsin v. Yoder, 406 U.S. 205, 216 (1972). Navajo beliefs have likewise held constant over the centuries that the Navajo have occupied the Southwest. *See infra* notes 86-93 and accompanying text.

21. Wisconsin v. Yoder, 406 U.S. 205, 210 (1972). It is equally so for the Navajos; "every daily act is colored by their conceptions of supernatural forces . . . ." C. KUCKHOHN & D.

to conclude that mandatory education placed a burden on the Amish's free exercise of religion,[22] despite the fact that education ranked "at the very apex of the function of the State."[23]

The Court looked to "the quality of the claims" to determine whether the Amish would merit exemption from the state law.[24] However, the Court noted that only a "few other religious groups" could make such a showing.[25]

Since its decision of *Wisconsin v. Yoder*, the Court appears to have narrowed the scope of free exercise protection in deference to the demands that an increasingly complex and diverse society has placed on the government. For example, the Court has held that the need for uniform crowd control prohibits the Krishna from being permitted to roam a state fair at will as their faith dictates.[26] It has also held that the need for a national comprehensive and mandatory Social Security system outweighs the Amish belief opposing contributions to such a system,[27] that the federal government's policy of eradicating racial discrimination nationwide outweighs a private religious university's claim that its discriminatory practices were protected by the first amendment,[28] and that the uniform dress regulation in the military outweighs the plaintiff's religious practice of wearing a yarmulke.[29]

However, the Court continued to grant free exercise protection in some cases, most notably where the individual had been put to a choice between employment and a religious practice.[30] The differing treatment afforded these cases suggested that the Supreme

---

LEIGHTON, THE NAVAJO 179 (1974).

22. Wisconsin v. Yoder, 406 U.S. 205, 219 (1972).

23. *Id.* at 213.

24. *Id.* at 215. "In evaluating those claims (of the Amish) we must be careful to determine whether the Amish religious faith and mode of life are, as they claim, inseparable and interdependent." *Id.*

25. *Id.* at 235-36.

26. Heffron v. International Soc'y for Krishna Conscience, 452 U.S. 640 (1981).

27. United States v. Lee, 455 U.S. 252 (1982).

28. Bob Jones Univ. v. United States, 461 U.S. 574 (1983).

29. Goldman v. Weinberger, 475 U.S. 503 (1986).

30. Hobbie v. Unemployment Appeals Comm'n, 107 S. Ct. 1046 (1987) (denial of unemployment benefits to Seventh-Day Adventist who refused to work on Saturday, her Sabbath, even though she became Seventh-Day Adventist after beginning employment, violated her free exercise rights); Thomas v. Review Bd., 450 U.S. 707 (1981) (denial of unemployment compensation benefits to Jehovah's Witness who refused on religious grounds to work in foundry that fabricated steel for military uses violated his free exercise of religion); Sherbert v. Verner, 374 U.S. 397 (1963).

Court was developing a two-tiered analysis. On the first tier were those claims in which the government compelled conduct that was inconsistent with religious beliefs. On the second tier were those claims in which government actions had an incidental impact on religious practices. This two-tiered analysis became evident in *Bowen v. Roy.*[31]

In *Bowen v. Roy*, the Court was faced with a claim by a Native American couple that the requirement to obtain a Social Security number for their minor child in order to be eligible for aid violated their religious beliefs and, therefore, their free exercise of religion.[32] In rejecting this claim, the Court characterized the requirement as having only an indirect and incidental effect on religious practice.[33] This requirement is different, the Court opined, from "government action or legislation that criminalizes religiously inspired activity or inescapably compels conduct that some find objectionable for religious reasons."[34]

Moreover, "[a]bsent a proof of intent to discriminate, the government meets its burden when it demonstrates a challenged requirement which is neutral and uniform in its application [and] is a reasonable means of promoting a legitimate public interest."[35] Therefore, if a claim is analyzed on the second tier, the government need not demonstrate a "compelling interest."

A clear reading of the Court's decisions over the past eight years indicates that three principal criteria appear to determine on which tier the free exercise claim will be analyzed. The first criterion is whether the plaintiff has been the subject of coercion. Thus, in *Thomas v. Review Board*,[36] the Court focused on the compulsory nature of the state regulation.[37] There must be some government conduct that forces the individual to act or not to act in accordance with his or her beliefs.[38] This leads to the second criterion, the relationship between the religious practice and the belief.

---

31. 476 U.S. 693 (1986).
32. *Id.* at 695.
33. *Id.* at 706.
34. *Id.*
35. *Id.* at 708.
36. 450 U.S. 707 (1981).
37. *Id.* at 717-18.
38. *Id.*

The importance of the religious practice to the religious belief appears to play an important role in determining whether the infringement impedes the free exercise of religion.[39] Requiring proselytizers to stay in a booth rather than mix with a crowd,[40] requiring that only certain hats be worn in the military,[41] or denying tax benefits to schools that discriminate[42] does not prohibit the practice of the religion.

The third criterion is whether there is some objective standard by which the Court is able to determine not only the importance of the belief but also the extent of the burden. This is exemplified by *Sherbert v. Verner* in which an individual refused to work because of a religious belief and thereby lost her job. It is in contrast to *Bowen v Roy* in which it was claimed that government action prevented the individual "from attaining greater spiritual power."[43]

B. *Native American Free Exercise Claims in the Lower Federal Courts*

While hundreds of Navajo families were being relocated, several individual Native Americans and their tribes struck out into the wilderness of the federal courts to assert their free exercise claims. The response of the lower federal courts to these free exercise claims has been almost universally unfavorable.[44] Therefore, a

---

39. Although the Court has never expressly adopted a requirement of centrality, "its holdings would seem to reflect it." L. Tribe, American Constitutional Law 1247 n.37 (1988).

40. Heffron v. International Soc'y for Krishna Conscience, 452 U.S. 640 (1981).

41. Goldman v. Weinberger, 475 U.S. 503 (1986).

42. Bob Jones Univ. v. United States, 461 U.S. 574 (1983). "Denial of tax benefits will inevitably have a substantial impact on the operation of private religious schools, but will not prevent those schools from observing their religious tenets." *Id.* at 603-04.

43. Bowen v. Roy, 476 U.S. 693, 696 (1986).

44. Crow v. Gullet, 541 F. Supp. 785 (D.S.D. 1982) (Native American claim that state operation and development of Bear Butte State Park violated free exercise rights was denied given strong state interest in preserving environment), *aff'd*, 706 F.2d 856 (8th Cir.), *cert. denied*, 464 U.S. 977 (1983); Hopi Indian Tribe v. Block, 8 Indian L. Rep. (Am. Indian Law. Training Program) 3073 (D.D.C. 1981) (Hopi and Navajo claims that development of San Francisco Peaks, sacred areas to both tribes, burdened their free exercise of religion were denied on grounds that development would not impair the plaintiffs' practices), *aff'd sub nom.* Wilson v. Block, 708 F.2d 735 (D.C. Cir.), *cert. denied*, 464 U.S. 956 (1983); Sequoyah v. Tennessee Valley Auth., 480 F. Supp. 608 (E.D. Tenn. 1979) (Cherokee claim that defendant's construction of Telico Dam would flood traditional grounds, thereby violating their free exercise rights, was denied), *aff'd*, 620 F.2d 1159 (6th Cir.), *cert. denied*, 449 U.S. 953 (1980); Badoni v. Higginson, 455 F. Supp. 641 (D. Utah 1977) (Navajo claim that de-

review of these opinions is necessary in order to more fully understand the obstacles facing the Navajo claims.

Although the Native American claims dealt with rights of access to their religious sites[45] rather than relocation, the legal reasoning in these decisions has application to the Navajo claims. The lower courts have focused on coercion, government interests, and centrality.

Generally, the lower federal courts have adopted a narrow definition of coercion. Government action that incidentally impedes a religious practice does not rise to the level of coercion.[46] This view of coercion, recently adopted by a plurality of the Supreme Court in *Bowen v. Roy*,[47] suggests that only affirmative government acts will be found to impose a burden on religious practices.[48]

The lower federal courts have also shown greater deference to government programs by expanding the scope of "compelling government interests." Therefore, assuring public access to a natural wonder,[49] developing energy resources,[50] and preserving the envi-

---

fendants' operation of Rainbow Ridge National Monument, a religious site to the plaintiffs, violated their free exercise rights was denied on grounds that park operation did not coerce plaintiffs to violate their beliefs), *aff'd*, 638 F.2d 172 (10th Cir. 1980), *cert. denied*, 452 U.S. 954 (1981). Native American claims have prevailed in only one case, United States v. Means, 627 F. Supp. 247 (D.S.D. 1985), which has been appealed and therefore is not discussed in this Comment.

45. For a detailed discussion of the Native American cases, see Barsh, *supra* note 9; Stanbor, *Manifest Destiny and American Indian Religious Freedom: Sequoyah, Badoni and the Drowned Gods*, 10 AM. INDIAN L. REV. 59 (1982); Comment, *supra* note 9.

46. Therefore, in Badoni v. Higginson, 638 F.2d 172 (10th Cir. 1980), *cert. denied*, 452 U.S. 954 (1981), the court noted that the "government here has not prohibited plaintiffs' religious exercises in the area of Rainbow Bridge." *Id.* at 178. In Wilson v. Block, 708 F.2d 735 (D.C. Cir.), *cert. denied*, 464 U.S. 956 (1983), the court held that where the government action is indirect, no burden is found unless the government action penalizes "adherence to religious belief." *Id.* at 741.

47. The plurality adopted the words of Justice Douglas that "the Free Exercise Clause is written in terms of what the government cannot do to the individual, not in terms of what the individual can extract from the government." Bowen v. Roy, 476 U.S. 693, 700 (1986) (quoting Sherbert v. Verner, 374 U.S. 398, 412 (1963) (Douglas, J., concurring)).

48. Although the plaintiff in *Bowen v. Roy* argued that the Social Security Act requirement to have Social Security numbers is an affirmative compulsory act by the government, the Court found the requirement to be an integral part of internal governmental procedures and therefore beyond first amendment reach. Bowen v. Roy, 476 U.S. 693, 703 (1986).

49. Badoni v. Higginson, 638 F.2d 172 (10th Cir. 1980), *cert. denied*, 452 U.S. 954 (1981).

50. Inupiat Community of Arctic Slope v. United States, 548 F. Supp. 182 (1982) (government's interest in developing oil reserves off north slope of Alaska outweighed Inupiat use of same area for religious purposes, as government conduct was not a "serious obstacle"

ronment, protecting park visitors, and improving public access to historical landmarks[51] have all been determined to be compelling government interests that outweighed Native American access claims. Although these policies and objectives are important, they do not appear to reach interests of the "highest order."[52]

The Supreme Court introduced the concept of centrality.[53] However, it was the lower federal courts that made it a part of the burden analysis.[54] Centrality requires the plaintiff to show that the religious practice or belief is indispensable[55] or, in the case of religious sites, that it could not be performed anywhere else.[56]

This requirement has been criticized.[57] It exceeds the Supreme Court's own requirements for demonstrating that a burden exists and imposes an almost impossible burden of proof.[58] Nonetheless, the Native American plaintiffs in *Northwest Indian Cemetery Protective Association v. Peterson*[59] were able to meet this burden.

The Chimney Rock area of the Six Rivers National Forest adjoins the Hoopa Valley Indian Reservation in northern California. This area has historically been used for religious purposes by the Yurok, Karok, and Tolowa Indians.[60] In 1982, the United States Forest Service decided to construct six miles of road into Chimney

---

to such use), *aff'd*, 746 F.2d 570 (9th Cir. 1984).

51. Crow v. Gullett, 541 F. Supp. 785 (D.S.D. 1982), *aff'd*, 706 F.2d 856 (8th Cir.), *cert. denied*, 464 U.S. 977 (1983).

52. *See* Wisconsin v. Yoder, 406 U.S. 205, 215 (1972).

53. The Supreme Court first used the concept in Sherbert v. Verner, 374 U.S. 397, 406 (1962), when it referred to the belief at issue as a "cardinal principle," and later expressly used the term in Wisconsin v. Yoder, 406 U.S. 205, 210 (1972), when it described the Amish beliefs at issue as "central." Subsequently, the Alaska Supreme Court in Frank v. Alaska, 604 P.2d 1068, 1073 (1979), found the Athabascan Indian practice of eating elk meat to be the "centerpiece" of their most important religious practice. In People v. Woody, 61 Cal. 2d 716, 719, 394 P.2d 813, 817-18, 40 Cal. Rptr. 69, 73-74 (1964), the California Supreme Court found that peyote was the "theological heart" of Navajo religion.

54. The Court of Appeals for the District of Columbia Circuit considered the centrality issue when it examined whether the government program would burden the religious practice. Wilson v. Block, 708 F.2d 735, 742 (D.C. Cir. 1983).

55. Sequoyah v. Tennessee Valley Auth., 620 F.2d 1159, 1164 (6th Cir.), *cert. denied*, 449 U.S. 953 (1980).

56. Wilson v. Block, 708 F.2d 735, 742 (D.C. Cir.), *cert. denied*, 464 U.S. 956 (1983).

57. Stanobor, *supra* note 45, at 67-72.

58. In Native American religions, "no one thing has absolute significance over another." G. REICHARD, NAVAJO RELIGIONS A STUDY OF SYMBOLISM 11 (1983).

59. 565 F. Supp. 586 (N.D. Cal. 1983), *aff'd*, 795 F.2d 688 (9th Cir. 1986), *rev'd sub nom.* Lyng v. Northwest Indian Cemetery Protective Ass'n, 108 S. Ct. 1319 (1988).

60. *Id.* at 591.

Rock.[61] This was after the Forest Service's own study on the impact of this road on the tribe's religious practices had concluded that the road should not be built because it would be "potentially destructive of the very core of Northwest [Indian] religious beliefs and practices."[62]

The Native Americans brought suit to enjoin the construction, alleging that it violated their first amendment free exercise rights.[63] The district court applied the centrality test and determined that the use of the land was "central and indispensible to the Indian plaintiffs' religion."[64] The court then determined that the state's interest in completing the road was not a "paramount interest necessary to justify infringement of plaintiffs' freedom of religion."[65] The district court granted the injunction.[66]

The Court of Appeals for the Ninth Circuit affirmed the district court's holding,[67] and admonished the government for failing "to take into account the free exercise standard that control[led] this case."[68] The Ninth Circuit distinguished *Bowen v. Roy* by noting, "logging and road construction on public lands . . . is not the kind of internal governmental practice that the Court found beyond free exercise attack in *Roy*."[69] The Supreme Court's response came with its decision of *Lyng v Northwest Indian Cemetery Protective Association*.[70]

C. Lyng v. Northwest

In writing for the majority,[71] Justice O'Connor conceded that the "government's proposed actions will have severe adverse effects on the practice of their [Indian] religion."[72] Justice O'Connor then

---

61. *Id.*
62. *Id.* at 595.
63. *Id.* at 590.
64. *Id.* at 594.
65. *Id.* at 596.
66. *Id.* at 606.
67. Northwest Indian Cemetery Protective Ass'n v. Peterson, 795 F.2d 688 (9th Cir. 1986), *rev'd sub nom.* Lyng v. Northwest Indian Cemetery Protective Ass'n, 108 S. Ct. 1319 (1988).
68. *Id.* 694-95.
69. *Id.* at 693.
70. 108 S. Ct. 1319 (1988).
71. Justice O'Connor was joined in her opinion by Justices Rehnquist, White, Stevens, and Scalia.
72. Lyng v. Northwest Indian Cemetery Protective Ass'n, 108 S. Ct. 1319, 1324 (1988).

turned not to an examination of whether the countervailing government interest was compelling[73] or reasonable,[74] but rather to a discussion of the plurality's opinion in *Bowen v. Roy*.[75] The Court rejected the Native Americans' argument that *Bowen v. Roy* was distinguishable, noting that "[t]he building of a road or the harvesting of timber on public land cannot meaningfully be distinguished from the use of a Social Security number in *Roy*."[76] The majority concluded that in *Lyng*, as in *Bowen*, there was no coercion to violate or penalize a religious belief[77] and readopted the *Bowen* reasonableness test: "[I]ncidental effects of government programs, which may make it more difficult to practice certain religions but which have no tendency to coerce individuals into acting contrary to their religious belief, [do not] require the government to bring forward a compelling justification for its otherwise lawful actions."[78]

In response to the issue of centrality, the court noted that such a requirement would necessitate weighing the value of every belief and practice that is threatened by government action.[79] This could lead to a finding that "sincerely held religious beliefs and practices are not 'central' to certain religions."[80] The majority sum-

---

73. The Native Americans, in their brief, argued that the government should be held to the higher standard of "compelling interest" in determining whether the conceded burden was justified under the first amendment. Respondent's Brief at 39, Lyng v. Northwest Indian Cemetery Protective Ass'n, 108 S. Ct. 1319 (1988) (No. 86-1013).

74. The government argued that a "showing of the reasonableness of the government action should be sufficient to justify a land management decision that is subject to scrutiny under the free exercise clause." Appellant's Brief at 18, Lyng v. Northwest Indian Cemetery Protective Ass'n, 108 S. Ct. 1319 (1988) (No. 86-1013).

75. 476 U.S. 693 (1986).

76. Lyng v. Northwest Indian Cemetery Protective Ass'n, 108 S. Ct. 1319, 1325 (1988). The Indians had argued that *Bowen v. Roy* was concerned only with internal government actions whereas this case did not and, in any event, presented a "significantly greater" religious liberty than in *Bowen*. *Id.* at 1322. In rejecting these arguments, the majority refused to examine the impact of the government acts on plaintiffs' beliefs and practices. *Id.* at 1323.

77. *Id.* at 1325. Justice O'Connor's utilization of *Bowen* might strike some as curious in that it was Justice O'Connor who dissented in part in *Bowen*, arguing that the plurality's "reasonableness" standard had no place in first amendment analysis, and concluded that the "government has failed to show that granting a religious exemption . . . will do any harm to its compelling interest in preventing welfare fraud." Bowen v. Roy, 476 U.S. 693, 728 (1986).

78. Lyng v. Northwest Indian Cemetery Protective Ass'n, 108 S. Ct. 1319, 1326 (1988).

79. *Id.* at 1329.

80. *Id.* at 1329-30.

marily dismissed centrality as an "approach [that] cannot be squared with the Constitution or with our precedents, [which] would cast the judiciary in a role that we were never intended to play."[81]

By equating *Lyng* with *Bowen*, the majority essentially equates Bowen's "harm to his daughter's spirit" with the tribe's damage to their spiritual development should the road be built.[82] This is consistent with the Court's tendency to reject free exercise claims where the Court fails to find objective evidence of a burden. Further, and more importantly, it reiterates the Court's emphasis on coercion as the key element in free exercise analysis.[83] Although the evidence supported a finding that there was a significant burden on the religious practice[84] and no countervailing, compelling government interest, the Court refused to find a first amendment free exercise burden because the element of coercion was missing.

The majority noted that if the law forbade the Indians from visiting the Chimney Rock Area "a different set of constitutional questions" would be raised.[85] Therefore, it appears that the *Lyng* Court has not precluded the use of a *Wisconsin v. Yoder* analysis in future cases.

II. THE NAVAJO

A. *The History of Navajo Relocation*

The ancestors of the Navajos migrated from Asia to North America sixteen hundred years ago.[86] Although it is impossible to determiney precisely when they arrived in the Southwest, it is clear that before the Spanish arrival in the early sixteenth century the Navajo were well settled in the Southwest. Navajo hogans have

---

81. *Id.* at 1330.

82. *Id.*

83. The majority construes *Wisconsin v. Yoder* as resting principally on the coercive impact of the state mandatory school attendance law. *Id.* at 1329.

84. The majority recognized this point. *Id.* at 1326. In addition, the appellate court had noted that there was virtually no evidence contrary to the argument that a substantial burden would result from the road construction. Northwest Indian Cemetery Protective Ass'n v. Peterson, 795 F.2d 688, 692 (9th Cir. 1986), *rev'd sub nom.* Lyng v. Northwest Indian Cemetery Protective Ass'n, 108 S. Ct. 1319 (1988).

85. Lyng v. Northwest Indian Cemetery Protective Ass'n, 108 S. Ct. 1319, 1327 (1988).

86. G. BAILEY & R. BAILEY, A HISTORY OF THE NAVAJOS: THE RESERVATION YEARS 11 (1986).

been dated to the eleventh and fourteenth centuries in eastern New Mexico, not far from the present relocation area.[87] Additionally, an examination of Navajo legends further substantiates their Southwest presence during this period.[88]

Following Spanish contact, the Navajos began their movement throughout New Mexico and Arizona.[89] Navajo settlement in the relocation area by the early seventeenth century is irrefutable.[90] As a result of this movement, there was increasing Navajo, contact and conflict with the Spanish,[91] Mexicans, and other tribes.[92]

Following the Mexican War in 1846, the United States took control of the Southwest and the Navajo land.[93] The Navajo were subsequently relocated to Bosque-Redondo in New Mexico.[94] This relocation, however, lasted only until 1868 when a new treaty was signed with the Navajo, and they were permitted to return to their traditional lands in eastern New Mexico and western Arizona.[95]

Navajo history, however, is only part of the necessary backdrop. The Hopi village, old Oraibi, is one of the "oldest continuously inhabited villages in the nation."[96] Although this does not

---

87. E. CAHN, BY EXECUTIVE ORDER: A REPORT TO THE AMERICAN PEOPLE ON THE NAVAJO-HOPI LAND DISPUTE 50-60 (1982).

88. *Id.*

89. Iverson notes that by the early 1600's, "The People" had "migrated westward, as far as The Black Mesa country of northern Arizona." P. IVERSON, THE NAVAJO NATION 3 (1981). Dutton observes that by the 1630's the Navajo's "had become a large and powerful people" living as far west as the little Colorado River in eastern Arizona. B. DUTTON, AMERICAN INDIANS OF THE SOUTHWEST 212 (1975).

90. Healing v. Jones II, 210 F. Supp. 125, 137 n.8 (D. Ariz. 1962), *aff'd per curiam*, 373 U.S. 758 (1963). After reviewing historical evidence as to occupation and use of disputed lands, the court held that the Navajo and Hopi tribes had joint ownership of the land. The court noted that archeological studies found 900 Indian sites in the executive order area most of which were Navajo sites dating from 1662 to 1939. *Id.*

91. Navajo-Spanish conflict can be traced as far back as the mid-17th century, and up to the more turbulent times of the early 1800's. G. BAILEY & R. BAILEY, *supra* note 86, at 17-18; B. DUTTON, *supra* note 89, at 68.

92. P. IVERSON, *supra* note 89, at 5.

93. *Id.* at 18.

94. Approximately 8,500 Navajo were relocated in Bosque-Redondo. *Id.* at 23.

95. There is no dispute that this first forced relocation was a complete failure. P. IVERSON, *supra* note 89, at 10; C. KLUCKHOHN & D. LEIGHTON, *supra* note 21, at 41.

The 1868 treaty gave the Navajo a reservation of 3.5 million acres. Given the nature of the land and the population growth of the Navajo, this area was clearly inadequate. C. KLUCKHOHN & D. LEIGHTON, *supra* note 21, at 43. It resulted in the expansion of the Navajo beyond their original western reservation boundary, and thereby closer to the traditional Hopi villages. Whitson, *supra* note 1, at 375.

96. P. IVERSON, *supra* note 89, at 11.

mean that the Hopis predated the Navajos in the Southwest[97] and thereby have a stronger claim to the disputed area,[98] there is no question that the Hopi have their own tradition. That tradition is, however, different from the Navajos. The Hopis have remained close to their villages on the prongs of Black Mesa[99] because of their agricultural economy,[100] their closely interwoven social structure,[101] religious practices,[102] and need for protection.[103] Therefore, unlike the Navajo, the Hopi have not ventured far beyond their villages.[104]

On December 16, 1882, President Chester A. Arthur signed an Executive order creating a Hopi Reservation of 2.4 million acres "for the use and occupancy of the Mogui [Hopi], and such other Indians as the Secretary of the Interior may see fit to settle thereon."[105] The reservation, created for curious reasons,[106] held within it the pattern of land use that was to predominate for the next century[107]—a tightly woven Hopi community and a growing

---

97. One author has concluded that the "Hopi arrival at Oraibi cannot be dated prior to the twelfth century. The Navajo presence at San Francisco Peaks in Arizona and Chaco Canyon in northwestern New Mexico and other localities goes back to 1200 or earlier." E. CAHN, supra note 87, at 75.

98. This was suggested by the district court in Healing v. Jones when it wrote that "[t]he recorded history of the Navajos does not extend as far back as that of the Hopis. From all historic evidence it appears that the Navajos entered what is now Arizona in the last half of the eighteenth century." Healing v. Jones II, 210 F. Supp. 125, 134 (D. Ariz. 1962), aff'd per curiam, 373 U.S. 758 (1963). Such statements are open to dispute and in the case of the Navajo, late eighteenth century arrival is simply incorrect. See supra note 89.

99. J. KAMMER, THE SECOND LONG WALK: THE NAVAJO-HOPI LAND DISPUTE 22 (1980).

100. Id.

101. B. DUTTON, supra note 89, at 77.

102. J. KAMMER, supra note 99, at 60.

103. B. DUTTON, supra note 89, at 34.

104. This is not to suggest that the Navajos were nomads without permanent villages or even residences. Rather, Navajos are best described as herdsman, not nomads. Id. at 77. "[T]hey are no more 'nomads' than well-to-do New Yorkers who commonly migrate twice yearly over greater distances than do the Navajos." C. KLUCKHOHN & D. LEIGHTON, supra note 21, at 39. In addition they too have a strong agricultural tradition. P. IVERSON, supra note 89, at 5.

105. Healing v. Jones II, 210 F. Supp. 125, 129 n.1 (D. Ariz. 1962) (quoting Exec. Order of President Arthur (Dec. 16, 1882)), aff'd per curiam, 373 U.S. 758 (1963).

106. The reservation was created to give the local Indian agent authority to expel two whites from the Hopi villages, who were thought to be meddling in Hopi affairs. J. KAMMER, supra note 99, at 27.

107. For a discussion of the legal, cultural and economic history of this dispute over this period, see J. KAMMER, supra note 99; Schifter & West, Healing v. Jones: Mandate for Another Trail of Tears, 51 N.D.L. REV. 73 (1974-1975); Whitson, supra note 1.

Navajo culture.[108] However, the Executive order did not vest any land in either tribe nor did it set forth who the "other Indians" were.[109] These issues became the subject of the decision in *Healing v. Jones*.[110]

In 1958, Congress passed legislation that authorized the district court to "quiet title" in the reservation created by the 1882 Executive order.[111] The district court's response was to find that the Hopis had exclusive interest in one-sixth of the reservation, and as to the balance, "the Hopi and Navajo Tribes have joint, undivided, and equal interests as to the surface and sub-surface . . . ."[112] This decision hardly "quieted" title; not long after, the Hopi set out to claim their share of what is now known as the Joint Use Area ("JUA").[113]

From 1972 to 1976, the district and appellate courts, in response to a Hopi writ of assistance, held that Navajo construction was to be restricted on the JUA and that Navajo grazing would be limited to one-half of the JUA.[114] Simultaneously, Congress began to consider a series of proposals to resolve the issue of ownership.[115] Congress enacted legislation,[116] which provided for a mediation process to partition the JUA.[117] If mediation proved unsuc-

---

108. Although there is evidence of Hopi movement out of their village core and into the balance of the 1882 reservation, it appears to have been minimal and principally the result of federal government influence rather than a natural development. J. KAMMER, *supra* note 99, at 30-32.

109. Healing v. Jones II, 210 F. Supp. 125, 137 (D. Ariz. 1962), *aff'd per curiam*, 373 U.S. 758 (1963).

110. *Id.*

111. Act of July 22, 1958, Pub. L. No. 85-547, 72 Stat. 403 (1958).

112. Healing v. Jones II, 210 F. Supp. 125, 137 (D. Ariz. 1962), *aff'd per curiam*, 373 U.S. 758 (1963). This conclusion would appear to ignore the fact that usage of the land outside the Hopi village area was almost exclusively Navajo. Schifter & West, *supra* note 107, at 99. The usual method of determining interest is to examine usage at the time of "treaty recognition," which in this case was 1958, when there was a predominantly Navajo usage stretching back centuries. *Id.* at 96.

113. J. KAMMER, *supra* note 99, at 47-48.

114. Sekaguaptewa v. MacDonald, 544 F.2d 396 (9th Cir. 1976), *cert. denied*, 430 U.S. 931 (1977); Hamilton v. MacDonald, 503 F.2d 1138 (9th Cir. 1974); Hamilton v. Nakai, 453 F.2d 152 (9th Cir.), *cert. denied*, 406 U.S. 945 (1972).

115. See J. KAMMER, *supra* note 99, at 91-137 for a discussion of the various proposals.

116. Navajo-Hopi Relocation Act, Pub. L. No. 93-531, 88 Stat. 1714 (1974), *amended by* Navajo Hopi Relocation Amendments Act, Pub. L. No. 96-305, 94 Stat. 930 (1980) (codified at 25 U.S.C. §§ 640d to 640d-28 (1982)).

117. The act set up a mediation process with negotiating teams of five members from each tribe approved by the respective tribal councils, giving the mediator and the negotiat-

cessful, the partition would be accomplished by the mediator and the district court.[118] This process ultimately resulted in the partition of the JUA.[119] Since then, 1,193 Navajo families have been relocated from Hopi land.[120] Although relocation was to be completed in 1986, there are 1,395 Navajo families and 10 Hopi yet to be relocated.[121] Many of these Navajo are the named plaintiffs in *Manybeads v. United States*, or members of the class;[122] they look to the federal courts for protection of their right to free exercise of their religion.

B. *Navajo Religion*

As with Native Americans generally, Navajo life is shaped by their beliefs.[123] In Navajo mythology, shortly after man's emergence onto the earth, the four clans were created.[124] Each clan was given a specific area within the four sacred mountains for which they were to be caretakers.[125] This caretaker relationship with the land continues today and is at the foundation of the Navajo claim that their forced removal violates their free exercise of religion.[126]

---

ing teams 180 days to settle the dispute. 25 U.S.C. § 640d-1 (1982). If the mediator and negotiating teams were unable to resolve the dispute, the mediator was to submit a plan to the district court. *Id.* § 640d-2. Given that the "dispute" over use of the JUA had existed since at least 1958, it is amazing that Congress thought that tribal members could resolve the matter in 180 days. Moreover, the councils who were to choose the negotiating teams were themselves not representative of the tribe's traditional people. Whitson, *supra* note 1, at 376. This is a continuation of the nineteenth century federal policy of creating Navajo political organizations that have no roots in the Navajo people. G. BAILEY & R. BAILEY, *supra* note 86, at 32. It was therefore also not surprising that the views of the traditional people were virtually ignored during the partition process so that their only present recourse is to seek relief by way of their own litigation.

118. 25 U.S.C. § 640d-3 (1982).

119. The partition was ultimately approved in an unpublished order signed February 10, 1977. *See* Whitson, *supra* note 1, at 380 n.73.

120. NAVAJO-HOPI INDIAN RELOCATION COMM'N, PROGRAM UPDATE AND REPORT FOR OCT. 1987, at 3 (Nov. 6, 1987).

121. *Id.*

122. Manybeads v. United States, No. 88 Civ. 0181 (D.D.C. filed Jan. 26, 1988).

123. Barsh, *supra* note 9, at 364.

124. P. IVERSON, *supra* note 89, at xxviii-xxix.

125. Affidavit of Mae Wilson Tso, in Support of Plaintiffs' Motion for Preliminary Injunction at 7, Manybeads v. United States, No. 88 Civ. 0181 (D.D.C. filed Jan. 26, 1988) [hereinafter Tso Affidavit]. The Four Sacred Mountains are Blanca Peak in the east, Mount Taylor in the south, San Francisco Peak in the west, and Hesperus Peak in the north. BIG MOUNTAIN COMM., BIG MOUNTAIN COMMUNITY REPORT 4 (June 10, 1982).

126. Memorandum of Points and Authorites in Support of Plaintiffs' Motion for a Pre-

Big Mountain, where Navajos have lived for more than four generations and from which they are now told to move,[127] is also a sacred place as it is the home of Be'goo chidi' or the "one that created man."[128] This site has no religious significance to the Hopi,[129] but has additional religious importance to the Navajo. The mountain has herbs and plants for Navajo ceremonies that can only be collected there;[130] Navajo burial grounds are located there;[131] and Red Yellow Spring, a sacred place of great significance is also located there.[132]

The importance of Navajo guardianship in such areas as Big Mountain cannot be overemphasized. Navajo faith commands that not only the clan but also the individuals stay in their traditional use area because of their responsibility to care for the land.[133] This caretaker role is not manifested once a week or even once a day but is reflected throughout the day of traditional Navajos as they offer prayers and offerings.[134] It is a constant and inseparable relationship. Removal from the land would be "cataclysmic."[135]

From the first moment of life this strong relationship to the land is created in the burying of the placenta in the traditional use area.[136] Each infant's cradleboard is made from a tall and straight tree representing that the child will grow up "with a good heart and mind."[137] This cradleboard is later buried beneath the same tree from which it came.[138]

---

liminary Injunction, Manybeads v. United States at 3, No. 88 Civ. 0181 (D.D.C. filed Jan. 26, 1988).

127. J. WOOD & K. STEMMLER, LAND AND RELIGION AT BIG MOUNTAIN: THE EFFECTS OF THE NAVAJO-HOPI LAND DISPUTE ON NAVAJO WELL-BEING 12 (1981). Big Mountain is an isolated Navajo community of 150 square miles whose residents are scheduled for relocation. *Id.* at 2-3.

128. BIG MOUNTAIN COMM., *supra* note 125, at 5.

129. J. WOOD & K. STEMMLER, *supra* note 127, at 12.

130. *Id.* at 13. *See also* BIG MOUNTAIN COMM., *supra* note 125, at 10-11.

131. J. WOOD & K. STEMMLER, *supra* note 127, at 12.

132. Affidavit of John Wood in Support of Plaintiffs' Motion for Preliminary Injunction at 10, Manybeads v. United States, No. 88 Civ. 0181 (D.D.C. filed Jan. 26, 1988) [hereinafter Wood Affidavit].

133. Tso Affidavit, *supra* note 125, at 18.

134. Affidavit of Thayer Scudder in Support of Plaintiffs' Motion for Preliminary Injunction at 6, Manybeads v. United States, No. 88 Civ. 0181 (D.D.C. filed Jan. 26, 1988).

135. Wood Affidavit, *supra* note 132, at 10.

136. J. JOE, THE EFFECTS OF FORCED RELOCATION OF A TRADITIONAL PEOPLE 120 (1985).

137. Tso Affidavit, *supra* note 125, at 8.

138. *Id.*

The Big Mountain area is covered with sacred places; one study found nineteen sacred sites. This study also observed that there "may be even more localities [sacred sites] of potential significance."[139] These sacred sites are natural areas, such as springs, where prayers or offerings are made.[140] Their relationship to this particular land led one writer to conclude that "Navajo religion is only capable of being practiced within specifically defined traditional areas."[141]

Myth, ceremony, sacred place, home, and obligation are all one arising from and turning back to the Navajo land. Such a relationship has led many scholars and Navajos to conclude that taking the people from their land is taking them from their religion.[142] Violet Ashkie is a seventy-four year old Navajo from Big Mountain.[143] She speaks with clarity:

> When you remove us away from our land, you take away our religion, our way of life. We cannot practice our religion anywhere else, only at our birthplace where we know the spiritual beings . . . . If you force us to go elsewhere we would get sick and we couldn't heal ourselves, we would not survive. You would be sentencing us to die.[144]

III. THE ARGUMENT

The traditional Navajo's first amendment free exercise claim will be argued in three arenas: whether relocation imposes a burden on first amendment exercise; whether there is a government interest supporting relocation; and whether the establishment clause is implicated in the plaintiffs' claims for relief.

---

139. J. WOOD & W. VANNETTE, A PRELIMINARY ASSESSMENT OF THE SIGNIFICANCE OF NAVAJO SACRED PLACES IN THE VICINITY OF BIG MOUNTAIN ARIZONA 12 (1979).

140. Wood Affidavit, supra note 132, at 8.

141. Affidavit of Jerome M. Levi in Support of Plaintiffs' Motion for Preliminary Injunction at 5, Manybeads v. United States, No. 88 Civ. 0181 (D.D.C. filed Jan. 26, 1988).

142. John Wood, following his initial study of the Navajo, concluded that there was a "symbiotic relation between belief, place, participation through use, and occupancy" that would be severed by a policy of relocation which allowed only access back to sacred sites. J. WOOD & W. VANNETTE, supra note 139, at 2. In Wood's subsequent study he concluded that "[i]f they [the Navajo] are forced to leave the land, they will be forced to leave their religion." J. WOOD & K. STEMMLER, supra note 127, at 4.

143. Affidavit of Violet Ashkie in Support of Plaintiffs' Motion for Preliminary Injunction at 6, Manybeads v. United States, No. 88 Civ. 0181 (D.D.C. filed Jan. 26, 1988).

144. Id.

A. *The Burden*

The key element in the burden analysis requires the court to find that an individual is being affimatively coerced to violate his or her religious beliefs.

In this context, the government's argument is that the Navajo-Hopi Relocation Act of 1974 ("Relocation Act")[145] does not directly coerce the Navajo to move. Many of the Navajo who have already moved have done so voluntarily.[146] Further, the Relocation Act itself is not aimed at discriminating against religious beliefs and, to the extent it impacts such beliefs, accommodation by way of access back to religious sites is provided.[147] Finally, the Navajo, who only recently appeared in the Southwest as compared to the Hopi, are traditionally nomadic and therefore have not established a strong religious connection to any particular place over a protracted period.[148] Therefore, the Relocation Act does not constitute an affirmative coercive burden on the traditional Navajo because their religion can be practiced elsewhere. To the extent that it cannot, access back to their sacred places is provided, leaving their religion intact.

The Navajo contend that the removal has not been voluntary; those who have left have done so because of the threat of forced removal, not because they wished to leave.[149] The Relocation Act

---

145. Pub. L. No. 93-531, 88 Stat. 1714 (1974), *amended by* Navajo-Hopi Settlement Act, Pub. L. No. 96-305, 94 Stat. 929 (1980) (codified at 25 U.S.C. §§ 640d to 640d-28 (1982)).

146. The voluntary nature of the program is supposedly evidenced by the fact that designated relocatees must apply for relocation benefits. By August of 1987, 1,225 families had been relocated, 1,445 families "were certified as eligible for relocation," and 30 Navajo families have not yet applied. CONGRESSIONAL RESEARCH SERVICE, NAVAJO-HOPI RELOCATION 10-11 (Oct. 9, 1987).

147. 25 U.S.C. § 640d-5(c) provides that "reasonable provision shall be made for the use of and right of access to identified religious shrines for the members of each tribe on the reservation of the other tribe where such use and access are for religious purposes." 25 U.S.C. § 640d-5(c) (1982).

This accommodation argument would follow Justice O'Connor's observation in *Lyng v. Northwest* that the Forest Service had taken many ameliorative measures to limit the impact of the road construction upon religious practices, suggesting that reasonable government responses to religious practices will meet the government's constitutional duties. Lyng v. Northwest Indian Cemetery Protective Ass'n, 108 S. Ct. 1319, 1328 (1988).

148. Healing v. Jones II, 210 F. Supp. 125, 135 (D. Ariz. 1962), *aff'd per curiam*, 373 U.S. 758 (1963). "[The Navajo] were semi-nomadic or migratory, moving into new areas at times . . . ." *Id.*

149. Affidavit of Brooke Phillips in Support of Plaintiff's Motion for Preliminary In-

requires removal; those who cannot leave because of their religious beliefs are faced with forced removal.[150] Providing access back to their sacred sites is insufficient for the practice of their religious beliefs.[151] Forced relocation has such a coercive impact on traditional Navajo religious practices and life[152] that it constitutes a burden deserving of constitutional protection.

In *Wisconsin v. Yoder*, the compulsory education statute threatened to "undermin[e] the Amish community and religious practice," thereby forcing the Amish to "abandon belief . . . or . . . to migrate to some other and more tolerant region."[153] The Navajo do not even have the option of migrating "to some other and more tolerant region." Their traditional lands are their religion. Moreover, the lands at issue are private Indian lands, not public lands as in *Lyng*.

The other criteria in the burden analysis are also met. The importance of these lands to the traditional Navajo religion cannot be contested. An objective measure of the burden, similar to that in the employment cases, is present. The Navajo believe that they are the caretakers of these particular lands. Therefore, they must choose between obeying the Relocation Act and practicing their religion.

B. *The Government Interest*

If the court finds coercion, the Navajo relocation may be justified by a compelling government interest. In the absence of coercion, the relocation may be upheld if the government action, in administering Indian lands, is reasonable.

A threat to public safety and order may constitute a compelling government interest.[154] Historically, there has been a dispute

---

junction at 2-3, Manybeads v. United States, No. 88 Civ. 0181 (D.D.C. filed Jan. 26, 1988). Additionally, limitations on Navajo construction and herd size in the JUA have significantly effected the ability of traditional Navajo to remain on the JUA, virtually assuring their removal. *See supra* note 111.

150. 25 U.S.C. §§ 640d-4(3); 640d-5(b); 640d-9(c); 640d-12(a), 640d-13(a) (1982).

151. J. Wood & W. Vanette, *supra* note 139, at 28.

152. Several studies have demonstrated the psychological and physical damage that has resulted from forced relocation. *See* J. Joe, *supra* note 136, at 19-25; T. Scudder, No Place to Go: Effects of Compulsory Relocation on Navajos 27-30 (1982).

153. Wisconsin v. Yoder, 406 U.S. 205, 218 (1972).

154. *See* Prince v. Massachusetts, 321 U.S. 158 (1944) (state child labor law prohibiting sale of magazines by children under age of twelve was not a violation of defendants religious

over ownership of the JUA,[155] which has been coupled with the violence allegedly characteristic of Navajo-Hopi relations.[156] Although individual acts of violence between Navajo and Hopi have been documented,[157] there is no evidence that this warrants forced relocation.[158] In fact, the violence appears to be due in large part to government policies[159] or the relocation itself.[160]

Without factual support for widespread violence, the government is left with a "lost money" argument.[161] However, government costs alone, as they relate to the claims of the traditional Navajo, do not appear to rise to the level of a compelling government interest, even under the expansive view adopted by the lower federal courts.[162]

---

practice to have their children sell religious magazines); Jacobsen v. Massachusetts, 197 U.S. 11 (1905) (state law requiring compulsory vaccination for smallpox was within the states power to protect public health and not a violation of any liberty preserved under the Constitution); Reynolds v. United States, 98 U.S. 145 (1878) (defendants religious belief that he had a duty to practice polygamy could not be asserted as a defense to a criminal charge of polygamy).

155. The concept of partitioning the JUA dates back to the mid-1930's. J. KAMMER, *supra* note 99, at 40.

156. It would appear that the court's ruling in Healing v. Jones II, 210 F. Supp. 125, 154 (D. Ariz. 1962), *aff'd per curiam*, 373 U.S. 758 (1963), was based at least in part on its finding that there was a Navajo "proclivity to commit depredations against the Hopis." This theme, that the tribal dispute made partition "the only practicable solution", was reiterated in Sekaquaptewa v. MacDonald, 575 F.2d 239, 245 (9th Cir. 1976), *cert. denied*, 430 U.S. 931 (1977).

157. J. KAMMER, *supra* note 99, at 67.

158. Whitson, *supra* note 1, at 382-83.

159. J. KAMMER, *supra* note 99, at 38-40.

160. Forced relocation has resulted in incidents of resistance by traditional Navajos. *Id.* at 1-5. There also appears to be substantial evidence that traditional Hopis, unlike their leadership, are in support of the traditional Navajo religious claims and a halt to relocation, thereby further undercutting the argument that continued close proximity of the tribes will result in conflict. J. KAMMER, *supra* note 99, at 198.

161. CONGRESSIONAL RESEARCH SERVICE, NAVAJO-HOPI RELOCATION 5-6 (Oct. 9, 1987). "[I]n addition to the $64 million spent to date, approximately $274 million will be necessary to complete relocation by 1993. This is an 824 percent cost growth for the program since 1974." *Id.*

162. It has been suggested that one of the reasons for the court's ruling in both Sequoyah v. Tennessee Valley Auth., 480 F. Supp. 608 (E.D. Tenn. 1979), *aff'd*, 620 F.2d 1159 (6th Cir.), *cert. denied*, 449 U.S. 953 (1980), and Badoni v. Higginson, 455 F. Supp. 641 (D. Utah 1977), *aff'd*, 630 F.2d 172 (10th Cir. 1980), *cert. denied*, 452 U.S. 954 (1981), was that the government projects were substantially completed. In this case, however, as the future budget estimates testify, relocation is far from substantially complete, and unlike the building of a dam, relocation is divisible. Therefore costs incurred here should not constitute a finding of a compelling government interest sufficient to overcome the provable burden. *See supra* note 161.

In fact, partition was not the only alternative available to Congress. Historically, Native American land claims have been resolved by cash payments or other means, but not relocation.[163] Forced relocation is a drastic departure from these prior policies, which may not only implicate a violation of Congress' trust obligation,[164] but also supports the plaintiffs' argument that less burdensome alternatives existed to relocation. This would compel a finding that forced relocation, as it burdens free exercise of religion, is not constitutionally permissible.[165]

If the standard is reasonable government action, the argument is that in the area of government regulation of Indian lands, the government is given plenary power.[166] Although this power is no longer premised on a blind faith in congressional good-faith,[167] judicial review of such actions is limited to determining whether there is a rational basis for the government policy.[168] In this case, there would arguably be grounds for finding such a rational basis because the government seeks to resolve a decades old dispute by exercising qualified plenary authority over Indian lands.

Acceptance, however, of such a doctrine would mean that based on the slender thread of rational basis[169] the federal government could strip Native Americans of their first amendment rights and relegate them to the non-citizen status they once held.

---

163. Whitson, *supra* note 1, at 410 n.256.

164. Plaintiffs' fourth cause of action asserts a violation of the federal trust responsibility. Manybeads v. United States, No. 88 Civ. 0181, slip op. at 53 (D.D.C. filed Jan. 26, 1988).

165. Sherbert v. Verner, 374 U.S. 397, 407 (1962).

166. Lone Wolf v. Hitchcock, 187 U.S. 553, 568 (1903) (congressional plenary authority over Indian relations not subject to judicial review). The Lone Wolf doctrine has been subject to severe criticism. Whitson, *supra* note 1, at 397 n.185.

167. United States v. Sioux Nation of Indians, 448 U.S. 356, 410 (1980) (where Native Americans allege that there is a taking of treaty-protected property, Congress' power to control such land is not absolute).

168. C. WILKINSON, AMERICAN INDIANS, TIME AND THE LAW 81-82 (1987); *see also* Delaware Tribal Business Comm. v. Weeks, 430 U.S. 73, 85 (1977).

169. Hobbie v. Unemployment Appeals Comm'n, 107 S. Ct. 1046 (1987). "[S]uch a test has no basis in precedent and relegates a serious First Amendment value to the barest level of minimal scrutiny . . . ." *Id.* at 1054 (quoting Bowen v. Roy, 476 U.S. 693, 730 (1986) (O'Connor, J., dissenting)).

C. *The Establishment Clause*

Although the establishment clause[170] is not the principal focus of this Comment, discussion of its application is necessary to the extent it impacts the free exercise claims.

The plaintiffs seek to enjoin forced relocation of themselves and other members of their class who "practice the traditional Dineh religion" and who are estimated to be more than 1,500 but whose "exact number and identity . . . will be determined upon further discovery."[171] The response is twofold: first, that the establishment clause mandates governmental neutrality, which itself is a compelling state interest sufficient to warrant the burden imposed on the plaintiffs; secondly, that the government's involvement in determining which of the remaining Navajo are practitioners and which are not constitutes excessive entanglement and thus violates the clause. Therefore, the argument is an attempt to have the establishment clause both ways: as a reason to support relocation and as a reason not to modify relocation.

It is well settled that the government cannot use the establishment clause to inhibit the rights protected under the free exercise clause.[172] Therefore, the only issue is whether an accommodation of free exercise rights would so entangle the government as to create an establishment clause violation. Determining which of the remaining Navajo practice traditional religion and which do not arguably puts the government in a position of determining which religion is to be protected and which is not. The government then becomes the arbiter of acceptable religious practices, and this violates the establishment clause.[173] However, by accepting the affida-

---

170. U.S. CONST. amend. I. The establishment clause provides in pertinent part: "Congress shall make no law respecting an establishment of religion . . . ." *Id.* The Supreme Court has devised a three prong test: "First, the statute must have a secular legislative purpose; second, its principal or primary effect must be one that neither advances nor inhibits religion, finally, the statute must not foster "an excessive government entanglement with religion." Lemon v. Kurtzman, 403 U.S. 602, 612-13 (1971) (citation omitted).

171. Manybeads v. United States, No. 88. Civ. 0181, slip op. at 32 (D.D.C. filed Jan. 26, 1988).

172. Wisconsin v. Yoder, 406 U.S. 205, 220-21 (1972) (the establishment clause cannot be used to prevent the protection of values promoted by the right of free exercise).

173. The Supreme Court has apparently held that a policy of excluding religious groups from school facilities would involve the government in "greater entanglement" as it attempted to determine "which activities fall within religious worship and religious teaching," and which do not. Widmar v. Vincent 454 U.S. 263, 272 n.11 (1981).

vits filed in the Navajos' suit[174] testifying to their religious beliefs, the government, and the court, can be easily satisfied as to who follows the traditional Navajo religion and who does not.[175] Further, as to whether the government would be placed in such a permanent and continuing relationship with the religion that it would violate the establishment clause,[176] once relocation is halted, there is no reason for a continuing government involvement.

Conclusion

Native American free exercise claims have not fared well in the courts. However, the Supreme Court's decision of *Lyng v. Northwest Indian Cemetery Protective Association* did not foreclose the possibility of a *Wisconsin v. Yoder* analysis should certain criteria be met. The claims of the Navajo in *Manybeads v. United States* appear to meet these criteria. The Navajo are being forced to leave their lands, yet their religious faith and these lands are "inseparable and interdependent." The government can offer no countervailing "interests of the highest order."

The Navajo have lived and practiced their beliefs in the deserts of the Southwest for hundreds of years. The first amend-

---

174. Affidavits of Mae Wilson Tso, Jack Hatathlie, Violet Ashkie, Mark Charley, Alice Benally, Kee Shay, Betty A. Tso, and Ella Bedonie in Support of Plaintiffs' Motion for Preliminary Injunction, Manybeads v. United States No. 88 Civ. 0181 (D.D.C. Jan. 26, 1988).

175. Where there is an identifiable religion, even a Native American one, the government record is one of acceptance rather than to challenge claims of religious belief. *See* Crow v. Gullett, 541 F. Supp. 785 (D.S.D. 1982), *aff'd*, 706 F.2d 856 (8th Cir.), *cert. denied*, 464 U.S. 977 (1983); Hopi Indian Tribe v. Block, 8 Indian L. Rep. 3073 (D.D.C. 1981), *aff'd sub nom.* Wilson v. Block, 708 F.2d 735 (D.C. Cir.), *cert. denied*, 464 U.S. 956 (1983); Badoni v. Higginson, 455 F. Supp. 641 (D. Utah 1977), *aff'd*, 638 F.2d 172 (10th Cir. 1980), *cert. denied*, 452 U.S. 954 (1981). *But cf.* Sequoyah v. Tennessee Valley Auth., 480 F. Supp. 608 (E.D. Tenn. 1979), *aff'd*, 620 F.2d 1159 (6th Cir.), *cert. denied*, 449 U.S. 953 (1980) (plaintiff's claims arose out of a concern for a loss of their culture and history and not out of religious concerns). However, such a result would not appear to have been warranted by the facts in that case, nor in the claims brought by the traditional Navajo. *See* Comment, *supra* note 6, at 166.

176. "[O]ne of evils 'against which the establishment clause was intended to afford protection' . . . [was an] active involvement of the sovereign in religious activity." The Court went on to find there was the threat of a continuing and expanding involvement in Rhode Island's statute that provides state salary supplements to non-public elementary school teachers. Lemon v. Katzman, 430 U.S. 602, 623-24 (1970) (quoting Walz v. Tax Comm'n, 397 U.S. 664, 668 (1970)).

ment right to free exercise of religion mandates granting their requested injunction to halt any further forced relocation.

CHARLES MILLER
Class of 1990

INDIAN RIGHTS: NATIVE AMERICANS VERSUS AMERICAN MUSEUMS—A BATTLE FOR ARTIFACTS†

*Bowen Blair**

Introduction

The degradation of American Indian culture is a familiar feature in United States history. By depriving Indians of artifacts which possess special religious and ceremonial significance, American museums are contributing to this cultural debasement. Several Indian groups have initiated formal, yet nonlegal, requests for the return of these relics. However, museums, often relying upon solid legal and practical grounds, have typically ignored these requests.

An analysis of two confrontations between Indians and museums, concerning Zuni War Gods and Iroquois wampum belts, clarifies the legal and moral issues involved. A further examination of the federal Antiquities Act[1] and its proposed replacement,[2] the first amendment to the United States Constitution,[3] and a recent Public Law,[4] reveals legal solutions available to assist Native American attempts to protect undiscovered artifacts and to reclaim those artifacts presently held by museums.

Case Studies

In the late sixteenth century,[5] members of the Iroquois Nation's Onondaga Tribe fashioned belts from purple and white clam and conch shells.[6] These wampum belts were an integral part of the Iroquois culture. Symbols woven into the belts constituted the Onondagas' only recorded history.[7] Furthermore, ac-

---

† Portions of this note were published in an earlier version in the *American Indian Journal*, Vol. V, No. 5, at pp. 13-21, and in Vol. V, No. 6, at pp. 2-6. These portions are reprinted in this version with permission from the *American Indian Journal*.

* J.D. expected 1980, Lewis and Clark Law School, Northwestern School of Law. Issue Editor of *Environmental Law*.

1. 16 U.S.C. § 431 (1976).

2. H.R. REP. No. 1825, 96th Cong., 1st Sess. (1979).

3. U.S. CONST. amend. I.

4. Act of Aug. 11, 1978, Pub. L. No. 95-341, 92 Stat. 469.

5. Akwesasne Notes, May 1970, at 1, col. 4. For historical account of the Iroquois wampum, *see* A. MOLLOY, WAMPUM (1977).

6. N.Y. Times, Mar. 11, 1971, at 44, col. 6.

7. ARTS ADVOCATE, Jan. 1975, at 1, col. 1.

cording to Chief Irving Powless, the belts "are our religion and our law combined."[8]

In 1898, under questionable circumstances,[9] the New York State Museum at Albany obtained twenty-six of the Onondagas' wampum belts. Among these belts was perhaps the Iroquois' most famous, the Hiawatha belt.[10] Although the Onondaga refuse to attach a price to the wampum belt, experts estimate its art value at $280,000.[11]

The Onondaga later demanded the return of the belts. Each demand was refused by the state museum. In 1971, public pressure resulted in the passage of an act[12] which provided for the return of five wampum belts to the Onondaga. However, this return was conditional. The first condition stipulated that facsimiles of the belts had to be displayed at the state museum, to replace the genuine articles.[13] The second prerequisite required the Indians to build an "appropriate," "fireproof" facility on their reservation to house the wampum belts.[14] The adequacy of the housing would be determined by the museum's council on the arts,[15] which also retained the power to institute a "special proceeding" to compel the return of the wampum belts should the Onondaga fail to comply with the Act's provisions.[16] This second prerequisite was a practical impossibility.[17]

The twin War Gods, Masewi and Oyoyewi,[18] like the Iroquois wampum belts, play an essential role in Zuni culture and religion. The War Gods symbolize courage, strength, and virtue.[19] The cult of the War Gods, or *A'hayuta,* is delegated to the bow priests in the Zuni Tribe,[20] who also constitute the executive arm of the Zuni religious hierarchy.[21] The annual ceremony of the

---

8. N.Y. Times, Mar. 11, 1971, at 44, col. 6.

9. See discussion in text at note 58, *infra.*

10. N.Y. Times, Apr. 17, 1970, at 40, col. 2.

11. *Id.* The Iroquois analogize the pricing of the wampum belts with Anglo-Americans setting a price on the Declaration of Independence. *See* ARTS ADVOCATE, *supra* note 7, at 2, col. 3.

12. N.Y. INDIAN LAW § 27 (McKinney).

13. *Id.* at (2).

14. *Id.*

15. *Id.*

16. *Id.*

17. This requirement has to date remained unfulfilled. See note 34, *infra.*

18. 47 U.S. BUREAU OF ETHNOLOGY ANN. REPORTS 64 (1932).

19. *Id.*

20. *Id.* at 525.

21. *Id.* at 562.

bow priests is held at the winter solstice,[22] and six days after the announcement of this solstice, men from the Deer and Bear clans start creating the images of the War Gods.[23] These images, known to the art world as actual War Gods, are wooden, pole-like carvings, frequently adorned with eagle feathers. The War Gods are used in Zuni kivas, sacred ceremonial chambers closed to non-Zunis.[24] After the ceremonies, the War Gods are placed on specific mountain peaks on Zuni land, where they continue to serve a religious purpose.[25]

The Zuni are currently negotiating with at least two museums, the Smithsonian Institute and the Denver Art Museum, for the return of War Gods stolen from the Zuni reservation at the turn of the century.[26] Neither museum has been receptive to the Zuni requests. The Smithsonian, following the lead of the New York State Museum, has offered to return the images if the Zuni will build an adequate museum.[27]

To fully appreciate the American Indians' desire for the return of these and similar artifacts, an understanding of Native American culture and religion is essential. However, that analysis exceeds the scope of this note, and a generalization must suffice: religion pervades every aspect of Indian life, particularly Indian art. Chief Oren Lyons of the Onondaga succinctly articulated this tenet; "Religion, as it has been and is still practiced today on the reservation, permeates all aspects of tribal society. The language makes no distinction between religion, government, or law. Tribal customs and religious ordinances are synonymous. All aspects of life are tied in to one totality."[28] Indian artifacts, therefore, can rarely be separated from Indian religion. Wampum, for instance, is art as well as religion; it also represents Iroquois culture, history, and current existence. Zuni religious leaders concur with the appraisal, and describe their artifacts as "the essence of our Zuni culture."[29] Moreover, the loss of these artifacts to museums has created for the Zuni "an imbalance in

22. *Id.* at 526.
23. *Id.*
24. *Id.* at 527.
25. *Id.*
26. Telephone conversation with Bryant Rogers, Director, Zuni Legal Aid, Aug. 8, 1978. *See also* Letter from Indian Pueblo Legal Services, Inc., to Bowen Blair, Oct. 2, 1978.
27. Telephone conversation with Bryant Rogers, *supra* note 26.
28. ARTS ADVOCATE, *supra* note 7, at 2, col. 4.
29. *See* Appendix A, at item 1, Statement of Religious Leaders.

the spiritual world,"[30] which can be rectified only by the return of the artifacts.

The Museum Position

The issue of Indian reclamation of Indian artifacts from museums is an extremely difficult one to resolve. Both sides possess cogent moral and legal arguments. Museums generally rely on four persuasive points: (1) their public responsibility to preserve and exhibit the artifacts for the benefit of all Americans; (2) their doubt as to specific Indian ownership; (3) their unwillingness to establish a precedent of returning a part of their collections to original owners; and (4) their legal claims to the artifacts.

The reason most cited by museums for refusing to return the Indian artifacts concerns their presumed public responsibility to preserve and exhibit the artifacts for the benefit of all Americans, not just the Indians.[31] The requisite corollary which follows this justification—that Indian tribal museums have inadequate facilities to similarly care for the objects—is largely true.[32] According to Martin Link, the director of the Navajos' excellent tribal museum for eighteen years, "there is not a single tribe, including the Navajo, that is properly equipped to take care of any large collections."[33] Museums also cite the poor locations of the reservation tribal museums as a reason to refuse Indian requests. These locations are considered to be inconvenient for the average visitor.[34]

There are several persuasive counter-arguments to museum assertions that they provide the best places to preserve and exhibit the Indian artifacts. Basically, Indians contend that because museums do not share the Indians' religious concern and

---

30. *Id.* at 2.

31. *See generally* MUSEUM NEWS, Mar. 1973, at 22.

32. Reservation Indians are not wealthy. Disease, poverty, and substandard education are realities in their life. The thought of raising enough money to build an "adequate" Tribal Museum, especially during a period when private funding is unable to support the larger, more affluent white museums must seem ludicrous to the Indians. (*See generally* MUSEUM NEWS, Mar. 1973, at 22).

33. Letter from Martin Link to Bowen Blair, Aug. 26, 1978.

34. N.Y. Times, Mar. 11, 1971, at 44, col. 5. "In the early 1970's, museums arrived at an ingenious solution to the problem of Indian requests for artifacts. Exemplified by the New York State Museum and Smithsonian actions, museums offered to return part of their collections to the Indians, if the Indians would build adequate housing for the artifacts. These acts bolstered the museums' images as concerned humanitarians, ensured the preservation of the artifacts, and effectively negated the Indians' reclamation attempts."

knowledge for these objects, the artifacts are not well cared for. The Zuni, for example, claim museums should not house the War Gods because the gods' proper religious location is on mountaintops.[35] Since the museums do possess the War Gods, however, the Zuni argue that the gods should be properly preserved. To them, proper preservation does not mean an annual lacquering of the War Gods, as might be correct with other museum collections, but involves leaving the War Gods completely untouched.[36] The gods are supposed to reside on mountain peaks, totally exposed to the elements. This idea of purposeful deterioration is alien to most museums, and Zuni efforts to prevent the unnatural preservation of their War Gods have been ignored.[37]

Indians are also worried that their sacred objects will be indiscriminately deaccessioned to private collectors or foreign countries. In 1975 the Iroquois discovered that the director of the Museum of the American Indian-Heye Foundation, Dr. Dockstader, who was apparently low on museum funds,[38] had "exchanged" two of the Iroquois' wampum belts for other items.[39] A few months later, the museum's deaccessioning policy was revealed in *Lefkowitz v. Museum of the American Indian-Heye Foundation*.[40] A trustee of this museum had become suspicious when an art dealer offered to sell him several artifacts which were listed in the museum's inventory.[41] The trustee soon discovered that "deaccessioning was almost entirely handled by the director, Dr. Dockstader, without comparative valuations, committee approval or consultation with the trustees."[42] The anxiety felt by many Native Americans regarding this type of indiscriminate deaccessioning was articulated by Iroquois Chief Oren Lyons: "Just because the museums happen to be having a financial crisis doesn't give them the right to sell and barter our sacred objects. We're having a survival crisis. Those belts are our history, our identity. They are beyond price."[43] Despite the superior facilities of the larger museums, therefore, Indian artifacts may be better preserved by Indians.

35. 47 U.S. BUREAU OF ETHNOLOGY ANN. REPORTS 527 (1932).

36. Telephone conversation with Bryant Rogers, *supra* note 26.

37. *Id.*

38. ARTS ADVOCATE, *supra* note 7, at 3, col. 1.

39. *Id.*

40. C.A. No. 41416/75 (D.N.Y. 1975). *See also* L. DUBOFF, THE DESKBOOK OF ART LAW 887 (1977) [hereinafter cited as DUBOFF].

41. C.A. No. 41416/75 (D.N.Y. 1975).

42. DUBOFF, *supra* note 40, at 887.

43. ARTS ADVOCATE, *supra* note 7, at 3, col. 1.

The second major argument used by museums to support their retention of Indian artifacts concerns the museums' uncertainty as to the identity of the legitimate Indian owners. The various tribal laws regarding private ownership of art objects are complex, especially to non-Indians. Hopi law is one of the clearest on this subject. Generally, the personal goods of a Hopi man are inherited by his sisters, brothers, and clanspeople.[44] Art objects and artifacts, such as ancient masks, medicine bundles, and animal figurines are clan property, usually controlled by the senior male of the clan.[45] After the passage of several generations, artifacts may change clans, may be claimed by several clans, or may be claimed by several members within the same clan—all of which raises difficult ownership questions.

Norman Ritchie, the chief ranger of the Navajo National Monument, was involved in a complicated situation concerning conflicting Indian ownership claims several years ago. The Monument had been displaying a Navajo medicine bundle which was claimed by a relative of the original owner. Ritchie was prepared to relinquish the bundle until several other relatives appeared and also claimed it. According to Ritchie: "As it stands now, we have the bundle, but the families involved have not determined to our satisfaction who actually should get the bundle. We have the bundle in safe storage, and will not exhibit it, and would be willing to return it, but heirship in cases like this, when it has once been sold, traded or given away becomes an interesting point in Navajo law."[46]

It is important to realize that the ownership question does not appear in all, or even most, Indian reclamation attempts. For instance, neither the New York State Museum nor the Smithsonian could justifiably plead unknown or conflicting ownership of the wampum belts and War Gods because these artifacts were indisputably created by the respective tribes, and the entire tribes—not individual members—are seeking reclamation. Furthermore, Zuni law is somewhat unusual in that very few religious artifacts are privately or clan-owned.[47] Therefore, conflicting claims of ownership among individual Zuni would be rare.

The third argument frequently presented by museums is that even a single return of an artifact would create a dangerous

---

44. Beaglehole, *Ownership and Inheritance in an American Indian Tribe,* 20 IOWA L. REV. 304, 307 (1934).

45. *Id.* at 308.

46. Letter from Norman Ritchie to Bowen Blair, July 13, 1978.

47. *See* Appendix A at item 2, Statement of Religious Leaders.

precedent which could lead to the depletion of the museums' collections.[48] This reasoning, which is valid to an extent, seems to underlie every Native American reclamation attempt.

Undoubtedly, successful tribal suits would encourage other Indian tribes to initiate their own actions. Perhaps those suits possessing similar factual and legal bases would also succeed, which might reduce the holdings of certain museums, particularly those specializing in Indian collections. In any case, museums should not fear Indian successes spreading to other miniorities. A victorious suit would probably be grounded upon the Indians' religious ties to these objects,[49] and few minorities possess similar art/religion connections. Furthermore, Native Americans have a more acute need for their artifacts than do other minorities because unlike these groups (with the exception of Mormons), Native Americans cannot return to the "old country" to regain sacred artifacts and lost religious traditions. American Indians have only the United States. Thus, despite the setting of precedent, the detrimental effects on Native Americans from not being able to worship and conduct their religion as in centuries past would seem to outweigh the occasional loss of artifacts by museums.

The fourth major argument proposed by museums is that they possess valid legal title to the artifacts. Certainly American property law, which confers ownership of all artifacts or objects found on private land in the landowners,[50] favors museums. The landowner may sell, destroy, or exploit any such object, regardless of who the original owner was.[51]

However, all museum property does not derive from private ownership. Much is illegally expropriated from public land, or land owned by Native Americans.[52] Clemency Coggins, a noted art historian, described a common museum attitude toward artifacts discovered on Indian land: "As far as many American museums are concerned, a bird in the hand is worth everything. Museum people are schooled in the acquisition, conservation, and practical esthetics of objects in relation to museum collections. They believe that any object which is acquired by a

---

48. Akwasasne Notes, *supra* note 5, at 1, col. 4. This argument was proposed by the New York State Museum, among others.
49. See discussion in text at note 99, *infra*.
50. Annot., 170 A.L.R. 708 (1947).
51. *Id.*
52. *See generally* 36 AM. ANTIQUITIES 374 (1971), for a discussion of the illegal antiquities trade.

museum is necessarily in a better place than it was before. . . ."[53]
Zuni religious leaders believe this attitude is directly responsible
for the theft of their artifacts: "The thefts and illegal selling of
these Zuni religious items and artifacts is based primarily on the
practice and willingness of museums, both private and public, . . .
to pay high prices for these items."[54]

Indian "gifts" to museums also should be scrutinized. For instance, according to the New York act which concerned the wampum belt return, the Iroquois in 1898 "duly elected" the University of the State of New York "to the office of wampum
keeper."[55] Closer inspection invites skepticism regarding this
"election."

At the end of the nineteenth century, the Regents of the New
York State Museum, apprehensive that the Iroquois tribes were
breaking up and would take the valuable wampum belts out of
New York, elected Harriet Maxwell Converse promoter of a drive
to "rescue" as much wampum as possible.[56] Despite the obvious conflict of interests, Mrs. Converse persuaded the Onondaga chiefs to appoint her their attorney in their efforts to
reclaim wampum held by John Thatcher, the mayor of Albany.[57]
She next convinced the chiefs their case would be improved if
they elected the Board of Regents "wampum-keeper with full
power to get possession and safely keep forever all wampums of
the Onondaga and Five Nations."[58]

In the ensuing court battle against Thatcher, commenced in
1898—only eight years after the battle of Wounded Knee, when
anti-Indian feelings inflamed the country—the Iroquois failed to
regain their wampum.[59] The court also ruled that the university
had never been selected wampum keeper.[60] The 1971 New York
legislature's actions declaring the "election" of the university to
"wampum keeper," therefore, appear inexplicable.

Considering the time period in which many museums received
Indian artifacts, and the continuing existence of prejudice against
Indians in parts of the United States, no museum's assertion of

53. Coggins, *Archeology and the Art Market,* 175 SCIENCE 263, 264 (1972).
54. *See* Appendix A, at item 4, Statement of Religious Leaders.
55. N.Y. INDIAN LAW § 27(1) (McKinney).
56. ARTS ADVOCATE, *supra* note 7, at 2, col. 2.
57. *Id.*
58. *Id.*
59. Onondaga Nation v. Thatcher, 29 Misc. 428, 61 N.Y.S. 1027, 169 N.Y. Rep. 584
(1901).
60. *Id.*

valid legal title should be accepted without suspicion. Kenneth Hopkins, the director of Olympia's State Capitol Museum, concurs with this postulate:

> As for materials that were not "stolen," I doubt their existence. The legalisms that confound the picture of Indian dispersal apply as well to Indian cultural relics. Here in our Northwest, we live on land "legally" acquired from the Indians. Yet as the history of the acquisition falls under scrutiny, we in local history find ourselves in the awkward position of trying to interpret events that we would prefer not to have to interpret.[61]

It should not be inferred, however, that all, or even the majority, of museums are unethical or refuse to entertain serious Indian requests for sacred artifacts. For instance, when Hopi elders demanded the return of deeply religious kiva masks on exhibit in Phoenix's Heard Museum, the director willingly complied.[62] Another encouraging incident occurred in Santa Fe in 1977, when the Wheelwright Museum returned eleven sacred medicine bundles to four Navajo medicine men.[63] Overall, the brightest future for Native American reclamation attempts rests upon the beliefs of men like Olympia's Director Hopkins, who declared, "Indian material belongs with Indians. I draw no lines around this, set up no perimeters, fall back on no qualifications. Indian material to Indians. Nothing less."[64] Because museums are generally not as cooperative as these southwestern ones, and their directors not as obliging as Hopkins, Native Americans must rely upon other methods to protect and procure their religious artifacts. United States laws provide some hope.

Pertinent Laws

The best way for Indians to secure their artifacts is to prevent their removal from Indian lands. The Antiquities Act of 1906[65] attempts to accomplish this. The third section[66] of this Act imposes a

61. MUSEUM NEWS, Mar. 1973, at 23.

62. ART NEWS, Dec. 1977, at 94.

63. Letter from Susan McGreevy, Director of the Wheelwright Museum, to Bowen Blair, July 14, 1978.

64. MUSEUM NEWS, Mar. 1973, at 23.

65. 16 U.S.C. § 431 (1976).

66. "Any person who shall appropriate, excavate, injure, or destroy any historic or prehistoric ruin or monument, or any object of antiquity, situated on lands owned or controlled by the Government of the United States, without the permission of the Secretary

$500 fine and/or ninety days imprisonment on anyone appropriating an "object of antiquity"[67] from federal land without permission. Since many remaining Indian sites existed on land in the public domain and within the purview of this Act,[68] the Antiquities Act seemed an ideal mechanism to protect Indian artifacts.

Unfortunately, the Act contains two major limitations. First, the Act does not protect artifacts from museums; in fact, it encourages museum exploitation. Permits will be granted "for examination of ruins, . . . excavation, . . . and the gathering of objects of antiquity"[69] upon these lands, "*Provided*, That the examinations, excavations, and gatherings are undertaken for the benefit of reputable museums, . . . with a view to increasing the knowledge of such objects, and that the gatherings shall be made for permanent preservation in public museums."[70]

Any "reputable" museum can acquire a permit through the Antiquities Act to collect sacred artifacts from federal land. The "reputable" restriction represents no consolation for Indians who have witnessed museums such as the Smithsonian appropriate artifacts from their lands.[71] The Act nevertheless does vicariously af-

---

of the Department of the Government having jurisdiction over the lands on which said antiquities are situated, shall, upon conviction, be fined in a sum of not more than $500 or be imprisoned for a period of not more than ninety days, or shall suffer both fine and imprisonment, in the discretion of the court." 16 U.S.C. § 433 (1976).

67. *Id.*

68. *See* Wilson & Zingg, *What is America's Heritage? Historic Preservation and American Indian Culture*, 22 KAN. L. REV. 413, 422 (1974).

69. 16 U.S.C. § 432 (1976).

70. *Id.*

71. Few, if any, tribes in the Southwest have escaped serious damage from the "pothunters" who roam tribal and federal lands seeking Indian relics. The size and organization of these illegal groups vary as much as their motives; the groups range from heavily armed, high-profit squads equipped with bulldozers and four-wheel drive vehicles, to the single tourist bumbling for an authentic souvenir of his vacation. The destruction wrought by the larger groups is particularly severe. Since a premium is placed upon speed in order to avoid detection, broken pots and crushed artifacts are the inevitable consequences of these well-organized raids. According to art historian Clemency Coggins, a more subtle yet equally pernicious damage accompanies the pothunters' incursions: "Once a site has been worked over by looters in order to remove a few salable objects, the fragile fabric of its history is largely destroyed. Changes in soil color, the traces of ancient floors and fires, the imprint of vanished textiles and foodstuffs, the relation between one object and another, and the position of a skeleton—all of these sources of fugitive information are ignored and obliterated by archeological looters." Coggins, *Archeology and the Art Market*, 175 SCIENCE 263 (1972).

Illegal pothunting and the resultant destruction of sites and artifacts has increased significantly the past few years [*see* 125 CONG. REC. E427 (daily ed. Feb. 8, 1979) (remarks of Rep. Udall)]; *see also* ARIZONA REPUBLIC, Mar. 6, 1978)]. A Tucson art dealer

fect museums by prohibiting excavations conducted by unscrupulous "pothunters,"[72] who frequently sell their illegal booty to museums.[73] Moreover, regulations adopted after the enactment of the Antiquities Act have attempted to restrict this liberal permit system.[74] For instance, permits may be granted only after obtaining the consent of Indian landowners, who may prescribe special conditions for the digging.[75] The concurrence of the Bureau of Indian Affairs official having jurisdiction over the property also is required.[76] Furthermore, once the permit has been issued and the excavation completed, the permittee must restore the land to the satisfaction of the individual Indian and the Bureau of Indian Affairs.[77]

The second and most serious limitations apparent in the Antiquities Act involves its failure to define what constitutes an "object of antiquity." Specifically, how old must an artifact be before it is included in this definition? The sparse legislative history supporting the Act[78] does not clarify this uncertainty. For instance, the Act's sponsor in the House, Congressman Lacey, declared the purpose of the Antiquities Act was to "cover the cave dwellers and cliff dwellers . . . [and] to preserve these old objects of special interest and the Indian remains in the pueblos in the Southwest."[79] Cases which interpret the Act are more illuminating with respect to this "object of antiquity" standard.

---

estimates that 80 percent of the Hopi pots presently being traded were illegally excavated on public lands [Hochfield, *Plundering Our Heritage*, ART NEWS, Summer, 1975, at 31]. Some experts recognize pothunting as the major cause of site destruction in the Southwest [*Id.*]. There seems to be no single basis for this pothunting proliferation. Several factors, including increased outdoor recreation by Americans, a new awareness and appreciation for Indian culture with a concomitant rise in the price of Indian art, and a greater availability of technically sophisticated machinery, such as metal detectors and four-wheel drive vehicles, probably have contributed. For a good article which discusses the problems created by pothunters, *see* Hochfield, *supra*.

72. Hochfield, *supra* note 71, at 30.

73. *See* 43 C.F.R. §§ 3.1-3.17 (1978), which details what applications for permits must specify; *i.e.*, time, place, persons involved, etc.

74. 25 C.F.R. § 132.2 (1977).

75. *Id.*

76. *Id.* at § 132.5.

77. Telephone conversation with Bryant Rogers, *supra* note 26. *See also* Letter from Indian Pueblo Legal Services, Inc. to Bowen Blair, Oct. 2, 1978.

78. H.R. REP. No. 2224, 59th Cong., 1st Sess. 3 (1906); S. REP. No. 3797, 59th Cong., 1st Sess. (1906). For a more detailed discussion of the congressional intent behind the Antiquities Act, *see* Cooper, *Constitutional Law: Preserving Native American Cultural and Archeological Artifacts*, 4 AM. INDIAN L. REV. 99, 100 (1976).

79. 40 CONG. REC. 7888 (1906).

The first criminal case to deal with this standard, *United States v. Diaz*,[80] represented a major setback for Indians' efforts to protect their buried artifacts. A United States magistrate convicted defendant Diaz of stealing Apache religious artifacts—"approximately twenty-two face masks, headdresses, ocotillo sticks, bull-roarers, fetishes and muddogs,"[81] from a medicine man's cave on the San Carlos Reservation, and fined him five hundred dollars.[82] On appeal, Diaz argued that since the artifacts were less than five years old, they did not constitute "object[s] of antiquity."[83] The appellate court, however, upheld the lower court's decision,[84] concluding: "The determination [of the meaning of 'object of antiquity'] can be made only after taking into consideration the object or objects in question, the significance, if any, of the object and the importance the object plays in a cultural heritage."[85]

This definition, because it accounts for the artifacts' cultural and religious value to the Indians, would have been ideal for Native Americans living on federal land. Unfortunately, in Diaz's second appeal,[86] the Ninth Circuit Court of Appeals reversed his conviction.[87] The court decided that the Antiquities Act, because it failed to define "ruin," "monument," or "object of antiquity," was unconstitutionally vague.[88]

The Ninth Circuit's decision was extended to an even more frustrating conclusion in *United States v. Jones*.[89] Jones allegedly violated the Antiquities Act, but the prosecutors, realizing that no conviction in the Ninth Circuit under the unconstitutional Act was possible, instead indicted him for violations of theft and malicious mischief statutes. The court dismissed the charges, holding it was Congress' intent that the Antiquities Act be the exclusive means through which the government could prosecute a defendant for activities encompassed by the Act, even though other statutes covered the same activities.[90]

As will be discussed,[91] Congress is presently attempting to cor-

---

80. 499 F.2d 113 (9th Cir. 1974).
81. United States v. Diaz, 368 F. Supp. 856, 857 (D. Ariz. 1973).
82. *Id.*
83. *Id.*
84. *Id.* at 859.
85. *Id.* at 858.
86. United States v. Diaz, 499 F.2d 113 (9th Cir. 1974).
87. *Id.* at 115.
88. *Id.*
89. 449 F. Supp. 42 (D. Ariz. 1978).
90. *Id.* at 46.
91. See discussion in text at notes 120-144, *infra.*

rect this unfortunate hiatus. Several western states[92] and Indian nations,[93] moreover, have anteceded congressional action by enacting their own antiquities acts which generally provide clearer definitions of "object of antiquity," promulgate stronger penalties for violations, and pertain to nonfederal land.

Despite the Ninth Circuit decisions, the Antiquities Act is not impotent. Other circuits are not bound by the Ninth. The Tenth Circuit,[94] for instance, has upheld the constitutionality of the Antiquities Act in cases involving Mimbres Indian artifacts.[95] These

92. For instance, Colorado defines an "object of antiquity" as "any historical, prehistorical, or archeological resource" [COLO. REV. STAT. ANN. § 24-80-409 (1973)], whereas New Mexico's definition includes "any object of historical, archeological, architectural or scientific value" [N.M. STAT. ANN. § 4-27-11 (1953)]. South Dakota promulgates the strictest penalty for violations of its antiquities act—a $1,000 fine and/or six months' imprisonment, in addition to forfeiture of all appropriated materials [S.D. COMP. LAWS ANN. § 1-20-35].

93. *See* Appendix B for the Navajo Antiquities Act. The reason for the Act's lenient penalties involves limitations to tribal jurisdiction, not a lack of desire by the Navajo to punish pothunters. The Hopi probably possess the most effective "antiquities act"; after a series of particularly devastating artifact losses, they simply closed their reservations to non-Hopis. *See* Hochfield, *supra* note 71, at 32.

94. The Tenth Circuit, which includes New Mexico, Colorado, Utah, Oklahoma, Kansas, and Wyoming, contains numerous and exceptionally valuable Indian sites and artifacts. This circuit is matched only by the Ninth, which includes California, Nevada, Idaho, Oregon, Washington, and Montana.

95. In October of 1975, three brothers were arrested by Forest Service officers while illegally excavating a Mimbres Indian ruin. [United States v. Quarrell, C.A. No. 76-4 (D.N.M. 1976) (criminal complaint)]. The artifacts in the Quarrell brothers' possession included "two metates, two grooved stone axes, other miscellaneous stone tools, three nearly complete Mimbres bowls, and a quantity of assorted sherds." [Collins, *A Proposal to Modernize the American Antiquities Act,* 202 SCIENCE 1055, 1057 (1978)] Trial testimony established the age of the pottery at between eight and nine hundred years. The court decided these artifacts qualified as "object[s] of antiquity," upheld the constitutionality of the Antiquities Act, and found the defendants guilty. For stealing these artifacts, worth approximately $2,700, and for causing irreparable damage to a rare Mimbres archeological site, two of the Quarrells were sentenced to one year of supervised probation, and required to perform forty hours of community service.

Two years after the *Quarrell* case, another Mimbres Indian ruin, this one in the Gila National Forest in Gila, New Mexico, was looted by pothunters [United States v. Smyer & May, C.A. No. 77-284 (D.N.M. 1977) (criminal complaint)]. The damage at this site was extensive; Forest Service officers found 800 sherds, an abundance of chipped stone artifacts, and severely damaged skeletal remains. Defendants May and Smyer admitted responsibility and confessed selling two of the bowls discovered at the ruin for $4,000. A search of the defendants' residences uncovered over 30 Mimbres black-on-white bowls, in addition to numerous other artifacts.

Smyer and May were charged with eleven counts of violating the Antiquities Act. The court decided the eight- to nine-hundred-year-old artifacts were protected by the Antiquities Act, and that the Act was constitutional. Judge Bratton elaborated: "While it may

courts ecided that the Act's "object of antiquity" standard was sufficiently precise for cases dealing with 800- to 900-year-old artifacts.[96] Even if the majority of courts were to uphold the constitutionality of the Antiquities Act, however, the Act applies exclusively to uncollected artifacts. For laws which would aid Indians in reclaiming artifacts held by museums, one must look elsewhere.

The first amendment to the United States Constitution declares that "Congress shall make no law respecting an establishment of religion, or prohibiting the free exercise thereof."[97] This amendment is binding on the states through the fourteenth amendment's due process clause,[98] and is also applicable to the states through their own constitutions.

Case law has extended this religious protection. In *Sherbert v. Verner*,[99] a Seventh Day Adventist was denied unemployment compensation because she refused, for religious reasons, to take jobs which would require her to work on Saturday.[100] In a landmark decision, the Supreme Court upheld her right to compensation and declared that the first amendment's free exercise clause protects religious practice, as well as religious belief.[101] In *Sherbert,* the Court also instituted a balancing test which weighed an individual's right to the free exercise of the practices of his chosen religion, against any compelling state interest in regulation of these practices.[102]

In *People v. Woody*,[103] the Supreme Court of California applied the *Sherbert* holding to a fact situation involving Navajo Indians. The *Woody* court dealt with the use of peyote in Navajo religious ceremonies.[104] The *Sherbert* test balanced the Navajos'

---

not be possible to state in the abstract a precise number of years that must pass before something becomes an 'object of antiquity,' such exactitude is not required. . . . The Antiquities Act must necessarily use words 'marked by flexibility and reasonable breadth, rather than meticulous specificity,' in order to accomplish its purposes." [Citations omitted.] *Id.* The Judge then sentenced Smyer and May to imprisonment for ninety days on each of the eleven counts, the terms to run concurrently. *Id.* The case is presently being appealed.

96. See discussion at note 95, *supra.*
97. U.S. Const. amend. I.
98. Cantwell v. Connecticut, 310 U.S. 296, 303 (1940).
99. 374 U.S. 398 (1963).
100. *Id.* at 399.
101. *Id.* at 404.
102. *Id.* at 406-409.
103. 61 Cal. 2d 716, 394 P.2d 813, 40 Cal. Rptr. 69 (1964).
104. *Id.*

right to practice their religion, of which peyote is an integral part, with the state's interest in prohibiting the use of hallucinogenic drugs. The decision of the court to protect the Navajos' rights hinged upon the importance of peyote consumption to the Navajos' religion as practiced in the Native American Church: "Although peyote serves as a sacramental symbol similar to bread and wine in certain Christian churches, it is more than a sacrament. Peyote constitutes in itself an object of worship; prayers are directed to it much as prayers are devoted to the Holy Ghost."[105]

Just as the Navajos' peyote does, wampum and War Gods constitute "object[s] of worship" to the Iroquois and Zuni. As explained earlier,[106] these artifacts represent the essence of Iroquois and Zuni life. Moreover, because of Native Americans' unique fusion of art and religion, a great percentage of Indian artifacts currently held by museums would be included as "object[s] of worship." By retaining these sacred artifacts, museums are, in effect, interfering with the Indians' right to practice their religion, as guaranteed by *Sherbert.*

To determine whether this first amendment protection should apply to the Indian artifact situation, the interests of both the Indians and the museums must be balanced within the context of the *Sherbert* test. For the Indians, the artifacts are needed to practice their religion, to rectify "an imbalance in the spiritual world."[107] Iroquois and Zuni religion without wampum and War Gods would be similar to Navajo religion without peyote.

The contravening "compelling state interest"[108] exists in the museums' reasons for retaining the artifacts: (1) their public responsibility to preserve and exhibit the artifacts for the benefit of all Americans; (2) their doubt as to specific Indian ownership; (3) their unwillingness to establish a precedent of returning a part of their collections to original owners; and (4) their legal claims to the artifacts. As explained earlier, all of these justifications have been at least partially eroded by a closer examination of their foundations.[109] Furthermore, assuming these assertions were valid, it is doubtful whether they would outweigh the Indians' right to practice their religion.

---

105. *Id.* at 721, 394 P.2d 813, 40 Cal. Rptr. 69 at 817.
106. See discussion in text at notes 29-36, *supra.*
107. See Appendix A at item 2, Statement of Religious Leaders.
108. Sherbert v. Verner, 374 U.S. 398, 406 (1963).
109. See discussion in text at notes 32-64 *supra.*

In *Woody*, prohibition of peyote did not constitute a "compelling state interest," despite the drug's possible "deleterious effects upon the Indian community, and even more basically, in the infringement such practice [peyote use] would place upon the enforcement of the narcotic laws . . . ."[110] If museums were forced to relinquish a few holdings, the effect on the community would be considerably less grave then the potential effects of the *Woody* decision. No possibility of flagrant disregard of drug laws, or a drug overdose epidemic, would exist. Actual physical harm is not involved. Therefore, it seems the state's interests in protecting its citizens are significantly less compelling in the Indian artifacts situation than in a situation such as that in the *Woody* case.

Furthermore, should the religious practices and the "compelling state interest" ever assume equal weight in the balancing test, the court must rule in favor of religious practices.[111] Once a plaintiff demonstrates that a statute imposes a burden on his religious practice, this showing brings him within the purview of the first amendment,[112] "and entitles his religious freedom to a 'preferred position' on the scales of the balance. This 'preferred position' rebuts the normal presumption in favor of the constitutionality of statutes. Moreover, it erects a contrary presumption in its place—a presumption favoring religious freedom."[113]

The problem with applying a first amendment solution to an Indian artifacts situation is that neither Congress nor the states have enacted many laws directly abridging Indian religious practices. One notable exception is the New York law which refuses to relinquish the wampum belts until the Iroquois build an "adequate" shelter to house the belts.[114] Since this law seriously interferes with the Iroquois' first amendment freedom to practice their religion, and because the counter-balancing "compelling state interest" is slight, an argument can be made that the New York law should be declared unconstitutional.

One museum which occupies a central position in the Indian artifacts controversy, and which may be more vulnerable to a first amendment attack, is the Smithsonian Institute. In addition

---

110. People v. Woody, 61 Cal. 2d 716, 722, 394 P.2d 813, 818, 40 Cal. Rptr. 69, 74 (1964).

111. Breslin, *Recent Developments: Statute Prohibiting Use of Peyote Unconstitutional as Applied to Religious Users,* 17 STAN. L. REV. 494 (1965).

112. *Id.* at 498.

113. *Id.*

114. N.Y. INDIAN LAW § 27 (McKinney).

to possessing numerous essential Indian artifacts,[115] the Smithsonian controls the actions of many other museums in this field. For instance, all museum applications for excavation permits on federal land must be referred to the Smithsonian for recommendation.[116] Of greater consequence, no Indian artifacts collected under the auspices of the Antiquities Act can be removed from a public museum without the written permission of the Smithsonian's Secretary.[117] Because Congress created the Smithsonian,[118] and it is controlled by members of Congress,[119] Congress should be held accountable for the Smithsonian's actions. Smithsonian acquisition policies which infringe upon Indians' religious practices are in this sense directed by Congress and thus are subject to first amendment attack. Considering the Institute's prestigious and authoritative position among American museums, even a partial relinquishment of its Indian artifact collection would establish a particularly persuasive precedent for other museums to follow.

Even where Congress and the states have enacted no laws directly abridging Indian religious practices, the first amendment serves as a solid foundation for a viable policy argument. Freedom of religion is perhaps the most important tenet supporting United States society. Museums should not be permitted to erode this doctrine by acquiring and retaining artifacts of fundamental religious significance to Native American people.

Recent Laws

Two recent actions by Congress should aid Native American attempts to protect or regain their artifacts from museums. Congress has recently passed the Archeological Resources Protection Act of 1979,[120] which modifies the Antiquities Act. This modification significantly strengthens the Act and should correct its constitutional deficiencies. The second congressional action produced Public Law 95-341 on American Indian Religious

---

115. Telephone conversation with Bryant Rogers, *supra* note 26. *See also* Letter from Indian Pueblo Legal Services, Inc. to Bowen Blair, *supra* note 26.

116. 43 C.F.R. § 3.8 (1977).

117. *Id.* at § 3.17.

118. 20 U.S.C. § 41 (1974).

119. *Id.* at § 42.

120. Pub. L. 96-95 (approved Oct. 31, 1979). To date this law is unpublished. However, the final text may be found at H.R. 1825, 96th Cong., 1st Sess., 125 CONG. REC. S14719-S14721 (daily ed. Oct. 17, 1979). For the original version, *see* H.R. 1825, 96th Cong., 1st Sess. (1979); the Senate version is S. 490, 96th Cong., 1st Sess. (1979).

Freedom,[121] which represents a crucial governmental policy shift toward the rights of Native Americans regarding the practice of their religions.

The Archeological Resources Protection Act, sponsored in the House by Congressman Udall[122] and in the Senate by Senators Domenici and Goldwater,[123] was formulated by the archeological community and Departments of Interior and Agriculture.[124] This bill should benefit Native Americans who seek to protect their artifacts in three important respects. First, the bill corrects the Antiquities Act's constitutional defect by clarifying the "object of antiquity" standard. The Archeological Resources Protection Act substitutes the term "archeological resource"[125] for "object of antiquity," and, unlike the Antiquities Act, proceeds to define "archeological resources":

> The term "archaeological resource" means any material remains of past human life or activities which are of archaeological interest, as determined under uniform regulations promulgated pursuant to this Act. Such regulations containing such determination shall include, but not be limited to: pottery, basketry, bottles, weapons, weapon projectiles, tools, structures or portions of structures, pit houses, rock paintings, rock carvings, intaglios, graves, human skeletal materials, or any portion or piece of any of the foregoing items. Nonfossilized and fossilized paleontological specimens, or any portion or piece thereof, shall not be considered archaeological resources, under the regulations under this paragraph, unless found in an archaeological context. No item shall be treated as an archaeological resource under regulations under this paragraph unless such item is at least 100 years of age.[126]

The particularity of this definition should satisfy the vagueness problem enunciated in the *Diaz* case.[127] Instead of being confronted with the nebulous "object of antiquity" standard, judges would be able to resort to the Archeological Resources Protection

---

121. Act of Aug. 11, 1978, Pub. L. No. 95-341, 92 Stat. 469.

122. 125 CONG. REC. H433 (daily ed. Feb. 1, 1979) (remarks of Rep. Udall).

123. 125 CONG. REC. S1798 (daily ed. Feb. 26, 1979) (remarks of Sen. Domenici).

124. Letter from Charles McKinney (Consulting Archeologist for the Department of the Interior's Office of Archeology and Historic Preservation) to Bowen Blair, Feb. 28, 1979.

125. Pub. L. 96-95 § 3(1) (1979), H.R. 1825, 96th Cong., 1st Sess., 96 CONG. REC. S.14719 § 3(1) (1979).

126. *Id.*

127. United States v. Diaz, 499 F.2d 113 (9th Cir. 1974).

Act's practically conclusive list and easily determine whether the particular artifact was included in the provision.

Although solving the vagueness problem, the bill's "archeological resource" standard contains a major drawback for Native Americans. Only objects "which are at least one hundred years of age"[128] are protected. Thus, a sacred Zuni War God, carved only forty years ago, could be essential to Zuni religion but would not be safeguarded by the act. In order to fully protect Native American culture, this arbitrary age criterion should be eliminated and a standard which emphasizes the cultural value of the artifact to its creators substituted.[129] Even with this limitation, however, the Archeological Resources Protection Act's "archeological resource" standard represents a notable improvement over the Antiquities Act.

The second major revision of the Antiquities Act contained in the Archeological Resources Protection Act concerns penalties for violators of the Act. The Antiquities Act's 73-year-old penalty provision—a $500 fine and/or 90 days' imprisonment, constitutes little more than a business expense for the modern pothunter[130] receiving up to thousands of dollars for a single pot.[131]

The Act advances two types of sanctions. For the occasional violator of this legislation, such as the "unwary tourist,"[132] the Federal Land Manager who oversees the applicable land may levy a civil penalty.[133] This penalty shall take into account: "(A) the archaeological or commercial value of the archaeological resource involved, and (B) the cost of restoration and repair of the resource and the archaeological site involved."[134] Should the same person again violate this legislation, similar computations would be made, but the fine could be doubled.[135]

---

128. *Id.* The 100-year limitation can be traced to an earlier proposal, 43 Fed. Reg. 14,975 (1978). This proposal, submitted by the Heritage Conservation and Recreation Service also concerned the revision of the Antiquities Act's "object of antiquity" standard, and suggested that protection should be given to artifacts which were older than a hundred years (*id.* at 14,976). The original bill before the House set the limit at fifty years. H.R. 1825, 96th Cong., 1st Sess., 125 Cong. Rec. H433 (daily ed. Feb. 1, 1979).

129. A good example of such a standard was enunciated by the trial court in United States v. Diaz, 368 F. Supp. 856, 858 (D. Ariz. 1973). See quotation in text at note 85.

130. *See generally* 125 Cong. Rec. H433 (daily ed. Feb. 1, 1979) (remarks of Rep. Udall).

131. Hochfield, *supra* note 71, at 31.

132. 125 Cong. Rec. H433 (daily ed. Feb. 1, 1979) (remarks of Rep. Udall).

133. Pub. L. 96-95 § 7(a)(1).

134. *Id.* at § 7(a)(2).

135. *Id.*

The Archeological Resources Protection Act also contains criminal penalties which are more appropriate for modern pothunters than the 1906 Antiquities Act. Any person who knowingly violates the new law will be subject to a $10,000 fine and/or one year imprisonment.[136] However, "if the commercial or archaeological value of the archaeological resources involved and the cost of restoration and repair of such resources exceeds the sum of $5,000," the offender will be subject to a fine of not more than $20,000 and/or two years' imprisonment.[137] Repeat offenders are susceptible to a fine not to exceed $100,000 and/or imprisonment not to exceed five years.[138] Certainly these new provisions provide a greater deterrent to pothunters than the Antiquities Act's $500 fine and/or 90 days' imprisonment condition.[139] As mentioned earlier,[140] once pothunters are deterred, many less scrupulous museums will lose their sources for Indian artifacts. Thus, while not directly pertaining to museums, the Act's stricter penalties should vicariously affect museum acquisitions.

The third significant modification of the Antiquities Act proposed by this bill entails an expansion of prohibited conduct. The Antiquities Act forbids the appropriation, excavation, injury to or destruction of any "object of antiquity,"[141] whereas the Act would, in addition, outlaw the selling, purchasing, exchanging, transporting, receiving, or offering to sell, purchase, or exchange any such objects.[142] This new addition is especially important because it would directly encompass those museums obtaining artifacts from pothunters. Moreover, all museums would be forced to scrutinize the origins of their Indian pieces acquired after the effective date of this Act, and relinquish those artifacts of questionable origin in order to avoid the possibility of harsh punishment under the Archeological Resources Protection Act.

The second recent congressional action which will have a dramatic effect on Indian efforts to reclaim artifacts, Public Law 95-341 on American Indian Religious Freedom,[143] was passed August 11, 1978. This law clarifies the Indians' first amendment

---

136. *Id.* at § 6(d).
137. *Id.*
138. *Id.*
139. 16 U.S.C. § 433 (1976).
140. See discussion in text at notes 65-71.
141. 16 U.S.C. § 433 (1976).
142. Pub. L. 96-95 § 5(b) (1979).
143. Act of Aug. 11, 1978, Pub. L. No. 95-341, 92 Stat. 469.

right to freedom of religion. Most importantly, the law does not seek to correct any express federal policy which infringes upon Indians' religious practices. Instead, it attempts to rectify injustices which occurred from a lack of federal policy.[144] As discussed *supra*, the first amendment protects Indians from laws which directly infringe upon their religious practices; this law protects these activities even when the infringement does not result from a specific law. Therefore, Public Law 93-341 is particularly beneficial with respect to Indian reclamation attempts, where the retention of the artifacts by museums is often not supported by laws susceptible to a first amendment attack.

The new law declares: "That henceforth it shall be the policy of the United States to protect and preserve for American Indians their inherent right of freedom to believe, express, and exercise the traditional religions of the American Indian, . . . including but not limited to access to sites, use and possession of sacred objects . . ."[145] To ensure compliance with this policy, "federal executive agencies are directed to evaluate their policies and procedures in consultation with Native religious leaders in order to determine appropriate changes which may be necessary to protect and preserve American Indian religious cultural rights and practices.[146] Furthermore, the law requires an annual presidential report to Congress detailing the determinations, administrative changes, and future recommendations made in conjunction with this new policy.[147]

In Public Law 95-341 the phrase, "use and possession of sacred artifacts" is most pertinent to the Indian-museum confrontation. The Chairman of the Senate Select Committee on Indian Affairs which recommended passage of this law, Senator Abourezk, described the Indians' relationship to the type of objects this law was meant to address: "To the Indians, these natural objects have religious significance because they are sacred, they have power. . . , they are necessary to the exercise of rites of religion, they are necessary to the cultural integrity of the tribe and, therefore, religious survival."[148] The Committee also accepted testimony from Lee Lyons, a member of the Onondaga Nation, regarding the New York State Museum's retention of the

144. *Id.*
145. *Id.*
146. *Id.* at § 2, 92 Stat. 470.
147. *Id.*
148. *Hearings on S.J.R. 102 Before the Senate Select Comm. on Indian Affairs,* 95th Cong., 2d Sess. 235, (1978) (Report to accompany S.J.R. 102).

Iroquois wampum belts.[149] This testimony further established the relationship between Indian artifacts and religion: "[The wampum] represents [the Iroquois'] way of life. It represents their religion. It represents their culture, and their language, their way."[150]

Because this law is so new, its effect on museums is unclear. Certainly, it does not mandate wholesale surrender of the artifacts to the Indians. This law should demonstrate its greatest strength in the area of federal funding of museums. Federal agencies are required to "evaluate their policies and procedures"[151] in order to implement changes necessary to protect American Indian religious practices.[152] Many museums that hold religious artifacts, thereby interfering with the Indians' "use and possession of sacred artifacts," are at least partially financed by the federal government. The Smithsonian Institute, for instance, is completely federally subsidized.[153] Numerous museums also have obtained federal tax-exempt status.[154] Federal agencies, in accordance with this law, should withhold funds and remove tax exemptions from museums that possess sacred artifacts to which Indians have valid claims. Once the artifacts are returned, the exemptions and special status could be restored. When confronted with the choice of losing substantial federal subsidies and benefits, or yielding a small part of their collection, museums would presumably select the latter.

Public Law 95-341 does not represent the pinnacle of legislative concern regarding Indian reclamation attempts. California, for instance, which Senator Abourezk called "light years ahead of the Federal Government,"[155] has an exceptionally progressive statute. This statute states:

No public agency, and no private party using or occupying public property, or operating on public property, under a public license, permit, grant, lease, or contract made on or after July 1, 1977, shall in any manner whatsoever interfere with the free expression or exercise of Native American religion

149. *Id.* at 115.
150. *Id.*
151. Act of Aug. 11, 1978, Pub. L. No. 95-341, § 2, 92 Stat. 470.
152. *Id.*
153. 20 U.S.C. §§ 54, 55 (1974).
154. DUBOFF, *supra* note 40, at 874.
155. *Hearings on S.J.R. 102 Before the Senate Select Comm. on Indian Affairs,* 95th Cong., 2d Sess. 235 (1978).

as provided in the United States Constitution and the California Constitution.[156]

Public museums, or private museums with public connections, which retain sacred Indian artifacts, are affected by this statute.[157] The museums' retention of these artifacts certainly would be encompassed by the statute's "in any manner whatsoever interfere with the free expression or exercise of Native American religion" clause,[158] and thus would be outlawed.

An amendment to this statute,[159] proposed by California's Office of Planning and Research, would immensely aid Indian efforts to control their artifacts. This amendment would assign California Indian artifacts discovered on public property to local Indian cultural groups or to a public trust administered by the Native American Heritage Commission.[160] The Commission consists of nine members appointed by the governor, the majority of whom must be "elders, traditional people, or spiritual leaders of Californian Native American tribes.[161]

The importance of this amendment derives from its specific determination as to the ownership of the discovered Indian artifact, an issue which currently puzzles American museums.[162] The amendment declares:

> In making such determination [regarding Indian ownership of the artifacts] the Commission shall consider and base its decision on the following factors: (i) the relationship of a proposed recipient to the creator of the artifact; and (ii) the ability of a proposed recipient to preserve the artifact from destruction or deterioration. In determining to which descendants a cultural artifact should be returned, the Commission shall give first preference to any descendants who reside in the locality where

156. CAL. PUB. RES. CODE § 5097.9 (West 1971). This statute is not as broad as it seems. Its major limitation is that "The public property of all cities, counties, and city and county located within the limits of the city, county, and city and county, except for all parklands in excess of 100 acres, shall be exempt from the provisions of this chapter." *Id.*

157. *Id.* Private museums with public connections include museums located on public property or those which have public leases. However, the limitations set out in note 156 must also be considered.

158. *Id.*

159. Cal. Proposal OPR—78-04. *See also Hearings on S.J.R. 102 Before the Senate Select Comm. on Indian Affairs,* 95th Cong., 2d Sess. 218 (1978).

160. *Id.*

161. CAL. PUB. RES. CODE § 5097.92 (West 1972).

162. See discussion in text at notes 44-47.

the artifact was discovered; second preference to any descendants who are residents of that state; and, third preference to other California Indians.[163]

Should no descendants of the artifact's creator be located, or should the descendants not want the artifact, it would be placed under the control of the Commission.[164] The Commission would preserve the artifact, occasionally lend it out, and return it to the descendants should they be located and desire the artifact.[165] Thus, the amendment not only requires ownership of Indian artifacts to be placed with the Indians instead of museums, but it clearly sets out the procedure through which this transfer will be effectuated.

Conclusion

Many American Indians rely today upon sacred artifacts created by their ancestors. By withholding these artifacts, American museums are disrupting essential Indian religious practices.

Indians have achieved little success in their efforts to reclaim these artifacts.[166] This is often because museums possess solid legal and practical grounds for retaining their collections. Recent legislative actions, however, have strengthened the Indians' position.

The Archeological Resources Protection Act represents a tremendous improvement over the Antiquities Act, and should discourage illicit museum appropriations of Indian artifacts. Public Law 95-341, the most progressive enactment regarding Indian religious freedom, was not passed until August of 1978. These laws, combined with older rights, such as the first amendment's freedom of religion clause, equip Indians with persuasive legal arguments to employ against museums. The future,

---

163. Cal. Proposal OPR—78-04. *See also Hearings on S.J.R. 102 Before the Senate Select Comm. on Indian Affairs,* 95th Cong., 2d Sess. 218 (1978).

164. *Id.*

165. *Id.*

166. According to James Nason, a member of UCLA's Department of Anthropology, these efforts will continue, as well as increase: "[Indian reclamation attempts are] not a fad so much as a representative facet of the growing interest of American Indians in their own cultural heritage and in their identity as contemporary residents of this country. Museum specimens are not only the physical respresentations of this heritage and identity, but also the symbols of the loss of American Indian autonomy and culture by military, legal and demographic processes." MUSEUM NEWS, March, 1973, at 20.

therefore, should reveal legal challenges brought by Indians against museums, greater Indian success, and a concomitant heightening of museum awareness and understanding for the religious needs of Native American people.

APPENDIX A

ZUNI TRIBAL COUNCIL
ZUNI, NEW MEXICO
RESOLUTION NO. M70-78-991

WHEREAS, the Zuni Tribal Council consisting of the Governor, Lieutenant Governor and six Tenientes, is declared to be the legislative authority of the Pueblo of Zuni by Article V, Section 1 of the Constitution of the Zuni Tribe; and,

WHEREAS, the Zuni Tribal Council is authorized by Article VI, Section 1, (d) of the Constitution and to act in all matters that concern the welfare of the tribe; and,

WHEREAS, The Zuni Tribal Council has for several years been aware of the increasing problems posed for the Zuni people by the loss, theft or unauthorized removal from Zuni lands of items of *sacred religious* significance to the Zuni people; and,

WHEREAS, on May 30, 1978, the Tribal Council initiated a formal process by which this problem and the related problem of securing proper care for and/or return of such items as may now be in possession of museums or other third parties might be addressed and resolved; and,

WHEREAS, it is recognized and stated by the Tribal Council in its May 30th memorandum that "because this effort ultimately involves protection and return of objects which are intimately bound up with the traditional religious practices and doctrines of the Zuni Tribe, the appropriate tribal religious leaders should have final control over the process of policy making and decision making in this matter"; and,

WHEREAS, the Zuni Religious leaders have thoroughly considered this problem in their religious councils of which detailed transcripts in the Zuni language have been prepared and from which the official Tribal Translator has abstracted a brief formal statement in the English language of the position of these religious leaders on this matter, said statement being attached hereto and dated September 20, 1978; and

NOW, THEREFORE, BE IT RESOLVED, that the Zuni Tribal Council does hereby formally adopt the attached statement of the Zuni religious leaders as the official position of the Zuni Tribe on this matter, and does hereby reiterate the Council's full support of the Zuni Religious leaders in their efforts to protect and to secure proper care for or return of items of religious significance to the Zuni people; and,

BE IT FURTHER RESOLVED, that the Zuni Tribal Council hereby request that all museums and other third parties as appropriate work with the Zuni Tribe to resolve the problems identified in this resolution by implementation of the recommendations attached hereto and dated September 21, 1978.

[Signed by]
Zuni Tribal Council:
Dorson Zunie, Lt. Governor
Virgil Wyaco, Teniente
Fred Bowannie, Sr., Teniente
Chester Mahooty, Teniente
Lowell Panteah, Teniente
Chauncey Simplicio, Teniente

Certification

I hereby certify that the foregoing resolution was duly considered by the Zuni Tribal Council at a duly called meeting at Zuni, New Mexico at which a quorum was present and that the same was approved by a vote of 7 in favor and 0 opposed on Sept. 23, 1978,

Edison Laselute, Governor
Pueblo of Zuni
Approved by
Edison Laselute, Governor Sept. 23, 1978

Statement Of
Religious Leaders of the Pueblo of Zuni
Concerning Sacred Zuni Religious Items/Artifacts

Prepared By
Wilfred Eriacho, Official Tribal Translator,
From a Written Transcript in the Zuni Language of
A Meeting of the Religious Leaders of
The Pueblo of Zuni
Held on May 9, 1978

September 20, 1978

We the Religious and Civil leaders of the Zuni people hereby develop this statement based on six basic premises/components/cultural ways, of the Zuni culture.

1. The Zuni religion originated with the creation of the world, and exists to protect all beings on the earth, and to provide fertility and abundance of goodness for the Zuni people and their neighbors throughout the world. Our priests and religious leaders take on responsibility for carrying out the intricate rituals and ceremonies that are the framework of our religion only after years of preparation and training. Dedication and seriousness of action is required by all involved in the Zuni religion to ensure its beneficial effects.

2. All religious items/artifacts/objects, no matter how insignificant it/they may seem to non-Zunis, are of very high/great religious value. They are in fact, the essence of our Zuni culture.

3. Very few items/artifacts of religious significance are created by knowledge and skill of any one individual. The majority of these items/artifacts were created by groups of religious orders, each having skill or expertise in a specific fact/aspect of the Zuni religious culture.

4. Very few items/artifacts of religious significance are privately/individually owned. The majority of these items/artifacts have been created for the benefit of all the Zuni people, and are communally owned.

5. No one individual or a group(s) of individual(s) has/have the right to remove communally owned religious items/artifacts from the Zuni land for any purpose/reason whatsoever. This is illegal according to traditional Zuni Law, and to do so is tantamount to theft. Privately owned religious items/artifacts can be sold by their owners although we call this selling your life and do not condone it.

6. The historical disruption of the Zuni religion by first the Spanish colonial government and later by the United States government; and by the theft and removal of sacred items/artifacts by museums and private collectors, has created an imbalance in the spiritual world. In order to restore harmony to all living things, this balance needs to be restored.

Meetings of and by the religious and civil leaders of the Zuni Tribe have identified the following problems as being very detrimental to the well being of the Zuni people. The foremost problem, the one that distresses the Zuni people the most is the removal of religious items/artifacts from the Zuni land. It hurts us that throughout the whole world, religious items/artifacts belonging to the Zuni people are displayed in museums, both public and private, and in private collections. These display places are far removed from Zuni land, for whose benefit these items/artifacts were created.

When a Zuni religious item is made/created, many religious orders participate in its creation. Every step of its creation is accomplished with prayer and instruction for the purpose. Its general purpose is to provide both a beneficial psychological and physical environment for the Zuni people. An environment that will cause the Zuni people to prosper in products, wisdom, skill, and all good things. Even though these items are created/constructed out of inanimate articles such as wood, leather, rock, and other such things, it is with and through religious prayers and instructions during the construction that it gains/achieves spiritual life to perform the benefits for the Zuni people. Thus each and every Zuni religious item is greeted/addressed as being one's father or mother, or child. The purpose of these religious items/artifacts has been defeated/destroyed by their removal from the Zuni land. Any beneficial qualities that they were to bestow upon their Zuni people, and, by extension, the whole world through their innate wisdom have been destroyed. Adverse effects have developed.

The theft/stealing of religious items/artifacts from their sacred places in and around Zuni land has diminished their effectiveness. Because of our cultural beliefs, many of these items/artifacts are not to be locked up but are to be placed at various locations in and around Zuni lands if they are to fulfill their purpose. These locations were determined in Ancient times. The thefts and illegal selling of these Zuni religious items and artifacts is based primarily on the practice and willingness of museums, both private and public, and private collectors to pay high prices for these items. The placing of monetary value on religious items/artifacts leads to theft of more religious items/artifacts for sale on world art markets. The display or storage of religious items/artifacts as art objects or ethnological curiosities helps to foster and sustain the market demand for religious items/artifacts.

Because of the many adverse effects and conditions that have been experienced by the Zuni people, we have made a decision to respectfully request the return of all our communal religious items/artifacts currently on display or in storage in the world museums and to try to stop the theft and sale of sacred Zuni religious items/artifacts. This decision is based on our desires to perpetuate our Zuni culture in its full/total context/totality with the blessing from our spiritual fathers, mothers, and children which are rightfully ours. In order to accomplish this very essential goal, we need your assistance and directions/instructions. We ask for your assistance in achieving this goal.

APPENDIX B

Resolution of the Navajo Tribal Council
ENACTING AN ANTIQUITIES PRESERVATION LAW
Passed January 27, 1972
(59 in favor: 0 opposed)

WHEREAS:

1. The Navajo Nation contains many ruins and excavation of Archaeological sites and objects of antiquity or general scientific interest, and

2. These sites and objects are irreplaceable and invaluable in the study of the history and preservation of the cultural background of the Navajo Nation, and

3. Large quantities of rare objects, pottery, petrified wood, fossils and artifacts have been sold to tourists and traders and these pieces of Navajo history and culture have been irretrievably lost to the detriment of the Navajo Nation as a whole.

NOW THEREFORE BE IT RESOLVED THAT:

1. After the date of this resolution, any Indian who shall intentionally appropriate, excavate, injure or destroy any object of historic, archaeological, paleontological, or scientific value, or any Indian who shall hold or offer for sale any historic or prehistoric object of archaeological, paleontological, or scientific value, without permission from the Navajo Tribal Council as

provided in Navajo Tribal Council Resolution CF-22-58 (16 NTC 233), shall be guilty of an offense and if convicted, punished by labor for not more than one month or a fine of not more than $500, or both.

2. After the date of this resolution the unauthorized buying, holding for sale or encouraging of illicit trade of objects of historical, archaeological, paleontological, or scientific value by any person or employee shall be good cause for withdrawing a business privilege pursuant to Navajo Tribal Council Resolution CMY-33-70 (5 NTC 51) or terminating a lease pursuant to Navajo Tribal Council Resolution CJ-38-54 (5 NTC 77 (b))

3. After the date of this resolution any non-Indian who shall intentionally appropriate, injure, destroy, buy, hold or offer for sale or encourage illicit trade of objects of historical, archaeological, paleontological, or scientific value may be excluded from Tribal land subject to the jurisdiction of the Navajo Tribe in accordance with procedures set forth in Navajo Tribal Council Resolution CN-60-56 and Resolution CN-64-60 and found in 17 NTC 971-976.

4. The Navajo Tribe's Department of Parks and Recreation and Navajo Tribal Museum shall be the lawful repository for and guardians of Navajo Tribal property of historical, archaeological, paleontological or scientific value.

Distributed courtesy MUSEUM AND RESEARCH DEPARTMENT, The Navajo Tribe Window Rock, Arizona 86515

ONE IS MISSING: NATIVE AMERICAN GRAVES PROTECTION AND REPATRIATION ACT: AN OVERVIEW AND ANALYSIS

*June Camille Bush Raines**

> *If human remains and burial offerings of Native people are so easily desecrated and removed, wherever located, while the sanctity of the final resting place of other races is strictly protected, it is obvious that Native burial practices and associated beliefs were never considered during the development of the American law of property . . . .*
> — Walter Echo-Hawk[1]

I. Introduction

In 1960, during an archaeological study, the remains of thirty-two Native Americans who had been buried for over 1000 years were disinterred. Over the next thirty years, various museums and universities across the country studied the remains of these people.[2] On Wednesday, November 6, 1991, they went home.

Tribes descended from those thirty-two Native Americans were finally allowed to rebury the remains of these people. These reburials are the first since Congress enacted federal legislation requiring the repatriation of Native American remains and grave goods.[3]

This comment begins with a brief introduction to this repatriation legislation and examines the historical movement toward excavating Native American grave sites under the guise of science. Next, the legislation is examined. This development includes an examination of the perspectives of museums, scientists, and Native Americans. The legislation does not address all aspects of repatriating remains and grave goods; therefore, this comment includes suggestions for amendments to the act. This comment concludes with the proposition that the rights of Native Americans to their dead can be protected while still providing contributions to the scientific and museum communities.

---

* Third-year student, University of Oklahoma College of Law.

1. Walter R. Echo-Hawk, *Museum Rights v. Indian Rights: Guidelines for Assessing Competing Legal Interests in Native Cultural Resources* 14 N.Y.U. Rev. L & Soc. Change 437, 448 (1986). Echo-Hawk is currently an attorney for the Native American Rights Fund (NARF) in Boulder, Colorado.

2. Alex Peltzer, *Native Americans Reclaim Remains of Ancestors*, Gannett News Service, Nov. 7, 1991, *available in* LEXIS, Nexis Library, Currnt File.

3. These remains are believed to have been of villagers of the Wakchumni tribe. *Id.*

This legislation does not have to mean an end to the archaeological study of our ancestors; alternatives do exist.

The Need for Legislation

Laws against grave-robbing exist in every state,[4] as do laws against tampering with human corpses.[5] Yet for centuries, scientists have been heralded for their work in disinterring the remains and grave goods of Native American people.

The federal government pays museums to house these remains and funds museum programs designed to locate, exhume, and display even more remains. The government has not drawn distinctions based on whether or not these long-dead people were on public, private, or Native American lands. The government's attitude toward the rights of Native Americans to their ancestors and their ancestors' possessions reflects the government's long-standing view of the Native American as someone generally less deserving of rights than the white man.

During the 1850s, many state governments enacted measures which forbade Native Americans from mingling with whites and which denied Native Americans access to legal protection.[6] In 1871, Congress decreed that "no Indian tribe shall be acknowledged or recognized as an independent nation, tribe or power . . . ."[7] America needed a justification for its expansion into Native American domain, and what better justification than portraying the Native American as a nonperson, undeserving of rights or protection. The government believed Native Americans needed to feel they were in the "grasp of a superior."[8] Congress apparently wanted to be that superior entity, and thus established laws and policies to ensure that it would be.

The images of Native Americans portrayed by the government for the purpose of keeping Native Americans inferior included the savage and the heathen; all portrayals were negative with regard to the Native American as a human being.[9] The most obvious "evidence" that Native Americans were subhuman was their failure or refusal to understand white man's law — certain proof that the Native American had no reasoning ability and was therefore not human.[10] The government viewed the Native American as "a relic of an earlier age who must be

---

4. For example, CAL. HEALTH & SAFETY CODE § 7052 (West 1988) makes disinterment of human remains, without legal authority, criminal.

5. For example, OHIO REV. CODE ANN. §§ 3763-3764 (1988) make tampering with corpses a crime.

6. RAY BILLINGTON & MARTIN RIDGE, WESTWARD EXPANSION 591 (5th ed., 1982).

7. Id. at 609.

8. LORING PRIEST, UNCLE SAM'S STEPCHILDREN: THE REFORMATION OF UNITED STATES INDIAN POLICY 1865-1887, at 242 (1961).

9. WILLIAM SAVAGE, INDIAN LIFE 6 (1977).

10. Id.

elevated or eliminated . . . a threat to an orderly Christian society.''[11]

From the arrival of the earliest Indian-European, the government justified expansion into Indian Territory by defining the Native American as a degraded race. This stereotype, which lasted long after any political usefulness the government could have claimed, continues to work to the benefit of the United States.[12] The Native Americans' ambiguous dual legal status has allowed the government to classify the tribes as dependent or independent nations, depending upon which position better serves the government's needs at a particular point in time.[13]

Because of the efforts of humanitarian groups, Congress finally granted Native Americans citizenship in 1924.[14] The rights that generally come with citizenship have been slow to develop for the Native Americans. "That Indians as a people survived at all is a testimony to their vitality and to their capacity to nurture their heritage in a hostile world.''[15] It is this vitality which likely provided Native Americans with the strength to fight the United States government once again. This time the battle would be for their dead.

Recently the federal government succumbed to pressure from numerous Native American groups and passed legislation concerning their ancestral remains. Groups such as the National Congress of American Indians and the Association on American Indian Affairs worked together as the driving force behind the passage of legislation which provides Native Americans some control over the remains and grave goods of their forefathers.[16] The Native American Graves Protection and Repatriation Act (NAGPRA or the Act),[17] passed in November 1990, provides strict federal standards regarding the treatment of both museum-housed remains and objects and newly discovered remains and objects.

The main purpose of NAGPRA is to protect Native American burial sites by regulating the removal of human remains, funerary, sacred, and cultural patrimonial objects.[18] This protection extends to remains and objects found on federal, Native American, and Hawaiian lands.[19]

---

11. BILLINGTON & RIDGE, *supra* note 6, at 19.

12. SAVAGE, *supra* note 9, at 7.

13. PRIEST, *supra* note 8, at 200.

14. Act of June 2, 1924, ch. 233, 43 Stat. 253.

15. BILLINGTON & RIDGE, *supra* note 6, at 601.

16. *Repatriation Act Protects Native Burial Remains and Artifacts*, NARF LEGAL REV. (Native American Rights Fund, Boulder, Colo.), Winter 1990, at 1, 3 (vol. 16. no. 1) [hereinafter *Repatriation Act Protects Remains*].

17. 25 U.S.C. §§ 3001-3013 (Supp. II 1990).

18. H.R. REP. No. 877, 101st Cong., 2d Sess. 8 (1990), *reprinted in* 1990 U.S.C.C.A.N. 4367, 4367.

19. *Id.*

The Act requires all federally funded museums, entities, and agencies to comply by compiling an inventory of these items and then repatriating[20] them, upon request, to the tribe of origin.

According to its legislative history, NAGPRA has two objectives. One is to provide the tribes with first rights to anything found on the designated lands. Persons wishing to excavate such items must apply for a permit, pursuant to the Archaeological Resources Protection Act (ARPA).[21] Any incidental discoveries made on federal land must be reported in writing to the federal land manager and to the appropriate tribe.[22]

The second objective of NAGPRA is to provide affected tribes with a complete inventory of remains and funerary objects held by federally funded museums and agencies. NAGPRA allows museums and agencies five years to complete the written inventories and notify the affected tribes.[23] The museums or agencies must include with this inventory a statement describing how, when, where, and from whom the agency received the items.[24]

II. Historical Movements

A. Excavation in the Name of Science

As early as the eighteenth century, the white man excavated Native American burial sites and mounds.[25] In 1784, Thomas Jefferson excavated the Native American burial mounds located on his Virginia property.[26] This excavation became known as the "first scientific excavation in the history of archaeology" and earned Jefferson the moniker of the "father of American archaeology."[27]

It is not surprising that with the President of the United States not only approving of but also participating in the disinterment of Native

20. Repatriation means to send back to the country of birth or citizenship. WEBSTER'S II DICTIONARY 592 (1984).

21. 16 U.S.C. §§ 470(aa)-470(11) (1988). The Act requires notice of excavation be given to tribes if excavation is to take place on non-Indian land and could harm cultural or religious sites.

22. H.R. REP. No. 877, *supra* note 18, at 9, *reprinted in* 1990 U.S.C.C.A.N. at 4368.

23. *Id.* The Act also makes provisions, discussed *infra* text accompanying note 54, for remains and objects which cannot be identified by tribe.

24. *Id.* The inventory is not required to be an item-by-item list. The Act allows museums and federally funded entities the option of submitting a summary of their inventory. If the inventory is in summary form, it must be completed within three years.

25. GORDON R. WILLEY & JEREMY A. SABLOFF, A HISTORY OF AMERICAN ARCHAEOLOGY 36 (1974).

26. *Id.* at 37. These mounds measured over twelve feet high and contained layers of skeletal remains.

27. *Id.* at 38.

American remains and funerary objects, the rest of the nation would soon become involved in "archaeology."[28] In 1846, the Smithsonian Institution opened its door and its "immeasurable impact on the dawning age of professional archaeology in the 19th century" began.[29] The Smithsonian, which became known as the "nation's attic," came to hold one of the largest collections of remains of Native Americans.[30]

Other museums quickly followed. In 1868, the United States Surgeon General ordered a "collection" of Native American crania.[31] The military used the crania in studies to determine whether the Native American was inferior to the white man, based solely on the size of the crania.[32] Army personnel took over 4000 skulls from battlefields, fresh graves, and burial scaffolds and placed them in the Army Medical Museum.[33] The Smithsonian's Museum of Natural History currently stores all but eighteen of these 4000 skulls.[34]

Presently the Smithsonian holds the single largest collection of Native American remains in this country; by the museum's own estimate, it holds over 18,500 skeletons of Native Americans.[35] This collection numbers far greater than its closest competitor, the Tennessee Valley Authority, which maintains approximately 13,500 Native American remains.[36] In this country, museum collections of Native American remains are estimated to total as high as 600,000.[37] Additionally, Native American remains have been found in museums as far away as London.[38] There may be as many as two million remains housed in

---

28. Willey and Sabloff do not state what Jefferson did with the objects and remains unearthed from these mounds.

29. WILLEY & SABLOFF, *supra* note 25, at 48. At its opening, the Smithsonian Institution was funded for the most part by Englishman James Smithson. He left a half million dollars to the United States to create an entity which would "increase and diffus[e] . . . knowledge among men." *Id.* at 41. It has since become federally funded.

30. *Repatriation Act Protects Remains*, *supra* note 16, at 1.

31. *Id.* at 2.

32. H.R. REP. No. 877, *supra* note 18, at 8, *reprinted in* 1990 U.S.C.C.A.N. at 4367.

33. *Repatriation Act Protects Remains*, *supra* note 16, at 2.

34. *Id.* The Army does not have an accurate count of the number of skeletal remains or funerary objects in its possession. H.R. 5237, 101st Cong., 2d Sess. 27 (1990).

35. *Repatriation Act Protects Remains*, *supra* note 16, at 1. As a Northern Cheyenne woman described it: "[W]e saw huge ceilings in the room [of the Smithsonian's National Museum of Natural History], with rows upon rows of drawers." The curator explained the drawers housed Native American skeletal remains. *Id.*

36. *Id.* at 2 n.3.

37. Steve Moore, *Federal Indian Burial Policy: Historical Anachronism or Contemporary Reality?*, NARF LEGAL REV. (Native American Rights Fund, Boulder, Colo.), Spring 1987, at 1, 1 (vol. 12, no. 2).

38. Anne Hazard, *Lawmakers to Act on Bill Requiring Museums to Return Indian Remains*, 1991 States News Service, Oct. 5, 1990, *available in* LEXIS, Nexis Library, Current File. The Pitts Rivers Museum in London has a collection of many early North American tribes' skeletons.

museums internationally.[39]

It is not only museums which keep large collections of Native American remains. Universities also maintain collections, often long after they have completed their studies of them. Western Washington University has in basement storage over eighty Lumi remains.[40] One tribe member who visited the university stated, "There were our people stacked in little boxes like cordwood."[41]

The methods museums and other entities employ are not different from those employed by Western Washington University. This lack of respect for ancestral remains fuels the fires that keep tribes like the Lumi pushing for the return of their ancestors' remains and possessions. While going through the boxes of remains, an elder discovered the skeleton of a young woman — the box shook and he said, "One is missing."[42] It was then that another tribe member felt the spirit of death:

> Anyone else would have thought it was the wind blowing across their shoulder. But I didn't ignore it. And I found the [young woman's] baby. . . . I wonder how many people that keep bones in boxes, drawers and museums walk by and think all they heard or felt was the wind.[43]

B. Science Must Take a Back Seat

The Smithsonian Institution, along with most federally funded museums and agencies, demonstrated great unwillingness to return even one of the sets of remains to the descendants who requested their return from the museum. In fact, when the government organized a task force to examine and make recommendations regarding the display and treatment of scared objects and remains, the Smithsonian Institution refused to participate.[44]

According to one museum curator, museums do not want to return Native American objects unless the museum can be assured the objects will receive proper care.[45] Based on the methods of storage many

---

39. Estimate given by Walter Echo-Hawk. Estimate includes universities, museums, tourist attractions, and government agencies. *Id.*

40. *Sidebar*, States News Service, Sept. 4, 1991, *available in* LEXIS, Nexis Library, Currnt File.

41. *Id.*

42. *Id.*

43. *Id.* (quoting Jewell James, a member of the Lumi Cultural Committee).

44. Echo-Hawk, *supra* note 1, at 440. The Smithsonian Institution claimed it was technically not a federally funded entity and, therefore, would not be affected by the recommendations. The government, however disagreed. *Id.*

45. M.S. Mason, *Ceremonial Mask Return Home*, CHRISTIAN SCI. MONITOR, June 12, 1991, at 14 (statement of Richard Conn, Curator of Denver Art Museum American Indian Collection).

facilities employ, such as the Smithsonian and Western Washington University,[46] it is ironic that museums worry that tribes will not take proper care of their ancestors.

Archaeologists at the Smithsonian fear that returning any of the bones would be to "forever alter, if not to end, the science of physical anthropology."[47] The chairman of the physical anthropology department at the Smithsonian's National Museum of Natural History stated that although there may be some social benefit in repatriating the remains of the affected tribes, the loss to science would be irreversible.[48] Proponents for Native Americans responded quickly by saying NAGPRA is evidence that, "[S]ociety has decided that when human remains and science collide, science has to take a back seat."[49]

The loss of which the chairman spoke is, to some extent, real. Repatriating the remains from all federally funded entities will severely limit anthropological research in the future. But alternatives exist to foregoing the research altogether. In fact, NAGPRA includes a provision which actually encourages tribes and museums to work together in meeting each other's needs.[50] Museums and tribes can negotiate rights to remains and funerary objects. For example, one museum, which had held an Iroquois tribes' wampum belts as part of its collection, negotiated a shared usage agreement with the tribe.[51] The parties agreed that the tribe has the right to use the wampum belts for religious and ceremonial purposes, and the museum may use the belts for study and education.

This type of agreement could easily be reached in regard to remains as well. Museums have considered making replicas of collections they will likely repatriate.[52] Reservation-site museums, which have recently opened in the United States and Canada, provide another option as well.[53]

46. *See supra* notes 40, 42. The Field Museum in Chicago kept remains of Blackfeet people in wooden crates. Steven Johnson, *Museum's Blackfeet Remains To Go Home*, CHI. TRIB., Oct. 20, 1991, at 1C.

47. Brigid Schulte, *Smithsonian Packs the First Large Shipment of Native American Remains to Return to Tribes*, 1991 States News Service, Sept. 5, 1991, *available in* LEXIS, Nexis Library, Currnt File.

48. *Id.*

49. *Id.*

50. H.R. REP. No. 877, *supra* note 18, at 16, *reprinted in* 1990 U.S.C.C.A.N. at 4375.

51. *Id.* at 4372.

52. But consider Governor Edgar of Illinois who refused to recommend replacing Dickson Mounds Native American remains with replicas, despite the Native Americans' belief that the display of the remains was insensitive. Governor Edgar said plastic bones are "goofy" and expensive. *Across the Nation*, USA TODAY, Sept. 4, 1991, *available in* LEXIS, Nexis Library, Currnt File.

53. Mason, *supra* note 45, at 14. These museums allow the tribes to maintain the remains and allow the public the opportunity to benefit from the education experience.

There is no question that NAGPRA'S repatriation requirement will limit future studies based on actual remains and grave goods. However, NAGPRA provides that museums may retain rights to unidentifiable remains and objects and may keep remains and objects which tribes do not request be repatriated to them.[54] Furthermore, it is possible that some tribes will not seek the return of all items on a museum's inventory list — tribes may have limited resources which would impede their ability to preserve the objects museums currently care for. Museums should expect to have fewer remains and objects to study, but museums' complete loss of all available means of scientific research is not likely.

III.   Legislative History of NAGPRA

A.   Case Law Development

Although the specific movement behind the proposals which eventually became NAGPRA took over five years to legislate,[55] the movement for recognition of Native Americans' rights to ancestral remains has existed almost since the first excavation.[56] It is only recently, however, that Native Americans have felt they were in a position to bring a white government to court.[57]

One problem Native Americans faced, and will likely continue to face even under NAGPRA, in suing the white man for tribal remains is standing. A party must have a direct, substantial interest which the court recognizes in the outcome of a suit in order to bring a claim against another.[58] Parties without standing cannot bring a court action.[59]

Native Americans generally believe they are connected spiritually and familially with their ancestral Native Americans and that this connection is sufficient for standing. Courts, however, generally require a more direct and substantial interest. For example, in *Bailey v. Miller*,[60] a Native American sought to prevent the disinterment of the remains of an aboriginal. The court refused to allow the action, stating that because the Native American was not a direct descendant or an authorized representative for the tribe of the dead person, he had no standing to sue to prevent the disinterment.[61] The court refused to

---

54. 25 U.S.C. § 3005 (Supp. II 1990).

55. *New Law Protects Human Remains and Cultural Items*, INDIAN AFFAIRS, Winter/Spring 1991, at 4 [hereinafter *New Law*].

56. *See supra* notes 25-27.

57. MARCUS F. PRICE, DISPUTING THE DEAD: U.S. LAW ON ABORIGINAL REMAINS AND GRAVE GOODS 21 (1991).

58. Sierra Club v. Morton, 405 U.S. 727, 730 (1972).

59. *Id.*

60. 143 N.Y.S.2d 122 (1955).

61. *Id.*

consider the Native American's belief that he had a spiritual relationship with the dead person, even though this relationship with the dead person is a recognized Native American religious belief.

This strict position continues to make it difficult for Native Americans to have tribal remains and grave goods returned to them, even under NAGPRA. Although the standing requirement is defined somewhat more loosely in NAGPRA,[62] the burden of proof is still on the Native American to prove a relationship, or standing, to the items requested.[63]

Perhaps NAGPRA should presume that grave goods and Native American remains are the property of the tribes or their representatives and, therefore, standing exists for repatriation requests. Museums, which have paperwork describing how they obtained each piece in a collection, are in a better position to meet a burden of proof of ownership than a tribe would be. Tribes would have no record of missing or stolen remains and grave goods.

Native Americans also faced the problem of semantics in American courts. In 1898, almost one hundred years after Jefferson's first "scientific excavation,"[64] an Ohio court addressed the issue of defining a "body" at law. Cemetery officials disinterred a body which had been buried for approximately forty years and reburied it in a common grave without the family's permission. The family sought damages based on the unlawful disinterment of a body. *Carter v. City of Zanesville*[65] ultimately held that the Native American skeleton was not a "body" in the eyes of the law because the governing statute prohibiting disinterment of bodies did not apply to decomposed persons.[66]

Because of the general lack of statutory or common law provisions pertaining to remains and grave goods of Native Americans, courts continued to interpret laws in a manner which discriminated against these people. In 1965, *Newman v. State*[67] held that a college student's removal of the skull of a Native American from a burial site did not constitute desecration under the state's grave robbing statute because there was no evidence of malice.[68] The court considered the fact that

---

62. 25 U.S.C. § 3001 (Supp. II 1990).

63. Consider, for example, the Shiloh Mounds in Tennessee. Investigators have not yet been able to determine which historic Native American tribes may have been descendants of the mound builders. FRANKLIN FOLSOM & MARY FOLSOM, AMERICA'S ANCIENT TREASURERS 246 (1971). How then can a Native American today prove to the park administration that he or she should have standing to claim the remains and objects at Shiloh?

64. *See supra* notes 25-27 and accompanying text.

65. 52 N.E. 26 (Ohio 1898).

66. *Id.*

67. 174 So. 2d 479 (Fla. Dist. Ct. App. 1965).

68. *Id.*

this particular burial was an unfamiliar and a secret custom. Therefore, the court said, the student could not have been acting with malice.[69] The dissent, however, took a different view, based upon the idea that a grave need not be familiar or of ordinary custom to be protected. "The sanctity of the final resting place of the Indian peoples . . . should be recognized and should be accorded highest respect."[70]

In 1971, an Ohio court determined that Native American remains did not qualify as a "body" under the state's grave-robbing statute. The court, in *State v. Glass*,[71] reasoned that the skeleton was no longer a body because a corpse ceased to remain.[72] The court reasoned that "body" was not the same as "remains of persons long buried and decomposed."[73] The court did not consider that the defendant in the case had paid someone to have the remains removed and reburied — a certain sign that a body of some kind remained.

In an equally chilling decision, a California court found that a Native American burial site, which had once contained remains of over 600 Native Americans, was not a cemetery under state law. In *Wana the Bear v. Community Construction*,[74] the court held that an ancient Miwok burial site did not constitute a cemetery and was, therefore, not protected by state law.[75] The court explained that in 1872, the state had outlined two means for creating a cemetery: dedication and prescriptive use.[76] The Miwok tribe had used the burial site in question as a cemetery since the early 1800s, but in 1850 the Miwok tribe was driven away. Therefore, the court reasoned, the site in question did not meet either of the prescribed methods for creating a cemetery.[77] The state allowed the land to be developed, unearthing numerous remains which ended in their destruction.

Decisions such as these seem to be the result of clever attorneys finding a loophole in existing statutory definitions. To differentiate between a dead body and a "corpse long dead and buried" seems reaching at best. It seems logical that if something remains of the

---

69. *Id.* at 483.

70. *Id.* at 484; *see also* Sequoyah v. TVA, 620 F.2d 1159, 1163 (6th Cir. 1980), *cert. denied*, 449 U.S. 953 (1981) ("Cherokees . . . have great reverence for their ancestors and believe places where they are buried have cultural and religious significance.").

71. State v. Glass, 273 N.E.2d 893 (Ohio Ct. App. 1971).

72. *Id.* at 896.

73. *Id.*

74. 180 Cal. Rptr. 423 (Ct. App. 1982).

75. *Id.* at 426.

76. A "dedicated" cemetery is a place dedicated to and used for permanent interment of humans. A "prescribed" cemetery is land used in or near a city as a cemetery for five uninterrupted years. CAL. HEALTH & SAFETY CODE § 8126 (West 1988).

77. *Wana the Bear*, 180 Cal. Rptr. at 426.

person buried, then does a body not exist? Further, if the body is buried in an area reserved for the burial of many people, a burial site or cemetery exists. NAGPRA does provide some guidance in that its definitional section broadens the interpretation of "burial site" and "remains."[78] Hopefully, these broader definitions will prevent future court findings such as those discussed in *Wana the Bear*, *Glass*, and *Carter*.

B. Governmental Policies

The government has been more willing to return land to the Native Americans than the rights to their dead. In 1946, Congress created the Indian Claims Commission, an entity designed to provide Native Americans restitution for lands taken from them by the white man.[79] Interestingly, Congress did not use this as an opportunity to provide Native Americans the additional right to have their ancestors returned. Instead, Congress allowed acts such as the Antiquities Act of 1906[80] and the Historic Sites Act of 1935[81] to continue to exist unchanged, despite the fact that these acts presented little or no recourse for Native Americans seeking the return of the remains of their ancestors.

The Antiquities Act of 1906, which has yet to be repealed,[82] gave exclusive jurisdiction and control of all prehistoric remains found on government-owned-or-controlled land to the federal government.[83] The Historic Sites Act of 1935, which was part of President Roosevelt's New Deal, is directed more at protecting historical sites than protecting or repatriating grave goods and aboriginal remains.[84]

The American Indian Religious Freedom Act (AIRFA),[85] passed in 1978, provided Indians some rights to repatriation of tribal remains and grave goods.[86] The AIFRA stresses Native Americans' religious freedom as protected by the First Amendment of the Constitution and requires federal agencies to consider the effect their acts might have on "Indian religious beliefs, objects, and practices."[87] While the statute

78. *See* discussion *infra* note 126.
79. 25 U.S.C. § 70v-3 (1988).
80. 16 U.S.C. §§ 431-433 (1988). Generally, the Act provides that excavations must be "undertaken for the benefit of reputable museums. 16 U.S.C.A. § 432 (West 1974). Additionally, 43 C.F.R. § 3.17 (1985) states that collections obtained under the Antiquities Act of 1906 cannot be removed from public museums without written consent of the Smithsonian.
81. 16 U.S.C. §§ 461-467 (1988). Generally, the Act provides for the protection of properties of national significance.
82. However, some provisions in this Act have been declared unconstitutionally vague because certain crucial terms were not defined. *See* United States v. Diaz, 368 F. Supp. 856 (D. Ariz. 1973), *rev'd*, 499 F.2d 113 (9th Cir. 1974).
83. PRICE, *supra* note 57, at 25.
84. *Id.* at 26.
85. 42 U.S.C. § 1996 (1988).
86. *Id.*
87. PRICE, *supra* note 57, at 30.

appears to protect grave goods and possibly burial sites, it does not. The Act requires only that agencies consider the effect; not that they act upon the effect.

Although our government may have been unwilling to repatriate the remains to Native Americans currently residing in the United States, it was very receptive to the idea of repatriating these remains to other countries. In 1971, the United States entered into a treaty with Mexico providing for the recovery and return of stolen archaeological, historical, and cultural properties.[88] The treaty defines "cultural properties" as "art objects and artifacts of the pre-Columbian cultures of the United States of America and the United Mexican States . . . that are property of federal, state, or municipal governments."[89]

Clearly, the United States government entered into this treaty based, at least in part, on its understanding of the importance that prehistoric remains have to their descendants, and likely in an attempt to strengthen or maintain good relations with a foreign government. It was nothing less than insulting for our government to refuse or neglect to provide this same courtesy and right to its own citizens. Native Americans certainly consider the remains and funerary objects housed by museums as having been stolen from them. The museums have no more right in keeping Native American stolen cultural objects than this country has in keeping objects stolen from the people of Mexico.

If the United States is willing to enter into such a treaty with a foreign government, should it not also be willing to enter into a similar treaty with the government of the Native Americans? Not only would such a treaty show Native Americans that the government recognized their sovereign rights, but it would also do much for government-tribal relations. The government's choice to deal with Mexico and not its own Native American citizens is a clear reflection of the second-class status that the United States grants Native Americans. Unfortunately, the United States took over fifteen years to offer similar protection to Native Americans.

C. The Evolution of NAGPRA

1. Overcoming the Opposition

Regulation in the area of repatriation has met with governmental resistance since first becoming a recognized issue. In 1986, Senator John Melcher (D-Mont.) introduced a bill which would have provided

88. Recovery and Return of Stolen Archaeological, Historical and Cultural Properties, July 17, 1970, 22 U.S.T. 494 [hereinafter Treaty of Cooperation], *reprinted in* FRANKLIN FELDMAN & STEPHEN WEIL, LEGAL & BUSINESS PROBLEMS OF ARTISTS, ART GALLERIES, AND MUSEUMS 23 (1973).

89. Treaty of Cooperation, *supra* note 88, 22 U.S.T. at 495, *reprinted in* FELDMAN & WEIL, *supra* note 88, at 24.

a means for dispute resolution between museums and Native Americans.[90] The bill was defeated, mostly because of pressure exerted on politicians by museum interest groups, who appear to have been more organized at the time than Native American groups.[91]

In 1988, the Senate Select Committee on Indian Affairs held hearings regarding repatriation legislation.[92] The committee postponed the bill to allow museums and Native Americans the opportunity to discuss the needs of both sides. This is likely the first time representatives from these groups were encouraged to meet. The Panel of National Dialogue on Museum-Native American Relations met for approximately one year before presenting its recommendations.

The panel — made up of museum professionals, college professors, anthropologists, archaeologists, and tribal and religious leaders — recommended that federal legislation be enacted. The panel felt that the legislation should take into consideration both the rights of Native Americans and the value of scientific study and education.

The Native American Burial Site Preservation Act of 1989 was introduced March 14 but was quickly defeated.[93] If passed, this Act would have prohibited the excavation of Native American burial sites and the removal of grave goods. Less than two weeks later, the Native American Grave and Burial Protection Act was introduced.[94] Although this Act did not provide for repatriation, it received the support of Native American groups as a step in the right direction.

In 1989, the National Museum of the American Indian Act (the NMAIA)[95] passed. The NMAIA established the museum which will house the Smithsonian's large Native American collection. The NMAIA, a great improvement from the boxes of stored remains, applies only to the Smithsonian and serves as a "living memorial to Native Americans."[96]

Most Native American communities again supported the NMAIA as a good beginning. The founding director of the museum, a Cheyenne, said the museum was designed to be a "collaborating partner" with Native Americans, a way to sustain their culture.[97] Perhaps, he said, it will even resolve the conflict between tribes and whites by providing a better understanding of Native American contributions.[98] Ironically,

90. *Repatriation Act Protects Remains, supra* note 16, at 3.

91. *Id.*

92. H.R. REP. No. 877, *supra* note 18, at 10, *reprinted in* 1990 U.S.C.C.A.N. at 4369.

93. *Id.*

94. H.R. 5237, 101st Cong., 2d Sess. 27 (1990).

95. Pub. L. No. 101-185, 103 Stat. 1337 (1989).

96. *Id.* at 1337. The museum is scheduled to open in the year 2000.

97. Zan Dubin, *O.C. Curator Helps Launch Museum in D.C.*, L.A. TIMES, Oct. 2, 1991, at 1F.

98. *Id.*

the NMAIA, which honors the first people in this country, will occupy the last space available in the National Mall in Washington, D.C.[99]

The legislative history of the NMAIA indicated the purpose of the act was to collect and preserve Native American remains and funerary objects.[100] The NMAIA does provide for repatriation of these objects, but only for those which can be identified by a preponderance of the evidence as belonging to a particular individual or as affiliated with a particular tribe or as having been removed from a specific burial site.[101] Obviously, Native Americans seeking repatriation of any items find themselves at the mercy of the National Museum of the American Indian. Native Americans can prove the affiliation or burial site generally only with the records and information kept by the museum.

Native Americans then have the burden of proof to show the museum has no rights to the requested items.[102] Once the individual making the request meets this burden, the museum may offer proof that it does have the rights to the items. This burden of proof requirement certainly seems contrary to 25 U.S.C. § 194, which does not put the burden of proof on the Native American.[103]

NAGPRA was introduced on July 10, 1990, by Representative Morris Udall (D.-Ariz.).[104] During hearings on the bill, Native American leaders testified that scientists quickly study and then rebury most non-Indian remains.[105] Indian remains, however, are sent to museums to be curated, and as one Native American so eloquently put it, "the cultural curation of mingled remains of various individuals [by museums] does not suggest reverence for the contents."[106] Some Native Americans believe the spirits of their dead cannot rest until they are returned to their homeland[107] and therefore, museums interfere with Native Americans' rights to religious freedom. "[The spirits of our

---

99. NMAIA, 103 Stat. at 1337.

100. H.R. REP. No. 877, *supra* note 18, at 8, *reprinted in* 1990 U.S.C.C.A.N. at 4367.

101. NMAIA, 103 Stat. at 1343.

102. H.R. REP. No. 877, *supra* note 18, at 19, *reprinted in* 1990 U.S.C.A.A.N. at 4378.

103. 25 U.S.C. § 194 (1988).

104. H.R. REP. No. 877, *supra* note 18, at 12, *reprinted in* 1990 U.S.C.C.A.N. at 4371.

105. As a member of the Blackfeet tribe said, "I don't think [white people] would appreciate it if their great-great-grandfathers were put on display in different reservations and had us handling them like a basketball or something." Johnson, *supra* note 47, at 1. Other analogies offered by Native Americans include the secret taping and public study of confessions given in a Catholic church. *Id.*

106. PRICE, *supra* note 57, at 16.

107. H.R. REP. No. 877, *supra* note 18, at 13, *reprinted in* 1990 U.S.C.C.A.N. at 4372.

ancestors] have been held hostage in museums and universities in the name of science."[108]

Museum supporters countered that all Americans have the right to history and if museums are forced to rebury Native American remains, they will not be able to use the remains later as new testing methods develop. Archaeologists believe useful information still exists in the remains.[109] However, museum supporters do see a need for legislation to protect burial sites from looting and desecration, presumably because they too stand to lose directly in such an event.

Apparently, museums do not believe all Americans have the right to bury their dead. Nor do they seem to believe that history can be gleaned as effectively from the remains of non-Indians. Fortunately, however, legislation ultimately favored the Native Americans in this battle, and NAGPRA gave Native Americans the right to the return of their dead.

Support for NAGPRA from various federal agencies has not been overwhelming. Prior to the legislation's passage, the House requested comments from agencies likely to be affected by NAGPRA. The Department of Army voiced concerns in two areas. First, the Army believed the provision which requires notice to and consent of tribes prior to excavation placed an "impossible burden" on the federal land managers.[110] Secondly, the Army believed NAGPRA presented an unnecessary overlap of the Archaeological Resources Protection Act.[111]

The Army apparently did not have even a general understanding of either NAGPRA or the ARPA; there is virtually no overlap at all between these acts. The ARPA basically replaced the Antiquities Act of 1906; it seeks to secure present and future benefits which archaeological resources and sites can provide for Americans.[112] The ARPA makes no distinction between Indian and non-Indian lands.

Under the ARPA, Native American complaints regarding the disinterment of Native American remains and objects are advisory only. The emphasis is on protecting Native American objects. Further, the ARPA effectively prevents repatriation and reburial of grave goods and remains — it requires that such items found on federal land be preserved in "suitable institutions."[113] NAGPRA, on the other hand, gives Native Americans the final say in disinterment of Native American remains and grave goods. It also provides for the repatriation of

108. Johnson, *supra* note 46, at 1C.

109. John E. Peterson, *Dance of the Dead: A Legal Tango for Control of Native American Skeletal Remains*, 15 AM. INDIAN L. REV. 115, 119 (1990).

110. H.R. REP. No. 877, *supra* note 18, at 23, *reprinted in* 1990 U.S.C.C.A.N. at 4382 (Letter from the Department of the Army).

111. 16 U.S.C. § 470(aa) (1988).

112. MARILYN E. PHELAN, MUSEUMS AND THE LAW 1113 (1982).

113. PRICE, *supra* note 57, at 30.

both remains and objects to the tribes, whether they were found on federal land or on Indian land. It will be interesting to see how these two provisions will be reconciled.

As to the Army's concern of undue burden, NAGPRA requires no more work from or by the federal land manager than the current method prescribed by the ARPA.[114] In fact, under the ARPA, the federal land manager can control the entire permit process. Because Native Americans only advise the ARPA, the whole decision-making process must be handled solely by the federal land manager. Under NAGPRA, the federal land manager must handle the permit process only when unauthorized finds are discovered on non-Indian lands.

The Department of Justice took the opportunity to voice its concerns over the effect the Takings Clause of the United States Constitution might have in regard to NAGPRA.[115] The Department felt uncomfortable with the idea that Congress would be exercising its spending power to accomplish an uncompensated taking of private property from museums and agencies.[116] The basis for this argument is somewhat confusing because the Takings Clause applies to private property. Federally funded entities currently possess the remains sought to be recovered; therefore, they would not be considered private property.[117]

And what about the illegal taking of property from the Native Americans? Very few of the objects and remains housed in museums were actually purchased from the tribes. It is true that some objects may have been purchased from art dealers or individuals, but most of the objects and remains were taken from Native American burial grounds without any authorization from the affected tribes. The constitutionality of museums and federal agencies ability to keep objects they know with some degree of certainty belong to the descendants of those buried is questionable.

The Department of Justice might also have been more concerned with the issue of whether remains and grave goods located on private property might legally be the property of the current land owner — Indian or non-Indian. American property law generally vests ownership of all objects found on private land in the land owner.[118] However,

---

114. 16 U.S.C. § 470 (1988).

115. U.S. Const. amend. V.

116. H.R. Rep. No. 877, *supra* note 18, at 25, *reprinted in* 1990 U.S.C.C.A.N. at 4384 (Letter from the Department of Justice).

117. *See* U.S. Const. art. IV, § 3, cl. 2. In reference to the Department of Justice's concerns, the Committee included language to the effect that its intent was not to provide for takings in violation of article 5. H.R. Rep. No. 877, *supra* note 18, at 15, *reprinted in* 1990 U.S.C.C.A.N. at 4374.

118. Echo-Hawk, *supra* note 1, at 445.

in white versus Native American trials regarding the right to property, the white person has the burden to prove ownership.[119]

The Department of the Interior suggested that the government maintain a stewardship role over any unidentifiable remains.[120] "Unidentifiable," according to NAGPRA, means it is not possible to determine the tribe of origin for remains or grave goods.[121] In conceding that the remains should be repatriated to the ancestral tribes, the government is admitting the government's right to the remains is subordinate to that of the tribes. However, the Department of the Interior did not explain why the government should maintain any control over these remains. This suggestion illustrates the government's desire to maintain at least some degree of control over Native American affairs — another example of the government's need to be the Great Father[122] to its wards, the Native Americans.

2. Provisions and Prostrations

Supported by tribes, the American Association of Museums, and the Society for American Archaeology,[123] NAGPRA finally passed in November 1990.[124] The definitions in the Act, for terms such as burial site[125] and cultural items,[126] should prevent courts and attorneys from using interpretations of terms as loopholes to avoid the application of the statute.[127] The committee that drafted the bill intended courts to read the definitions literally and took care to clarify meanings.[128] The Act

---

119. 25 U.S.C.S. § 194 (Law. Co-op. 1983). However, it should be noted that individual tribe members have neither title nor right to communally owned property which is held for common use by the tribe. Echo-Hawk, *supra* note 1, at 442. This point, while proper in relation to the Takings Clause argument, is moot. Congress designed NAGPRA to regulate findings of remains and objects on federal, Hawaiian, and Indian lands only.

120. H.R. REP. No. 877, *supra* note 18, at 30, *reprinted in* 1990 U.S.C.C.A.N. at 4389 (Letter from the Department of the Interior).

121. 25 U.S.C. § 3001 (Supp. II 1990).

122. FRANCIS PRUCHA, THE GREAT FATHER: THE UNITED STATES GOVERNMENT AND THE AMERICAN INDIANS 2 (1984).

123. *New Law*, *supra* note 55, at 1.

124. 25 U.S.C. §§ 3001-3013 (Supp. II 1990).

125. *Id.* § 3001(1). The definition of "burial site" includes natural and prepared locations, either above or below the surface, where human remains are deposited. This definition should prevent decisions like *Glass* from recurring.

126. *Id.* § 3001(3). The definition of "cultural items" includes human remains and associated or unassociated funerary objects, sacred objects, and objects which have an ongoing traditional, historical, or cultural importance.

127. *See supra* notes 67, 71, 74.

128. For example, the Committee explained that "cultural affiliation" is a method of ensuring the claimant has a reasonable connection with the requested materials. H.R. REP. No. 877, *supra* note 18, at 14, *reprinted in* 1990 U.S.C.C.A.N. at 4373.

also includes an in-depth explanation of "ownership,"[129] likely included to prevent standing problems as discussed above.

Sections 3003 and 3004 of the Act stipulate action that museums and other federally funded agencies which house aboriginal remains must take. Basically, these sections require these entities to take inventory of all aboriginal remains and funerary objects and to file the inventory list for publication in the Federal Register.[130] The Act describes which remains and objects must be repatriated and how to do so.[131] In general, museums must repatriate upon request of the Native American tribe or organization associated with the remains.[132] However, if a museum determines it needs a specific object for a specific scientific study or major benefit to the United States, it may keep the object for the duration of the study but must return it within ninety days of the study's completion.

The Act also establishes a review committee whose function is to "monitor and review the implementation of the inventory and identification process and repatriation activities . . . ."[133] Parties failing to comply with NAGPRA or with the review committee's findings will be penalized, after notice and opportunity for hearing under the Act.[134] Each violation is considered a separate offense and is subject to penalty.[135]

The government included provisions whereby both Native American tribes and museums can apply for grants for the purpose of assisting in either enforcing or complying with NAGPRA.[136] It seems ironic that the government, which put off enacting this type of statute for so long, would include language, which states that the Act reflects the

---

129. 25 U.S.C.S. § 3002 (Law. Co-op. Supp. 1991). "Ownership" is defined in terms of order of priority, with lineal descendants being first, tribes being next, and the federal government following. The Committee explained that "right to possession" was not intended to usurp state law. H.R. REP. No. 877, *supra* note 18, at 14, *reprinted in* 1990 U.S.C.C.A.N. at 4373.

130. 25 U.S.C § 3003(d)(3) (Supp. II 1990). Museums have five years in which to complete and file this inventory.

131. *Id.* § 3005.

132. *Id.* § 3005(a)(5).

133. *Id.* § 3006(a). The committee is made up of seven members: three nominated by tribes, two of who are traditional religious leaders, three nominated by museum communities, and one appointed by consent of the others. H.R. REP. No. 877, *supra* note 19, at 19, *reprinted in* 1990 U.S.C.C.A.N. at 4378.

134. 25 U.S.C. § 3007 (Supp. II 1990).

135. *Id.* § 3007(a). Civil penalties are assessed by the Secretary of the Interior. Criminal penalties are available for the illegal trafficking of Native American human remains and cultural items in violation of NAGPRA. These penalties range from up to one year in prison and/or fines for the first offense and up to five years and fines for the second offense. 18 U.S.C § 1170 (Supp. II 1990).

136. 25 U.S.C. § 3008 (Supp. II 1990).

"unique relationship between the Federal Government and Indian tribes."[137]

NAGPRA includes authorization of funds "as may be necessary to carry out this Act."[138] The Congressional Budget Office estimated the cost of enacting NAGPRA would be from $200 million to $500 million over a five-year period.[139] Congress allotted $5 million to $10 million for grants to tribes to aid in repatriation.[140] The main costs are anticipated to be the preparation of inventories. This figure is based on the estimate that federally funded museums hold between 100,000 to 200,000 Native American remains which will each cost fifty to one hundred fifty dollars to inventory.[141] Based upon earlier estimates, NAGPRA failed to account for at least 400,000 to 500,000 remains — those likely held by privately funded museums and agencies, collectors, and art dealers. Although the newly enacted penalties[142] should keep these numbers from growing, they provide little motivation for the numbers to decrease. There is nothing in NAGPRA to encourage or protect private entities or individuals from facing criminal charges for trafficking, should they want to come forward with their remains or grave goods.[143]

Finally, NAGPRA vests the United States district courts with jurisdiction over actions brought under the Act.[144] There is no explanation given as to why the Act did not vest Native American tribal courts with this jurisdiction. Tribal courts generally have jurisdiction over actions, even by non-Indians, occurring on Indian land. NAGPRA should be no different. The Act, in distinguishing between remains found on tribal lands versus those found on federal lands, should provide tribal courts with jurisdiction even over those remains found on federal lands. There should at least be a distinction made as to the lands upon which the remains or grave goods were found.

Overall, NAGPRA fills many of the gaps left by earlier acts such as the AIFRA, the ARPA, and the NMAIA. NAGPRA provides some explicit definitions of crucial terms, sets up a review committee to handle remains and objects which do not fit into any identifiable

137. *Id.* § 3010.

138. *Id.* § 3012.

139. H.R. REP. No. 877, *supra* note 18, at 21, *reprinted in* 1990 U.S.C.C.A.N. at 4380. This figure is far lower than that estimated by private individuals. *See supra* note 40.

140. H.R. REP. No. 877, *supra* note 18, at 22, *reprinted in* 1990 U.S.C.C.A.N. at 4381.

141. *Id.*

142. *See supra* note 124.

143. *See infra* note 167 and accompanying text (discussing the American Indian Ritual Objects Repatriation Foundation).

144. 25 U.S.C. § 3013 (Supp. II 1990).

categories, and protects both remains and grave goods. What the courts will do with this Act — how they will interpret it, how they will apply it — remains to be seen.

IV. The Outlook

The museum and archaeological communities knew it was only a matter of time until Native American groups could force the passage of this type of legislation. In 1973, the following quote appeared in *Museum News*:

> [Indian reclamation attempts are] not a fad so much as a representative facet of the growing interest of American Indians in their own cultural heritage and in their identity as contemporary residents of this country. Museum specimens are not only the physical representations of this heritage and identity, but are also the symbols of the loss of American Indian autonomy and culture by military, legal and demographic processes.[145]

Since the passage of NAGPRA, over thirty tribes from across the United States have sought the return of tribal remains from the Smithsonian Institution alone.[146] NAGPRA appears to have provided Native Americans not only with the standing to seek the return of tribal remains and grave goods, but also with the courage to challenge federal entities. As museums complete and file their collection inventories, this number will likely rise. However, unless all museums and people in associated fields do their best to comply with NAGPRA, actions litigating the ambiguities and loopholes of NAGPRA will soon reach the courtroom.

Consider, for example, actions in other states which had previously enacted legislation similar to NAGPRA. In 1989, in Nebraska, the state historical society claimed it was not a state agency because of its nonprofit corporate status. Therefore, the historical society stated it did not have to comply with the state statute and public records law requiring it to provide tribes with a list of its inventory and to return all identifiable remains upon request.[147] The Pawnee tribe learned that

---

145. Bowden Blair, *Indian Rights: Native Americans Versus American Museums — A Battle for Artifacts*, 7 Am. Indian L. Rev. 125, 148, (1979).

146. Schulte, *supra* note 47.

147. Unmarked Human Burial Sites and Skeletal Remains Protection Act, Neb. Rev. Stat. § 12-1201-12 (1989).

the historical society intended to honor only partially the tribe's request for tribal remains and objects. The historical society intended to return just the prehistoric Pawnee remains, rather than all identifiable Pawnee remains.

The court received evidence that the state had appropriated over $21 million to the historical society in the last ten years, accounting for seventy-five percent of the historical society's operating budget. Based on this information, the court ruled the historical society was a state agency and, accordingly, had to provide the requested documents to the Pawnee tribe.[148]

This case illustrates the problem that could arise in determining exactly which museums and agencies qualify as "federally funded." It is unclear as to whether the federal government must completely fund a museum or agency in order for the museum to fall into this category or whether a museum or agency qualifies if it receives a one-time-only federal grant. If so, would that museum or agency be bound by NAGPRA for only the year the grant was received or forever? If not, how much funding means "federally funded"? This ambiguity presents federal agencies and museums with a loophole which could be used to stall compliance or even form the basis of a lawsuit. NAGPRA should be amended to define exactly what makes a museum or entity "federally funded" for purposes of the Act. Any museum or other entity which must rely on federal funds to remain in operation should be considered federally funded for purposes of NAGPRA — if the government provides the means for maintaining operations, the government should also have a say in what collections that entity retains.

Idaho has had a law similar to NAGPRA in effect since 1984.[149] It mandates reburial, prohibits willful disturbances of graves, and prohibits individual possession of grave goods or remains.[150] A separate provision states any violation of the statute is a felony and may result in imprisonment or fines up to $10,000 per violation.[151] The problem: Native Americans report that the statutes are not effective because of the light punishments courts choose to impose. In one case, a violator who robbed Native American graves and sold the artifacts received only a five-year probation and was ordered to pay restoration costs for the burial grounds he robbed.[152] Native Americans in the state did not believe the punishment fit the crime nor that it would deter others from committing the same act.

148. Pawnee Tribe Prevails in Nebraska Historical Society Lawsuit 1, NARF News Release, July 12, 1991 (Native American Rights Fund, Boulder, Colo.).

149. IDAHO CODE §§ 27-501 to 27-504 (1990) ("Protection of Graves").

150. *Id.* § 27-502.

151. IDAHO CODE § 18-7028 (1987) ("Unlawful Removal of Human Remains").

152. PRICE, *supra note* 57, at 61.

NAGPRA provides for similar penalties[153] but, like those in the Idaho statue, the punishments are discretionary. The Secretary of the Interior determines the punishment and "may" assess civil penalties. Once a museum or agency has been assessed a penalty, even if it fails to pay, the next punishment is still discretionary.[154] Punishments should be mandatory under NAGPRA if they are to constitute an effective deterrent. If violators receive a "slap on the wrist," as did the party in the Idaho case, museums will not have a great deal of motivation to comply; in fact, museums may have less to lose by keeping remains if they face only small fines.

A case that illustrates just how far a party will go to avoid returning Native American remains or grave goods is *People v. Van Horn*.[155] During a 1987 archaeological survey for the city, Van Horn uncovered an ancient grave which contained two skeletons, each with a millstone[156] on its chest. Van Horn contacted the coroner about the skeletons and kept the millstones at his corporation's laboratory. Several Native American groups learned of the find and sought to have the millstones returned to be reburied with the skeletal remains. Van Horn refused, claiming that the Native Americans based their claim to the millstones on race rather than on kinship, that he did not have actual possession of the stones, that the stones were not grave goods or artifacts, and that the statute applied to Native Americans only — not to Indians.

Van Horn attempted to persuade the court that his corporation, not he, possessed the millstones and that these stones could not be considered artifacts because he personally believed that the stones had been placed on the bodies to weight them down and not as associated burial objects. Further, stated Van Horn, even if the stones were used as funerary objects, they were "Indian" objects, not "Native American" objects. The court was not convinced by this "purpose determines artifact" argument or by Van Horn's possession argument. The court saw Van Horn's distinction between "Indian" and "Native American" as helpful to the state's case.[157] By attempting to make the distinction between "Indians" and "Native Americans," a difference courts do not recognize, Van Horn admitted that an Indian would have rights to the millstones.

The California statute at issue made it illegal to possess Native American artifacts or human remains taken from a Native American grave.[158] Van Horn claimed that this statute was so vague that it

---

153. 25 U.S.C. § 3007(a)(5) (Supp. II 1990).

154. *Id.* § 3007(a), (c).

155. 267 Cal. Rptr. 804 (1990).

156. A millstone is one of a pair of thick, heavy disks used for grinding something such as flour. FUNK & WAGNALL'S NEW PRACTICAL STANDARD DICTIONARY 847 (1956).

157. *Van Horn*, 267 Cal. Rptr. at 808.

158. CAL. PUB. RES. CODE § 5097.99 (West 1987).

violated the due process clause of the Fourteenth Amendment. His basis for this claim was that the statute did not define "Native American" or "grave." The court, relying on a "simple" reading of the statute, did not agree.[159] Despite Van Horn's attempt to argue every word of the statute, the court found against him and ordered him to return the millstones for reburial.[160] Van Horn's claims, although not victorious, had enough merit to keep the action in court for three years.

Similar ambiguities exist within NAGPRA. Many of the same issues facing courts prior to NAGPRA's passage will likely be raised again and again until the statute incorporates them. Decisions distinguishing between a cemetery and an abandoned burial site, which tested standing, and which refused to equate "remains" with "body" for grave-robbing purposes have not been handed down for the last time.

Along the same lines, an attorney could argue that while remains were placed in the burial site, what is in the site now can no longer be considered "remains" because of decomposition or passage of time. NAGPRA's definition of "remains" does not specifically include "decomposed bodies" or "as existing after long periods of time."

As to the standing issue, NAGPRA requires only a reasonable showing of affiliation, either to historical or prehistorical groups. The relationship which must be traced is that of a "shared group identity."[161] This phrase is vague at best, and leaves room for an argument over what constitutes a "shared group identity" and a "reasonable" relationship. A better definition would include the kinds of evidence that are sufficient. It might require a showing of tribal papers, museum documents, oral testimony, and such evidence must show, for example, blood relation, religious connection, or tribal orientation. While the vagueness provides a greater opportunity for Native Americans to meet the standing requirement for making their repatriation request, it also provides many opportunities for museums and other entities to defeat that standing, depending on how a court might interpret it.

Perhaps the most obvious shortcoming of NAGPRA, and the weakness most difficult to correct, is that NAGPRA applies to federally funded entities. Private museums and collectors may still legally possess Native American remains, grave goods, and cultural items; NAGPRA does not provide any incentive for private museums or collectors to comply voluntarily with its mandates.

In 1990, Sotheby's, a world-renowned private auction house, announced plans to include in its May Indian art auction three Native American masks. Tribal representatives took immediate action, writing

159. *Van Horn*, 267 Cal. Rptr. at 816.
160. *Id.*
161. 25 U.S.C. § 3001(2) (Supp. II 1990).

the New York auction house to express their view that the sale of the ceremonial masks was sacrilegious.[162] Sotheby's had identified two of the masks as Hopi and one as probably Navajo. Requests by these tribes to examine the masks, which represent life spirits, were denied.[163] Sotheby's left the masks on its auction list.

Fortunately, Elizabeth Sackler, of the Arthur M. Sackler Foundation, learned that Sotheby's intended to auction these masks against the wishes of the affected tribes.[164] Sackler purchased the masks at the auction and announced she intended to return the masks to "the Indian nations to whom they belong."[165] With this, Sackler launched the American Indian Ritual Objects Repatriation Foundation (AIROF).[166]

Sackler hopes that the AIROF will be able to act as a middle man for art dealers, collectors, and others who want to return items to the tribes of origin. AIROF will help make this return possible by providing tax relief to the persons wishing to return the items[167] and guaranteeing the return of the items to the rightful owners.[168] Additionally, Sackler sees the AIROF as a liaison between museums and tribes seeking the repatriation of grave goods, cultural items, or remains. Sackler believes she can help repatriate goods by helping museums decide whom to contact within tribes, what to expect from the tribes that come to collect their goods, and by communicating with tribes seeking repatriation from museums.

Sackler says many Native Americans still have trouble communicating with white people about legal issues. Said one Hopi chief, "White man law and Indian law are different. White man law is changeable. Indian law is not."[169]

What has been called the "last major battle in the bitter controversy over Native American remains and funerary objects"[170] is taking place at Dickson Mounds, Illinois. The museum, built around a Native American burial site, is the last remaining museum to display Native American remains publicly. Despite attempts by Oklahoma tribes to

---

162. Nancy Ross, *Mask of Uncertainty*, NEWSDAY, Aug. 15, 1991, at T5.

163. Amei Wallach, *No More Auction Block for 'Life Spirit,'* NEWSDAY, Nov. 7, 1991, at 113.

164. Elizabeth Sackler is president of the Arthur M. Sackler Foundation, which exhibits her father's collection of Asian and Middle Eastern antiquities and art. Her father founded the Arthur M. Sackler Gallery in Washington. *Id.*

165. Ross, *supra* note 162.

166. *Id.*

167. Persons wishing to donate the items back to the tribes would receive tax credit for the auction value of them. *See* Wallach, *supra* note 163.

168. *Id.*

169. *Id.*

170. Lauren Ina, *Indian Burial Site Focus of Controversy*, WASH. POST, Nov. 10, 1991, at A24.

have the site closed, the once privately owned museum refuses either to return the remains or to rebury them.[171] Museum curators claim the remains are of Mississippians, a tribe whose lineage has yet to be traced to any specific tribe in existence today.[172] The Oklahoma tribes protesting the display claim they are related to the Mississippians. Regardless of the standing issue, the museum is not legally required to return the remains or grave goods. The museum is state funded and Illinois currently has no law similar to NAGPRA which requires repatriation of such Native American items.

Organizations like AIROF provide little hope to Native Americans in cases such as the Dickson Mounds. Board members of Dickson Mounds take pride in their local museum, claiming the dispute is an economic issue. One board member went so far in his defense of the museum as to say there just are not that many places to spend money in the town — presumably the $2000 annual revenue represents money spent by people seeking entertainment at the Dickson Mounds. Said another, "It's not like we're looking at dirty pictures here."[173]

However, these displays offend Native Americans. Their protests, one of which included an attempt to rebury some of the remains, have been ignored by those in the position to close the display. Moreover, the state governor made a campaign promise to keep the site open. Those protesting the display have no hope of changing or closing the site unless Congress enacts federal law similar to NAGPRA which would apply to private museums like the Dickson Mounds.

V. Conclusion

NAGPRA provides Native Americans with more protection for their grave goods and ancestral remains than all the related legislation combined. NAGPRA gives Native Americans ownership rights in their own tribal and cultural property — to their history. NAGPRA furnishes Native Americans a foothold in the courtroom in actions to compel violators of the Act to comply. It serves as an indication that the government may finally be ready to put Native American rights above the research performed by a select group of the population, even over something so important as science.[174]

NAGPRA is not without its flaws. It leaves enough ambiguities for the stubbornest of people to find a claim which is contrary to the

---

171. *Id.*

172. The Mississippians are believed to have lived from 900 A.D. to 1250 A.D. They were responsible for the raised platform earth mounds found in the Illinois area. *Id.*

173. *Id.*

174. As one commentator has noted with regard to change within our legal system: "The progress of science raised the authority of the test tube over the [cross]." WILL & AURIEL DURANT, THE LESSONS OF HISTORY 39 (1968).

Act's intent and also strong enough to get them into the courtroom. However, NAGPRA is a very good beginning of what can become one of the most meaningful pieces of legislation passed for Native Americans.

Museums and other federal entities that house the remnants and remains of the Native Americans' cultural and religious history have already begun the task of returning these objects to tribes. Whatever the tribes decide to do with the objects — house them in reservation museums, share them with federal museums, utilize them in ceremonies, rebury them — should serve as solace that the repatriated items and remains will return to Native Americans part of their history that has long been owed to them.

Employment Division, Department of Human Resources v. Smith: A Hallucinogenic Treatment of the Free Exercise Clause

I. INTRODUCTION

In 1990, the United States Supreme Court drastically altered the traditional protections afforded religiously motivated conduct under the Free Exercise Clause of the first amendment. The Court, in *Employment Division, Department of Human Resources v. Smith* (*Smith II*),[1] held that the Free Exercise Clause did not prohibit applying state drug laws to ceremonial ingestion of peyote, a mild hallucinogen. Furthermore, states may deny unemployment compensation based on the use of the drug, even if the drug was ingested for religious purposes.[2] In reaching this result, the Court refused to recognize religious peyote use as a protected right.

This Note contends that the *Smith II* Court engaged in a stilted and ultimately destructive interpretation of the Free Exercise Clause. *Smith II* marks a radical departure from traditional free exercise jurisprudence. This Note criticizes the Court's failure to protect freedom of religion, one of the most fundamental of rights. Finally, this Note asserts that the Supreme Court should have constitutionalized peyote use in the context of rites associated with the Native American Church,[3] despite state laws prohibiting its use. The Court's decision is an ominous sign that minority religions, those whose practices exist outside of mainstream religions, are now vulnerable to the whim and caprice of majoritarian sentiments.

II. BACKGROUND

A. The Setting—Sacramental Use of Peyote

The flickering glow of the evening fire radiates through the tepee's buckskin walls and invites the Native American Indians to enter,

---

[1] 110 S. Ct. 1595 (1990) (*Smith II*).

[2] *Id.* at 1606.

[3] The tradition of eating peyote as a religious ritual dates back perhaps 10,000 years before the discovery of America to the Native American Indians' ancestors, the aborigines. *See* STEWART, PEYOTE RELIGION 17, 30 (1987). Today, the practice is retained by 300,000 members of the Native American Church. *See* Nelson, *Native American Religious Freedom and the Peyote Sacrament: The Precarious Balance Between State Interests and the Free Exercise Clause*, 31 ARIZ. L. REV. 423, 424 n.4 (1989).

leaving behind the cosmopolitan, complex world.[4] Gentle drum rhythms dance in the air creating a serene, formal mood. No one speaks as twenty male Indians,[5] jeweled and painted, humbly enter, one by one, and reverently sit on blankets sprinkled with ceremonial sagebrush. When everyone is settled, the all-night sacramental meeting begins.

The drum beat deadens and the Chief stands, drawing everyone's attention, as he slowly moves to the center of the tepee. Members immediately kneel around a moon-shaped mound and begin to pray.[6] The Chief places a large decorative peyote "button"[7] upon sprigs of sagebrush in the center of the crescent-shaped altar. This button represents the "Father Peyote" to whom all prayers and songs are directed.[8] The Chief hovers over the alter, removes ground cedar from his incense bag, and sprinkles the fragrant substance into the climbing flames. White wisps of sweet smoke curl into the air. The peyote bag is then blessed and passed around the tepee clockwise until each member has collected four peyote buttons.[9] The buttons taste bitter making some men vomit.[10]

When all have eaten the "Divine Cactus,"[11] the Chief violently shakes a gourd rattle in the smoke and initiates the Opening Song.[12] Confined within the walls of the buckskin structure until the first rays of dawn, the participants sing and pray for anyone who is sick or in need of help.[13] Prayers, songs, and quiet contemplation, enhanced through the effects of peyote, frequently lead to personal revelations.[14] These are often in the form of visions and audible messages directly from Father Peyote, the "Divine Spirit."[15] Peyote often speaks to the participant and promises him forgiveness of his sins. Believers are "confident that Peyote will overcome both bodily and

---

[4] *See generally* E. ANDERSON, PEYOTE: THE DIVINE CACTUS 45-48 (1980).

[5] Usually only the men participate in the religious peyote consuming ceremony; women and children are sometimes allowed to watch. *Id.* at 49.

[6] *Id.*

[7] Peyote buttons are the harvested top of the peyote plant. E. ANDERSON, *supra* note 4, at 42.

[8] *Id.* at 45-46.

[9] *Id.*

[10] *Id.* at 46.

[11] *See generally* E. ANDERSON, *supra* note 4, at xv. There are several names given to peyote. The author has chosen the term "Divine Cactus." *Id.*

[12] Peyotists sing four songs: the Opening Song, the Midnight Song, the Dawn Song, and the Quitting Song. *Id.* at 47-48.

[13] *See generally id.*

[14] *Id.* at 41.

[15] E. ANDERSON, *supra* note 4, at 41 (citing J.S. SLOTKIN, THE PEYOTE RELIGION 77 (1980)).

spiritual ills, for it is their 'comfort, healer, and guide . . . .' "[16] Following the Dawn Song and the Ceremonial Breakfast, the Indians end their religious ritual and exit the ceremonial tepee to "welcome the sun."[17]

Members of the Native American Church do not view peyote as merely the means to communicate with their Deity; rather, peyote *is* the Divine Spirit.[18] Although peyote serves as a sacramental symbol similar to the Christian's bread and wine, it is more than a sacrament. Peyote is an object of worship that embodies the Divine Spirit and those who partake of it enter into direct contact with their Deity.[19] Without peyote, the religion of the Native American Church dies.

B. *A Synopsis of Free Exercise Cases*

In the 1878 landmark decision of *Reynolds v. United States*,[20] the Supreme Court refused to recognize the free exercise claim of George Reynolds, a Mormon charged with polygamy in violation of federal law.[21] Noting that polygamy was offensive to Western cultural norms, the Court determined that prohibiting polygamy was constitutionally permissible.[22] In essence, the Court ruled that a citizen may not be able to participate in a proscribed activity irrespective of its religious significance.[23] The Court's holding in *Reynolds* drew a distinction between religious beliefs and religious practices. While prohibiting interferences with religious beliefs, the Court permitted interferences with religious practices.[24]

The notion that government legitimately could interfere with religious practices remained a tenet of Supreme Court doctrine for nearly 100 years until another landmark decision, *Sherbert v. Verner*.[25] This case introduced a shift in the Court's interpretation of the Free Exercise Clause. The *Sherbert* Court established a balancing test for analyzing first amendment claims: weighing a person's reli-

---

[16] *Id.* at 41.

[17] O. STEWART, PEYOTE RELIGION 330 (1987).

[18] Amicus Curiae Brief for the American Jewish Congress in support of Respondents at 22, Employment Div., Dep't of Human Resources v. Smith, 110 S. Ct. 1595 (1990).

[19] *See* People v. Woody, 394 P.2d 813, 817-18 (Cal. 1964).

[20] 98 U.S. 145 (1878).

[21] *Id.* at 166-67.

[22] *Id.* at 164-66.

[23] The Court was concerned that religious beliefs could assume superiority over the law of the land, "permit[ting] every citizen to become a law unto himself." *Id.* at 167.

[24] *Id.* at 166-67.

[25] 374 U.S. 398 (1963).

gious liberties against a state's interest.[26] If an individual's religious interest is burdened, the state must show a compelling reason to justify the infringement of religious liberty.[27]

In *Sherbert*, a Seventh Day Adventist was fired from her job for refusing to work on Saturday.[28] South Carolina denied her unemployment benefits because she rejected suitable work offered by her employer.[29] In analyzing the case, the Court recognized that a substantial burden upon the exercise of the plaintiff's religion existed.[30] The government was then obligated to justify this burden by showing that a compelling state interest outweighed the interference imposed on the plaintiff's exercise of religion.[31] After hearing the facts, the Court found the denial of benefits unconstitutional.[32]

Only nine years later, in *Wisconsin v. Yoder*,[33] the Court reiterated the need for a compelling interest test when state statutes infringe on religious beliefs.[34] In *Yoder*, the Court struck down a Wisconsin law requiring that Amish parents send their children to public schools after they completed eight years of Amish education.[35] The Court concluded that the state's interest in universal education was not entirely free from a balancing process when it impinged on other fundamental rights. These rights include the free exercise of religion and the parental interests of raising children according to certain religious precepts.[36] Furthermore, enforcement of the compulsory formal education requirement would gravely endanger, if not destroy, the free exercise of Amish religious beliefs.[37]

The *Yoder* Court noted that the religious sect had been identified as a successful and self-sufficient segment of American society for three centuries. Furthermore, the Amish demonstrated the sincerity of their religious beliefs; the interrelationship of belief with their

---

[26] *See id.* at 403-04.

[27] *Id.* at 406-07.

[28] *Id.* at 399. Seventh Day Adventists believe that Saturday is the Sabbath Day according to Biblical teachings.

[29] *Id.* at 401.

[30] *See Sherbert*, 374 U.S. at 403-06.

[31] *Id.* at 406.

[32] *Id.* at 410.

[33] 406 U.S. 205 (1972).

[34] *Id.* at 215.

[35] *Id.* at 234. The Old Order Amish believe that a public high school education would threaten their culture and jeopardize their salvation. In strict adherence to *Romans* 12:22, "be not conformed to the ways of the world", the Amish avoid the modern secular world, including public education. *Id.* at 216.

[36] *Id.* at 213-15.

[37] *Id.* at 215-19.

mode of life; the vital role that belief and daily conduct play in the continuing survival of Old Order Amish communities; and the hazards presented by Wisconsin's enforcement of a generally applicable statute.[38] Thus, it was incumbent on the State to show with particularity how granting an exemption to the Amish would adversely affect the State's admittedly strong interest in compulsory education.[39] The Court found that accommodating the Amish religion would neither impair the physical or mental health of Amish children, nor impair their ability to become productive, self-supporting members of the Amish community. Moreover, the accommodation of the Amish religion would not discharge the duties and responsibilities the Amish owed as citizens or in any other way materially detract from the welfare of society.[40]

In *Hobbie v. Unemployment Appeals Commission*,[41] a case factually analogous to *Sherbert*, the Court again embraced a strict standard of scrutiny for free exercise claims. *Hobbie* involved the firing of a Seventh Day Adventist for her refusal to work on Saturday, her Sabbath.[42] She was denied unemployment compensation because she refused to work certain scheduled shifts.[43] The Court concluded that Florida's refusal to award unemployment compensation benefits to the appellant constituted an actionable abridgment of her free exercise rights.[44] The Court reasoned that the State's denial of benefits because of an individual's religious belief, pressured the individual to violate her religious beliefs, thereby burdening her practice of religion.[45] The Court explicitly reaffirmed *Sherbert* and *Yoder* and determined that only an overriding state interest could justify this infringement of the Free Exercise Clause and no such interest existed.[46]

III. THE *Employment Division, Department of Human Resources v. Smith (Smith II)* DECISION

A. *Facts and Procedural History*

Alfred Smith, a Klamath Indian, was fired from his job as a counselor for a non-profit corporation that provided treatment for alcohol

---

[38] *Yoder*, 406 U.S. at 219, 234.
[39] *Id.* at 221, 235-36.
[40] *Id.* at 234.
[41] 480 U.S. 136 (1987).
[42] *Id.* at 138.
[43] *Id.* at 138-39.
[44] *Id.* at 139, 146.
[45] *Id.* at 139-40, 144.
[46] *Hobbie*, 480 U.S. 141-42.

and drug abusers. Smith was terminated after taking a small portion of peyote while off-duty at a Native American Church service.[47] The employment policy required him to abstain from the use of alcohol as well as other mind-altering drugs.[48] The Employment Appeals Board denied Smith's claim for unemployment insurance because he was terminated for "misconduct."[49] Oregon did not dispute that Smith was a Native American Church member, that his beliefs were sincere, or that acting on those beliefs resulted in the "misconduct" that led to his discharge.[50] Smith did not contest his termination. Rather, he challenged the ruling that denied him unemployment compensation. The benefits were denied because Oregon law disqualifies individuals discharged for "misconduct" from receiving unemployment benefits.[51]

The Oregon Court of Appeals reversed the Employment Appeals Board's decision and remanded for reconsideration.[52] The Oregon Supreme Court affirmed and remanded the case to the Board for entry of an order allowing benefits.[53] The United States Supreme Court, however, vacated the judgment and remanded to the Oregon Supreme Court for a determination of whether the Oregon's controlled substance law prohibited the sacramental use of peyote.[54] Pending

---

[47] Smith v. Employment Div., Dep't of Human Resources, 721 P.2d 445, 446 (Or. 1986).

[48] *Id.* at 446.

[49] *Id.*

[50] Employment Div., Dep't of Human Resources v. Smith, 485 U.S. 660, 667 (1988) (*Smith I*).

[51] *Smith*, 721 P.2d at 446. The statute applicable at the time provided in part:

An individual shall be disqualified from the receipt of benefits until the individual has performed service in employment subject to this Chapter, or for employing unit in this or any other state or Canada or as an employee of the Federal Government, for which remuneration is received which equals or exceeds four times the individual's weekly benefit amount subsequent to the week in which the act causing the disqualification occurred, if the authorized representative designated by the assistant director finds that the individual:

(a) Has been discharged for misconduct connected with work . . . .

OR. REV. STAT. § 657.176(2) (1985).

The administrative rule provided:

Under the provisions of ORS 657.176(2)(a) and (b), misconduct is a wilful violation of the standards of behavior which an employer has the right to expect of an employee. An act that amounts to a wilful disregard of an employer's interest, or recurring negligence which demonstrates wrongful intent is misconduct. Isolated instances of poor judgment, good faith errors, unavoidable accidents, absences due to illness or other physical or mental disabilities, or mere inefficiency resulting from lack of job skills or experience are not misconduct for purposes of denying benefits under ORS § 657.176.

OR. ADMIN. R. 471-30-038(3) (1985).

[52] Smith v. Employment Div., Dep't of Human Resources, 709 P.2d 246 (Or. Ct. App. 1985).

[53] Smith v. Employment Div., Dep't of Human Resources, 721 P.2d 445, 451 (Or. 1986).

[54] *Smith I*, 485 U.S. at 673-74.

that determination, the United States Supreme Court refused to decide whether the Constitution protected such use.[55]

On remand, the Oregon Supreme Court reaffirmed its earlier conclusion that "the First Amendment prevents enforcement of prohibitions against possession or use of peyote for religious purposes in the Native American Church."[56] The Oregon Supreme Court stated that it was unconstitutional to withhold unemployment compensation to one whose unemployment resulted from their exercise of religion.[57] The State of Oregon then appealed to the United States Supreme Court for a second time.[58]

B. *The Supreme Court's Holding*

In *Employment Division, Department of Human Resources v. Smith (Smith II)*,[59] the Court reversed the Oregon Supreme Court, stating that an exemption for the religious use of peyote was not constitutionally required.[60] The Court dismissed *Sherbert's* compelling state interest test, asserting that in recent years the Court had declined to apply the *Sherbert* test at all. Justice Scalia, writing for the majority stated that "[e]ven if we were inclined to breathe into *Sherbert* some life beyond the unemployment compensation field, we would not apply it to require exemptions from a generally applicable criminal law."[61] Scalia wrote that the government's ability to enforce criminal law should not be dependent on a " 'religious objector's spiritual development.' "[62] Requiring an exemption from the Oregon criminal law for the religious use of peyote would create, in Scalia's mind, "a private right to ignore generally applicable laws."[63] Therefore, the Court determined that the Free Exercise Clause does not require a generally applicable drug law to provide an exemption for the sacramental use of peyote so long as the law is rationally related to the legitimate state interest of curbing illicit drug traffic.[64]

Justice O'Connor, in concurrence, lambasted the Court's rationale,

---

[55] *Id.*

[56] Smith v. Employment Div., Dep't of Human Resources, 763 P.2d 146, 150 (Or. 1988).

[57] *Id.* at 149-50.

[58] Employment Div., Dep't of Human Resources v. Smith, 109 S. Ct. 1526 (1989) (granting certiorari).

[59] 110 S. Ct. 1595 (1990) (*Smith II*) (Justice Scalia wrote the opinion and was joined by Rehnquist, C.J., and White, Stevens, and Kennedy).

[60] *Id.* at 1606.

[61] *Id.*

[62] *Id.* (citing Lyng v. Northwest Indian Cemetery Protective Ass'n, 485 U.S. 439, 451 (1988).

[63] *Id.* at 1604.

[64] *Smith II*, 110 S. Ct. at 1605.

arguing that the same result could have been attained by an application of the strict scrutiny test.[65] Because religion is "a preferred constitutional activity . . . [a] law that makes criminal such an activity triggers constitutional concern—and heightened judicial scrutiny—even if it does not target the particular religious conduct at issue."[66] O'Connor argued that Oregon had a compelling interest in eliminating the drug trade sufficient to survive the strict scrutiny test and that allowing an exemption, even for religious purposes, would have undermined the law's effectiveness.[67]

Justice Blackmun's stirring dissent, joined by Justices Brennan and Marshall, endorsed O'Connor's criticism of the Court's rationale.[68] Blackmun wrote that the Court's decision "affectuated a wholesale overturning of settled law concerning the Religion Clauses of our Constitution."[69] The dissenters charged that providing an exemption from Oregon criminal laws for the sacramental use of peyote by members of the Native American Church would not unduly impede the state's goal of reducing the flow of illegal drugs.[70]

IV. ANALYSIS

The first amendment's Free Exercise Clause provides that "Congress shall make no law respecting an establishment of religion, or prohibiting the free exercise thereof . . . ."[71] The fourteenth amendment's Due Process Clause applies this guarantee to the states.[72] The Supreme Court has recognized that an allowance for the performance of, or abstention from, certain acts is implicit in the Free Exercise Clause.[73] Furthermore, the first amendment excludes all "governmental regulation of religious beliefs as such."[74] Therefore, the Free Exercise Clause encompasses the right to believe, profess and perform certain acts according to one's religious doctrine.[75]

---

[65] Id. at 1606 (O'Connor, J., concurring).

[66] Id. at 1612.

[67] Id. at 1614-15.

[68] Id. at 1616 (Blackmun, J., dissenting).

[69] Smith II, 110 S. Ct. at 1616.

[70] Id. at 1622-23.

[71] U.S. CONST. amend. I.

[72] See Cantwell v. Connecticut, 310 U.S. 296, 303 (1940).

[73] Free exercise of religion includes " '[t]he practice and performance of rites and ceremonies, worship, etc; the right or permission to celebrate the observances (of a religion)' and religious observances such as acts of public and private worship, preaching, and prophesying." Smith II, 110 S. Ct. at 1607-08 (quoting A NEW ENGLISH DICTIONARY ON HISTORICAL PRINCIPLES 401-02 (J. Murray, ed. 1897)).

[74] Sherbert v. Verner, 374 U.S. 398, 402 (1963) (citing Cantwell, 310 U.S. at 303).

[75] Id. at 404; Wisconsin v. Yoder 406 U.S. 205, 219-20 (1972) ("[B]elief and action cannot be

Until *Smith II*, the Supreme Court consistently applied the same standard to determine the constitutionality of a state statute burdening the free exercise of religion. Traditionally, first amendment jurisprudence mandated that any statute burdening first amendment rights be subject to a compelling interest test, provided that less restrictive means could not serve a state's compelling interest.[76] *Smith II* rendered the strict scrutiny test, in the free exercise context, a constitutional anachronism.

A. *Narrowing the Free Exercise Clause*

The peyote ceremony is so fundamental to the practice of the Native American religion, that to prohibit the ritualistic ingestion of peyote would eliminate the religion.[77] There can be no question that the act of ingesting peyote should be deemed presumptively protected conduct under the first amendment.[78] The Native American Church's peyote ceremony is conduct stemming from sincere religious beliefs. That conduct mirrors belief itself and thus, should be protected under the Free Exercise Clause.[79]

In the majority opinion, however, Justice Scalia asserts that the free exercise of religion means only "the right to *believe* and *profess* whatever religious doctrine one desires."[80] Justice Scalia refuses to include as protected free exercise any "conduct" that violates a valid,

---

neatly confined in logic-tight compartments."). For example, the government may not compel affirmation of religious belief, *see* Toracoso v. Watkins, 367 U.S. 488, 495 (1961); punish the expression of religious doctrines it believes to be false, *see* United States v. Ballard, 322 U.S. 78, 86-87 (1944); impose special disabilities on the basis of religious view or religious status, *see* McDaniel v. Paty, 435 U.S. 618, 639 (1978); or lend its power to one or the other side in controversies over religious authority or dogma, *see* Presbyterian Church v. Hull Church, 393 U.S. 440, 445-52 (1969).

[76] *See* Hernandez v. Commissioner, 109 S. Ct. 2136, 2148 (1989) ("The free exercise inquiry asks whether government has placed a substantial burden on the observation of a central religious belief or practice and, if so, whether a compelling governmental interest justifies the burden."); Hobbie v. Unemployment Appeals Comm'n, 480 U.S. 136, 141 (1987) (State laws burdening religions "must be subjected to strict scrutiny and could be justified only by proof by the State of a compelling interest."); United States v. Lee, 455 U.S. 252, 257-58 (1982) ("The state may justify a limitation on religious liberty by showing that it is essential to accomplish an overriding governmental interest."); Thomas v. Review Bd. of Ind. Sec. Div., 450 U.S. 707, 718 (1981) ("The state may justify an inroad on religious liberty by showing that it is the least restrictive means of achieving some compelling state interest.").

[77] *But cf.* United States v. Rush, 738 F.2d 497, 512-13 (1st Cir. 1984), *cert. denied*, 470 U.S. 1004 (1985) (holding that, unlike the peyote ceremony, marijuana use is not an integral part of the religious doctrine and practice of the Ethiopian Zion Coptic Church for equal protection purposes).

[78] *See supra* text accompanying notes 18-20.

[79] *Smith II*, 110 S. Ct. at 1608 (O'Connor, J., concurring).

[80] *Id.* at 1599 (emphasis added).

religion-neutral state provision.[81] The Court admits that a state would be " 'prohibiting the free exercise [of religion]' if [the state] sought to ban such acts or abstentions only when they are engaged in for religious reasons, or only because of the religious belief that they display."[82] Yet, the Court does not acknowledge that the first amendment prohibits state laws that *indirectly* impact religion by banning such acts when they are engaged in for any reasons.[83] Justice Scalia argues that it would be unconstitutional for the government "to ban the casting of statues that are to be used for worship purposes, or to prohibit bowing down before a golden calf."[84] However, it is not unconstitutional to indirectly annihilate a whole religion through "neutral" state statutes. Justice Scalia further states that "the right of free exercise does not relieve an individual of the obligation to comply with a 'valid and neutral law of general applicability on the ground that the law proscribes (or prescribes) conduct that his religion prescribes (or proscribes).' "[85]

The Court justifies this position by relying on *Reynolds v. United States.*[86] This case held that to exempt conduct "because of one's religious belief . . . would be to make the professed doctrines of religious belief superior to the law of the land, and in effect to permit every citizen to become a law unto himself."[87] For instance, if a religious adherent believes war is a sin, and if a certain percentage of the federal budget can be identified as devoted to war-related activities, such individuals would have a valid claim to be exempt from paying that percentage of the income tax.[88] If individuals were allowed to challenge the tax system because tax payments violated a religious belief, then the tax system could not function.[89]

However, the *Smith II* Court incorrectly defined religious freedom because the first amendment does not specifically distinguish between direct and indirect attacks on religion.[90] To state that a generally applicable law that indirectly prohibits religiously motivated

---

[81] *See id.* at 1600.

[82] *Id.* at 1599 (citations omitted).

[83] *See id.* at 1600.

[84] *Id.* at 1599 (citations omitted).

[85] *Id.* at 1600 (quoting United States v. Lee, 455 U.S. 252, 263 n.3 (1982) (Stevens, J., concurring)).

[86] 98 U.S. 145 (1879).

[87] *Id.* at 158.

[88] *Smith II*, 110 S. Ct. at 1601 (quoting United States v. Lee, 455 U.S. 252, 260 (1982)).

[89] United States v. Lee 455 U.S. 252 (1982); *cf.* Hernandez v. Commissioner, 109 S. Ct. 2136 (1989) (rejecting free exercise challenge to payment of income taxes alleged to make religious activities more difficult).

[90] *Smith II*, 110 S. Ct. at 1608 (O'Connor, J., concurring).

conduct does not at the very least implicate the first amendment is subterfuge of the highest order. Furthermore, the Supreme Court has ruled that certain conduct cannot be regulated through generally applicable laws.[91] Chief Justice Berger, writing for the majority in *Yoder*, stated:

> [O]ur decisions have rejected the idea that religiously grounded conduct is always outside the protection of the Free Exercise Clause. It is true that activities of individuals, even when religiously based, are often subject to regulation by the States in the exercise of their undoubted power to promote the health, safety, and general welfare, of the Federal Government in the exercise of its delegated powers. But to agree that religiously grounded conduct must often be subject to the broad police power of the State is not to deny that there are areas of conduct protected by the Free Exercise Clause of the First Amendment and thus beyond the power of the State to control, *even under regulations of general applicability.*[92]

At a minimum, the *Smith II* Court should have recognized that the first amendment allows exemptions to generally applicable laws based on religious conduct alone. "[W]e cannot assume, merely because a law carries criminal sanctions and is generally applicable, that the First Amendment *never* requires the State to grant a limited exemption for religiously motivated conduct."[93] The Court should have interpreted the Oregon statute as requiring an exemption for religious use of peyote. By requiring this exemption, the state's broad powers to regulate conduct would not have been infringed on, and the Indian's first amendment rights would have been protected.

B. *Scalia's "Hybrid" Scheme*

Justice Scalia cleverly evades the Court's previous holdings in *Yoder* and *Cantwell v. Connecticut*,[94] by categorizing them as "hybrid" cases.[95] Justice Scalia asserts that the only decisions in which the Court determined that the first amendment bars application of a neutral, generally applicable law to religiously motivated action "have involved not the Free Exercise Clause alone, but the Free Exercise Clause in conjunction with other constitutional protections, such as freedom of speech and of the press . . ., the right of parents to direct the education of their children . . . and freedom of associa-

---

[91] Yoder v. Wisconsin, 406 U.S. 205, 220 (1972).
[92] Yoder v. Wisconsin, 406 U.S. 205, 219-20 (1972) (citation omitted) (emphasis added).
[93] *Smith II*, 110 S. Ct. at 1611 (O'Connor, J., concurring) (emphasis in original).
[94] 310 U.S. 296 (1940).
[95] *Smith II*, 110 S. Ct. at 1602.

tion . . . ."[96]

Assuming, *arguendo*, that Justice Scalia's interpretation is correct, *Smith II* qualifies as a hybrid case and should be analyzed according to the compelling interest test. The facts of *Smith II* parallel the facts of *Yoder* and involve the same type of claim under the Free Exercise Clause. *Smith II* and *Yoder* both involve the "parental right" to direct the religious upbringing of children—yet different results are obtained in each case. Although Native American Indian children do not consume the peyote buttons in the religious ceremony, the adults have a vested interest in preserving this ritual which is essential to their religion, their way of life, and their posterity. Thus, *Smith II* should be deemed a "hybrid" case. Justice Scalia himself noted that "when the interests of parenthood are combined with a free exercise claim . . . more than merely a 'reasonable relation to some purpose within the competency of the State' is required to sustain the validity of the State's requirement under the First Amendment."[97] The Amish parents in *Yoder* desired to educate their children in the home to inculcate in their children traditional Amish religious values. The Supreme Court respected their wish.[98] Certainly, the 300,000 members of the Native American Church deserve as much consideration. Consequently, the Court should have applied the traditional strict scrutiny test utilized in *Yoder*.[99]

C. *Minority Religions: The Luxury We Cannot Afford*

The settled doctrine prior to *Smith II* was that only an overriding state interest could justify an infringement on free exercise. "The compelling interest test effectuates the First Amendment's command that religious liberty is an independent liberty, that it occupies a preferred position and that the Court will not permit encroachments upon this liberty, whether direct or indirect, unless required by clear

---

[96] *Id.* at 1601. *See also*, Cantwell v. Connecticut, 310 U.S. 296 (1940) (invalidating a licensing system for religious and charitable solicitations under which the administrator had discretion to deny a license to any cause he deemed nonreligious); Murdock v. Pennsylvania, 319 U.S. 105 (1943) (invalidating a flat tax on solicitation as applied to the dissemination of religious ideas); Follett v. McCormick, 321 U.S. 573 (1944); Wooley v. Maynard, 430 U.S. 705 (1977) (invalidating compelled display of a license plate slogan that offended individual religious beliefs); West Virginia Bd. of Educ. v. Barnette, 319 U.S. 624 (1943) (invalidating compulsory flag salute statute challenged by religious objectors).

[97] *Smith II*, at 1601 n.1 (quoting *Yoder*, 406 U.S. at 233).

[98] *Yoder*, 406 U.S. at 208.

[99] *See Smith II*, 110 S. Ct. at 1609 (O'Connor, J., concurring) Justice O'Connor stated that in other "hybrid" cases, the Court has rejected the particular constitutional claims only after carefully weighing the competing interests. *Id.*

and compelling governmental interests 'of the highest order.' "[100] Only a narrowly tailored important governmental interest justifies a denial of first amendment freedoms.[101]

Justice Scalia claims that our cosmopolitan nation is made up of "almost every conceivable religious preference."[102] He relies on this pretext to justify his denigration of minority religions:

> [W]e cannot afford the luxury of deeming presumptively invalid, as applied to the religious objector, every regulation of conduct that does not protect an interest of the highest order. [To] rule [in respondents'] favor would open the prospect of constitutionally required religious exemptions from civic obligations of almost every conceivable kind—ranging from . . . manslaughter and child neglect laws . . . to animal cruelty laws.[103]

Admitting that his philosophy disadvantages minority religions, Justice Scalia nonetheless characterizes this result as an "unavoidable consequence."[104] It is this aspect of the *Smith II* decision, the cavalier dismissal of minority religions, that sounds the death knell for the Free Exercise Clause as a protector of religious liberty.

Justice Scalia's dismissal of the Native American religion and culture as a luxury "we cannot afford,"[105] and its annihilation as an "unavoidable consequence"[106] of democratic government, makes a mockery of the framers' intent and the purpose of the first amendment.[107] In *United States v. Ballard*,[108] the Court stated that "the fathers of the Constitution were not unaware of the varied and extreme views of religious sects, of the violence of disagreement among them, and the lack of any one religious creed on which all men would agree."[109] The Court further noted that the constitutional framers "fashioned a charter of government which envisioned the widest possible toleration of conflicting views."[110] The Bill of Rights' purpose was to place certain subjects beyond the vicissitudes of political controversy.[111]

---

[100] *Yoder*, 406 U.S. at 233.

[101] Bowen v. Roy, 476 U.S. 693, 728 (1986) (O'Connor, J., concurring in part and dissenting in part).

[102] *Smith II*, 110 S. Ct. at 1605.

[103] *Id.* (citations omitted).

[104] *Id.* at 1606.

[105] *Id.* at 1605.

[106] *Smith II*, 110 S. Ct. at 1605.

[107] *Id.* at 1613.

[108] 322 U.S. 78 (1949).

[109] *Id.* at 87.

[110] *Id.*

[111] West Virginia Board of Educ. v. Barnette, 319 U.S. at 638 as *quoted in Smith II*, 110 S. Ct. at 1613 (O'Connor, J., concurring).

D. *Religious Peyote Use is a Reasonable Exemption to State Criminal Laws*

Although the Supreme Court may have feared the danger of allowing an exemption for the religious use of peyote, the Court erred in letting that speculative fear interfere with the protections of the Free Exercise Clause.[112] "The Court must not ignore the danger that an exception for a general [law] . . . may run afoul of the Establishment Clause, but that danger cannot be allowed to prevent any exception no matter how vital it may be to the protection of values promoted by the right of free exercise."[113] Twenty-three states and the federal government have allowed religious peyote use exemptions for a number of years and have not been overwhelmed by claims to other religious exemptions.[114]

Unlike other religious groups, the Native American Indians are granted special privileges not given to others solely based on their unique cultural heritage and political status. For example, Indians have been allowed to kill eagles and use their body parts in religious ceremonies and to take game out of season for use in certain ceremonial rites.[115] Indians are further protected under the American Indian Religious Freedom Act which states:

> [I]t shall be the policy of the United States to protect and preserve for American Indians their inherent right of freedom to believe, express, and exercise the traditional religions . . . including but not limited to access to sites, use and possession of sacred objects, and the *freedom to worship through ceremonials and traditional rites.*[116]

Certainly this Act offers evidence that Congress intends to protect the religious traditions of Native Americans. Implicit in such a grant of protection is an acknowledgement that traditional Native American religious ceremonies have cultural significance and must be preserved. For members of the Native American Church, peyote symbolizes sacredness and is the embodiment of the healing power. Therefore, the peyote ritual is essential to the preservation of Indian cultural heritage and to the maintenance of the Native American

---

[112] *Smith II*, 110 S. Ct. at 1621 (quoting *Yoder*, 406 U.S. at 234 n.22) (Blackmun, J., dissenting).

[113] *Id.*

[114] *Id.* at 1618 n.5, 1620 (Blackmun, J., dissenting).

[115] *See e.g.*, United States v. Thirty-Eight Golden Eagle Parts, 649 F. Supp. 269 (D. Nev. 1986), *aff'd*, 829 F.2d 41 (9th Cir. 1987) (holding that the Native American Religious Freedom Act allows Indians with permits to possess eagle parts).

[116] 42 U.S.C. § 1996 (1987). (emphasis added).

religion.[117]

One commentator noted that it seems only rational "to treat Indian members of the Native American Church not as members of a distinct racial group, but as members of a people 'set apart' culturally and politically who owe no duty to conform to American customs, especially where the failure to follow those customs causes no disruption of White society."[118] The Native American Church significantly differs from mainstream religions in this country. Although the fundamental tenets of the Native American Church are completely foreign to any mainstream religious way of thinking, the Court should aggressively protect the cultural and religious heritage of Native Americans; particularly since the isolated and restricted use of peyote in Native American Church ceremonies in no way threatens to disrupt mainstream American culture.

History demonstrates that majority religions have succeeded in procuring exemptions from generally applicable laws that impacted their doctrinal practices. For example, during Prohibition, the federal government exempted the Roman Catholic Church's religious use of wine from its general ban on possession and use of alcohol.[119] Congress recognized that without wine, there would be no communion. Similarly, without peyote there would be no Native American religion, no Deity.

E. *Justice O'Connor Pushes Fear While Justice Blackmun Prescribes Tolerance*

Justice O'Connor defines Oregon's primary compelling state interest as fighting the war on drugs.[120] She claims that "drug abuse is 'one of the greatest problems affecting the health and welfare of our population' and thus 'one of the most serious problems confronting our society today.' "[121] She argues that peyote has a "high potential for abuse . . ." and that possession and use of peyote, "even by only one person, is inherently harmful and dangerous."[122] Justice O'Connor further asserts that "[b]ecause the health effects caused by the use of controlled substances exist regardless of the motivation of

---

[117] 1978 U.S. Code Cong. & Admin. News, pp. 1262, 1263.

[118] Nelson, *Native American Religious Freedom and the Peyote Sacrament: The Precarious Balance Between State Interests and the Free Exercise Clause*, 31 Ariz. L. Rev. 423, 439 (1989).

[119] *Smith II*, 110 S. Ct. at 1618 n.6.

[120] *Id.* at 1613-14 (O'Connor, J., concurring).

[121] *Id.* at 1614 (quoting Treasury Employees v. Von Raab, 109 S. Ct. 1384, 1395 (1989)).

[122] *Id.* at 1614.

the user, the use of such substances, even for religious purposes, violates the very purpose of the laws that prohibit them."[123]

However, fighting drug abuse and trafficking clearly was not the motivating factor behind Oregon's actions because Smith was not arrested for criminal behavior; rather, he was denied unemployment benefits due to the practice of his religion.[124] It appears that Oregon's real interest centered on minimizing its financial commitment in paying unemployment benefits.[125] When balanced against the burden placed on the Native American Church as a result of the criminalization of peyote, Oregon's financial interest clearly should not prevail.

As Justice Blackmun points out in his dissent, Justice O'Connor's fears of peyote and its potential effect on the public welfare are both speculative and wrong.[126] Noted peyote historian Maurice H. Seevers studied peyote and its effects extensively and concluded that while peyote is a narcotic, it is relatively non-addicting.[127] Furthermore, there is practically no illegal traffic in peyote primarily because peyote is a rare plant,[128] with such a bitter, pungent taste that it has never been popular.[129] The Drug Enforcement Agency records on seizures of illegal narcotics chronicles that in the period between 1980 and 1986, the government seized only 19.4 pounds of peyote; in contrast, during that same period, the government confiscated fifteen million pounds of marijuana.[130] Therefore, it is a safe assumption that peyote distribution for use in religious rituals has "nothing to do with the vast and violent traffic in illegal narcotics that plagues this country."[131]

Unlike alcohol and other drugs, peyote does not endanger the public when consumed in accordance with the tenets of the Native American Church. Native American members take peyote in a traditional

---

[123] Id.

[124] Smith II, 110 S. Ct. at 1596.

[125] Nelson, supra note 118, at 443. See also Smith v. Employment Div., Dep't of Human Resources, 721 P.2d 445, 450-51 (Or. 1986).

[126] Smith II, 110 S. Ct. at 1618.

[127] E. ANDERSON, PEYOTE: THE DIVINE CACTUS 160 (1980). "Seevers calculated the 'addicting liability' of a number of drugs found in United States society by constructing an index based upon the factors of tolerance, physical dependence, and habituation. He concluded, . . . that alcohol was the most addicting (an index factor of 21), followed by the barbiturates with an index of 18, opium and its derivatives (16), cocaine (14), and marijuana (8). Peyote, according to Seevers, had a liability of only 1, and this single value was due solely to the fact that some of his experimental subjects showed a slightly increased tolerance during the testing." Id.

[128] See O. STEWART, PEYOTE RELIGION 3, 12-16 (1987).

[129] Smith II, 110 S. Ct. at 1620 (Blackmun, J., dissenting).

[130] Id. (citing Olsen v. Iowa, 808 F.2d 652, 656 (8th Cir. 1986).

[131] Id.

all-night meeting in which members are confined to the tepee until the effects of the drug have worn off.[132] In contrast, alcohol and drug users are not physically restrained from driving and are free to inflict severe, often fatal damage to innocent persons. Furthermore, peyote consumption outside of religious ceremonies and rituals is sacrilegious.[133] The Native American Church refuses to allow the presence of non-members at its rites and vigorously opposes the sale or use of peyote for non-religious purposes.[134] Finally, religious peyote use, sale, and distribution was under strict federal regulations immediately prior to *Smith II*.[135] Therefore, even if the United States Supreme Court had allowed a sacramental exemption from Oregon's criminal laws, the religious use of peyote would never unleash Justice O'Connor's feared avalanche of illegal drug trafficking or abuse.

V. Conclusion

Any threat to the precious and fundamental rights explicit in the Free Exercise Clause should demand that a compelling governmental interest test be applied. As Justice O'Connor acknowledged, "[t]here is nothing talismanic about neutral laws of general applicability or general criminal prohibitions, for laws neutral toward religion can coerce a person to violate his religious conscience or intrude upon his religious duties just as effectively as laws aimed at religion."[136] The Supreme Court should have recognized the importance of the Native American Church's sacramental use of peyote and extended the same deference historically granted Christian sacramental practices. Without this recognition, Native American Indians are denied their first amendment freedoms.

The *Smith II* decision is tragic for two humanistic reasons. First and most obviously, the Court's ruling effectively destroys the doctrinal foundations of the Native American Church. Second, this deci-

---

[132] *See* O. STEWART, *supra* note 128, at 327-30.

[133] People v. Woody, 394 P.2d 813, at 817-18 (Cal. 1964).

[134] *See* E. ANDERSON, *supra* note 127, at 15.

[135] *Smith II*, 110 S. Ct. at 1620 (Blackmun, J., dissenting). *See also* 21 U.S.C. §§ 1307.31 (1989) (stating registration requirements for the distribution of controlled substances):

The listing of peyote as a controlled substance . . . does not apply to the non-drug use of peyote in bona fide religious ceremonies of the Native American Church, and members of the Native American Church using peyote are exempt from registration. Any person who manufactures peyote for or distributes peyote to the Native American Church, however, is required to obtain registration annually and to comply with all other requirements of law.

21 C.F.R. 1307.31 (1989).

[136] Employment Div., Dep't of Human Resources v. Smith (Smith II), 110 S. Ct. 1595, 1612 (1990) (O'Connor, J., concurring).

sion constitutes a significant diminution of a vanishing culture, a unique facet of America's rich and diverse heritage. But more significantly, from a legal standpoint, *Smith II* has emasculated the first amendment and subverted congressional policies, making them "hollow promises."[137]

The drum no longer sounds in the ceremonial tepee. The ancient chants no longer echo around the glowing embers. The communal fire has died.

RASHELLE PERRY

---

[137] *Smith II*, 110 S. Ct. at 1622.

Trouble In High Places
Erosion of American Indian Rights to Religious Freedom in the United States

Vine Deloria, Jr.

The First Amendment to the Constitution declares that Congress shall make no law respecting the establishment of religion or prohibiting the free *exercise* thereof. The Fourteenth Amendment has rendered the legislatures of the states as incompetent as Congress to enact such laws. The constitutional inhibition on the subject of religion has a double aspect. On the one hand, it forestalls compulsion by law of the acceptance of any creed or the practice of any form of worship. Freedom of conscience and freedom to adhere to such religious organization or form of worship as the individual may choose cannot be restricted by law. On the other hand, it safeguards the *free exercise of the chosen form of religion.* Thus the amendment[s] embrace two concepts—freedom to believe and freedom to *act* (emphasis added).

Cantwell v. Connecticut
310 U.S. 296, 1940

Two recent Supreme Court cases, *Lyng v. Northwest Indian Cemetery Protective Association* (108 S. Ct. 1319 (1988)) and *Employment Division, Department of Human Resources of Oregon v. Smith* (110 S. Ct. 1595 (1990)), have stripped American Indians of the protection of the federal courts and the American Constitution insofar as the practice of traditional religions is concerned. Although the two cases are viewed in tandem as attacks on Indian rights, they only coincidentally come together. *Lyng* attempts to deal with Indian rights as defined following the passage of the American Indian Religious Freedom Resolution, and *Smith* confronts the question of the relationship of religion and the state. Thus, while *Lyng* can be cited as precedent in federal Indian law, *Smith* examines much broader questions of constitutional law. The latter case was considered in order to determine whether the state of Oregon held a constitutional right to impose either civil or criminal penalties upon members of the Native American Church for their traditional use of sacramental peyote simply because use of the substance was legally denied to everyone else. The high court held that the state did in fact possess such rights. But, as the dissenting justices put it in *Smith:*

> The Court today—interprets the [Free Exercise] Clause to permit the government to prohibit, without justification, conduct mandated by an individual's religious beliefs, so long as the prohibition is generally applicable. But a law that prohibits certain conduct—conduct that happens to be an act of worship for someone—manifestly does prohibit that person's free exercise of his religion. A person who is barred from engaging in religiously motivated conduct is barred from freely exercising his religion. Moreover, that person is barred from freely exercising his religion regardless of whether the law prohibits the conduct only when engaged in for religious reasons, only by members of that religion, or by all persons.[1]

The high court opinion in *Smith* therefore voids long-settled interpretations of the constitutional protections extended over the free exercise of religion—not only with regard to Indians, but to everyone else as well—and throws them in the same "community standards" arena covering pornography and other forms of obscenity.[2] *Lyng*, on the other hand, provides an opportunity to examine the three major paths that federal Indian law has taken in the course of American history: 1) the treaty relationship, 2) the Trust Doctrine, and 3) property ownership of the public domain by the federal government. Many practitioners of federal Indian law, including, unfortunately, most of the judges and justices who write decisions, tend to use these ideas interchangeably or as complementary theories that bolster a vague belief that Indians are and must always be at the mercy of the United States government. But these interpretations of the Indian relationship are actually exclusive of one another, and therefore any effort to combine them in a decision or legal brief inevitably adds to rather than reduces the confusion and mystery of federal Indian law.

The Treaty Relationship

It was the custom of European powers to enter into diplomatic relationships with powerful Indian peoples who controlled large areas of the interior of the continent. Since there was intense rivalry between the colonizing powers, no nation seeking possessions in the New World dared deal with native peoples in a manner that would leave open the question of legality for another nation to exploit.[3] With the exception of Spain—which conquered the Indians of Central and South America, including Mexico—Great Britain, France, and even Russia[4] sought some kind of legal formality in their relations with the Indians.[5] Dutch settlers in New York ensured that they had a deed, properly signed by the local Indian leaders before they began land speculation, and as late as 1847 a colony of German settlers in Texas entered into a formal agreement with the Comanches.[6] Spain and later Mexico signed numerous treaties with indigenous nations occupying the Gulf coast, Texas, and the American Southwest.

Treaties gave institutional structure to the expanding field of international law, which started to emerge in the generation after the discovery of the New World. Debates among Spanish theologians inspired thinkers of other countries particularly the Dutch, to articulate principles that should govern nations in their relations with one another.[7] European history became a fertile source of data for deriving these principles, and since small nations and minor principalities had often been the subject of larger territorial and dynastic wars, it was not unusual for large and small states to have agreed upon peaceful arrangements that would govern their activities even though it was apparent to all that the larger nation could easily seize and absorb the smaller one.[8]

Once such status had been recognized for small nations, it was no problem to transfer that concept to the North American situation and make it applicable to Indian nations.[9] Consequently, formal diplomatic relations were established with the various indigenous peoples and international political status was accorded them. The difficulty, however, was one of perception. European mini-states had family relationships with the rulers of larger nations, they were contiguous to the powerful countries of Europe, and they represented long-standing historical traditions going back to the time of original settlement when the barbaric tribes had divided the Roman Empire.[10] Indians could not claim this history and since they were of a different "race," and had different religions, languages, and cultures altogether, their political rights, even when phrased in European terms, were always considered to be intellectually suspect.[11]

France adopted the Indian custom of holding councils, reaching an agreement, and holding to the agreement until conditions changed and another council was warranted. Russia, Spain, and England, with some bureaucratic perversity, insisted on written documents to mark the negotiations with the Indians. The early colonial treaties are actually transcripts of councils held and discussions undertaken to clarify the points of conflict. The United States, after following this format for the first three years of the Revolution, in 1778 adopted the formal written document as evidence of the treaty and, consequently, the vast majority of diplomatic documents recording American relations with Indians fall into a formal set of legal instruments.[12]

From 1778 to the present time, the United States has generally used a diplomatic format with carefully worded texts and has not regarded the actual discussions and presentations made during the negotiations as part of the agreement, except insofar as courts have allowed transcripts to be entered into evidence to indicate the intent of the negotiators.[13] With this obsession with legality, the three branches of government have had to devise a vocabulary with which to interpret the status of the treaties and agreements. Here the legislative and judicial branches looked to the judiciary for guidance and the lower federal courts produced two interpretations of the status of treaties that have since been adopted by the federal government (with the exception of reactionary politicians and bureaucrats who have convinced themselves that Indians have no rights whatsoever).[14]

In *Turner v. American Baptist Missionary Union* (24 Fed. Cas. No. 14251 (C.C. Mich. 1852)), a Michigan federal district court rebutted the argument that Indian treaties had a different status than did those made with larger and foreign countries:

> *It is contended that a treaty with Indian tribes has not the same dignity or effect as a treaty with a foreign and independent nation. This distinction is not authorized by the constitution.* Since the commencement of the government, treaties have been made with the Indians, and the treaty-making power has been exercised in making them. *They are treaties, within the meaning of the constitution, and as such are the supreme laws of the land* (emphasis added).[15]

Thus, whatever other arguments might be made by the people seeking to dilute Indian rights, attacking the right articulated by a treaty or agreement is not within the realm of legality. The only alternative to granting the rights and privileges spelled out in treaties is to invoke another doctrine or to use rhetorical arguments to change the meaning of words, narrowing the content of ideas to a restricted, technical legal sense. Both of these tactics have been used on occasion but the general principle holds: treaties and agreements made with the Indians are the supreme law of the land.

The other major doctrine of interpretation relating to the diplomatic documents dealing with Indians was articulated in *U.S. v. Winans* (1905) by the Supreme Court. "The treaty was not a grant of rights *to* the Indians, but *a grant of rights from them*—a reservation of those not granted (emphasis added)."[16] This doctrine means that unless a specific subject matter becomes part of the negotiations and the exercise of powers relating to it is allocated to the United States, or occasionally to a private party, as in the case of education and other social services, the subject matter *and* the power to deal with it remain with the Indians.

The treaty or agreement with the Indians thus has precisely the same effect on the relationship of Indians to the United States as does the Tenth Amendment to the Constitution, which states: "The powers not delegated to the United States by the Constitution, nor prohibited by it to the States, are reserved to the States, respectively, or to the people." There are, consequently, some very large areas in which it is believed that a political vacuum occurs, and the federal government and the states often try to rush in and lay claim, arguing that nature abhors a vacuum, and that if a political power is not being exercised it does not exist or that they have the right and responsibility to fill it.[17] But such actions are a violation of the law since the subject matter and the power to deal with it must pass from the Indians to the federal government only as a matter of negotiated agreement.

In recent decades, Congress has adopted the format of the negotiated "settlement act" as a vehicle for resolving disputes that would otherwise involve extensive and prolonged litigation on the part of Indians, states, and the federal government.[18] These "settlements," in which the contending parties bring their proposed solution to Congress for final adjustment and approval, range from ancient land claims[19] to water rights[20] and child welfare agreements.[21] Except for the formalities of giving presents and being restricted to approval by the United States Senate alone, these settlement acts have all the status and legality of the old treaties and agreements. There is no question that the government should have informed the Indians in the

Lyng case of their right to seek a legislative solution in the same manner as did the Taos Pueblo, which secured return of its sacred Blue Lake area in 1970.[22]

It is important to bear in mind that formulating a settlement for use of the sacred California "High Country" at issue in *Lyng* was a reasonable and logical alternative to the litigation that took place. But it was apparent that the emphasis on the Trust Doctrine precluded all other considerations—by the Indians, by their attorneys, and by the federal agencies involved. Since settlement was never suggested at any time during the controversy, we must turn to the Trust Doctrine itself to see if it provided protections more reliable than a negotiated settlement.

The "Trust" Doctrine

The so-called Trust Doctrine is a strange creature composed of long-standing themes prevalent during the first century of "discovery" of the "New World": the need to find some operative principle to describe the internal location of Indian nations within the area claimed by the United States and for a practical guideline for the administration of services promised to the Indians in treaties and agreements. No single source can be found for the Trust Doctrine outside of the historical and political situations in which it has been invoked as a measure of federal performance. Consequently, it stands outside the constitutional framework as a moral presence much as does the idea of freedom with respect to American citizenship.

The justification for laying claim to lands in the Western hemisphere and for entering into political relationships with inhabitants was grounded in the idea that the Pope was Christ's representative in matters spiritual and temporal, and that all institutions were justified and validated if they functioned within the broad moral framework of Christian religion. The Pope could therefore "grant" rights to lands in the Western hemisphere to Christian sovereigns with the condition that they bring the natives thereof to a full understanding and acceptance of Christianity.[23] Although the Pope's authority was rejected by Protestant countries a few decades after this pronouncement, all European nations based their colonial claims on the "pagan" status of the natives of lands they were discovering, and some effort, however sporadic and minimal, was made to provide Christian religious teachings to people they were busy subduing.[24]

A series of what were virtually world wars originating in European dynastic struggles meant a juggling of claims in North America, and it was presumed that as the losing nations ceded their colonial possessions, their rights to exclusive intercourse with the natives were also transferred.[25] The alleged "Doctrine of Discovery," as the mature form of this practice came to be known, was interpreted by European colonial powers as vesting in the discovering country the legal right to acquire title over the lands described in the process of exploration.[26] Thus an explorer, landing on a remote headland of a North American coast, might claim all acquisition rights to lands encompassed by the watershed of the river at whose mouth he stood for his sovereign. It was then up to the sovereign to provide for the settlers and for administrative officials to establish the presence of the nation in that locale. As long as the natives did not eject the colonists, the claim was supposed to be respected by other European nations during times of peace. The Spanish, for example, landed on and claimed Cape Flattery but were rudely dispelled by the Makahs, and hence their claim came to naught.[27]

Following the Treaty of Paris (8 *Stat.* 80, September 3, 1783), which closed the American Revolution, Americans believed they had inherited the discovery claims of Great Britain to that area of North America where the British had recognized their independence—the Atlantic seaboard and vaguely identified areas of the Ohio Valley, excluding the region of Canada and some of the Great Lakes shorelines. The Indians were left in a diplomatic wasteland between 1783 and 1815 because they were able to make treaties, and did with *both* the United States and Great Britain, and yet lived within the territory now claimed by the United States as its own.[28] There is no question about the international status of Indians during this period, since Spain was also making treaties with the Indian nations living in the southeastern United States.[29]

In 1823, in a strange case involving the validity of a land sale made while Great Britain was the primary sovereign west of the Mississippi, *Johnson v. McIntosh,* the Supreme Court outlined its own version of the Doctrine of Discovery, which it admitted was illogical and preposterous but, since it was maintained by force, was the operative law regarding land titles. Therefore, according to the Supreme Court, "the Indian inhabitants are to be considered as merely occupants, to be protected, indeed, while in peace, in the possession of their lands, but to be deemed incapable of transferring the absolute title to others."[30] The perceived legal incapacity to transfer land title then gave justification for the federal government to assert that it held the legal title, that the Indians possessed the equitable title, and that a kind of trust existed within the relationship.[31]

John Marshall, in writing his two *Cherokee* opinions less than a decade later, sought to transfer the concept of incomplete title to lands to the political status of Indians as well. We can see in retrospect that Marshall was placed in an untenable position from which he had to extricate himself. In 1829 and 1830, the state of Georgia passed a series of statutes purporting to give the state jurisdiction within the borders of Cherokee Nation thereby nullifying Cherokee laws and political existence. The Cherokees filed an original action in the Supreme Court seeking to secure a writ of prohibition blocking enforcement of these Georgia laws. The choice was clear: accepting the Cherokee petition and granting relief would have opened the Supreme Court to numerous future filings by a wide variety of Indian nations, some not even as large as the Euroamerican's backwoods settlements. Marshall therefore described the status of Indians and the United States as resembling that of a ward and guardian relationship, referring perhaps to the handicap he had already imposed upon Indians in reference to the passage of valid land titles.[32]

Thus, the initial approach of the Cherokees was thwarted. A year later Reverend Samuel Worcester and a group of missionaries, convicted under a Georgia statute, approached the court with the argument that they had been active within Cherokee

Nation and had followed Cherokee laws because of the U.S. treaty relationship with the Cherokees, and because their services were understood as authorized activities under a federal statute. Faced now with the question of ruling whether a federal law, passed in accordance with the Commerce Clause that gave exclusive jurisdiction to Congress, overruled or took precedence over a state statute, the Chief Justice immediately ruled in favor of the federal position.[33] Unfortunately, subsequent Supreme Courts and lower federal courts seized upon the phrases "ward" and "guardian" and elaborated on them to suggest that a rigid "trust" relationship exists between the United States and American Indian nations.

Application of this doctrine varies considerably, however, depending on the forum in which it is presented. When Indians sued the United States in the Court of Claims and Indian Claims Commission, consistent application of the Trust Doctrine would have meant the awarding of exceedingly high sums as compensation for the many land cessions made during the 19th century. Again, the difficulty was conceptual. The United States wore two hats in the claims process: it had been the trustee of the Indian nations and, at the same time, was supposed to be making some land purchases as an impartial buyer. In general, the Indian Claims Commission took the position that the government was the buyer in good faith in a series of transactions in which the Indians acted as wholly competent legal sellers.[34]

Today the Trust Doctrine has been cited as the basis for providing a wide variety of social services to Indians, and is also cited as the excuse for high-handed bureaucratic manipulations of reservation resources. Most often the doctrine is brought into play when tribal governments wish to use their lands in a manner that conflicts with policies of the Bureau of Indian Affairs (BIA). Then the excuse is that Indian governments, under the supervision of the federal government, must secure the highest cash income from their resources, rather than use them in alternative ways that might be more beneficial and productive over the long term—particularly for the Indians, themselves. "Trust" thus leads directly to the question of property law and ultimately to the conflict between legal and equitable titles to public domain lands.

The Power of Property Rights

In 1883, the Supreme Court was faced with the question of determining the nature of criminal jurisdiction over crimes committed by one Indian against another on an Indian reservation.[35] Revised Statutes, Sections 2145 and 2146, passed in 1873, gave the basic jurisdiction to the federal government but preserved jurisdiction to an Indian nation that had, through treaty negotiations, reserved such powers to itself. In 1881 Crow Dog, a Brûlé Lakota, had killed Spotted Tail, a chief of the Brûlés and a favorite of the government. Resolving the killing through traditional Lakota condolence procedures, by compensating Spotted Tail's family, Crow Dog was neither in prison nor sentenced to death. The BIA, which had been agitating for extension of federal criminal jurisdiction for over a decade, immediately secured a special congressional appropriation to take the case to the Supreme Court. Crow

Dog, indicted and convicted in the Dakota Territory federal district court, became somewhat of a national celebrity as a result.

The Supreme Court upheld the *Revised Statutes* since it was clear that this situation had been adequately examined and approved by Congress. The ensuing outcry of the newspapers upon hearing the decision, coupled with intense lobbying by the Interior Department, resulted in the passage of the "Seven Major Crimes Act" in 1885. Actually, this radical change in criminal jurisdiction was not given proper hearing by Congress. It was, instead, attached to the annual appropriation act for the Bureau of Indian Affairs as a small paragraph purporting to extend federal jurisdiction over all reservations. In fact, it was never applied to the Five Civilized Tribes in Oklahoma or to smaller, scattered groups in other parts of the country. But, was the act constitutional in view of the previous reluctance of Congress to take such a step,[36] and in view of the treaty relationship that already defined the matter of jurisdiction quite adequately, particularly with respect to the Lakota poeple of the Great Plains ?[37]

The answer was not long in coming. Then pending from the California district court was an appeal dealing with a murder conviction of two Indians on the Hoopa Reservation. The district court had certified six questions to the Supreme Court, the third and sixth of which referred specifically to the recently passed statute. The decision in *United States v. Kagama* (1886) is so illogical that it should be reproduced, at least in part:

> The mention of Indians in the Constitution which has received the most attention is that found in the clause which gives Congress "power to regulate commerce with foreign nations and among the several States, and with the Indian tribes." This clause is relied on in the argument in the present case, the proposition being that the statute under consideration is a regulation of commerce with the Indian tribes. But we think it would be a very strained construction of this clause, that a system of criminal laws for Indians living peaceably in their reservations, which left out the entire code of trade and intercourse laws justly enacted under that provision, and established punishments for the common-law crimes of murder, manslaughter, arson, burglary, larceny, and the like, without any reference to their relation to any kind of commerce, was authorized by the grant of power to regulate commerce with the Indian tribes. While we are not able to see, in either of these clauses [the taxation clause being the other clause cited in the argument] of the Constitution and its amendments, any delegation of power to enact a code of criminal law for the punishment of the worst class of crimes known to civilized life when committed by Indians...[38]

Departing from all previous case law, the high court rejected the tax and representation clause of the First Article and Fourteenth Amendment, as well as the Commerce Clause, which had previously been the major constitutional moorings enabling Congress to deal with Indians. Instead Justice Miller, writing the unanimous opinion, went back to geography, noting that "Indians are within the geographical limits of the United States. The soil and the people within these limits are under the political control of the Government of the United States, or of the States of the Union."[39] Moreover, Miller then argued that:

[T]his power of Congress to organize territorial governments, and make laws for their inhabitants, arises not so much from the clause in the Constitution, in regard to disposing of and making rules and regulations concerning the Territory and other property of the United States, as from the ownership of the country in which the Territories are, and the right of exclusive sovereignty which must exist in the National Government and can be found nowhere else.[40]

In support of this novel reasoning, which suggested that a federal statute could be constitutional by appealing to a power or attribute outside the Constitution, Justice Miller cited Chief Justice Marshall's opinion in *American Insurance Co. v. Canter* (1 Pet. 511 (1827)). This dealt with the territorial status of the people of Florida after it had been acquired by the United States: "Perhaps the power of governing a Territory belonging to the United States, which has not by becoming a State, acquired the means of self-government, may result necessarily from the fact that it is not within the jurisdiction of any particular State. The right to govern may be the inevitable consequence of the right to acquire Territory. Whichever may be the source whence the power is derived, the possession of it is unquestioned."[41]

Miller, like many of his successors, was irretrievably lost in the complexities of American history. Florida was acquired from Spain in 1819 by purchase and treaty, and the United States then acquired *political jurisdiction* over the territory. It was not acting in the capacity of a private landowner. Thus the property rights argument, when applied to the United States in any of its constitutional capacities, does not bring with it political powers that originate outside the Constitution in the *fact* of landownership, and which are not subject to limitations imposed by the Constitution. To argue otherwise would vest the federal government in a set of ultra-constitutional powers of unlimited scope. Additionally, the United States holds its lands, the public domain, on behalf of its citizens, and this ownership is not held against the citizens as if the United States were a competing private landholder.

The *Lyng* Case

The *Lyng* case is typical of much contemporary litigation over the use of federal lands. The Forest Service, which managed the Six Rivers National Forest, primarily for the benefit of the timber industry, proposed to build a six-mile paved road—known as the "G-O Road"—that would link two existing roads leading respectively to Gasquet and Orleans, California. The proposed road would run through the Chimney Rock section of the forest and would severely disrupt the solitude of a remote area known to the Yurok, Karok, and Tolowa Indians as the "High Country," a place used for untold hundreds of years for Vision Quests, gathering of medicine roots, and other ceremonial purposes. Prior to the controversy generated by the Forest Service proposal, the religious leaders of these Indian groups had conducted their religious ceremonies without disturbance or interruption.

A number of non-Indian conservation and environmental groups were also interested in this area and wanted it kept as a wilderness. Consequently, when the case was filed in the Northern District federal court in California, an impressive number of plaintiffs joined suit. In addition to an Indian coalition called the Northwest Indian Cemetery Protective Association, the Sierra Club, the Wilderness Society, California Trout, Siskiyou Mountain Resource Council, Redwood Audubon Society, Northcoast Environmental Society, and State of California acting through and by the Native American Heritage Commission and State Resources Agency all became plaintiffs. It is very difficult to determine, without being privy to pre-litigation conferences among the respective plaintiffs, whether the Indians initiated the suit or were drawn into it by other groups. The question is interesting in this respect: if the Indians initiated the suit, their theory of the spiritual value of the lands should have been the primary argument; if not, the secular perspective of the other plaintiffs may have determined the arguments that were used. Thus, the religious question might or might not have been foremost in the minds of the attorneys who directed the litigation.

At any rate, the complaint against the Forest Service should have made its director blush and withdraw the proposal immediately. The agency was accused of violating the First Amendment (Indian religious freedom exercise), the American Indian Religious Freedom Act, the National Environmental Policy Act, the National Historic Preservation Act, the Federal Water Quality Control Act, the Porter-Cologne Water Quality Control Act (a California state statute), Hoopa Indian Water and Fishing Rights (allegedly protected under the self-proclaimed "trust responsibility" of the federal government), the Wilderness Act, the Administrative Procedure Act, the National Forest Management Act of 1976, and the Multiple Use, Sustained Yield Act. This impressive list of federal and state statutes is in some ways more indicative of the inability of the United States Congress to adopt an intelligent comprehensive plan for management of public resources than it is an indictment of Forest Service practices. One could, however, argue that this endless list of efforts actually footnotes the indifference found in federal agencies fulfilling their responsibilities.

Now we enter the twilight world of administrative procedures and entrenched attitudes. The Forest Service had authorized a study of the impact of the proposed road on Indian religious beliefs and practices and had made an effort to devise an alternative route that would have minimized the impact both visually and audibly. Ten different routes were considered, including the possibility of not building the road at all. The Forest Service had also prepared two reports for the Advisory Council on Historic Preservation and had held a meeting at its request. In arguments before the courts, it was pointed out that aside from not building the road, none of the plaintiffs had suggested a route that had been neglected or overlooked by its study. Yet, the Forest Service frankly admitted that it had something of a trust responsibility to the Indians.

Prior to the trial, the district court denied the motion for a preliminary injunction with the understanding that the road would not be started until a full hearing could be held on the merits of the argument.[42] The trial then commenced, and during the course of the presentations the religious arguments began to have some weight. A document entitled the *Theodoratus Report*, which dealt with Indian religious practices, had outlined a comprehensive understanding of what the Indians did ceremonially and also pointed out that the ultimate plan was to build 200 miles of logging roads in the vicinity of the sacred area, close to their three most important mountains: Chimney Rock, Doctor Rock, and Peak #8.[43]

There was no question that the proposed road and ultimate management plan would destroy the area for religious and recreational purposes, dump an unknown quantity of dirt and gravel into streams (thereby destroying local salmon spawning beds) and serve little useful purpose by simply eliminating this part of an old forest. Under then-prevailing case law, the Forest Service was required to demonstrate a "compelling interest" to the federal government, at least sufficiently important to justify substantially burdening the practice of religion. But the court could find only miniscule bureaucratic justifications for the proposed road. It is useful to recount the Forest Service's understanding of what constitutes a compelling interest because it illustrates the difficulties involved in applying constitutional tests to the actions of federal agencies. The justifications were:

- The road would increase the quantity of timber accessible for harvest.
- It would stimulate employment in the regional timber industry.
- It would provide recreational access to the Blue Creek unit.
- It would allow for further efficient administration of Six Rivers National Forest.
- It would increase the price of the bids on future timber sales by decreasing the cost of hauling timber to the mills.
- It would increase timber production, thereby stimulating the timber industry.[44]

It does not take a genius to survey this list and realize that it is a set of excuses rather than compelling interests. The values of Forest Service personnel who rank possible increases in future timber bids and ease of administration against Indian rights, and the welfare of the forest itself, tend to speak for themselves. The courts, once they are allowed into the process, can do little but credit this reasoning and the commercial values represented by the Forest Service and its clients with a higher purpose.

The three possible theories of Indian relationship to the federal government—treaty, trust, and property—now come into focus. In order to use the treaty relationship, it would have been necessary for the Indians to approach Congress when the Forest Service first began its survey and seek special congressional action to set aside that part of the Six Rivers National Forest for their use. The Taos Pueblo effort at Blue Lake could have been cited as a precedent, and even if no legislation had been passed immediately, raising the issue of the preservation of sacred sites while the *Theodoratus Report* was being written would have radically changed the emphasis in that document, giving the Indians considerably more leverage in articulating their point of view.

The Forest Service admitted the existence of a trust relationship in its first court appearance, but the nature of this trust was not adequately explained by either the Indians or the Forest Service during the actual trial. The decision in 1983 favored the Indians. Yet, as we shall see when we discuss the appeals, this issue quickly fell by the wayside. What is important to note at this point, however, is that "trust" exists as a viable factor only at the very highest level of the administrative pyramid, that is, at the secretarial and presidential level, as part of the "climate" of responsibility. When trust appears at the lowest administrative level, it becomes merely one factor of many to be considered. And since the efficient and generally acceptable way of doing business is the real context within which administrative decisions are made, the trust responsibility is far too abstract a notion to have impact on the decisions made by forest managers.

Congress has had to confront this propensity of bureaucrats to sidestep policy considerations and the plenitude of other federal acts, which the Forest Service had been accused of violating, requiring that various steps be taken so that the intangible factors of forest preservation, historic preservation, clean water, and other goals be considered in the management of the national forests. However, these requirements are generally viewed by bureaucrats as mere stumbling blocks, hurdles to be surmounted in their quest for managerial control over lands and trees they consider to be their own property. Under existing federal law, while the Forest Service is required to file environmental impact statements and deal with the question of historic preservation, its personnel are really the directors of all administrative procedures. They, consequently, are in a position to determine the content and ultimate conclusions of all these reports and formal statements. Once a federal agency has decided on a course of action, litigation is a farce because the important issues that might have weighed heavily in the minds of judges and justices have already been neatly packaged in language that the federal agency has created.

At trial, however, the Forest Service did not do so well. It conceded the road construction would not materially improve access to timber resources.[45] It became abundantly clear that the road would not increase the number of jobs in the timber industry.[46] Increased recreational use of the area meant increased environmental degradation.[47] The road would increase sediment in Blue Creek, thus reducing the salmon spawning grounds and violating the trust responsibility for Indians downstream at the Hoopa Reservation.[48] It also became apparent that the Forest Service actions since 1960 had created a situation in which the construction of the road seemed inevitable—the "administrative symmetry" argument.[49] The six factors cited by the Forest Service as constituting the "compelling" federal interest devolved down to the simple proposition that the agency wanted to build the road. Period.

The federal district court therefore issued a permanent injunction against the building of the road and prohibited the Forest Service from engaging in any actions that would allow commercial timber harvesting in the High Country until a supplemental Environmental Impact Statement (EIS) could be made and circulated for public comment. Indians and environmental groups breathed easier with this ruling but the real meaning of it was again only too clear. The Forest Service had not done an adequate job of burying the arguments raised by the other side and, therefore, needed to go back and put some more nails in the coffin. Thus, as 1983 closed, the larger issues of an ancient forest, the religious freedom of three groups of American Indians, the national historic heritage, and concern for the environment were now prisoners of a process of technical readjustment to an environmental impact statement *that was to be written by the Forest Service.*

The case went to the Ninth Circuit Court of Appeals in July 1984, and was decided in June 1985. The Forest Service had raised three issues the court felt bound to address:

- Whether the district court erred in enjoining road construction and timbering in the High Country of the Blue Creek unit on the ground that such activity would impermissibly burden the Indian plaintiffs' first amendment right to free exercise of their religion;
- Whether the district court erred in holding that the EISs prepared for the road and the land management plans failed adequately to discuss the effects on water quality of the proposed actions;
- Whether the district court erred in holding that the Forest Service's proposed actions would violate the Federal Water Pollution Control Act and state water quality standard.[50]

Two of these issues, dealing with the technical aspects of water, were obviously close calls since predictions concerning the improvement or degradation of water constitute an inexact science subject to alteration as political and other considerations warrant. Thus, the real question on appeal was the religious freedom issue. And the key to this issue was whether the proposed actions would "impermissibly burden" the Indian's free exercise of religion. The Forest Service clearly did not prevail when it attacked the religious rights of the three Indian groups. Its basic argument was that the government's action *had* to penalize a religious belief or practice. The nuance here is that the action had aspects of deliberate intent which could be better satisfied with some other procedure. Here the Indians were rescued by the holding in the *Sherbert* case in which the Supreme Court ruled that an injury might be described as indirect, that is, without a clear intent to commit injury but having the effect of an injury.[51]

The discussion of the Establishment Clause was more enlightening. The Forest Service argued that managing the forest so that it would not intrude on the practice of Indian religion would be tantamount to establishing a religious shrine. While the appeals court also rejected that argument, pointing out to the Forest Service that it had far overstepped its own logical conclusions, the response noted that only one of the proposed uses of this part of the national forest—commercial harvesting of timber—was rejected. Other purposes, including outdoor recreation, range, watershed, wildlife, fish habitat, and wilderness uses were all upheld.[52] Presumably the establishment of a religious preserve for a single group, which is how the Forest Service described the religious argument, would exclude all of these other uses entirely.

The Forest Service logic really ended abruptly at this juncture, and it is useful to note that the other multiple uses—recreation, various habitats, and wilderness—actually had no more standing or value in that agency's perspective than did the Indian religious use. While the agency was bound to consider all of these other uses, and the multitude of federal laws cited by the plaintiffs in their initial appearance in court testified to the intent of Congress with respect to public lands, the fact is that federal lands are managed for the benefit of private commercial parties. The average citizen, informed that one of many uses he or she wanted to see on a tract of land was prohibited, might be content to exclude that use and get on with enjoyment and care of the land. Not so the Forest Service, since the agency's actions following this decision—*not* existing laws or congressional intent—define its real sense of purpose and mission.

Dealing with the violation of environmental laws at the circuit level was merely a matter of reviewing the procedures used by the Forest Service. Tiptoeing carefully among the various findings of the district court regarding the Basic Management Plan and the Environmental Impact Statement, the circuit court vacated the portion of the injunction that precluded timber harvesting or construction and upheld the rest of the decree.[53] The decision pleased no one and the case was given a rehearing in July 1986. At issue were the religious freedom arguments of the Indians, the portions of the EIS that had been found inadequate, and whether or not the National Environmental Policy Act and Wilderness Act required the Forest Service to evaluate the impact of the road on the wilderness potential of the region.[54]

If the logic of the case seemed to be established—pitting the congressional intent of protecting Indian religious freedom and ensuring that wilderness areas receive special consideration in the management of federal lands against the mission and administrative practices of the Forest Service in spite of its clear preference for commercial timber harvesting over the many other more benign uses of the area—it would have required a sophisticated judge or justice to decide the case. Coincident with this prolonged litigation, however, was an unexpected development that surely had the potential to moot the question of road construction. In 1984, Congress had passed the California Wilderness Act (98 *Stat.* 1619), which placed in a wilderness status about 19,000 acres of the Eightmile Creek area and 26,000 acres of the Blue Creek area—areas closely adjacent to sacred sites important to the Indians. But with a perversity known only in a government too large to be coordinated, this act had preserved the corridor in which the proposed road was to be located until other decisions were made regarding construction.

Thus, external events had created a novel situation. Obviously wilderness had become a primary value for both Congress and the state of California. According to popular definitions of wilderness, its primary value is as an area in its pristine natural state, because this represents some intangible and difficult-to-define spiritual aspect of nature that has a superior value to commercial use of the area. In a sense, we have a generalized secular use, albeit one that represents a recognition of intangible values no matter how shallow they might be emotionally, now holding a greater value than a specific religious use of the same region. The question here is whether the Indian argument is to be considered inferior to the wilderness argument because of a racial distinction.

Unfortunately, at the circuit court level and later with the Supreme Court, the close parallel in motive and perspective was neither recognized nor understood. This neglect should be a warning to Indians and non-Indians alike that the popular belief prevailing that non-Indians can somehow absorb the philosophical worldview of American Indians and inculcate "reverence" for the land into their intellectual and emotional perspectives is blatantly false. Inherent in the very definition of "wilderness" is contained the gulf between the understandings of the two cultures. Indians do not see the natural world as a wilderness. In contrast, Europeans and Euroamericans see a big difference between lands they have "settled" and lands they have left alone. As long as this difference is believed to be real by non-Indians, it is impossible to close the perceptual gap, and the substance of the two views will remain in conflict.

The rehearing of the case was basically a rehash of the previous hearing except that Judge Canby dealt a bit more thoroughly with the establishment question. But his language was not clear, as evidenced by his treatment of the articulation of the government's "paramount interests" in building the road:

> There was testimony that completion of the road and logging in the high country would increase employment in Del Norte County, but that this benefit would simply represent a shift of work from elsewhere in the state. Thus, there would be no statewide net gain in employment. There was evidence that forest management functions would be made easier by the road. There was evidence that the road would also provide greater recreational access to the area, but the projected use was not large.[55]

This was a fine analysis, but what was the real bottom line to be drawn? Canby needed to conclude that nothing was to be gained by this road, that its impact would simply be to rearrange pre-existing activities in a minor fashion so that even predictions of benefits were suspect. Consequently, the real issue was whether or not the Forest Service could act apart from the rest of the federal government. The Forest Service obviously has no argument to be considered if Canby's decision spells out what is actually at issue in this case.

Mild as Canby's opinion was, it drew a dissent from Judge Beezer, who otherwise agreed with his conclusions regarding the environmental issues. Yet, he felt that the Indians had not established a first amendment violation satisfactorily. Culling his objections from recently published law review articles that called into question some of the Indian arguments, Beezer concentrated on the *Theodoratus Report* and sought to distinguish between the actual presence of the road and the audible and visual side-effects that the road would create. This method of attack was reminiscent of the logic of the last century in which federal courts divided commerce into its constituent parts, arguing that there was no violation of the Commerce Clause by shipment of goods across country because the goods were always in one state or another, and hence subject to state regulation wherever they were located.

Beezer would have allowed construction of the road, assuming that no important archaeological sites were disturbed, and then encouraged the Indians to seek an injunction against the logging if it placed a burden on their religious practices. But then Beezer argued that logging activities were irrelevant to the analysis anyway because the issue was the construction of the road.[56] How the road, whose sole purpose for existence was commercial logging, could have been separated from logging for purposes of analysis and then put back together for purposes of administration without becoming a ludicrous exercise in abstract logic was never explained by the judge.

About all the rehearing had produced was a dissenting judge, a further fragmentation of substantial arguments into smaller subsets of complaints, and the identification of the religious issue as one to be decided by the Supreme Court if it wished to take the case. Judge Beezer had clearly identified the issue under consideration with respect to the federal-Indian relationship. If this decision was upheld, it would mark the first time since the passage of the American Indian Religious Freedom Resolution that Indian religious freedom could be used to enjoin development of the public lands.[57] The Indians and the environmental groups were unable to get the Ninth Circuit Court to look at the California Wilderness Act as an intervening statement by Congress that the whole area was to be treated as a wilderness, regardless of the Indian religious freedom issue. All previous efforts to put teeth into the Religious Freedom Resolution had failed because the question was that of the protection of spiritual activities as weighed against the investment made by federal agencies. In this case alone was there intervening evidence that Congress had a broader policy concern that mooted the question of building the road.

Here the specificity of the California Wilderness Act gave the case a bizarre twist. The section of land through which the road was to be built was preserved from wilderness until the pending case was resolved. Consequently, Congress was sending a mixed message: there *would be* a wilderness designation but there *could be* a road. The most obvious interpretation of the situation was that Congress did not want to deal with the politics of the road and hoped that things would be resolved locally without any further direction or involvement at the Washington level. Since the federal government is often perceived as a monolithic creature with a central, coordinated purpose, the confusion left by the vagueness of the California Wilderness Act meant that the property argument, which could be construed as ultra-constitutional, would become a powerful presence in the subsequent Supreme Court examination of the case.

Enter the Reagan Court

The Forest Service appealed the Ninth Circuit Court ruling and the case, now known formally, with replacement of Max Petersen with Lyng as head of the Forest Service, as *Lyng v. Northwest Indian Cemetery Protective Association* (108 S.

Ct. 1319 (1988)), was handed down in 1988. The high court had granted *certiorari* on the basis that the lower courts had not clearly explained whether they had determined a decision based on the First Amendment was necessary because this might have given the Indians relief beyond what they could have expected from the statutory claims they had made.[58] Such reasoning seemed to place minor statutory relief above the freedoms granted by the Bill of Rights and, therefore, gave prophetic forecast to how the majority would view and resolve the issue.

Justice Sandra Day O'Connor, writing the majority opinion, put the construction of the road in perspective; it was the final link of a seventy-five-mile paved road that had been gradually completed over the years by the Forest Service. Leaving the road unfinished would then have left two segments coming to a dead end in what was now a designated federal wilderness area with timber harvesting prohibited in much of the area. The majority of the Ninth Circuit Court had upheld the religious freedom claims, but the fact that there was a dissenting judge encouraged O'Connor to use that dissent to imply a degree of slippage the Supreme Court could not overlook: "These differences in wording suggest, without absolutely implying, that an injunction covering the Chimney Rock area would in some way have been conditional, or narrower in scope, if the district court had not decided the First Amendment as it did."[59] But what would have made the injunction "narrower in scope" apart from the First Amendment? Every other factor was environmental in nature and involved possible degradation of the area. So, O'Connor identified a nonexistent danger and promptly sought to deal with it.

The majority opinion then went down the line of traditional reasoning that government activities could not be disrupted by the religious claims of citizens because of the great variety of possible religious beliefs and activities inherent in American society. The basic "threat" perceived by the high court was that of a "sudden revelation" of sacredness to individuals, as well as the equally necessary task of recognizing and accommodating beliefs. O'Connor seized on the most remote possibility, a revelation at the Lincoln Memorial to one individual, and pretended that this was comparable to the continuing religious practices of three groups of Indians which extended back perhaps thousands of years. Her basic logical structure appeared to be: "Socrates is a man. Socrates is insane. All men are therefore insane." Such thinking is applicable perhaps to the netherworld inhabited by the current Supreme Court justices, but is hardly relevant to the issue at hand.

The thrust of O'Connor's opinion was aimed directly at the previous holding in *Sherbert v. Verner*, the indirect but easily identifiable burden on religion. "Whatever may be the exact line between unconstitutional prohibitions on the free exercise of religion and the legitimate conduct by the government of its own affairs," O'Connor argued, "the location of the line cannot depend on measuring the effects of a governmental action on a religious objector's spiritual development."[60] The measuring test, however, was precisely the line that *had* to be drawn, and when O'Connor admitted that "the government does not dispute, and we have no reason to doubt, that the logging and road-building projects at issue in this case could have devastating effects on traditional Indian religious practices," the issue should have been resolved.[61] As Justice Brennan put it in a dissent in which he was joined by Justices Marshall and Blackmun:

> The Court does not for one minute suggest that the interests served by the G-O Road are in any way compelling, or that they outweigh the destructive effect construction of the road will have on [the Indians'] religious practices. Instead, the Court embraces the Government's contention that its prerogative as land-owner should always take precedence over a claim that a particular use of federal property infringes religious practices. Attempting to justify this rule, the Court argues that the First Amendment bars only outright prohibitions, indirect coercion and penalties on the free exercise of religion. All other "incidental effects of government programs," it concludes, even those "which may make it difficult to practice certain religions but which have no tendency to coerce individuals into acting contrary to their religious beliefs," simply do not give rise to constitutional concerns. [Ever since] our recognition nearly half a century ago that restraints on religious conduct implicate the concerns of the Free Exercise Clause, [this Court has] never suggested that the protections of the guarantee are limited to so narrow a scope.[62]

At this point in discussing the opinion, it is important to note that O'Connor was using what is called the "old fact situation" to justify her reasoning, since the California Wilderness Act had rendered moot the question of whether or not there would be logging in the area: there would not be. With commercial logging virtually eliminated as a justification for building the road, the issue then became simply a question of whether the Forest Service had to give Indian religious freedom its due. O'Connor decided negatively on this point, arguing that the federal government as a landowner had certain rights that could not be infringed upon by either its wards or its citizens.[63]

In this, O'Connor finally committed the high court to a formal position on a question it had studiously avoided addressing through a whole series of cases involving Indian spiritual rights to land during the past half-century. Examples include the submersion of traditional Cherokee burial grounds in the Tennessee Valley behind the Tellico Dam,[64] flooding of much of the Allegheny Seneca Reservation in Pennsylvania behind the Kinzua Dam,[65] flooding of Lakota burial sites on the Standing Rock Reservation as part of the Missouri River Project,[66] submersion of the Rainbow Bridge formation, sacred to both the Navajo and the Hopi, behind the Glen Canyon Dam in southern Utah,[67] and destruction of Hopi and Navajo sacred sites on the San Francisco Peaks (near Flagstaff, Arizona) during construction of a ski resort.[68] Further, the Supreme Court's ruling in *Lyng* destroyed the basis for several promising religious freedom cases brought by Indians during the 1980s in the effort to protect or regain use of sacred lands. Notable in this regard were Lakota efforts to ensure unrestricted access to and spiritual use of the Black Hills,[69] and litigation designed to prevent wholesale strip mining of sacred areas within the former Navajo-Hopi Joint Use Area in northeastern Arizona.[70] At this point, such endeavors in attaining due process through U.S. courts appear to have been gutted by the "G-O Road Decision."

Stripped of peripheral issues, the matter before the high court was to weigh the government's trust responsibility toward Indians against its right to manage its own affairs. Undeniably, part of those affairs, a very important part, was execution of the trust responsibility itself. Hence, the question *should* have been academic. But the context in which trust responsibility was conceived to be important was back at the local level with the *Theodoratus Report*. When the Forest Service decided to proceed in spite of the religious question, then the integrity—and independence—of federal agency decision-making powers became the issue and the Supreme Court felt impelled to protect them.[71] To quote Brennan:

> "[T]he Free Exercise Clause," the Court explains today, "is written in terms of what the government cannot do to the [group or] individual, not in terms of what the individual [or group] can exact from the government." [Claiming] fidelity to the unremarkable constitutional principle, the Court concludes that even where the government uses federal land in a manner which threatens the very existence of a Native American religion, the government is simply not "doing" anything to the practitioners of that faith. Instead, the Court believes that Native Americans who request that the government refrain from destroying their religion effectively seek to exact from the government de facto beneficial ownership of federal property. These two astonishing conclusions follow naturally from the Court's determination that federal land-use decisions that render the practice of a given religion impossible do not burden that religion in a manner cognizable under the Free Exercise Clause.[72]

Once the idea of trust responsibility was negated, and this neutralization could only occur by conceiving of the Indians as a private party petitioning the government, rather than as a people to whom a trust responsibility is owed, it became necessary to attack the practice of religion itself. Consequently, O'Connor had to destroy the religious issue in order to deny the Indians. The minority opinion dwelled a bit on Indians and then defended previous doctrine on religious freedom. The dissenting justices objected to the twist that O'Connor had given to constitutional law. "The court's coercion test turns on a distinction between governmental actions that compel affirmative conduct inconsistent with religious belief and those governmental actions that prevent conduct consistent with religious belief," Brennan argued.[73] The distinction is important. With this new test the federal government, state, or municipality can deliberately oppress a minority religion as long as it is not apparent in the legislative record that there was an overt attempt to do so. *Lyng* thus leads directly to *Smith* and the variety of cases following *Smith* that place the religious body, of whatever persuasion, under the auspices of the state.

Felix S. Cohen once remarked that Indians serve as a sort of miner's canary on the American domestic scene. The idea is that oppression of indigenous peoples indicates at an early stage the general tightening of the administration of justice to exclude and restrict the rights of all citizens.[74] The basis for this statement is the nature of the trust responsibility. Trust requires that the United States act with the highest moral standards in its treatment of a small group of people who have placed themselves or have been placed under its protection. If a special and specific responsibility cannot be discerned and met, there is not much hope that broader and more universal responsibilities are going to be upheld. The minority opinion adequately described the meaning of the *Lyng* decision in its closing remarks: "[T]oday's ruling sacrifices a religion at least as old as the Nation itself, along with the spiritual well-being of its approximately 5,000 adherents, so that the Forest Service can build a 6-mile segment of road that two lower courts had found had only the most marginal and speculative utility, both to the Government itself and to the private lumber interests that might conceivably use it."[75]

Trouble in High Places

The tremendous irony of *Lyng* is that the road construction was later abandoned, as it should have been, so that the case need never have been heard in its own right. In upholding the principle that no citizen or group of citizens—or "wards," if that is what the Indians are—can tell a federal agency through court injunction how it is supposed to manage public lands, the Supreme Court has openly elevated the federal government to a dictatorial position over its citizens, legitimizing it as an entity with oppressive powers instead of a government of, by, and for the people. Three major questions arise from this litigation: 1) What is the nature of the trust responsibility of the federal government toward American Indians and what primacy does it have in the pyramid of federal values and decision making? 2) What is the nature of the relationship between the practice of religion and the administration of government? 3) What is the real nature of government in the United States today? The first question involves Indians primarily and non-Indians only secondarily, but the second and third questions are pivotal inquiries that must be resolved if American citizens are to maintain (or recover) their individual and collective freedoms.[76]

For American Indians, the message is especially clear. With the shunting aside of the trust responsibility in the *Lyng* case and the propensity of federal courts to interject the property doctrine when it is most convenient as a defense for the actions of government agencies, the most fruitful course of dealing with the U.S. government now seems to be in negotiated settlements. In other words, what is required is a modernization of the old diplomatic treaty relationship between Washington and the various Indian nations. *Lyng* may have been a necessary step in replacing the Trust Doctrine with the treaty settlement process, thus reversing a century-long trend of making the treaty right a function of the willingness of the federal entity to fulfill its promises. To the extent that this materializes over the next few years, and there is some indication that it will, *Lyng* may ultimately be remembered as an positive legal landmark by Indian people, regardless of the Supreme Court's intent in rendering its decision in the case.[77]

However, the high court's property argument is far greater than its application to Indians. Charged with multiple-use responsibilities for the Six Rivers National Forest, the Forest Service promptly opted for its traditional client, the timber industry, thus making public lands a reserved resource for private exploiters. Conservation and ecological groups, concerned about federal land management must now articulate their interests in a much more aggressive manner than has previously been the case. They must confront the emotional reality of federal agency existence, which is that government bureaucrats and employees deeply believe that the property they are charged with managing belongs to them *personally,* and that any effort by the public to participate in management is a personal affront. The more than 35 percent of the United States that is comprised of public lands belongs, in theory at least, to the public as a whole, not to federal employees and their favored clientele.[78] Until we can force a clear statement regarding limitations on the rights and powers that property ownership bestows on the federal government, we will *all* have the sword of Damocles hanging over our heads.

Notes

1. The opinion is reprinted in full in Clinton, Robert N., Nell Jessup Newton, and Monroe E. Price, eds., *American Indian Law: Cases and Materials,* The Michie Co. Law Publishers, Charlottesville, VA, 1991, pp. 46-65; quote from p. 55.
2. As concerns Indian peyote use specifically, *Smith* reversed the precedent that this was a protected activity established in *People v. Woody* (61 Cal. 2d 716, 394 P.2d 813, 40 Cal. Rptr. 69 (1964)).
3. See Lindley, Mark Frank, *The Acquisition and Government of Backward Territory in International Law,* Longmans Green Publishers, London, 1926.
4. An interesting reading in this connection is Belch, Stanislaus F., *Paulus Vladimiri and His Doctrine Concerning International Law and Politics,* Mouton Publishers, The Hague, 1965.
5. Several examples may be found in Davenport, Francis Gardener, ed., *European Treaties Bearing on the History of the United States and Its Dependencies,* Vols. I and II, Carnegie Institution of Washington, Washington, D.C., 1917.
6. See Neighbors, Kenneth, "The German-Comanche Treaty of 1847," *Southwestern Historical Quarterly,* No. 52, July 1948, pp. 32-48.
7. See generally, Williams, Robert A., *The American Indian in Western Legal Thought: The Discourses of Conquest,* Oxford University Press, London/New York, 1990 for background information. Also see Washburn, Wilcomb E., *Red Man's Land, White Man's Law,* Charles Scribner's Sons Publishers, New York, 1971 (esp. first two chapters).
8. See von Gierke, Otto Friedrich, *Natural Law and the Theory of Society, 1500-1800,* Cambridge University Press, Cambridge, MA, 1934 and *The Development of Political Theory,* W.W. Norton Publishers, New York, 1939.
9. See, for example, Canny, Nicholas P., "The Ideology of English Colonization: From Ireland to America," *William and Mary Quarterly,* No. 30, October 1973, pp. 575-98.
10. This is well covered in the introductory chapters of Bullough, Donald A., *The Age of Charlemagne,* Elek Books, London, 1965. Also see Hay, Denys, *Europe: The Emergence of an Idea,* University of Edinburgh Press, Edinburgh, 1968.
11. Although there are numerous examples of smaller states aligning themselves with larger states in the European example, the geographical setting of the New World plus the cultural differences made it impossible for Europeans to attribute political status of any substance to Indians. Justice Johnson in the first *Cherokee* case tried to establish an incipient or expectant status for the Cherokees akin to the Israelites wandering in the wilderness (i.e., a people *about* to achieve national and international status—but not yet).
12. The most instructive example of the use of treaty negotiations to indicate intent of the principals was in the *United States v. Washington* (384 F. Supp. 312 (W.D. Wash. 1974)) fishing rights case when anthropologist Barbara Lane gave extensive testimony on what fishing meant to the Northwest Indians and the role as commercial supplier of fish to the settlers that Isaac Stevens intended to play. Otherwise, the tendency of the courts has been to accuse Indians of having such a vested interest in the outcome of a case that they would lie to affect the course of a trial, an accusation that has never remotely been proven.
13. One need only compare the Treaty of Pittsburg (September and October 1775) between the U.S.

and the Iroquois Six Nations, Delawares, and Shawnees with the 1778 Delaware Treaty. The 1775 treaty consists of more than 100 pages of dialogue, primarily discussions concerning each point in contention. The 1778 treaty is several pages long and has sterile articles written in legal language that clearly outline benefits and responsibilities. The 1775 treaty can be found in Downes, Randolph C., *Council Fires on the Upper Ohio*, University of Pittsburg Press, Pittsburg, 1940, pp. 25-127. The text of the 1778 treaty appears as the first entry in Kappler, Charles J., *Indian Treaties, 1778-1883*, Interland Publishers, New York, 1973.

14. Good readings in this regard may be found in Cohen, Felix S., *The Legal Conscience: Selected Papers*, Yale University Press, New Haven, CT, 1960.

15. *Turner v. American Baptist Missionary Union*, at 346.

16. *United States v. Winans*, at 380-1.

17. This sequence of reasoning is what is really at stake in cases involving exercise of Indian self-governing rights although it is technically classified as an "infringement test" in *Williams v. Lee*, 358 U.S. 217 (1959).

18. This act first became an acceptable way of resolving Indian claims with the Alaska Native Claims Settlement Act in 1970. It was understood as a means of avoiding prolonged and complicated litigation. Thereafter, when confronted with complex claims and rights and the prospect of decades of litigation, both Indians and the federal and state governments decided to work out compromises and have them approved by Congress. The prospect of settlement is now an increasingly popular way of handling disputes that covers subjects of major importance as well as small annoyances.

19. See Rhode Island Indian Claims Settlement Act of 1978, P.L. 95-395, 92 *Stat.* 813.

20. See Southern Arizona Water Rights Settlement Act of 1982, P.L. 97-243, 96 *Stat.* 1274.

21. As of 1991, more than twenty indigenous nations have signed agreements under provision of the Indian Child Welfare Act of 1978.

22. Act of December 15, 1970, P.L. 91-550, 84 *Stat.* 1437. For context, see Gordon-McCutchan, R.C., *The Taos Indians and the Battle for Blue Lake*, Red Crane Books, Sante Fe, NM, 1991.

23. For discussion of these ideas, see Hanke, Lewis, *The Spanish Struggle for Justice in the Conquest of America*, University of Pennsylvania Press, Philadelphia, 1949.

24. See Quinn, David Beers, *England and the Discovery of America, 1481-1620*, Alfred A. Knopf Publishers, New York, 1974.

25. France, through a clever scheme, ceded Louisiana to Spain at some point before it signed the peace treaty with Great Britain closing the last of the "French and Indian Wars" (1756-1763). Later, Spain ceded Louisiana back to France and, in 1803, Napoleon sold it to the United States. But what the U.S. actually received in this purchase was the exclusive right to buy land within the boundaries of the Louisiana territory from the various Indian nations which owned it. Thus, many treaties after 1803 dealing with the Transmississippi West are purchase treaties wherein Indians sell some portion of their lands to the U.S. See Alvord, Clarence Walworth, *The Mississippi Valley in British Politics: A Study of the Trade, Land Speculation and Experiments in Imperialism Culminating in the American Revolution* (2 Vols.), Russell and Russell Publishers, New York, 1959.

26. Marshall used a variant of this treaty to void a land sale made by Indians at a public transaction conducted by the British a year before the American Revolution broke out. His application, in *Johnson v. McIntosh*, was to claim that the United States had good legal title in spite of British-Indian activity. Perhaps more strange, British-Indian land transactions in the Great Lakes region were almost always held to be valid even though some of them took place *after* the 1783 Treaty of Paris by which England admitted defeat at the hands of its dissident North American colonists.

27. The only remaining trace of Spanish presence in the area is a name, the Strait of Juan de Fuca.

28. The Treaty of Ghent (8 *Stat.* 218, TS 109, December 24, 1814), ending the War of 1812, required the United States and Great Britain to make peace treaties with the Indian allies of the other party so as to foreclose intertribal warfare started as a result of Indian nations aligning with one or another of the larger warring states, and to ensure that each of the larger countries would treat its former enemies justly. For background, see Horsman, Reginald, *Expansion and American Indian Policy, 1783-1812*, Michigan State University Press, Lansing, 1967.

29. See, for example, the treaty between Spain and the Creek Confederacy (May 20-June 1, 1784) at Pensacola, Florida, in *American State Papers: Foreign Affairs*, Vol. I, U.S. Government Printing Office, Washington, D.C., pp. 278-9. In fact, after the independence of the United States,

Spain and/or representatives of the King of Spain made some thirty treaties with Indian nations now regarded as domestic to the U.S. The indigenous principals in these international agreements ranged from the Choctaw, Creek, and Chickasaw of the Southeast, to the Comanches, Navajos, and Apaches of the Southwest, to several peoples in the San Francisco Bay area.

30. For a full elaboration, see *Johnson v. McIntosh* at 591-2.
31. Further discussion may be found in Cohen, Felix S., "Original Indian Title," *Minnesota Law Review*, No. 32, 1947, pp. 28-59.
32. *Cherokee Nation v. Georgia* (1831) gives a broad view of Marshall's use of the term. It was an analogy he was not quite capable of completing since it would have raised substantial questions about the amount of money the U.S. was offering Indians for their lands. Therefore, the comparison is qualified by use of the word "resembles," which, in this and other contexts, can mean almost anything.
33. In *Worcester v. Georgia* (1832), Marshall bolstered the status of federal statutes permitting missionaries to enter Cherokee lands, under Cherokee laws. In doing so, he brought the full measure of constitutional citation to bear (at 559): "[T]hat instrument confers on Congress the powers of war and peace; of making treaties; and of regulating commerce with foreign nations, and among the several States, and with the Indian tribes. They are not limited by any restrictions on their free actions; the shackles imposed on this power, in the confederation, are discarded."
34. See Vance, John T., "The Congressional Mandate and the Indian Claims Commission," *North Dakota Law Review*, No. 45, 1969, pp. 325-36.
35. *Ex Parte Crow Dog* (1883).
36. The BIA had tried but failed to get Congress to enact a similar law for nearly a decade. On May 20, 1874, the Senate Committee on Indian Affairs rejected the Bureau's overtures, stating, "The Indians, while their tribal relations subsist, generally maintain laws, customs, and usages of their own for the punishment of offenses. They have no knowledge of the laws of the United States and the attempt to enforce their own ordinances might bring them in direct conflict with existing statutes and subject them to prosecutions for their violation." See U.S. Senate, Committee on Indian Affairs, *Senate Report 367*, Vol. II, 43rd Cong., 1st Sess., U.S. Government Printing Office, Washington, D.C., 1874.
37. Article 1 of the 1868 Fort Laramie Treaty between the U.S. and the Lakota, Cheyenne and Arapaho nations made specific provisions for criminal jurisdiction to remain with the Indians. The latter agreed to surrender a person who committed a crime against non-Indians, or pay compensation for his or her crime, but the U.S. had no jurisdiction of its own within the boundaries of the "Great Sioux Nation."
38. *United States v. Kagama*, at 378-9.
39. Ibid., at 379.
40. Ibid., at 380.
41. *American Insurance Co. v. Canter* at 542.
42. *Northwest Indian Cemetery Protective Association v. Petersen*, 552 F. Supp. 951 (1982).
43. *Northwest Indian Cemetery Protective Association v. Petersen*, 565 F. Supp. 586, 592 (1983).
44. Ibid., at 595.
45. Ibid.
46. Ibid., at 595-6.
47. Ibid., at 596.
48. Ibid., at 605.
49. Ibid., at 601 (footnote).
50. *Northwest Indian Cemetery Protective Association v. Petersen*, 764 F.2d 581, 585 (1985).
51. *Sherbert v. Verner*, 374 U.S. 398 (1963).
52. *Northwest Indian Cemetery Protective Association v. Petersen*, 764 F.2d 581, 586 (1985).
53. *Northwest Indian Cemetery Protective Association v. Petersen*, 795 F.2d 688 (9th Cir. 1986).
54. Ibid., at 589.
55. *Northwest Indian Cemetery Protective Association v. Petersen*, 795 F.2d 688, 695 (1986).
56. Ibid., at 702.
57. Ibid., at 701.
58. *Lyng v. Northwest Indian Cemetery Protective Association*, at 1320.
59. Ibid., at 1324.
60. Ibid., at 1326.
61. Ibid.

62. Ibid., at 1338.

63. Ibid., at 1339.

64. On Tellico Dam, see Ensworth, Laurie, "Native American Free Exercise Rights to the Use of Public Lands," *Boston University Law Review*, No. 63, 1983, pp. 141-79. Also see Matthiessen, Peter, *Indian Country*, Viking Press, New York, 1984, pp. 103-126.

65. On Kinzua Dam, see U.S. Senate, Committee on Interior and Insular Affairs, *Hearings Before the Committee on Interior and Insular Affairs: Kinzua Dam Project, Pennsylvania*, 88th Cong., 1st Sess., U.S. Government Printing Office, Washington, D.C., May-December 1963.

66. On the Missouri River Project, see Lawson, Michael L., *Dammed Indians: The Pick-Sloan Plan and the Missouri River Sioux, 1944-1980*, University of Oklahoma Press, Norman, 1982.

67. This is the *Badoni* case; see "Table of Key Indian Laws and Cases" in this volume. Also see Ensworth, op. cit.

68. On San Francisco Peaks, see Lovett, Richard A., "The Role of the Forest Service in Ski Resort Development: An Economic Approach to Public Lands Management," *Ecology Law Quarterly*, No. 10, 1983, pp. 507-78.

69. *United States v. Means, et al.*, Civ. No. 81-5131, D.S.D. December 9, 1985.

70. One such suit, *Manybeads v. United States*, was dismissed by U.S. District Judge Earl Carroll on October 20, 1989, largely because of the high court ruling in *Lyng*.

71. An interesting discussion of the unsavory principles enshrined as doctrine by the *Lyng* decision may be found in Chambers, Reid D., "Discharge of Federal Trust Responsibility to Enforce Claims of Indian Tribes: Case Studies of Bureaucratic Conflict of Interest," *American Indian Law Newsletter*, Vol. 4, No. 15, 1980, pp. 1-20.

72. *Lyng*, op. cit., at 1336.

73. Ibid., at 1335. For further discussion, see Morris, Glenn T., "The 'G-O Road Decision': A Frontal Assault on American Indian Religious Freedom," in Ward Churchill, ed., *Critical Issues in Native North America*, International Work Group on Indigenous Affairs (IWGIA), Copenhagen, 1989, pp. 77-8.

74. Cohen, Felix S., "The Erosion of Indian Rights, 1950-53: A Case Study in Bureaucracy," *Yale Law Journal*, No. 62, 1953, p. 390.

75. *Lyng*, op. cit.

76. An interesting discussion of certain of the issues raised may be found in Clayton, Richard P., "The Sagebrush Rebellion: Who Should Control Public Lands?" *Utah Law Review*, 1980, pp. 505-33.

77. In any event, resumption of *de facto* treaty-making was one of the recommendations advanced by Senator Daniel Inouye's Special Committee on Investigations in its 1989 final report. See U.S. Senate, Select Committee on Indian Affairs, *Final Report and Legislative Recommendations: A Report of the Special Committee on Investigations*, 101st Cong., 2d Sess., U.S. Government Printing Office, Washington, D.C., November 20, 1989, p. 17.

78. For background, see Public Land Review Commission, *One Third of the Nation's Land*, Public Land Review Commission, Washington, D.C., 1970.

Acknowledgments

Inouye, Daniel K. "Discrimination and Native American Religious Rights." *University of West Los Angeles Law Review* 23 (1992): 3–19. Reprinted with the permission of the *University of West Los Angeles Law Review*.

Loesch, Martin C. "The First Americans and the 'Free' Exercise of Religion." *American Indian Law Review* 18 (1993): 313–77. Reprinted with the permission of the *American Indian Law Review*.

Doty, Peggy. "Constitutional Law: The Right to Wear a Traditional Indian Hair Style—Recognition of a Heritage." *American Indian Law Review* 4 (1976): 105–20. Reprinted with the permission of the *American Indian Law Review*.

Woodward, David. "The Rights of Reservation Parents and Children: Cultural Survival or the Final Termination?" *American Indian Law Review* 3 (1975): 21–50. Reprinted with the permission of the *American Indian Law Review*.

Laurence, Robert. "The Bald Eagle, the Florida Panther and the Nation's Word: An Essay on the 'Quiet' Abrogation of Indian Treaties and the Proper Reading of *United States* v. *Dion*." *Journal of Land Use and Environmental Law* 4 (1988): 1–21. Reprinted with the permission of the *Journal of Land Use and Environmental Law*.

Ensworth, Laurie. "Native American Free Exercise Rights to the Use of Public Lands." *Boston University Law Review* 63 (1983): 141–79. Reprinted with the permission of *Boston University Law Review*.

Stambor, Howard. "Manifest Destiny and American Indian Religious Freedom: *Sequoyah, Badoni,* and the Drowned Gods." *American Indian Law Review* 10 (1982): 59–89. Reprinted with the permission of the *American Indian Law Review*.

McAndrew, Stephen. "*Lyng* v. *Northwest*: Closing the Door to Indian Religious Sites." *Southwestern University Law Review* 18 (1989): 603–29. Reprinted with the permission of the *Southwestern University Law Review*.

Miller, Charles. "The Navajo-Hopi Relocation Act and the First Amendment Free Exercise Clause." *University of San Francisco Law Review* 23 (Fall 1988): 97–121. Reprinted with the permission of the University of San Francisco, School of Law.

Blair, Bowen. "Indian Rights: Native Americans Versus American Museums—A Battle for Artifacts." *American Indian Law Review* 7 (1979): 125–54. Reprinted with the permission of the *American Indian Law Review*.

Raines, June Camille Bush. "One Is Missing: Native American Graves Protection and Repatriation Act: An Overview and Analysis." *American Indian Law Review* 17 (1992): 639–664. Reprinted with the permission of the *American Indian Law Review*.

Perry, Rashelle. *"Employment Division, Department of Human Resources* v. *Smith*: A Hallucinogenic Treatment of the Free Exercise Clause." *Journal of Contemporary Law* 17 (1991): 359–76. Reprinted with the permission of the *Journal of Contemporary Law*.

Deloria, Vine, Jr. "Trouble in High Places: Erosion of American Indian Rights to Religious Freedom in the United States." In *The State of Native America: Genocide, Colonization, and Resistance.* Edited by M. Annette Jaimes (Boston: South End Press, 1992): 267–90. Reprinted with the permission of South End Press.